THE UNFINISHED CENTURY

53441

E   Leuchtenburg, William Edward,
741   1922-
.L48   The unfinished century; America
        since 1900. General editor: William
        E. Leuchtenburg. Contributors:
        Richard M. Abrams [and others]
        Boston, Little, Brown [1973]
          xiv, 970 p. illus. 24 cm.

           Includes bibliographical refer-
        ences.

           1. United States--History--20th
        century. I. Abrams, Richard M.
           II. Title.

E741.L48   917.3'03'9
                                        72-14216
                                           MARC
Library of Congress
06268   ]   575972   B   © THE BAKER & TAYLOR CO.   4219

CONTRIBUTORS

UNIVERSITY OF CALIFORNIA, BERKELEY RICHARD M. ABRAMS

UNIVERSITY OF CALIFORNIA, LOS ANGELES STANLEY COBEN

INDIANA UNIVERSITY ROBERT H. FERRELL

UNIVERSITY OF CALIFORNIA, SANTA BARBARA OTIS L. GRAHAM, JR.

COLUMBIA UNIVERSITY WILLIAM E. LEUCHTENBURG

STATE UNIVERSITY OF NEW YORK, STONY BROOK DAVID F. TRASK

UNIVERSITY OF NORTH CAROLINA, CHAPEL HILL SAMUEL F. WELLS, JR.

THE UNFINISHED CENTURY
America Since 1900

GENERAL EDITOR
WILLIAM E. LEUCHTENBURG COLUMBIA UNIVERSITY

LITTLE, BROWN AND COMPANY BOSTON

Library of Congress Catalog Card No. 72-14216

First Printing

Published simultaneously in Canada
by Little, Brown & Company (Canada) Limited

Printed in the United States of America

E
741
.L48

CREDITS AND ACKNOWLEDGMENTS

Cover photographs:

Back cover, left to right: Culver Pictures; Library of Congress; The Cincinnati Historical Society.
Spine: Culver Pictures.
Front cover, left to right: Steve Schapiro from Black Star; Culver Pictures; United Press International.

Chapter opening and closing photographs:

Pages 2–3: Historical Pictures Service, Chicago.
Page 112: State Historical Society of Wisconsin.
Pages 116–117: Brown Brothers.
Page 252: Culver Pictures.
Pages 256–257: The Granger Collection.
Page 354: United Press International.
Pages 358–359: Thomas McAvoy, LIFE Magazine, © Time Inc.
Page 460: United Press International.
Pages 464–465: Culver Pictures.
Page 572: Culver Pictures.
Pages 576–577: Roger Malloch, Magnum.
Page 672: United Press International.
Pages 676–677: Andreas Feininger, LIFE Magazine, © 1950 Time Inc.
Page 798: Shel Hershorn from Black Star.
Pages 802–803: Wide World Photos.
Page 942: United Press International.

Permission to use excerpts from works by the following authors is gratefully acknowledged:

W. H. AUDEN. Quotation on page 429 from "New Year Letter (January 1, 1940)" in *The Collected Poetry of W. H. Auden* (Random House, 1945). Quotation on page 860 from "Whitsunday in Kirchstetten" in *About the House* by W. H. Auden (Random House, 1965). Both reprinted by permission of the publisher.

Preface

Of the writing of prefaces there is no end, and, many would say, no need. As the proof of the pudding is in the eating, so the test of a book is in the reading. Anterior statements that seek to alter this fact fall somewhere between a public relations gambit and an *apologia*. Nor does the writing of a history of the United States in the twentieth century require any justification. We are now in the eighth decade of this tumultuous age, which has seen more rapid change than any other epoch, and all of our lives have been deeply affected by the earthshaking movements of these years.

The twentieth century has a particular importance in the history of the United States, because for the first time this republic took a pre-eminent position in the world. It began the century in 1900 as a country of 76 millions tentatively edging into the international arena and by the 1970's was a world power of more than 200 millions with far-flung foreign interests. The most technologically advanced of any country, the United States nurtured the assembly line and the sky-scraper, television and the computer, was, indeed, as Gertrude Stein said, the first nation to enter the twentieth century. "Americans adapted naturally to the modern environment," observed a French commentator. "They seem to be born into this age, born to make long-distance calls, hop international flights or act in films." When the century began, few had any reason to know of Kitty Hawk, North Carolina, but before the seventh decade had ended, Americans had left their footprints on Tranquility Base, the Moon. The story of what Sir Alan Bullock has called this "Promethean Age," an era of wars and depressions, of material progress and cultural achievement, of vast population movements, and of technological innovation, is one of the most compelling sagas in the history of mankind.

Yet if the significance of twentieth-century history needs little elaboration, the organization and emphases of this particular volume are so different that a word of explanation may be in order. To be sure, it is the conceit of every new textbook that it is unique. This one is. We have taken advantage of that characteristic twentieth-century trait, specialization, and divided the history of these years among seven authors. There are, however, eight chapters, because the editor, notoriously more verbose than his collaborators, has required an extra chapter to meet his assignment. Each "chapter" is in a sense a discrete essay. This format has permitted each writer to analyze at length a period and subject in which he has concentrated much of his research and where he is familiar with the most recent scholarship to an extent that most generalists are not. Since diplomatic historians have staked out foreign affairs as a separate enterprise, we have respected this demarcation in our arrangements. At the same time, those responsible for the chapters on diplomatic history have been alert to the domestic influences on foreign policy, and the contributors on domestic matters have been conscious of the ever-increasing impact of the world on events in America.

In a book of this character it is essential that the separate efforts coalesce in a single whole. The authors are men of strong convictions, not always in agreement with one another. But we have taken pains to achieve a desirable degree of coordination. The editor read every draft of every chapter and inflicted his suggestions up to the point of, and sometimes beyond, human tolerance. Our editors at Little, Brown, especially Charles H. Christensen and Jane E. Aaron, made numbers of helpful suggestions. Contributors also read at least the early drafts of one another's chapters and were generous with their comments. They were particularly free with criticisms of the editor's drafts. We have not sought to impose a false homogeneity on the book. Rather we have attempted to develop themes that run through more than one chapter.

Inevitably, we have been concerned with the growth of that leviathan, the twentieth-century state, but our interests run well beyond what is usually connoted by "political history." In addition to analyzing legislation, government agencies, and the warfare of political parties, we have been engrossed by the social, economic, and, in a broad sense, the cultural history of the times. The contributors have recognized the importance of the role of women, of blacks, of Chicanos, and of diverse ethnic groups. We have explored violence as well as harmony, not just elites but the multitudes. The book is not preoccupied with Washington or the Eastern seaboard but gives attention to every section of the country. We have not hesitated to make judgments or to stress uniformities. But we have also tried to be sensitive to the discerning comment that Martin Duberman made about David Potter: "To read Potter is to become aware of a truth that only the greatest historians have been able to show us: that the chief lesson to be derived from the study of the past is that it holds no simple lesson, and that the historian's main responsibility is to prevent anyone from claiming that it does."

In inviting historians to participate in this project, the editor was especially attracted to those who were at the cutting edge of research in their specialities as well as being gifted writers. As historians measure age, several of the participants are in the youthful bracket of the profession. The contributors teach at institutions in many regions — the East, the Midwest, the South, and the Far West. Their scholarly interests range from the role of the American corporation in overseas investment to the transit of nuclear physics to the United States, from the history of diplomacy to the inhibitions on collectivism in modern America, from the nature of Anglo-American relations in the early years of this century to the vicissitudes of the cold war.

Like more than one character in a novel of the Great Depression, we have incurred many debts, and we are happy to acknowledge them. Our creditors are legion: archivists, librarians, graduate assistants, typists, proofreaders, members of our families — the list is endless. But two debts require special mention. Without the labors of our fellow historians who in their monographs and articles have made of recent history a worthy discipline, this book would not have been possible. Our greatest debt, however, is to our students who have contributed to our learning and compelled us to sharpen our formulations. To them, to their contemporaries, and to those who will follow them go our good wishes for the years that remain in this troubled, exciting, and as yet unfinished century.

William E. Leuchtenburg

Contents

Maps

Charts and Tables

1

Reform and Uncertainty

America Enters the Twentieth Century, 1900–1918

RICHARD M. ABRAMS

When, at the age of twenty-two, Theodore Roosevelt announced to a Harvard classmate that he planned to enter politics in order to promote the cause of good government in New York, his friend wondered if he had lost his mind. In 1879, "everybody" knew New York politics was in the hands of liquor interests, labor bosses, and gangsters, supported by unscrupulous lawyers and *nouveaux* businessmen expert in making dirty deals with scoundrels like themselves. "Teedie" (the youthful Theodore's affectionate family sobriquet) was born an aristocrat—heir to old New York Dutch wealth and to civic leadership but conditioned by his class origins to hold himself aloof from the squalor of mid-nineteenth-century politics. He had nothing of the physical bearing of a leader. Although he stood a respectable five feet nine inches tall, a narrow frame made

him appear undersized. He was nearsighted in the extreme. The small, metal-rimmed glasses perched on his nose often trailed a long, black silk cord, in the upper-class fashion of the day. When he smiled, he showed large and prominent teeth, and when he spoke, his voice came out piping high and thin. All in all, as a friend later recalled, to the politicians of the day Roosevelt seemed "a joke, a dude, the way he combed his hair, the way he talked — the whole thing."

Roosevelt entered politics with a zeal that became his trademark. If the men in politics really were rough and vulgar, that only meant, he said, "that the people I knew did not belong to the governing class, and that the other people did." "I intended to be one of the governing class," he later wrote, "and if they proved too hard-bit for me I supposed I would have to quit, but I certainly would not quit until I had made the effort and found out whether I really was too weak to hold my own in the rough and tumble."

Eventually Roosevelt achieved what he had set out to do: He gained access to "the governing class," and in significant measure he regained it for the patrician class to which he belonged. More than that, he helped make politics an attractive career for the talented, the educated, the earnest, and the goodwilled. Above all, he removed from social reform the stigma of effeteness that had attached to it in the nation's adolescence.

There was surely nothing effete (or "unmanly," to use the new century's preferred word) about Roosevelt. Despite his moderate stature, his myopia, and the asthma from which he suffered until his early twenties, Roosevelt led a robust, even heroic, life. He became an expert marksman and horseman as a teenager, and was a member of the boxing and wrestling teams at Harvard. In the 1880's he put such skills successfully to test by riding herd with ranchers in the Dakota Territory, brawling with a thug in a saloon, leading a posse to capture two armed and wanted men, and matching sharpshooting skills with Indians in Wyoming. Meanwhile, his po-

Theodore Roosevelt poses in about 1881 in his Dakota clothes (top), wearing boots and a pearl-handled revolver far more expensive than the typical "cowboy" could afford, and uncharacteristically without his glasses. Although he may have looked and sounded like a "dude," Roosevelt was probably a better shot and horseman than any of the ranchers he met. TR as President sits with his family (bottom). Left to right: Quentin (who was killed in action in World War I); Theodore, Jr.; Archie; Alice; Kermit; Mrs. (Edith Carew) Roosevelt; and Ethel.

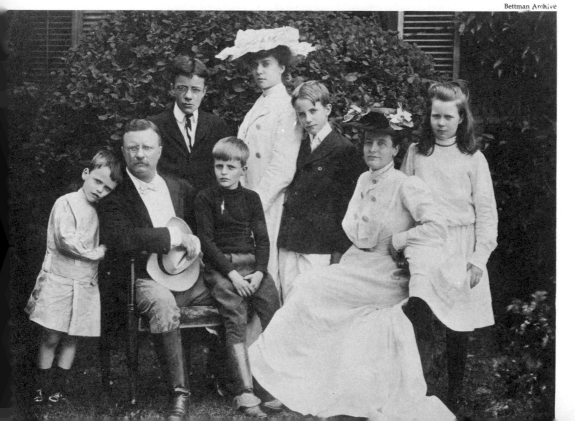

litical career took him to Albany three times as a member of the New
York legislature, to Washington for six years as a member of the
United States Civil Service Commission, to New York City in 1895
as police commissioner, and back to Washington as assistant secretary of the navy. When war with Spain erupted in 1898, he quit
the Navy Department and organized a volunteer cavalry unit,
dubbed the "Rough Riders," which saw heavy action in Cuba. By
the time New Yorkers elected him governor, upon his return from
Cuba, Roosevelt was already an American folk hero.

TR's nomination to the vice-presidency in 1900 resulted from the
efforts of New York's politicos to rid themselves of a leader with so
much popular strength that he could not be controlled for the usual
boodling and partisan purposes. They declined to heed warnings
that in recent years royalty and presidents had been falling victim
to assassins with terrifying frequency — President Carnot of France
in 1894, Prime Minister Canovar del Castillo of Spain in 1897, the
Empress Elizabeth of Austria-Hungary in 1898, King Humbert
of Italy in 1900 — and that Roosevelt, their nemesis, might thus accede
to the presidency. Social and political tensions agonized major
societies throughout the world, from Peking to Paris, from Pretoria
to Petrograd. Disciples of the Russian anarchists Michael Bakunin
and Prince Peter Kropotkin seemed to be everywhere. In the United
States, the misnamed Gay Nineties had produced a four-year
economic depression, brutal industrial warfare, the merging of scores
of corporations into gigantic trusts, and racial upheavals that would
culminate with the disfranchisement of nearly all black Americans.
In 1896, in cold fear of apparent signs of revolution, the country's
principal industrialists and bankers had stowed their traditional
party differences and united to put down an agrarian rebellion led
by William Jennings Bryan of Nebraska. Two years later, conflict
with Spain to free Cuba had offered mock-heroic diversion, but that
soon evolved into a wretched war against Filipino independence,
which some Americans by 1900 began to believe was costing
America its unique heritage. "To puke up its ancient soul, and the
only things that gave it eminence among nations . . . without a wink
of squeamishness," groaned William James during the presidential
campaign that year, ". . . is what the Republicans would commit us
to in the Philippines." Passions ran high, but "McKinley Prosperity"
prevailed. Bryan, campaigning as an anti-imperialist, lost for the
second time, and TR came down to Washington resigned to boredom
and oblivion as Vice-President. He felt, he said, as if he were "taking
the veil."

Six months later, in September 1901, Leon Czolgosz's bullet at the Pan American Exposition in Buffalo, New York, put an end to the McKinley era. The era of Theodore Roosevelt began.

"He is not an American, you know," John Morley said, "he *is* America." Young, expansive, self-confident, optimistic, moralistic (though unwilling to let mere principle stand in the way of "what needs to be done") — Roosevelt embodied all these qualities as did the nation he came to lead at the age of forty-two. His exuberance and impulsiveness reminded some of his escapades as a cowboy and led others to describe him as a child not more than about twelve years old. These characterizations miss his keen intelligence and abilities, as well as the careful attention he devoted to every major decision. With his education, his experience, his patrician sense of disinterested responsibility, Roosevelt entered the presidency better prepared than any man since John Quincy Adams. His preparation, as well as his energy and flexibility, would serve him well. They would also be well tested, for the country was entering a period as trying as any before, except that of the Civil War.

It is comfortable to see Roosevelt's seven-and-a-half year leadership as inaugurating the twentieth century in the United States. But the Roosevelt era may also be regarded as the finale of the nineteenth century. TR's adminstration (1901–1909) bought time while Americans reexamined their progress, reassessed their objectives, ruminated on their newly acquired international role, and began to discover flaws in their conception of the national character. The world was passing beyond the easy assertion of righteousness that Roosevelt could still successfully use to justify policy. It was about to move past the belief that integrity, honesty, and manliness would suffice to save civilization. The attributes that made Roosevelt so appealing would soon take on the aspect of romantic simplicity.

1901 in Perspective

The United States in 1901 was a nation of about 76 million people. Almost nine of every ten Americans were Caucasian — that is, of European origin, predominantly from the United Kingdom, Germany, and Scandinavia. Probably eight of ten professed some form of Protestantism. Not surprisingly, most American observers referred to the nation as white, Anglo-Saxon, and Protestant. Although nonwhites, non-Anglo-Americans, and non-Protestants might have denied that such racial, ethnic, and religious characteristics were

Alice Roosevelt, the President's daughter, portrays the "Gibson Girl" look in this 1904 photograph. The illustrator Charles Dana Gibson created in 1895 the popular model of urbane, clean-cut American womanhood: head held high, chin thrust upward, eye lids at half-mast, hair tied together above the shoulders. According to a contemporary *New York World* editorial: "Before Gibson synthesized his ideal woman . . . there was no type of her to which one could point and say, 'That is the typical American girl.' As soon as the world saw Gibson's ideal it bowed down in adoration." Gibson also created a male type — square-shouldered, square-jawed, and (perhaps most important) clean-shaven.

indispensable ingredients of Americanism, few contemporaries asserted the contrary on behalf of blacks, Indians, Jews, Catholics, Armenians, Slavs, Celts, Orientals, Latins. The denials of dissenters usually argued that religious and ethnic matters had no place in the country's politics. This view would eventually prove untenable.

Traditionally, laws had compelled businesses to be closed on Sundays regardless of proprietors' religious convictions. Mormons faced sanctions, including exclusion from elective office, if they practiced polygamy. Public schools might require readings from Protestant versions of the Bible. Anti-miscegenation laws and legally enforced segregation according to race confirmed long-standing social policies that dictated "racial purity." Civil service examinations deliberately gave advantages to those raised in the Anglo-American heritage. In 1901, these conditions were mostly taken for granted, even by many who suffered inequities because of them. By 1915, Americans would begin, for better and for worse, to acknowledge the existence, and assert the legitimacy, of social policies expressed in law that were premised on religious and ethnic preferences and on racial preconceptions.

The growing size and self-consciousness of the nation's immigrant population were in part responsible for the new emphasis. As of 1900, about one in every seven Americans—10.2 million in all—had been born abroad; and another 15.6 million—about one in five—had at least one foreign-born parent. Between 1880 and 1910, about one-third of the nation's population growth came from foreign immigration. Beginning in the 1880's, most immigrants came from southern and eastern Europe and not only did not speak English but professed "alien" religions such as Roman Catholicism, Eastern Orthodoxy, and Judaism. In addition to Europeans who failed to meet normative ethnic tests, there were 8.8 million native-born Negroes (about 12 percent of the population), 250,000 American Indians, and about 120,000 Chinese and Japanese.

Most recent immigrants and their children settled in a few agricultural states, such as the Dakotas and Minnesota, and in the nation's largest cities. At the turn of the century thirty-seven cities had populations of 100,000 or more. In ten of these cities at least three-fourths of the residents were first- or second-generation Americans, and in another ten the figure exceeded two-thirds. Such concentrations gave newer Americans a greater impact than their minority status might otherwise suggest.

The nation was still mostly rural in 1901. As much as 63 percent of the population lived in places with fewer than four thousand people: Some of these places were unincorporated tax refuges in the midst of metropolitan regions, and others had been enveloped by the growth of nearby cities, so that they were really more urban than rural. All the same, most Americans had had the experience of growing up in

Immigration to the United States, 1870-1930

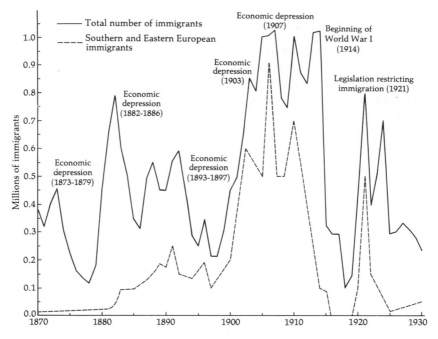

Sources: *Statistical History of the United States from Colonial Times to the Present* (Stamford, Conn.: Fairfield Publishers, 1965); and the report presented by Senator William P. Dillingham, Senate document 742, 61st Congress, 3rd session, December 5, 1910: Abstracts of Reports to the Immigration Commission.

small country communities. They knew the seasonal rhythms of life, the isolation and stillness of a snowbound countryside, the intimate, deep joy of spring thaw, the scorching heat of the sun in a planted field, the expectant tumult of harvest time, the regular reappearance of fairs, circuses, holidays, preacher evangelists, and stump-speaking politicians, the familiar closeness of horses and livestock, the snug camaraderie at the village church, the general store, the drugstore soda fountain, the saloon. They had seen horseshoes and other hardware fashioned by blacksmiths and butter churned at the local creameries. Baking bread, filling oil lamps, fetching coal and wood, watering horses, knitting, mending and washing clothes, accounted for much of each household's daily rounds.

There was an integral orderliness to rural life that served as the model for nearly every plan for social reform proposed in the early twentieth century. Indeed, in the opinion of some who believed the city beyond salvation, the decline of country life foretold the demise of organized society. Even those who spoke enthusiastically of the metropolis' potential for progress and a higher civilization implicitly sought to restore the vitality of the primary face-to-face relationships they imputed to life in farm communities. According to Robert Park, an originator of urban sociology, the source of the malaise of city life could be found in the replacement of "the more intimate and permanent associations of the smaller community" by the casual and occasional relationships that prevail in big cities. Jane Addams, raised in a small town in Illinois where her father had known Abraham Lincoln, never discarded her hope that Hull House, the settlement she helped to found in Chicago in 1889, would provide

By the turn of the century, the general store with its pot-bellied stove and checkerboard philosophers was on its way out, replaced as a kind of social center by the combination drugstore and ice-cream palace that featured elegant marble and brass ice-cream and soda-fountain accoutrements. By 1902 everything was up to date in the Loeb and Hollis store in Kansas — electric lights and ceiling fans and (mostly) clean-shaven salesmen.

Pennell Collection, University of Kansas, Lawrence

the nucleus to enable people in the city to regain the collective morale, left behind in their native villages. John Dewey's revolutionary theory of progressive education owed much to his recollections of rural life in Burlington, Vermont, where he was born in 1859. Society, Dewey wrote in *School and Society* (1899), "is a number of people held together because they are working along common lines, in a common spirit, and with reference to common aims." In a farming community everyone in the family had something to do, and something always had to be done. The young were initiated early into habits of order, industry, and mutual responsibility. Work had an immediacy connected with sustenance and comfort. The division of labor and impersonality of modern industrial activities destroyed that environment and the motivations and life purposes it inspired. Like the program at Hull House, in which Dewey was active before he moved to New York in 1905, Dewey's scheme for progressive schools centered on restoring children's acquaintance with "the primal necessities of life."

The rural model was not always drawn accurately. The stability of small-town communities in the nineteenth century has probably been exaggerated. Agricultural towns seem to have shared much of the impermanence that observers commonly noticed about big-city neighborhoods. Industrialism helped unhinge social structures everywhere: Railroads and the telegraph reduced the isolation of the Great Plains and of the remote valleys of New England and the Appalachians; machinery, some of it steam powered, made plowing, sowing, and harvesting many times more productive than they were with hand labor. New technology inspired new ideas for wealth and spoiled advantages once thought secure. It was hard to keep children down on the farm when machines made their labor superfluous and when opportunities beckoned at the end of the railroad tracks in Chicago, Cleveland, Pittsburgh, and New York.

However, transience seems to have characterized agricultural communities for reasons having little to do with industrialism. Hamlin Garland, the literary chronicler of midwestern life, wrote poignantly of his family's constant migrations and of his own vain craving for permanence. Perhaps some subtle compulsion implicit in the Puritan work ethic drove men such as the elder Garland to move on again and again even though they found success each time they settled. Possibly transience was endemic in the commercialism of American agriculture. Americans' consideration of their land as a commodity like the crops they raised on it seems to have been unique among nineteenth-century farmers anywhere. To people like the Garlands, writes Lewis Atherton, "America was never more than ten years old." Few things remained long enough for local traditions to grow. Even those who tried to put down roots found them weakened by the constant stream of newcomers passing through and by their children's choice of careers that took them physically and spiritually to distant soil.

By 1901, farming no longer occupied the majority of American workers. Less than 38 percent of the work force (including children aged ten to fourteen) was employed on farms, down from about half of the work force in 1880. Another 38 percent of the work force consisted of craftsmen, factory and mine operatives, and nonfarm laborers. Proportionately fewer farmers owned their own farms than ever before. Farm tenancy was up from 25 percent of all farms in 1880 to 35 percent in 1900, and it would rise to nearly 40 percent by 1920. Only half of the acreage in the country was wholly owned by the operators. As corporate farm ownership ate up the country's most fertile land, the figure would continue to diminish even though tenancy figures would also decline after 1930. To meet shrinking cost-price margins, farmers had to increase productivity by means of expensive machinery, irrigation, and heavy use of chemicals for fertilizer and insecticides. Small farmers had no capital for such investments, and given the vagaries of crop prices, banks generally declined to grant them credit. Thus much of the most cultivable land came into the hands of syndicates, which hired managers — occasionally as part-owners — to operate farms.

In the South, sharecropping imprisoned at least a half-million farm families. The arrangements varied considerably. Usually the landlord supplied tools, animals, and feed, as well as the land that the tenant worked, in return for one-half or three-fourths of the crop. Sometimes 'croppers worked the landlord's fields for a specified number of days each week, not unlike in the medieval manorial system, but unlike his feudal counterpart, a 'cropper usually had no assurance that he could stay on the land from year to year. Ninety percent of the nation's black people lived in the South, most of them seeking a livelihood in agriculture. Almost three-fourths were farm tenants, and more than a third of all black farmers worked on a sharecrop basis. By 1900 about 100,000 blacks had migrated to cities to work in service industries, on the waterfront, or in factories, but in the fifty years after the Civil War most migration remained within southern agricultural areas, gravitating westward, especially to

Arkansas, Texas, and Oklahoma — where once again conditions merely defied expectations. One analyst in 1895 probably exaggerated only slightly when he suggested that thirty years of emancipation had netted the average freedman about a dollar a year in increased real income.

As southerners, Negroes suffered more than economic hardship, and the new century did not soon offer them relief. During the 1890's the remnants of support for the freedman's civil rights crumbled as northern liberals shifted their attention to other political priorities, wearying of a cause they never fully believed in. This left the course clear for the South's practical repeal of the Fifteenth Amendment and most of the Fourteenth Amendment as well, at least for individuals having even one black grandparent. Homer Plessy, for example, though native-born and Caucasian in appearance, had "one-eighth African blood" and was therefore adjudged by the United States Supreme Court (in *Plessy* v. *Ferguson*, 1896) to be lawfully required by the state of Louisiana to travel exclusively in railroad coaches specially provided for members of "his race." Southern whites employed direct action to enforce Jim Crow laws, which proliferated during the 1890's, and they achieved the complete disfranchisement of southern blacks by 1910 similarly with the aid of violence and bloodshed.

Mayhem, lynchings, and murder were not the worst features of life for blacks. That resided in the daily humiliations imposed not merely by the threat of wanton violence but also by the law itself. Courts in the South scarcely made a pretense of treating Negroes and whites as equals. No black person could testify against a white or could safely (or perhaps in any fashion) bring charges against a white. Crimes, including the most brutal murders, if perpetrated by whites against blacks, would almost invariably be unpunished and even unprosecuted. However, a mere "discourtesy" by a black toward a white — sometimes no more than a glance, especially if directed toward a white woman — could become a capital offense. A system in which county sheriffs earned much of their income in proportion to the number of prisoners they held in jail inspired roundups of Negroes, who might then be leased to labor contractors.

That such abominations did not drive Negroes out of the South in significant numbers before 1915 suggests that they could not perceive an altogether better life in the North or West. The fact that Negroes remained predominantly in southern agriculture helped isolate them from the renascent humanitarianism emerging in the cities after the turn of the century. But there were more important barriers. Despite the demand for unskilled labor required by industrialization, few blacks found a welcome in the factories of the North. Interracial work forces were more common in Atlanta and Birmingham than in northern workshops or on the waterfronts. By 1901, Samuel Gompers, president of the American Federation of Labor, had just about given up his efforts to persuade member unions to accept nonwhites. In the guise of labor laws, moreover, states such as Illinois forbade employers to recruit Negroes from the South. Although northern courts and politics accorded more humane treatment than did those in the South, contemporary informed opinion in both North and South held Negroes to be inherently inferior to whites. This belief permitted even northern liberals at best only a condescending concern about what happened to black people; most seemed to share a greater anxiety about the injury blacks might inflict on their bright hopes for an orderly, progressive society. So, until the needs of war after 1915 threw open job opportunities to Negroes in northern factories, nearly all American blacks endured conditions of malice and brutality in the South, from which even the most ebullient years of the progressive era offered little relief.

Although most black farmers faced problems that economic gains would not solve, a number of developments around the turn of the century made the years from 1900 to 1914 the golden age of agriculture. The international market for foodstuffs and other staple crops improved sharply. Inflationary pressures caused by the increase in urban population overcame the deflationary force of late-nineteenth-century agricultural expansion. Commodity prices rose as a consequence. The relationship of the prices of staple crops to the prices of industrial goods from 1909 to 1913 would become the base in the 1930's for federal subsidies designed to restore "parity" to farm incomes.

The reduction in the proportion of workers earning their living from agriculture helped raise per capita incomes. It also facilitated organization for collective economic activities and thereby strengthened farmers' political leverage. State and federally financed irrigation projects made speedy headway when supported by singleminded groups that could afford lobbyists to tend to their interests and that could ally with related forces such as land developers and speculators. State governments promoted the standardization of grading, appropriated funds for research, applied controls on warehousing and railroad practices, and in other ways assisted the farm industry to reduce waste in cultivation, handling, and distribution. With such changes taking place, banks that had declined to risk loans to individual "dirt farmers" unfolded their resources to large farming operations capable of improving productivity according to modern needs. A. P. Giannini would build his Bank of Italy into the gargantuan Bank of America by specializing in agricultural loans in California when the business first began to appeal to financiers. All in all, for the 3 million Americans who owned their farms, and for probably most of the 2.5 million who rented or partly owned their land, the rewards of American life bore a realistic relationship to the promise.

On the other side of the coin, a growing number of those who made their living in agriculture did so as migrant farm laborers. This was especially so in states like California, Mississippi, and Florida, which featured labor-intensive crops, requiring much seasonal hand labor, such as cotton, hops, fruits, and vegetables. Perhaps no sector of the American work force was more exploited than migrant farm workers. Mostly they were single males, unskilled, and unable or unwilling to hold regular jobs. Some were confirmed hoboes who worked only as long as necessary to earn a stake that would carry them through a winter or enable them to join a hobo "jungle" for a while. Others lacked families because of abandonment or misfortune. Still, almost a third of the migrant or casual farm labor force was composed of families, a small but growing proportion of whom lived perpetually on the road in search of a livelihood. In California, Chinese and Japanese families made up as much as 15 percent of the migrant force in 1901; Mexicans began to immigrate in substantial numbers only after 1910. Contemporary studies found that about half of the migrant workers were "native whites." In America, where nonwhite and alien groups were expected to fill the most wretched jobs, the high proportion of "Anglos" suggests that the employment problem, even in the land of gold and honey, was no marginal matter. Railroad companies claimed that about half a million hoboes regularly hung around stations awaiting the chance to jump aboard trains. That nearly five thousand persons were killed annually between 1901 and 1905 and an equal number severely injured while "riding the rails" tends to confirm such estimates of the size of the transient work force.

But twentieth-century America would become a predominantly urban society, a fact for which few contemporaries were prepared. The 1870's was the last decade in which the population growth in rural districts and small towns exceeded that in metropolitan areas. Between 1900 and 1910, 53 percent of the growth of the national population was in the metropolises, an expansion rate more than twice that of the nonmetropolitan regions. Between 1910 and 1920, metropolitan areas accounted for 67 percent of the nation's population growth, more than three times the growth rate of the nonmetropolitan areas. Without modern technological innovations, which had increased agricultural productivity and provided long-distance, high-speed transportation, it would have been impossible to feed the millions of people engaged in the nonfood-producing activities of urban workers. But the same technology that made urban concentration possible increased individuals' dependence on forces beyond both their own control and the natural restraints of the marketplace.

Indeed, no sector of the society had more intimate experience with the inadequacy of the marketplace as an adjudicator for social policy than the city, where the mutually exclusive character of diverse interests was endemic. Literally and figuratively, people trod on each others' toes. If an individual's life style neglected sanitary habits, the diseases that might infect him more likely than not would infect his more fastidious neighbors. Careless construction of one house necessarily jeopardized others nearby. One man's recreation tried another's moral sensibilities.

As the boundaries of urban population widened, people came to depend more heavily on government than they had grown used to. Businesses and shoppers required rapid transportation to get from home to work or to stores. The selection of the routes of street railways — mostly drawn by horses until electrification arrived early in the 1890's — became a contentious issue among various interest groups and their political allies at city hall and in the state legislatures. The trolley car made possible the development of real estate far beyond the center of the city, while sometimes injuring interests immediately along or too remote from its route. The extension of city development, moreover, made obsolete the arrangements whereby neighborhood guilds contracted privately for garbage disposal and street maintenance, just as it rendered impractical volunteer firefighters, who often competed among themselves for the fees and booty they usually received for their services.

Despite the centrifugal spread of cities, space was always at a premium. This meant great pressure from business groups for the maximal commercial use of every square inch of land — whether for mercantile and manufacturing purposes or for rental housing —

leaving little room for trees, lawns, parks, and playgrounds. The declining years of the nineteenth century had produced some exceptional work toward planning livable cities. In 1898 Robert Wood of Boston's South End settlement house believed he saw hope for "the principle that the modern city . . . must more and more minister directly to the comfort and pleasure of its inhabitants." Boston and Philadelphia led the way in preserving and designing woods and meadows in miniature; Brooklyn owes its lovely Prospect Park, Manhattan its Central Park, and Chicago its Lincoln Park to the forethought of landscape architects such as Frederick Law Olmsted. But such arboreal islands, meant to be reminiscent of a rural environment—to provide citizens with the opportunity for "a day in the country"—were exceptions. They were located away from the most congested parts of the city, and they failed to offer relief from the pestiferous, odoriferous, nerve-jangling, claustrophobic experience that the average urbanite had to learn to cope with. The inadequacy of recreational areas especially in the cities that grew to substantial size before 1910 cannot be ascribed to oversight. But one cannot expect that people accustomed to taking rural surroundings for granted, and often regarding residence in the city as an interim arrangement preceding the purchase of a farm, would brood on the social, psychological, or physiological consequences of asphalt and granite enclosure.

To house the millions who poured into the cities from farms as well as from abroad, builders had invented the tenement—a four-, five-, and sometimes six-story walk-up designed to make maximum use of minimal space. Naturally, water facilities, light, and air were as minimal as the space. Toilet facilities consisted of single hallway "water closets" rarely available on more than one or two floors of the building. Tenants in buildings with rear courtyards used what were called "school sinks"—a single broad plank with a series of seat holes placed over a trench that might or might not be flushed out a couple of times a day by the house custodian or superintendent. Usually the school sinks served tenants of several buildings with common rear courts. Many tenements were completely closed off on three sides, so that the only air and light available to rear apartments came from an air shaft. This was the feature usually chosen by tenement residents as the most obnoxious of all. As one explained to a New York state commission investigating housing conditions in 1901:

The air shaft is so narrow that the kitchen windows in two houses adjoin one another. In most houses the air shafts are the only means of light and air for at least two out of every three rooms, and the only means of lighting the staircases. The first thing that awakens one in the morning is the loud voices of the various tenants, intermingled with the odors that arise from the kitchen windows. It is, indeed, wonderful that you can distinguish any one voice among them all.

The shaft was the source of more than cooking odors. "You see" said one housekeeper of a five-story tenement, "it's damp down there, and the families, they throw out garbage and dirty papers and the insides of chickens, and other unmentionable filth. The housekeeper before me wasn't so particular, and I just vomited when I first cleaned up the air shaft. Then it's so hard to get into, you know. I have to crawl through the window, and in that other air shaft I have to climb down a ladder." For the tenants, tossing garbage into the air shaft often seemed a necessity, given the alternatives. "It is much easier than climbing the dark stairs and running the risk of breaking one's legs," remarked one resident. Not surprisingly, many tenement dwellers sealed up the air shaft window of their apartment. Better the darkness than the noises, the odors, and the diseases that exuded through the window.

The halls were another blight. Coming in from sunlight, one felt swallowed up by the dense, stifling darkness—like "the black mouth of a mine shaft," said one inspector. "The only light and ventilated halls," he reported, "are in the oldest houses, of little depth, with a window to the yard." Newer houses were longer and deeper, with two or four families on each floor and a single window at the middle to light the stairwell but not the halls. "This light and air," the inspector wrote, "comes from the air shaft; hence even the stairway of the lower two or three stories is dark." "Imagine," he concluded, "dense fumes of frying fat and boiling vegetables. . . . Fancy that these are blown inward until they meet another body of dead air left by two or four adults or eight or ten adults, eight to sixteen children (two or four apartments remember) who have slept there for eight hours . . . [and] damp, foul bedclothes . . . also waiting for a chance to catch the least particle of fresh air . . . and you have somewhat of an idea of a tenement hall."

More affluent families, of course, could find more commodious housing. Much of it contrasted in no special way with nonurban abodes except for their more limited grounds and their uniform exteriors. Attached homes had been common in villages for centuries, but in the cities three-story rowhouses sometimes achieved elegance—New York's brownstones, for example, and many of the red brick and white stone–trimmed houses of Baltimore and Bos-

Woman's Work, painted about 1911 by John Sloan, an American who lived from 1871 to 1951. Sloan was one of a small group of American painters known as "the ash-can school" who broke with the tradition of painting romantic subjects and emphasized instead "everyday" scenes of life in the United States. Clothes hanging to dry on roof tops and from attachments on fire escapes were common features of the urban landscape until laundromats and automatic driers began to make the clothespin an archaeological wonder for Americans born after 1950.

Culver Pictures

The Cornelius Vanderbilt mansion at West 58th Street and 5th Avenue, New York City, about
1900. The very rich no longer build chateaux in the cities. They
live there instead in duplex suites in high-rise condominiums and luxury
hotels. The structure shown here was one of several Vanderbilt-family palaces
built along 5th Avenue during the last quarter of the nineteenth century.
"The Vanderbilts," remarked high-society pundit Hans Knickerbocker in 1889, "have
come nobly forward and shown the world how millionaires ought to live."

ton. Central heating from a furnace in the basement, a bathroom and
flush toilet with drains leading out of the building to sewer mains
or to a tank under the garden, possibly electric but more likely gas
lighting fueled by means of pipes built into the walls and leading to
the main under the paved street in front, and a hot water heater for
each sink, all distinguished modern city homes from any one was
likely to find in the country.

The extravagantly rich adorned their cities with fantastic mansions, such as the one Charles Schwab, president of Carnegie Steel Company built in 1901 on Manhattan's 72nd Street and Riverside Drive. Designed to be the largest of them all, it occupied a full city block and stood four stories high, not counting the 116-foot lookout tower. It had a wine cellar, gymnasium, bowling alley, sixty-foot swimming pool, and its own steam and electric power plant in the basement. Like transplanted country chateaux, such places provided accommodations for great numbers of guests. Schwab's had ninety bedrooms and a laundry room that could meet the daily needs of a hundred people.

More typical of urban housing was the multiple-unit building—the "block of flats," or apartment house—which varied in elegance and amenities from those of a residence hotel to those of a spacious middle-class family home complete with maid's quarters and "hall boys" among whose duties it was to deliver visitors' calling cards to the residents. In his novel *A Hazard of New Fortunes* (1890), William Dean Howells offers an incomparable description of apartment houses in New York City just before the turn of the century as he recounts the house-hunting efforts of a couple (modeled on himself and his wife) about to move from Boston to Manhattan. He records the common lament about the impersonal, superficial quality of big-city life. According to Mrs. Basil March, the apartments she visits would have benefited if the money spent on marble entrance halls, pretentiously decorated drawing rooms, and oversized bedrooms had been used to provide a true living room "where the family can all come together and feel the sweetness of being a family." "Why," she goes on, "those tenements are better and humaner than those flats! There the whole family lives in the kitchen, and has its consciousness of being." The flat destroyed that feeling. "It's confinement without coziness; it's clutter without being snug."

Like Mrs. March, many Americans seemed to believe that there was something terribly disconcerting about the modern urban environment, but few were prepared to recognize that city life required new concepts of social order. The fact that an urban society had to concern itself with the private sanitary habits of its citizens bewildered many. "Bathing," complained one reformer, "is a necessity in the crowded city; in the country it is not. The enhancement of land values and the necessity of artificial cleanliness or bathing lead back to the same common root as their cause; namely, the forced, artificial, anti-natural concentration of population." Building codes

This slum dwelling in New York City's East Side, around 1905–1912, illustrates Mrs. Basil March's statement in Howells' *A Hazard of New Fortunes* that in the tenement everyone lived in the kitchen. One wonders, however, if the virtues she attributed to such familial intimacy outweighed the obvious discomforts. It was hard not to romanticize the poor even in an age of realism and reform.

would be needed to preserve some decency for people living in egregious juxtaposition and to protect the health of the rest of the population. (Among other things, they would have to require a bathroom in every apartment.) But to make the necessary regulations effective, policy makers would have to wrench themselves from the notion that rural life provided the norm toward which to orient reforms. More than that, they would have to discover that the profit motive and the marketplace would not serve to produce ade-

quate housing and livable cities. It would require government planning and public revenues to do the job.

For millions of Americans, city living meant not only tenement
houses but also the saloon. What better place did most wage earners
have to go when not working? What better refuge from the tense
household activities in the cramped quarters of a flat? What more
congenial place to "be with the boys" and to get tips about money
opportunities, jobs, and politics? On the other hand, Andrew Sinclair, whose *Era of Excess* is generally hostile to the prohibitionist
movement, has observed, "For every decent saloon that filled a
need in the community, there were five that increased poverty and
crime among working people." By 1910 it was estimated that there
was a liquor bar or tavern for every three hundred Americans living
in the cities. Moreover, breweries and distilleries owned as much as
70 percent of the saloons, which meant that if a barkeeper did not use
every device — from free lunches to "free" women — to encourage his
clients to drink, he stood to lose his franchise.

Not surprisingly, the saloon was early targeted as a prime enemy
of American life. One prohibitionist campaign song implored voters
to

> Think of sisters, wives, and mothers;
>   Of helpless babes in some low slum;
> Think not of yourself but others;
>   Vote against the Demon Rum.

Beyond the familial problems aggravated by demon rum lay the
frustrated hopes of civic reformers. It escaped none who were intent
upon reducing the soaring costs of government incurred by the upward curve of urban growth that alcohol contributed to the expense
of crime control, produced inefficiency among civil employees, and
sometimes created young widows and orphans who became burdens on the state. In addition, few businesses were more closely
tied to the political machines that stood athwart the path to clean
and efficient government than were the liquor interests. The alliance
was a natural one: The politicos needed the money that the liquor
business could provide, and the saloons needed the licenses that the
politicos controlled.

Still, this does not get to the nub of the liquor issue in the daily
experience of contemporaries. Temperance campaigns struck at more
than personal and political corruption and at more than individuals'
claim to their own private choice of refreshment and recreation. They

Ten United States Cities (Population of 100,000 or More) with Highest Percentages of Foreign Born or Foreign Born and Second Generation Residents, 1900–1910

	Foreign born				Foreign born and second generation			
	1900		1910		1900		1910	
	City	Percentage of total population	City	Percentage of total population	City	Percentage of total population	City	Percentage of total population
1.	Fall River, Mass.	47.8	Fall River, Mass.	42.6	Fall River, Mass.	86.4	Fall River, Mass.	86.3
2.	Paterson, N. J.	36.8	Lowell, Mass.	40.9	Milwaukee, Wis.	83.0	New York, N. Y.	80.7
3.	New York, N. Y.	36.7	New York, N. Y.	40.4	Chicago, Ill.	79.1	Lowell, Mass.	80.5
4.	Boston, Mass.	34.8	Paterson, N. J.	36.1	Detroit, Mich.	78.5	Chicago, Ill.	79.6
5.	Chicago, Ill.	34.5	Boston, Mass.	35.9	New York, N. Y.	78.5	Milwaukee, Wis.	78.9
6.	Detroit, Mich.	33.6	Chicago, Ill.	35.7	Worcester, Mass.	78.5	Paterson, N. J.	77.4
7.	Cleveland, Ohio	32.6	Bridgeport, Conn.	35.5	Paterson, N. J.	77.3	Boston, Mass.	76.5
8.	Worcester, Mass.	31.7	Cleveland, Ohio	34.9	Cleveland, Ohio	77.0	Cleveland, Ohio	76.4
9.	Providence, R. I.	31.5	New Haven, Conn.	32.0	Minneapolis, Minn.	76.0	Cambridge, Mass.	75.6
10.	Milwaukee, Wis.	31.2	Detroit, Mich.	33.5	San Francisco, Cal.	75.6	Detroit, Mich.	75.3

Source: Data compiled from the 1900 and 1910 census returns by the Bureau of the Census.

served as a substitute focus for a social controversy that most Americans preferred not to face head on. There was almost an instinctive fear that to do so would jeopardize the fragile consensus on which peace and order depended in a nation of such ethnic diversity. Alcohol, rather than color, religion, or national origin, became the ostensible test of a person's character, his morality, his Americanism —even though it was indeed color, religion, and national background that troubled the testers. Frequently enough, temperance enthusiasts made this clear in bluntly phrased speeches or editorials. Said one, in 1908:

> Our boast has been that we are a Christian people, with Morality at the center of our civilization. Foreign . . . conquest is rapidly making us un-Christian, with immorality enthroned in power. Besodden Europe, worse bescourged [by drink] than by war, famine, and pestilence, sends here her drink-makers, her drunkard-makers, and her drunkards, or her more temperate but habitual drinkers, with all their un-American and anti-American ideas of morality and government; they are absorbed into our national life, but not assimilated; with no liberty whence they came, they demand unrestricted liberty among us, even to license for the things we loathe; and through the ballot-box . . . their foreign control or conquest has become largely an appalling fact; they dominate our Sabbath, over large areas of the country; they have set up for us their own moral standards, which are grossly immoral; they govern our cities . . . [and] the great cities govern the nation; and foreign control or conquest could gain little more, though secured by foreign armies and fleets.

Despite the noisome and discomfitting elements of urban life, the availability of jobs continued to lure more and more people to the city. Even in commercial port cities such as New York and San Francisco, employment opportunities were increasingly industrial, principally in manufacturing and construction. Big-city industry typically consisted of fabricating, assembling, and processing—bottling, clothes-making, sheet-metal work. Factories were small. Many were sweatshops—rooms or storage lofts never intended for industrial activities. Much manufacturing, notoriously of cigars and cheap clothing, was done in the tenements.

Industry provided opportunities for thousands of small entrepreneurs who brought food, fuel, and services to the urban work force. Success in America, at least for thousands of the nation's recent immigrants, meant not riches, which most were practical enough to discount as unreachable, but self-employment. The pushcart peddler selling fruit, vegetables, bottled drinks, used clothes, services such as scissors-and-knife sharpening and umbrella repair, was the low man on the ladder whom success by any definition eluded. But there were also thousands of tiny shops, often no larger than twelve by thirty feet (perhaps including a kitchen in the back and a bedroom and "parlor" upstairs), which served as neighborhood groceries, fruit and vegetable stores, tailors, jewelers, shoe repair and barber shops, laundries, drugstores, kitchen hardware outlets, florists, and the now all-but-defunct candy stores, general stores for children that dispensed pulp magazines, ices, rubber balls, string, kites, as well as candy. Such shops sustained with remarkable dignity whole families

This view of Hester Street in the Lower East Side of New York City, one of the broader streets running east to west in the "Jewish ghetto," was taken about 1900. Hundreds of thousands of Russian and Galician Jews settled in this corner of Manhattan, and also in the Williamsburg and Brownsville districts of Brooklyn, during the 1880's and 1890's. The picture suggests something of the crowded living conditions of urban life, and perhaps a little of the powerful cultural ferment that took place there. These people were refugees, dispossessed and poor, but not demoralized.

History Division, Los Angeles County Museum of Natural History

whose living standards must otherwise have been classified with abject poverty. Better-established entrepreneurs owned and operated catering services, funeral parlors, restaurants, hairdressing salons, bakeries, lumber yards, stables, and high-fashion clothing stores. In an age witnessing the decline of the family farm and the ascendancy of corporate consolidations, the city sustained the institution of "private enterprise" and perhaps also the illusion that the marketplace was a fair arbiter of one's life chances.

To millions of people, neither the metropolis nor the rural village or farm was home. The development of heavy industry in the last third of the nineteenth century had caused a proliferation of company and factory towns. In some cases such communities arose spontaneously at mining locations. The availability of water, for power and disposal of refuse, determined other town sites. Sometimes a big corporation settled in an already established town and became the chief employer there. Often state and county governments reached out for companies – because of the economic benefits they would presumably bring with them — by granting them land, tax breaks, and a legal standing amounting to political autonomy. Such towns, Republican statesman Henry Stimson observed even in 1922, needed "only castles, drawbridges, and donjon keeps to reproduce to the physical eye a view of the feudal days."

It is not hard to imagine what life in a town dominated by a single corporation or industry was like, especially in an age when few gave thought to limiting the prerogatives of property owners. The despotism was all the more complete because of the general assumption that industry inevitably brought social benefits. Especially in the South and in parts of the West, which self-consciously sought to escape from economic dependence on staple crops, industrialists enjoyed the pretense — as the historian of two North Carolina counties put it — of building "an orderly community of happy, God-fearing, working people, enjoying all the conveniences and comforts of improved social conditions." "We make American citizens," said a textile manufacturer when he was asked what his factory did, "and run cotton mills to pay the expense."

The typical factory hand worked fifty or sixty hours a week. In the steel industry, where unionism had been obliterated after the failure of the Homestead Strike in 1892, 20 percent of the work force did a twelve-hour shift seven days a week, and to gain a Sunday holiday every other week workers would take "the long shift" — twenty-four hours without a break. (Of course, at times during the shift there

Women and Children in the Labor Force, 1880–1930

			Children gainfully employed, nonagricultural work		
Year	Percentage of women gainfully employed		Total number of children aged 10–15 (in millions)	Total number of children employed (in millions)	Percentage of children employed
	Aged 10 and over	Aged 10–15			
1880	14.7	9.0	6.6	1.1	16.8
1890	17.4	10.0	8.3	1.5	18.1
1900	18.8	10.2	9.6	1.7	18.2
1910	21.5	8.1	10.8	1.6	15.0
1920	24.1	5.8	12.5	1.4	11.3
1930	22.0	2.9	14.3	0.7	4.7

Source: *The Statistical History of the United States from Colonial Times to the Present* (Stamford, Conn.: Fairfield Publishers, 1965).

was little to do, and some workers could sleep, as company spokesmen took pains to explain.) Because it was assumed that the conditions an employee accepted (or suffered) were strictly a matter of voluntary agreement between him and his employer according to the principles of private contract, the courts ruled that government could not legitimately interfere. After the turn of the century, the courts did begin excepting women and children from this principle on the grounds that they were not fully competent to exercise their liberty of contract as responsible, independent, intelligent human beings. In industries such as textiles, where women and children often made up most of the work force, some state laws did effectively reduce the work week to as little as fifty-four hours, though such laws were uncommon until after 1910.

Compulsory school-attendance laws, especially in the North, did more than maximum-hours legislation to limit the employment of children in factories and mines. But one ceased to be a child in most states after the age of fourteen and, in many cases, ten or twelve. Only 8 or 9 percent of the fourteen to seventeen age group was attending public day schools in 1900, and only 13 percent was attending ten years later. Merely 6.4 percent of the seventeen-year-old population in 1900 was in high school.

In the South, where textile and jute mills and mines absorbed some of the white labor force fleeing unprosperous farms, the long hours, persevering work habits, and family employment, which had characterized life on the farm, were easily transferred to factory life in the typical company town. The custom of families working side

These children were employed as "breakers" in a coal mine. In 1900, 1.75 million children between the ages of ten and fifteen were "gainfully employed," in a total workforce of 29 million. That was the highest number recorded in the history of the United States. The child labor reforms of the progressive era would bring the figure down by 1920 to 1.4 million in a workforce of 42.4 million.

by side, as they had done in the fields, was kept intact not only by the paternalism of employers ostensibly concerned with the moral cohesion of the home but also by the fact that parents needed the wages of their children to maintain themselves.

Companies in a factory town employed most of the people in the town, commonly owned the houses that the workers lived in, and ran the stores that supplied them. Although in the late 1890's some state laws began to forbid the practice, companies often paid workers in scrip or chits, thereby eliminating any options they might have had for spending their earnings outside of the corporation-run enterprises. Pension benefits and periodic bonuses, sometimes in the form of company stock, reinforced employees' dependence on the company, especially since the company specifically excluded employees who had not demonstrated their "loyalty" to the corporation for a specified number of months.

The despotism of life in a company town was often quite unintended and unperceived. In 1900, probably most factory and mine operatives had agricultural backgrounds. Whether they had been farm owners or tenants, they found in the factory an opportunity — often illusory, to be sure — to escape from the poverty and drudgery they had experienced as farmers. (Prosperous farmers generally did not leave agriculture, though some of their children probably did.) The factory also may have provided a haven from burdensome and sometimes bewildering responsibilities. The studied paternalism of company towns seems often to have been received as beneficence by operatives lacking sophistication as members of a wage-earning class. Company housing, for example, was usually better than the housing most of the workers had ever seen, and so were wages and medical, sanitation, and educational facilities. To be sure, employers believed, and asserted, that their generosity eliminated the causes of labor unrest. But this candor seems only to have enhanced the effectiveness of the beneficent posture. In 1900 America was a society in which one could dismiss reformers, socialists, and unionists as purveyors of a culture of discontent. One could still support the stewardship of the rich and cite the wonders of American industrial progress, without serious embarrassment or fear of derision. This would change soon after 1900, when the standard for judgment would shift from the comparative wretchedness of the past to the promise of American life.

The assumption of benevolence tended meanwhile to justify the most brazen tyranny. Unionism usually met with prompt repression and the brutal expulsion of "troublemakers." Many companies, such as United States Steel, had "secret service" divisions that carried on espionage among the workers in the factories, stores, saloons, and fraternal lodges. At election times, factory foremen and shop stewards directed voter recruitment activities. Although by 1900 most states supposedly guaranteed the secret ballot, one steelworker remarked to an investigator in 1908: "These men have been so long dominated by the Corporation that they dare not disobey. They have a sort of superstitious feeling that somehow the boss will know if they vote wrong." Even if the boss could not know how individuals voted, company threats to close the plant if the district voted wrong could often assure compliance.

These circumstances help explain why less than 4 percent of all nonagricultural workers were members of labor unions at the turn of the century. But there were technological, demographic, and ethnic reasons as well. Unions were strongest in industries that required skilled workers whose crafts gave them a basis for comradeship with their peers and bargaining leverage vis-à-vis their employers. Technological changes removed the need for many skills, thus decimating unions based on them. Even so, scarcely a fifth of skilled labor was unionized in 1900. The threat that machines would replace workers if they became too expensive or troublesome probably deterred unionization. So did the influx of immigrants, who provided employers with an alternative and sometimes more docile labor supply. So too did the rivalry of ethnic groups, upon whose mutual animosities employers successfully played to break strikes.

The weakness of unions meant that collective bargaining would have to wait two generations to gain legitimacy as a technique for allocating shares of the social surplus, but it did not mean an absence of labor conflicts. One might say that American industrial relations were typically governed by despotism mitigated by recurrent riot. Coeur d'Alene, Idaho; Ludlow, Silver Springs, and Cripple Creek, Colorado; McKees Rocks and Homestead, Pennsylvania; Lawrence, Massachusetts; and Paterson, New Jersey, are names, mostly of mining and factory towns, that have gained international renown as scenes of industrial warfare that took scores of lives from 1892 to 1914. The railroad brotherhoods, the United Mine Workers, and the American Federation of Labor generally failed to organize the masses of eastern and southern Europeans, who had begun to outnumber all other immigrants by a four-to-one margin after 1885. The newcomers, however, usually had ethnically oriented fraternal associations that in times of economic duress served effectively as labor organizations. The ethnic character of such organizations could be a source of both strength and weakness. On the one hand, it inspired an intense internal solidarity; on the other, members were vulnerable to external competition—"scabbing" —by workers belonging to rival ethnic groups.

Union membership increased briefly to a pre–World War I high of 7 percent of the nonagricultural work force around 1904. This change can probably be attributed to three things. First, prosperity after 1897 augmented the demand for steady labor, giving workers the money to pay union dues and stiffening their resistance to company truculence. Second, the National Civic Federation—a progressive organization arising in 1901 from efforts to reduce industrial strife—gave respectable and well-publicized encouragement to union organization; its chief officers were Mark Hanna, Republican national leader and industrialist, and Samuel Gompers, president of the AFL. Third, President Theodore Roosevelt encouraged the principle of collective organization of industrial resources in the interest of economic efficiency. He frequently spoke of the utility of unions for bringing order and discipline to the nation's work force and for providing a counterweight to the growth of corporate power.

The remarkable consolidation of industry after 1897 made its own contribution to organized labor, albeit indirectly. In many of the combinations, organizers inflated the capitalization of the resulting corporations. To realize on the added capital, investors and the bankers who had underwritten the mergers depended on several years of steady production, uninterrupted by work stoppages. Rising prices (partly a planned consequence of the mergers) encouraged accommodation to labor's demands in the expectation that higher costs could be passed along to consumers. For a time, the financiers who dominated many of the new corporations pursued a policy of amity, occasionally in the face of the old-line factory managers whose producer habits had made union-busting a virtual pastime.

The near-doubling of union ranks between 1900 and 1904 soon met with an effective counterattack. The National Association of Manufacturers (NAM), dominated by relatively small midwestern industrialists of an old-fashioned breed, found an elusive unity in a vigorous nationwide anti-union campaign. Union-busting in the name of individualism, the open shop, and the right to work gained a resurgent popularity after 1904, buttressed by Supreme Court decisions that found unions susceptible to prosecution for violation of the anti-trust laws, upheld local court injunctions against picketing, boycotts, and similar strike organizing activities, and made union leaders personally liable in some cases for damages to struck companies. Meanwhile, the Bankers' Panic of 1903 ended the boom in business mergers and weakened the resources and will of bankers to buy industrial peace with concessions to labor. Finally, the wave of immigration that brought 2.8 million newcomers to the United States between 1900 and 1904, and a total of 8.8 million by the end of the first decade of the twentieth century, helped undermine once more the bargaining leverage of union labor.

Immigrants arrive at Ellis Island, two of them clasping all-important entry papers in their teeth. (They probably disembarked first at Hoboken or Jersey City, where they received their papers. The ferry in the picture could not have made an Atlantic voyage.) Between 1903 and 1912, almost 900,000 Europeans each year were given health examinations and processed for admission to the country on the twenty-seven-acre, federally owned island in New York harbor. The massiveness of the migration to the United States offered impressive evidence of the nation's remarkable success.

Years of Confidence

Although much about American society at the turn of the century was sordid and depressing, what plainly impressed most contemporary observers and what historians have generally remarked on was the atmosphere of ebullience and expectation and hope. Partly it was the simple psychological effect of entering a new century, perhaps made all the greater because the country had recently emerged from a devastating depression. Prices rose sharply after 1897 — a sign of good business prospects, reflected in briskly rising employment. Although an unconscionable number of workers toiled for less than a dollar a day, despite higher prices a full and nutritious dinner could be prepared for twenty-five cents, wool sweaters could be bought for ten cents, and a pair of new top-quality shoes could be had for about three dollars.

Still more striking was the confidence that things would be getting better. A keen faith that science and the accelerating accumulation of knowledge would soon obliterate evil motivated thousands of young men and women to join reform clubs and associations, to do "social research," to bring order and efficiency to the institutions that seemed to be faltering under the burden of blindly coping with the complexities of modern times. Scientific and technological changes had perhaps disrupted whole communities, thrown into doubt whole systems of thought and value, and produced considerable suffering and waste; yet science and technology promised solutions even to the problems they had seemingly produced. If there was still hunger, new machinery and chemicals would soon increase agricultural productivity and new managerial methods would improve distribution to end privation in a future most commentators already claimed to see. If there was still ignorance, progressive educational techniques employed in the mass-oriented public schools would soon overcome it. If there was still disease — hookworm, tuberculosis, typhoid — medical science would soon find cures, as it already had for diphtheria and smallpox. If there was still crime, modern psychology, sociology, and criminology offered hope of rendering it to insignificant dimensions. If society contained too many members "unfit" to survive on their own, new inquiries into chromosomes and heredity suggested to some the means for an efficient and humane final solution.

A partial catalog of advances that contemporaries witnessed offers ready explanations for the era's ebullience. The period abounded in revolutionary scientific achievements. Only a few years before the turn of the century, in 1895, Wilhelm Konrad Roentgen had detected X-rays, and in 1898 fellow Europeans Pierre and Marie Curie had observed the phenomenon of radioactivity. In 1900, Max Planck inaugurated the study of quantum physics; five years later Albert Einstein introduced his Special Theory of Relativity; and during the course of the era, Ernest Rutherford made exciting progress toward demonstrating the feasibility of atomic fission. Few contemporaries understood these achievements, yet their implications about the destructibility of matter and the relativity of time slipped into the consciousness of a society already alert to the possibilities of fundamental change.

A young person in 1901 already had come to accept as commonplace marvels such as telegraphy, the telephone, celluloid film and the portable Kodak camera, the phonograph, and the electric railway. Electric lighting promised the early doom of gas illumination, itself only a recent phenomenon. Other wonders had appeared whose potentials were not yet widely appreciated. Charles Duryea had built the first operable American automobile in 1892; Thomas Edison had introduced his "vitascope" movie projector in 1895; and a number of individuals believed they had the mastery of air transportation within their grasp. These efforts as yet seemed frivolous or chimerical. Few people discerned the profound effect they would have on the physical and social environment within the next twenty years. A spirit of high expectancy nevertheless pervaded the country, making it hard to think that anything was impossible. Invention had become a part of the American way of life. Edison had even made it a commercial enterprise—surely not his least contribution to modern change.

Thomas Alva Edison, fifty-four years old in 1901, stood as the paragon of American inventive ingenuity. More than that, he was the myth incarnate of the old-fashioned, self-made, practical man. No invention was worthwhile, he repeatedly asserted, unless it had commercial possibilities. Although that did not entirely describe his own motivations, it expressed the kind of hardheadedness that Americans seemed to prize. The seventh and last child of a Canadian insurrectionist who had fled Ontario in 1837, young Alva had grown up in the small, declining town of Milan, Ohio, where he had experienced poverty and isolation but where the wonderment of science and modern machinery had seemed much the bigger for it all. When he was twenty-two, he quit employment as a telegrapher and entered business to produce "inventions to order." In 1876 at Menlo Park, New Jersey, he established the world's first industrial research laboratory. Although several Americans in the nineteenth century could claim credit for more than one major achievement (notably George Westinghouse, who followed his invention of the air brake with pioneering work in alternating current and electric generators), one has to remark even today on the extraordinary number of products that Edison originated or helped inspire, from gummed envelopes to the discovery of electronic phenomena and the subsequent development of radio. Perfection of the telephone owed much to Edison's improvements in voice transmission, and in 1894 he began marketing an electric automobile that remained in manufacture for twenty years.

Of all his inventions, the motion picture camera and projector probably had the greatest social consequences. Although in 1901 it

Thomas Edison, the poet and naturalist John Burroughs, Henry Ford, and Harvey Firestone, whose Tire & Rubber Company supplied the Ford Motor Company, pose by an ancient mill during an automobile excursion through New England in the summer of 1918. "We will get away from fictitious civilization," Edison wrote to Burroughs when planning the first such expedition in 1914. Remarkably, Edison and especially the sentimental Ford personally experienced a painful nostalgia for rustic, pre-industrial life that their own work so effectively obliterated. They thus expressed the nation's deep-lying ambivalence about the "progress" it had witnessed during the progressive era.

Courtesy of the Ford Archives, Dearborn, Michigan

scarcely seemed credible, movies would profoundly influence twentieth-century life not only as entertainment but as a means of communication and as an art form. At first, motion pictures were shown in a nickelodeon, where for five cents one could find usually puerile and sometimes prurient titillation. Not until 1903 and *The Great Train Robbery* did audiences see a film with a reasonably serious, coherent plot. By 1910, traveling movie shows, known as "black tops" because the tents had darkened interiors to keep out light, were common features of the rural scene. The film as an art form owes much to D. W. Griffith, who in 1907 began working with techniques such as the close-up, the fade-out and dissolve, and the flashback. From Europe came the first full-length picture in 1912, a four-reel presentation of Queen Elizabeth's life produced by Adolph Zukor, with Sarah Bernhardt in the lead. Zukor thereby simultaneously launched the feature film and the star system. But it was

Ku Klux Klansmen ride to the rescue of Southern white womanhood in *Birth of a Nation,* D. W. Griffiths' 1915 motion picture epic, which grossed $18 million on its first tour. Based on Thomas Dixon's novel *The Clansmen* (1905), the film expressed the by-then popular revisionist view of the Civil War and Reconstruction, namely, that it was all a great mistake. "My only regret," said President Wilson after a private preview showing, "is that it is all so terribly true"; and Supreme Court Chief Justice Edward White confided to Dixon: "I was a member of the Klan, sir. . . . You've told the true story . . . of outraged manhood."

Culver Pictures

Griffith who summoned in the modern movie era with two extrava-
ganzas, *Birth of a Nation* in 1915 and *Intolerance* in 1916. By then the
industry was well on its way toward inspiring startling changes in
Americans' life styles and expectations.

Not Edison but a twenty-seven-year-old Italian gave the world
its most exciting scientific event in 1901. Nothing could have
dramatized technological potentialities so well as Guglielmo
Marconi's demonstration of transatlantic wireless telegraphy. The
feat linked the unimaginable, fantastic world of electrons and elec-
tromagnetic waves with the pragmatically comprehensible. The
young Bolognese, working with British capital, had already put his
invention to practical use in 1898 to report daily to Queen Victoria on
the health of her son, the Prince of Wales, who was recovering from
a knee ailment on his yacht, and to give a minute-by-minute account
of the Kingstown Regatta to the Dublin *Daily Express*. Eight years
later, on Christmas Day in 1906, Nebraska-born Lee De Forest,
working from somewhat different principles, broadcast voice for
the first time. In the following year, De Forest provided twenty-six
sets of equipment to the United States navy for use when President
Roosevelt sent the Great White Fleet on its journey around the world,
and in January 1910, the airwaves carried the first complete opera
performances—the Metropolitan's double bill, *Cavalleria Rusticana*
and *I Pagliacci*, featuring the great Enrico Caruso.

The commercial and military potential of the wireless made an
immediate impression, but it was not so with flying machines. When
Wilbur and Orville Wright "conquered the air" in December 1903
at Kitty Hawk, North Carolina, with the first successful heavier-
than-air, self-propelled flight, the achievement earned scant notice.
Only the Norfolk *Virginian-Pilot* gave it front-page coverage; the
prestigious New York *Tribune* buried it in the sports section. Even
five years later, most aviation experts believed that at best the airplane would provide entertainment for sporting racers or a means for
adventurers to explore inaccessible regions. Then the military took
an interest, and air transportation gained a sure though slowly developed future.

One may attribute the small interest in aviation, as Walter Lord
has, to Americans' preoccupation with the automobile. Earlier in
1903, E. T. Fetch and M. C. Krarup's continental crossing from San
Francisco to New York in fifty-two days won headlines and acclaim.
There were already a dozen or more different kinds of vehicles on the
market, including the Edison Electric, the Stanley Steamer, and the

December 17, 1903, was cold, gray, and windy on Kitty Hawk beach, North Carolina. At 10:25 A.M., thirty-two-year-old Orville Wright—dressed as usual in a dark business suit, starched white collar, and tie, although he lay prone between the two wings of the kite-like contraption—lifted off in his airplane from a wooden track made of two-by-fours, and flew 100 feet across the sands. Orville and his thirty-six-year-old brother Wilbur flew their machine four times that day. The last time, with Wilbur at the controls, it stayed in the air almost a full minute. It was not until 1908, however, that the Wright brothers' achievement became widely known. "I have come to the conclusion," Orville wrote in 1925, "that almost no one ever really believed [it] who had not actually seen [one of our flights]. It amuses me that practically everyone now thinks he has always believed in its possibility."

Packard that Fetch and Krarup drove. "The horse is doomed," Edison had declared in 1895. Others maintained that the automobile would never be more than a conspicuous prestige commodity ("Oats are too cheap," Duryea had said), but in the next fifteen years it was on its way toward making "horse-and-buggy" synonymous with "old-fashioned" and "backward."

Henry Ford was the man most responsible for that. Born on a farm near Dearborn, Michigan, in 1863, Ford fled the drudgery of farm life at the age of sixteen to work as a mechanic in Detroit, eventually with the Edison Illuminating Company. In his free time he assembled his first automobile in 1894, and by 1901 he was recognized as something of a pioneer in the automobile industry, having constructed three serviceable cars. By then the principle of assembling had already been established by Ransom Olds, while Henry Leland, who originated the Cadillac and later the Lincoln, had perfected the use of standard, interchangeable parts. Ford exploited these techniques in building the Model-T in 1909. Within five years, more than a half-million of the small, simple, inexpensive, easily repaired machines were rolling on the roads. In 1914, Ford introduced the moving assembly line in his new Highland Park factory, and in the public's mind the name Ford came to represent modern, mass-production efficiency. Ford's introduction of the five-dollar-a-day wage in 1915—which he claimed would make it possible for his workers to buy the product they manufactured, thereby expanding the market for his automobiles—enhanced his popularity. The gesture, moreover, marked the degree to which industry in the twentieth century would depend on consumer goods, rather than on capital goods as in the nineteenth century.

The social consequences of the automobile were as great as those of the railroad three-quarters of a century earlier. Not only did the motor vehicle provide the means for privacy and mobility previously unavailable to most people, it gave an enormous fillip to economic growth just as the stimulus of the railroad industry had begun to fade. The steel, rubber, and petroleum industries enjoyed the most direct impact, and road and bridge construction, machine tools, some plastics, and chemicals were not far behind. The demand for gasoline stations and auto repair shops offered new opportunities to small enterprise, as did the need for quick-order restaurants to serve the growing mobs of tourists and joyriders.

The airplane, radio, motion picture, and automobile all depended on two sources of energy that were novelties at the turn of the century—the electric generator and the internal-combustion engine. During the course of the progressive era, each provided millions of people who would never know riches with a remarkable array of conveniences that quickly became necessities as defined by new standards of living comfort. Two inventions by Croatian immigrant Nikola Tesla—the alternating current motor and the principle of the rotary magnetic field, which made possible long-distance power transmission—ensured the future of electricity. The development of the steam-turbine electric generator after 1896 by George Westinghouse and others made feasible low-cost electric power for house-

Taking the Model-T for weekend and holiday excursions along the fast-improving country roads became a popular pastime, though sometimes punctuated by exasperating, back-wrenching efforts to restart a stalled flivver with a hand crank. The electric self-starter had been introduced in 1912, but when this photograph was taken around 1915 they were not yet commonly included as "standard equipment."

hold consumption. Almost half of the nonfarm residences in the country had electricity by 1920, and dynamos powered more than 30 percent of the industrial machinery in the country, compared with less than 2 percent in 1900. The raising of telephone lines across the continent made possible instantaneous communication with remote village communities and helped reduce the isolation of the nation's farms. There were 1.4 million telephones in the country in 1900 and ten times that many by 1920. The gasoline-driven tractor was unknown in 1900; farmers were using almost 3 million twenty years later.

Business innovations played a role at least as important in sustaining contemporary optimism as did technological advances. For three decades American merchants and industrialists had been experimenting with new forms of business organization in order to take advantage of mass-market opportunities afforded by the completion of the national railroad network, population growth, and the increasing concentration of consumers in metropolitan areas. The dimensions of the market made large earnings possible on small profit margins, but they also required unprecedented levels of capital investment and the centralized administration of widely dispersed units of enterprise. Advantage lay with the companies that gained an edge in efficiency or productivity, because entry into the mass market depended most of all on the ability to offer goods or services at the lowest price. The downward curve of prices from 1873 to 1897 indicates the rigor of the competitive struggle. Both the quest for cost savings and the need to protect investments by safeguarding supplies and market outlets led to the integration into single corporate units of diverse stages of the industrial process such as resource procurement, manufacturing, processing or fabricating, and distribution. The old-style family firm, which had typified merchant and manufacturing enterprises through the first three-quarters of the nineteenth century, proved unable to meet the extended managerial and capital requirements. By the turn of the century, the large, publicly held business corporation enjoyed unusual popularity, not only among businessmen but among advanced thinkers in the community at large. Its most evident virtue was its ability to provide the administrative and financial flexibility necessary to govern the vast operations of businesses servicing nationwide and international markets. New-style corporate management seemed to promise the efficient employment of economic resources to reduce deprivation and concomitant social discontent.

The ascendancy of the modern corporation did not take place without a number of innovations in law and public policy. One was implicit in a series of court decisions that (a) redefined "property" to include not merely the land or tangible objects that a person might possess but what a person might expect to earn by commercial use of what he possessed, and (b) gave to corporations legal standing as "persons," thereby qualifying them for the privileges, protections, and immunities guaranteed by the Constitution under the Fifth and Fourteenth Amendments. These changes gave corporations security against attempts to restrain business activities in the interest of competing claims of social policy. A rewriting of state incorporation laws, beginning in New Jersey in 1889, meanwhile enabled corporations to possess other corporations, a privilege that the courts usually had denied. Businesses could merge their interests through holding companies without necessarily violating anti-trust laws. Because large, long-range capital commitments suggested the need to stabilize earnings, and because the anti-trust laws forbade rival companies to fix prices or set market quotas toward that end, mergers of competing companies became the popular alternative.

The great consolidation movement that climaxed in the period from 1897 to 1903 took place in large measure through the auspices of John Pierpont Morgan. Morgan's dominance had three basic sources: The British-born son of Junius Spencer Morgan, a British banker, had unusually good European banking connections, giving him access to sources of money unavailable to most other American investment houses. He had an aggressive interest in business consolidation, manifested in his mostly successful reorganization of the southern railroad system during the 1890's. The fact that President Grover Cleveland had sought Morgan's direct assistance in saving United States gold supplies during the financial crisis of the 1890's gave Morgan a special glamor in financial circles and contributed to the almost unique trust he enjoyed among leading industrialists seeking salvation from "destructive competition." General Electric, United States Steel, and International Harvester were among the giants organized with Morgan as broker.

Aided by permissive changes in state incorporation laws, Morgan and other securities underwriters invented new forms of corporate stocks to lure public savings into capital enterprises. Most attractive were preferred stocks, which were securities more in the nature of debentures than of equity shares. Preferred stock represented a claim against a company's anticipated earnings rather than against its tangible assets. Like a bond it carried no voting rights, thereby assuring company owners against their loss of control, but unlike a bond it did not count as debt and therefore evaded debt restrictions often prescribed by corporate charters or state laws. Because it usually offered a minimum percentage return on the face value and had claim to assets immediately after bonds in case of bankruptcy, preferred stock gave the appearance of removing much of the risk conventionally associated with industrial investments and thus attracted traditionally conservative capital. Through this and other promotional devices, investment bankers began introducing a broader sector of the society to securities trading and direct capital investment. Modern speculative trading in industrial securities, which would reach scandalous dimensions in the 1920's, may properly be dated from 1901, when Wall Street publications first began listing quotations on publicly sold "industrials."

For some, the corporate reorganization of American business enterprise was the most significant development of the previous century. "I weigh my words," averred Columbia University President Nicholas Murray Butler, "when I say that in my judgment the . . . [business] corporation is the greatest single discovery of modern times. . . . Even steam and electricity are far less important . . . and they would be reduced to comparative impotence without it." This was hyperbole by any standard. But there was little doubt that without the corporation, expeditious recruitment of capital and efficient allocation of resources for the production and distribution of goods and services would have been long delayed. Moreover, many progressive observers saw in the management techniques developed by the corporate giants for the administration of their far-flung, sometimes international, empires a promise of a vast new integration of the nation's political and economic energies. "Concentration," "consolidation," and "control" came to be the bywords of anticipated social efficiency.

This is to stress some of the gains. But there were also costs. The publicly held corporation undermined the principle of private, proprietary business enterprise on which the country had once staked its political institutions and justified the permissiveness of its laws governing business behavior. "It is the difference," said Andrew Carnegie in 1896, "between individualism and communism applied to business, between the owners managing their own business . . . and a joint stock concern of a thousand shifting owners ignorant of the business." American social theorists had usually assumed that proprietary business enterprise was the principal institution on which individual character and self-reliance could be built and on which, in turn, the practice of self-government depended. But the large publicly held corporation threatened to both preempt opportunities for individuals to engage in business and doom the nation's young to a dividend-collecting or a salaried rather than an entrepreneurial future.

In addition, corporate ownership tended to institutionalize callousness and unscrupulousness in business. Corporate managers could and did excuse brutal price and labor policies with the argument that their obligations were to "the corporation" and that they had no authority to interpose their personal ethics or social policies. Indeed, the courts insisted that a corporation's management could not sacrifice potential dividends in the interest of some putative public good. In a stockholder suit in 1919, for example, the Michigan Supreme Court decided that Henry Ford could not set wages or prices to benefit workers or to help redistribute the gains produced by technological advance; management's prime obligation, the court declared, was to make the largest profits for the benefit of stockholders.

Corporate giantism, the product of the very facility for recruiting capital that counted as one of the corporation's virtues, by 1900 presented a direct threat to the continued viability of the nation's political processes. It had become a commonplace that a single corporation might have greater assets and might directly control the lives of more citizens than the city and county governments under which it operated. But by the turn of the century many corporations were richer than whole states and than many European countries as well. Directly and indirectly, such power inevitably corrupted electoral and legislative processes. Any countervailing force had to emanate from coalitions, which could only be ad hoc and ephemeral, offering little relief from the prevailing power of a few corporation directors.

Thus corporate consolidation at the turn of the century appeared on the one hand to herald a new, progressive order and on the other to pose a triple threat to the nation's major institutions. No issue was more central to the politics of reform then spreading out from the cities and states onto the national scene than the effect of corporate consolidation on American life. Progressivism, the chief reform movement of the new century, had many aspects, but its political form consisted largely of the attempt to reconcile the country's resurging commitment to principles of human dignity, individual liberty, and democratic self-government with Americans' still vigorous commitment to economic objectives, for which the corporation offered such promise of fulfillment.

Progressive Stirrings

It was an exciting time in which to be alive. Every generation of Americans has had to adjust to profound changes. But the basic character of the innovations with which Americans would have to cope in the new century set the progressive era apart. For all the disorder that attended the nation's transformation in the nineteenth century, as Henry Steele Commager has noted in *The American Mind* (1950), the process of adjustment "took place within an economic and social framework that was reasonably stable and a political and moral framework that was almost entirely so. . . . The institutions of property, family, school, church, and state, although subjected to continuous buffetings were never seriously challenged." By the end of the century, "the rhythm of change became impetuous and erratic." It had reverberations in the nation's most important philosophical premises. For the first time the confidence that had been characteristic of the American spirit would appear threatened. Americans were not unaccustomed to a transmuted environment; but, writes Commager, "they were unprepared for the crumbling of their cosmic scheme."

That scheme owed its design mainly to the country's Protestant heritage. It continued to give comfort to those driven upon the winds of change, though some also found inspiration in it to exert themselves against social iniquity. Mostly, however, the philosophical premises on which the nation grew worked to impede effective responses to new conditions and to frustrate the new awareness which science brought forth. The scheme would ultimately give way, and none so assuring would ever replace it.

Nineteenth-century American Protestantism prescribed rigorous tests for an individual's worth. The old-time religion required hard work and even suffering as part of the discipline a man needed for the cultivation of good character and the moral virtues essential for salvation. If a man failed to overcome suffering, more likely than not it signified his unworthiness. Moreover, to attempt to use the state to assist those who suffered went counter to "God's way." Said one typical church leader:

> The staple which Providence has to deal with in the races of men is ignorance and indolence interstratified with sin—stupidity made heavy, solid, opaque, and gritty with a wicked will. . . . Unpitying poverty, absolute and severe want, must be allowed to force action, to sharpen instincts, to strengthen the will. . . . The loitering, unambitious poor still reserve for themselves the lash of necessity. [They] are checked in increase . . . by hardship and disease, and left under the severe hand of physical law [from which they suffer] according to the dulness [*sic*] and sin that is in them.

By the late nineteenth century, Darwinian theory could have offered a radical alternative to the moral absolutes of the Calvinist heritage. Certainly religious leaders protested often enough that it did. If at the Creation nothing had appeared in its final form, one could reasonably assume that the "truths" gleaned from ancient religious doctrines might have questionable relevance for the more finely evolved human species. Yet to the absolutistic mind of the nineteenth century, Darwinism merely suggested its own absolutes — the determinism of the "laws of Nature." The tests of virtue prescribed by the Calvinist God became indistinguishable from the tests of fitness imposed by Nature. Guardians of the new scientific intelligence warned away all interference with the evolutionary process by man's will and sympathy. Only gradually would the notion that environment determines behavior as well as genetic traits capture the imagination of a society increasingly impressed by its ability to overcome Nature, or at least to use the intelligence Nature had provided in order to shape the environment. The experience of the 1890's, which featured a severe economic depression, massive distress, and extensive social violence far beyond what anyone could reasonably attribute to "the loitering unambitious poor," contributed substantially to convincing many Americans that they might improve social behavior by improving the conditions in which people lived. After 1900 Darwinism would suggest not so much the benign fatalism of long-term evolutionary progress, but rather the exhilarating possibilities of social engineering, with the state providing the chief resources and sanctions. The progressive era dawned at the awakening to such possibilities.

It would be too much to say that the new century witnessed a distinct realignment of priorities. The force of inertia was too great. Throughout the nineteenth century most Americans had assumed that economic growth was the key to maintaining republican institutions, reasonably equal life chances, and optimal conditions for liberty. Nothing was permitted to retard growth, for it was presumed to control all else. Most people seemed to agree that one had to trade off equality for growth. Without the rich, there could be no savings, capital formation, or investment. (Some would add, without the poor, there would be no one to work for low wages to make production cheap enough to service expanding consumer markets.)

Nevertheless the last quarter of the nineteenth century witnessed a stiffening resistance to the unspoken policy of granting all the priorities to economic growth. The dimensions of suffering that had become evident late in the century had convinced many that, whatever their faith in the ultimate harmony of the universe, there was a poor correlation between sin and failure, or for that matter between virtue and success. Indeed, many seemed inclined to believe that poverty caused sin rather than that sin underlay poverty. The "deserving poor" appeared as too large a proportion of the society to be discounted as the accidents of an otherwise perfectly functioning social system. Thus the cause of human welfare would make some small but palpable gains.

The rise of Social Christianity (usually called the Social Gospel movement after 1900), the founding of settlement houses, the proliferation of civic and social reform associations, the development of progressive education, the dramatic emergence of modern feminism, the growing impetus of the temperance movement, all were indications of a rising sensitivity to the cause of welfare and social justice. Each movement pressed the demand that the prerogatives of private property yield to minimum standards of quality, public safety, commercial ethics, and living and working conditions. The progressive movement drew its force and essence from these thrusts. All had begun by the 1890's and were intimately connected both in spirit and in personnel. Stirred by a nagging sense of Christian responsibility, thousands of young men and women launched into strenuous campaigns to make "the moral law," as Jane Addams put it, something other than "a far-off abstraction utterly separated from [one's] active life."

Troubled because their churches were becoming middle- and upper-class institutions, a few Protestant ministers began a struggle to make the church "relevant" once again to the millions of American workers for whom religion in general and Protestantism in particular had come to represent little more than "pie in the sky when you die." "Religion, to have power over an age," wrote Walter Rauschenbusch, "must satisfy the highest moral and religious desire of that age." Protestantism had failed to respond to the growing consciousness that the evils manifest in the world had a social origin and were not merely evidence of the failings of individuals. "The chief purpose of the Christian Church in the past," said Rauschenbusch, "has been the salvation of individuals. But the most pressing task of the present is not individualistic. Our business is to make over an antiquated and immoral economic system; . . . to create just and brotherly relations between great groups and classes of society; and thus to lay a social foundation on which modern men individually can live and work in a fashion that will not outrage all the better elements in them."

Rauschenbusch was in a minority, even among the Social Christians, in locating the source of social evil in the capitalist system. But they all shared the sense that the nation's priorities needed readjustment and that the poor and wage-earning classes deserved the state's special attention even though it might cost "industry" some profits. Actually, most of the Social Christianity movement had no more ambitious an objective than eliminating the overt signs of a sinful society—conventional signs such as gambling, hard drinking, prostitution, and the petty corruption of daily life, rather than the consequences of economic and social oppression. But as in so many reform movements, causes that began with limited goals activated reformers who inevitably discovered new evils and demanded more reforms. The Social Gospel turned the attention of the nation's religious institutions away from a conveniently complacent preoccupation with individual salvation and toward a renewed concern for the social content of Christianity. In the progressives' quest for social justice, it was an indispensable achievement. The organization in 1908 of the Federal Council of Churches marked the maturation of the movement "to secure larger combined influence for the churches of Christ in all matters affecting the moral and social condition of the people, so as to promote the application of the law of Christ in every relation to human life."

The message of the Social Christians was intended not only for the rehabilitation of the poor but for the uplifting of their benefactors as well. Good works would help prepare the soul for grace. Beginning in the late 1880's, many young, religiously motivated, middle-class Americans—directly inspired by Toynbee Hall in London—began settling themselves in large old houses located in run-down sections of big cities. "The subjective necessity for Social Settlements," wrote Jane Addams of Hull House, "is . . . identical with that necessity which urges us on toward social and individual salvation." Objectively, their purpose was to establish personal liaison with the foreign-born and wage-earning classes and to shape the neighborhood into the unit of social cohesion that the big city seemed so distinctly to lack. The settlement houses thus developed as colonies of middle-class virtue amid the poor to serve as leavening for the alien and unlucky; they simultaneously gave justification and an education to the missionaries and social workers who gathered there. Their participants sought "the joy of finding the Christ which lieth in each man, but which no man can unfold save in fellowship."

The first settlement was founded in New York by Stanton Coit in 1886, in collaboration with Felix Adler and the Ethical Culture Society. Within ten years there were seventy-four, by 1905 over two hundred, and by 1910 more than four hundred. Chicago's Hull House, founded by Ellen Gates Starr and Jane Addams in 1889, was the most vigorous, inventive, and influential, though Lillian Wald's

Jane Addams, here sitting on the terrace steps of Hull House in 1932, spent over half a century in a career devoted to the poor and the disadvantaged. The settlement houses bred a small army of social reformers who became prominent in business and government in the twentieth century, but they never succeeded in getting the government to take on the responsibilities needed to solve the social problems that the settlement workers confronted.

Henry Street Settlement in New York and Robert Woods' South End House in Boston earned comparable renown. In addition, dozens of settlements took root in conjunction with universities. One can infer the remarkable spontaneity of the movement from the fact that many of the original settlement workers were initially unaware of their counterparts in other places.

A quick glance at the movement might suggest the limits of its influence. Although western and southern cities, such as San Francisco and New Orleans, had some settlements, most were located in relatively few northeastern cities, especially New York, Boston, and Chicago. The background of settlement residents was scarcely more representative of the nation, and still less of the neighborhoods they sought to uplift. The workers were predominantly of old American ancestry, with college degrees and of Protestant persuasions; and at least until 1905, they had only partly secularized evangelical motivations. Moreover, they were overwhelmingly young (under thirty), female, unmarried, and with little staying power (in the mean, under three years).

Yet even discounting these seeming handicaps, the settlement movement had an enormous impact. The biographies of the non-political leaders of reform during the progressive era, and in the New Deal as well, reveal the extraordinary number who had spent at least one year with a settlement, usually early in his or her career. At settlement houses most of them gained their first close understanding of what it was like to live as the working classes did in the modern, industrial city. The shock of that exposure evoked from this extraordinary, articulate group of individuals a torrent of social tracts. Before S. S. McClure, Ida Tarbell, and Lincoln Steffens entered the business of journalistic exposés (on which Theodore Roosevelt later bestowed the "muckraking" moniker), the settlements had already begun to inspire investigations into nearly every element of urban life—not only housing and working conditions but the psychology of child development, juvenile delinquency, penal procedures, pauperism and poverty, the demoralization of the foreign-born, the generational gap between the foreign-born and their children, the exploitation of women, the archaic quality of public school education, family planning, the special travail of urban blacks. Although scores of urban and industrial reform organizations arose independently, the settlements and the social experts they produced usually provided the data needed for effective action. And indeed the power of that expertise and the agitation it aroused proved great enough to move even the typically obtuse legislators of the era to revise police practices, housing codes, schools, court procedures, prison conditions, mine and factory regulations, and labor laws.

Much of what the social workers did had a nostalgic quality. They tried to train workers in traditional crafts, in an age that had made the artisan superfluous. There was much pure romanticism in the "cultural" programs they often inflicted upon their clientele. Moreover, at least initially they sought to accomplish their objectives by voluntaristic means, especially by fostering a community spirit of brotherhood and classlessness to be channeled in neighborhood guilds. They eventually sought political help and even challenged the political institutions they discovered rotted with corruption or clogged by vested interests, but basically they relied on a kind of community-wide spiritual renascence.

In at least three respects, however, the settlement workers pointed the way out of the nineteenth century and toward a twentieth-century appreciation of social problems. In the first place, in their efforts to rehabilitate the often demoralized immigrants they encountered, many settlement workers—especially at Hull House—learned to appreciate the value of the immigrants' ethnic heritage. From their experience, John Dewey, who had worked with Hull House residents, developed the idea of cultural pluralism—the coexistence of diverse groups cherishing divergent value systems and ethnic preferences—not merely as a viable social arrangement but as embodying the most important qualities of a democratic society.

Second, in an era thoroughly convinced of Negroes' inherent racial inferiority, the settlement workers counted among the very few whites who attempted to place the special plight of black people in the public forum. The overwhelming force of contemporary racial assumptions affected the settlements as it did everything else in the progressive era; so that one should not be astonished that insofar as the settlements worked with Negroes at all, they usually did so in segregated facilities. ("Our settlement," averred a spokesman in 1910 for a segregated house in Philadelphia, "has its unique problem for it deals not with a race that is intellectually hungry, but with a race at the sensation stage of its evolution and the treatment demanded is different.") But it was three settlement workers—Mary White Ovington (whose study *Half a Man: The Status of the Negro in New York*, 1911, yields only to W. E. B. DuBois's *The Philadelphia Negro*, 1897, as the best contemporary investigation of urban black people), William English Walling, and Henry Moskowitz—who initiated the organization of the National Association for the Advancement of Colored People (NAACP) in 1909. It would take a tremendous effort merely to correct the misinformation embodied in the prevailing Darwinist theories about "race evolution," to say nothing about overcoming the baser sorts of racial prejudices, before the abysmal racism that stood in the way of social progress could even begin to abate. The research done by settlement workers, especially their emphasis on the role of environment in shaping personality (or "character"), gave crucial impetus to such change.

Finally, the settlement workers were among the few who chose their model of the livable city not from nostalgic rural ideals but from their vision of what city life had to offer civilization. "The reason the poor like to live in New York," Mary Simkhovitch told a national conference in 1909, "is because it is interesting, convenient, and meets their social needs. They live there for the reason that I do; I like it." It is no wonder that of all the leaders of progressive reform who stayed active through Franklin Roosevelt's New Deal, the urban social workers almost alone remained uniformly enthusiastic about reform. Unlike so many other progressives who were motivated by nostalgia for rural life, by their apprehension of dangers to preferred but already doomed cultural qualities, and by their sense of loss, the urban workers faced up to problems that would remain central to the nation's adjustment to the twentieth century.

The prohibitionists best illustrate the defensive and nostalgic qualities of reform in the era. The prohibition movement must not be identified with progressivism, though the two reform thrusts overlapped significantly. Both sought the moral regeneration of society through the uplifting of individuals, and both were prepared to use the state to enforce moral law. The prohibitionists, however, were more certain than typical progressive reformers about what the moral law was. Both began by assuming nationwide consensus on the primary features of that law, generally identifying it with Protestant values. But whereas the progressives lapsed into confusion — and some even altered their objectives — when they discovered that the consensus did not exist, the prohibitionists merely redoubled their determination to enforce their version of moral truth.

The identification of anti-liquor activism with militant Protestant churches — acting through organizations like the Women's Christian Temperance Union (WCTU), founded in 1874, and the Anti-Saloon League, founded in 1893 — helps explain this zealousness. The temperance movement began essentially as an effort to induce wayward individuals to adapt themselves to the dominant American mode. By the end of the nineteenth century, however, it had become clear that the "wayward" would not necessarily accept their designation as objects of reform. They came to be viewed as stubborn proponents of competing cultures, which those who were strenuously affirmative about their own values could scarcely tolerate. Circumstances demanded that the state repress the aberrants.

There was a curiously radical ingredient in this conservative objective. Voting and ethnic statistics show a high correlation not only between anti-liquor militancy and native rural Protestantism but between such zeal and political (especially agrarian) insurgency throughout the 1875–1915 period. The early leadership of the WCTU, which functioned as a major component of the feminist movement, further illustrates the coincidence of insurgent pressures with the retrospective, defensive character of the temperance movement. (The coincidence in this case may say something about the conservatism of the women's movement at the time.) Temperance also found an ally in modern science, which indicated that serious medical ailments result from heavy drinking. "Scientific" surveys showing a sensational increase in the consumption of alcohol (especially beer) from 1900 to 1915 helped persuade an increasing number of Americans, fearful as they were of the social transformations they were witnessing, that prohibition was the only practical if not moral way to preserve national stability.

There was of course a difference between "blue laws" designed to enforce temperance and total prohibition. It was one thing to point out that intemperance ruined human beings and threatened social order; it was another to argue that drink itself was unsavory and ought to be forbidden by any society purporting to be moral. The Prohibition Party for more than half a century had implicitly included in its definition of The Good Society an abstaining citizenry. But not until 1900 did the WCTU convert to prohibition; the Anti-Saloon League did so in 1907.

As of 1900, only five, decidedly rural, states had prohibited the sale and manufacture of intoxicating beverages. Altogether 18 million people, or about 23 percent of the population, lived in "dry" wards, towns, counties, or states. In six years the percentage almost doubled. By the end of 1918, on the eve of national prohibition, more than 75 percent of the American people were not able to buy alcoholic drinks in their own communities. Not nearly that percentage can be said to have favored prohibition, for state legislatures and county governments notoriously overrepresented rural districts and in 1918 perhaps as many as 2 million adult males were essentially disfranchised by Selective Service and the American Expeditionary Force. The imposition of prohibition on unwilling cities and industrial counties would lead to law enforcement nightmares in the 1920's. But meanwhile the tensions of the age rose to proportions approaching hysteria, causing usually judicious individuals to identify teetotalism with patriotism and imbibers with the forces of sedition.

The movement acquired such momentum that by 1917 "the noble experiment" of prohibition converted men like Supreme Court Justice Louis D. Brandeis, an outstanding civil libertarian, and former President William Howard Taft, who in 1913 had vetoed Congress' act to prohibit the transportation of liquor into dry states for private use. (Congress overrode the veto.) The sense of crisis goaded even the nonpartisan leadership to accept the popular placebo, and the politicians, like easy-living and hard-drinking Warren G. Harding, fell over themselves in their rush to get aboard the dry bandwagon. ("There is only one side to the moral, economic, political, or patriot phase of the question," said Harding's political manager in 1917, anticipating a little of his protégé's happy verbal ineptitude.)

In sum, the mounting power of the anti-liquor movement seems to have reflected the anxieties aroused by the failure of government to restore a social equilibrium favorable to those groups that had experienced the erosion of certain accustomed advantages. The early successes of modern prohibitionism corresponded closely with the decline of the Populists' effort; the culminating successes would coincide with the failure of progressivism to offer significant solutions to domestic problems or to avoid the compounded apprehensions brought on by World War I. Edgar Lee Masters captured this point in a few acerbic lines of his *Spoon River Anthology* (1916):

> Do you remember when I fought
>   The bank and the courthouse ring . . .
> And when I fought the water works . . .
>   And when I fought the business men . . .?
> Then do you remember
>   That staggering up from the wreck of defeat . . .
> I slipped from my cloak my last ideal . . .
>   And smote the bank and the water works,
> And the business men with prohibition
>   And made Spoon River pay the cost
> Of the fights that I had lost?

Social Revolution

The progressive period was one of those eras that seem to occur about every half-century in modern times in which personal values, life styles, and the collective sense of social purpose undergo major challenges and in which the accepted premises of conventional thought and action confront insistent questioning. The traumas of industrialization, city growth, ethnic challenge, and World War I were disturbing enough to anyone who longed for the return of a social mix favorable to traditional values, but there were equally disconcerting "internal" changes—changes in attitude and out-look—that depended as much on the momentum of intellectual inquiry and discovery as on the structural developments of the age. Although most traditional institutions and values would survive, seemingly none was spared the challenge—not the political system, the profit motive, religion, the family, marriage, sexual mores, education, even the concept of childhood.

After more than a half-century of slow growth, the feminist movement—the somewhat ambiguous rubric given to women's demands for equal opportunities as citizens, as jobholders, and as intelligent and passionate human beings—began to take on imposing form. The suffrage campaign formed the principal salient, but it screened many more consequential changes. Indeed, the identification of voting rights with "equality" seems to have diverted reforming energies and to have exhausted the imagination of those who had led the struggle up to that time. Beyond politics were signs of a liberation far more significant. The advent of comfortable clothes, the elimination of cumbersome petticoats, the recession of skirt hems from the ankle almost halfway to the knee, the growing popularity of bobbed hair, all beginning before 1910, indicated women's determination to participate actively in life without the symbolic and physical encumbrances imposed by the Victorian China-doll ideal of femininity. Women were entering prestigious professions in small but telling numbers, and by 1910 nearly half of the college degrees in the country were being awarded to women. (However, less than 3 percent of all adults completed college, and a college education was still widely viewed as a hindrance to a successful business career.) Meanwhile, "solid" middle-class and upper-class women—even such as Alice Roosevelt Longworth, Theodore Roosevelt's daughter—had begun scandalizing traditionalists by smoking cigarettes in public and by discussing birth control, venereal diseases, and the sexual act in their social clubs and in public forums.

Psychological and cultural encumbrances were not so readily shaken. It is likely that at least nine of every ten Americans born in 1900, male or female, were taught that sexual intercourse was at best a necessity sanctioned only by matrimony exclusively for the pro-

The growth of modern, corporate business offered new kinds of occupations for women. Like Theodore Dreiser's heroine in *Sister Carrie* (1900), thousands of young women left the farms and small towns for employment in the big cities (though probably not many experienced lives as eventful as Carrie's). Very few gained such attractive positions as the young lady pictured here in a spacious, big-city, skyscraper office. In 1890 only about 4 percent of women employed in nonfarm occupations were classified as clerical workers. By 1910 the number had risen only to 10 percent; almost 80 percent in 1910 still found jobs only in domestic or personal services and in home or factory manufacturing.

creation of the species and that any "unnecessary" (not to say "unusual") sexual activity was evil, debilitating, and physically dangerous. That caveat included masturbation as well as mutual forms of erotic satisfaction. Physicians and preachers alike spoke of the draining of vital body fluids, and children were warned that "self-abuse" would cause insanity.

The proscriptions on women were particularly severe. The civilized man was supposed to keep his natural sexual appetites under control. The genteel woman was not supposed to have natural sexual desires. In Robert Herrick's novel *Together*, the heroine's thoughts as she yields to her lover probably measured the proper contemporary woman's perception of sexuality:

She was cold, tranquil beneath her lover's kisses. . . . She could not meet him wholly in this inmost intimacy, and her heart was troubled. . . . This other thing was the male, the something which made all men differ from all women in the crisis of emotion—so she supposed—and must be endured. . . . She began to assume that . . . the passionate desire was something desired by the man and to be avoided by the woman. . . . She never dreamed that some day she herself might change, might be waked by passion.

For suggesting in 1908 that the heroine would indeed find fulfillment in awakened passion, Herrick was roundly assailed. Even William Dean Howells, ostensibly a leader of the "realist" school in literature, in effect apologized for Herrick, writing in a review of Herrick's work: "I will still believe that with the one break noted in 'Together' Mr. Herrick's fiction is a force for the higher civilization."

Herrick was one of the first major novelists to join contemporary sociologists and psychologists in asserting with approval the sexual nature of the female of the species. The appearance of the motif in literature reflected modifications in the social ethos. Alfred Kinsey's studies of sexual behavior indicate that the first noteworthy change in erotic experiences among American women seems to have occurred around 1915. The change included a marked increase in premarital relations and in the experiencing of orgasm. Although the guardians of culture, male and female, continued to assail suggestions that women might legitimately enjoy and expect erotic satisfaction, by 1910 it had become permissible to acknowledge that, despite their mothers, ministers, and school marms, even the "best" young girls very likely knew the essentials of all there was to know by the time they entered puberty, and, what was more, they were notably untroubled by what they knew. By 1920, "good girls" in their teens and twenties would be dancing with boys face to face and cheek to cheek, discussing how far to go with petting, and wondering aloud what was wrong with the girl who had never been kissed.

The social revolution implicit in such developments was the consequence of no single movement but represented rather confused crosscurrents of many kinds of questioning. For example, although some feminists by 1910 had begun to argue that women have as much right and as much capacity to enjoy sex as do men, probably most leaders of the women's movement continued to reject "sexual exploitation" in such terms as virtually to reject sex itself. The fact that by 1910 women were being divorced at twice the 1880 rate, and evidently with less social and economic anxiety than divorce had previously incurred, signified for some women liberation from "legal prostitution" and perhaps also from the powerful nineteenth-century notion that a woman could find no worthy social fulfillment out-

side of marriage. However, to most members of the women's movement, especially to those prominent in the suffrage and temperance
campaigns, divorce represented a serious blow to civilization. Like
birth control, it suggested "race suicide," a phrase that appeared
frequently in the utterances of the day from the same social critics
who deplored "excessive individualism" and who viewed the general trend toward increased sexual freedom as further confirmation
of how industrialism and urbanization were subverting the foundations of America. Altogether, the mostly middle-class and upper-
class women who dominated the women's movement, especially the
suffrage campaign, generally sought to enlarge their role in society
in order to aid in the defense against the horde of "inferior races"
inundating the country and undermining its moral quality. They
were not interested in furthering a sexual revolution, though many
of the arguments they used for political equality served the cause
of increased sexual freedom.

There were still other forces eroding the received sexual mores.
The new discipline of psychoanalysis, which had been evolving in
Europe under the auspices of Sigmund Freud since the 1880's, and
the "New Psychology" developed by G. Stanley Hall and William
James in the United States had pointed to childhood experiences,
particularly sexual training, as the source of adult neuroses. By
1905 it was becoming as unsatisfactory to attribute mental disorders
to inherited biological defects as a century earlier it had become to
ascribe dementia to moral weakness or to the intrusion of demonic
spirits. Following the lead of the older science of biology, the new
psychological studies placed a forceful emphasis on the environmental determination of personality. In retrospect, from the findings
of psychoanalysts, it seems clear that the stresses underlying mental
disorders, at least in the United States and in Western Europe early
in the twentieth century, had much to do with the self-denying discipline demanded by modern industrial processes and the acquisitive motif of mature capitalism. The "capitalist spirit" required
savings—pecuniary, energetic, and emotional. The middle classes
felt the burden most strongly. To achieve or maintain middle-class
status required lengthy technical or professional training, which in
turn suggested late marriage. Indeed, from 1870 to 1910 the average
marriage age rose strikingly, from the late teens to the early twenties,
and middle-class families began deliberately to reduce the number of
children they produced. In the absence of reliable birth control
methods, this meant not merely continence but virtually total ab-

stinence—at least for women. Since it was not expected that men of any class had the moral strength to deny their indisputably virile natures, the responsibility for birth control fell mainly on the women.

The astonishingly rapid acceptance of psychoanalytic theories about sex, most particularly in the United States after 1910, may have reflected the contemporary reaction against the determination of life styles by economic goals. Economic needs do not dictate sexual mores, and there is no convincing evidence that capitalism or industrialism has increased mental disorder in any society or that mental disorder is most prevalent in capitalistic, industrialized societies. But there does seem to be a relationship between the emergence of open criticism of traditional sexual discipline in America and the lessened force of the country's preoccupation with economic growth.

For somewhat related reasons, attitudes toward children and education underwent a drastic transformation. By about 1905 it had become "old-fashioned" to regard children as moral vessels likely to be filled with evil unless force-fed on virtue. In accord with the new confidence that what was natural had at least as much potential for good as for evil, the progressive approach to education asserted the need to seek and cultivate the child's natural aptitudes. The rationale underlying traditional, catechistic teaching suffered further from the disintegration of the traditional consensus about fixed moral values, especially as those values had been tied to the industrial discipline then being questioned.

As in the case of the women's movement, much of the impetus for progressive education came from the desire to meet the challenge to conventional values posed by demographic and industrial changes. "The idea," writes Lawrence Cremin in *The Transformation of the School* (1961), "had its origin during the quarter-century before World War I in an effort to cast the school as a fundamental lever of social and political regeneration." Civic reformers and efficiency enthusiasts had long envisaged educational requirements to be the answer to corrupt and wasteful government. In the nineteenth century, such reformers had sought primarily to attach educational tests to the civil service, but after the turn of the century the emphasis shifted to cultivating skills and intelligence through improved schools, in order to make more efficient use of the nation's human resources. Educators began encouraging vocational training, while they deemphasized "classical" education as the model preparation for the worthwhile life. John Dewey believed progressive education should serve as an "embryonic community life, active with types of occupations that reflect the life of the larger society and permeated throughout with the spirit of art, history, and science." In its class-rooms, assembly halls, workshops, laboratories, music rooms, gymnasiums, and even in its cafeterias, the school was to make edu-cation part of the experience of living. Children were to participate in its various activities as they would have in the productive routine of the household in the pre-industrial environment. School facilities were to be a true center of neighborhood activity, used by the whole community, and attracting persons of all ages throughout the year.

The use of public schools as instruments of social policy appealed to conservatives as well as to social innovators. Which social policy remained a matter of little concern until the various reformers dis-covered the divergence of purposes among them. The failure to reckon with the issue left them unprepared for some of the more important social developments of their day. Those perplexed by the flood of immigrant children into the cities, for example, sought to use the public schools as agencies for Americanization. The effort to explain democracy to the refugees of Europe's despotism and to develop "good character," "individualism," and "self-reliance" had at least two unexpected consequences: It raised profound ques-tions about what such things meant in a complex, largely corporatized industrial society, and it laid out in detail as never before the civil rights and privileges belonging to all citizens in a liberal democracy such as the United States purported to be. In this as in many other instances, progressives wrought more than they had intended or would even well understand.

In seeking to repair the damage that industrialism had inflic-ted on human values, reformers revealed that a free society concerned with individual dignity, self-reliance, and personal liberty required a greater variety of life styles and social preferences than they had imagined or in the last resort many were willing to tolerate. The crisis of the World War would come along in time to veil this un-welcome fact. For at least the duration of the war, the cause of na-tional security would serve to repress the emerging schisms, enabling Americans to avoid recognizing the failure of reform efforts to re-store the conditions that had once made life seem secure.

The new psychology and educational theory had counterparts in law, economics, philosophy, anthropology, and political theory. Each system of inquiry in its own way helped undermine the con-ventional faiths. Although this effect was largely incidental to the independent momentum of each discipline, unquestionably the stirrings all around provided mutual stimulation. Whatever the theorists' specific purposes, their work helped dissolve confidence in principles that had traditionally served as moral anchors for social policy.

This is most evident in what was slowly happening in legal theory. Judges may pretend, or even persuade themselves, that rules of reason and precedent predetermine their decisions, remarked Oliver Wendell Holmes, Jr., in *The Common Law* (1881), but that neither is nor ought to be the fact: "The life of the law has not been logic; it has been experience. The felt necessities of the time, the prevalent moral and political theories, intuitions of public policy . . . even the prejudices which judges share with their fellow-men, have had a good deal more to do than the syllogism in determining the rules by which men should be governed." The path of the law in the long run follows the course of social preference; thus its legitimacy, said Holmes (on another occasion), resides not with some mythical body of eternal principles but in the degree to which the law expresses "the will of the *de facto* supreme power in the community."

After his appointment to the Supreme Court by Theodore Roosevelt in 1902, Holmes waged a constant fight against judges' habitual reference to archaic moral assumptions to justify their obstruction of social legislation. His dissent in the notorious *Lochner* case (1905) became the classic reference for what Roscoe Pound called "the sociological movement in jurisprudence, the movement for the adjustment of principles and doctrines to the human conditions they are to govern rather than to assumed first principles, the movement for putting the human factor in the central place and relegating logic to its true position as an instrument." The Court majority in that case decided that a New York act to establish a ten-hour day for bakers deprived both employers and employees of their liberty and property "without due process of law," by which they meant not that the legislative process had been vitiated in some way but that the statute outraged five Justices' view of the morality of a state's interference with the wage-bargaining process. Liberty of contract, the Court had come to claim (and reasserted to an extreme in this instance), was a natural and therefore inalienable right. No legislature could legitimately abridge it unless the Court itself found such abridgment "reasonable." Holmes objected that the majority had reasoned from "an economic theory which a large part of the country

Oliver Wendell Holmes, Jr. (1841–1935), was an Associate Justice of the Supreme Court from 1902 to 1932. "The men I should be tempted to commemorate," he once said, "would be the originators of transforming thought."

does not entertain." He suggested that the Court's decision might have been correct if it had derived from a consensus on the validity of classical or laissez-faire economic theory, but he denied that such a consensus prevailed.

The implications of Holmes' view badly frightened conservatives, who set about deliberately to pack the Court with "reliable" judges hostile to such relativistic heresy. And they made no mistake. The new jurisprudence, which Holmes' *Lochner* dissent exemplified, pointed a loaded cannon at the structure of privilege conventionally blessed by social favor. Where would be the stability, the continuity, the predictability that law should provide if it came to be accepted that law merely reflects a society's dominant preferences at a particular moment in history? What guidance would a society have in choosing its preferences? In Holmes' view, law ceases to serve as the measure of good judgment and moral policy; it becomes a mere function of power, "mitigated," as Holmes put it, only "by sympathy, prudence, and all the social and moral qualities." Like his contemporaries whose work also punctured the old absolutes, Holmes was remarkably confident that "the social and moral qualities" would suffice to prevent any radically inhumane policy changes. But in any event, there was a harder imperative to which he hearkened. Holmes' opposition to judicial interference with social legislation came not from a commitment to democracy and innovation—he had no such commitment—but from a fear that to thwart the expression of substantial power by those who in fact possess it would virtually destroy the law's primary function as the mechanism by which society may resolve conflict peacefully. Law thus had preeminently pragmatic rather than normative value.

Thorstein Veblen, in *The Theory of the Leisure Class* (1898) and *The Theory of Business Enterprise* (1904), did for economics what Holmes and Pound did for law. One wonderful thing about the classical model that Adam Smith and his disciples had fashioned, Veblen noted, was that it left the essentially moral decisions about the distribution of wealth and the allocation of life chances to the impersonal, divinely guided mechanism of the free market. The trouble was that the model had little relationship to attainable conditions, so that it neither described nor could usefully prescribe a workable economic order. When necessities were scarce, Veblen conceded, there was some cause for believing that the laws of supply and demand operated to encourage efficiency, stimulate productivity, and fill consumers' preferences at fair prices. But, said Veblen, the United States and much of Europe had reached an age of surpluses. Whereas in the old system the "captain of industry" or entrepreneur could profit most by maximizing production, in the new order the entrepreneur becomes saboteur; he must seek to limit production and create artificial scarcities in order to maximize his gains. Hence the need for businesses to combine, in order to control prices, quality, market quotas, and the number of firms newly entering an industry.

Having demonstrated the inadequacy of the market for achieving a just or moral distribution of social rewards, Veblen turned the problem over to politics. That is, the state must intervene to define what constitutes a fair share of whatever any particular groups may covet. And, as in the Holmesian analysis, insofar as fairness becomes subject to determination by law and law is the outcome of political bargaining, justice becomes dependent on power.

John Dewey's effort to reconstruct philosophy to make use of the remarkable advances of nineteenth-century scientific thought further chipped away at old certainties. Philosophy, Dewey insisted, had to shake off its ancient, burdensome, metaphysical quest for transcendent truth: "The abandonment by intelligence of a fixed and static moral end [is] the necessary precondition of a free and progressive science [of society]." Illuminated and guided by scientific method, philosophy had to turn to the tasks of defining social directions, of locating the sources of evils, and of seeking "to free men's minds from bias and prejudice and to enlarge their perceptions of the world around them."

If one recognizes, said Dewey, that philosophy has not been an insulated, self-generating system of thought but has been integral with the history of civilizations, then "instead of the disputes of rivals about the nature of reality, we have the scene of human clash of social purpose and aspirations." Like the new jurisprudence and the new economics, Dewey's linking of philosophy to the interplay of social forces reduced Truth to truths that were ultimately dependent on the preferences that triumph in any particular historical context. The mark of a liberal civilization is the degree to which the struggle for ascendancy is governed by a creative intelligence that extracts from everyday experience the real and current needs of human beings. Dewey left unstated the inevitable conclusion that insofar as the test of social excellence or truth depends on mutable preferences, a liberal civilization is not provably superior to any other social system.

Herbert Croly, author of *The Promise of American Life* (1909) and in 1914 one of the founding editors of the progressive journal *The New Republic*, made a precocious effort to grapple with the political implications of the new thinking. He traced the disturbances facing America in the new century to the constriction of economic opportunities. The industrial revolution, said Croly, realized the hopes of generations of pioneering Americans. "Democracy," he wrote in 1912, "has always meant to Americans a political system which contributed by whatever the means to their individual economic well-being. . . . To the [post–Civil War] generation of business men . . . it seemed like the order of nature . . . and its success was so considerable that it was accepted as a matter of course by the dominant mass of opinion." From the beginning, Americans acted on the theory that an individual's profits were indistinguishable from social gain: "The public interest, which government was supposed to promote, was conceived chiefly as a collection of individual interests." As long as the country provided an apparently "inexhaustible store of natural opportunities," the theory served well. "But those natural resources are now in large measure passed into the hands of individuals," Croly observed, and political leaders could no longer count on abundance to fulfill the promise of success and independence, which had become "an essential part of the American national idea."

The disappearance of the frontier and the advent of large-scale business consolidations thus posed serious threats to the promise of American life. Ideals proclaimed as "American" set forth the value choices of a dwindling segment of the society. Moral preference tended to become increasingly dependent on mutually exclusive interests. Every group claimed justice and righteousness for itself but meant only what suited its own advantage. Constricted opportunities meanwhile altered expectations and confronted Americans with alternative evils: "They could not withdraw the . . . privileges which business had been enjoying without disturbing confidence and checking expansion, yet they could not perpetuate the advantages enjoyed by certain kinds of business without making the state increasingly responsible for flagrant economic inequalities." Conservatives would be "obliged to countenance many grave abuses"; reformers would be "obliged to injure many innocent people, disappoint the immediate expectations of many more," and launch programs of "dangerous economic and political reorganization."

In the strictest sense, Croly observed, there is no such thing as impartial legislation; every law necessarily discriminates in favor of some interest and against some other. The appeal to "fair play," he argued, is usually a plea for some kind of privilege. This was true even when the plea was made in the name of "the people." Thus he refused to endorse most of the popular government measures of the day, including the initiative, recall elections, and direct primaries. To have faith in "the people," he said, meant to trust special interests to check special interests.

Croly's solution was the creation of a national faith of selfless-

President Theodore Roosevelt, in a characteristic pose, addresses a Flag Day crowd, probably in 1907 or 1908. Congress created Flag Day in 1895. The 1890's, troubled by economic crises, urban blight, and an increasingly polyglot population, produced an outpouring of nationalist, patriotic enthusiasm. None championed such zeal more heartily than Roosevelt. Deprived of a monarchical symbol of enduring nationhood, Americans pressed the flag into service. In 1916, amidst renewed social anxieties, President Wilson would officially proclaim as the national anthem the unsingable ballad that Francis Scott Key wrote in 1814 to honor "The Star Spangled Banner."

ness, a "New Nationalism" that overrode self-centered, parochial, and occasional interests for the higher, common interest. Like Dewey, Croly placed his hopes on the creative potential of education and intelligence. He made it evident that there were no institutional remedies for the fragmentation of life and amoral social drift. Only a regenerated spirit of nationhood, shaped by the knowledge that science makes available for setting feasible national purposes and fashioning effective means for reaching them, could restore the force of common standards of right, decency, justice, and morality. "A people which becomes more of a nation," he wrote, "has a tendency to become for that very reason more of a democracy." The extent of citizens' agreement on values determines the responsiveness of a government's policies; the more the nation functions as an integral, corporative whole, the more likely that its members will share in a moral consensus.

With the retrospect of half a century and the experience with totalitarian nationalism, which Croly lacked, one may fairly cringe at the dangers of an all-dissolving devotion to The Nation. Croly assumed that American tradition and democratic institutions would effectively brake any tendencies toward oppression. "The American democracy," he wrote, "can trust its might to the national interest, because American national cohesion is dependent, not only upon certain forms of association, but upon fidelity to a democratic principle. . . . American patriotism combines the imaginative projection of an ideal national Promise with loyalty to historical tradition and precedent."

Like nearly all his contemporaries who helped shoot down the conventional absolutes, Croly was not seriously troubled by assigning to the power of prevalent interest the determination of social decisions that traditionally were constrained by moral force. It was characteristic both of their optimism and of their limitations that they in effect placed their faith on the continuing influence of the very moral sensibilities that their own analyses declared derivative and impermanent. While asserting that right and justice are functions of power and politics, they could not imagine that such relativism might breach all limits. To paraphrase William James' essay on "determinism," they never doubted that the possibilities which might tempt the will of a dominating interest were far fewer than the possibilities one could coldly fancy.

The Politics of Social Justice

Although it should be plain that progressivism had more to do with profound cultural developments than with politics, the most conspicuous feature of the progressive movement was the revitalization of government—especially at the federal level—as a positive instrument for social policy-making. Ultimately, indeed, only government could make possible many of the policies that reformers urged. For most of the nineteenth century, the state had mostly contributed to the making of social policy by gradually abdicating responsibility for it in favor of privately negotiated contracts among individuals and voluntary associations in the supposedly open market. The emphasis of law-making had been to enlarge the permissive areas in which private economic energies could follow their natural and presumably beneficent course. Toward the end of the century it had become evident, especially to the losers, that certain "special interests" had gained the power to skew the market mechanisms in their own favor. The movement for government regulation, which took form in agencies such as the Federal Trade Commission, the Children's Bureau, and the Pure Food and Drug Administration, represented progressivism's chief effort to set things right.

The appeal to government for the redress of various economic and social disadvantages inevitably had its effect on the political

William Jennings Bryan, here pictured making a speech in 1907, is the only major party candidate to lose three tries for the Presidency: 1896, 1900, and 1908. But more than any political leader of his time, the silver-throated Nebraskan forced the American political system to deal with the economic problems created by the industrial revolution. Unfortunately, the fears he raised among conservatives in both parties, as well as his inability to communicate successfully with the nation's industrial, urban, and recent immigrant voters, gave the Democratic Party a minority status that even Woodrow Wilson's victories in 1912 and 1916 did not erase.

Brown Brothers

system. At the turn of the century, American political parties stood as independent interest groups much like private social clubs that also, almost incidentally and always imperfectly, reflected the political pressures generated by public need. In the 1890's, the Populists had worked to force the political parties to commit themselves to specific government programs. The nomination of William Jennings Bryan for President on the Populist and Democratic tickets in 1896 constituted a substantial move toward constructing an issue-oriented political system. It had its counterpart in Mark Hanna's efforts, as the "power behind the throne" in the McKinley administration, to subdue the fraternity-order qualities of the Republican Party and to turn the GOP into an agency that would serve the country's business interests. Theodore Roosevelt's objective became the transformation of the Republican Party into an agency on behalf of a broader definition of the public's interests.

When Roosevelt became President, "the trusts" led the list of major national issues. By 1901, the greatest consolidation movement in the nation's history was already four years old. In 1899 alone there had been more than twelve hundred mergers of manufacturing and mining firms; until the 1960's and with the exception of 1929, this was by far the largest number of combinations recorded in any year in the country's history. By 1903, concentration characterized just about every major industry; that is (in the standard definition of "concentration"), the top four companies in most industrial categories accounted for 50 percent or more of the business in their category. To some this presented no problem, but to unorganized interests that had to compete or deal with the consolidated giants — and the unorganized plainly made up the majority — business concentration appeared an unmitigated disaster brought on by collusion and corruption, by illicit and unfair trade practices, by special favors bought from legislatures, and by privileged access to the country's closely held credit structure.

Roosevelt gained his greatest popularity as a trustbuster, although there was some irony in this. TR counted himself among those who believed consolidation would modernize the economy and who stressed the technological and economic imperatives that underlay the movement. He once said that rather than forbidding all combinations, laws should distinguish between combinations that do good and combinations that do evil. The law, he urged, should not be so construed "that the business of the country cannot be conducted without breaking it."

Election of 1900

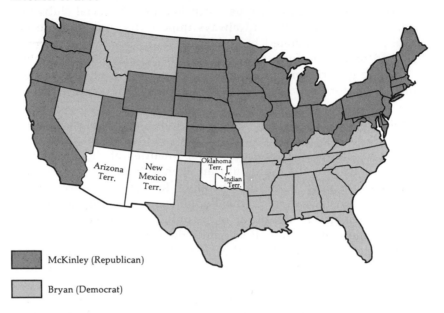

McKinley (Republican)

Bryan (Democrat)

Election of 1904

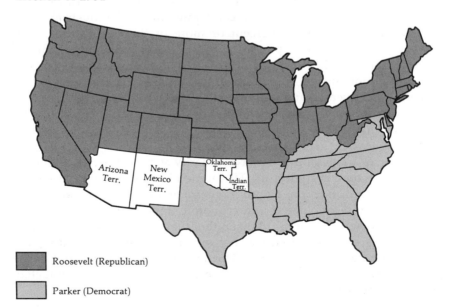

Roosevelt (Republican)

Parker (Democrat)

The Great Consolidation Movement, 1897-1903

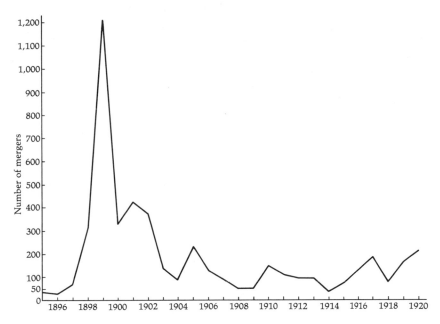

Source: Ralph Nelson, *Merger Movements in American Industry, 1895-1956* (Princeton: Princeton University Press, 1959), p. 37.

In politics, symbols are more important than realities. The President's dramatic attacks on certain trusts counted for more than his reservations about trust-busting. He struck at those, such as Standard Oil, that had long tried the tolerance of a public that liked to believe it knew, even in the absence of formal prescription, the difference between fair and unscrupulous competitive behavior. He struck too at those, such as the big meat packers, who had tested the public's sensibilities by (quite literally) failing to keep their houses clean. But more important than such attacks, Roosevelt endeared himself to the public by reasserting the dignity of the federal government in the face of the corporations' self-arrogated autonomy. More than anything else, this held the significance of his triumph over the Morgan-Hill-Harriman alliance in the Northern Securities Company anti-trust suit in 1904, which first established TR's anti-trust credentials.

Roosevelt's presidency produced a spate of regulatory measures designed to impose minimal constraints on the most obnoxious abuses of private power. The first important federal meat inspection and food and drug regulations emerged from his administration. The first federal law to limit the power of a private industry (the railroads) to set its own prices also owed much to his efforts. Roosevelt himself counted as his greatest work the inauguration of the country's first program for the conservation of natural resources. Although that program made only small headway during his own and the immediately succeeding administrations, it at least established the principle of the need for a nationally directed conservation effort.

In a general way, Roosevelt sought to outline a national policy that would balance the broad prerogatives traditionally accorded to private decision-making against the need for a governmentally determined concept of *national interest.* It is wise, the President said in 1905, to conserve "the national virtue of self-reliance, of independence in initiative and action . . . and to provide for its fullest exercise." Yet, he added, "it is also true that where there is not governmental restraint or supervision some . . . exceptional men use their energies not in ways that are for the common good." Of all TR's accomplishments, the most significant was his reintroduction into government of its ancient function of taking a primary role in the shaping of social policy. This indeed was the most remarkable political feature of the progressive era.

Roosevelt's efforts in the nation's capital gave special focus to the reform impulses emanating from diverse parts of the country. On the city and state levels, reformers fought vigorously to gain control of the political mechanisms that commanded the orientation of social and economic priorities. To overcome the advantages held by incumbents—that is, the "Old Guard" who had tied their political options to the ascendant or vested interests—reformers sought changes in the political system. Thus were born laws to require nominating elections for party candidates (primaries), the initiative and referendum ("I & R"), which bypassed the formal legislative process altogether, popular recall of public officials and, in a few cases, of judicial decisions, and the reorganization of city governments to give dominant governing power to nonpartisan commissioners and managerial experts. William U'Ren of Oregon and Hazen Pingree as mayor of Detroit and as governor of Michigan helped spotlight such reforms before 1900. Robert "Fighting Bob" La Follette, as governor of Wisconsin, inspired progressives through-

The trusts were the major national issue in the new century, and the Hearst press vied with *McClure's Magazine,* which featured writers such as Lincoln Steffens, Ida Tarbell, and Ray Stannard Baker, to lead the clamor against them. In F. Opper's cartoons, such as this one published in 1902, "The Common People" were not usually pictured as laborers or farmers but as consumers and taxpayers.

Culver Pictures

out the country as the movement gathered impetus after the turn of the century.

The "Wisconsin Idea," as La Follette's program came to be known, featured most of the political innovations that would eventually define progressive politics on the national scene—a legislative reference service that introduced expertise into the shaping of social legislation, commission regulation of public service corporations, labor laws, and in general the positive use of the state to assist certain disadvantaged groups. Not all of it was new to the American scene. Some older eastern states such as Massachusetts had been enjoying comparable institutions and government services before La Follette discovered the problems they were designed to meet. But

La Follette's attacks on the "bosses" and "vested interests" did dramatize the growing rejection of old priorities and old leadership.

The political insurgency in the states and on the national political level as well drew strongly from that impulse. Thus the "Iowa Idea," upon which progressive Republican Albert B. Cummins built his political career after 1901, in a certain sense amounted to little more than a campaign for tariff revision. But at a time when high-level protectionism constituted a test of GOP loyalty, revisionism represented not merely disenchantment with the high cost of tariffs; it struck a deliberate blow at orthodoxy and thus against eastern domination of the Republican Party and the distorted allocation of economic opportunities that such domination implied. Neither Roosevelt nor his successor William Howard Taft fully grasped the significance of that element in the party insurgency they faced, and Taft in particular fell victim to it.

In many ways Taft exemplified the new politics of the Roosevelt era. Educated at Yale and studious in jurisprudence, he had served ably as a federal judge, as first governor-general of the Philippines, and as secretary of war under Roosevelt before he became TR's candidate for President on the Republican ticket in 1908. He was a man of intellect and experience and lacked the deep conditioning in small-time partisan politics that had shaped every President's outlook during the quarter-century from Hayes to McKinley. But Taft's career in the White House demonstrated that intellect, experience, and even goodwill were not sufficient.

First, he encountered a rebellion against Joe Cannon, the Speaker of the House whose tightfisted control and obtusely conservative politics had enraged numerous Congressmen of both parties. Although the revolt against "Uncle Joe" had no clear sectional character, nor even a distinct basis in political philosophy, it did manifest the substantial sentiment of the Congress and the country against the techniques of bossism and political obstructionism. Taft personally stood for a contrasting style of leadership, and he stoutly disliked Cannon as an individual. Yet he declined to support the insurgents because he feared that deposing Cannon would create a schism within the Republican Party and jeopardize his hopes to carry forward the gains of progressive reform achieved during the previous eight years. Taft probably assessed the politics of the situation accurately, but in acting on that appraisal, he incurred the distrust of those who had looked to him, as they had to Roosevelt, to defeat the crotchety leadership that Cannon represented. In this as in subsequent issues during his single-term administration, Taft chose sides unwisely. His program could have had no meaning except insofar as it might have contributed to the realignment of advantages within his party, among the constituencies that the party factions represented, and among competing economic and regional groups throughout the country.

His difficulties with the tariff issue illustrate the point. Taft had been an active revisionist within the party as early as 1903, and his first move as President was to call a special session of Congress to lower tariff rates. His effort met with frustration at the hands of Old Guard Senate leader Nelson Aldrich, whose amendments to the administration and House's version of the tariff bill raised the rates on most important items even above those of the previous tariff. Taft signed the Payne-Aldrich tariff bill anyway because, as he remarked at the time, he did not care to gain popularity at the expense of men such as Aldrich, whom he personally respected, to the advantage of insurgents such as Cummins and La Follette, whom he distrusted.

Election of 1908

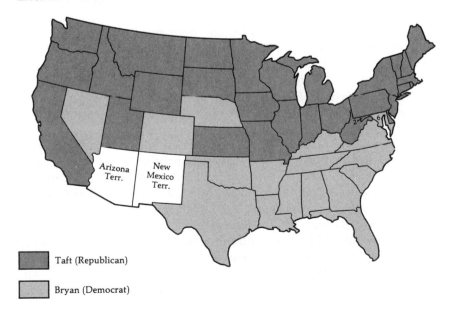

Taft (Republican)

Bryan (Democrat)

The last two, he noted, had voted for tariffs to protect their own states' products even while denouncing the high rates that Aldrich and allies had inserted on behalf of their constituents.

When the long and laboriously negotiated Canadian Reciprocity Treaty came before the Senate for approval in 1911, Taft could again remark caustically on the insurgents' seeming hypocrisy. As Taft saw it, the treaty not only gained for the United States unprecedented trade advantages within the British imperial system, it also looked toward a measurable check on the rising cost of living by admitting Canadian foodstuffs into the United States free of duty in exchange for a lowering of Canadian tariff barriers against American manufactured goods. It seemed an eminently sensible measure; yet the insurgents, who generally had stood for consumers' interests and other causes they identified with "social justice," voted against the treaty.

The crux of the issue, in both the Payne-Aldrich tariff and the Reciprocity Treaty, lay in which interests gained what and at whose expense. It was perhaps not Taft's fault that he missed the point. The insurgents' rhetoric implicitly argued that the rightness or wrongness of a political position could be measured by reference to some common standard of decency abstracted or standing apart from interest. In sharing this assumption, Taft had lots of company from all political camps. But whatever their rhetoric, the insurgents in fact used a standard that related directly to the preponderance of advantages enjoyed by rival interests: Both the treaty and the tariff act offered few prizes and many penalties to the insurgents' primarily agricultural constituents and gave extensive benefits to the same eastern industrial interests that had long and effectively supported the Old Guard leadership of the Republican Party. For "social justice," one sometimes had to read "readjustment of regional, commercial, or political advantages."

Conservation offers another example of the political nature of social justice and also of Taft's hapless inability to see the interests at stake. Anxiety about the potential exhaustion of the country's natural resources had emerged in the 1890's when Americans realized the frontier era was over. The report by the United States Census Bureau in 1891 that new settlements no longer advanced along any discernible line within the continental boundaries had inspired deep concern among both economists and political theorists about the implications of resource scarcity. (Plenty of "free land" was still available, but this did not affect the import of the bureau's observation.) Without the open options that the abundance of unsettled regions had apparently afforded, American democratic institutions seemed headed for perilous strain. The idea of rational, conservative use of resources arose before the turn of the century among agronomists, geologists, engineers, and other professionals. As a social idea born of the shift away from the prerogatives of individual enterprise and reliance on marketplace decisions to the long-term needs of the collective society, conservation came to life as the child of the Roosevelt administration.

The Ballinger-Pinchot controversy of 1910 again revealed Taft's weakness for giving personalities and political expediency greater attention than current demands for realignment of social priorities. The dispute arose over the opening, or rather reopening, of a coal region in Alaska to private development. The area lay within the public domain and had been set aside by conservationists during the Roosevelt administration. Taft's secretary of the interior, Richard Ballinger, abruptly reversed the earlier policy in order to permit the Guggenheim mining interests to exploit the deposits there. Revelations of Ballinger's action by departmental investigator Louis Glavis promptly raised a scandal, and Chief Forester Gifford Pinchot, a Roosevelt confidant and renowned publicist for conservation, vigorously assailed Ballinger, who was his immediate superior. So far as Taft could understand the issues, it seemed a matter of whether Ballinger and the Guggenheim interests had in fact violated any law (Taft decided they had not) and whether Pinchot and Glavis had been insubordinate (they had been, indisputably). But that was to turn merely to the easiest of issues. A feasible conservation program required much more assiduous attention to what was at stake in shaping a program that might "fairly" accommodate the competing interests of nature lovers, entrepreneurs, consumers, ranchers, vacationers, and farmers. The issue went far beyond personalities, law enforcement, or administrative discipline.

To preserve or restore resource abundance, conservationists urged planning for the wise use and, where possible, replenishment of the country's mineral, soil, timber, and water resources. Some stressed the establishment of national parks and forests to prevent exploitation by monopolistic commercial interests. Others, including Pinchot, emphasized regulating the use of resources by leasing sections of the public domain on specified terms, including the payment of fees to make conservation programs self-sustaining. Most agreed on the need to develop multiple-purpose programs that would deny to any single interest a monopoly of a particular resource. For example, the construction of dams would control flooding, generate electric power, and provide lakes for recreation, while regulating the flow of water downstream for drinking, sewage, and the irrigation of dry but otherwise arable lands. Implicitly, the conservation movement required interstate or regional programs directed from Washington; the federal government would serve as the chief coordinating agency.

Therein lay the rub. It became evident that though Americans might agree on the general objectives, they agreed remarkably little on methods and priorities. Regional and state rivalries conditioned much of the ensuing conflict. Most of the leading conservationists were easterners, such as Pinchot and Roosevelt. Disturbed by the wanton destruction of resources inflicted on the country's older states, reformers hoped to avoid a similar fate for the West. But many westerners regarded the conservation movement as a threat to the rapid development of their region and to the growth of opportunities for wealth that development implied. Taft's very selection of Ballinger as his secretary of the interior reflected his obtuseness. He came to Ballinger because he had heard "good things" about his "integrity" from westerners who claimed conservationist credentials, and he thought it "just" to give the West a turn at the helm of the Interior Department. Of course, both easterners and westerners could probably agree that lawbreakers and those who irresponsibly squandered resources had to be stopped. But westerners such as Ballinger were inclined to let the "free market" dictate priorities in the uses of land and to resist encroachments of federal power. For Pinchot and Roosevelt, and ultimately for Taft as well, this approach subverted the need for careful coordination of multiple-purpose and regional conservation programs.

In the end, Taft had to fire Ballinger precisely because of such differences, but it is not clear that he (or many others) ever fully recognized that the resolution of the conservation issue required the sacrifice of some, wholly legitimate, interests to the advantage of others. The right of Americans to use the public domain for private profit, which traditionally had been undisputed, had to be sharply qualified. The right to cut timber even on one's own land had to be regulated to prevent the destruction of watersheds. Property rights had to give way to the construction of dams that would flood some people out on behalf of the broader public interest. The right to dump wastes into waterways and oceans had to be weighed against the costs of impure drinking supplies and depleted fishlife. Americans could settle issues such as these only politically; the society had to determine policy directions by resorting to political procedures — elections and legislative action — as distinguished from the activities of administrative and judicial agencies, the effectiveness of which depends on policy consensus. The inclination of political leaders to delegate responsibility for the hard decisions to the courts and to the regulatory agencies would lead only to grief. Indeed, the difficulty would continue to afflict the entire movement to regulate big business.

The Regulation Movement

The complexities the progressives faced in their efforts to establish a just policy even for a single industry can be seen in the case of the railroads. That industry produced the first truly big businesses. Quite naturally it served as the target of the earliest campaigns for federal regulation. The political rhetoric of the last third of the nineteenth century was full of farmers' grievances against railroad practices, and numerous agricultural states passed regulatory measures dubbed "Granger Laws." But farmers were scarcely unique in their desire to use government leverage to improve their bargaining position; the regulatory laws were not the product of their agitation alone. Merchants and shippers as much as farmers suffered from rate pools, cuts in services, discriminatory rates, and arbitrary grading standards and high prices at the railroad-owned grain elevators and warehouses. Stockholders, moreover, sought protection against company directors who manipulated securities for their private gain at the expense of the company. Many spokesmen for railroad management also began seeking federal controls to reduce the hazards of rate wars, to eliminate the power of certain shippers (for example, Standard Oil) to extort rebates, to bypass the multitude of changing state regulations, and to deter the slowly growing sentiment for government ownership.

Congress responded to these pressures in 1887 with the Interstate Commerce Act, but its inadequacies were quickly demonstrated. The issue remained a major one throughout the administrations of Theodore Roosevelt, William Howard Taft, and Woodrow Wilson. Under Roosevelt, Congress passed two measures, one (the Elkins Act) aimed primarily at rebates and the other (the Hepburn Act) to allow the Interstate Commerce Commission (ICC) to fix *maximum* railroad rates. The latter was not a negligible power in an inflationary age. But neither act touched the heart of the problem, because both dealt only with the question of the ostensible immorality of rate-gouging and deceptive business practices.

At stake in the fight for regulation of the railroad industry was what kinds of goods should flow from what shipping points and to what destinations. By setting special *low* rates for certain goods tagged for favored destinations, railroads often could influence the prosperity of entire sections of the country. In effect, the traffic managers — whose whole interest was to maximize the traffic and profits of their private railroad companies — had the power, by determining transportation costs, to decide that shoes should be made in Boston rather than in Richmond, that Buffalo rather than New York should be a major flour-producing center, that bicycles should be shipped to Detroit from eastern manufacturers and to the East from Detroit manufacturers, that San Francisco rather than Reno or Salt Lake City should become the major shipping center for the West. To be sure, the decisions were not altogether the traffic managers' to make; pressures from the railroads' clientele — shippers, jobbers, manufacturers — often forced the managers to adjust rates when they might have preferred not to. In any event, the issue concerned whether goods were to flow as the market directed, according to the patterns developed through the multitude of private shipper-carrier negotiations, or as some public policy determined, according to the decisions of a government agency like the ICC.

In 1910, Congress empowered the ICC to fix rates by requiring railroads to justify in advance all rate differentials — that is, to explain to the ICC's satisfaction why, for example, the total cost by rail from St. Louis to San Francisco was lower than the cost from St. Louis to Reno or why steel shipped west to Cincinnati should travel at a different rate than steel shipped east from Chicago or north from Birmingham. For a variety of reasons — not least, the paucity of criteria for deciding what constituted a "fair" traffic pattern — the ICC exercised its new power with such restraint that a chief effect of the Mann-Elkins Act was merely to confirm (and give legitimacy to) the rate and traffic patterns already established. Still, in the confusion of the period, the regulatory legislation had the appearance of making a major contribution to "social justice." The ascendant groups within the railroad industry might continue to enjoy many of the same advantages that their power had won for them in the previously undisturbed economic arena, but the de jure transfer of power to government meant that policy decisions would gain the justification of having been subject to the outcome of contests within the political arena. Economic power, it was thought, would bow to democratic power.

The reformers sought, however, not merely to substitute political power for economic power but to exchange rationality, efficiency, and expertise for the waste and injustice implicit in the undirected market economy. There was an implicit faith that "science," or at least "the scientific method," would provide the answers to nettlesome questions of public policy. And up to a point the optimism was not misplaced. Among the era's noteworthy accomplishments was the exposure of the wastefulness of permitting private interests, governed primarily by the profit motive, to exploit the nation's resources without the guidance of some well-defined concept of the public's long-term welfare. Yet the issue of waste, like the issues of extortionate prices and dishonesty in business and the abuse of the prerogatives of private property, diverted attention from the problem of reassessing priorities concerning the award of advantages to competing social interests. And this was a matter that technical experts could not solve without policy guidance.

An economist could ascertain, for example, that the maintenance of steel-wire manufacturing in New England necessitated the most inexcusable waste in the cross-hauling of resources and of the finished products. There were no iron or coal deposits in New England, and the principal market for steel wire, especially barbed wire, lay even farther west than did iron and coal. But an agency faced with deciding whether to remove the favorable transportation rates that made wire manufacturing economically feasible in New England had to consider more costs than those of cross-hauling. How heavily should the experts weigh the human costs of dislocation for the thousands of families dependent on wire manufacturing who might be forced to move? If the region lost its wire manufacturing, would the economic loss to the railroads servicing both the industry and the thousands of individuals dependent on it for their livelihoods be of such dimensions as to impair the railroads' ability to service the region's other industries? Would setting the rates to favor the statistically optimal location of an industry result in an undesirable concentration of population in particular resources-rich areas? How heavily should a regulatory commission weigh the costs—especially to the principle of government regulation by commissions—that would surely follow from antagonizing political interests in Con-

gress whose constituents stood to pay the price of decisions pre-
dicated mainly on economic efficiency?

It is scarcely surprising that the era handled such questions with
resolute inconsistency. For example, after 1900, ICC decisions tended
to reflect the growing political power of midwestern merchant-
shipper groups by denying the major railroads' petitions for higher
rates despite the marked rise in operating costs throughout the
period. On the other hand, the ICC's general ratification of rate differentials favorable to eastern as opposed to southern and western
business groups seemed to reflect the eastern origins of the majority
of the commissioners more than it did the application of expertise.
When the United States entered the World War in 1917 and the federal
government took control of the railroads, the new Railroad Administration came to define "efficiency" as the railroad managers did —
probably because President Wilson chose a railroad man to head it —
thus sacrificing a variety of services that shippers had come to
enjoy over the previous fifteen years with the blessing of favorable
ICC decisions. (Wilson would pay for that policy in 1918 when it
contributed to the Republicans' sweep of the congressional elections in the middle and far west.) By 1920, twenty-five years of poor
railroad management, the inconsistency of regulatory policy, and
the advent of competition from trucks had made the railroads a sick
industry. In the Transportation Act of that year, Congress rejected
labor's plea for nationalization and gave the railroads exemption
from the anti-trust laws in the misguided hope that, under federal
supervision, rival shipper and railroad interests (but not labor, passenger, or consumer interests) could resolve among themselves the
questions of public policy and efficiency to which the government
had failed to give definition.

The railroads were only a special case of the conundrum presented
by the ascendancy of big business and the giant corporation. On the
one hand, traditional economic theory had emphasized the role of
vigorous competition in maximizing economic efficiency; unless
pressed by competitors, business normally could not be expected to
adopt cost-saving practices or to improve the quality of goods and
services. On the other hand, corporate consolidations seemed to be
demonstrating that the efficient use of resources required the integration of procurement, manufacturing, fabrication, and distribution processes. That implied "giantism," and insofar as every
market has a limited capacity, it meant that industries supplying
each market had room for only a limited (small) number of maxi-

mally efficient companies. In a word, it signified the practical legitimacy of monopolistic power.

To deal with this dilemma, the progressives experimented with a number of devices. In line with the initial optimism that the market economy suffered from nothing more fundamental than fraud and truculence, the Roosevelt administration adopted a program designed to expose corporate activities to public scrutiny. For these purposes, Congress in 1903 founded the Department of Commerce and Labor, within which it placed a Bureau of Corporations charged with data-gathering. It was intended in this approach that a common sense of decency would force corporations to be good—not only to be honest but to avoid unscrupulous, even if strictly legal, practices. Roosevelt went even further. By means of informal understandings with corporate leaders (most particularly with J. P. Morgan), TR essentially assured corporations of immunity from anti-trust prosecutions if he could be satisfied, from information gathered by the Bureau of Corporations, that their activities were honestly conceived and promised to be beneficial to the community. When he was not so convinced, Roosevelt proceeded, with his usual flare for the dramatic, to "bust the trusts"—as when he attacked the "meat trust" with both an anti-trust suit (*Swift & Co.* v. *United States*, 1905) and the Meat Inspection Act (1906) and broke up the merger of the chief transcontinental railroad lines (*Northern Securities Co.* v. *United States*, 1904).

This approach foundered on the rock of President Taft's determination to enforce the law despite the presumed merits of the corporations and the ostensible advantages of specific monopolistic business practices. Taft explicitly rejected Roosevelt's preference for deciding between "good" and "bad" trusts on an ad hoc basis. Indeed, so vigorously did Taft attack monopolistic arrangements that for a time the Old Guard stirred into activity to dump him when he came up for renomination in 1912. Meanwhile, the Supreme Court—perhaps in response to mounting protests from business that the government could charge any agreement among competing companies with being a "contract, combination, or conspiracy in restraint of trade"— ruled in 1911 (*Standard Oil Co.* v. *United States*) that Congress could not have intended the Sherman Anti-Trust Act to outlaw all restraints of trade but only "unreasonable" ones. This meant that the judiciary replaced Roosevelt as the arbiter of "good" and "bad" trusts.

The Court's "rule of reason" did not settle the issue. Some advocates of consolidation rejoiced that they had won a great victory, but others feared that the uncertainty inherent in leaving it up to the Court seriously inhibited business planning and investment. The sharp rise in the cost of living from 1897 to 1912 focused attention on the power of the giant corporations to fix prices and otherwise to render everyone's income, wealth, and life chances subject to the dictates of a corporate elite. The Panic of 1907, the recession that followed, accompanied by a resumption of rising prices, and the extraordinary political power-play that turned the Payne-Aldrich tariff "reform" of 1909 into one of the highest tariffs in United States history, successively heightened the public's concern over corporate power. Then in 1912 a congressional subcommittee headed by Arséne Pujo of Louisiana gained attention with hearings on the so-

In an age of fabulous and flamboyant millionaire moguls, J. P. Morgan was the king of them all. He is shown here in 1912 arriving at the Capitol Building to testify before the Pujo Committee, which was then investigating the "Money Trust." He is accompanied by his daughter, Mrs. Herbert Satterlee, and J. P. Morgan, Jr.

Brown Brothers

called Money Trust. The Pujo Committee revealed a closely inter-locking relationship among the leading financial institutions and implied that the nation's credit structure lay in the grip of a small clique of bankers.

This was the setting for the three-cornered national campaign of 1912. Despite a long series of presidential primary contests—the first such campaigns in history—anti-Taft Republicans failed to head off the President's bid for renomination. TR threw his hat in the ring in February and at first seemed sure to recapture the party, but his endorsement of the right of the electorate to reverse state court interpretations of the Constitution by referendum promptly frightened away his conservative support. Taft took the nomination. Roosevelt bolted the GOP, and a hastily assembled Progressive Party, with roots in reform associations and insurgent political groups throughout the country, named the Old Rough Rider its candidate. Expostulating that he felt "as fit as a bull moose," TR gave the new party its durable nickname. The Democrats chose Woodrow Wilson, New Jersey's crusading new governor who after only one year in office had gained a national reputation for leading a vigorous fight against big corporate interests and overthrowing the old-guard leadership of the state Democratic Party.

Roosevelt presented a genuinely different approach to govern-ment policy on concentrated power. His program effectively repu-diated the marketplace as a useful regulator of economic forces. He called Taft's legalistic anti-trust posture "rural toryism" and urged that government actively coordinate the nation's enterprises to ex-ploit the efficiency of consolidated, integrated economic units. He proposed boards of experts—"commission government," both friends and enemies called the plan—to reduce waste "scientifically" and to enhance the fruitfulness of human and material resources. The program boldly called for government assistance to groups that the marketplace had served poorly. This would incur some risks, but Roosevelt promised to make use of the potentials of concentrated power while overcoming its dangers. Although particular interests would necessarily enjoy the government's favor, a new, powerful, progressive consensus would preserve the interest of the nation as a whole over any individual or narrow group interest. Borrowing directly from Herbert Croly, TR labeled the consensus the spirit of a "New Nationalism."

Roosevelt lacked major party support, but he rather than Taft provided the chief opposition to the Democrats' remarkable nominee.

Thomas Woodrow Wilson's rise in politics had been more spectacular than any man's in the history of the country. Scarcely three years before he became President of the United States he had neither engaged actively in organized politics nor anticipated doing so. He had been born in Virginia in 1856 and raised in Georgia. His father had served as the minister of a Presbyterian church. His English-born mother was the daughter of a Presbyterian minister, as was his first wife, Ellen Axson, who remained his most devoted companion until her death in 1914. Wilson's personal sense of religious obligation remained exceptionally powerful throughout his life. After completing degrees at Princeton and at the University of Virginia law school, he briefly practiced law but gave it up to earn a Ph.D. at the new Johns Hopkins University, publishing his thesis, *Congressional Government,* in 1885. In the next twenty years he became one of the country's leading historians and a professor of jurisprudence and political economy, teaching at Bryn Mawr, Wesleyan, and Princeton. He was selected president of Princeton University in 1902. In 1910, New Jersey Democratic leaders, threatened by progressive insurgency within the party, turned to Wilson, a skilled and practiced orator but a political amateur, to heal the party rift by heading the state ticket. Nationwide impatience with Republican conservatism helped give Wilson a surprising victory in the normally Republican state. Although his own views were conservative, Wilson sensed the political mood in New Jersey. He renounced the machine that had promoted him and led a sensational reform campaign against "the interests" in the state whose corporation laws in the 1890's had made it the birthplace of the corporate revolution and the home of the trusts. Then, in July 1912, at the Democratic National Convention, a since-discarded rule that a candidate had to have two-thirds of the votes to win nomination enabled Wilson to overcome the lead of House Speaker Champ Clark of Missouri on the forty-sixth ballot.

Although he had once faulted the Roosevelt administration for placing too much emphasis on trust-busting, Wilson countered the New Nationalism with warnings about the perils of concentrated power, whether in private hands or exercised by government. He offered instead to use federal resources to secure a "New Freedom" from the corporatization of American life. Like Roosevelt, he had long seen the necessity for state intervention in the social process. "It is not in being let alone by government that my liberty consists," Wilson had written in 1891, "but in being assisted by government to maintain *my equal place* among my fellows." In 1912, he reiterated the point. "Freedom today," he said, "is something more than being let alone. Without the watchful . . . resolute interference of the government, there can be no fair play between individuals and such powerful institutions as the trusts." Unlike Roosevelt, however, Wilson saw the danger to individual liberty coming from the very organization of society that was implicit in the "concentration and control" program Roosevelt and many advanced progressives were advocating. He reminded his audiences of the nation's basic premise and faith that the success of American democracy lay in the independence and character of its people. How, he asked, could Americans continue to be free if their development was stunted by overbearing organizations that decided for them in advance the terms of "the common good"? "Benevolence," he noted, "never developed a man or a nation. We do not want a benevolent government. We want a free and a just government." "The next generation of youngsters," he declared, "[have to] be free to go about making their own lives as they will." They must not be born into a country where they have to be employees or nothing, in a land of supervised monopoly, where the conditions of industry are determined by small groups of men in business or government.

The disruption of the Republican Party gave Wilson the presidency. He topped his opponents with only 42 percent of the popular vote. Although he won many states by a plurality, he amassed fewer votes than William Jennings Bryan had polled in any of his three presidential campaigns, and he won absolute majorities in only those counties that Bryan had carried in his 1908 campaign against Taft. The vote, in other words, showed that the normal Republican majority had endured. It consisted of industrialists, most of the financial interests, most urban and suburban voters, a sizable share of the industrial work force (which continued to favor tariff protection), and most northern and western agricultural interests. Roosevelt divided this coalition at a 4 to 3 ratio with Taft. He took with him most of the leading progressives, including urban civic reformers and settlement workers; western and midwestern Republicans who had had their fill of eastern domination of the party; industrialists and financiers, especially some usually associated with the Morgan interests who had become dismayed by Taft's trust policies; finally, an indeterminate though probably large number of Republicans for whom the Roosevelt name was magic. Democratic strength remained in the South, in big city wards with strong Irish-American and other ethnic leadership, among the less prosperous farmers throughout the country, and among certain financial and commercial groups in whose concerns "free trade" weighed

Election of 1912

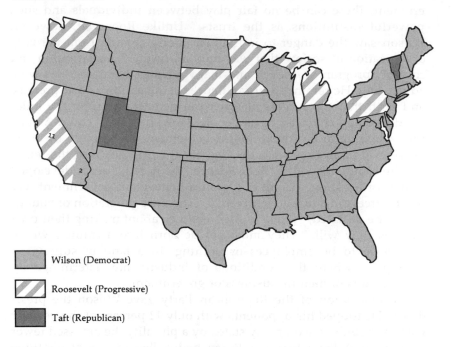

- Wilson (Democrat)
- Roosevelt (Progressive)
- Taft (Republican)

heavily. Wilson owed his election to this mostly conservative constituency.

Whatever the reasons people may have had for voting as they did, Wilson brought into office a mandate to reduce the power of the trusts and to end the uncertainties confronting business—uncertainties that emanated from the ambivalence of government policy and from the threat of arbitrary power wielded by the giant corporations. Wilson had promised to subdue the trusts and to revitalize the marketplace. He now had to try to perform the trick. Unfortunately, the President-elect had also promised not to disturb the consolidations and holding company structures already operating. Since the great consolidation movement had climaxed a decade earlier, for the chief executive to concede the prevailing noncompetitive system meant that very little indeed could be done to restore a salubrious environment for a free market.

With passage of the Clayton Anti-Trust Act and the establishment of the Federal Trade Commission (FTC) in 1914, the Wilson adminis-

President-elect Woodrow Wilson and out-going President William Howard Taft pose for photographers at the White House on Inauguration Day, March 4, 1913. His election, Wilson said in his address that day, represented the second thoughts of the American people on the material achievements of the nation at the cost of "lives snuffed out, of energies overtaxed and broken, the fearful physical and spiritual cost to the men and women and children upon whom the dead weight and burden of it all has fallen pitilessly the years through."

tration did the best it could (given its self-imposed limits) to prevent economic concentration from getting much worse. The new legislation included an effort to give a modern, relevant definition to collusive practices (for example, interlocking directorates among two or more ostensibly competing companies) and proscription of practices that were not monopolistic but appeared plainly designed to produce monopoly (for example, discriminatory pricing, whereby a company with many branches set low prices only in locations where it had competitors). The FTC's chief purpose was to keep pace with the inventiveness of the American entrepreneur by examining each new business technique and by defining and enjoining what it decided were "unfair trade practices."

The first Wilson administration (1913–1917) pushed through two other measures designed to reduce the concentration of "private power." The first was a drastic lowering of the protective tariff. For generations the Democratic Party had considered the tariff the "Mother of Trusts" because it excluded competition from abroad and effectively subsidized large domestic producers. The scandal of the Payne-Aldrich tariff in 1909 had occurred just when Americans seeking to improve the quality of life had become most acutely sensitized by experience in their own communities to the power of entrenched, remotely owned corporate interests. It also came after more than a decade of sharply rising prices, which had hit wage earners as well as those in the middle class who subsisted on relatively fixed incomes. The Underwood tariff bill of 1913, the first measure to be passed in Wilson's term, was a symptom of the public's reaction. It put scores of items on the "free list," drastically reduced all other schedules, and for the first time used the income tax—made constitutionally lawful by the Sixteenth Amendment in 1913—to make up needed revenues. The tariff was never fully tested, however, for the outbreak of war in Europe revived nationalist protective sentiments and set Democrats to worrying about the menace of European "dumping" on the American market when the war ended. The result was the Tariff Commission Act of 1916, which foreshadowed the resumption of full protectionism by 1921.

The second and more important measure was the Federal Reserve Act of December 1913. The act established twelve regional banks to provide reserve resources for private banks throughout the country. The reserve banks were authorized to convert into currency, in the form of Federal Reserve Notes, certain kinds of assets held by private banks, such as government bonds and commercial paper representing loans to businessmen. The assets served as backing for the issuance of the notes. In the past, the nation's money supply had mostly depended on private bank notes backed by gold and by Treasury bonds held by the issuing banks. By adding commercial paper to the note-issuing power, the act introduced some flexibility into the money supply by permitting the currency to increase when business transactions and loans increased, and vice versa. These features of the Federal Reserve System (FRS) appealed to small businessmen and farmers who were prey to the rising costs of loans precisely when they needed cash for harvesting and moving their products and whose remoteness from the credit centers of the country placed them at an additional disadvantage.

Wilson's administration fell far short, however, of reducing the power of the small group of private bankers who possessed the main strategic positions in the economy. The FRS did nothing to separate investment banking functions from commercial banking; the Glass-Steagall Act of 1933 would do that, after the stock market crash exposed major banking abuses. More important, the FRS made only the feeblest gestures toward reducing the interlocking control of all kinds of financial institutions by a small number of individuals each of whom sat on several corporate and banking directorates simultaneously. Finally, the act did nothing to redeem President Wilson's vow to equalize the chances of small and new businesses in their competition for credit with the giant corporations.

The inadequacy of the Wilsonian program lay in a contradiction between its objectives and the premises on which most of the progressives, including Wilson, continued to act. In a general way the progressives sought to emancipate American life from the tyranny of industrialism, especially from the corporatization it had imposed upon the society. But they could never liberate themselves adequately from the assumption that the foundations of a free society were essentially economic. Thus, they always trembled to tamper with the very economic institutions that required subordination. Implicitly they sought radical change but struggled to preserve the roots of the past. As a result, their reforms did little to alter the structure of advantages among the contending forces of the era.

War's Impact on Wilsonian Reform

The political and economic changes that did occur had almost certainly more to do with the outbreak of war in 1914 than with the progressive movement as it was manifested in the Wilson administration. For example, in the first three years of his administration, Wilson sided with conservatives by refusing to permit the federal government to underwrite amortized loans backed by farm land. But by 1916, Wilson became seriously concerned about the possibility of a shortage of foodstuffs unless farmers gained access to capital to develop marginal farm lands. He also may have worried about the startling growth of the Nonpartisan League, a north-central farm-state organization that advocated state ownership of railroad, insurance, warehouse, and credit facilities; the League had great appeal among credit-hungry farmers in undeveloped and marginal agricultural areas. The war issue, however, provided a sufficient reason and became the explanation for Wilson's sudden policy reversal. In February 1916, he threw his support to a rural credits program that established, with federal capital, twelve regional land banks that would help finance farm credit institutions.

At least two other measures can be attributed to the war crisis. Fear of clogged transportation lines at a time when the country might have to mobilize at any moment also persuaded Wilson to shelve his compunctions about "class legislation" and to dictate by statute the settlement of a threatened railroad strike. The Adamson Act of 1916 mandated an eight-hour day, with time and a half for overtime. This was the first instance of federal intervention in wage bargaining in a private industry. Establishment of the Tariff Commission similarly represented Wilson's obeisance to the war situation. By 1916, even free traders recognized the need for some protection against postwar flooding of markets when European producers revived and added their goods to what the war-expanded American industries were shipping.

As the carnage ground on in Europe, Wilson developed a fervor for mediating the peace, an ambition strongly enhanced by his extraordinary sense of religious purpose. The whole meaning of America, its historical mission to serve as herald for a new world order, and indeed the whole significance of Woodrow Wilson's own existence and rise to power, seemed suddenly close to realization. To say this amidst the prevailing skepticism three-quarters of the way through the twentieth century risks making a fanatic of Wilson. Certainly the man felt his religious obligations deeply, perhaps in some respects more intimately than his average contemporary did, but there was nothing unbalanced or unreasonable about him. Unlike the plastic religiosity that would become so common by mid-century, religion in the early part of the century still conveyed a literal force.

In 1916, it contributed to Wilson's earnest determination to participate in the negotiations that would shape the postwar world.

One prerequisite was that he win reelection in a contest against
a Republican Party reunited behind the candidacy of Supreme Court
Justice Charles Evans Hughes. Toward this end Wilson reversed
himself on a number of issues and in some cases compromised
dearly held principles. To construct a winning coalition required
splitting off at least a half-million votes from the normal Republican
majority. Wilson set his sights especially on those who had left the
GOP for Roosevelt in 1912. The rural credits legislation helped
enormously with the usually Republican agricultural interests of the
Middle and Far West. So too did the Tariff Commission Act, for even
dissident Republicans were protectionists and had remained unimpressed with the "free trade" tariff act that Wilson had put
through in 1913. To attract the generally Republican social workers
of the big cities, Wilson reversed himself on a federal child labor
act, although he continued to insist (correctly, as it turned out) that
the courts would find it unconstitutional, and on a federal workman's

Election of 1916

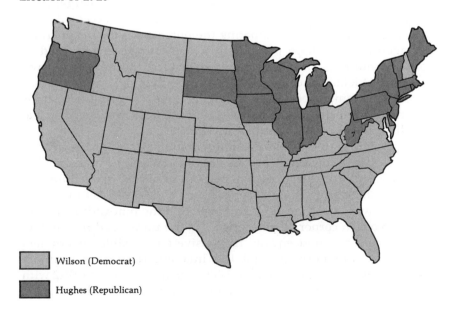

Wilson (Democrat)

Hughes (Republican)

compensation act, which he also expected (this time wrongly) the courts to void.

Although many historians have argued that Wilson abandoned his New Freedom for Roosevelt's New Nationalism in 1916, federal policies in that election year resembled TR's 1912 program only superficially. Wilson did digress from the principle that government's only legitimate function was to guarantee "a free and fair field" — that is, to maintain the efficacy of the marketplace. The rural credits legislation, the Tariff Commission Act, and especially the Adamson Act, all did suggest that special interests could henceforth apply to the government for benefits beyond what the marketplace offered. What was missing was the spirit of a lasting national purpose — something larger and more enduring than the specific circumstances brought on by the war and Wilson's heightened desire to gain reelection. Only the atmosphere of crisis made it possible to claim that the 1916 measures contributed to the national interest above and beyond what they offered to the special interests that had come to the trough.

Once the United States entered the war, indeed, much more would follow. Americans would submit to the federally directed allocation of foodstuffs and material resources and to government operation of the telephone, telegraph, and railroad systems. Businesses doing work on war contracts faced sanctions if they failed to bargain collectively with their employees, and most industries accepted price and wage controls. By coordinating the purchase of the major crops, war agencies fixed farm prices, partly to encourage greater production. In addition, the government suspended the anti-trust laws, and both officially and unofficially (by abetting vigilante activities) discouraged employees from changing jobs or going on strike. Superficially all this could be called socialism as well as New Nationalism, but of course none of it was either.

The evolution of the Wilson administration's position on government assistance to various private sectors is worth further scrutiny. The burden of Roosevelt's argument, both in his use of the Bureau of Corporations during his own presidency and in his call for "commission government" in 1912, had been that the innovative capabilities of modern corporate enterprise and the unrealized potential of other sectors required equally responsive and flexible government regulations. Commissions, not the inherent rigidity of statutory prescriptions, could provide that. Wilson had countered in 1912 with the warning that unless rigid guidelines were established by statute, it would be impossible to prevent the interests to be regulated from controlling the regulators. The inexorable logic of both positions would be fully proved during the next ten years.

At first Wilson was confident about the efficacy of statutory law. In presenting his anti-trust program in 1913, he asserted that after more than a decade of debate it had become plain enough which corporate practices the law should permit and which contravened conventional standards of legitimacy. But he did not reckon with the continuity, or indeed with the acceleration, of change. By the end of 1914, a serious business recession and the outbreak of war in Europe persuaded him that extensive statutory prescriptions would unduly aggravate business uncertainties. Each new provision of the anti-trust laws had to be tested in court, and the courts had amply demonstrated their whimsical ways. The FTC was one consequence of Wilson's new reckoning, but it was a minor one. Until Calvin Coolidge packed the commission a decade later with men favorable to business consolidation and corporate autonomy, the FTC functioned largely as intended, to make independent investigations of illegitimate corporate practices, to expose illegal behavior, and to obtain cease-and-desist orders. In other words, it worked to protect competition, not to foster and regulate combinations. (Its anti-trust activities, indeed, would get the commission into deep political trouble with the reactionary Republican Congress of 1919–1921.) The Wilson administration made far more serious concessions to the need for flexibility than creating a regulatory commission.

First, the Justice Department began accepting "consent decrees" instead of pressing anti-trust charges through the courts. A "consent decree" permitted a corporation to elude prosecution upon the abandonment of the disputed business practice and the promise not to do it again, without conceding that what it had done was illegal — and without losing the trade advantages its (probably illegal) behavior had gained for it. The war and the Wilson administration's fear of rocking business' boat in times of "crisis" served as sufficient justification.

The war brought about a more thorough liaison between government and the ascendant interests of the business community. By 1916 as American intervention appeared to grow more likely, "preparedness" groups arose among some businessmen to coordinate military ordnance requirements with business capabilities. Again, the logic of the development was indisputable. Without coordination, mobilization would become a nightmare of chaotic waste. Moreover, the long-neglected military establishment, led by men of poor or at least badly tested administrative abilities, could not be expected to meet its needs. In fact, except for the leaders of the big business corporations, no one in America had the training to handle the massive problems of national resource allocation, interagency administrative organization, the integration of economic factors, and the economics of intracorporate transfer payments. The country had nothing comparable to the relatively disinterested educational establishment that would begin to emerge in policy-making circles during Franklin Roosevelt's New Deal. In August 1916, the National Defense Advisory Committee (NDAC), consisting of seven private business leaders appointed by members of Wilson's Cabinet, began operating virtually as a contracting agency hired by the government to provide war matériel and services. Inevitably, business interests that felt excluded by the NDAC advisers began to protest, so that by July 1917 Congress found it necessary to replace the NDAC with the more officially structured War Industries Board (WIB). But just as inevitably, lacking any national system of regulatory offices, the WIB turned to the private United States Chamber of Commerce (USCC) to form "war service committees" throughout the country. These committees consisted of businessmen elected by the dominant trade association in each industry or, in industries with no functioning trade association, by groups named by the USCC itself.

The war service committees were private commercial bodies certified by the federal government to represent the collective interests of each industrial or mercantile sector and authorized to operate outside the anti-trust laws. They made crucial decisions concerning which companies could obtain which materials, which contracts, and virtually at what prices. Their decisions were, practically speaking, subject only to the veto of Bernard Baruch, the chairman of the WIB, who self-consciously operated as a supreme arbiter of the national good. As approvingly summarized by Grosvenor Clarkson, erstwhile secretary of the NDAC and later "official" historian of the WIB, through the scores of war service committees, "industry imposed its own emergency laws and regulations and assumed ninetenths of the burden of responsibility for enforcing them." Contemporary mythology averred that the businessmen who so served stoutly put their private interests behind them for the duration. But the extent to which Americans believed that would testify only to the innocence of an age that lingered on the assumption that the nation's interests could be identified with the voluntary arrangements worked out by private business enterprise.

When the war ended, the Wilson administration made haste to cut loose nearly all the putative New Nationalist paraphernalia it had adopted. Suspicious of each other, the politicians and business leaders who had participated in the WIB's experiment with industrial cooperation promptly dismantled the machinery they had constructed during the previous two years. Agricultural supports were abandoned with a suddenness that contributed substantially to the farm disasters of 1920 and 1921. The War Labor Board's policies of supporting collective bargaining dissolved in the federal government's panicked reaction to the spread of strikes in 1919 (caused by the government's precipitous abandonment of price controls while attempting to use its wartime powers, still technically operative because there was no peace treaty, to enforce a wage freeze). Congress and the administration moved to shelve the steeply graduated income tax and the excess profits tax, deflating expectations that at least those would prove not merely war measures but durable achievements of the progressive movement that the society might use to bring about a more equitable distribution of wealth. In sum, the retreat from progressive achievements usually attributed to Harding and Coolidge actually began in the closing years of the Wilson administration. The Wilsonian progressives had never regarded them as more than war measures.

The Demise of Confidence

The apparent exigencies of war and the mania for protection against internal subversion eventually justified far more than the close regulation of Americans' economic activities. The Post Office would decide what literature Americans could not read; the Justice Department would prescribe, under the authority of the Sedition and Espionage Acts, what Americans could not say; and the War Department, through the Selective Service, would take on the awesome task of deciding which young men might have to surrender their lives. This was done in the name of national security. If it had anything to do with the spirit of progressivism that Roosevelt had addressed back in 1912, it was only in the sense that the war itself came to be clothed in the garb of a crusade for progressive, democratic ideals. The garb proved to be a disguise, as many by 1919 discovered. The cause of national security brought to America only an illusive, superimposed unity, which the progressive movement, for all its small successes and large enthusiasms, had failed to achieve. It would channel the panicked energies of a nation undergoing a profound social revolution not in the manner that the capping of an oil well allows for controlled distribution of the pressure below but in the way that a hose nozzle narrows and intensifies the heedless flow behind it.

Panic had been building for a long time before the war. Growing evidence of radical social change had produced increasingly passionate mobilization in defense of conventional institutions. At the same time, some who had enjoyed few advantages in American society began to show impatience with the continued neglect of their interests. The two extremes only occasionally clashed head-on; more usually they vented their rage on imagined or convenient enemies.

The defenders represented themselves as the stalwarts of civilization, and on its behalf they plainly prepared to use any and all means available, not least violence and intimidation. Roman Catholics, traditional targets throughout American history, once more became marks. The animus of the 1890's, when the American Protective Association spread its bile, was restored in 1911 with the organization of the Guardians of Liberty, headed by former Commanding General of the Army Nelson Miles as "Chief Guardian," and with the launching in the same year of *The Menace,* a pathologically anti-Catholic weekly from Aurora, Missouri, which within four years achieved a national circulation of 1.5 million. But every other minority or nonconforming group sooner or later aroused the wrath of "patriots" in different parts of the country. Negroes, who had mostly been subdued by 1910, became subjected to mass violence once more as they began in 1915 the first large migration to northern and western cities in response to the wartime demand for industrial labor. Few southern outrages compared with the intensity of the race riot in East St. Louis, Illinois, on July 2, 1917. Police and national guardsmen stood by and watched or participated in an assault on the black section of town that left hundreds of homes burned and thirty-nine blacks and nine whites dead.

Until 1914, the "official" reaction in the country to vigilantism and hate groups was mostly negative, but the rise of the Industrial Workers of the World (IWW) made such a posture increasingly uncomfortable. Even in California, where traditions of civil liberties were about as insubstantial as in the deep South, Progressive Governor Hiram Johnson, TR's vice-presidential running mate in 1912, at first exercised a restraining influence on the efforts of employers' groups to prevent IWW organizers from holding meetings, distributing literature, and making speeches. By 1914, even Johnson declined to stake his influence any longer on attempts to defend constitutional principles of free speech and assembly. Organized in 1905 by William ("Big Bill") Haywood, leader of the Western Federation of Miners, and by Eugene V. Debs, head of the Socialist Party of America, the "Wobblies" made a point of rejecting government authority and of dedicating themselves to the destruction of capitalism by any means necessary. Haywood's advocacy of "a little sabotage in the right place at the proper time" gave them a self-defeating reputation for treachery; it aroused popular belligerence grossly disproportionate to anything the Wobblies ever accomplished. In 1912, even the Socialists expelled them; Debs repudiated "any tactics which involve stealth, secrecy, intrigue and necessitate acts of industrial violence for their execution." The IWW gave expression to the frustrations of those who had the least stake in organized society—miners, lumberjacks, and migratory workers. In 1912 and 1913 they achieved a few remarkable successes in eastern industrial cities like Lawrence, Massachusetts, and Paterson, New Jersey, and won a "Free Speech" battle in San Diego. But, as Roger Baldwin, later director of the American Civil Liberties Union, observed, these victories may only have stimulated further the already demonstrated eagerness of conservatives to use foul means to control the forces that threatened them. Convinced of the absolute rightness of their own interests, the self-appointed defenders of American institutions believed there was too much at stake to observe "legal niceties." Most Americans were not prepared to honor the principle of equal treatment before the law for any whom they regarded as "enemies of civilization."

Even before the United States officially entered the war in April 1917, "patriotic" ardor had risen to a fevered pitch. Upon American entry, near-hysteria took over. Outrages to constitutional law and to human decency, to say nothing of offenses to common sense, were abundant. Hundreds of men and women—possibly thousands—were boldly abused, and some were murdered. Their assailants went unmolested and often uncriticized. At times there were scenes reminiscent of Old World pogroms. In Flat River, Missouri, in mid-July 1917, scores of immigrant workers were suddenly expelled from town by local "patriots" eager for their jobs. A *New York Herald* dispatch from the town a few days later reported:

Today weary mothers carrying babes, with older children trudging along in the dust, lined almost every road out of town. They were going to join their husbands, who were driven out yesterday or the day before, but many of them did not know just where to go. . . . Reports of pillage continue to be made.

In a few extraordinary incidents people were shot by zealots for failing to rise during the playing of the National Anthem. Many more were arrested for speaking "disrespectfully" of the flag or simply for declining to display it on demand. Convictions for such offenses came swiftly, and sentences were meted out in months and years. Patriots attacked especially Americans of German descent and subjected them to a variety of humiliating gestures, such as making

Elizabeth Gurley Flynn, twenty-three-year-old organizer for the Industrial Workers of the World, addresses silk workers during the strike in Paterson, New Jersey, from February to July 1913. The daughter of Irish immigrants, Flynn began her career as a radical when she was sixteen. Being a woman in an era of strident "male chauvinism" gave her (for a time) certain advantages as a labor agitator. In 1909, a Spokane jury that sent a coorganizer to prison for "criminal conspiracy" freed Flynn because, as the foreman told the prosecutor, no jury "is goin' to send that pretty Irish girl to jail merely for bein' bighearted and idealistic, to mix with all those whores and crooks down at the pen."

Brown Brothers

demonstrations of their "loyalty" by publicly kneeling and kissing the flag.

Vigilantism had not merely racial and xenophobic elements; it had distinctly economic and class overtones. Employers and business associations exploited the widespread malaise to discipline their labor force and beat down labor "agitators." The race riot in East St. Louis as well as subsequent disorders in New York, Chicago, and elsewhere, followed the use of black workers as strikebreakers (though one must not conclude that that was the sole reason for the riots). Anti-syndicalist laws, ostensibly aimed at the IWW, camouflaged the railroading of labor organizers of any sort and suppression of speech, free assembly, and the press wherever labor relations were tense. In the name of law and order, police, militia, and federal troops frequently rode roughshod over citizens whose economic grievances were thought to jeopardize the national security. Arizona witnessed its own "Armenian incident" when vigilantes and local authorities near Bisbee kidnaped twelve hundred striking miners, put them on board a cattle train without food or water, and abandoned them in the New Mexico desert in mid-July 1917. In this case, federal troops were belatedly dispatched to the rescue, but most Americans seemed to consider the action justified because the strikers had "sabotaged" the copper mines by refusing to work for the wages offered.

The worst of it was that the hysteria had the official support of the government. Sedition and anti-syndicalist laws cropped up in many states, making it a crime to do virtually anything that in the judgment of local as well as federal authorities might "hinder the war effort." The country's leading political figures, not least President Wilson himself, endorsed the motto "He who is not with us is against us and is to be punished." None exceeded the shrillness of Theodore Roosevelt, who warned: "The Hun within our gates masquerades in many disguises; he is our dangerous enemy; and he should be hunted down without mercy." The United States attorney general congratulated the Illinois Bar Association for declaring disloyal any lawyer who took the case of someone charged with draft evasion and he warned that "an outraged people and an avenging government" would have no mercy on those who opposed the war.

With the encouragement of the War and Justice Departments, vigilante groups sprang up in every corner of the nation. The American Defense Society, the National Security League, and the American Protective League led the list. There were also the Sedition

Slammers, the Terrible Threateners, the American Vigilante Patrol, the Knights of Liberty, and the Boy Spies of America. The most important was the American Protective League, which the Justice Department officially sponsored. For a small registration fee, one could become a member of the league and thus deputized to make "secret service" investigations of one's neighbors. Nearly every state, city, and town had its Council of Defense, dedicated to the harassment of every "slacker" or "traitor," which usually meant anyone who suggested that the United States should not have entered the war, who objected to conscription, who thought conscription of wealth was at least as justifiable as the drafting of men, who protested conditions of employment, or who had the horrendous misfortune to intimate in public that the Allies' treatment of their imperial subjects in Africa, Ireland, and India was probably as brutal as the Germans' treatment of the Belgians. George Creel, who as the federal director of the Committee on Public Information during the war contributed substantially to the hysteria in his own right, reflected thirty years later on the obnoxious shrillness of the principal loyalty, defense, and security leagues. "At all times," he remembered, "their patriotism was a thing of screams, violence, and extremes, and their savage intolerances had the burn of acid."

Denunciations of dissent did not stop with the argument that the opponents of war, of conscription, or of particular labor policies were wrong: they insisted that opposition was degenerate and

Every community was eager to demonstrate its loyalty to the nation, its devotion to the war effort, its willingness to serve. This Junior Red Cross Parade in St. Paul, Minnesota, probably in the early fall of 1917, is an example of how the Red Cross' mission of mercy mingled easily with "100 Percent Patriotism" and veneration of the flag.

Minnesota Historical Society

treasonous. Thus, newspapers such as the *Los Angeles Times* excoriated President Wilson himself in April 1917 for having "unpatriotically" aided and abetted "the sleeping treason that would avoid the righteous sacrifices of war" by resisting intervention until then. One must not dismiss this phenomenon as a political tactic or as a consequence of "natural wartime excitement." The ease with which charges of treason flowed followed logically from the prevailing assumption that only someone morally obtuse could fail to recognize that the Germans were really barbarians—"Huns" and "Tartars" and "Goths." The frequency with which the "patriots" raised the image of saving civilization points to precisely what appeared to be at stake. At the same time, the extremism of the attacks suggests the hyperbole used by those who have begun to doubt that they are right. Those who reiterated to themselves and to others their belief that "the German Government is the inveterate foe of all the ideals which we hold sacred" (from Secretary of State Robert Lansing's 1916 diary) cannot have failed to perceive, even if only subconsciously, that by 1914 many things once held "sacred" had already become objects of searching skepticism. Inevitably, the treason bag held not merely opponents of the war but socialists, pacifists, aliens, atheists, unionists, wets, "uppity" blacks, disinterested intellectuals, and anyone else whose apparent nonconformity exposed the weaknesses of the social fabric.

End of an Era

The progressive era, which had begun secure in the confidence of the nation's moral soundness, drew to a close in a condition that one can only describe as panic. As Henry F. May has observed in *The End of American Innocence* (1959), "Most of the custodians of culture, beset already by intellectual attack and worried by signs of sexual, racial and other kinds of insurrection, linked the Allied Cause with the defense of all they valued, and thereby added the last element needed to produce a really big explosion." In an article for *The New Republic* in 1915, historian James Harvey Robinson put into the category of obsolete ideals a variety of once-dependable verbal formulas, including "sound doctrine, consistency, fidelity to conscience, eternal verities, immutable human nature, and the imprescriptible rights of man." Woodrow Wilson successfully brought to bear the force of precisely such formulas in mobilizing Americans for war. "It would be impossible," he said in 1917, "for men to go through the dark night of this terrible struggle if it were not that they believed they were standing for some eternal principles of right." Nevertheless, the emotional excesses of the war and post-war years sharply indicated the uncertainty nagging at the American spirit.

The outbreak of war in Europe in midsummer 1914 had produced an instant trauma throughout most of the western world. For the

Although still in their infancy, the movies had already produced a few big name "stars" by the time the United States entered World War I. A huge crowd gathers to hear Douglas Fairbanks, Sr., speak the cause of patriotism as he promotes Liberty Bonds on the steps of the Subtreasury Building, Wall Street, New York. Fairbanks, like Mary Pickford whom he married in 1920, established himself first as a stage actor before entering films in 1915.

great civilized nations to have fallen upon each other with the brute violence so many westerners had come to believe was reserved for the lesser peoples of the world seems to have burst all at once some of the more important illusions about progress that both Europeans and Americans had cherished over the previous decade and more. Memoirs as well as surviving letters and editorials abound in expressions of unfathomable shock and suggest the somber, dazed, immediate certainty that something fine had been shattered forever.

At the same time, a distinct exhilaration seems to have accompanied the sense of tragedy. It had, in part, something to do with a lingering of the same optimism that had fueled the era's reform movements. War, some people quickly rationalized, could perfect the advances humanity had made over the previous century. Had not the progressive Indiana congressman, Albert Beveridge, once described war as "the divine instrument of progress"? "War, when you are at it," conceded Oliver Wendell Holmes, Jr., in 1895, "is horrible and dull. It is only when time has passed that you see that its message was divine." "We need it," added the twice-wounded Civil War veteran and future Supreme Court Justice, "that we may realize that our comfortable routine is no eternal necessity of things." William James had thought in 1906 that martial attributes and the thrill of conquest had lost their popular favor; they seemed "no longer morally avowable motives." The sudden reality of war appears to have restored their appeal. "Is not peace an element of civil corruption?" asked Thomas Mann, the German novelist. "The German soul," he declared, "is opposed to the pacifist ideal of civilization." War, he exulted, would prove "a purification, a liberation, an enormous hope," and the expected German triumph would be a victory for excellence and spirit over numbers. On the other side, Henri Bergson, the great French philosopher, expressed his confidence that an Allied victory would bring "the rejuvenation and enlargement of France [and] the moral regeneration of Europe," so that "France and humanity" could "resume the march forward . . . toward truth and justice." Rupert Brooke, the British poet who would soon gain martyrdom in a Flanders field, proclaimed in 1914 his own gladness "To turn . . . from a world grown old and cold and weary."

> Honor has come back. . . .
> And Nobleness walks in our ways again,
> And we have come into our heritage.

"If this war had not come, we should all have been rotten!" the American journalist and reformer, Ray Stannard Baker, recorded in his diary. "I thought once it could be done by some voluntary revolt from comfort and property. . . . But it was not enough. . . . At moments I fear lest this war be over too soon — before the people are scourged into an awakening." The progressive American journal, *The New Republic,* was impelled to remark in October 1915: "Instead of the thankfulness that we are providentially escaping the storm, one finds on every hand the sense that we are missing something."

In retrospect, militant nationalism's triumph over reason and human sympathy became one of the more disillusioning features of the war era. Or at least it was disappointing to those who had entered the progressive era optimistic that scientific rationalism could make civilization more humane. Perhaps Holmes was right when he said in 1916: "It seems to me so useless to be confident when again and again we are given proof that only the inbred qualities of men really count, and that you spread those by selecting them for survival, and not by building Polytechnics or starting settlements in the slums." With determined effort the social reformers could stimulate concern (largely, to be sure, by appealing to self-interest) about human beings who suffered deprivation, maltreatment, and injustice. But if there were 20 million Americans who subsisted in poverty, there were 80 million who enjoyed substantial comfort. It was a fact that continued to speak to the nation's remarkable success. Eventually the 80 million, or a major portion of them, became bored with reform. There were movies, baseball and prize-fighting, the new syncopated music called "ragtime" and the new-style, up-close dancing that went with it, cigarettes (for women, too), nightclubs and vaudeville shows, automobiles one could buy cheap that could take the family for a time on the town or for an excursion in the country. There were things to do, to enjoy. For a short time at least, the war became one of them.

The "boredom of being at peace" and "the peacefulness of being at war" explain much about the excessive enthusiasm that sustained the mindless carnage for more than four years, and that disrupted the return to "normalcy" afterward. "There was one potent intoxicant," writes British historian Arthur Marwick in *The Deluge* (1965), "which helped even intelligent men to accept the indescribable suffering and sorrow long after the sentiments of honour and duty were becoming tarnished. . . . This was the feeling that here indeed was *the* Great War, a time of historical intensity such as had never been lived through before." The war added a dimension of largeness, of splendor and worthwhileness, to the lives of ordinary men and women. It allowed them to postpone the tough, humdrum decisions about living in favor of dramatic concerns about death. It made the distinction between good and evil simple once more. It forgave them their unwillingness to tolerate those who challenged their choices in such matters.

And then it was over.

SUGGESTED READINGS

Every student of the early twentieth-century United States ought first to peruse Mark Sullivan's marvellous six volumes, *Our Times* (1926–1934), a journalist's collection of photographs, sketches, cartoons, contemporary advertisements, paintings, and even sheet music, illustrating mainly the social history of the Roosevelt and Wilson eras, with an extensive running commentary that is often uniquely perceptive. Lewis Atherton, *Main Street on the Middle Border* (1954), and Robert H. Walker, *Life in the Age of Enterprise, 1865–1900* (1967), will further familiarize readers with the flavor of turn-of-the-century life. Samuel P. Hays, *The Response to Industrialism, 1885–1914* (1957), and Robert H. Wiebe, *The Search for Order, 1877–1920* (1967), offer interesting historical syntheses. For more specialized treatments of the nineteenth-century background, see Henry F. May, *Protestant Churches and Industrial America* (1949); Richard Hofstadter, *Social Darwinism in American Thought* (1955 ed.); James Willard Hurst, *Law and the Conditions of Freedom in the Nineteenth Century United States* (1956); Edward C. Kirkland, *Industry Comes of Age, 1860–1897* (1961); Blake McKelvey, *The Urbanization of America, 1860–1915* (1964); and Fred Shannon, *The Farmer's Last Frontier: Agriculture, 1860–1897* (1961). Harold U. Faulkner, *The Decline of Laissez Faire, 1897–1917* (1951), is a sometimes dry but always informative account of economic and technological developments. Matthew Josephson's detailed biography, *Edison* (1959), and Keith Sward's provocative *The Legend of Henry Ford* (1948) cover much more than just those two inventors' careers. Erik Barnouw, *A Tower in Babel: A History of Broadcasting in the United States to 1933* (1966), is poorly written but contains the best available coverage of that subject. Thomas Cochran's survey, *The American Business System* (1957), is presently being rewritten; watch for it.

For social winds of change, the following titles are generally self-explanatory: William L. O'Neill, *Everyone Was Brave: The Rise and Fall of Feminism in America* (1969), which is a little tendentious; Andrew Sinclair, *The Better Half: The Emancipation of American Women* (1965), a fast, easily read survey; Aileen S. Kraditor, *The Ideas of the Woman Suffrage Movement, 1890–1920* (1965); David M. Kennedy, *Birth Control in America: The Career of Margaret Sanger* (1970), a brilliant essay that examines much more than the subtitle indicates; Rush Welter, *Popular Education and Democratic Thought in America* (1962), covers the country's whole history but is especially stimulating for the progressive era; so too is Lawrence Cremin's *The Transformation of the School: Progressivism in American Education, 1876–1956* (1961); Raymond

Callahan, *Education and the Cult of Efficiency: A Study of the Social Forces That Have Shaped the Administration of the Public Schools* (1962); Richard Hofstadter's *Anti-Intellectualism in American Life* (1964), like Welter's tome, starts from the beginning; Nathan G. Hale, Jr., *Freud and the Americans: The Beginnings of Psychoanalysis in America, 1876–1917* (1971), a brilliant, exhaustive study. Morton White, *Social Thought in America: The Revolt Against Formalism* (1957 ed.), has become a classic. It should be read in conjunction with Charles Forcey, *The Crossroads of Liberalism: Croly, Weyl, Lippmann and the Progressive Era, 1900–1925* (1961); Samuel J. Konefsky, *The Legacy of Holmes and Brandeis: A Study in the Influence of Ideas* (1956); James Willard Hurst, *Justice Holmes on Legal History* (1964); David Riesman, *Thorstein Veblen: A Critical Interpretation* (1953); and the chapters on William James and John Dewey in Paul K. Conkin's *Puritans and Pragmatists* (1968). Henry F. May, *The End of American Innocence: A Study of the First Years of Our Own Time: 1912–1917* (1959), makes the difficult nuances of cultural change clear.

For the progressive movement, Richard Hofstadter's *The Age of Reform* (1956) is still the most stimulating analysis despite innumerable efforts to pick it apart. George Mowry, *The Era of Theodore Roosevelt* (1958), and Arthur S. Link, *Woodrow Wilson and the Progressive Era* (1954), are both excellent surveys, although they are heavily weighted on the political coverage. John Morton Blum's *The Republican Roosevelt* (1954) and *Woodrow Wilson and the Politics of Morality* (1956) are both especially perceptive and well written. Roy Lubove, *The Professional Altruist: The Emergence of Social Work as a Career, 1880–1930* (1965); Allen F. Davis, *Spearheads of Reform: The Social Settlements and the Progressive Movement, 1890–1914* (1967); Samuel P. Hays, *Conservation and the Gospel of Efficiency* (1959); Samuel Haber, *Efficiency and Uplift: Scientific Management in the Progressive Era, 1890–1920* (1964); Paul Carter, *The Decline and Revival of the Social Gospel* (1954); Mel Scott, *American City Planning since 1890* (1969); Roy Lubove, *The Progressives and the Slums* (1962); Joseph R. Gusfield, *Symbolic Crusade: Status Politics and the American Temperance Movement* (1963); Andrew Sinclair, *Era of Excess: A Social History of the Prohibition Movement* (1962); and Robert H. Bremner, *From the Depths: The Discovery of Poverty in the U.S.* (1956), will all help the student to cover the vital nonpolitical elements of progressivism.

On the Regulation Movement, it might be well to start with R. M. Abrams' brief documentary essay, *The Issue of Federal Regulation in the Progressive Era* (1963). Gabriel Kolko's *The Triumph of Conservatism* (1963) and *Railroads and Regulations* (1964) have had great appeal to a generation of students disillusioned with the American liberal heritage, but they both misuse evidence and have to be read with caution for the interesting information they contain. Albro Martin, *Enterprise Denied: Origins of the Decline of American Railroads, 1897–1917* (1971), the mirror opposite of Kolko's efforts, blames regulation for the destruction of a valuable industry. K. Austin Kerr, *American Railroad Politics, 1914–1920* (1968); Robert H. Wiebe, *Businessmen and Reform: A Study of the Progressive Movement* (1962); Marver Bernstein, *Regulating Business by Independent Commission* (1955); and Melvin I. Urofsky, *Big Steel and the Wilson Administration* (1969), should help to correct Kolko's and Martin's one-dimensional approaches.

Marc Karson, *American Labor Unions and Politics, 1900–1918* (1958), is not convincing when he stresses workers' Catholicism as a conservative influence against unionism, but otherwise it presents an extremely stimulating account. Melvyn Dubofsky, *We Shall Be All: A History of the Industrial Workers of the World* (1969), is an exhaustive labor of love. James Weinstein, *The Decline of Socialism in America, 1912–1925* (1967), must be read together with Daniel Bell, *Marxian Socialism in the United States* (1967 ed.), because they offer contradicting theses. John Laslett, *Labor and the Left: A Study of Socialist and Radical Influences in the American Labor Movement 1881–1924* (1970), offers some sharply drawn case studies. John Higham, *Strangers in the Land* (1955), is still the best survey of American nativist attitudes. Oscar Handlin's *The Uprooted* (1949) is a valuable attempt to present the immigrant's view of the assimilation problem. August Meier's *Negro Thought in America, 1880–1915: Racial Ideologies in the Age of Booker T. Washington* (1963) remains the most thorough study of the subject.

H. C. Peterson and Gilbert C. Fite, *Opponents of War, 1917–1918* (1957); William Preston, Jr., *Aliens and Dissenters: Federal Suppression of Radicals, 1903–1933* (1963); Zachariah Chaffee, Jr., *Free Speech in the United States* (1941); and Richard Hofstadter and Walter Metzger, *The Development of Academic Freedom in the United States* (1957), help to demonstrate the difficulties of dissent. Joan M. Jensen, *The Price of Vigilance* (1968), is a useful account of the American Protective League.

Some of the best treatment of vital subjects, such as black resistance to oppression, the war economy, and the rise of the corporation, is contained in scholarly articles. Students can find many of them in anthologies, notably, R. M. Abrams and L. W. Levine, eds., *The Shaping of Twentieth-Century America* (1971), which also contains the R. M. Abrams' "The Failure of Progressivism," not printed elsewhere; A. S. Link, ed., *The Impact of World War I* (1969); and S. Fine, ed., *Recent America* (1967). Arthur M. Schlesinger, Jr., and Morton White, eds., *Paths of American Thought* (1963), contains extremely useful articles not available elsewhere, such as Richard Hofstadter, "The Revolution in Higher Education," Alfred Kazin, "The Realistic Novel," Morton White, "Pragmatism and the Scope of Science," and Paul Samuelson, "Economic Thought and the New Industrialism." Similarly, Seymour E. Harris, ed., *American Economic History* (1961), has Lloyd Ulman's "The Development of Trades and Labor Unions" and "Unionism and Collective Bargaining in the Modern Period," and other original essays by different scholars on population, immigration, natural resource policies, and transportation.

Significant Statistics

	1900	1920
Population	76,094,000	106,466,000
Percentage urban	39.7	51.2
Percentage rural	60.3	48.8
Percentage non- white	12.0	10.0
Life expectancy		
White	47.6	54.9
Nonwhite	33.0	45.3

Gross national prod-
  uct (current
  dollars)		

Total (billions of dollars)	17.3	88.9
Per capita (dollars)	231	835

Defense spending
  (millions of
  dollars)[a]
	332	4,329

As percentage of GNP	1.9	5.0
Military personnel on active duty	125,923	343,302
Labor union mem- bership	791,000	5,034,000
Birth rate (per 1,000 live births)	32.3	27.7

Advertising expendi-
  tures (millions
  of dollars)
	542	2,935

Motor vehicle registrations	8,000	239,161
Persons lynched		
White	9	8
Nonwhite	106	53

High school grad-
  uates (as percent-
  age of all
  persons over
  16 years old)
	6.4	16.8

Sources: *Historical Statistics of the United States, Colonial Times to 1957; Statistical Abstract of the United States,* 1970; and *Digest of Educational Statistics,* 1970.

[a] Includes veterans spending; excludes interest.

2

The Challenges of Power
American Diplomacy, 1900–1921

SAMUEL F. WELLS, JR.

It is difficult for Americans who came to international awareness after World War II to comprehend the limited interests and the parochial point of view of United States foreign relations at the turn of the century. In 1900 the nation was just beginning the international involvement that would be vastly accelerated by two world wars and would lead to the feeling after 1945 that Americans had an interest in every significant shift of power around the globe. The distance from the diplomacy of William McKinley to that of Richard Nixon is immense, despite a number of striking personal and political similarities between the two men.

One might assume that a nation with over 1.2 million troops and 399 major military installations overseas in 1970 had an established tradition of foreign commitment. Yet the international orientation

of the United States in 1900 showed only a dim outline of what it would become. At that time the only American troops on foreign soil were 5,728 engaged in the stabilization and reform of Cuba and 2,140 remaining in Peking as a legation guard after the Boxer expedition. The diplomatic establishment was equally modest. Whereas in 1970 the personnel of the State Department working in the United States totaled 12,050 (including over 4,000 members of the Peace Corps and the Agency for International Development), in 1900 the department had 98 employees. In 1970 the Department of State received or sent more than three thousand telegrams a day; in 1900 one man, Second Assistant Secretary Alvey A. Adee, read and sorted every message coming into the department and personally drafted most of those being dispatched. The foreign policy bureaucrat of today must envy but can never achieve the coordination and continuity that Adee provided in his forty-two years as an assistant secretary of state.

By 1900 American diplomacy had begun its great transformation; World War I would highlight many changes already under way and initiate others. Although most of the basic alterations in foreign relations became permanent only after 1941, the definition of interests as well as the creation of precedents and rhetoric that would shape much of the future occurred in the first two decades of the century as the United States adjusted to the responsibilities of being a great power.

Turning Outward

For the origins of America's expanded international activity one must look to the 1890's. During that decade numerous reasons, some irrational but no less persuasive, induced Americans to turn outward. After devoting a generation to industrial expansion and conquering the West, they wanted to assert beyond the borders the new strength of their nation and its traditional humanitarianism. For some the most attractive opportunities now lay abroad. A vocal group of business leaders, convinced that industrial production exceeded the nation's capacity to consume, insisted that the only way to prevent overproduction and the recurrence of financial panics like that in 1893 was to gain secure markets and sources of raw materials overseas. Many Americans, pointing to the revival of imperial expansion during the 1880's, felt the European powers had shown the way to resolve this problem. In addition to providing markets and raw materials, colonies would remove the difficulties posed by the disappearance of the frontier, announced by the superintendent of the Census in 1890. They would create a compelling reason to develop a large battle fleet and a chain of naval stations, which some industrialists and advocates of power politics wanted for reasons of their own. An empire would also stimulate and protect the rapidly growing Protestant missionary effort.

Critics of expansionism argued in vain that by the mid-1890's many perceptive European leaders were rejecting imperialism because it created more difficulties than it solved. Workers' demands for higher wages so that they could purchase supposedly excess goods were futile. Would-be imperialists were not moved by the argument that because the Census Office had defined the frontier as a continuous line of unsettled land, the proclamation of the frontier's end overlooked vast tracts of inexpensive land still available. The current of opinion ran too strongly against these thoughts from traditional America. The new attitudes fed heavily on the ideas of Social Darwinism, and Americans increasingly believed that the nation could prove its fitness to survive only by joining the great powers of Europe in their imperial contests.

Burgeoning aspirations for an expanded role in the world strongly conditioned Americans' view of Cuba's revolt against Spain in 1895. The McKinley administration sought a pacified, autonomous Cuba in order to protect extensive American investments on the island and maintain a high level of trade, but the intransigence of both Spain and the rebels prevented any resolution of the guerrilla warfare. Propaganda from rebel juntas or councils in several large United States cities stimulated humanitarian sympathy for the Cuban people, and the sinking of the battleship *Maine* in Havana harbor, with the loss of over 260 American lives, created a widespread clamor for intervention on behalf of the rebels. Although he used every diplomatic means to persuade Spain to grant the rebels' demands, McKinley ultimately chose to yield to the widespread pressure for war rather than risk disruption of the Republican Party and likely political defeat. Citing "the large dictates of humanity" and "many historical precedents," the President sought and on April 19, 1898, gained congressional authority to intervene forcibly to stop the fighting and ensure Cuban independence. After an episodic but exhilarating campaign of less than four months, these ends were gained. Cuba received at least technical independence, and the

Philippine rebels who were reluctant to accept the blessings of American guidance, May 11, 1899. These poorly equipped insurgents formed part of General Antonio Luna's army, which promised to be the best among the Filipino forces until Luna was assassinated in June 1899. Aguinaldo later dropped Luna's idea of full unit resistance to the United States and perfected guerrilla warfare.

United States, having annexed the Hawaiian Islands during the war, went on to take Puerto Rico, Guam, and the Philippines from Spain.

The United States found itself in 1900 on a new course in international affairs. For the first time the nation had forcibly annexed noncontiguous territory. Within the next few years, the government would develop a constitutional status for unincorporated possessions, putting citizens of the new territories under the full sovereignty of the United States but denying them citizenship and many of the procedural rights guaranteed by the Constitution and the Bill of Rights.

As befit a great power, America faced a full-fledged colonial insurrection. In February 1899 Filipino nationalists sparked a revolt in the hope of forcing the Americans to accept independence for the

Philippines as they had for Cuba. This revolt dragged on for over three years and took the lives of four thousand Americans and probably as many as twenty thousand Filipinos. Seventy-five thousand American troops—almost three-fourths of the United States army—were needed to suppress the rebellion, and the McKinley administration resorted to a variety of drastic measures, including tactics for which Americans had criticized the Spanish in Cuba. The administration view was put coarsely but accurately by Colonel Frederick Funston, leader of the dramatic raid in which the rebel leader Emilio Aguinaldo was captured, effectively ending the insurrection. Funston described America's military activities in the Philippines as an attempt to remove "these bullet-headed Asians" from the path of "the bandwagon of Anglo-Saxon progress and decency."

Other Americans were not so confident about the justice of United States actions. One of the most biting assessments came from Mr. Dooley, the widely read newspaper character created by Finley Peter Dunne. Commenting on "The Philippine Peace," the sardonic Irish saloon-keeper explained to his friend Hennessy some of the civilizing effects of the water cure:

It is not always nicessry to kill a Filipino American right away. Me desire is to idjacate thim slowly in th' ways an' customs iv th' counthry. . . . A Filipino . . . niver heerd iv th' histhry iv this counthry. He is met be wan iv our sturdy boys in black an' blue . . . who asts him to cheer f'r Abraham Lincoln He raytuses. He is thin placed upon th' grass an' given a dhrink, a baynit bein' fixed in his mouth so he cannot rejict th' hospitality. Undher th' inflooence iv th' hose that cheers but does not inebriate, he soon warrums or perhaps I might say swells up to a ralization iv th' granjoor iv his adoptive counthry. One gallon makes him give three groans f'r th' constitchoochion. At four gallons, he will ask to be wrapped in th' flag. At th' dew pint he sings Yankee Doodle. Occasionally we run acrost a stubborn an' rebellyous man who wud sthrain at me idee iv human rights an' swallow th' Passyfic Ocean, but I mus' say mos' iv these little fellows is less hollow in their pretintions.

The Philippine insurrection ended dreams of a greater American empire. From the start, a substantial number of Americans had objected to intervention in Cuba and even more strenuously to the annexation of territories overseas. For them and for many others who had uncritically accepted the republic's new ventures, the Filipino revolt provided a harsh lesson in the problems of maintaining colonies. Revulsion from this experience convinced American leaders that the acquisition of distant lands was not a suitable way to expand the nation's influence. With the exception of the purchase in 1916 of the Danish West Indies (now the American Virgin Islands), the United States has continued to eschew territorial annexation.

Despite imperial problems shared with the European powers, many Americans held a unique vision of their role in international politics. To a greater extent than in most dynamic, youthful nations, expansionists in America believed they had a special mission to reshape the world by spreading republicanism, democracy, and free enterprise. They expected that the acceptance of these principles by other countries would lead to the adoption of America's traditions of party politics, Protestant Christianity, and private property— institutions thought by Americans to be universally applicable and acceptable. Underlying this idea of mission was an entrenched assumption of Anglo-Saxon racial superiority as well as the belief that the United States represented the most free and efficient society within the Anglo-Saxon community. In an era when the harsher aspects of Darwinian competition were being modified for social ends, Americans, in demonstrating their superiority, felt an obligation to help less fortunate peoples improve their condition.

The sense of mission at the start of the twentieth century flowed naturally from the progressive movement. Rejecting the idea that the United States could achieve world leadership by example alone, progressive expansionists wanted the government to be active in spreading American institutions. Just as domestic reformers endeavored to assimilate recent immigrants into Anglo-Saxon ways, so progressives active in international affairs worked to Americanize other societies, from Cuba to China. Sharing the progressive belief in the primacy of economic forces, diplomats frequently concentrated their attempts to reform other nations on the regulation of business and financial institutions in an effort to prevent corruption and limit monopoly. If given the opportunity, Americans would seek to establish honest, efficient government based on democratic procedures and free from the domination of special interests and to construct schools, highways, and sanitation systems modeled on those in the United States. The final step in reshaping a society would be the creation of an orderly judicial system shielded from political manipulation. The conviction that the new institutions would uplift and morally improve their recipients permeated progressives' efforts at home and overseas.

There were some limitations to this American dream. Because the social and economic systems of Europe appeared too established and tradition-bound to accept the American system readily, progressive expansionists focused their attention on Latin America, where they had special responsibilities, and on East Asia, the only remaining undeveloped area not already divided by the powers. Once they had limited their energies geographically, the expansionists agreed that their main thrust should be economic. At the core of the attempt to export a business civilization was the belief that economic expansion could establish the conditions under which other American institutions would be adopted and would flourish.

As the early years of the twentieth century unfolded, progressive America's expansionist vision encountered numerous obstacles. Businessmen insisted on investing their capital where they could gain maximum returns. The United States could not reshape foreign nations without undertaking major political obligations. Indeed, most undeveloped countries did not welcome American institutions and influence. Most serious, the committed expansionists represented only one part—albeit the most energetic and vocal part—of a minority of the American people concerned with and knowledgeable about foreign affairs. The great mass of the population, interested only in domestic matters, instinctively opposed costly overseas activities. The success of the expansionists' drive to create an informal economic empire depended on the extent to which they could win mass support for their idea of America's mission.

When the statesmen of the great European powers looked at the United States in 1900, they did not notice the extensive limits on the nation's international actions that virtually all Americans accepted. Instead they saw America ranking in the top three, and most often first, in every statistical measurement of national strength—area and population, the production of coal, iron, steel and agricultural commodities, railroad mileage, the value of accumulated capital and manufactures, and naval strength and defense expenditures. The events of 1898 had added the only missing qualification to make the United States a great power. During that year Americans showed a willingness to use their immense resources to play an expanded role in the world, and their subsequent handling of the Philippine insurrection indicated a determination not to turn back. Henceforth diplomatists unanimously accorded the powerful republic full status as a great power. International analysts spoke frequently of "the American peril," and the British journalist William T. Stead in his book *The Americanization of the World: or The Trend of the Twentieth Century* (1901) advised his countrymen to establish a firm connection with the nation that would be the predominant force of future international politics. The emergence of the United States as the first non-European great power highlighted the diplomatic revolution under way and caused each nation to examine anew its global position.

In prestige and power Great Britain was foremost of the seven great powers at the turn of the twentieth century. British pre-eminence in economic, naval, and imperial strength had been un-challenged since 1815. In the last decades of the nineteenth century, when other nations developed heavy industry and entered the race for empire, they invariably came into conflict with Britain. The choice colonies and strategic sites from Gibraltar and Suez to South Africa, India, and Singapore were all firmly in John Bull's hands. By 1900 British leaders had started a search for alliances to lessen their vulnerability before the expanding desires of the other powers.

Statesmen of the day would probably have ranked Russia, the United States, and Germany as the next strongest powers. Despite an inefficient government and the lack of industry, Russia presented an awesome image of strength by combining vast area and popula-tion with an inclination toward aggressive, expansionist diplomacy. Some analysts might have hesitated to put the United States in third place because of doubts about the government's continued readiness to use its admittedly great strength. Changes in American political leadership, however, soon removed these reservations. Germany had risen to a position of world power somewhat earlier than the United States and almost as rapidly. Military prowess and the Kaiser's dis-position to take risks made Germany greatly feared, but there were also critical weaknesses. In addition to fragile national unity, diplo-matists often cited the inadequacies of Germany's food production and navy as well as the minimal strategic and economic value of its empire.

Of the three remaining powers France was the most respected. Although suffering from diminished military potential as a result of the overwhelming defeat by Germany in 1870 and the Dreyfus epi-sode, France possessed an expanding economy, a widespread em-pire, and a diplomatic corps of unmatched excellence. The other two great powers probably owed their status more to their capacity to create problems for their associates than to actual strength. Austria-Hungary was split by ethnic factionalism and burdened with limited resources and a declining economy. Italy, divided and poor, seemed incapable of dealing with its domestic problems or restoring its reputation after defeat by the Ethiopians in 1896.

Although these rankings had important effects on international alignments and decisions, they contained elements of bias and subjective judgment. Indeed, it is distressing to realize that these basic assessments of national strength were formulated and modified in a way similar to the manner in which modern sportswriters select the top ten college football teams. The case of Japan is a useful example. In 1900 the Japanese had just begun to play the game of international politics. They were presumed to be racially inferior; they were in the wrong region of the world; and their only noteworthy victory had been over China, which had replaced the Ottoman Empire as the doormat of nations. International pundits ignored the fact that Japan, by most yardsticks of national power, was clearly superior to Italy and Austria-Hungary. The Japanese remained unranked until they attacked second-ranked Russia and literally blasted that prestigious power out of the contest on land and on sea. As a result of the Russo-Japanese War, Japan moved to fifth place and Russia dropped to sixth. From that point forward, diplomatists acknowledged that there were eight great powers.

Within the context of increasingly intense national rivalries, some of the established powers moved quickly to gain the support of the new entrants. Both Germany and Great Britain considered developing an understanding with the United States. In the summer of 1898 German officials discussed a proposal for cooperation with America, but when leaders in Washington objected to commitments that might lead to conflict with Britain, German interest cooled. Britain, on the other hand, set out at the same time to create as close a friendship as the United States would accept. Proceeding cautiously to resolve all outstanding issues without attempting to reach a broad political agreement, Britain achieved a firm understanding with America by 1904. As a further protection against the ambitions of the continental powers, Britain concluded an alliance with the other rising power, Japan, in 1902. With the signature of an Anglo-French agreement two years later, the main outlines of the restructuring of great power relationships became clear.

The United States surveyed numerous diplomatic opportunities as the new century opened. All the powers desired cordial relations with the American republic, and Great Britain, the nation with the most seriously conflicting interests, showed the strongest desire for cooperation. Even though William McKinley won reelection by a thumping majority in 1900, questions remained about the course American leaders would choose in international politics and the obligations the American people would be willing to accept. Through a quirk of fate, Theodore Roosevelt became the man to shape the answers.

Roosevelt, Mahan, and Great Power Behavior

Not since John Quincy Adams had the United States possessed a chief executive better prepared to manage international relations than Theodore Roosevelt. Only forty-two, he nonetheless had thought extensively about America's position in world affairs and had clear objectives. His first task was to gain the confidence and support of the nation, but Roosevelt had plans to increase diplomatic activity.

The young President had derived many of his ideas on international affairs from the writings of his respected friend Captain Alfred Thayer Mahan. Having retired in 1896 after forty years of naval service, Mahan developed a second career as an essayist and historian of the importance and appropriate uses of sea power. He related the lessons of past international struggles to present conditions—a technique he had found successful in his first major work, *The Influence of Sea Power upon History, 1660–1783*, published in 1890. Before his death in 1914, Mahan published more than fifteen volumes of history, biography, and essays.

Mahan viewed the oceans not as barriers but as avenues of trade and communication. In analyzing how America should utilize its great potential, he searched the history of England to learn how sea power had advanced British national interests almost without interruption for over two centuries. The ultimate goal of sea power, he concluded, was a flourishing foreign commerce carried in American merchant ships and protected by a powerful battle fleet. His program for the United States required American domination of the Caribbean through the construction and fortification of an isthmian canal and through control or neutralization of the major strategic sites protecting the planned canal—Cuba, the Danish West Indies, and Hawaii.

From the base of power created in the Western Hemisphere, the United States, Mahan urged, should extend its missionary and trading interests into China and other parts of East Asia. In *The Problem of Asia* (1900) he argued that "in the wide movement of expansion which has characterized the last quarter of the closing century, the Pacific Ocean in general and eastern Asia in particular are indicated as the predominant objects of interest, common to all

Captain Alfred Thayer Mahan, U.S.N. (1840–1914), pictured here in about 1906. In addition to outlining the strategic program for the United States, Mahan achieved great influence in all the naval nations. His books were translated into six languages, and the German and Japanese governments placed them in schools, libraries, and on all their warships. According to a leading scholar, the historian of sea power "became practically the naval Mohammed of England."

nations, both in the near and in the remote future." As a means of dealing with this challenge, he called for the cooperation of the Teutonic sea powers—Britain, Germany, and the United States—with Japan to limit the steady expansion into China of Russia, the leading land power. This proposal continued to fascinate Americans until Russia ceased to be viewed as an important threat in 1905.

Although Europe consumed fully three-quarters of America's exports, Captain Mahan did not rate European affairs as high in his priorities for positive strategic action as Latin America, which took 16 percent, and East Asia, which used almost 5 percent. Mahan focused his program on the areas open to the greatest possible economic expansion. He recognized the overwhelming importance of trade with Europe, but he believed that it and America's other interests in Europe would be protected by the balance of power in operation since the end of the Napoleonic wars. Great Britain had functioned as the crucial element in the balance, and Mahan assumed that common interests would allow Britain to continue to serve as America's first line of defense in Europe. The United States had a fundamental concern in any significant shift in the European balance; thus Mahan urged a policy of close cooperation with Britain, stopping short of formal alliance, which he felt would be politically dangerous and unnecessarily restrictive.

In Mahan's international program for the United States in the twentieth century, two themes stand out. Politically, the foundation of his system was a cordial understanding with Great Britain, necessary for American control in the Western Hemisphere as well as for equal opportunity in Asia and continued influence in Europe. Geographically, his top priority was an American-controlled canal, which would ensure the superiority of the United States in the Caribbean and would provide, along with Hawaii, Guam, and the Philippines, an advantage in the international competition for Asian wealth.

Mahan's influence, noteworthy in the 1890's, increased tremendously when a vigorous advocate of his overall strategic program became President of the United States. Roosevelt had carefully followed the development of Mahan's ideas from his first major publication in 1890, and as President he maintained a lively exchange with the retired officer on matters ranging from world politics to naval design and tactics. In March 1901, less than six months before becoming President, Roosevelt had showed his enthusiasm for Mahan's proposals when he wrote the scholarly officer that he had read *The Problem of Asia*

with the greatest interest . . . and, in the main, with entire agreement. I feel that the United States and England should so far as possible work together in China, and that their co-operation and the effective use of sea power on behalf of civilization and progress which this co-operation would mean in the valley of the Yangtze Kiang, is of the utmost importance for the future of Asia, and therefore of the world. But I do not have to tell you, with your wide and profound historical research, that while something can be done by public men in leading the people, they cannot lead them much further than public opinion has prepared the way. They can lead them somewhat further; but not very much.

Roosevelt's comment on the effect of public opinion illuminates the main constraint on the government's diplomatic activity. While welcoming the prestige that came with recognition as a great power, most Americans continued to cling to traditional notions of non-entanglement and isolationism. Statesmen in Washington could not ignore the fact that the treaty of peace with Spain had won Senate approval with only one vote to spare after heated debate on the propriety and legality of America's annexation of the Philippines. A majority of the American people opposed involvement in the rivalries of the powers in Europe and Asia, and any proposal for cooperation with Britain met automatic resistance from virtually all citizens of Irish and many of German origin. The international orientation of the average American in 1900 reflected a hearty acceptance of the Monroe Doctrine with its prohibition of European meddling in the Western Hemisphere and a pledge of American noninvolvement in the affairs of Europe. The chief practical result of this climate of opinion was that American diplomatists could anticipate relative freedom to pursue a large view of United States interests in the Caribbean and in adjoining regions, but they felt pressure to advance overwhelming justification for even minor activities in Europe and Asia.

A masterful politician, Roosevelt naturally modified programs such as Mahan's to suit political exigencies. He pushed hard to gain control and stability in the Caribbean and to expand Asian trade, but difficulties in gaining support at home and abroad frequently forced him to shift his policy or reduce his expectations. Nonetheless, the program Mahan had developed by 1900 provided a strikingly accurate blueprint for Roosevelt's diplomacy, and, despite great differences in style and rhetoric, both William H. Taft and Woodrow Wilson would follow the general lines of the international program that Roosevelt established. The area of greatest continuity would be the Western Hemisphere, where the range of action was largest.

Hegemony in the Western Hemisphere

American leaders assumed that control of the Western Hemisphere required domination of the Caribbean region. They made an important distinction between the degree of United States interest in the Caribbean and that in the remainder of Latin America south of the Orinoco River. Although willing to accept in the more distant section a slow growth of American influence and an assurance of no territorial acquisitions by any nation outside the hemisphere, Washington officials insisted on unassailable predominance in the Caribbean itself. They planned to achieve this command through extensive economic ties and by possession or neutralization of critical strategic sites. Economic expansion would advance, they believed, on private initiative with a minimum of formal leadership and planning, but strategic decisions had to be made. When Roosevelt entered office in 1901, he found that steps were being taken to secure part of the Danish West Indies and establish American control of the proposed isthmian canal. And in Cuba, where the McKinley administration had encountered its greatest problems, the new President took over an inventive policy already being implemented.

The United States had difficulty deciding the appropriate extent of freedom for Cuba. After the victory over Spain many imperialists had sought to evade the restrictions of the Teller Amendment by which Congress had disclaimed any intention "to exercise sovereignty, jurisdiction, or control over . . . [Cuba], except for the pacification thereof." But the desire to annex Cuba soon waned as Americans became aware of the island's problems of economic stagnation, illiteracy, and disease. After the repugnant ordeal of the Philippine insurrection, the United States explored all ways to avoid a similar clash with the larger Cuban nationalist movement. Early in 1900, at the urging of Secretary of War Elihu Root, McKinley decided on the establishment of an independent Cuba with provisions for close regulation by the United States.

McKinley had selected Root for the Cabinet in August 1899, claiming he had to have, as Root later reported it, "a lawyer to direct the government of these Spanish islands." It was the brilliant lawyer Root who, drawing on ideas from General James H. Wilson, Senator Orville H. Platt of Connecticut, and others, developed the method of gaining for the United States effective direction of Cuba with only limited political responsibility. Root's solution took the form of the Platt Amendment to the Army Appropriation Act, which McKinley signed into law on March 2, 1901.

The Platt Amendment authorized the President to end the military government of Cuba when a civil government had been established under a constitution containing a specific set of assurances. The five most important guarantees were that the government of Cuba would not make any diplomatic agreement which might impair Cuban independence or permit any foreign power to gain control over any

Elihu Root (1845–1937): corporation lawyer, Cabinet member, and leader of the Republican Party. As secretary of war (1899–1904) and secretary of state (1905–1909), Root designed many of the techniques used in managing America's empire without colonies. For his efforts to strengthen international law and promote arbitration, Root won the Nobel Peace Prize in 1912; and in 1917, at age 72, he led a special mission to Russia to convey United States good will to the new Provisional Government.

portion of the island; that it would not incur any public debt for which its ordinary revenues would be inadequate to make reasonable payments of interest and principal after the discharge of current government operating expenses; that it would grant "that the United States may exercise the right to intervene for the preservation of Cuban independence [and] the maintenance of a government adequate for the protection of life, property, and individual liberty . . ."; that it would ratify and accept all acts of the United States military government; and that it would sell or lease to the United States land for coaling and naval stations to be negotiated later.

To ensure that these obligations were firmly established, Root insisted that they be included in the domestic law of both nations as well as in a treaty. In the United States the terms appeared as part of the Army Appropriation Act; and after the exercise of various forms of persuasion, the Cubans placed them unchanged in their constitution and in a treaty with the United States signed on May 22, 1903. In conferences with Cuban leaders Secretary Root gave the assurance that the United States would intervene only to prevent foreign attacks on Cuban independence or to deal with a state of complete anarchy. And Senator Platt informed the Cubans that the amendment bearing his name had been carefully "drafted with a view to avoid any possible claim that its acceptance . . . would result in the establishment of a protectorate or suzerainty, or in any way interfere with the independence or sovereignty of Cuba."

Most foreign observers and some Americans declined to accept these assurances at face value. Many agreed with the Parisian paper *Le Temps,* which concluded: "Of the independence of Cuba nothing remains; of the promises of the United States equally little." In truth the Platt Amendment had effectively established an American protectorate over Cuba. The restrictions on Cuban independence were substantial, and the United States alone was left to judge when any violation justified intervention. Still, within these confinements, the United States acted magnanimously toward Cuba. The American military administration greatly improved the island's education, sanitation, government, and transportation. When a satisfactory Cuban government was formed, American troops withdrew in May 1902. The United States granted Cuba favorable terms in the lease of two naval bases and in the negotiation of a commercial treaty. And, even when the Cubans encouraged American intervention in 1906, Roosevelt authorized American troops' return to Cuba only with great reluctance and made certain that all troops were withdrawn shortly after he left office in 1909. By comparison with European imperial policies, American practices in Cuba were enlightened and almost permissive.

Under Roosevelt and Root, Cuban policy can best be described as a generous paternalism operating within clearly defined controls. The potential for widespread intervention in Cuban affairs was, however, always present. When less judicious men were in charge of American diplomacy, such intervention would occur on several occasions before Franklin D. Roosevelt abrogated the Platt Amendment in 1934 as part of the Good Neighbor Policy.

In contrast to its actions in Cuba, the United States demonstrated considerably less restraint in its zealous efforts to gain an interoceanic canal. One of the obstacles to an exclusively American canal was well on the way to removal when Roosevelt became President. In 1850, when their relative power was quite different, Great Britain and the United States had concluded the Clayton-Bulwer Treaty in which each nation agreed not to seek total control over any isthmian canal and to keep any such canal unfortified and neutral. During the war with Spain the dramatic voyage of the battleship *Oregon* from Puget Sound around Cape Horn to the Caribbean had emphasized the value of a canal that could reduce by at least one-third the time needed to transfer a fleet from coast to coast. This realization, added to the need to defend the new island possessions in the Pacific, had convinced McKinley and his advisers by December 1898 that an American canal was a national necessity. Secretary of State John Hay set out to gain British approval. He signed a treaty in February 1900, but Roosevelt and his strategy-conscious friends made the agreement unacceptable to Britain by leading a successful fight to add three amendments ensuring complete American direction and the right to fortify the canal. Negotiations for another treaty had begun when McKinley was assassinated.

Eager to avoid a clash with the outspoken new President, the British government quickly determined that concession to American demands was necessary and could be turned into a positive act of friendship. On November 18, 1901, the two nations signed a second Hay-Pauncefote Treaty that expressly abrogated the Clayton-Bulwer Treaty, approved American construction and management of an isthmian canal, and tacitly accepted fortifications. The United States pledged to keep the canal neutralized and "open to the vessels of commerce and of war of all nations . . . on terms of entire equality," a clause that would later be the subject of some dispute. This treaty marked a notable victory for the United States and was a major step in the development of close Anglo-American cooperation.

Having won British consent, American leaders faced only the selection of a route and the negotiation of construction rights before work on the canal could begin. Lobbying and intrigue characterized the choice of a site for the waterway. Three separate commissions since 1895 had chosen the Nicaragua route, and the House of Representatives had recently passed the Hepburn bill approving this proposal and authorizing funds for construction. But Roosevelt became convinced in January 1902 that a route through Panama was preferable because it would be cheaper to build and maintain and because harbors and a railroad in Panama would allow construction to begin a year earlier than in Nicaragua. A problem developed, however, in gaining construction rights: a French corporation, the New Panama Canal Company, owned the canal rights through Panama. This company was the successor to that led by the great French engineer, Ferdinand de Lesseps, who had failed in his attempt to cut a canal through Panama and declared bankruptcy in 1888 with the task only two-fifths finished. The New Panama Canal Company now wanted to sell its rights and rusty machinery to the United States for the inflated sum of $109 million. When it appeared that Washington might choose Nicaragua due to the extra cost of the Panama rights, the company dropped its price to $40 million, a figure which made the estimated cost of rights and construction roughly $5 million cheaper through Panama.

Roosevelt hastened to take advantage of this change. He had Senator John C. Spooner of Wisconsin introduce an amendment to the Hepburn bill under which the United States would switch to the Panama route if the New Panama Canal Company would accept $40 million for its assets. If this transaction and a treaty of authorization with Colombia, which controlled the Panama territory, could not be concluded within a reasonable time, the Spooner amendment directed the President to proceed with the Nicaragua route. The administration received invaluable assistance in lobbying for the Panama route from two leading figures in the New Panama Canal Company—William Nelson Cromwell, a prominent New York lawyer and large contributor to the Republican Party, and Philippe Bunau-Varilla, the former chief engineer of the de Lesseps company. After a tremendous struggle in both the Senate and the House, Roosevelt's leadership won passage of the Spooner amendment authorizing the Panama route in June 1902.

The United States then applied strong pressure to get Colombian agreement for a canal through its province of Panama. But the Colombian government, in a weak political position and unwilling to encourage charges of sacrificing national rights to the North Americans, hesitated to grant the terms that the United States considered vital for management of a canal. When the Colombian minister in Washington refused to sign a treaty without definite instructions from home, Hay dealt with his more willing chargé d'affaires, Dr. Tomás Herrán, and finally exacted an agreement from him on January 22, 1903, after threatening to turn to Nicaragua. The Hay-Herrán Treaty granted the United States a one-hundred year lease on a strip across Panama six miles wide for an initial payment of $10 million and an annual rental of $250,000.

The treaty immediately became a leading issue in the election of a new Colombian congress. The nation had just emerged from a costly three-year civil war that had claimed over 100,000 lives, and before the elections in March 1903 the aged president, José Marroquín, declared that the new congress would have to bear full responsibility for ratification of the treaty. Although the nation desperately needed the income a canal would provide, widespread opposition to the treaty appeared during the campaign. The Colombians had valid objections to the Hay-Herrán terms. The treaty placed very substantial restrictions on Colombian sovereignty in the canal zone, and it contained a clause to prevent Colombia from gaining any part of the $40 million due to the New Panama Canal Company for its machinery and canal rights, rights originally granted by the Colombian congress. (This clause, of such benefit to the New Panama Canal Company, was the handiwork of Cromwell, who would later take his share by claiming $832,449 in legal fees.) Marroquín did suggest to the American minister that opposition to the treaty might be reduced by the payment of more money, and the Colombian senate insisted on amendments to gain this and other changes. When the United States responded curtly that it would consider no amendments, Marroquín boldly submitted several tactless and offensive American notes to a public session of the upper house on August 12. The angry senate reacted immediately by voting unanimously to reject the treaty.

In his eagerness to start on the canal Roosevelt saw no merit in any of the Colombian arguments. Instead he pictured Marroquín as a dictator who could have gained approval of the treaty at will and Colombia's request for more generous terms as blackmail. Refer-

ring at times to the Colombians as "those contemptible little creatures in Bogotá" and "foolish and homicidal corruptionists," Roosevelt declared on August 17 that "we may have to give a lesson to
those jack rabbits." But as he perceived the situation, his alternatives were quite limited. His view of Colombian motives rendered
the negotiation of a more liberal treaty totally unacceptable, and his
public commitment to Panama as the better route made a return to
Nicaragua undesirable. The solution that clearly appealed to
Roosevelt was the use of an 1846 treaty between Colombia and the
United States (known in the United States as Bidlack's Treaty)—
which authorized the United States to intervene in Panama to maintain free transit and to protect Colombian sovereignty and the neutrality of the isthmus—as a pretext to seize the isthmus from Colombia and build the canal. The President even drafted a message to
Congress in October asking for a decision on whether to open negotiations for a canal in Nicaragua or to go ahead in Panama "without any further parley with Colombia," and he strongly recommended the Panama plan. But, fortunately for the United States and
for Roosevelt, a revolution for the independence of Panama from
Colombia broke out before this message was sent to Congress.

When Roosevelt drafted his message, he knew about plans among
prominent Panamanians and officials of the New Panama Canal
Company to stage a revolution. Initiated early in 1903, arrangements
for the revolt had taken shape when Bunau-Varilla arrived in New
York in September to talk with leaders of the plot. The energetic
Frenchman supplied the Panamanians with $100,000 to bribe
Colombian officials and otherwise advance the revolt, and in
October he went to Washington, where he described plans for the
revolution in detail to Roosevelt and Hay. Although the President
made no pledge of assistance to Bunau-Varilla, he did speak very
definitely of his intention to build the canal in Panama with or without Colombian approval. From Roosevelt's remarks and from his
own knowledge about the distribution of American naval forces in
the Caribbean, Bunau-Varilla concluded that the United States
would intervene to ensure the success of a revolt if the Panamanians
could seize Panama City and Colón. In describing later to a friend
how Bunau-Varilla had reached his conclusion about American
assistance, Roosevelt declared that "he would have been a very
dull man if he had been unable to make such a guess."

Proceeding on the basis of this "guess," Bunau-Varilla persuaded
his colleagues to stage the revolt as soon as possible. And on No-

vember 2 the Navy Department in Washington directed several warships in the Caribbean and Pacific to proceed to Panama to "maintain free and uninterrupted transit" across the isthmus. Although appearing to authorize action against any force—government or insurgent—that might interrupt the operation of the Panama Railroad, the orders plainly sought to prevent the landing of a force of Colombian troops reportedly en route to Panama. The basis for these orders was Bidlack's Treaty. Its use to justify actions aiding the overthrow of Colombian sovereignty in Panama demonstrates the capacity of determined men for rationalization.

The revolt occurred on November 3, although not as planned because 474 Colombian troops got ashore at Colón before the United States naval authorities received orders to prevent their landing. But American forces prevented suppression of the revolt on the Caribbean side, and officials of the Panama Railroad (fortunately owned by the New Panama Canal Company) refused to transport the Colombian soldiers to the main site of the revolution in Panama City on the Pacific coast. The successful revolt was over in a few hours, the only violence being a short bombardment by a Colombian gunboat which killed a Chinese laborer and a donkey. The rebels declared the independence of Panama on November 4 and through the judicious use of Bunau-Varilla's gold persuaded the Colombian troops to depart on a British steamer the following day. The United States hastily recognized the new Panamanian government on November 6. Hay and Bunau-Varilla, now Panama's minister in Washington, signed a treaty on November 18 granting the United States the right to build and control a canal through Panama and establishing an American guarantee of Panama's independence. The new treaty contained the same financial arrangements as the Hay-Herrán agreement, but it provided the United States more complete authority (as if "it were the sovereign") over a strip ten miles wide and a lease in perpetuity. The government of Panama accepted the treaty, and the United States Senate, after angry debate, also approved it on February 23, 1904.

As one of the most blatant examples of high-handed treatment of Latin nations, the Panama episode earned tremendous ill will for the United States. While doing no more than encouraging a revolt already in the planning stage and providing support after it began, the Roosevelt administration guaranteed the success of the Panama revolution. Moreover, by tactful, patient diplomacy the United States could have gotten Colombian permission for a Panama canal with

The Panama Canal Zone
(construction began May 1904; opened for traffic August 1914)

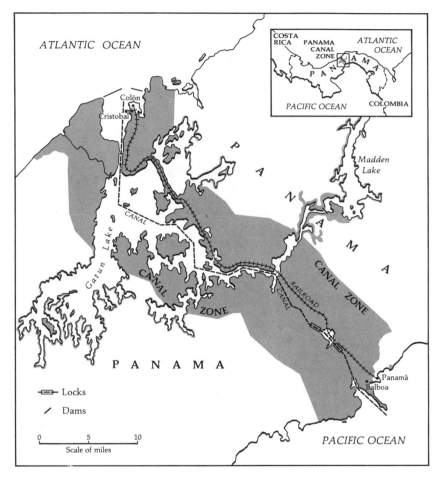

only a slight increase in time and money. Although Roosevelt won
the approval of the Republican press as well as a good proportion of
the Democratic, independent, and anti-imperialist papers, a number
of influential journals were highly critical. *The New York Evening
Post* charged that "this mad plunge of ours is simply and solely a
vulgar and mercenary venture, without a rag to cover its sordidness
and its shame." *The New York Times* agreed, declaring that the United
States had followed "the path of scandal, disgrace, and dishonor."
The Springfield Republican, accusing the government of "shocking

hypocrisy," described the episode as "one of the most discreditable performances in our history."

Roosevelt would later boast, "I took the canal zone," but at the time he devoted great effort to justifying his actions. He prepared a detailed special message to Congress emphasizing the perfidy and unreasonable demands of Colombia. He arranged publication in *Scribner's Magazine* of "Panama," a poem by the well-known Irish-American journalist James Jeffrey Roche celebrating the opportunity created by Roosevelt's diplomacy for that "child of destiny" (the United States) to "guard a hemisphere" in the interests of civilization. There is a story, perhaps apocryphal, that Roosevelt at a meeting of his Cabinet launched into a lengthy defense of his policy and in conclusion turned to Elihu Root to ask if he had answered the charges against him. The secretary of war, whose wisdom and restraint had been notably absent during the Panama incident while

President Theodore Roosevelt visits the Culebra cut of the Panama Canal in November 1906. In inspecting his favorite project, TR became the first President to leave the United States while in office. He enthusiastically reported to his son Kermit that the canal was "the greatest engineering feat of the ages. . . . I went over everything that I could possibly go over."

Underwood & Underwood

he was in England serving on the Alaskan Boundary Tribunal, replied with a mischievous smile: "You certainly have, Mr. President. You have shown that you were accused of seduction and you have conclusively proved that you were guilty of rape."

Although Roosevelt would temper his conduct in the future, he remained convinced of his righteousness during the Panamanian revolution, calling it "the most important action I took in foreign affairs." He had operated on what were to him sound reasons: the belief that an American-controlled canal was the nation's foremost need; the intense desire to begin construction of the canal before the 1904 elections; and the feeling of racial superiority to the Colombians, which made it impossible to treat them as equals. Yet in pursuing this course Roosevelt had violated the lesson of his favorite West African proverb: "Speak softly and carry a big stick, you will go far." At considerable cost to the republic's reputation, he had used the big stick. Although this image of forcefulness undoubtedly proved useful, Roosevelt would never again in his tenure as President wield the stick. In dealing with important questions he would show greatly increased sophistication in his diplomatic techniques. His public postures would revive and exploit the "big stick" image, but his diplomatic behavior would be uniformly calculated and restrained.

Construction of the Panama Canal began in May 1904, and the canal opened for traffic in August 1914. It cost about $375 million, and it involved the United States intimately in the affairs of Panama, which for all practical purposes became another American protectorate. Although Americans took great pride in the canal, there was also a feeling of guilt toward Colombia. The Taft administration initiated attempts to placate the Colombians, and the Democratic administration of Woodrow Wilson succeeded in signing a treaty with Colombia in April 1914, which apologized for America's part in the Panama revolution and offered a $25 million indemnity. But Senator Henry Cabot Lodge, Roosevelt's closest friend, assembled a group of the Rough Rider's supporters in the Senate sufficient to block the treaty. Only in 1921 when the United States sought entrance to newly discovered oil fields in Colombia, and Roosevelt had been dead for two years, did Lodge reverse himself and bring about approval of this treaty minus the expression of apology.

After the creation of protectorates to guard America's vital interests in Cuba and Panama, Roosevelt followed more flexible, informal roads to strategic dominance at other points in the Caribbean. With regard to the Danish West Indies, the United States employed Mahan's concept of denying the use of desirable bases to potential enemies. The Roosevelt administration resorted to such a policy only after an attempt to purchase the islands had failed. In 1897 private citizens in Denmark and the United States had revived the idea of selling these islands to America, and after much behind-the-scenes maneuvering representatives of the two nations signed a treaty in January 1902 providing for sale of three islands for $5 million. The United States Senate had refused to approve a similar treaty of 1867, and now it was Denmark's turn. For a variety of reasons — desire for more money, factional disputes, and pressure from friends of Germany — the upper house of the Danish parliament rejected the treaty by one vote.

The United States then relied upon the prerogatives of power. On several occasions Roosevelt and Hay informed the Danes in unmistakable terms that the United States would not allow the islands to be sold to any other nation. And, when the problems of World War I heightened American desire to have the islands, Denmark decided in August 1916 to sell the three large islands and many smaller ones for the inflated sum of $25 million. The United States completed the purchase and then occupied its last overseas possession in 1917. At other times during this period, with reference to Samaná Bay in the Dominican Republic, the Galápagos Islands of Ecuador, Magdalena Bay on the Pacific coast of Mexico, and other locations, the United States made it clear in various ways that it would not allow the lease or transfer to foreign powers of sites suitable for naval bases.

The Venezuelan furor in the winter of 1902–1903 disclosed the need for other methods to ensure American command of the Caribbean. The situation had become critical when Cipriano Castro, the dictator-president of Venezuela whom Roosevelt described as "an unspeakably villainous little monkey," refused to make payments on the large bonded debt he had floated with European investors. The United States did not object when informed that Britain, Germany, and Italy intended to establish a naval blockade of Venezuela to force payment of the debt. The blockade began early in December 1902, and as part of their campaign of persuasion the European powers captured several Venezuelan gunboats, landed troops at one port, and bombarded forts at another. To the surprise of international observers, the American public viewed these acts of force as violations of the Monroe Doctrine. When the State Department responded

An artist's impression of German warships off Venezuela in February 1903. Anxiety about German motives reached even the historian Henry Adams, who wrote a friend from Washington: "All is chaos. The Germans are trying our patience very badly indeed. . . . My own real uneasiness is that . . . [the Kaiser] may not be sane. In a dynamite magazine lunatics are dangerous."

to public pressure by urging a peaceful resolution of the dispute, the blockading powers decided to accept Castro's appeal for arbitration.

As negotiations on lifting the blockade proceeded, violence erupted again late in January 1903. A Venezuelan fort fired without warning on a German ship, and a few days later three German ships returned and demolished the fort. A new outburst of public feeling swept the United States, focused this time exclusively on German ambitions in the Caribbean. Roosevelt acted quickly to prevent a major crisis with Germany by issuing an informal ultimatum to Berlin to accept arbitration and refrain from acquiring any Venezuelan territory. The furor soon subsided as the powers lifted the blockade on February 14, 1903, and submitted the issue for arbitration by a panel of judges from the International Court of Arbitration at The Hague.

Wanting to dissociate itself from the aggressive impressions that

Germany had made, the British government assured the United States that it had no hostile intentions in the Caribbean region. On the very day the blockade was lifted, Prime Minister Arthur J. Balfour declared in a speech at Liverpool:

We welcome any increase of the influence of the United States of America in the Western Hemisphere. We desire no colonization, we desire no alteration in the balance of power, we desire no acquisition of territory. We have not the slightest intention of interfering with the mode of government in any portion of that continent. The Monroe Doctrine, therefore, is not really in question at all.

This bold statement for all practical purposes represented British acceptance of the Monroe Doctrine, and it was an integral part of the developing Anglo-American understanding. But the British did not stop there. Public and private spokesmen shrewdly argued that the American position on Venezuela carried with it important new responsibilities. As *The Times* of London had explained, "the Power which holds a shield over the weaker States is under an obligation to compel them to observe their duties in regard to others."

Roosevelt found the British argument quite persuasive, and announcement of The Hague decision on the Venezuelan case and events in the Dominican Republic moved him to act quickly to ensure "responsible" behavior among the Latin American republics. When on February 22, 1904, the judges directed Venezuela to pay its creditors, they gave preference in payment to citizens of those nations engaged in the blockade. This decision, as a leading American diplomatist said, "put a premium on violence"; in light of the widespread debts and unstable governments of the Caribbean area, it confronted the United States with the grave possibility of repeated European interventions in the Western Hemisphere.

Deteriorating conditions in the Dominican Republic created a threat of early intervention. The revolution-wracked Dominican government owed a large debt to citizens of eleven nations, and during the spring and summer of 1904 an intense rivalry developed over who would get first claim to the government revenues. The most heated competition was between the Santo Domingo Improvement Company, an American financial group that had previously been under contract to collect the customs revenues for the Dominican government, and representatives of French, Belgian, and Italian bondholders. Despite increasing European talk of intervention and an appeal from the new Dominican president for American assistance, Roosevelt hesitated to launch any important innovation in foreign policy until he had won election in his own right.

In November, 56 percent of the popular vote endorsed Roosevelt's performance as President. On December 6, in his annual message to Congress, Roosevelt announced his new approach to American responsibilities in the Western Hemisphere. In doing so he took care to link these obligations to the Monroe Doctrine, to which the American people had shown such emotional attachment during the Venezuelan blockade. After an evangelical appeal for righteous international behavior and the vigorous discharge of duty, Roosevelt declared:

If a nation shows that it knows how to act with reasonable efficiency and decency in social and political matters, if it keeps order and pays its obligations, it need fear no interference from the United States. Chronic wrong-doing, or an impotence which results in a general loosening of the ties of civilized society, may in America, as elsewhere, ultimately require intervention by some civilized nation, and in the western hemisphere the adherence of the United States to the Monroe Doctrine may force the United States, however reluctantly, in flagrant cases of such wrong-doing or impotence, to the exercise of an international police power.

To the President's considerable pleasure, the new policy came to be known as the Roosevelt Corollary to the Monroe Doctrine. This happened despite comment at the time on the corollary's broad, and some said unwarranted, extension of the duties imposed by the original principles of 1823, which in the Western Hemisphere had sought only to preserve the independence of the South American states and prevent any cession of territory to European powers. But, although there was some criticism of the police power that Roosevelt arrogated to the United States in Monroe's name, a sizable majority of those concerned with the issue preferred to reserve judgment and see whether the policy would improve the stability of Latin nations and what such entanglements would cost.

The United States did not delay in implementing the Roosevelt Corollary in the Dominican Republic. In February 1905 the Dominican government agreed to a protocol authorizing the United States to collect the customs and disburse the receipts to the government's creditors, with at least 45 percent of the total going for the government's current operating expenses. Although some Dominicans were suspicious of American motives, their government had originally suggested the customs receivership and was pleased with its creation. When in Washington Democratic members of the

THE WORLD'S CONSTABLE.

This 1905 cartoon shows Roosevelt prepared to use arbitration and his big stick (labeled "The New Diplomacy") to resolve problems in the Western Hemisphere and beyond. Both the great powers and the smaller nations appear eager to sample America's newest service for the world.

Senate strongly opposed the plan for financial supervision, the President kept the treaty from coming to a vote and worked out an executive agreement with the Dominicans for operation of the customs receivership.

The task of managing this new form of what William Appleman Williams has called "non-colonial imperial expansion" fell to none other than Elihu Root, who returned to Washington as secretary of state in July 1905, following the death of John Hay. Root took great pains to allay Dominican fears of interference in their internal affairs; he sought to adjust the debt equitably without excessive payment to speculators or grafters; and he altered the form of the United States government's responsibilities to make it more acceptable to the Senate. Finally, in February 1907, he negotiated a new convention with the Dominicans incorporating these changes, and the United States Senate approved it that same month.

By all short-range standards the customs receivership was a substantial success. After payment of its debts, the Dominican government gained more income from its share of the customs receipts than it had ever received previously. Dominican internal politics were relatively calm, and the government initiated a program of public works. Yet each month the United States became increasingly responsible for maintaining stability, and the logic of this would ultimately require American military occupation in 1916.

The implications of the Roosevelt Corollary assumed a different form when revolution broke out in January 1908 in Haiti, which shares the island of Hispaniola with the Dominican Republic. Although the revolt itself was short-lived, unrest continued and began, with encouragement from the elderly Haitian president, to assume anti-foreign tones. In March rumors spread that a massacre of foreigners was planned, and many of the foreign community spent a night hiding in the forest. In order to protect themselves in the future, the diplomatic representatives of Germany, France, and Britain developed a plan to take turns providing a permanent European guard ship in Haitian waters. Because they were jealous of the expanding American role in the Caribbean and desired to antagonize the American minister in Port au Prince, whom they disliked, the Europeans did not ask the United States to join them.

Once it learned of the guard ship proposal, the State Department immediately sought to have it quashed. Calling in the counselor of the British Embassy, Assistant Secretary Robert Bacon emphasized the special interest of the United States in a stable government in Haiti because of its common border with the Dominican Republic, a state in which the United States had important obligations. Bacon expressed the fear that foreign guard ships might lead to European intervention in Haitian affairs, and he assured Britain that the United States could provide whatever protection foreign lives and property required. In turning initially to the British, Bacon showed sound instinct, for the Foreign Office denounced any association with the guard-ship plan and rebuked the British minister for taking independent action in violation of his standing instructions. After a short time Germany and France also abandoned the project. On this occasion, by exercising diplomatic pressure through the understanding with Great Britain, the United States acted to limit the opportunity for any possible European intervention in the Caribbean area.

During his presidency, Theodore Roosevelt created in the Western

Hemisphere an American empire without colonies. When he arrived in office, Roosevelt found his nation restructuring Cuba under the Platt Amendment and possessing Puerto Rico without plans for its development. The United States had a growing navy and large aspirations, but there was no consensus among Americans on the degree to which national power should be coordinated and utilized in world politics. Selecting from proposals already under discussion, Roosevelt put together an international program based on command of the Caribbean. He achieved firm control over the crucial strategic sites of Cuba and Panama through the establishment of protectorates and began construction of the Panama Canal. Relying on the advice of Hay and Root, the Rough Rider perfected American dominance in the Caribbean by a variety of other techniques, ranging from the denial of naval bases to foreign powers to the formal acceptance of the obligation to maintain financial responsibility and public order among the Latin republics. With the defeat of the Haitian guard-ship proposal, the United States established its objection to any forcible intervention in the Caribbean by a foreign power. By 1909 the United States had achieved an unchallenged ascendancy in the Caribbean with only minimal involvement in the administration of dependent states. From this center of power American influence penetrated the remainder of Latin America sufficiently to guarantee hegemony throughout the hemisphere.

   Although there would be some shifts in policy under Taft and Wilson, United States dominance continued to be the objective in the Latin American diplomacy of Roosevelt's successors. The critical American relations with Cuba and Panama remained the same, as did the goals of preventing foreign intervention and ensuring the financial responsibility of Latin governments. Changes occurred in the means, or policies, used to reach these goals, such as the development of new methods to exercise financial supervision or maintain stability. But these modifications by the next two administrations reflected altered circumstances and personalities rather than fundamental departures in hemispheric relations.

   By all reasonable expectations William Howard Taft should have proved an able successor to Roosevelt, who had hand-picked him to carry on his policies as President. Taft brought to office almost unmatched experience in foreign affairs, having served as the first civil governor of the Philippines and having carried out as secretary of war delicate diplomatic missions in Cuba, Panama, and Japan.

The Creation of an American Empire: The Caribbean, 1898-1917

LESSER ANTILLES

ATLANTIC OCEAN

Purchased from Denmark, 1916

VIRGIN IS.

PUERTO RICO

Captured by U.S., 1898; Ceded to U.S. by Spain, 1898

Customs receivership established, 1905; Occupied by U.S. troops, 1916

DOMINICAN REPUBLIC

BAHAMAS

HAITI

Occupied by U.S. troops, 1915; Customs receivership and Platt Amend. provisions established, 1915

Caribbean Sea

Guantanamo Nava. Base

JAMAICA

CUBA

VENEZUELA

FLORIDA (U.S.A.)

Occupied by U.S. troops, 1898-1902; Tied to U.S. by Platt Amendment, 1901; Guantanamo leased to U.S., 1903; U.S. intervention, 1906-1909

U.S. assisted revolution, 1903; Hay-Bunau-Varilla Treaty, 1903

PANAMA CANAL ZONE

COLOMBIA

PANAMA

500

400

300

200

100

Scale of miles

0

BRITISH HONDURAS

HONDURAS

NICARAGUA

COSTA RICA

MEXICO

GUATEMALA

EL SALVADOR

U.S. armed intervention, 1910 and 1912; Unofficial customs receivership, 1911; Bryan-Chamorro Treaty approved, 1916

Veracruz occupied by U.S., 1914; U.S. punitive expedition, 1916-1917

Veracruz

PACIFIC OCEAN

The new President shared both Roosevelt's objectives and his methods in foreign affairs and saw his duty to be merely continuing and perfecting these policies. Unfortunately he lacked the flexibility, energy, and forcefulness to adapt to the complex situations that developed, and his major assistants were equally incapable of meeting the challenge. On Root's suggestion Taft chose Senator Philander C. Knox of Pennsylvania as his secretary of state. Before going to the Senate, Knox had had a very successful career as a corporation lawyer in Pittsburgh and had served as Roosevelt's attorney general. Although unquestionably able, Knox approached his diplomatic tasks with an arrogance and narrow legalism that proved a distinct handicap. In addition the secretary shared many of Taft's limitations. Neither man showed the attention to detail or the sensitivity to larger issues and the feelings of other nations that had been the basis of success for Roosevelt and Root.

The Taft administration fully accepted the critical importance of the Panama Canal and continued Roosevelt's policies in Cuba and Panama. The main innovation attempted by Taft and Knox was a refinement of the Roosevelt Corollary, which relied on financial reorganization of the Latin governments to maintain stability. Feeling that the major threat to the security of the canal lay in the possibility of foreign intervention in the Caribbean to collect defaulted debts, Taft sought to remove the danger by renegotiating the foreign debts of each government and replacing them with American loans. Under the Taft-Knox plan, which was a modification of an investment program initially used in China, private American bankers, with only minimal supervision by the State Department, would supply these loans and organize the collection of customs duties.

In presenting this policy of financial reorganization, administration officials assured the public that the program's benefits would extend beyond the investors. All Americans, they claimed, would profit from the increased trade that was certain to follow investment into stable areas. And the Latin people themselves would be, in Taft's phrase, "the immediate beneficiaries," for the flow of American funds and goods would improve the condition of their lives. As Knox grandly declared in December 1911: "If the American dollar can aid suffering humanity and lift the burden of financial difficulty from states with which we live on terms of intimate intercourse and earnest friendship . . . , all I can say is that it would be hard to find better employment." Still, critics quickly labeled this new approach "dollar diplomacy," and with his poor sense of public relations Taft accepted the name and asserted that his purpose was "substituting dollars for bullets."

Taft's new path to stability met its fullest test in Nicaragua. When a revolution broke out in 1909 against the pugnacious Nicaraguan dictator José Santos Zelaya, the United States did not hesitate to indicate its support for the rebels. After Zelaya resigned under public American pressure, Taft found it necessary to use bullets before dollars could be introduced. Officially protecting foreign lives and property, the United States landed sailors and marines to prevent the capture of the rebel headquarters at Bluefields by government forces. But when the rebels with American aid eventually won control of the government in August 1910, they had difficulty forming an effective government of their own. The new president soon fled the country, elevating his vice-president, Adolfo Díaz, to the top post. Díaz had previously served as secretary of the United States–Nicaragua Concession, a Pittsburgh-owned mining corporation that was the largest American interest in Nicaragua. Since this corporation was a former client of Knox's law firm, Taft and Knox not unnaturally found Díaz an entirely suitable leader to establish order in Nicaragua.

If anything, Díaz wanted too much American guidance. He sought an American protectorate on the Cuban model, which involved substantially greater responsibilities than Taft wanted to assume. Knox and the Nicaraguan minister in Washington eventually developed a compromise plan in the form of the Knox-Castrillo Convention, signed on June 6, 1911. This agreement provided that the Nicaraguan government should negotiate a loan of about $15 million from American banks for the purpose of refunding existing internal and foreign debts. Customs receipts would service the loan, and the collector general of the customs would be named by the Nicaraguan government from a list drawn up by the bankers and approved by the President of the United States. The agreement included various guarantees that could be used to justify forcible American intervention. When the United States Senate refused to approve the treaty, the two governments and the bankers worked out an unofficial agreement for the collection and disbursement of the customs revenue. Without the guarantees of a treaty, however, the bankers declined to advance more than a small part of the proposed loan, and the foreign debt was never refunded.

Despite the failure of the treaty, American obligations in Nicaragua increased dramatically under the Taft administration. Con-

A machine gun platoon of United States marines in Nicaragua, 1910. This unit was part of the Panama garrison battalion commanded by swashbuckling Major Smedley D. Butler, who landed his 250 marines on May 30, 1910, to neutralize Bluefields and protect the rebel command post. In commenting later on his troops' purpose in Nicaragua, Butler with characteristic exaggeration declared: "It didn't take a ton of bricks to make me see daylight. It was plain that Washington would like the revolutionists to come out on top." With assistance from the U.S.S. *Paducah,* the marines guided the rebels to victory and then returned to Panama at the end of September.

fronted with a revolution led by his secretary of war, Díaz in July 1912 appealed to the United States for aid. The State Department responded with a declaration of firm support for Díaz, and when this proved inadequate, Taft sent in 2,700 marines to quell the revolt. After restoring order the United States left a "legation guard" of about 100 marines in Nicaragua, and with only one brief withdrawal this force remained until 1933. The American presence did provide a level of political and financial stability that Nicaragua had not previously known, but it was achieved by military rather than by economic means.

The 1911 assassination of the president of the Dominican Republic demonstrated the inability of over five years of American financial supervision to strengthen the political system. When the new chief executive showed himself powerless to stem constant anarchy, the United States intervened with economic pressure to force him from office in favor of its candidate, the archbishop of Santo Domingo. The new prelate-president was, however, totally unsuited to the demands of the job, and after a hectic four months in office he fled for Europe in March 1913, mailing his resignation as he boarded ship.

Taft's attempt to use private resources to rehabilitate the finances of the Caribbean states and thereby maintain stability proved a dismal failure. Difficulties with self-serving and inept Latin politicians and the reluctance of American bankers to invest without assurances of backing from Washington hampered the administration's efforts in Honduras and Guatemala. When the State Department did complete treaties with Nicaragua and Honduras, the United States Senate rejected them because of partisan politics and disapproval of the obligations to be assumed by the American government for the benefit of a small number of investors.

In his last annual message to Congress in December 1912, the President blamed the collapse of "dollar diplomacy" in the Caribbean—and the Nicaraguan revolution of the preceding summer— on the Senate's refusal to endorse the Knox-Castrillo Convention. Taft's charges, coming after his loss to Woodrow Wilson in the November elections, rang a bit hollow. He had not shown the flexible leadership required by shifting political currents at home and in the Latin republics. In particular, he had not paid adequate attention to the progressive sentiment against vested economic interests which was growing rapidly among the American people and in Congress. The President's remarks were symbolic of the defeatist tone of his whole administration, a tone most vividly expressed in May 1912 when Taft began to respond to Theodore Roosevelt's charges against him in the fight for the Republican nomination. Then, in speaking to an audience at Hyattsville, Maryland, Taft declared: "I am a man of peace, and I don't want to fight. But when I do fight I want to hit hard. Even a rat in a corner will fight." With such leadership what program could succeed?

When Woodrow Wilson entered office in March 1913, he found a baffling range of Caribbean problems confronting him. There was unrest in Cuba and a developing civil war in Mexico. Haiti and the Dominican Republic stood on the brink of political and economic chaos, and only an American legation guard maintained relative order in Nicaragua. Despite his expressed desire to devote full energy to his program of domestic reform, Wilson had good reason to anticipate important problems in foreign affairs.

The Wilson administration showed a strong desire to launch a new diplomatic program, especially in Latin America. The President and his secretary of state, the long-time Democratic leader William Jennings Bryan, denounced "dollar diplomacy" and called for a new era of cordiality and cooperation with the Latin republics. As one step in this direction, the administration negotiated the abortive treaty with Colombia that apologized and provided an indemnity for the role of the United States in the Panama revolution. Bryan also labored zealously to complete a series of "cooling-off treaties," the popular name for conciliation agreements that pledged the signatories to delay hostilities in any dispute for one year to allow an impartial investigation and a reduction of tensions. The United States signed thirty Treaties for the Advancement of Peace, as they were formally called, and many of them were with nations of the Western Hemisphere. Numerous diplomats considered them unrealistic and none of the pacts was ever invoked, but Bryan viewed the "cooling-off treaties" as his life's greatest achievement.

Wilson's primary goal in Latin America became the spreading of democratic institutions. Convinced that this was the best way to ensure stability, he declared on March 11, 1913, that his administration "would have no sympathy with those who seek to seize the power of government to advance their own personal interests or ambition." Later in the year the President told a British diplomat, "I am going to teach the South Americans to elect good men." And when critics contended that the Latin states were not ready for democratic institutions, Wilson responded, "When properly directed, there is no people not fitted for self-government." The issue came to be how far the United States should go to provide "proper direction," although very few Americans then, or since, questioned the propriety of extending such direction.

Revolutionary Mexico provided an early trial for Wilson's program of expanding democracy. In 1911 a broadly based social revolution led by Francisco Madero had overthrown the dictator Porfirio Díaz, who had ruled with only one brief interruption since 1877. The United States had dealt with Madero's government correctly but without enthusiasm. The new Mexican president was not able to mold an effective government, and in February 1913 conservative elements ousted Madero and soon murdered him and his vice-president. The leaders of the new counterrevolutionary government were General Félix Díaz, a nephew of the former dictator, and General Victoriano Huerta, who had served as Madero's leading military commander. By a complicated series of arrangements worked out at the American Embassy with the full complicity of the ambassador, Huerta became provisional president and pledged to hold elections in the near future in which he would throw his support for president to Félix Díaz. The Taft administration clearly intended to recognize Huerta's regime but held out for concessions on several issues pending between the two nations. When these did not quickly materialize, Taft decided to leave the matter for his successor.

For Woodrow Wilson the Mexican situation presented an opportunity for moral instruction. His denunciation on March 11 of those who seized power "to advance their own personal interests or ambition" was aimed directly at Huerta. Throughout the spring and summer, the President resisted all pressure to recognize Huerta's government as he gathered information from private agents, consuls, and businessmen that would help him determine how best to "safeguard constitutional rights and methods of action" for Mexico. Finally he decided that the United States should not recognize any government that came to power by force and in violation of its nation's constitution. Wilson's denial of recognition to a government which had substantial control of its territory and population was a decided break with American and international practice. (The United States continued to use nonrecognition as a means of diplomatic pressure until 1930, and it has, of course, revived the practice in recent years with regard to the People's Republic of China and some other Communist governments.) While the Wilson administration postponed recognition and the development of a clear policy, virtually all of the other great powers, including Britain, France, and Germany, recognized the Huerta regime as the de facto provisional government of Mexico.

By early August Wilson had formed two strong opinions which would shape his future policy. He decided that Huerta's administration, which he characterized as "a government of butchers," was unacceptable and should be replaced. And he believed, quite erroneously as he later learned, that the British government, from a desire for a large oil concession and other favors, was keeping Huerta in power through its recognition and suspected financial aid. Wilson's task was to remove Huerta and find a suitable replacement. The most promising substitute appeared to be Venustiano Carranza, an early supporter of Madero and governor of Coahuila, who had begun a revolt against Huerta in late March. Backing from the south had joined the original revolt in the north, and Carranza had named his movement "Constitutionalists," a step certain to appeal to Wilson.

To obtain a change of government and a return to constitutional methods, Wilson designed a mediation plan that former Minnesota Governor John Lind delivered to Huerta's government in August. The plan included proposals for an armistice, early elections in which Huerta would not be a candidate, and a pledge by all Mexican factions to accept the results of the vote. In return the United States promised to recognize the government chosen under these conditions. Misleading and inept reports from Lind persuaded Wilson that Huerta had accepted the proposal for elections already scheduled for October 26 and had pledged not to be a candidate. Huerta, however, shattered this expectation on October 10 when, faced with increasing opposition from the legislators, he arrested 110 deputies, dissolved congress, and announced rule by executive decree.

Huerta's action convinced Wilson that the Mexican dictator had to be forced from office by whatever means necessary. The first step was to isolate Huerta diplomatically, with Britain the primary object of the campaign. The President personally drafted a harsh note asking the powers to stop maintaining Huerta's regime with diplomatic recognition and financial aid. Although cooler heads convinced Wilson not to send this note, someone high in the administration leaked it to the press, where its publication unofficially conveyed the message to other governments. Leading newspapers carried stories on October 24 declaring that Washington was "seething with indignation" over British policy in Mexico. On October 27 the President followed this with his dramatic speech at Mobile, Alabama, denouncing foreign economic exploitation of Latin America and promising the assistance of the United States to see that in the coming era "material interests [are never] made superior to human liberty and national opportunity."

Wilson did gain British backing for his program, and he made his intentions known to the world in a circular note to all diplomatic posts on November 24. In this unusually direct statement Wilson declared:

It is the purpose of the United States, therefore, to discredit and defeat such usurpations [as Huerta's] whenever they occur. The present policy of the

Government of the United States is to isolate General Huerta entirely; to cut him off from foreign sympathy and aid from domestic credit, whether moral or material, and so to force him out.

It hopes and believes that isolation will accomplish this end, and shall await the results without irritation or impatience. If General Huerta does not retire by force of circumstances, it will become the duty of the United States to use less peaceful means to put him out. . . .

Beyond this fixed purpose the Government of the United States will not go. It will not permit itself to seek any special or exclusive advantages in Mexico or elsewhere for its own citizens, but will seek, here as elsewhere, to show itself the consistent champion of the open door.

The President's pledge to support equal economic opportunity through an open door policy in Mexico helped gain the powers' acceptance of his plan, but diplomatic isolation did not weaken Huerta's position. Wilson then moved to increase pressure on the Mexican ruler. In February 1914 he raised the embargo on the export of arms to Mexico, and shipments of arms soon began to flow to the Constitutionalist forces in the northern states. He strengthened the United States naval squadron stationed in Mexican waters to protect American lives and property. Finally, on April 9, an incident occurred at the port of Tampico which gave Wilson the pretext he desired for military intervention. On that day an American naval officer and seven bluejackets went ashore to buy gasoline and were arrested by a Huertista officer for being in a prohibited area. Even though they were quickly released with proper apologies, the commander of the American naval squadron, Admiral Henry T. Mayo, demanded a twenty-one gun salute to the American flag. Later, on learning of the demand, President Wilson supported it. Huerta was willing to approve the salute on the condition that the United States return it. Although Wilson initially considered exchanging simultaneous salutes, his position soon hardened and he rejected even this concession.

Meanwhile Wilson had ordered the entire Atlantic fleet to Mexican waters. On April 20 he delivered a special message to Congress, in which he cited the Tampico incident and two less significant affronts and asked Congress for authority to use the armed forces to gain from Huerta "the fullest recognition of the rights and dignity of the United States." As Congress considered his proposal, Wilson moved to implement a plan to blockade both coasts of Mexico, occupy Tampico and Veracruz, and possibly send an expedition to Mexico City. Before this plan went into effect, news reached Wash-

A squad of bluejackets from the U.S.S. *Michigan* pose on the dock in Veracruz, 1914. After the poorly planned seizure of the customhouse resulted in unexpected and unwanted violence, American forces remained for seven months operating the port, improving health and sanitation conditions, and exerting pressure on the various Mexican political factions. Although it helped eliminate Huerta, the United States occupation of Veracruz did not advance democracy and it seriously damaged American influence in Mexico.

ington that the German steamer *Ypiranga* was approaching Veracruz with a cargo of guns and ammunition for Huerta's forces. Wilson made a quick decision to occupy the customhouse at Veracruz to prevent the arms from reaching Huerta. On April 21 American sailors and marines landed in Veracruz and, to Wilson's complete surprise, met stiff Mexican resistance. American casualties totalled 19 dead and 47 wounded, while the Mexicans lost at least 200 dead and more than 300 wounded. On April 22 the United States Congress approved the use of the armed forces against Huerta's government.

Even though opinion in the United States supported the intervention and many leaders felt that American troops should proceed on to Mexico City, Wilson recoiled in horror at the bloodshed caused by his decision to occupy Veracruz. He was further surprised when

Carranza roundly denounced the landing and demanded the withdrawal of American forces. Now eager to avoid war, Wilson accepted the offer of Argentina, Brazil, and Chile to mediate the dispute with Mexico. But the President was adamant in his intent to keep United States troops in Veracruz until Huerta either retired or was forced from power. The American brigade grew to over 7,000 men, and it managed to remain in Veracruz for seven months without further hostilities with any Mexican faction. When the *Ypiranga,* in violation of her captain's pledges to American naval officers, circled back in late May to deposit her cargo of arms at Puerto México, the United States made no attempt to prevent the arms from reaching Huerta.

As it developed, these supplies arrived too late to help the provisional president. Although the mediation effort proved unsuccessful, largely due to Carranza's refusal to participate and accept an armistice, the combination of Constitutionalist military pressure and the loss of his major source of revenue and supplies at Veracruz increasingly weakened Huerta's position. Accepting the inevitable, he resigned on July 14, 1914, and fled to Europe. The Constitutionalists occupied Mexico City on August 20, and Wilson's policy appeared to be on the verge of success.

Carranza soon demonstrated, however, that he was even less willing than Huerta had been to accept Woodrow Wilson's version of a new constitutional order for Mexico. The Constitutionalist coalition soon broke apart, and with civil war again raging Carranza found reason to refuse Wilson's entreaties to hold early elections. For a time Wilson supported the guerrilla chieftain Francisco (Pancho) Villa against Carranza, feeling that Villa would provide the greatest opportunity for democracy in Mexico. But when Carranza's forces gained a series of victories and the European war provided deepening complications for the United States, Wilson determined that the civil war had to be ended and stability restored. Seeing Carranza as the only leader capable of uniting the nation, Wilson reversed his policy in the summer of 1915 and declared American neutrality in the civil war. In October he completed this shift when the United States, acting with six Latin states, extended de facto recognition to Carranza's government.

Villa then showed his true colors as he began a campaign of terror against American lives and property. He hoped to lure Wilson into a military response, which would result in an American clash with Carranza, and this is precisely what occurred. Villa's destruction of Columbus, New Mexico, in March 1916, resulting in the deaths of

Brigadier General John J. Pershing crosses the Rio Carmen near El Valle, Mexico, in pursuit of
Pancho Villa, probably in March 1916. Pershing was at this point over 130 miles from
United States territory, and troops of the Punitive Expedition went as far as 350 miles into
Mexico before clashes with Carranza's forces led to their concentration nearer the border.
Although they killed over a hundred of Villa's raiders, the Americans failed
to crush his guerrilla army in an episode that historian Arthur S. Link calls, "the unhappiest
chapter in the history of Mexican-American relations since the war of 1846–1848."

nineteen Americans, led to the so-called Punitive Expedition commanded by Brigadier General John J. Pershing. Against Carranza's
desires, Pershing led a force of almost 7,000 men nearly 350 miles
into Mexico in pursuit of Villa.

Mexico and the United States stood on the brink of war, but Wilson
and Carranza both drew back. Negotiations ran from September
1916 through the following January. As pressure mounted from
Germany, Wilson decided to withdraw Pershing's force. Without
ever coming to grips with Villa, the last American troops left Mexico
on February 5, 1917. On the same day Carranza presented a new
constitution to the Mexican people, and under the new law the first
chief won a decisive victory in March elections. With Carranza's

inauguration on May 1, constitutional government returned to Mexico for the first time since Madero's overthrow. Wilson had misgivings about Carranza's radical program, but after receiving assurances that American investments, particularly in oil, would be protected, the United States extended full de jure recognition to Carranza's government on August 31, 1917. Ever since his initial dealings with Huerta, Wilson's assumptions about how to effect change in Latin nations had proved to be greatly flawed; he especially underestimated the vigor and resistance to external guidance of revolutionary nationalism. Despite widespread evidence that the Mexican people did not want American institutions or moral instruction, Wilson continued to believe that the democratic principles of the United States could be extended throughout the Western Hemisphere and beyond.

In Nicaragua the Wilson administration developed American techniques of managing an informal empire to their highest form. The President and Secretary Bryan adopted without substantial change the financial regulations and legation guard that Taft had established. Bryan even renegotiated and strengthened a treaty Knox had signed giving the United States exclusive rights to build a canal through Nicaragua. The Bryan-Chamorro Treaty, signed on August 5, 1914, contained provisions for American naval bases at either end of the canal on the Great and Little Corn Islands and on the Gulf of Fonseca. In return for these extensive rights, the United States pledged to pay $3 million to Nicaragua. Senate opposition forced the administration to delete provisions giving the United States broad control over Nicaraguan external affairs and internal order along the lines of the Platt Amendment, and after further delay the Senate approved the treaty in February 1916. Despite the loss of these formal constraints the United States treated Nicaragua as a protectorate. It chose Emiliano Chamorro, the friendly Nicaraguan minister in Washington, to be Díaz's successor as president and guaranteed his election by persuading his opponent to withdraw from the race. American leaders used the legation guard and special naval missions to reinforce extensive political and economic advice. Yet all of the American supervision and encouragement was inadequate, for the roots of democracy were unable to catch hold in Nicaraguan soil.

On the island of Hispaniola Wilson intervened to maintain order in both Haiti and the Dominican Republic. In Haiti, where the United States had fewer interests and exercised less direction, revolution followed revolution every few months after 1910, and in 1914 the United States strongly suggested financial supervision as a means of preventing outside intervention. Before this could be arranged, however, a bloody massacre of political prisoners in July 1915 led Wilson to decide that the United States must, as he wrote Secretary of State Robert Lansing, "take the bull by the horns and restore order." Wilson sent in a force of marines to quell the fighting, and in September 1915 the Haitian government signed a treaty with the United States setting up a protectorate that added a customs receivership and other restraints to the basic Platt Amendment provisions. With its troops remaining until 1934, the United States established more complete control of Haiti than of any other Caribbean republic.

The mechanisms of the American customs receivership had proved insufficient to maintain order in the Dominican Republic, and the United States confronted an unstable political situation. The logic of the initial intervention led Wilson to use economic pressure and threats of force to urge broad political reforms on a succession of Dominican governments after 1913. Resistance by the Dominican congress and continued disputes among the main political factions prevented success for the American proposals. When the ambitious Dominican secretary of war prepared to overthrow the government in April 1916, Wilson sent in marines to occupy critical positions in the capital and prevent a revolution. The Dominican president resigned, and no prospective new government would accept the American reform plan. Since the United States was already deeply involved in Haiti and since the Dominicans refused to be led toward democracy, Wilson saw no alternative to ordering the creation of an American military government for the Dominican Republic in November 1916. For the next six years the United States navy governed the republic, and American troops remained until 1924. The United States continued to exercise substantial control over the finances of both the Dominican Republic and Haiti until 1941.

Along with its achievement of political hegemony in the years after 1900, the United States steadily won command of Latin American trade and investment from Great Britain, which had dominated the region throughout the nineteenth century. Customs receiverships and "dollar diplomacy" considerably assisted this economic advance by simultaneously discouraging European investments and stimulating those of the United States. By the outbreak of war in 1914, the United States possessed roughly 50 percent of Latin trade and was rapidly developing a strong position in long-term investments. With Britain locked in a fight for survival that demanded all its resources, the United States established firm control of Latin American trade during the war years. The total value of United States trade with Latin nations, exports and imports, increased sharply from $798 million in 1914 to $1,801 million in 1917 and reached a peak of $3,393 million in 1920. At the same time, bankers and officials in Washington were engaged in a concerted drive to have New York replace London as the financial center of the world, and American investments showed noteworthy increases in Cuba, the West Indies, and the larger nations of South America. Although the United States did not surpass Britain in capital investment in Latin America until the mid-1930's, the trade expansion of the war years indicated that American predominance in investment was only a matter of time.

In addition to accelerating United States economic supremacy in the Western Hemisphere, World War I encouraged the start of a new American policy of disengagement from the responsibilities assumed under the Roosevelt Corollary as "the policeman of the West." Wartime cooperation put Great Britain permanently in America's political and economic debt and thereby ensured continued British acceptance of American hegemony in the hemisphere. Perhaps more important, the war removed the only potential challenge to American authority by crushing Germany and dismantling its empire. The disappearance of serious external threats diminished the need to guarantee Latin financial responsibility as a means of preventing foreign intervention. The importance of the Monroe Doctrine in shaping diplomatic actions also declined, although opponents of the League of Nations would still use the doctrine as a weapon in their fight against Wilson. Adjusting to these reduced demands, the Wilson administration began in 1918 to withdraw from the daily obligations of supervision in the republics where the United States had intervened. As commitments declined, American leaders sought to maintain stability through indirect means; and as part of a new spirit of cooperation, they began to work toward a policy of nonintervention. Although it would be violated on numerous occasions, nonintervention as initiated by Wilson would continue to be a preferred diplomatic guideline under his Republican successors and would ultimately be used by the administration of Franklin D. Roosevelt as an essential principle of the Good Neighbor Policy.

During the two decades after 1898 the United States perfected its control over the Caribbean region, a power base from which American leaders believed they could maintain primacy throughout the Western Hemisphere. All three Presidents of the progressive period pursued the objective of American hegemony, and they relied on similar policies with adjustments to meet new circumstances. After 1904, Washington officials attempted to ensure stability by replacing strategic with economic measures such as Roosevelt's customs receivership and Taft's refunding of foreign-held debts. When financial supervision proved inadequate to keep order, Roosevelt and Taft used force in Cuba and Nicaragua, respectively. Although Wilson entered office denouncing "dollar diplomacy," he found no alternative to continuing the programs of financial regulation in the Dominican Republic and Nicaragua. And he ultimately resorted to military means in Mexico, Haiti, Nicaragua, and the Dominican Republic. Wilson's desire to spread democratic institutions reflected a greater aspiration for social change than Roosevelt or Taft had shown, and it represented a new diplomatic objective. But events at home and abroad prevented the changes necessary to export democracy, and in its practical manifestations Wilson's Latin American diplomacy before 1918 differed little from that of his predecessors. Although he seldom talked directly about it, Wilson followed the basic policy of protecting the Panama Canal and preventing foreign intervention. The innovation in Wilson's Latin diplomacy came with the policy of disengagement. Yet the nation's goals in the hemisphere remained hegemony and stability, and if threats to these vital objectives arose, the United States would not hesitate to abandon disengagement and revive intervention.

A complex blend of political and economic forces shaped American diplomacy for the Western Hemisphere. The political and economic purposes of American leaders did not conflict, but tended to run parallel to one another as reinforcing lines of national influence. Although all three administrations of the progressive era shared the political aim of strategic domination and the economic aim of expanded trade and investment, each placed political factors foremost in determining and justifying actions. Leaders of each administration utilized economic means of stabilization, but they did so only after strategic dominance was relatively secure and with the understanding that they would employ force or political restrictions if economic methods proved unsatisfactory.

Economic interests did not determine United States diplomacy for

Latin America, even though businessmen and some politicians discussed extensively the need to increase overseas trade and investment. Progressive leaders like Roosevelt and Wilson, with their cultivated anti-business appearances, desired economic expansion, but they opposed any economic action abroad that could not be justified by its benefits to the security and welfare of all citizens. Taft, who was more fully committed to economic diplomacy, had little success because his program called for the use of capital in areas of limited profitability, and under the sluggish economic conditions before 1914 the most attractive investment opportunities lay in Europe. In contrast, American intervention occurred, with the exception of Cuba and Mexico, only in countries where actual and prospective trade and investment were small. The interventions came at points of real or supposed strategic importance in the defense of the Panama Canal.

Cuba, better than any Latin nation, demonstrates how inextricably meshed were the political and economic interests of the United States. The sugar trade had tied Cuba economically to the United States well before the island revolted against Spain in 1895. Yet the American decision to intervene in Cuba, insofar as it had rational roots, stemmed from political concern about the future security of the United States. With its proximity to the Florida coast and its position as the most valuable strategic site for command of the Caribbean, Cuba remained primarily of political interest to Americans. To protect this interest the United States designed the Platt Amendment, gained authority for two naval bases on the island, and granted favorable terms in the reciprocity treaty of 1902 in order to revive the island economy. These basically political actions worked in turn to increase America's economic stake in the island as United States investments grew from about $50 million in 1898 to over $500 million in 1920 and trade jumped from $57 million in 1900 to an unusual high of $1,237 million in 1920. Although Cuba continued to grow in economic importance until the 1950's, the United States made its major decisions concerning the island republic on political grounds. And in the two instances of military action regarding Cuba in the early 1960's, the motivation of United States leaders was almost exclusively strategic.

The sharp increase in American military intervention during the progressive era resulted from the effort to establish hegemony in the Caribbean. This exercise of strength marked the nation's willingness to assume the position of a great power within its sphere of influence. It also reflected the attitudes of Americans toward their purpose in the world and the rights of other countries within the United States sphere to achieve independent development. The insensitivity of American statesmen to the needs of the Latin republics for distinctive national goals and institutions is striking. Yet some of the interventions of the progressive period were justified as a means to prevent the establishment of a foreign power in the Western Hemisphere, an objective that remains valid today. The intrusions in Cuba and the Dominican Republic, for example, were necessary to guarantee vital positions for the United States and to eliminate foreign threats. Other interventions, such as those of Roosevelt in Panama and Wilson at Veracruz, demonstrated a needless use of force and were unjustifiable attempts to dominate other peoples. Most of the remaining episodes, from the Punitive Expedition into Mexico to the occupation of Haiti, fall in a gray area where judgments differ widely. These actions had only a limited bearing on American security, and evaluations of them will be determined largely by one's view of the proper obligations of a great power in maintaining order and limiting oppression. The Punitive Expedition appears to have been a necessary protection of American lives and property along the border, but the United States should have avoided the other interventions since they had little chance of establishing lasting order or preventing oppression.

During the progressive years the overwhelming majority of Americans accepted a large view of great power responsibilities and defended the interventions of the United States in its area of paramount interest. By comparison, agreement on a general expansion of American interests into East Asia was vitiated by confusion on the means to be used and reluctance to undertake entangling ventures.

A Limited Role in East Asia

Competition among the great powers for control of Chinese resources and territory dominated East Asian international politics from the end of the Sino-Japanese War in 1895 through World War II. Although Japan won a decisive victory over China, Russia along with Germany and France intervened in 1895 to limit the victor's gains and especially to prevent the annexation of any mainland territory. All of the powers except Austria-Hungary and Italy had extensive commercial ambitions in China, and the contest for economic concessions and imperial prestige turned into a scramble for leased ports and spheres of influence when Germany gained a 99-year lease on Kiaochow Bay in March 1898. In this race Russia and Japan had the largest immediate aims; the British, who controlled 80 percent of China's foreign trade, had the most to lose.

Despite a deep interest in the future of China, the United States stood aside during the initial competition for concessions because of its involvement in the Cuban question and ultimately the war with Spain. For some Americans the Philippine Islands provided the means to expand interests in Asia by serving as a stepping-stone to the vast market of four hundred million Chinese. But for the McKinley administration the protests of the anti-imperialists and the problems posed by the Philippine insurrection cooled any plans for an active Far Eastern policy. Further, trade with China was small — in 1899 slightly over 1 percent of United States exports went to China — and Chinese obstacles to expanded commerce combined with the apathy of American businessmen to prevent the development of the China market. During the Russo-Japanese War, in 1905, exports to China rose to 3.5 percent, but they quickly fell back to the lower level and were only 1.7 percent in 1920. In short, American goals in China were largely economic but remained unrealized in the first twenty years of the century.

Concerned about the threat to increased trade posed by the growing spheres of influence, McKinley and his advisers sought a way to maintain an "open door" for equal access to commercial opportunities in China. They wanted to respond to the demands of those such as Brooks Adams who called on the United States "to enter upon the development of Eastern Asia, and to reduce it to a part of our economic system." In March 1898 and again the following January Great Britain made overtures to gain American cooperation in preserving the "open door," a phrase already widely used. The Cuban problem prevented serious consideration of the first British offer, and McKinley rejected the second because he feared joint action with England would pull the United States into unnecessary complications with other powers. He also knew that any step resembling an alliance would generate serious political opposition among Anglophobes. During the summer of 1899, after the Senate approved the peace settlement with Spain, William W. Rockhill, the State Department's Asian expert, advanced a proposal that McKinley and Hay accepted with only a few minor changes. This initiative reflected the administration's desire to take a public position on the threats facing

East Asia in 1900

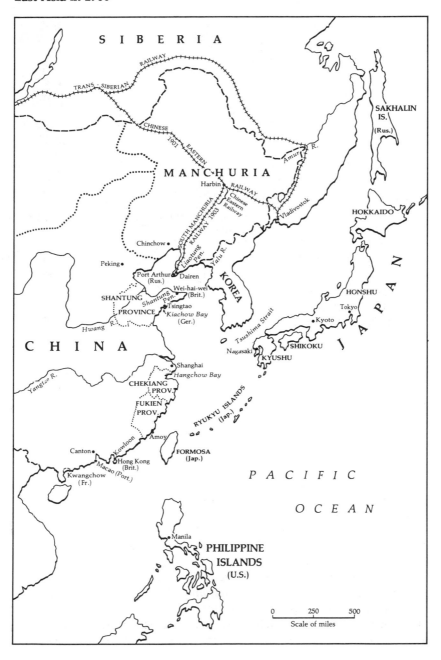

The Promise of China. The caption to this 1900 cartoon read: "THE OPEN DOOR TO CHINA! Uncle
Sam Has Distanced All Competitors in Gaining Access to the Riches of the Flowery
Kingdom." The welcoming smile of the Chinese and the powers' admiring glances reflect
the buoyant optimism of Americans contemplating the treasures of the China trade.

China without committing American resources to a specific line of
action.

John Hay dispatched the first Open Door notes to Britain, Germany, and Russia on September 6, 1899. Similar notes to France,
Italy, and Japan followed on November 17. Explicitly accepting the
spheres of influence with their special privileges for investment, the
notes requested the powers to join in supporting the principles of
equal treatment for all foreign trade throughout China and of continued Chinese control of the customs duties. Most of the nations
received even this limited suggestion coolly, and only Italy accepted
the American proposal without major qualification. Nevertheless,
Hay announced in May 1900 that the powers had given satisfactory

The Problem of China. The body of United States Army Captain Henry J. Reilly, killed by the Boxers, August 15, 1900. For two months Western nations followed with great interest international attempts to rescue the legations from the combined attacks of the Boxers and the Chinese Imperial army. Reilly was shot the day after the siege was broken as he directed the fire of his artillery battery in support of troops assaulting the inner Imperial City. His body lies near where he fell in the Chien Men, the huge central gate through the Tartar Wall normally opened only for the passage of the emperor.

assurances that they accepted the Open Door, thus giving the impression that action by the United States had prevented the partition of China.

Within a month, Hay's assessment of the Open Door notes received a stern test from the Boxer Rebellion. For over a year scattered anti-foreign nationalists known in the west as Boxers had disrupted

China with outbursts of violence. In the spring of 1900 the Boxer movement spread across the country, and the killing of westerners and Chinese Christians and the destruction of property increased sharply. The rebellion reached a peak in June when a large group of the militants laid siege to some four hundred western diplomats, missionaries, and businessmen in the compound of the British legation in Peking. Despite the restraints dictated by military involvement in the Philippine insurrection and the approaching national elections, the McKinley administration felt it had to act to protect American lives and property in China. The President therefore ordered United States troops (ultimately over 6,300) to join the international expeditionary force forming to raise the siege.

Meanwhile, on July 3, Secretary Hay sent a circular telegram, which became known as the second Open Door note, to the powers emphasizing the limited mission of the military force and America's opposition to any partition of China. In the message Hay declared that, beyond rescuing the endangered Americans and preventing the spread of the disorders, it was the purpose of the United States to "preserve Chinese territorial and administrative entity . . . and safeguard for the world the principle of equal and impartial trade with all parts of the Chinese Empire." The expeditionary force reached Peking and broke the siege on August 14. The rescuers found sixty-five of the defenders, including seven American marines, dead. Although there was no subsequent partition of China, this was not, as most Americans chose to believe, because of Hay's July circular. Instead, the prospect of conflict among the powers in addition to Chinese resistance persuaded the most ambitious nations that partition would be too costly.

The Open Door policy represented a cautious approach to the chaos of a disintegrating empire. As expressed in the 1899 notes and in the circular of the following July, the policy consisted of two principles: equal treatment for all foreign trade and preservation of China's administrative and territorial integrity. Containing no provisions for action beyond diplomatic cooperation, the Open Door policy sought to establish a verbal shield for the protection of future, mainly economic, interests. The July circular, announced the day before the meeting of the Democratic National Convention, had many of the qualities of a campaign document. It contained something for everyone concerned with Asia and America's position in the world, and it was quite useful in blunting the charges of the Democratic anti-imperialists. It was, however, much less effective overseas. When, early in 1901, Japan asked for American assistance in upholding the Open Door against Russian incursions in Manchuria, Hay replied in February that the United States was "not prepared singly, or in concert with other Powers, to enforce these views in the east by any demonstration which could present a character of hostility to any other Power." The following July, Rockhill, now minister in Peking, noted how the Open Door had not diminished the competition of all the powers for concessions in China but had involved America in their machinations. "I trust it may be a long time," he complained, "before the United States gets into another muddle of this description."

When he acceded to the presidency in September 1901, Theodore Roosevelt concentrated his attention on the things he deemed most important in gaining election in his own right in 1904. Foremost among these were a responsible and energetic domestic program and a vigorous Caribbean diplomacy focused on an American-controlled isthmian canal. The new President viewed East Asia as a region of less importance to the United States and believed with John Hay that the preferred policy was to keep America's options open for future expansion by encouraging a balance of power in the Far East. Russia loomed as the main threat to such a balance, and Hay's policy was to cooperate with Japan and Britain in restraining Russia and other ambitious powers. But when Japan again sought American support to block Russia, Hay repeated his earlier refusal. The Japanese then turned to the British, who were seeking ways to reduce overseas obligations, and in January 1902 these two island empires concluded the Anglo-Japanese Alliance for defensive purposes in Asia only. Under Roosevelt, as earlier, the Open Door in China remained an objective, but not one for which the United States would undertake any substantial commitment.

As the twentieth century opened, China began to emerge from centuries of parochial division and warlord rule and to develop a nationalism that would reach new heights in the 1970's. Contrary to American mythology, a large number of Chinese leaders saw the Open Door as a rationale for hated economic imperialism, and largely because of the methods used to suppress the Philippine insurrection, they viewed Americans as more objectionable expansionists and concessionaires than other westerners. Many Chinese resented the suppression of the Boxers and the expansion across their country of railroads constructed and controlled by foreigners. Their new nationalism caused them to feel particularly insulted by the exclusion of Chinese laborers, known then as coolies, from the United States. When the treaty that had authorized the exclusion of coolies approached expiration, the Chinese government came under heavy pressure not to renew it. So, with Roosevelt's approval, Congress in 1904 passed a unilateral act excluding all Chinese working-class immigrants. Many Chinese merchant communities responded with a boycott of American goods and services and a refusal to work for American families and firms in China. The boycott spread rapidly, reaching a peak in 1905 and creating much tension and hostility between Americans and Chinese. Outraged by this violation of American "rights," Roosevelt at one point threatened (one suspects mainly for domestic consumption) to use American troops to force the lifting of the boycott. This proved unnecessary as the boycott lost the support of merchants and came to an end after the imperial court issued an edict in March 1906 condemning anti-foreign activity. China tacitly accepted exclusion of its laborers from the United States, but the nationalist stirrings of the boycott indicated portentous shifts in Asia. It should have been evident to perceptive men that China would resist, to use Brooks Adams' phrase, being reduced to a part of the American economic system.

Japan, in contrast, viewed the United States more favorably and believed the two nations' Asian interests to be complementary. Russian expansion into Manchuria and Korea, areas the Japanese saw as necessary and logical parts of their empire, posed Japan's leading foreign problem. Japanese leaders tried to negotiate a compromise settlement with Russia, but the tsarist government, plagued by factionalism and inefficiency, could not reach a decision. Tired of waiting and mistrustful of Russian intentions, the Japanese government gave in to military pressure for action and opened hostilities in February 1904 with a surprise attack on the Russian fleet at Port Arthur. To the amazement of western military experts, the Japanese army gained a series of early victories, and by June 1905 Japanese forces had soundly defeated the Russian army and wiped out the Russian fleet. By this impressive performance, Japan gained recognition as the first nonwestern nation to become a great power. But while she had decisively beaten the world's second most feared nation, Japan found herself on the verge of bankruptcy and unable to continue hostilities. In the summer of 1905, Japanese leaders secretly asked Theodore Roosevelt to initiate peace discussions.

During the later stages of the war, the United States took part in a fundamental reshaping of Asian international politics. Although sympathetic with Japan, Roosevelt continued his policy of seeking a balance of power that would provide protection for the Open Door during and after the hostilities. The President enthusiastically confirmed the understanding negotiated by his secretary of war, the Taft-Katsura Agreement of July 1905, in which Japan declared that it had no aggressive intentions toward the Philippines and the United States in response stated its approval of the aims of the Anglo-Japanese Alliance and acceptance of Japanese control of Korea. (The United States was the first nation to recognize Japan's protectorate over Korea, thus helping to close the door on that former part of the Chinese empire.) In revising and renewing the Anglo-Japanese Alliance, signed in August 1905, Britain took pains to inform the United States of changes regarding Korea and plans for renewal, and the British foreign secretary explicitly declared to Japan that his nation would never allow the alliance to be directed against the United States in Asia or elsewhere. Through these diplomatic maneuvers the United States clarified its policy in East Asia and established as close a connection with Britain and Japan as it could without actually joining their alliance.

Acting on Japan's request, Roosevelt invited Japanese and Russian delegates to meet for peace talks at Portsmouth, New Hampshire. When a deadlock developed in negotiations, the President adroitly intervened to bring about a peace settlement in September 1905. Roosevelt's efforts in restoring peace to Asia won him international acclaim and the 1906 Nobel Peace Prize.

Cordiality with Japan soon ended, however, because the Japanese government encouraged its people to believe that pressure from Roosevelt, not Russian resistance and Japan's own economic weakness, had denied them better peace terms. When in October 1906 the San Francisco school board insulted the Japanese by ordering the segregation of Japanese students, anti-American sentiment quickly swept Japan. Underlying the deep-seated feelings on both sides was a strong movement among Americans on the West Coast to bar all further working-class immigrants from Japan. For two years this tension between the United States and Japan was punctuated by Japanese talk of war and American demands, particularly on the Pacific slope, for exclusion or other discriminatory legislation.

Roosevelt realized that the proud and recently victorious Japanese would not be as easily appeased as China had been during the

Delegates to the Portsmouth Conference pose with President Theodore Roosevelt. Left to right: Count Sergei Witte, former Russian minister of finance; Baron R. R. Rosen, former Russian minister to Japan and newly named ambassador to the United States; Roosevelt; Baron Komura, Japanese minister of foreign affairs; Minister Takahira, Japanese minister to the United States. With negotiations stalemated, Roosevelt wrote his son Kermit on August 25, 1905: "I am having my hair turned gray by dealing with the Russian and Japanese peace negotiators. The Japanese ask too much, but the Russians are ten times worse than the Japs because they are so stupid and won't tell the truth." Despite his frustrations, TR wrung from each side concessions that made peace possible.

Chinese immigration crisis. With the resourceful assistance of Elihu Root the President fashioned a flexible, moderate solution. Roosevelt and Root persuaded San Francisco authorities to revoke the segregation order, and then in the autumn of 1907 they devised a gentlemen's agreement in which Japan pledged to prevent voluntarily the emigration of any further laborers. To hold the Japanese to their word, Roosevelt used such means as diplomatic pressure and sending the Great White Fleet of sixteen battleships on a cruise around the world with a stop in Japan. The American strategy worked; tension over immigration faded so rapidly that within five weeks of the fleet's departure from Yokohama Secretary Root was able to sign an executive agreement with Japan that became the capstone of the Roosevelt administration's diplomacy for East Asia. In the Root-Takahira Agreement of November 30, 1908, the United States and Japan pledged to maintain peace and the status quo and to respect each other's possessions in the Pacific area. They also promised to support "the independence and integrity of China" (Japan refused to include "administrative entity" as stated in the second Open Door note) "and the principle of equal opportunity for commerce and industry of all nations in that Empire." In the event that these principles were threatened, they agreed to consult on action to be taken.

The Root-Takahira Agreement represented Roosevelt's restriction of American goals in East Asia to reflect the nation's actual interests and capabilities for defending them. In recognizing the status quo, the United States approved Japan's exclusive investment rights in southern Manchuria, an infringement of the Open Door principle. Roosevelt's willingness to accept Japanese dominance in Korea and southern Manchuria was, however, in return for a general agreement to maintain peace and protect the Philippines and a promise of equal opportunity to develop commerce in the rest of China, especially the Yangtze Valley. In carrying out this restrained policy, American naval planners decided that the Philippines could not be defended with the forces likely to be available, and in November 1909 they recommended and the Taft administration approved the establishment of the main Pacific naval base at Pearl Harbor rather than in the Philippines. Roosevelt remained convinced of the wisdom of his policy, and in December 1910 he declared to President Taft that the Open Door policy was excellent "so far as it can be maintained by general diplomatic agreement; but . . . [it] completely disappears as soon as a powerful nation determines to disregard it, and is willing to run the risk of war rather than forego its intention."

Roosevelt lectured his successor on the limitations of the Open Door because he was distressed by the extent to which Taft and Knox had abandoned the policy of balanced ends and means that they had inherited. Although Taft did not pretend that Asia outweighed Latin America in importance to the United States, he did allow his past associations with Asia to expand sharply his administration's diplomatic activities and hopes for an increased American role in the east. The Taft administration made two important policy changes: it took a much more active financial part in China, and it began a concerted attempt to confine Japanese expansion in Manchuria. And to these shifts in policy it added a new moralistic tone that would become a standard element of American diplomacy in Asia. In a speech at Cincinnati in November 1910, Secretary Knox stated this element clearly, if somewhat misleadingly, when he declared: "When we support the 'open door' in China, that is not the so-called 'dollar diplomacy,' but the recognition of a high moral duty." Although it was easy to adopt an attitude of moral superiority in asking for equal treatment in areas outside America's own region of vital interests, detached observers would have noted very few differences in the Taft administration's handling of economic diplomacy in Asia and in Latin America.

Taft and Knox adopted the program of two energetic young diplomats, Willard Straight and Francis M. Huntington Wilson, who had unsuccessfully opposed the Roosevelt policy of conciliating Japan. During the Taft years Straight served as the representative to the government for bankers and railroad builders interested in Asian investment, and at the age of thirty-three Huntington Wilson moved up from a junior post to reorganize and manage the Department of State as first assistant secretary under the indolent Knox. With the persuasive advice of Straight and Huntington Wilson, the Taft administration sought to protect the integrity of China as a means of maintaining the Open Door for American trade, and it believed that the political influence necessary to counter threats to Chinese integrity could best come through increased American investment. To advance this ambitious diplomatic strategy Taft and Knox developed two projects: They arranged for American bankers to be included in a consortium planning to build railroads in south and central China, a project known as the Hukuang loan; and Knox proposed the neutralization of Manchurian railroads through a large multinational loan to China for the purchase of all the railroads in this distant province. Such a loan, Knox reasoned, would guarantee the territorial integrity of China by removing the instrument used by Russia and Japan to expand their economic and political rights in Manchuria.

Both projects, however, bore little relation to political and economic realities, and Knox's indelicate handling only doomed them more rapidly to failure. Taft and his advisers overlooked the fact that little excess capital was available in the United States and better investments existed in Europe and Latin America than in Asia. They ignored changes in East Asian politics, such as the rapid decline of the Manchu dynasty in China and the spread of hostility to foreign exploitation. American diplomatists had no knowledge of the 1907 agreement between Russia and Japan that had divided Manchuria into spheres of influence. And increasing European tensions, which had brought about a significant settlement of issues between Britain and Russia in 1907, further complicated all Asian questions. When, in November 1909, Knox asked Britain to support and urge upon the Japanese his scheme for neutralization of the Manchurian railroads, the Foreign Office understandably declined to offer its assistance. Russia and Japan, after completely rejecting Knox's proposal, proceeded in July 1910 to sign another secret understanding pledging "common action" to defend their Manchurian spheres of influence.

In the meantime Taft, through a direct appeal to the Chinese prince regent, had gained access for the American banking group to the consortium floating the Hukuang loan. When problems developed in negotiating the loan, the American group's interest declined. The consortium finally forced the weakened Chinese regime to accept its terms, only to see the loan itself help spark a revolution that overthrew the Manchus and led to creation of the Republic of China in February 1912. As the bankers added representatives from Japan and Russia to become a six-power consortium and began to negotiate another loan with the republican government of China, the American group lost its remaining interest. By the end of 1912 even Taft's strongest partisans conceded that, whether "a high moral duty" or not, the extension of "dollar diplomacy" to Asia had proved a total failure. It had unwittingly encouraged Japan and Russia to increase cooperation in dividing Manchuria, alienated their British and French allies from the United States, weakened Chinese integrity, and shown American diplomacy to be both naive and heavy-handed.

The Wilson administration made a concerted effort to establish a new policy for East Asia. Wilson and Bryan denounced "dollar diplomacy," pressed the willing American bankers to withdraw from the consortium, and made the United States the first nation to extend diplomatic recognition to the new Chinese republic, which reversed Taft's policy of cooperation with the powers in delaying recognition until concessions were granted. Yet these changes were relatively

minor, and on the more fundamental issues Wilson's policy followed trends begun under Taft. Although the techniques and rhetoric of "dollar diplomacy" did disappear, Wilson strongly encouraged increased trade and investment in China and in 1918 even
sponsored a new four-power consortium to aid China in economic
rehabilitation. The new administration continued the tone of moralism regarding the Open Door in China, and it explored new ways of
restraining Japan.

The emergence of the United States as the leading opponent of
Japanese expansion in China marked the most significant development in Asian policy during the Wilson years. Immediately after
entering office Wilson faced difficulty with Japan over a bill introduced in the California legislature to prevent Japanese residents
from owning land. The bill was enacted despite efforts from Washington to modify it, and a violent reaction occurred in Japan. Wilson
took steps to prevent a war scare in the United States, and tension
gradually ebbed even though a new element had entered to increase
Japanese-American estrangement.

Japanese ambitions during World War I introduced new problems for the United States. Entering the war against the wishes of
its British ally, Japan proceeded to capture the German islands in
the north Pacific and to occupy the German leasehold on the Shantung
Peninsula. In January 1915 the extent of Japan's intentions became
clear with the delivery to China of a secret memorandum known as
the Twenty-One Demands. Realizing that acceptance of these demands would make China a protectorate of Japan, Chinese officials
informed the United States of their plight and sought assistance.
Initially Wilson was slow to take a stand, but as Japanese pressure
increased the President stiffened, declaring to Bryan on April 14
"that we should be active as the circumstances permit in showing
ourselves to be champions of the sovereign rights of China." American protests did force Japan to modify some of the more extreme
claims, but confronted with a Japanese ultimatum China acquiesced
in the rest of the demands early in May. Secretary Bryan then announced that the United States would not recognize any agreement
between China and Japan that impaired American treaty rights, the
political and territorial integrity of China, or the Open Door policy.
The nonrecognition declaration had no effect at the time beyond
irritating the Japanese, but it would be important in efforts to restrict
Japan in the 1930's.

After declaring war on Germany, the United States sought to retreat from the high principle of nonrecognition and establish a temporary working agreement with Japan that would stabilize the situation in Asia until a peace settlement could be drawn. After several weeks of negotiation the two nations signed the Lansing-Ishii Agreement on November 2, 1917. Beyond restating the traditional pledge to maintain the Open Door and protect the territorial integrity of China, Japan and the United States made the apparently conflicting declaration that "territorial propinquity creates special relations between countries, and consequently the Government of the United States recognizes that Japan has special interests in China, particularly in the part to which her possessions are contiguous." In an additional protocol, kept secret at Japanese insistence, the two nations attempted to minimize the contradiction between Japan's special interests and the Open Door by promising not to "take advantage of the present conditions to seek special rights or privileges in China which would abridge the rights of the subjects or citizens of other friendly states." As a modus vivendi the Lansing-Ishii Agreement could have worked, but in practice the Japanese immediately disregarded the restrictions of the secret protocol and the Americans began to ignore the entire exchange. Unfortunately for the future of Japanese-American relations, duty-driven men on either side could locate what they wanted to find in this ambiguous agreement. In addition to continuing difficulties over rights in China, the Wilson administration would confront serious problems caused by Japanese desires during the Siberian intervention and the Versailles Conference.

United States diplomacy for East Asia followed a capricious course in the two decades after the enunciation of the Open Door notes. American diplomatists consistently recognized Asia as an area of secondary importance and generally agreed that American interests were limited to protecting the Philippines and maintaining Chinese integrity and the Open Door for American trade. Yet they varied greatly in estimates of how those interests could best be protected and the rate and manner by which they could be advanced. Roosevelt and Hay clearly wanted to follow a more active policy, but they limited their diplomacy to steps that could be justified by actual American interests and the current willingness of the American people to defend them. Roosevelt sought to conciliate Japan in Korea and Manchuria in order to head off expansion toward the Philippines or further immigration crises. In contrast, Taft abandoned realities, injected a new note of moralism into Asian policy, and tried to use economic pressure to restrain Japan and protect China for American trade. Wilson also worked to limit Japan but placed less reliance on economic measures and more on moral rhetoric. Although he would ultimately accept Japanese demands at Versailles, he fought compromise at every turn and helped create a deep animosity in both nations.

A shift in the meaning of the Open Door policy accompanied the dramatic changes in Asian politics in this period. Initially concerned mainly with the protection of American trade, the Open Door policy grew to focus more on the integrity of China as Russian and Japanese interests expanded. Later it incorporated the desire for equal opportunity for American industry and then investment. As the United States began to concentrate on restricting Japanese expansion, a new moralistic rhetoric developed to preach American responsibilities in East Asia. This line of argument, which dwelt on the threats to Chinese integrity from Japanese rapacity, sought to prevent Japan's creation of a sphere of control such as the United States had developed in the Caribbean under the principles of the Monroe Doctrine. The American people drew a sharp distinction between their beneficent actions in the Caribbean and the avaricious goals of Japanese militarists in China. But this was a difference the Japanese could not understand and would never accept. In the years after 1908 the former friendship between Japan and the United States was reversed, and by 1921 each nation viewed the other as its most likely foe in a major war. Since Japan remained committed to an empire on the Asian mainland and the United States increased its determination to protect Chinese integrity, the initial downhill turn on the road to Pearl Harbor can be located in the diplomacy of Taft and Wilson.

European Involvements and Anglo-American Friendship

Despite preponderant cultural and economic ties in Europe, American diplomatists before 1914 paid markedly less attention to European developments than to those in Latin America and Asia. A century of American isolation from European political rivalries had created a diplomatic tradition that statesmen refused to violate for anything short of a major threat to the nation. Throughout most of the nineteenth century the United States had relied on the balance of power in Europe to protect the republic's interests. Even after becoming a great power, the United States continued to depend on the maintenance of an equilibrium that prevented any single nation from gaining predominance in Europe. American policy makers appreciated and sought to maintain Britain's function as the balance wheel in the European system. Theodore Roosevelt was highly interested and knowledgeable about European affairs, and he involved the United States in several widely publicized mediation efforts at the Algeciras Conference on Morocco and during the Anglo-German naval rivalry. But even then the United States occupied only a minor position and accepted no continuing obligations. The Taft and early Wilson administrations took virtually no interest in Europe, and there was very little diplomatic contact beyond economic relations and a series of arbitration and conciliation treaties. After five years of diminished contact and ineffective diplomacy, represented most vividly by Knox's neutralization scheme and Wilson's Mexican policy, European diplomatists by 1914 could with good reason question America's continued willingness and capacity to fulfill the position of a great power.

The firm though tacit understanding that the United States had developed with Great Britain, however, assured American concern with any European shift that threatened British power. Relations with Britain had provided the republic's most important international connection since winning independence, and from 1895 to 1903 the two nations consummated "the Great Rapprochement" in which they resolved all serious differences between them. Instrumental in completing the rapprochement, Theodore Roosevelt made the resulting understanding (or entente) with Britain the foundation of his international program for the United States, just as Captain Mahan had urged.

The Anglo-American understanding reflected the fundamental realization that the two nations had similar or complementary interests in most regions of the world. As Roosevelt wrote England's King Edward VII in March 1905: "In matters outside our own borders, we are chiefly concerned, first with what goes on south of us, second with affairs in the orient; and in both cases our interests are identical with yours." The new friendship also demonstrated Britain's need to abandon its century-long policy of isolation in order to gain support in areas where the empire was particularly vulnerable. British strategists concluded that they could not possibly defend their possessions in Canada and the Caribbean in case of war with the United States, so they decided to follow a conciliatory policy toward the powerful republic that would protect their territories and investments in the Western Hemisphere. American leaders were generally favorable to a closer tie with Britain because they viewed the cooperation as a means to extend their subtle reliance on British power for the purpose of spreading superior Anglo-Saxon civilization around the world. The most enthusiastic was John Hay, once ambassador to London, who declared in 1899 that while he was secretary of state the United States would not act "contrary to my conviction that the one indispensable feature of our foreign policy should be a friendly understanding with England."

Statesmen in both Great Britain and the United States, aware of the American people's continued opposition to entangling alliances as well as their widespread suspicion of English motives, proceeded with caution in developing the rapprochement. They began slowly with expressions of good will, limited cooperation in China, and mutual encouragement in their respective wars against Spain and the Boer republics of South Africa. The most critical stage came in resolving the isthmian canal and Alaskan boundary questions. The Hay-Pauncefote Treaty of 1901, in which Great Britain gave the United States full authority to construct and fortify an interoceanic canal, guaranteed American strategic dominance of the Caribbean. Coming as an unqualified concession, this accord diminished American hostility toward Britain and made cooperation a more acceptable policy for the Roosevelt administration to pursue.

Settlement of the Alaskan boundary dispute rounded out the Anglo-American understanding. This issue between the United States and Canada was important less for economic or security reasons than for what it indicated about political intentions. Americans on the West Coast wanted to see how tenaciously the administration in Washington would defend their interests, while all Americans and Canadians were eager to know what course Great Britain would follow. (The British government continued to direct Canadian foreign relations until 1911, when the dominion assumed this authority.) The dispute stemmed from the vagueness of the boundary between the Alaskan panhandle and Canada. The unclear boundary had posed no problem for over seventy years until the discovery of gold along Canada's Klondike River in 1896. The gold clearly lay in Canadian territory, but the best access route and the opportunity to manage development of the gold fields were in a region that the

Prominent advocates of Anglo-American friendship were John Hay (left) and Arthur James Balfour (right), both pictured in about 1903. Hay (1838–1905) admitted that an alliance with England was "an unattainable dream" but worked to achieve as complete an understanding as American political conditions would permit while serving as United States ambassador to London, 1897–1898, and secretary of state, 1898–1905. Balfour (1848–1930) continually backed close cooperation with the United States as England's first lord of the treasury and leader of the House of Commons, 1895–1905; Prime Minister, 1902–1905; first lord of the admiralty, 1915–1916; and foreign secretary, 1916–1919.

United States had nominally controlled for thirty years but that Canada now claimed. Negotiations dragged, and as the Canadians found their contention taken seriously they became adamant.

Theodore Roosevelt entered the White House determined to put to rest the Canadian claim, which he termed "an outrage pure and simple." A forceful stand, backed behind the scenes by Hay's skillful diplomacy, enabled the Rough Rider to obtain British agreement to have the boundary determined by a commission of "six impartial jurists of repute," three to be appointed by the President and three by the King of England. Although the evidence heavily favored the

American claim, Roosevelt left nothing to chance. He selected three highly partisan Americans for the commission and launched a vigorous campaign of public and private pressure, even threatening at one point to have American troops run the boundary if the commission did not make the proper decision. The two Canadian commissioners could not be moved, but Lord Alverstone, the chairman of the commission and Lord Chief Justice of England, appreciated the force of the American argument as well as his own government's desire to conciliate the United States. Alverstone voted with the three Americans, and in October 1903 the commission announced its decision to award the United States virtually all it had claimed. The bitterly disappointed Canadian representatives refused to sign the award, but Americans rejoiced at the favorable decision and correctly perceived Britain's posture of friendship. Resolution of the Alaskan dispute firmly cemented the Anglo-American understanding, for, as Roosevelt several years later wrote Mahan, it "settled the last serious trouble between the British Empire and ourselves, as everything else could be arbitrated."

Working out the implications of the understanding took almost two years after the Alaskan award. While the boundary tribunal was being formed, American objections to the blockade of Venezuela raised questions about the nature of American domination in the Caribbean. The Germans and more directly the British contended that, if they were not allowed to use pressure to collect debts and resolve other just grievances, the United States should intervene to see that the Latin nations met their responsibilities. Continued British urging and the development of serious financial problems in the Dominican Republic persuaded the American government to adopt the Roosevelt Corollary to the Monroe Doctrine. And Britain, facing the rising German naval threat, decided in October 1904 to withdraw to home territory all combat naval and military forces from Canada and the Caribbean on the premise that, as a government spokesman described it, "war with the United States was a contingency so remote that it might for defence purposes be neglected." In the hope of expanding cooperation in the Pacific, British leaders in January 1905 considered asking the United States to join the alliance with Japan, then in the process of revision and renewal. But after Roosevelt indicated privately that an alliance was politically impossible for the United States, Britain decided not to extend a formal invitation.

By the end of 1905 events had clarified the nature of the Anglo-

American understanding. As this tacit division of interests applied to the Western Hemisphere, Great Britain granted political and strategic predominance to the United States in return for the assurance of equal commercial opportunities and assistance in protecting British citizens and possessions from civil disturbances or foreign attack. The two nations also agreed that a similar division of interests could be worked out in regions such as the Near East, where Britain had predominant concern, and that in China they would pursue a policy of cooperation in maintaining the Open Door. The understanding was nothing more than a delicate series of shared assumptions, and its continued existence and growth required patient effort and forbearance plus a willingness to adjust to the partner's needs. These qualities were abundant in the diplomacy of Roosevelt and Root. There was extensive cooperation during the Russo-Japanese War, and Britain kept the United States from being a potential opponent in revising the Anglo-Japanese Alliance. Britain and the United States signed an arbitration treaty in 1908 that omitted questions of vital interest, and Root and British Ambassador James Bryce began a series of negotiations to "clean the slate" of all outstanding issues between their nations. A number of these, involving land and water boundaries, extradition, and the perennially troublesome Newfoundland fisheries dispute, were resolved under Root's imaginative direction; others, including open-sea sealing and pecuniary claims, were resolved under Knox.

Early in the Taft administration, however, suspicion and discord began to plague the new understanding. Taft highly valued British friendship, but his legalistic methods and his delegation of most diplomatic responsibilities to men like Knox and Huntington Wilson who had no special regard for the rapprochement led to immediate difficulty when combined with the effects of "dollar diplomacy" on British trade and investment. The seemingly innocuous process of refunding the debts of the Caribbean republics in fact injured British economic interests in two ways. First, since British investors held the largest portion of the bonded debt in all the Central American countries and substantial amounts in the island republics, refunding with American loans denied Britain a substantial amount of investment. Second, and more important since the loans often were not repaid on schedule, loss of the loan often meant loss of the more profitable trade that normally followed the bonds. As early as July 1909, a senior British diplomat in Washington could declare when discussing American policy in Central America and the Dominican

Republic: "I expect the Foreign Office is pretty well irritated at the want of consideration that Mr. Knox has shown." And by January 1911, British Foreign Secretary Sir Edward Grey complained of the "great difficulty" Britain was having in negotiating Open Door commercial agreements in Latin America. "We are constantly finding," he explained, "that the difficulty is caused by a belief amongst Central and South Americans that the United States are not favourable to the open door." In contrast, the extension of "dollar diplomacy" to Asia in the form of the consortium and neutralization plans did not injure British interests as much as it demonstrated a disturbing lack of American diplomatic finesse.

The British would have had reason for greater concern had Taft succeeded in his attempt for reciprocal tariff reduction with Canada. The Republican Party had traditionally advocated high protective duties to stimulate industry, but progressive opposition to favors for special interests and the need to increase exports fueled a growing movement for lower tariffs. Convinced that a less restricted flow of trade would benefit both Canada and the United States, Taft sought to satisfy the demands for reform by leading the fight for a reciprocity agreement with the dominion. The administration reached terms with Canadian representatives in January 1911, and each government set out to put the accord into operation through concurrent legislation rather than by a treaty. Responding to the objections of farm, fishing, and lumber groups, a majority of Republicans in the Senate opposed the President's bill. But with the support of the Democrats and an odd group of previously high-tariff Republicans, Taft won the approval of Congress and in late July signed the bill, which he had called "the most important measure of my administration." Unfortunately, the struggle for reciprocity in the United States had led to comments there which assisted the already powerful opposition in Canada. Several times Taft had asserted that the people of the dominion were "coming to the parting of the ways," when they would have to choose between commercial friendship and isolation from United States markets. And Champ Clark, Democratic Speaker of the House and presidential aspirant, declared that he favored lower duties because he hoped to see the day "when the American flag will float over every square foot of the British North American possessions clear to the North Pole."

Using these statements to bolster the argument that reciprocity would lead to annexation by the United States, the Canadian Conservative Party forced the Liberal government to dissolve parliament and call a national election. In an emotional campaign the Conservatives, heavily financed by railroad and manufacturing interests, capitalized on suspicion of the United States and rising national feeling to win a decisive victory in September 1911. The new Conservative majority then defeated the reciprocity bill in parliament. The reduction of tariffs in North America would have harmed British trade, but the government in London declined to interfere or express an opinion on the issue because it desired to maintain both Canadian loyalty to the empire and American friendship. The Taft administration lacked this degree of perception and discipline. Although Canadian nationalism was the main reason for the failure of reciprocity, the President and his supporters had offended dominion sensibilities with their ill-advised remarks and helped to create what became a serious embarrassment for the United States.

Taft's effort to win the backing of liberal internationalists by negotiating general arbitration treaties with Great Britain and France met a similar fate. The President strongly advocated these broad pacts, which covered all "justiciable" differences that were "susceptible of decision by the application of the principles of law or equity," including questions of national honor and vital interest. If completed and carried out in the appropriate spirit, these agreements would in the future require the arbitration of issues such as the Alaskan boundary, and their passage would mark an important advance in the movement for peace and the rule of international law. Although designed as a model for extension to other governments, the pact with Britain was the primary objective. France was included mainly to tame Anglophobic sentiment. During the drafting process Britain proved highly cooperative, and France accepted the results. With the signature of the treaties on August 3, 1911, great enthusiasm swept the international peace movement. This excitement was premature, however, for Taft and Knox had not laid adequate groundwork with the Senate, which had wrecked important arbitration agreements with Britain in 1897 and 1905 and remained extremely jealous of its power to consent to treaties. Theodore Roosevelt, Senator Lodge, and now Admiral Mahan led the opposition, contending that no powerful state with expanding interests could pledge itself to arbitrate questions of national honor or fundamental concern. Although emphasizing that a general arbitration accord with England raised no dangers, critics attacked its use as a model for any other country. And on the ground that the pacts denied the Senate its right to set the terms of every arbitration, the opponents added so many unfriendly amendments in approving the agreements that the President refused to ratify them. Several years later Taft, who with all his limitations could turn the light of humor on himself, declared wistfully that in dealing with the treaties the Senate had

truncated them and amended them and qualified them in such a way that their own father could not recognize them. . . . So I put them on the shelf and let the dust accumulate on them in the hope that the Senators might change their minds, or that the people might change the Senate; instead of which they changed me.

A final dispute with Britain over the tolls to be charged for the Panama Canal stemmed less from lack of consideration or the side effects of an ill-conceived policy than from the chauvinism and pettifogging legalism of Taft and his chief advisers. By the terms of the Hay-Pauncefote Treaty the United States was pledged to keep the canal, scheduled for completion in 1914, open to vessels "of all nations . . . on terms of entire equality." In computing the tolls the Taft administration interpreted this clause to mean all nations other than the United States and submitted a bill, which Congress passed in August 1912, exempting from tolls American ships engaged in the coasting trade (that is, trade from one coast to the other as distinguished from foreign commerce). Administration officials claimed the schedule of tolls was both fair and within the terms of the treaty since they had excluded the projected American usage of the canal in calculating tolls and since the United States by paying the construction and maintenance costs was using this exemption simply as a subsidy to its coasting trade. The British, however, were in no mood for hair-splitting arguments or sharp bargaining. Appalled by the attacks on the arbitration treaty and involved in an intense dispute over refunding the Guatemalan debt, they wondered if all their concessions on the canal and other strategic issues had been in vain. The British government decided to make a stand, and the Foreign Office composed a long note of protest asking that the question be submitted to arbitration under the terms of the 1908 treaty. Knox, in what Walter Hines Page called a "wretched lawyer's note," replied that since the canal had not opened, no injury had occurred to Britain and there was nothing to arbitrate. By this time Taft had suffered defeat in the November elections, and Britain, in disgust at the diplomatic ineptitude of his administration, decided to postpone all further discussion of the tolls issue for the incoming Wilson administration.

The British had good reason to delay for Woodrow Wilson. They knew the President-elect had reconsidered his prior endorsement of the tolls exemption and had pledged in January 1913 to take "the right stand" when the appropriate time came. Wilson placed first priority, however, on his "New Freedom" domestic reforms and decided not to open the tolls question until he had guided his tariff and banking bills through Congress. He recorded a notable victory in early October when he signed into law the Underwood Tariff with its substantially reduced rates. But heavy opposition delayed the banking proposal in committee.

As Britain waited patiently for action on the tolls immunity, a crisis developed between the United States and Mexico that threatened to undermine future Anglo-American cooperation. In combating the Huerta regime, Wilson directed considerable hostility toward the British government, which he incorrectly believed to be providing essential diplomatic and financial backing for the Mexican dictator in return for new oil concessions. British officials felt Wilson's goal of putting the Mexican government on "a moral basis" was totally unrealistic because, as Sir Edward Grey dryly remarked, "It would require about 200,000 soldiers to put Mexico on a 'moral' basis." Nevertheless, realizing the intensity of the President's feeling, Britain decided to avoid any impression of assisting Huerta against the United States. In a prominent speech during November, Prime Minister Herbert H. Asquith pledged British cooperation on Mexico. Grey provided extensive explanations at the Foreign Office and had his private secretary Sir William Tyrrell, who was visiting Washington for other purposes, convey unqualified assurances of support in private discussions with Wilson and Secretary of State Bryan. By the end of November these efforts had persuaded Wilson of the purity of British motives in Mexico. In response, the President affirmed his intention to protect British investments and maintain the Open Door for British trade in Mexico. He also tacitly accepted a linkage between the Mexican and Panama tolls issues by assuring Tyrrell that he would soon act to remove the exemption for the American coasting trade.

Once suspicion of British policy in Mexico was dispelled, resolution of the tolls question and other issues proceeded rapidly in the first half of 1914. Wilson publicly called for revocation of the tolls exemption on February 5, and strong presidential pressure influenced Congress to pass the repeal bill in June. Meanwhile the Senate had approved a five-year renewal of the 1908 arbitration treaty with Britain, and despite a succession of disappointments over arbitration the British quickly ratified it. With the repeal of the tolls immunity, Britain finally consented to begin talks on Secretary Bryan's pet project, a conciliation agreement. Although the start of the European crisis that led to World War I delayed negotiations, Great Britain and the United States signed a "cooling-off treaty" on September 15, 1914. Then, unknown to American diplomatists, Britain designated this conciliation pact a general arbitration agreement, which by the terms of the 1911 revision of the Japanese alliance made it certain that Britain could not be dragged into any future Japanese-American dispute.

Thus, in the early weeks of a general European war, Britain underlined again for its oldest ally the great value placed on friendship with the United States. From the start of "the Great Rapprochement" in the 1890's, Great Britain had made many concessions to her American offspring. The United States had responded regularly with increased cooperation until the Taft administration engendered ill will and suspicion by taking British support for granted. Although a bit slow to act, Woodrow Wilson had restored the quality of the Anglo-American understanding just before the outbreak in 1914 of the conflagration in Europe. Despite some actions by the Senate and Taft's officials, American diplomacy in the Western Hemisphere, Asia, and Europe had since 1903 rested squarely on the assumption of continuing British friendship. Reliance for over a decade on the understanding with Britain would have a marked effect on American behavior in crises over neutral rights during World War I.

America and the Great War

During the first week of August 1914 all but one of the European great powers toppled into an unwanted war. The immediate origin of the struggle was the assassination on June 28 of Archduke Franz Ferdinand, heir to the thrones of Austria and Hungary, by a Serbian nationalist. But the fundamental causes lay much deeper in over a generation of competition for empire, prestige, and markets. The growth since 1905 of an intense rivalry between opposing alliance systems virtually guaranteed that a war involving one of the powers would automatically grow into a general conflagration. The hostile coalitions included the Triple Entente of France, Russia, and Great Britain—known during the war as the Allies—and the Triple Alliance of Germany, Austria-Hungary, and Italy — known as the Central Powers. Although allied with Germany and Austria-Hungary since 1882, Italy remained on the sidelines when fighting began and after bargaining with both sides for concessions joined the Allies in May 1915. Of the two non-European powers, Japan ignored British attempts to discourage participation and entered the war late in its first month on the side of the Allies. The United States, disclaiming any direct interest in the Old World's conflict, declared neutrality with a mixture of relief and anxiety.

Seldom in modern history have expectations about the duration and nature of a war proved more false than they did during the Great War of 1914–1918. Leaders in all the belligerent nations anticipated brief hostilities with only limited mobilization of resources and moderate destruction. British statesmen felt their navy would bear most of the fighting, and Sir Edward Grey told the House of Commons on August 3 that "if we are engaged in war, we shall suffer but little more than we shall suffer even if we stand aside." Everyone expected the boys to be home by Christmas. But these hopes were soon dashed. The fighting dragged on for over four years, nations mobilized completely for a struggle of attrition, and from the ablest young men of all belligerents over nine million were killed and many additional millions maimed. Yet each nation based initial plans on the assumption of a short war, and its thinking about America naturally reflected these views.

United States leaders considered no course except neutrality, although many citizens did have preferences among the belligerents. In a population that totaled ninety-two million in 1914, enthusiasm for the Central Powers came from those of German, Austro-Hungarian, and Irish stock. These included over eight million recent immigrants or children of immigrants from Germany and four million from Ireland. Most of the remaining Americans endorsed the Allied cause, and the large number of English origin matched the Germans and Irish in their fervor. Still sympathy did not breed a desire to become involved in the war, and few Americans objected to Woodrow Wilson's exhortation on August 19 to "be neutral in fact as well as in name" and "impartial in thought as well as in action."

The technical limits of neutrality, however, left a wide range of actions open to the United States. Although a neutral government could not provide a belligerent direct aid such as training troops or sheltering warships in its ports, a neutral state could through private transactions sell weapons, munitions, and other supplies to belligerents, and banks could extend loans to private companies or to the government of a combatant nation. Thus the latitude of neutrality easily allowed a nation to show a distinct preference among the warring states.

Although most Americans sought to follow Wilson's injunction to be impartially neutral, basic forces soon led the United States to favor the Allies. The American economy was just emerging from a slump, and the immense demand for war supplies led to the return of prosperity. Between 1914 and 1916 American trade in munitions alone jumped from $40 million to $1.3 billion, an increase of over thirty times; the sales for 1916 represented almost 24 percent of all United States exports. Due to Britain's vigorous command of the seas, the overwhelming proportion of war trade flowed to the Allies, thereby creating an important economic tie that would limit the Wilson administration's capacity to treat both groups of belligerents equally. After an initial prohibition on loans dictated largely by concern for stability of the domestic economy, the administration reversed its position in September 1915 and tacitly approved private loans to belligerent governments. By the time the United States entered the war in April 1917, American loans to the Allies totaled over $2.2 billion compared with only $27 million to the Central Powers.

The general attitudes of the two leading belligerents became even more important in determining America's posture. Great Britain, hoping to draw upon the strength of a decade's rapprochement, made the maintenance of American friendship one of its foremost diplomatic objectives. From the outbreak of war until his resignation in December 1916, Sir Edward Grey was guided by the premise that, as he wrote his ambassador in Washington, Britain should "do nothing which will be a cause of complaint or dispute as regards the United States Government; such a dispute would indeed be a crowning calamity . . . and probably fatal to our chances of success" in the war. Although Grey did not always have his way after the first year of war and difficulties did arise over blockade policy, the British tried to minimize objections and demonstrated a continuing awareness of American strength. Germany, on the other hand, frequently showed an insensitivity to American interests and values that seemed to reflect the belief that the United States would not enter the war even under extreme provocation. German leaders felt they had to use the submarine to counter British naval power, and

A German U-boat halts an American steamer. When British merchant ships began using hidden guns and false neutral flags to evade submarines, German naval commanders stopped surfacing to inspect vessels before attacking. The German policy of sinking without search or notification became the most important single factor in bringing the United States into World War I.

problems quickly developed over neutral shipping. The impact on Americans of U-boat warfare and the outrages committed during the German invasion of Belgium heightened the image of the Kaiser's Reich as a ruthless nation without respect for international law.

The international orientation of key American diplomatists also helped form decisions in Washington. Wilson and his advisers, with the exception of Bryan who remained deeply suspicious of everything English, felt that American principles were much closer to those represented by the British Liberal government than to those advanced by the Central Powers. Bryan was the most single-minded in his insistence on absolute impartiality and sought to avoid all situations that might drag the United States into war. Indeed, the secretary of state believed America should pay almost any price to bring peace through mediation. Bryan's chief associate was Robert Lansing, counselor of the Department of State until he succeeded Bryan as secretary in June 1915. As an international lawyer concerned with questions of maritime neutral rights, Lansing drafted many of the protests to Britain and Germany. Convinced by the autumn of 1915 that America should enter the war to support Britain, Lansing carefully developed the distinction between British violation of property rights, always subject to compensation and thus negotiable, and German violation of human rights, often fatal and fundamentally unnegotiable. Like Lansing, Colonel Edward M. House, Wilson's confidant and personal emissary, viewed the war in terms of balance of power and saw American interests as similar to Britain's. Although he shared the President's desire to enhance American prestige, House held more traditional ideas on the methods of diplomacy and subtly worked to bring Wilson to his position. Walter Hines Page, Wilson's old friend who served as ambassador in London, had direct access to the President, but he became so decidedly pro-British that, according to a recent scholar, by the spring of 1915 Washington officials received his reports with either "disinterest or disgust."

Wilson's political goals proved to be vitally important in shaping American neutrality. In contrast to his handling of the crises with Mexico and Japan, the President this time made all the important decisions and often drafted diplomatic notes on his portable typewriter. In defending American rights to trade with the belligerents, he sought to maintain his nation's status as a great power. From the start Wilson visualized the United States exerting leadership in the world through superior example. The United States would be the principled neutral without selfish interests, the outside power capable of mediating among predatory European states. America had a mission, the President believed, to mold the peace settlement as the impartial reformer from the New World. As the war advanced, however, Wilson began to understand that superior example alone would not gain significant influence for the United States. The changes in neutrality reflected, in part, the President's gradual realization that America had to intervene in the war in order to affect the peace.

Beyond the growth in the United States of a benevolent neutrality toward the Allies, diplomats and strategists had to confront an array of new issues created by the war. These problems stemmed, at least initially, from the techniques Great Britain used in applying an economic blockade to continental enemies. The German response with extensive use of submarines further complicated legal and diplomatic practices.

In the years immediately before the war, the powers had made a futile attempt to anticipate some of these issues by modernizing international law. Under traditional practice, a sea power could intercept and confiscate neutral trade with another belligerent if the goods were contraband (items exclusively for military use). And if the sea power had established a blockade of enemy ports, it could prevent all trade—contraband and noncontraband—with its enemies. The development of ironclad, steam-powered warships during the nineteenth century caused many of the established rules of neutrality to become obsolete, and disputes over the nature of a blockade and the definition of contraband increased. To establish a modern code of maritime law, Great Britain invited the naval nations to a conference, and after weeks of negotiating they signed the Declaration of London in February 1909. This treaty represented a significant victory for the rights of neutrals. It included both a substantially reduced list of absolute contraband items and broadened categories of free goods (clearly noncontraband materials that were not subject to capture if shipped by a neutral to an unblockaded belligerent port). The new maritime code also specified that a blockade was legal only when effective, meaning when the blockading ships were placed close enough to the port and in sufficient numbers to make interception of all maritime traffic reasonably certain. The restrictions placed on a blockading fleet were serious enough to cause the British government, although its delegation had signed the code at the end of the conference, to refuse to ratify the declaration.

When war broke out in 1914, the United States attempted to persuade the belligerents to adopt the new rules on neutral rights set forth in the Declaration of London. The Central Powers indicated a willingness to accept the declaration if the Allies did so without qualification. Despite numerous attempts by Wilson and Lansing to gain an unconditional acceptance, Great Britain insisted on modifications so fundamental that the Central Powers rejected them. The United States finally acquiesced in the British plan, which included some of the declaration's provisions but altered two important areas. One was the classification as absolute contraband of items such as copper, iron, aluminum, rubber, gasoline, and oil that had been listed previously as free goods or conditional contraband (materials such as food and clothing not exclusively for military use but subject to capture if proven to be destined for enemy armed forces). The other innovation was the addition of regulations to prevent neutrals from carrying contraband to neutral ports on the European continent, from which it would be shipped overland to the Central Powers.

With grudging American approval, Britain proceeded early in November 1914 to establish at considerable distance from German ports an undeclared blockade that utilized an expanded list of contraband. Seeking to deny the use of the North Sea to any other nation, the Admiralty declared it a "military area" and sowed it with mine fields more extensive than any previously used. British leaders claimed that these steps of economic coercion were necessary to equalize the advantages Germany had gained through the surprise attack on France. As the war turned into a stalemate during the winter, Britain moved to tighten the blockade further. The goal of British diplomacy was, as Grey wrote in his memoirs, "to secure the maximum of blockade that could be enforced without a rupture with the United States."

German policy makers, insisting that British naval actions violated the new requirements of international law, searched in early 1915 for a way to improve their position. Their strategy of a rapid conquest of France with the Schlieffen Plan's sweep through Belgium had not worked. Their army had ground to a halt at the Marne and confronted growing pressure from Russia in the east, and their navy had been bottled up in port by the superior British fleet. An important group of German naval leaders began to press for the unrestricted use of submarines against British commerce, citing Britain's use of an illegal blockade and extensive mining and emphasizing the dangers for Germany of a war of attrition. The navy argued for this fateful departure even though Germany had only twenty-one usable submarines and only a third of them could be operative at one time. Furthermore, the submarine at that stage of development was a flimsy craft with limited cruising radius and maneuverability—an easy target for opposing destroyers or fast cruisers.

Although Navy Minister Grand Admiral Alfred von Tirpitz, Chancellor Theobald von Bethmann Hollweg, and others had grave doubts about the effectiveness of submarines and fears concerning the response of important neutrals, they gave in to the need for a new approach to the war. Encouraged by a few chance submarine sinkings of British cruisers, naval leaders even assured the Kaiser that

British and German Naval War Zones, 1914-1918

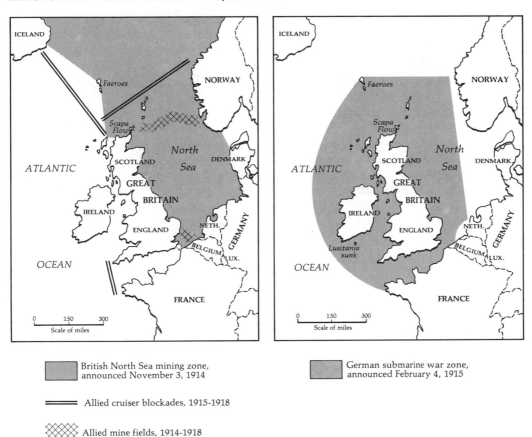

British North Sea mining zone, announced November 3, 1914

German submarine war zone, announced February 4, 1915

Allied cruiser blockades, 1915-1918

Allied mine fields, 1914-1918

a submarine blockade would force Britain to peace terms within six weeks. These glowing prospects convinced the Kaiser to act. On February 4, 1915, the German foreign minister declared that in two weeks the waters around Great Britain and Ireland would become a war zone in which German submarines would seek "to destroy every enemy merchant ship" without being able to ensure protection of persons and cargoes. "Neutrals," the foreign minister continued, "are therefore warned against further entrusting crews, passengers and wares to such ships." Moreover, since English vessels at times traveled illegally under neutral flags, neutral ships should avoid entering the war zone. This German blockade, announced without a thorough evaluation of its chances of success or its effects on neutrals, became the first in a chain of events that culminated in the unforeseen, and for Germany undesired, entry of the United States into the war.

When added to Britain's new methods of blockade, the unrestricted use of German submarines within an arbitrary war zone had tremendous impact on the unstable structure of international law and on the form of American neutrality. In response to the German use of submarines without warning and search, Britain began to arm merchantmen. The United States, accepting a finely drawn British distinction between offensive and defensive armament, allowed defensively armed merchantmen to enter American ports. Germany then started to sink all types of ships, including passenger liners, which led to several important diplomatic crises. Caught between these unprecedented extralegal actions, the United States asserted a new version of neutral rights in the form of the right of American citizens to travel safely on belligerent ships. The German announcement of submarine warfare in February 1915 thus set the stage for a major confrontation. And given the American attitudes favoring the Allies, the likely result was an important German-American clash that would involve the Wilson administration in anguished debate over possible reactions.

The crisis came with the sinking of the British liner *Lusitania* on May 7, 1915. German leaders had some reason to expect American criticism, for on February 10, less than a week after German announcement of the submarine blockade, Wilson had issued a stern warning that Germany would be held to a "strict accountability" for the loss of any American lives and property under this policy. Surprised by the President's harsh response, the German

The disaster of the *Lusitania* — shown here leaving New York harbor on her last voyage, May 1, 1915 (top), and, in a drawing, sinking beside fleeing passengers off Kinsale, Ireland, May 7, 1915 (bottom) — sparked the first serious American clash with Germany over submarine warfare. The explosion of munitions aboard the ship caused her to sink so quickly that it is remarkable that over 760 people survived. Recent evidence indicates that the liner not only carried a cargo of ammunition but also was armed with twelve concealed six-inch guns and received no protection while sailing through an area where submarines were known to be operating. Nevertheless, the new findings are not adequate to support their English author's suggestion that the British government lured the Germans into attacking the *Lusitania* in order to win American assistance in the war.

government had directed its submarine commanders to avoid attacking American merchant vessels. In the following weeks, however, American concern over the submarine blockade seemed to wane. When the German sinking of the British liner *Falaba* on March 28 first raised the issue of the safety of neutral passengers through the death of one American citizen, the United States made no protest. And Colonel House, then touring European capitals in his first mediation attempt, minimized German-American differences in an effort to involve the belligerents in negotiations. Under pressure from the naval staff for increased results, German submarine commanders successfully fought to have the restrictions on them lifted. When the captain of the submarine U-20 discovered a large four-stack liner steaming leisurely through the Irish Sea, he did not hesitate to fire his last torpedo. The shot hit its mark, and somewhat to his surprise the large ship exploded and sank within eighteen minutes. With elation he read from the large golden letters on the stern of the sinking ship that his victim was the prized queen of the Cunard fleet, the *Lusitania.* It was a significant blow to Britain, since the *Lusitania* carried almost two thousand passengers and crewmen as well as hundreds of cases of small-arms ammunition and fuses. Unfortunately for Germany, among the 1,198 dead there were 128 United States citizens.

Although Wilson agonized over his response, he knew from the start that he had to take a stand against Germany's testing of his "strict accountability." The destruction of the British liner horrified the American people, and in an attempt to moderate demands for action the President declared in Philadelphia three days after the sinking: "There is such a thing as a man being too proud to fight. There is such a thing as a nation being so right that it does not need to convince others by force that it is right." While he attempted to calm popular feeling, Wilson still intended to deal firmly with Germany. Deciding not to link submarine policy with British violations of neutral rights, the President in a stern protest note demanded German disavowal of the sinking. When the Imperial government made a noncommital reply, Wilson concluded that stronger language and an implicit threat of war were required to make the Germans understand his position. On June 9 he therefore dispatched a second *Lusitania* note, again insisting on disavowal and adding demands for the payment of reparations for injuries and a pledge to cease submarine attacks on passenger liners. To impress German leaders with his earnestness, Wilson asserted that the United States was not concerned even primarily with the rights of property but was "contending for nothing less high and sacred than the rights of humanity."

The second *Lusitania* note caused reverberations at home and abroad. Secretary Bryan, believing that the United States ought to restrict the travel of Americans on belligerent ships rather than risk war, resigned in protest the day before the note was sent. Robert Lansing was named his successor. The German government, unwilling to back down publicly, issued secret orders to its U-boat commanders to avoid attacking large passenger liners. When these instructions failed to prevent the sinking of the British liner *Arabic* on August 19, with the loss of two American lives, the German ambassador in Washington offered an indemnity and pledged that German submarines would not attack unarmed passenger ships without warning unless the ships resisted or tried to escape. Although this "*Arabic* pledge" went beyond the ambassador's instructions, the government in Berlin accepted it and in February 1916 even apologized for the sinking of the *Lusitania* and offered an indemnity. Germany refused to admit, however, that the sinking was illegal. Early in 1916 Wilson's resolute stand against Germany seemed to have gained success, but as the pressures of stalemated trench warfare grew, this achievement proved ephemeral.

Great Britain, meanwhile, took advantage of America's embroilment with Germany to expand economic warfare. In August 1915 Britain declared cotton, used in munitions as well as in uniforms, to be absolute contraband, but to minimize American objections the British government bought large quantities at an artificially high price. The response of the Wilson administration showed the distinction it placed on violations of property rights compared to breaches of human rights. The State Department drafted long, legalistic protests to Britain (the note of October 21 ran to seven thousand words) establishing bases for claims after the war. But there was neither threat of war nor economic reprisal.

A more important indicator of the Wilson administration's grudging acceptance of British policy came with the reversal of its ban on loans to belligerents. As early as the second month of the war, the United States had modified Bryan's statement discouraging all loans to allow the use of short-term treasury notes to finance French and Russian purchases of war supplies. But by the summer of 1915 the rapid expansion of war trade showed the need for more stable credit arrangements. Representatives of the Allies and American

financiers persuaded Secretary of the Treasury William G. McAdoo
that unless a public loan was allowed Britain would have to curtail
purchases sharply and pay for the remainder by sale of American
securities held in London, actions that would cause a drop in the
stock market and a reduction of industrial production. These arguments convinced Lansing, who put the case for approving a loan to
the Allies in a long letter to the President on September 6, 1915.
Emphasizing America's interests rather than Allied needs, the secretary of state concluded his appeal by asking: "Can we afford to
let a declaration as to our conceptions of the 'true spirit of neutrality' made in the first days of the war stand in the way of our national
interests which seem to be seriously threatened?" While he would
not formally remove the ban, Wilson authorized private assurances
to American bankers that the administration did not object to the
flotation of a $500 million bond issue for Britain and France. To the
great relief of the Allies and most American businessmen, the ban
on United States loans thus came quietly to an end.

Convinced that the war was likely to drag on for months, Wilson
decided during the autumn of 1915 that he should strengthen America's capacity to defend neutral rights. The *Lusitania* crisis had forced
officials in Washington to realize that they would be unable to make
effective use of the republic's power if diplomatic and economic
pressure failed. The President asked the War and Navy Departments
in July to draft proposals for improving the nation's defense capabilities. Wilson began to present his preparedness program in
November by calling for a substantial increase in the army. In St.
Louis in January he declared that the United States should have
"incomparably the most adequate navy in the world." Many progressives and pacifists, including a sizable group of Democratic
Congressmen from the South and West, opposed the administration
measures and contended that preparation for war was not a way to
protect neutrality. Wilson, advocating preparedness as essential to
safeguard the Western Hemisphere against unnamed (assumed by
the public to be German) threats, won the endorsement of Congress
during the spring of 1916 for significant increases in the army and
a large shipbuilding program for the navy.

As a political counterweight to his preparedness campaign and
with a sincere desire for peace, the President meanwhile initiated
an important effort to end the war through American mediation.
He sent Colonel House on a second mission to Europe in January
1916 to use the influence of the United States to stop the fighting

before either side was completely exhausted. During a similar mission the preceding January and February, the colonel had found none of the powers willing to compromise for peace. Now he discovered leaders in Paris and Berlin willing to listen, but only in London was any statesman ready to undertake so much as a limited commitment. House succeeded in signing an agreement with Sir Edward Grey on February 22, 1916, stating that whenever the Allies chose the time as appropriate, Wilson would call a peace conference. If Germany either refused the invitation or rejected reasonable terms, the United States would, House agreed, enter the war on the Allied side. Wilson modified this House-Grey memorandum to make it conform to constitutional requirements by adding "probably" before the pledge to join the Allies. Recent research indicates that in fact the British were not willing to accept American mediation, but simply wanted to show an openness to Wilson's peace move. They were successful in making their point, because House returned home convinced that the United States would ultimately have to enter the war against Germany.

While hoping for mediation, Wilson continued his defense of the full rights of neutrals by fighting the Gore-McLemore resolutions that warned American citizens not to travel on armed belligerent ships. A passenger ban of the sort advanced in these congressional proposals seemed an ideal means of minimizing involvement in the war, since a guarantee of safe travel on a belligerent ship was a novel legal interpretation of neutral rights and since most physical injuries came on such voyages. During the whole period of neutrality over 175 United States citizens would be killed traveling on Allied ships compared to three killed on American vessels. The Gore-McLemore suggestions generated widespread public support, and some observers believed that congressional sentiment ran three-to-one in favor of a passenger ban. Despite possible damage to his chances for reelection, Wilson adamantly opposed such a compromise of American prerogatives. Late in February 1916, he undertook a campaign of persuasion to defeat the resolutions by conferring with congressional leaders, using members of his Cabinet as lobbyists, and by publishing an emotional appeal to Senator William J. Stone, chairman of the Foreign Relations Committee. In his letter to Senator Stone, the President said that the United States should not allow "any abridgement of the rights of American citizens in any respect," declaring in an exaggerated tone, "once accept a single abatement of right and many other humiliations would certainly follow, and the whole fine fabric of international law might crumble under our hands piece by piece." Administration supporters succeeded in killing the Gore-McLemore resolutions, but within a month the *Sussex* crisis led to such a sharp restriction of American freedom of action that it underlined the potential value of a passenger ban.

In light of the subsequent impact of submarine operations, it is intriguing to speculate whether Wilson could have accepted a passenger ban, kept the United States at peace, and still have gained his objectives in reforming world politics. Knowing what intervention cost, one is tempted to believe that America could have avoided war. Yet it counters the weight of historical evidence to contend that the United States had more than a slender chance of remaining neutral in February 1916. The respective coalitions refused to compromise on war aims while their leaders became more desperate in search of victory; Wilson insisted on a resolute defense of American rights; and, as events of the spring would show, increasing nationalism made the people of the United States willing to back the President's stand. A passenger ban would not have defended the interests that the administration and an expanding number of Americans considered vital, and it would surely have served to diminish Wilson's influence as peacemaker.

The head-on clash with Germany over the *Sussex* greatly reduced whatever possibility the United States had of staying out of war. On March 24 a U-boat torpedoed the unarmed French passenger steamer *Sussex* in the English channel, and although the battered hulk minus its bow was towed to Boulogne, about eighty passengers were killed or wounded, including four Americans injured. To the United States the expanded use of submarines appeared an overt violation of the "*Arabic* pledge," and Secretary Lansing was sufficiently outraged to call for breaking diplomatic relations with Germany. Wilson determined to take a strong stand but, with General Pershing's expedition more than three hundred miles deep into Mexico in pursuit of Pancho Villa and with the American people still deeply divided over the war, he chose a stiff response with a long fuse. On April 18, 1916, the President sent a forceful but tempered note to Germany threatening to break relations "unless the Imperial Government should now immediately declare and effect an abandonment of its present methods of submarine warfare against passenger and freight-carrying vessels." After a lengthy debate, the German government replied on May 4 promising that its U-boats would not sink merchant ships without warning and without caring for passengers and crew. This "*Sussex* pledge" contained, however, a time bomb set against American neutrality, for the pledge was contingent on Britain's ceasing what the Germans contended were illegal practices, especially the food blockade. Although Wilson refused to accept the condition, it remained an ominous warning to America. This confrontation narrowed the issue with Germany to the point where any renewal of unlimited submarine warfare would leave the United States no honorable course but severing relations and probably war.

As the United States engaged in lengthy negotiations with Germany over neutral rights, Great Britain intensified economic pressure on the Central Powers and showed less concern for American sensibilities. Officials in London disregarded the intense public criticism in the United States of Britain's suppression of the Irish Easter Rebellion during April. Faced with dwindling manpower and supplies in a battle of attrition, British leaders searched for any means to bring their enemies to terms. In July 1916 the government moved toward a more comprehensive blockade by announcing a "blacklist" of some fifteen hundred firms, including nearly one hundred in the United States. British citizens were forbidden to trade with these firms, which had allegedly engaged in business with the Central Powers. The blacklist offended many Americans, not the least President Wilson, who exclaimed to Colonel House: "I am . . . about at the end of my patience with Great Britain and the Allies. This blacklist business is the last straw." The British also made clear that they were not interested in American mediation. The Foreign Office put aside suggestions to carry out the House-Grey memorandum. David Lloyd George, the powerful minister of munitions soon to replace Herbert Henry Asquith as Prime Minister, called on September 28 for a "knockout" of Germany and added pointedly, "There can be no interference at this stage."

American hostility toward Britain's vigorous prosecution of the war increased the importance of the peace issue in the presidential election of 1916. With the disintegration of the Progressive Party, the Republicans sensed a good opportunity to unite their normal majority and recapture the White House. Realizing the intense desire of most Americans to avoid war, party leaders passed by the ultranationalist advocates of intervention against Germany led by Theodore Roosevelt. Instead, the Republican convention nominated Charles Evans Hughes, who as an Associate Justice of the Supreme

Wilson campaigned on peace and progressivism in 1916. After a hard race besmirched by rumors about the President's personal life (he had remarried in December 1915 after the death of his first wife in August 1914), Wilson won the closest election since 1876. The outcome was certain only forty-eight hours after the last polls closed, when it became clear that the President would carry California by a little over 3,700 votes.

Court since 1910 had made no statements on foreign affairs. The Democrats renominated Wilson by acclamation and adopted a platform calling for advanced progressive social legislation and continued efforts for peace. The strength of antiwar sentiment impressed the President, and although uneasy with the implied promise that he could prevent "some calculated outrage" from dragging the United States into the European holocaust, Wilson accepted and exploited the Democratic slogan "He kept us out of war." Hughes denounced the inefficiency and weak Mexican policy of the administration and asserted that he would maintain peace while defending "all the rights of American citizens on land and sea." But, in refusing to disavow Roosevelt's bellicose speeches, the Republicans could not escape appearing the more warlike of the parties. While Hughes carried virtually all of the East and upper Midwest, Wilson's successful combination of peace with progressivism won the remaining Midwest, the South, and the West. The President received a narrow electoral majority of 277 to 254. This nonetheless represented an increase of almost three million votes over his total in 1912, and the returns convinced Wilson that peace advocates provided his margin of victory.

When assured of another term, Wilson launched his third and most extensive mediation attempt. Germany had sought peace talks in September and October, and when the President did not act soon after the elections, German leaders on December 12 announced their willingness to discuss conditions of a settlement with their enemies. Still hoping to arrange a peace conference, Wilson modified his plan and on December 18 asked each of the belligerents to declare its aims in the struggle. In reply the German government, declining to state terms, said it wanted direct negotiations with the opposing coalition and saw no part for neutrals in ending the conflict. The joint response of the Allies was more encouraging. Although they had defiantly rejected the German proposal, the Entente powers in their answer to Wilson specified peace terms similar to those discussed in the House-Grey memorandum. But the British, after advancing conditions agreeable to Washington, privately conveyed the opinion that their acceptance would require the defeat of Germany. On the basis of the German refusal to state war aims and the Kaiser's warning in October that his government might revive full submarine operations if negotiations did not succeed quickly, Wilson was convinced that the primary obstacle to peace rested in Berlin.

Desiring to encourage German moderation, the President presented his conception of an appropriate settlement in the "Peace Without Victory" speech of January 22, 1917. Appearing before the Senate, he stressed the need for a stable world order in declaring, "Only a peace between equals can last." Among the important conditions for ending the war he included: "government by the consent of the governed," a united and independent Poland, autonomous development for all peoples under alien rule, freedom of the seas, and the limitation of armaments. A settlement based on these principles would, the President asserted, justify United States "adherence to a League for Peace" to guarantee its permanence.

That Wilson defined terms satisfactory to America and announced them to the Senate indicated his increasing determination to have a hand in shaping the peace.

Wilson's proposals failed to influence Germany, because the Kaiser's government had already decided to resume unrestricted submarine warfare starting February 1. The military and naval commanders had begun pressing for revival of undersea operations the previous October, and the momentous decision came at a crown council at Pless on January 9. With army leaders insisting that only naval action could break the stalemate on land, the chief of the naval staff assured the Kaiser that the unhindered attacks of his fleet of over a hundred U-boats would crush England in six months or less. The generals countered Chancellor Bethmann Hollweg's warnings about the American response by contending that the anticipated entry of the United States into the war could have no significant effect before the Allies were forced to make peace. Field Marshal Paul von Hindenburg had declared on January 8: "We are counting on the possibility of war with the United States, and have made all preparations to meet it. Things can not be worse than they are now." Realizing that these arguments had convinced the Kaiser, Bethmann withdrew his opposition and Wilhelm II announced his decision to unleash the U-boats. On January 31 the German ambassador in Washington informed the United States that submarine operations would resume without restriction the next day. At the same time the ambassador crassly left a statement of the expansionist terms Germany "would have been willing" to accept if the Allies had attended the proposed conference.

On the grounds that the submarine decree violated the "*Sussex* pledge," Wilson broke diplomatic relations with Germany on February 3, 1917. But he continued to hope for peace and emphasized that the United States would not go to war over the sinking of Allied ships alone. Only "actual overt acts," he declared to Congress, would persuade him that Germany refused to respect American rights. Wanting to avoid any provocation, the President resisted demands from American shippers and nationalists to arm merchant vessels. As U-boat attacks increased, however, owners kept their ships in port and goods clogged the docks along the Atlantic coast.

British disclosure of the Zimmermann telegram on February 24 removed Wilson's doubts about German intentions. In this message, intercepted and decoded by British naval intelligence, Arthur Zimmermann, the German foreign minister, proposed to offer Mexico a military alliance if the United States entered the war against the Central Powers. He authorized his minister in Mexico City to promise, when victorious, to restore Mexico's "lost provinces" of Arizona, New Mexico, and Texas. The telegram deeply angered Wilson, especially because the Germans had been audacious enough to send it over the cables made available as a courtesy by the State Department when Britain severed German telegraphic connections with the Western Hemisphere early in the war. Convinced by this ill-conceived maneuver that Germany planned to continue submarine attacks regardless of Washington's reaction, the President moved to protect American commerce.

On February 26, Wilson asked Congress for authority to arm merchant ships, and when strong opposition to the bill developed in both houses, he released the Zimmermann telegram to the press. Published across the country on March 1, it generated a wave of anti-German protest that led the House of Representatives to pass quickly the authorization to arm merchant vessels. But in the upper chamber a dozen Senators, led by George W. Norris and Robert M. La Follette, began a filibuster against the bill that consumed the time until adjournment on March 4. Furious at what he called "a little group of willful men" for preventing the overwhelming majority of Congress from acting to defend American rights, the President on the legal advice of Lansing and the attorney general proceeded on March 9 to order the arming of American merchant ships.

Despite the virtual certainty of further conflict with Germany, Wilson still hoped to avoid war. For two weeks after Congress adjourned he secluded himself in the White House debating the alternatives before the nation. When news reached Washington on March 18 that German submarines had sunk three United States merchant vessels with the loss of fifteen lives, the President realized that armed neutrality would prove an ineffective means of protecting American lives and property. The whole course of his policy of strict accountability now left the United States no honorable choice but war. Reports the previous week of the revolutionaries in Russia overthrowing the tsar and proclaiming democratic principles made the American decision easier, for now the nature of the struggle could be clearly defined as democracy versus autocracy. On March 20, Wilson emerged from privacy to consult the Cabinet. To the surprise of several members, and probably the President, the advisers unanimously favored war and urged early government action. With his own conclusions reinforced, the President made his decision for

This drawing by Victor Perrard shows Wilson asking Congress for a declaration of war against Germany on April 2, 1917. The members of both houses and the packed galleries received the address with enthusiastic approval. Robert Underwood Johnson expressed the views of many in his poem "The Leader": "Beleaguered Liberty takes heart again, / Hearing afar the rescuing bugles blow; / And even in the strongholds of the foe / His name becomes the whispered hope of men."

war on the day of the Cabinet meeting but disclosed it to no one for a week. Then on March 21 he called a special session of Congress "to receive a communication concerning grave matters of national policy."

On the evening of April 2, Woodrow Wilson went before a packed joint session of Congress to request recognition of the existing state of war with Germany. Men around the world were moved by what the diplomat William Phillips called "the magnificence of the President's address." Wilson prescribed America's purpose in the war in these ringing phrases:

We are now about to accept gage of battle with this natural foe to liberty and shall, if necessary, spend the whole force of the Nation to check and nullify its pretensions and its power. We are glad, now that we see the facts with no veil of false pretense about them, to fight thus for the ultimate peace of the world and for the liberation of its peoples, and the German peoples included: for the rights of nations great and small and the privilege of men everywhere to choose their way of life and of obedience. The world must be made safe for democracy. Its peace must be planted upon the tested foundations of political liberty. We have no selfish ends to serve. We desire no conquest, no dominion. We seek no indemnities for ourselves, no material compensation for the sacrifices we shall freely make. We are but one of the champions of the rights of mankind. We shall be satisfied when those rights have been made as secure as faith and the freedom of nations can make them.

The Senate voted 82 to 6 on April 4 that a state of war existed between Germany and the United States, and early in the morning of April 6 the House joined by a vote of 373 to 50. For the first time in its history the United States entered a major war on another continent.

The American people did not approach war with the unity and enthusiasm the congressional vote might seem to imply. Articulate opinion was deeply split, with aroused peace advocates almost as numerous and active as the proponents of intervention. Sentiment for war, led by Roosevelt and Hughes as well as by backers of the President, was strongest in the East and parts of the South and Midwest, especially among business groups, progressive Republicans, and internationalist Democrats. Peace supporters were most heavily concentrated in the upper Midwest and West with particular strength among farmers, Socialists, and citizens of German and Irish origin. Leaders of antiwar opinion included the Socialist Eugene V. Debs, progressive Senators Norris and La Follette, Bryan, and Democratic Representative Claude Kitchin of North Carolina. The great silent mass of the population, which comprehended less fully than most groups what belligerency would mean for them, apparently combined an attitude of distaste for the war with a willingness to follow the President. Public opinion did not, however, have a great influence on Wilson. Although aware of the profound divisions over the war, he was determined not to be pushed toward an improper choice by an emotional populace. He probably felt that prompt action for war would help unite the majority of Americans, and he certainly made the decision to ask Congress to join the hostilities after painful solitary deliberation, not widespread consultation.

German submarine policy forced Wilson to choose between surrender and war. After rejecting surrender and exploring every other alternative to war, he concluded that belligerency was the only way to defend America's rights as a neutral and its prestige as a great power. The strong economic ties to Britain and the overthrow of tsarist despotism in Russia facilitated joining the Allies, but it took pressure from Germany to bring Wilson to a repugnant decision. Although not concerned with protecting the European balance of power—German victory appeared quite unlikely in the spring of 1917—the President did want to influence the peace settlement. Feeling the struggle was in its final phase, Wilson sought to achieve the goals set forth in his "Peace Without Victory" speech. He distrusted Allied aims almost as much as German and knew that the only means of winning a position at the peace table was participation as a belligerent. For the President, the desire to shape the postwar world thus added a positive dimension to the fight against German aggression.

In another sense, Wilson's decision for war signified a realization that America's objectives in the world, its mission as a great power, could not be attained solely by superior example. If one wanted specific results from a war, "being too proud to fight" was not an effective way to gain them. The President's message of April 2 represented a commitment to play great power politics by the prevailing rules in order to gain the opportunity at the peace conference to reform the entire system.

Yet to the extent that Wilson sought to commit the American people to this ambitious program of international reform, he moved into dangerous waters. His reelection had been extremely close, his control of Congress was rapidly shrinking, and although they might endorse intervention, many Americans did not share Wilson's broad aspirations. Senator William E. Borah of Idaho reflected this view when he declared during the debate on the declaration of war: "I join no crusade; I seek or accept no alliances; I obligate this Government to no other power. I make war alone for my countrymen and their rights, for my country and its honor." As sacrifices later mounted, this nationalistic attitude spread and should have served as a warning to the administration in its planning for international cooperation after the war.

The President's idealistic purposes also seemed out of place overseas in the atmosphere of a harsh struggle for survival that confronted the Allies. As the experienced British diplomat, Thomas B. Hohler, commented on March 23, 1917:

It looks as if W. [Wilson] would in fact help us pretty *well:* almost all he can: but I think he will try not to be *technically* an ally. He's the most agile pussy-footer ever made, and when any serious decision is taken, always tries to unload the responsibility on to someone else, and has been doing so this time again. But it does seem as if the Huns had fairly driven him into a corner out of which he can't possibly wriggle!

This suspicious view of the President and his war aims, an opinion that was soon widely shared in London and Paris, would pose problems for Wilson in attaining his goals in the peace settlement.

America entered the war with an enthusiasm based, in part, on the expectation of limited military involvement. Even the most knowledgeable Americans felt that their country's contribution would consist of massive financial and material aid, some naval assistance against submarines, and a token troop contingent to show the flag. American leaders soon learned, however, that the plight of the Allies required a greater commitment. Arthur J. Balfour, the British foreign secretary and former Prime Minister whom Ambassador Page described as "personally the most distinguished member of the Government," led a special mission to Washington that arrived on April 22. Balfour revealed that Britain was on the verge of exhaustion. The British army in France was short of troops and supplies, and German U-boats threatened to starve the home islands into submission. Since resuming unrestricted warfare, U-boats had claimed 540,000 tons of merchant shipping in February, 593,000 tons in March, and were in the process of destroying a total of 881,000 tons in April. The civilian population had food for only about two more months, and the government had overdrawn its account with J. P. Morgan and Company of New York by $400 million and had no cash reserves. Balfour and his colleagues called on the United States for large amounts of supplies and credits, for extensive cooperation in breaking the submarine threat, and for a force of 500,000 troops to be amalgamated into the British army. Missions with similar if

REMEMBER THE LUSITANIA

THE JURY'S VERDICT SAYS:
"We find that the said deceased died from their prolonged immersion and exhaustion in the sea eight miles south south-west of the Old Head of Kinsale on Friday, May 7th, 1915, owing to the sinking of the R.M.S. Lusitania by a torpedo fired without warning from a German submarine.

"That this appalling crime was contrary to international law and the conventions of all civilized nations, and we therefore charge the officers of the said submarine, the Emperor and Government of Germany, under whose orders they acted, with the crime of wilful and wholesale murder before the tribunal of the civilized world"

IT IS **YOUR DUTY** *TO* **TAKE UP THE SWORD OF JUSTICE TO AVENGE THIS DEVIL'S WORK.**

ENLIST TO-DAY

Brown Brothers

The call to duty. International law, civilization, and Old Testament justice all line up on the side of the Allies in this United States recruiting poster. During World War I the United States engaged in its first full-scale attempt at news management and propaganda under the direction of the Committee on Public Information.

less extensive requests soon arrived in Washington from France, Italy, and Belgium.

While the United States prepared for land warfare, a critical struggle occurred on the high seas. The British did most of the fighting, but the American navy responded well to the demands placed upon it. In addition to transporting large amounts of supplies and later almost half of the American Expeditionary Force (AEF), ships of the United States navy assumed important duties in the expanded anti-submarine campaign. The most significant American naval contribution was in helping to organize the convoy system for merchant shipping. Lloyd George pressed this plan upon the royal navy at the end of April 1917, and he received strong backing from Admiral William S. Sims, the commander of United States naval forces in Europe. When Sims' superiors at the Navy Department raised objections to convoys, he won American endorsement by an appeal to Wilson, who had favored the concept even before the British adopted it. The convoy system, augmented by increased anti-submarine patrols, proved effective in meeting the U-boat challenge. Monthly shipping losses fell below 440,000 tons by December 1917, and after the following April they never went above 200,000 tons. The navy's effort kept open the supply lines to Britain and allowed American troops to provide the essential reinforcements to meet Germany's last land offensive.

The final year of war on the Continent became a race against time for the Allies. The United States sought to have a million fighting men in France by May 1918, while the German general staff worked desperately to achieve victory before American manpower could become effective. Major General John J. Pershing, named commander of the AEF fresh from his duties as head of the Punitive Expedition in Mexico, led the first detachment of American soldiers in a parade through Paris on July 4, 1917. But before any meaningful number of troops arrived from the United States, twin disasters shook the Allies. In late October the Italian army crumbled under a joint German-Austrian attack near Caporetto, losing over 700,000 men as casualties or prisoners. Two weeks later the Bolsheviks seized control of Petrograd and began moving toward a separate peace with Germany.

The Allies responded in November 1917 by establishing unified command of their military forces through the Supreme War Council, composed of the heads of government and supported by a permanent committee of military representatives in continuous session in Paris. Colonel House represented President Wilson on several occasions at the Supreme War Council, and General Tasker H. Bliss served as the permanent military representative. When a German offensive strengthened by forty divisions from the Russian theater began in March 1918, the Allies named French General Ferdinand Foch the supreme Allied commander for the western front. Under the pressure of this desperate assault Wilson abandoned his general rule of leaving all military decisions to his field commander and directed Pershing to allow American troops to be used as replacements in British and French units until they arrived in sufficient numbers to form an independent force. This policy of amalgamation proved successful. In late May a German thrust was stopped about

The Yanks Are Here: General Pershing receives the colors from the President of France at the Invalides in Paris, July 4, 1917. In an attempt to raise French morale, a battalion of American troops participated in a ceremony with a French unit at this national war museum containing the tomb of Napolean and marched to the tomb of Lafayette. As Pershing wrote in his memoirs: "This first appearance of American combat troops in Paris brought forth joyful acclaim from the people. . . . Many . . . dropped on their knees in reverence as the column went by. These stirring scenes conveyed vividly the emotions of a people to whom the outcome of the war had seemed all but hopeless."

forty miles from Paris, and by mid-July the Allies were able to launch a counteroffensive.

Fresh American troops provided the essential power to blunt the German attack and create the Allied momentum that forced the Central Powers to seek peace. They arrived from the United States in large numbers through the spring, increasing from 300,000 in March to a million by July 1 and two million by the armistice in November. American deaths in battle and from other causes during the war totaled over 116,000. The loss was small compared to the 1,700,000 Russians, 1,357,000 French, and 900,000 Britons who died. But the cost was high for less than a year of combat service. Although

The American Expeditionary Force, 1918

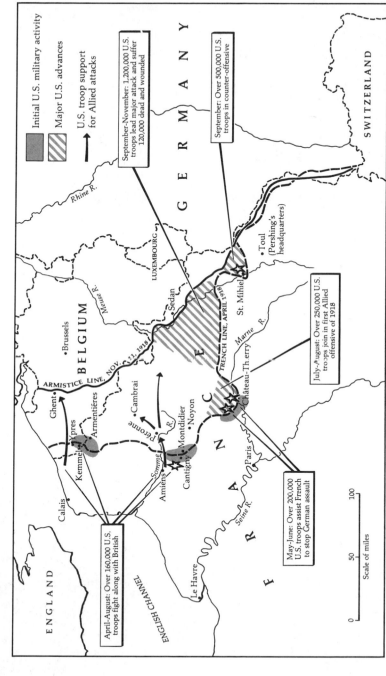

Initial U.S. military activity

Major U.S. advances

U.S. troop support for Allied attacks

September–November: 1,200,000 U.S. troops lead major attack and suffer 120,000 dead and wounded

September: Over 500,000 U.S. troops in counter-offensive

July–August: Over 250,000 U.S. troops join in first Allied offensive of 1918

May–June: Over 200,000 U.S. troops assist French to stop German assault

April–August: Over 160,000 U.S. troops fight along with British

GERMANY

SWITZERLAND

Rhine R.

LUXEMBOURG

•Brussels

BELGIUM

Meuse R.

Sedan

•Toul (Pershing's headquarters)

St. Mihiel

TRENCH LINE, APRIL 1918

ARMISTICE LINE, NOV. 11, 1918

Ghent•

Kemmel• Ypres

Armentières

Cambrai•

Péronne

Somme R.

Montdidier

•Noyon

Cantigny

Amiens•

Château-Thierry

Marne R.

F R A N C E

Paris•

Seine R.

Calais•

Le Havre•

ENGLISH CHANNEL

E N G L A N D

0   50   100

Scale of miles

Source: Redrawn by permission of The Macmillan Company, New York, and Weidenfeld and Nicolson Limited, London, from *The First World War Atlas* by Martin Gilbert. Copyright © 1967 by Martin Gilbert.

U.S. War Department General Staff from the National Archives
U.S. Signal Corps from the National Archives

the Allies probably would not have suffered military defeat without them, American contributions to the war on land and sea did make the decisive difference between a stalemate and an Allied victory.

In the complexities of wartime diplomacy, Woodrow Wilson had different goals from those of other leaders in the Allied coalition. The United States sought neither special advantages nor territory, and because of this divergence of war aims Wilson declined to join the Allies formally, keeping the United States as an "Associated Power." Throughout America's participation in the war, Wilson worked to avoid involvement in Allied intrigue and political maneuvering so that he might approach the peace conference with a free hand. He still clung to the principles enunciated in his "Peace Without Victory" speech of January 22, 1917, believing that a stable peace could not be built on total victory or harsh terms. Before the United States entered the war Wilson had been aware of the existence of secret treaties among the Allies pledging territory and economic advantages, and if the President had not then known the details, Balfour gave him copies of most of the treaties in May 1917. Yet Wilson never publicly admitted his knowledge of these secret obligations, because he wanted to maintain a completely independent posture from which to advance his own plan for the peace settlement. As he wrote Colonel House in July 1917: "England and France have not the same views with regard to peace that we have by any means. When the war is over we can force them to our way of thinking, because by that time they will, among other things, be financially in our hands; but we cannot force them now."

The economic superiority over the western Allies that the President anticipated became one of the salient results of the war. American business leaders and government officials set out to employ the profits generated by war manufactures to make New York the leading financial center of the world. Through the creation in

The glory and the sorrow of war. The troops of the 165th Infantry, 42nd Division, here enthusiastically boarding a train in New York City prior to sailing for France in October 1917 (top), saw some of the hardest fighting of the war at Lunéville, Reims, and the Meuse-Argonne offensive. The funeral (bottom) is being held for an unidentified soldier, probably of the 2nd Division, near Limey, southeast of Verdun, September 12, 1918. He fought with a unit engaged with the 42nd Division in the reduction of the St. Mihiel salient from September 12 to 15, 1918. The Americans won a notable victory and proved to skeptics their ability to launch a successful, coordinated attack. They captured 16,000 prisoners, but the cost was a little over 7,000 American lives.

1916 of a tariff commission, designed to remove the issue of tariffs from political logrolling, the administration hoped to negotiate entry into European markets as well as to protect developing industries at home. When foreign tariffs did not decline as rapidly as expected, Wilson backed modification of the anti-trust laws in the Webb-Pomerene Act of 1918 and in the Edge Act of 1919 allowing industrialists and bankers respectively to combine in trusts to gain maximum influence in foreign markets. Americans also formed branch factories and banks overseas to avoid the handicaps of foreign tariffs. This coordinated effort for economic expansion produced not only a significant advance in investment and command of Latin American trade but also a shift in America's net foreign investment position from debtor to creditor nation. In 1897 foreigners had invested $2.7 billion more in the United States than Americans had placed abroad, and despite a five-fold increase in American capital going overseas foreigners increased their favorable balance to $3.7 billion by the end of June 1914. But under conditions of war, these positions dramatically reversed; by 1919 Americans owned $3.7 billion more overseas investments than foreigners possessed in the United States. Appreciating its new leverage, the Wilson administration sought to use financial power to bring an early peace on American terms and to harness revolutionary movements such as the one sweeping Russia.

The success of the Bolshevik Revolution had a profound impact on wartime diplomacy and the development of war aims. On November 8, 1917, the very day the revolution was consummated in Petrograd, the Second All-Russian Congress of Soviets of Workers', Soldiers', and Peasants' Deputies approved and released to the press the Decree on Peace. Through this declaration, drafted by Lenin several weeks earlier, the new Bolshevik government proposed "to all the warring peoples and their governments that they immediately enter into negotiations for a just, democratic peace," which it characterized as "an immediate peace without annexations . . . and without indemnities." The Soviet leaders also called for an armistice of at least three months and made no secret of their hope that during that time their revolution would spread to other industrial nations, particularly to Germany. Denouncing secret diplomacy, Leon Trotsky, the commissar for foreign affairs, began to publish all the tsarist government's secret treaties with Britain, France, Italy, and Japan. These techniques of propaganda and the supposed popular control of foreign affairs, which came to be known as the "new diplomacy," put pressure on all governments to abandon their methods of elite statecraft and power politics.

The prospect of peace raised by the Bolsheviks, coupled with the disclosure of the selfish ends for which the war continued, forced the Allies to formulate a more idealistic statement of purpose as their exhausted nations approached the fourth winter of war. When, in December 1917, representatives of all the Allies meeting in Paris as the Interallied Conference deadlocked on the issue of war aims, Wilson decided to seize the initiative and make an independent statement. But before he could do so the British Prime Minister made his own declaration of war aims before the Trades Union Congress in London on January 5, 1918. Although there was no coordination of these speeches, the objectives that Lloyd George listed for Britain differed very little from those Wilson had already drafted and would announce in three days. The two statements varied sharply, however, in tone and purpose. Lloyd George, adopting the form but not the substance of the "new diplomacy," sought only to issue an elevated response to the public demands of the Bolsheviks and the private overtures of Austria-Hungary and had no intention of making these terms the basis of peace. Wilson, on the other hand, saw his speech as a definition of the liberal, democratic principles on which he hoped to form a just and lasting peace.

With the Fourteen Points Address, Wilson expected to claim moral leadership of the world for the United States. In replying to the Bolshevik declarations, he hoped not only to persuade the new Soviet government to continue the war for more liberal ends but also to encourage sentiment for peace among socialists and leftists in Germany and Austria. He wanted, in addition, to convey to the Allies the imperative need to abandon the advantages promised in their secret treaties. At the President's request, Colonel House had been at work since December 18 putting together suggestions for this address. He had drawn heavily on the research of the Inquiry, a group of experts working out of New York since September to assemble data and write papers on the important subjects to be dealt with at the peace conference. House brought recommendations and extensive supporting material with him to Washington, and he and the President drafted the main proposals of the American peace plan on January 4 and 5.

Without any advance notice of his subject, Wilson delivered the Fourteen Points Address to a joint session of Congress on Tuesday morning, January 8, 1918. Focusing his attention on the peace talks between Germany and the Bolsheviks at Brest-Litovsk, the President attempted to encourage moderate opinion in Germany and Austria-Hungary by asking for whom the negotiators from the Central Powers spoke—the expansionist military leaders who sought harsh terms from Russia and had demanded the resumption of unrestricted submarine warfare, or the more liberal majority of the Reichstag that had backed the peace initiatives. He had high praise for the courage and vision of both the new Soviet government and the great Russian people, declaring: "It is our heartfelt desire and hope that some way may be opened whereby we may be privileged to assist the people of Russia to attain their utmost hope of liberty and ordered peace." The President then enumerated the elements of America's program for world peace. Starting with five general points such as open covenants, freedom of the seas, and an impartial settlement of colonial claims, he proceeded to specific territorial issues in points six to thirteen and laid particular stress on the evacuation of all Russian territory and assistance to allow Russia the opportunity to determine its own political development. The final point was a call for "a general association of nations . . . [to guarantee] political independence and territorial integrity to great and small states alike." In conclusion Wilson stated in grandiloquent fashion the premise on which this plan rested and the value that he claimed the American people placed upon it:

An evident principle runs through the whole program I have outlined. It is the principle of justice to all peoples and nationalities, and their right to live on equal terms of liberty and safety with one another, whether they be strong or weak. Unless this principle be made its foundation no part of the structure of international justice can stand. The people of the United States could act upon no other principle; and to the vindication of this principle they are ready to devote their lives, their honor, and everything that they possess. The moral climax of this the culminating and final war for human liberty has come, and they are ready to put their own strength, their own highest purpose, their own integrity and devotion to the test.

The President rounded out his catalog of the conditions necessary for a lasting peace in three more addresses between February and September. In these speeches he set forth thirteen additional points, four of which restated previous ideas. The basic Wilsonian program thus consisted of twenty-three principles. Wilson's call for the shaping of "every territorial settlement . . . in the interest and for the benefit of the populations concerned" and for an attempt to

The Wilsonian Peace Program

The Fourteen Points
1. "Open covenants of peace, openly arrived at" and an end to secret diplomacy.
2. "Absolute freedom of navigation upon the seas . . . alike in peace and in war."
3. "The removal, so far as possible, of all economic barriers" to free trade.
4. Reduction of armaments "to the lowest point consistent with domestic safety."
5. An "absolutely impartial adjustment of all colonial claims" giving equal weight to the interests of the colonial populations and "the equitable claims" of the imperial governments.
6. "The evacuation of all Russian territory" and cooperation to allow Russia "the independent determination of her own political development and national policy and assure her of a sincere welcome into the society of free nations under institutions of her own choosing."
7. German evacuation of Belgium and restoration of full sovereignty.
8. "All French territory should be freed" and Alsace-Lorraine, taken by Prussia in 1871, should be returned to France.
9. "A readjustment of the frontiers of Italy . . . along clearly recognizable lines of nationality."
10. Autonomy for the peoples of Austria-Hungary.
11. Evacuation of Rumania, Montenegro, and Serbia; international guarantee of the political and economic independence of the Balkan states; and Serbian access to the sea.
12. Autonomy for the subject nationalities within the Turkish Empire and free passage through the Dardanelles for ships of all nations.
13. An independent Poland with "free and secure access to the sea."
14. "A general association of nations."

Supplementary Points
15. Base "each part of the final settlement . . . upon the essential justice of that particular case and upon such adjustments as are most likely to bring" a permanent peace.
16. An end to bartering "peoples and provinces . . . as if they were mere chattels and pawns."
17. Determine "every territorial settlement . . . in the interest and for the benefit of the populations concerned," and not as a compromise "amongst rival states."
18. Attempt to satisfy "all well-defined national aspirations."
19. "The destruction of every arbitrary power anywhere that can . . . disturb the peace of the world."
20. Conduct of nations "to be governed . . . by the same principles of honor and of respect for the common law of civilized society that govern the individual citizens."
21. Special interests "not consistent with the common interest of all" nations cannot become the basis for any settlement.
22. No alliances or special understandings will be allowed within "the League of Nations."
23. "There can be no special, selfish economic combinations" or economic boycotts except as used by the League of Nations for discipline.

satisfy "all well-defined national aspirations" comprised his declaration for "self-determination," a term that the President did not actually use but one that had been in wide use before the war. Wilson's advocacy gave it a special appeal for the nationalistic peoples of Eastern Europe and the Near and Middle East. Considering the difficulty of applying such a general principle, many of these hopes were certain to be frustrated.

The Fourteen Points and other liberal statements proved insufficient to keep the Bolshevik government in the war. On March 3, 1918, Soviet representatives signed the harsh Treaty of Brest-Litovsk with Germany, in which Russia pledged to demobilize its army and cease propaganda against the Central Powers and gave up Finland, the Baltic provinces, Poland, and the Ukraine. As German troops poured from the east to bolster the spring offensive in France, pressure rapidly built among the Allies for intervention in Russia. Britain and especially France wanted to reopen the eastern front in order to tie down several German divisions, and they viewed Japan and the United States as the obvious nations for this task. All of the Allies sought to prevent Bolshevism from spreading westward, and they desired to keep the large amounts of supplies in northern Russia and Siberia out of the hands of both the Germans and the Bolsheviks. From the first weeks of 1918, when it appeared that Russia would leave the war, the Allies repeatedly urged the United States to intervene. As a means of setting the precedent, Britain was the first to go into Russia by sending, on March 7, 1918, a small unit to Murmansk on the White Sea to protect supplies.

Despite Allied pleas, Wilson was highly reluctant to intervene. He did not want to arouse the hostility of the Russian people and still hoped to encourage the revival of liberal elements remaining from supporters of the Provisional Government. Moreover, he suspected Allied motives, seeing ideological reasons for their opposition to Bolshevism and territorial ambitions for Britain and France in the Middle East and for Japan in Siberia. The President also wanted to follow the advice of his military leaders and keep American troops in Europe to form an independent army. And, most important, he sought to continue his policy of standing free of political decisions that might limit his influence at the peace conference.

Arguments from General Foch that Allied success depended on American involvement in Russia forced Wilson to acquiesce in June 1918. He chose a limited form of action in the White Sea, sending a force that eventually grew to five thousand men to Archangel to guard supplies under British command. As it developed, the Bolsheviks had moved most of the materiel into the interior of the country before the troops arrived, and the Americans spent most of their time providing security for a variety of anti-Bolshevik groups. The United States contingent withdrew from Archangel in July 1919 with almost nothing to show for its efforts except the continuing hostility of the Soviet government.

Developments in Siberia persuaded Wilson in July 1918 to reverse his decision against intervention there as well. The stakes were higher in Siberia, for the Bolsheviks did not have control of the region and counterrevolutionary forces appeared strong. The Chinese had been the first to intervene in the east when they took over Manchuria and the adjacent area with a force of 3,500 men in December 1917. Japan now sought American approval to land troops to guard supplies and keep the Trans-Siberian Railway open. It was, however, the plight of the Czechoslovak legion that transformed the Siberian situation for Wilson. Seventy thousand Czech soldiers, who had previously fought with the Russian army against Germany, had been moving along the Trans-Siberian Railway to Vladivostok for shipment to the western front when misunderstandings developed and hostilities broke out with the Bolsheviks on May 26, 1918. The Czechs managed to seize much of the central portion of the railroad and a group of about eighteen thousand got through to Vladivostok, but there was a long gap in their control from the port city westward to Irkutsk. The Czechs on the coast announced their intention of fighting to reopen the railroad for their countrymen and contended that those preventing free transit were former German and Austrian prisoners whom the Bolsheviks had armed. This argument had great appeal with the Allies, who were inclined to see the Bolsheviks as agents of German imperialism, but in fact most of the Czechs' opponents were Hungarian and Russian Communists. Wilson had great admiration for the Czech people and was attracted to the idea of aiding the Czech soldiers in their attempt to enter the war against Germany on the western front.

The issue of the Czech legion provided the occasion for Wilson to respond to the Allies' entreaties for American intervention in Siberia in a way that did not involve the United States in the coalition's political schemes. The President declined a request from the Supreme War Council to join a Japanese-led force of one hundred thousand men for the purposes of aiding the Czechs and reopening

Allied and American Intervention in Russia, 1918

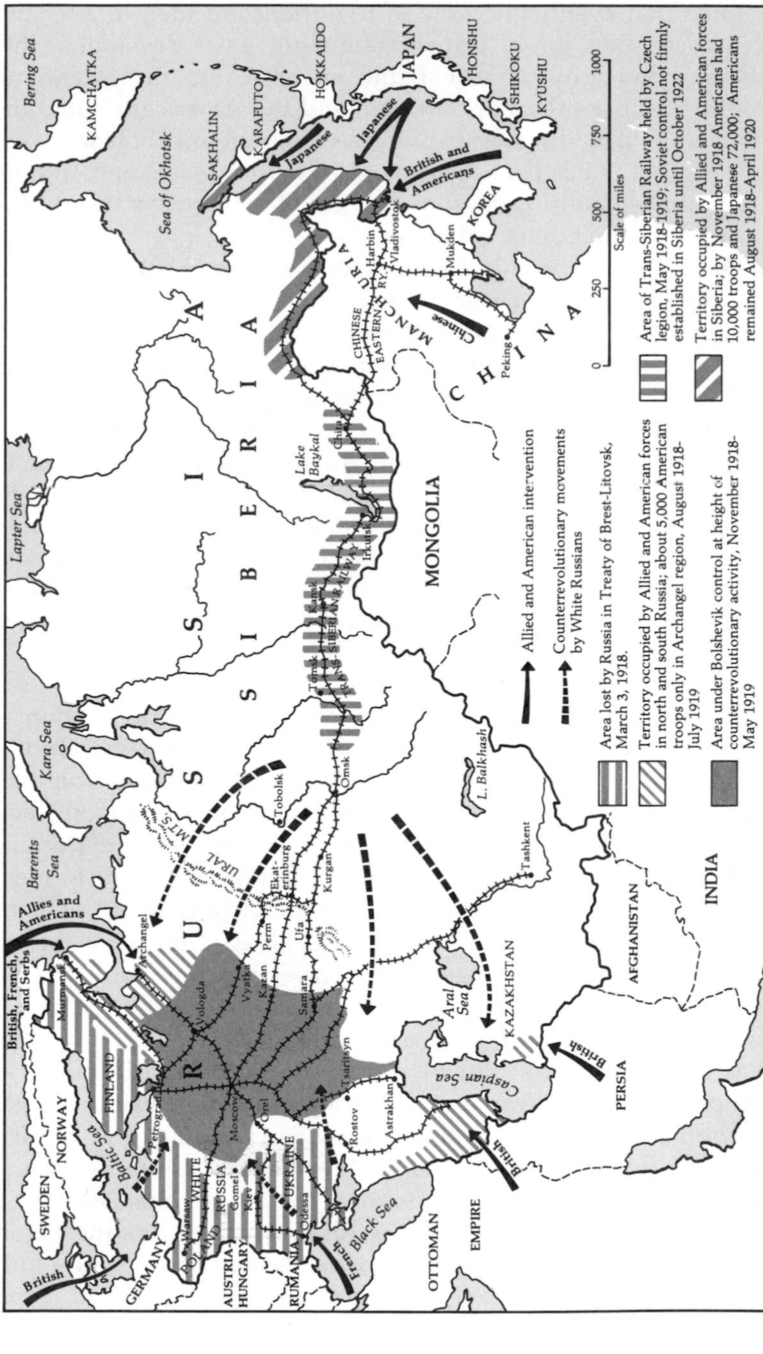

a second front against Germany. Instead, maintaining that a revived eastern front was totally unfeasible, Wilson proposed on July 6, 1918, a limited intervention of fourteen thousand men, half Japanese and half American. He further insisted that all statements clearly show that the expedition sought only to aid the Czechs, not to threaten Russian independence or territory. Although irritated by Wilson's narrowing of the purpose of the Siberian incursion, the western Allies had no choice but to accept it. The Japanese endorsed the President's plan but reserved the right to send additional men if necessary. The first group of Americans arrived in Vladivostok on August 16, and they soon numbered almost ten thousand. The American force, under the strict command of Major General William S. Graves, confined its activities to guarding the Trans-Siberian Railway and aiding the Czechs. The Americans would withdraw from Siberia in April 1920 having earned the distinction of being the only Allied unit intervening in Russia not to show overt hostility to the Bolsheviks.

Despite his ability to limit American actions in Siberia, Wilson saw his hopes for the expedition frustrated. He was not able to restrict or co-opt for his liberal purposes the Japanese, who built up a brigade of 72,000 men, seized northern Manchuria, and remained in Siberia until October 1922. Nor did he assist the Czech departure, for the two groups had rejoined the day before the main American contingent arrived in Vladivostok. Then, to make matters worse, the Czechs decided not to leave Russia for the western front but, with Allied urging, chose to stay in Siberia and oppose the Bolsheviks. Wilson could not even contend that the United States had not threatened Russian independence or territory, because by guarding supplies and railroads American troops did aid the counterrevolutionary cause in the civil war. The President's claims of neutrality aside, the American public and most Russians believed the actions of the United States were anti-Bolshevik, and the Soviet government has used this charge extensively in its propaganda since that time.

Although it was clear by September 1918 that his goals would be thwarted, Wilson refrained from pulling American troops out precipitously because he wanted to turn cooperation in Siberia to advantage at the peace conference. As it developed, American intervention at Archangel and Vladivostok earned little Allied gratitude. The United States was badly used in the whole episode. The most appropriate evaluation of this venture is that of the scholar and diplomat George F. Kennan, who declares "never, surely, in the history of American diplomacy has so much been paid for so little."

When, in September 1918, it appeared that the Allied and American counteroffensive might break through into Germany, the leaders of the German army demanded that the government approach President Wilson to arrange an armistice based on the Fourteen Points. The other Central Powers—Turkey, Bulgaria, and Austria-Hungary—were all eager for peace, and some had already opened secret negotiations. Since the summer of 1916 the German high command under Field Marshal Paul von Hindenburg had effectively ruled Germany, and the dynamic Quartermaster-General Erich Ludendorff held the real power behind Hindenburg. Ludendorff initiated the armistice move to gain time to reorganize his armies. He did not expect to end the war unless Wilson could arrange extremely generous terms with the Allies. On October 3 the new German chancellor, Prince Max of Baden, working through Swiss diplomatic channels, asked President Wilson to end hostilities and make peace on the basis of the Fourteen Points and his subsequent addresses.

Perceiving both the dangers and the opportunities in the German proposal, Woodrow Wilson moved shrewdly, and without consulting his Allies, to terminate the war. In two exchanges of notes he forced German leaders to accept the Fourteen Points completely and to pledge to evacuate Belgium and France before the peace conference, to cease U-boat attacks, and to allow Allied military leaders to dictate the detailed conditions of the armistice. Finally, the President insisted on the Kaiser's abdication and the creation of a democratic government in Germany. Ludendorff and his military colleagues found the terms of this pre-armistice agreement so harsh that they wanted to resume hostilities. But Wilson had correctly sensed the strong thirst for peace among the German people, including members of the military forces. Once the news of peace negotiations had spread through Germany there was no way to persuade the people to continue their wartime sacrifices. After a week of confused debate, the civilian leaders on October 20 asserted their control over the discredited military and accepted Wilson's conditions. Over his strong objections, Kaiser Wilhelm II was forced to abdicate on November 9. He fled to Holland, where he remained in rustic exile until his death in 1941.

Wilson next faced the problem of persuading the Allies to accept an armistice and make the Fourteen Points the basis of the peace settlement. With their own nations almost as depleted as Germany, Allied leaders welcomed the prospect of ending hostilities. But they had significant objections to the Fourteen Points and related principles. Britain insisted on retaining the right of blockade and thus opposed freedom of the seas; France wanted reparations and substantial territory from Germany; Italy had territorial ambitions on the eastern shore of the Adriatic that conflicted with self-determination; and, most ominously, both France and Italy lacked enthusiasm for the proposed league of nations and felt it should not be part of the peace treaty.

To bring the Allies into line, Wilson sent Colonel House on his fourth wartime mission to Europe. While the Supreme War Council worked out the military and naval conditions of the armistice, the President's confidant engaged in a grueling week of negotiations with top Allied leaders in Paris. House broke the deadlock by declaring on October 30 that, if the Allies maintained their excessive demands, the President would have to inform Congress of the terms for which they wanted to continue the war and ask if the United States should prolong hostilities to gain these ends. By November 4 the negotiators developed a compromise in which they agreed with two reservations to make peace on the principles announced by Wilson in his speech of January 8, 1918, and later addresses. These reservations essentially stated that freedom of the seas would be defined and discussed at the peace conference and that Germany would pay compensation (actually reparations) for damage to Allied civilians and their property.

The Supreme War Council designed the military and naval terms of the armistice in such a way that Germany would not be able to resume the war. These requirements compelled the German army to withdraw east of the Rhine and surrender roughly half its heavy arms and supplies, and forced the navy to send most of the battle fleet for internment in Allied ports. When presented with these stringent conditions on November 8, the German representatives objected, but with revolutionary outbursts occurring at home they had to end the war. They signed the armistice early in the morning of November 11, and the fighting ceased several hours later at 11 A.M. Great rejoicing swept all the Allied nations and the United States. In Germany there was an immense feeling of relief.

In later years both German and Allied leaders would be critical of the way the war ended. Most of the German charges against the

Allies had a basis in fact. The armistice terms were harsh, and in each of the three periodic renewals before the peace treaty was signed, the French successfully insisted that even more severe conditions be imposed. The peace treaty violated the German understanding of the Fourteen Points in numerous ways, and, most offensive, the Allies maintained the food blockade of Germany, over Wilson's strong protests, until July 12, 1919, three days after Germany ratified the Versailles Treaty. During these eight months after the armistice, thousands of Germans died of starvation and diseases complicated by malnutrition. But the charges, mainly from the German army, that the civilian government and German Communists and Jews ended the war prematurely by a "stab in the back" (*Dolchstoss von hinten*) of the army lacked foundation. The German high command had demanded an armistice as a play for time, and when it appeared that negotiations might bring peace, the generals found themselves unable to reverse the process they had initiated. If there was a "stab in the back," Ludendorff had wielded the dagger.

The Allied complaint that Wilson's intervention deprived them of total victory is negated by the fact that Colonel House had given the Allies the opportunity on October 30, 1918, to continue the war without the United States if they objected strongly to Wilson's terms. The Allied leaders chose to end the war and pledged themselves, with varying degrees of sincerity, to accept the President's principles as the basis of peace.

Woodrow Wilson played the central role in bringing the Great War to an end, and his diplomacy certainly stopped the fighting several months earlier than it would otherwise have ceased. As the peace conference approached, the impact of the United States on the European balance of power was everywhere apparent. The British statesman Lord Curzon, writing to Lloyd George the day after the armistice, commented apprehensively on America's new influence. The whole atmosphere in Paris tended, he complained, "to put us in the background. On the other hand the Americans abound: in the streets, in flagwaving, everywhere. For every Englishman I see 100 or 200 Americans. Talking about Shantung, waving flags, and kissing every Frenchwoman they meet. . . . Tremendous cheering outside as I write—probably the Americans."

At the end of 1918 Wilson appeared able to shape the peace settlement. But the forces of resistance and reaction were strong, in Europe and in America, and Wilson would have done well to take them into account.

Celebration of the armistice in Paris, November 11, 1918. In London, Rome, Washington, New York, and Paris, the people surged through the streets all day and through the night rejoicing at the end of the fighting with bonfires, gun salutes, bells, prayers, snowstorms of paper, and millions of instant friendships. A British soldier voiced the feelings of many in shouting, "Now this bleeding war is over, no more soldiering for me."

Negotiating a New World Order

In the extensive preparations for the peace conference, Wilson and his advisers made several decisions that, it was later charged, contributed to the Senate's defeat of the treaty. Most of these criticisms seem invalid, however, if one evaluates each decision with regard to what was known or could reasonably have been expected when it was made. The President's determination to honor the French request to move the conference from Geneva to Paris is reasonable in light of the weight of French sacrifice in the war and the humiliating terms imposed by Germany after the Franco-Prussian War in 1871. Wilson's insistence on heading the American delegation appears sound given the fact that all the other delegations would be led by their heads of government. The President, furthermore, had shown himself to be a highly skilled diplomatist in his handling of the submarine crises and the armistice negotiations, and at this critical hour he simply did not trust anyone else—not even Colonel House—to present his program for peace. And Wilson's call in the autumn of 1918 for the election of a Democratic Congress can be justified on the basis of precedent, although it did indicate that he was dangerously out of touch with prevailing political currents.

But after the elections of November 5, Wilson made a serious error in not adjusting his strategy to accommodate his domestic opponents. The vote gave the Republicans a majority of forty-six in the House and two in the all-important Senate, and it meant that Wilson's despised rival Senator Henry Cabot Lodge would become majority leader and chairman of the Senate Foreign Relations Committee. Yet Wilson resolutely refused to consult or court leading Senators, especially Republicans. And when he announced the composition of the American delegation to Paris on November 29, there were no Senators and no prominent Republicans. In addition to Wilson, the delegates included Secretary of State Robert Lansing, Colonel House, General Tasker H. Bliss, and Henry White, a career diplomat and nominal Republican. Moreover, none of these men was a strong leader, and Wilson clearly wanted it that way. One scholar has referred to the delegation as Wilson and "his errand boys." On the basis of tradition and feelings at the time, a very good case can be made that Wilson should have included in the delegation distinguished Republicans such as former President Taft and Elihu Root as well as two Senators.

The peace program Wilson took to Paris contained three themes that connected the specific points he had enunciated over the preceding year. First, any permanent settlement had to be a peace without rancor—a peace that removed the main causes of past wars including secret alliances, arms races, thwarted nationalism, and economic rivalry. Second, Wilson believed that the United States should serve as a model for the entire world; it represented the wave of the future. All peoples, the President felt, aspired to American institutions such as democratic government, broad suffrage, a capitalistic economy, and a liberal bourgeois society. Finally, the settlement should rest upon a world-wide peace organization energized by moral force. Enthusiasm for a league of nations had grown rapidly during the war, taking institutional form with the founding in June 1915 of the League to Enforce Peace, of which many prominent Americans including Taft and Lodge were members. Wilson publicly committed himself to the creation of a league of nations in May 1916 and quickly became its leading advocate. Wilson conceived of the new league primarily as a forum for compromising differences through the use of moral suasion. Only as a last resort would a voluntary armed force from the member states be formed. All nations, including the Central Powers and Russia, would be members.

These themes and the President's detailed proposals constituted the blueprint for a new world order. It was a basic plan of reform — in some ways analogous to the New Freedom reforms at home — that the New World took to the Old. With this program Woodrow Wilson advanced a liberal alternative to Lenin's call for world-wide socialist revolution. The President was fully aware of his competition with Lenin for the leadership of the Left. Only through the success of his new order, Wilson believed, could the world avoid the excesses and destruction of socialism and, at the same time, enlist the loyalty and the energy of the toiling masses. Viewing the peace conference in these elevated terms, one can appreciate why Wilson insisted on leading the American delegation, why he resisted compromise to the limit, and why he came to appear to so many of his critics a self-appointed messiah.

The attempt of the American delegates to serve as detached mediators for all types of issues would complicate the task of reform at the conference. The Inquiry stood at the center of this problem, for scores of members of this research staff went to Paris armed with mountains of reports and maps. The United States contingent was by far the best prepared at the conference, and the members were eager to resolve disputes among what they saw as predatory European powers. Wilson shared this view, and on the voyage to Europe he declared in a speech to the Inquiry members: "Tell me what's right and I'll fight for it." In reality the questions at Paris were not so simple, and frequently the Americans would encounter difficulties created by pursuit of the dual role of principled reformer and disinterested mediator.

The American delegation sailed for France on the S.S. *George Washington* on December 4, 1918. The President, the first chief executive to visit Europe while in office, received a tumultuous reception in Paris, where he was showered with roses and violets from a crowd of over two million and passed beneath a huge banner reading, "Honour to Wilson the Just." During brief visits the British people gave the President a warm but less enthusiastic welcome, and the Italians wildly cheered, "Viva Wilson, god of peace."

Taking these greetings as endorsements of his peace plan, Wilson convinced himself that he represented the aspirations of the peoples of Europe better than their own rulers. This was distinctly not the case, as the President might have understood had he noticed the critical comments that greeted his firm refusal of French and Belgian invitations to visit the devastated areas and pay homage to the thousands of white crosses lining the hills. Europeans did want peace, but they also wanted to force sacrifices from Germany, which had fought its battles on foreign soil.

At the peace conference Wilson found himself negotiating in small groups with very powerful men. Initially the Council of Ten,

President Wilson is driven to Paris City Hall to be made a citizen of the city on December 16, 1918. Two days after his triumphal welcome to Paris, Wilson drove with French President Raymond Poincaré through vast crowds and a glittering array of troops to be greeted formally by city officials. The people of Paris remained warm and enthusiastic toward President and Mrs. Wilson, but the attitude of government representatives and the press cooled as negotiations began.

Culver Pictures

composed of the premier and foreign minister of each of the five great powers in the Allied coalition, performed the basic work of the settlement. But as Japan restricted its interest to Asian questions, only four nations remained concerned with each problem. Plenary sessions of the delegations from all thirty-two nations attending the conference (including the five British dominions) met only periodically at Versailles to approve the decisions hammered out by the powers. Four national leaders determined every important issue, acting on the basis of reports drafted by a host of subcommittees of officials and experts. Among the Big Four, Wilson received most frequent support from David Lloyd George, a skilled debater and master of compromise who believed, with the President, that a stable peace required the continued presence of a strong Germany in the center of Europe. The greatest opposition came from the French Premier, Georges Clemenceau, whose foremost aim was to leave Germany too weak to menace France again. In the process Clemenceau hoped to make Germany pay in reparations much of the cost of the war. The genial Italian Premier, Vittorio Orlando, reserved his influence to advance his nation's interests in a few territorial questions. These European statesmen, including Lloyd George on many fundamental points, had a common cause against Wilsonism in their diplomatic tradition and their secret treaties. Moreover, while Americans had rejected Wilson's call for a Democratic Congress, Lloyd George had won an impressive victory in his December national elections largely on the issue of forcing Germany to pay for the war, and the French Chamber of Deputies had given Clemenceau a resounding vote of confidence two weeks later when he called for a peace based on revival of the balance of power with France dominant. As the conference opened, victory for Wilson's program was far from certain.

During the first phase of the conference, from January 12 until February 14, 1919, the delegates concentrated on drafting the covenant of the league of nations. At Wilson's insistence the covenant became the first article in the treaties of peace with all the Central Powers, and the President was named chairman of a subcommittee to draft the document. The first substantial problem arose from the desire of Japan and the dominions of South Africa and Australia to annex the German colonies in Shantung, Southwest Africa, and New Guinea, respectively. After a bitter fight, General Jan Christian Smuts of South Africa offered a compromise plan similar to one that Wilson had developed independently. This solution created three classes of mandates, depending on the colony's readiness for self-government. The mandatory power would administer the territory as a trustee for the league until it was prepared for independence. With responsible supervision, this plan provided a means for the liquidation of the empires of the Central Powers.

The form of the league of nations itself became the other serious dispute of the initial period of the conference. Clemenceau, arguing that it would take a full century for Wilson's idea of collective security to become effective, demanded that the great powers maintain peace through a general staff and league army. With Lloyd George's backing, the President successfully insisted that the league operate through public persuasion with arms as only a last resort. Thus, article 10 of the covenant, which Wilson would call "the heart of the League," bound members to consult on measures to take against aggressor nations. On February 14 the President reported the completed draft to a plenary session of the conference and gained acceptance of the league covenant as an integral part of the peace settlement.

The next day Wilson departed for a month-long visit to the United States to sign bills from Congress and explain the covenant to the American people. Already there was growing criticism of the new course on which the administration proposed to launch the nation. To his distress, the President proved unable to quell the opposition through a series of speeches and a long session of tedious cross-examination by the members of the House and Senate committees on foreign affairs. On February 28, in a fighting mood, Wilson called on the Democratic National Committee for help in silencing his critics, who he declared were "of all the blind and little, provincial people, . . . the littlest and most contemptible. . . . They have not got even good working imitations of minds." These harsh words, supposedly spoken in confidence, quickly reached the President's opponents. With malicious pleasure, Senator Lodge introduced a resolution on March 4 stating flatly that the league covenant was not acceptable "in the form now proposed." This statement, known as the Round Robin, soon had the signatures of thirty-nine Republican Senators or Senators-elect, six more than the number needed to defeat the treaty. The President still refused to compromise. Although he would seek certain clarifying amendments, he asserted just before returning to Paris that he intended to have the covenant so interwoven with the rest of the treaty that it could not be separated without "destroying the whole vital structure."

In the delegates' efforts to resolve the critical issues of reparations and territorial settlements during the second phase of the conference from March 14 until June 28, they faced increasing anxiety over social unrest spreading across Europe. The specter of Bolshevism, given new life by Béla Kun's seizure of power and creation of a Communist government in Hungary on March 21, became the leading object of concern. In late March and early April it appeared that Bolshevism might sweep through western Europe. A Soviet Republic was established in Bavaria, strikes broke out in Saxony and the Ruhr valley of Germany, and labor disputes increased in France, Italy, and Great Britain. In Russia the Soviets won several victories over counterrevolutionary forces. The successes of Bolshevism caused some Allied leaders to call for more stringent terms against Germany and full military intervention in Russia and Hungary, and it reduced support for Wilson's liberal peace program. Ray Stannard Baker, director of the American Press Bureau in Paris and later the President's biographer, analyzed the situation perceptively:

The President struggles almost alone to secure some constructive result out of the general ruin. If these old leaders only knew it, Wilson is the only strong bulwark left in the world against a wild Bolshevism on the one hand and a wilder militarism on the other. He would save the present democratic political system in the world by making it just, decent, efficient. . . . But what these old leaders are doing, with their greedy demands and selfish interests, is to give new arguments to Lenin and new force to Foch.

Yet before Wilson could press his battle for a just peace, he had to acknowledge his diminished authority with the American people by asking for reconsideration of the covenant and approval of four amendments designed to meet domestic criticism. After extensive negotiating, he had provisions added to the covenant stating that a member could withdraw from the league on two years' notice, that no nation would be required to accept a mandate without its consent, that domestic questions would be exempt from league jurisdiction, and that regional understandings such as the Monroe Doctrine were acceptable under the covenant. Neither Wilson nor the Allied statesmen felt these amendments made significant changes, but the Allies took advantage of the President's embarrassment to seek small advantages on other points. France reiterated its concern for security, and Japan requested an amendment recognizing the equality of all races. Wilson strongly objected to the Japanese proposal, feeling it did not belong in the covenant and knowing it would cause further trouble with the Senate. The racial

The Big Four in Paris, 1919. Left to right are Orlando, Lloyd George, Clemenceau, Wilson. Although the European statesmen pressed hard for economic and territorial privileges, the President won more concessions than he granted. The resulting treaty represented essentially a Wilsonian peace.

equality amendment received eleven votes in the plenary session, but six nations did not vote affirmatively and the President declared that the motion failed because it had not gained the usual unanimous backing. Although Wilson was technically correct, the Japanese were quite angry at his opposition and his refusal to call for the vote in a manner which separated the abstentions from the nays. On a matter of such importance to the United States, Wilson could prevail but only at considerable cost to his prestige. Finally on April 28, to the great relief of the American delegation, the full conference approved the revised covenant.

Wilson had to accept an unsatisfactory compromise on the issue of reparations. Both Britain and France wanted high reparations to provide income for their hard-pressed treasuries, and France wanted to keep Germany weak for years to come. At the suggestion of the young John Foster Dulles of the American delegation, Wilson advanced the "war guilt clause" stating that Germany and her allies were responsible for all the costs of the war. But this did not satisfy the French, and General Smuts again came up with a compromise. Germany would pay for war damages to civilians and the after effects, which were defined to include veterans' pensions. The delegates did not set a monetary figure for reparations but established a commission to measure the costs against Germany's ability to pay. The total bill would ultimately come to $33 billion, of which pensions alone composed more than half.

The dispute over Germany's frontiers became still more envenomed. Clemenceau demanded the cession to France of Alsace-Lorraine and the Saar Basin, the creation of an autonomous buffer state in the Rhineland, occupation of the Rhine bridgeheads for thirty years, and the establishment of a large Poland. With assistance from Lloyd George, Wilson vigorously resisted the French claims, arguing that they violated the principle of self-determination and would prevent a lasting peace. When the President threatened to leave the conference, Clemenceau finally acquiesced in a permanently demilitarized Rhineland to be occupied by France for fifteen years and League administration of the Saar for fifteen years (with French use of the coal mines), after which a plebiscite would determine whether the area remained with Germany or became French. The Big Four agreed upon an enlarged Poland with access to the sea through a corridor that cut Germany into two parts. In order to ease French fears about security, Britain and the United States signed separate treaties of guarantee pledging to aid France if Germany attacked again without provocation. These accords became binding only if both were ratified, and the refusal of the Senate to approve the American commitment would undermine the peace settlement's protection of France.

In other territorial matters, the conference granted Italy some land in the South Tyrol and an area around Trieste on the Adriatic but denied the more important request for control of the port of Fiume. Japan sought to annex the Shantung peninsula in China but was willing to settle for Germany's former economic concessions. After leading the opposition to the racial equality clause, Wilson felt compelled to sanction this transfer of economic rights to Japan. Riots broke out in China, marking the start of the May 4 movement, in

European Territorial Changes of World War I

Scale of miles: 0 — 150 — 300

——— International frontiers in 1924

Territory lost by the Central Powers

Territory lost by Russia

protest of Japanese expansion and the President's failure to enforce self-determination. The concessions in the Tyrol and Shantung would cause Wilson to lose the support of many American liberals in the forthcoming fight over the treaty.

The Allied and Associated Powers presented the completed treaty to German representatives on May 7 to allow them to study it and make written proposals for changes. The Germans objected bitterly about the severe terms, which, they claimed, violated the armistice agreement to abide by the Fourteen Points. Several minor alterations were made at German request, but when the Berlin government still refused to accept the settlement, Marshal Foch prepared to move his armies across the Rhine. The Germans then yielded and on June 28, 1919, five years after the assassination of Archduke Franz Ferdinand, they signed the treaty in the Hall of Mirrors at Versailles, where the French Republic had surrendered to Bismarck and Kaiser Wilhelm I in 1871.

The Treaty of Versailles without doubt represented a bundle of compromises. Wilson had gained the League of Nations and had substantially carried out most of the pledges in his Fourteen Points and later statements. But there had been many costly sacrifices on matters such as reparations, South Tyrol, and Shantung. The treaty caused much rancor in Germany, and it did not notably aid the spread of democratic government. The settlement was, furthermore, unrealistic in its expectations: it redrew the map of central Europe without taking Russia into account, and it assumed too much of the United States.

Yet the treaty accomplished much that would have been impossible had Wilson not raised men's hopes so high. As the British diplomat and man of letters Harold Nicolson aptly declares: "Given the atmosphere of the time, given the passions aroused in all democracies by four years of war, it would have been impossible even for superman to devise a peace of moderation and righteousness." Within what was possible, Wilson probably got the best terms attainable. And we must remember that, despite the imperfections of the treaty, Wilson relied on the League of Nations to make adjustments in the settlement and remove injustices that remained or occurred in the future. In all, Wilson's performance at Paris must be rated a success for his peace program and for America. It is unfortunate that he was not able to demonstrate the same persuasiveness and flexibility in his dealings with the United States Senate.

The Senate debate over the Treaty of Versailles ostensibly centered upon whether the United States should assume the responsibilities of collective security as defined in the League covenant, but in fact it was dominated by personal ambition and partisan intrigue. Although mass meetings, polls, and newspaper estimates indicated that a majority of the American public favored approving the treaty when it was signed, enthusiasm waned as the argument dragged on and problems multiplied in Europe. And, more vital, Senators with long terms in office and knowledge of the brevity of popular memory could disregard the desires of their constituents on this issue, especially if they managed to cloud the debate and represent their actions as a defense of the fundamental principles of the republic.

Within these lines, hostile Senators charted their strategy for defeat of the treaty while Wilson was still in Paris. As its core the opposition had a band known as the "irreconcilables," composed of fourteen Republicans and two Democrats led by the Republican and former Progressive William E. Borah of Idaho. These men totally rejected the League concept and would use any legal means to prevent American participation. A shifting combination of about twelve "mild reservationists" sought to add minor clarifying reservations (which, unlike amendments, did not require renegotiation of the treaty) but essentially favored the settlement. And the important group of about twenty "strong reservationists," led by Senator Henry Cabot Lodge, wanted either basic modifications or defeat of the treaty. Although Lodge himself would accept a restructured League, he had more faith in the balance of power with strengthened international law than in the new form of collective security. Lodge's attitude was, however, complicated by his intense partisanship and by his equally intense hatred of Woodrow Wilson. If the treaty was to be defeated, the Senator from Massachusetts wanted the Democrats, including the President, to bear part of the responsibility. Lodge thus pursued the strategy of holding lengthy hearings on the settlement in which every opponent could voice his objections and then advancing a series of amendments and reservations to chip away at the powers of the League. He gambled on the hope that Wilson would proudly refuse to accept any modifications designed by Lodge and would, in the end, kill his own creation.

Wilson rose to the bait. On July 10, in presenting the treaty to the Senate for approval, the President called on the upper house for prompt and unqualified acceptance of "this great duty." Earlier that day, when asked by a reporter if he believed the settlement would be approved with reservations, Wilson curtly replied: "I do not think hypothetical questions are concerned. The Senate is going to ratify the treaty." Had the President been able to control the timing of the Senate vote, his full-throttle approach of tying the League covenant to the treaty of peace and calling for rapid endorsement of both might have worked. But as the weeks passed, confusion and new-found objections to the treaty eroded his support in the Senate. To bring pressure on the legislators, Wilson decided to make a speaking tour on behalf of the League through the Midwestern and Western states. Starting on September 4, the already-fatigued President set out on an eight-thousand-mile trip to deliver thirty-two addresses in twenty-two days. It proved too much for his health, and Wilson collapsed from exhaustion after an appearance at Pueblo, Colorado, on September 25. His train roared back to Washington, but a few days after his return the President suffered a serious cerebral thrombosis that paralyzed his left side, impaired his speech, and almost took his life. Incapacitated for six months, the President was kept in virtual isolation by his wife and was unable to lead or properly assess the fight for the League. Although Wilson's stroke was probably not the decisive factor in the treaty's defeat, it certainly impaired the energy and alertness of the League's foremost advocate. This together with the fact that his wife protected him from all bad news only increased Wilson's sense of rectitude and made it certain that he would reject compromise.

During the President's western tour, the Senate Foreign Relations Committee reported the treaty to the floor, recommending approval after the addition of forty-five amendments and four reservations. When loyal Democrats and moderate Republicans defeated all the amendments, Lodge introduced another resolution of approval with fourteen reservations. The most significant new qualification, the second, stated that only Congress could authorize the use of the armed forces in the defense of another state. Although this clause could have slightly restricted the executive branch's freedom to cooperate under article 10, none of the reservations would have seriously hampered the operation of the League.

When the President refused to accept any of the Lodge reservations, the treaty appeared doomed. Wilson did allow the introduction of four clarifying reservations he had drafted earlier plus five offered by the Democratic minority leader, Senator Gilbert M.

Hitchcock. The Republicans defeated this slate of substitute reservations, and since the President remained adamant, the stage was set for two ballots. On November 19, 1919, the Senate refused to approve the Versailles Treaty with reservations or without. Most Democrats followed the President's orders to vote against the treaty with reservations. On the vote for the treaty with the Lodge reservations the Democrats and "irreconcilables" combined to defeat the motion, and on a subsequent ballot for the treaty without qualification the Republicans joined with the "irreconcilables" and seven Democrats to vote it down.

Efforts for compromise seemed on the verge of success in January. A group of Senators including Lodge worked out a slate of reservations satisfactory to two-thirds of their body, only to have the project killed by the "irreconcilables," who threatened to bolt the Republican Party in the 1920 elections. Still, prominent leaders in both Great Britain and France let it be known that their governments would accept the Lodge reservations in order to gain American membership in the League. The Senate voted to reconsider the treaty, and the Foreign Relations Committee reported another resolution of approval, this time with fifteen reservations. Wilson instructed Democrats to hold the line, declaring that if this group of restrictions were accepted, "these senators will merely offer new ones, even more humiliating." "These evil men," he charged, "intend to destroy the League." The second effort to pass the treaty came on March 19, 1920. The only ballot was for approval with reservations, and it failed by seven votes to gain the necessary two-thirds (forty-nine for, thirty-five against). Although twenty-one Democrats violated the President's directive and voted for the treaty with reservations, they were overpowered by the twenty-three loyalists who obeyed the embittered chief executive.

Wilson challenged the American people to make the presidential election of 1920 a "great and solemn referendum" on the League of Nations. Instead, the voters gave a solemn majority of seven million votes to Warren G. Harding, who ran an issueless campaign from his front porch in Marion, Ohio, and so masked his indifference to the League that some observers thought he would accept a modified form of the international organization. The mandate of the voters in 1920 was for a return to a simpler, more private style of life like that they believed they had known before what Otis Graham refers to as "The Great Campaigns" of progressivism and war had occurred. With Lodge rejoicing that the League was dead, the Harding administration proceeded to end the state of war with Germany by congressional resolution on July 2, 1921. Then on August 25 the administration signed the Treaty of Berlin with Germany, which provided the United States with all the rights and assurances included in the Treaty of Versailles. In this anti-climactic way, the Great Crusade for Democracy ended.

The competition for primary responsibility in the defeat of the Treaty of Versailles is indeed heavy. By refusing all compromise with the Senate, Woodrow Wilson surely engaged in what historian Thomas A. Bailey calls "The Supreme Infanticide." Wilson could have taken the United States into the League with the loss of a little prestige. But he fell short by only seven votes, and one must place considerable blame on those Democrats who believed in the League but blindly followed the President's orders on the final ballot. In the ultimate analysis, however, the greatest responsibility must rest with Henry Cabot Lodge and those who resolutely backed him. And it lies mainly with Lodge, for he dreamed up the strategy of delay and obfuscation, he designed the various series of redundant reservations, and he led the fight for them with every conceivable political tactic. The costly defeat of this treaty stemmed from a tragic clash of personal pride and vanity between two national leaders that has seldom been matched.

Challenges and Responses

In any analysis of American foreign relations in the first two decades of this century, the men whose contributions stand out are Theodore Roosevelt, Alfred Thayer Mahan, and Woodrow Wilson. Drawing on Mahan's synthesis of the nation's economic and strategic requirements, Roosevelt designed an international program that prevailed in all essentials throughout the period and in many ways until the start of World War II. The basic elements in this program included predominance in the Western Hemisphere, cooperation with Great Britain, maintenance of a limited commitment in East Asia, and a high level of economic involvement with Europe while avoiding Continental political problems unless the balance of power was seriously endangered. The weight given to these objectives shifted with the personnel of each administration and, more importantly, with the willingness of the American people to assume overseas obligations. The main variable, therefore, in the nation's acceptance of great power responsibilities was the leaders' capacity to gain and hold public support.

Before 1914, progressive expansionists proved unable to generate broad endorsement of their view of America's mission. The capital was not available to stimulate trade and investment abroad. Developing nations from the Dominican Republic to China did not welcome American institutions, and even in the Philippines, where the United States exercised full colonial supervision, these processes and organizations did not take root. Most seriously, the majority of the American people showed no sustained interest in foreign affairs and generally opposed actions that caused increased spending or political entanglement. The practical result was that for most of this period American leaders, while seeking to expand the republic's influence, felt constrained to avoid any significant financial or political obligations not directly related to the security of the Caribbean.

World War I became the greatest innovator in American diplomacy during the progressive era. It removed threats to the Caribbean and allowed Americans to look at their interests beyond the Western Hemisphere. It provided the prosperity and the capital that permitted economic expansion to succeed as a positive diplomatic technique. And it forced the United States to consider on a daily basis the full challenges of power. Both in Asia and in Europe Wilson abandoned the limited policies of Mahan and Roosevelt. In the East he continued Taft's course of resisting Japanese expansion; although not accepting any large commitments, he did place the United States in a moral position where a choice between retreat and significant involvement would be inevitable if Japan continued its drive for predominance in the region. The nature of the naval conflict in Europe led Wilson to accept belligerency in defense of American rights and in order to help make the peace.

The war also gave Wilson an opportunity to win public approval of increased international action by the United States. To justify the sacrifices of a struggle he believed to have been forced upon the nation, the President created an evangelical rhetoric about making the world safe for democracy and advocating the expansion of American ideals and institutions. Wilson devised a peace plan to reform international politics in a way that would both protect America and establish the conditions for Open Door expansion in accepted progressive fashion. By following his program, the United States could achieve security and peaceful penetration of the world's markets.

Wilson's call for a new world order failed to persuade many Americans. The public went along with the war, but its faith in a reformed world was not as strong as its desire to return to limited responsibility. Americans accepted entering the war to right the European balance and to demonstrate their willingness to protect the republic's interests, but they declined to bear the continuing burden of managing European and Asian problems. As the selfish ends of the Allies and the threat of Bolshevism became evident, people realized that the peace structure would entail further obligation and sacrifice. A large number wanted to make the new system work but doubted its chances of success. Some believed the nation could enjoy the benefits of economic expansion without the difficulties of collective security. Others rejected the League of Nations as entangling and dangerous. Basically Wilson misdirected his energies in trying to mobilize an enthusiastic public to press for Senate approval of the settlement, and the legislators, divided and losing interest themselves, allowed partisanship to determine the fate of the treaty. Even if the President, by accepting Lodge's reservations, had won endorsement of the treaty, the current against further international cooperation and involvement ran increasingly strong. All too many Americans, both in and out of the Senate, held the attitude expressed in the song popular with the doughboys in France:

> We drove the Boche across the Rhine,
> The Kaiser from his throne.
> Oh, Lafayette, we've paid our debt,
> For Christ's sake, send us home.

The Great Crusade showed that the United States would respond, albeit reluctantly, to defend its interests against actual attack and insult. But the American people through their representatives refused to answer the prophet Wilson when he called for continued participation in European affairs. It would take further crises and another war before Americans learned that political responsibility was both the challenge and the price of power.

SUGGESTED READINGS

Among works on the conflict with Spain and America's venture into formal empire, Ernest R. May, *Imperial Democracy: The Emergence of America as a Great Power* (1961), provides the best international setting. H. Wayne Morgan, *America's Road to Empire: The War with Spain and Overseas Expansion* (1965), gives a concise account of the war and its results. Lively studies of McKinley and domestic politics are H. Wayne Morgan, *William McKinley and His America* (1963), and Margaret Leech, *In the Days of McKinley* (1959). Walter LaFeber, *The New Empire: An Interpretation of American Expansion, 1860–1898* (1963), presents the background of the outward thrust with emphasis on economic forces. Useful on the opponents of empire are Robert L. Beisner's award-winning *Twelve Against Empire: The Anti-Imperialists, 1898–1900* (1968) and E. Berkeley Tompkins, *Anti-Imperialism in the United States: The Great Debate, 1890–1920* (1970).

Highly readable general studies that argue the "realist" case are Robert E. Osgood, *Ideals and Self-Interest in America's Foreign Relations* (1953), and George F. Kennan, *American Diplomacy, 1900–1950* (1951). A widely-read revisionist work that traces the development of Open Door imperialism since the 1890's is William Appleman Williams, *The Tragedy of American Diplomacy* (1962). Compact and valuable estimates of the secretaries of state are in Norman A. Graebner, ed., *An Uncertain Tradition: American Secretaries of State in the Twentieth Century* (1961). For matters of global strategy see William D. Puleston, *Mahan* (1939); William E. Livezey, *Mahan on Sea Power* (1947); and John A. S. Grenville and George Berkeley Young, *Politics, Strategy, and American Diplomacy: Studies in Foreign Policy, 1873–1917* (1966).

For coverage of the Presidents and their diplomatic policies, well-researched analyses of the Rough Rider are in Howard K. Beale, *Theodore Roosevelt and the Rise of America to World Power* (1956), and Raymond A. Esthus, *Theodore Roosevelt and the International Rivalries* (1970). These volumes and William H. Harbaugh, *Power and Responsibility: The Life and Times of Theodore Roosevelt* (1961), present TR as a vigorous but careful diplomatist, whereas Henry F. Pringle, *Theodore Roosevelt: A Biography* (1931), depicts an immature enthusiast for power. John A. Garraty, *Henry Cabot Lodge: A Biography* (1953), adds interesting information about Roosevelt and his closest political friend. The fullest treatments of Taft and foreign affairs are in Henry F. Pringle, *The Life and Times of William Howard Taft* (2 vols., 1939), and in Walter V. Scholes and Marie V. Scholes, *The Foreign Policies of the Taft Administration* (1970). For Wilson, the most compelling account is Arthur S. Link's magisterial biography *Wilson* (5 vols., 1947–1965), which ends with the decision for war in 1917. Link has written shorter treatments of events during and after the war: *Wilson the Diplomatist* (1957) and *Woodrow Wilson: A Brief Biography* (1963). A well-written full biography is Arthur Walworth, *Woodrow Wilson* (1965), and useful information on Wilson and his first secretary of state is in Paolo E. Coletta, *William Jennings Bryan: Progressive Politician and Moral Statesman, 1909–1915* (1969).

The Western Hemisphere receives general examination in Samuel Flagg Bemis' nationalistic study, *The Latin American Policy of the United States* (1943). Dexter Perkins summarizes his life's work on the "Principles of 1823" in the superb volume, *A History of the Monroe Doctrine* (1955). An indispensable work that minimizes the importance of economic motives is Dana G. Munro, *Intervention and Dollar Diplomacy in the Caribbean, 1900–1921* (1964). David F. Healy, *The United States in Cuba, 1898–1902* (1963), and Dwight C. Miner, *The Fight for the Panama Route* (1940), are useful monographs on the two leading strategic points in the hemisphere. Recent scholarship on relations between the United States and Mexico is extensive and generally of high quality. Howard F. Cline, *The United States and Mexico* (1963), gives a brief introduction to the problems of the progressive era. Robert E. Quirk, *An Affair of Honor: Woodrow Wilson and the Occupation of Veracruz* (1962), provides a good case study of the difficulties of moral instruction. Valuable recent works include: Peter Calvert, *The Mexican Revolution, 1910–1914: The Diplomacy of Anglo-American Conflict* (1968); Kenneth J. Grieb, *The United States and Huerta* (1969); and P. Edward Haley, *Revolution and Intervention: The Diplomacy of Taft and Wilson with Mexico, 1910–1917* (1970). Hans R. Schmidt, *The United States Occupation of Haiti, 1915–1934* (1971), discusses the acceptance of new obligations. A fine analysis of the influence of the Great War in restructuring diplomacy for the hemisphere is Joseph S. Tulchin, *The Aftermath of War: World War I and U.S. Policy Toward Latin America* (1971).

On Asian policy the standard survey, now quite dated, is A. Whitney Griswold, *The Far Eastern Policy of the United States* (1938). Akira Iriye, *Across the Pacific: An Inner History of American–East Asian Relations* (1967), presents a stimulating examination of informal relationships. Useful works that emphasize economic influences are Thomas J. McCormick, *China Market: America's Quest for Informal Empire, 1893–1901* (1967); Charles S. Campbell, Jr., *Special Business Interests and the Open Door Policy* (1951); and Jerry Israel, *Progressivism and the Open Door: America and China, 1905–1921* (1971). Marilyn B. Young, *The Rhetoric of Empire: American China Policy, 1895–1901* (1968), and Paul A. Varg, *The Making of A Myth: The United States and China, 1897–1912* (1968), give more weight to political and cultural factors than to economic. Excellent coverage of the Roosevelt years is in Raymond A. Esthus, *Theodore Roosevelt and Japan* (1966); Charles E. Neu, *An Uncertain Friendship: Theodore Roosevelt and Japan, 1906–1909* (1967); and Eugene P. Trani, *The Treaty of Portsmouth: An Adventure in American Diplomacy* (1969). John A. White, *The Diplomacy of the Russo-Japanese War* (1964), examines the interaction of all the concerned powers. William R. Braisted provides meticulous treatment of strategic affairs in *The United States Navy in the Pacific, 1897–1909* (1958) and *The United States Navy in the Pacific, 1909–1922* (1971). For the Wilson administration, see Tien-yi Li, *Woodrow Wilson's China Policy, 1913–1917* (1952); Roy W. Curry, *Woodrow Wilson and Far Eastern Policy, 1913–1921* (1957); and Burton F. Beers, *Vain Endeavor: Robert Lansing's Attempts to End the American-Japanese Rivalry* (1962).

America's critical relationship with Great Britain is the topic of Bradford Perkins' sensitive study, *The Great Rapprochement: England and the United States, 1895–1914* (1968). Soundly researched works on the creation of the understanding are Alexander E. Campbell, *Great Britain and the United States, 1895–1903* (1960), and Charles S. Campbell, Jr., *Anglo-American Understanding, 1898–1903* (1957). R. G. Neale, *Great Britain and United States Expansion: 1898–1900* (1966), minimizes British influence on American imperialism and the Open Door. Samuel F. Wells, Jr., analyzes the relative importance of economic and political elements in his forthcoming volume *The Tenuous Entente: Anglo-American Strategy and Diplomacy, 1904–1914*. Helpful on their special subjects are Kenneth Bourne, *Britain and the Balance of Power in North America, 1815–1908* (1967), and Alan J. Ward, *Ireland and Anglo-American Relations, 1899–1921* (1969).

From the rich literature on American neutrality, the most complete, balanced treatments are contained in Ernest R. May's multinational study, *The World War and American Isolation, 1914–1917* (1959), and Link, *Wilson,* vols. III–V (1960–1965). Ross Gregory, *The Origins of American Intervention in the First World War* (1971), presents the most recent brief account, and Daniel M. Smith, *The Great Departure: The United States in World War I, 1914–1920* (1965), provides the best synthesis of developments during neutrality and the peace conference. Valuable works emphasizing the concept of national interest are Daniel M. Smith, *Robert Lansing and American Neutrality, 1914–1917* (1958), and Edward H. Buehrig, *Woodrow Wilson and the Balance of Power* (1955). Of the revisionist studies critical of the decision to intervene, the most thoroughly researched is Charles C. Tansill, *America Goes to War* (1938). Also useful is Paul Birdsall, "Neutrality and Economic Pressures, 1914–1917," *Science and Society,* 3 (1939). Otis L. Graham, Jr., argues provocatively in *The Great Campaigns: Reform and War in America, 1900–1928* (1971) that Wilson should have stayed out of war, by using a passenger ban and a munitions embargo, in order to perfect progressive reforms at home. John M. Cooper, Jr., *The Vanity of Power: American Isolationism and the First World War, 1914–1917* (1969), analyzes the development of domestic sentiment against the war. Other helpful monographs include Karl E. Birnbaum, *Peace Moves and U-Boat Warfare* (1958); Barbara W. Tuchman, *The Zimmermann Telegram* (1958); Gaddis Smith, *Britain's Clandestine Submarines, 1914–1915* (1964); and Ross Gregory, *Walter Hines Page, Ambassador to the Court of St. James's* (1970). For new evidence and a provocative if unconvincing argument, see Colin Simpson, *Lusitania* (1973).

For wartime diplomacy, David F. Trask, *The United States in the Supreme War Council* (1961), and W. B. Fowler, *British-American Relations, 1917–1918: The Role of Sir William Wiseman* (1969), ably demonstrate from different perspectives how the United States maneuvered to gain maximum influence at the peace conference. Carl P. Parrini, *Heir To Empire: United States Economic Diplomacy, 1916–1923* (1969), makes an uneven argument on the important topic of America's drive for economic supremacy. Arno J. Mayer, *Political Origins of the New Diplomacy, 1917–1918* (1959), discusses the competition between Wilson and Lenin in the forming of war aims. N. Gordon Levin, Jr., *Woodrow Wilson and World Politics: America's Response to War and Revolution* (1968), presents an impressive analysis of Wilson's effort to spread American liberal capitalism, especially in his policies toward Germany and Russia. George F. Kennan has written two distinguished volumes on Soviet-American relations: *Russia Leaves the War* (1956) and *The Decision to Intervene* (1958). Also of value are Thomas A. Bailey, *The Policy of the United States toward the Neutrals, 1917–1918* (1942); Laurence W. Martin, *Peace Without Victory: Woodrow Wilson and the British Liberals* (1958); Betty M. Unterberger, *America's Siberian Expedition, 1918–1920* (1956); and Harry R. Rudin, *Armistice, 1918* (1944).

Among writings on the peace settlement, the most comprehensive are Thomas A. Bailey, *Woodrow Wilson and the Lost Peace* (1944) and *Woodrow Wilson and the Great Betrayal* (1945), and Paul Birdsall, *Versailles Twenty Years After* (1941). American planning is carefully examined in Lawrence E. Gelfand, *The Inquiry: American Preparations for Peace, 1917–1919* (1963).

David F. Trask, *General Tasker H. Bliss and the "Sessions of the World," 1919* (1966), describes the frustrations of one of Wilson's "errand boys," and Harold Nicolson, *Peacemaking, 1919* (1933), presents in sprightly style the views of a disillusioned young British diplomat. Helpful on the territorial settlements are Louis L. Gerson, *Woodrow Wilson and the Rebirth of Poland, 1914–1920* (1953); Victor S. Mamatey, *The United States and East Central Europe, 1914–1919* (1957); and Joseph P. O'Grady, ed., *The Immigrants' Influence on Wilson's Peace Policies* (1967). The impact of the Russian revolution and the fear of Bolshevism is explored in Arno J. Mayer, *Politics and Diplomacy of Peacemaking: Containment and Counterrevolution at Versailles, 1918–1919* (1967), and in John M. Thompson, *Russia, Bolshevism, and the Versailles Peace* (1966). Seth P. Tillman, *Anglo-American Relations at the Paris Peace Conference of 1919* (1961), emphasizes cooperation between the two English-speaking Allies, while Louis A. R. Yates, *The United States and French Security, 1917–1921* (1957), shows America's conflicts with the French. Warren F. Kuehl, *Seeking World Order: The United States and International Organization to 1920* (1969), and Sondra R. Herman, *Eleven Against War: Studies in American Internationalist Thought, 1898–1921* (1969), indicate how Wilson's views on collective security were too advanced for many informed Americans. Valuable works on the fight over the Versailles Treaty include Denna F. Fleming, *The United States and the League of Nations, 1918–1920* (1932); Selig Adler, *The Isolationist Impulse: Its Twentieth Century Reaction* (1957); and Ralph A. Stone, *The Irreconcilables: The Fight Against the League of Nations* (1970).

Significant Statistics

	1900	1920
Foreign trade (millions of dollars)		
Exports		
Americas	227	2,553
Europe	1,040	4,466
Asia	68	872
Australia and Oceania	41	172
Africa	19	166
Total	1,499	8,664
Percentage of GNP	8.6	9.3
Imports		
Americas	224	2,424
Europe	441	1,228
Asia	146	1,397
Australia and Oceania	29	80
Africa	11	150
Total	930	5,784
Percentage of GNP	5.3	5.9
Balance	+570	+2,880
Investment (billions of dollars)		
U.S. investments abroad	0.7[a]	7.0[b]
Foreign investments in the U.S.	3.4[a]	3.3[b]
Net investment position	−2.7[a]	+3.7[b]
Department of State budget (millions of dollars)	3.3	13.5
Diplomatic missions	42	47
Alliances in force	0	0
Overseas travel (travelers in thousands)	120	157

Sources: *Statistical Abstract of the United States; Historical Statistics of the United States, Colonial Times to 1957; and Treaties and Other International Agreements of the United States of America, 1776–1949.*

[a] Data for 1897.

[b] Data for 1919.

3

The First Years
of Modern America
1918–1933

STANLEY COBEN

It was an easy, quick adventurous age, good to be young in," Malcolm Cowley recalled, and a large number of other American commentators on the 1920's agreed. F. Scott Fitzgerald called it "the greatest gaudiest spree in history . . . , a whole race going hedonistic, deciding on pleasure." Frederick Lewis Allen, trying to capture the essence of the period in *Only Yesterday*, remembered "those charming, crazy days when the radio was a thrilling novelty, and girls wore bobbed hair and knee length skirts, and a transatlantic flyer became a god overnight, and common stocks were about to bring us all to a lavish utopia." This seemed—to use Fitzgerald's term—a "jazz age" to high school and college students who danced the fox-trot or, if they lived in Chicago or New York, the daring black

Motor vehicle registrations jumped from 468,500 in 1910 to over 15,000,000 in 1923, when this picture was taken. Large industries were created as a consequence, including a new type of retail store—the gas station. The number of billboard advertisements also multiplied, as traffic past previously inaccessible places increased.

bottom at parties that would have scandalized their Victorian grandparents. It soon became a jazz age also to many of these students' parents, who adopted their children's carefree attitudes along with their music and dances; also to bohemians, not only in Paris, Greenwich Village, and the south of France, but in small colonies in cities throughout the United States, even in Sinclair Lewis' creation Zenith, where George Babbitt enjoyed a brief fling almost as deeply satisfying to him as driving a powerful car or buying bootleg liquor.

The status of automobile ownership and the delicious ability to direct the movements and speed of these mighty vehicles extended far down the economic ladder from the upper middle class Babbitts. New car registrations for the year 1929 reached a total of 4,445,178, and the Automobile Manufacturers' Association estimated that Americans owned one car for every six people. A galaxy of home appliances changed the life patterns of millions: refrigerators, radios, washing machines, automatic ovens, vacuum cleaners, electric toasters, and dozens of other marvels. The number of telephones in use more than doubled, to over 20 million between 1915 and 1929. Talking movies, electric phonographs, and sports events in gigantic new stadiums provided entertainment for tens of millions. Effective contraceptives and a changing morality, with some aid from speakeasies and motorcars, made sex a formidable competitor to commercial entertainment. Among the consequences of this widespread hedonism were a decline in the number of newspapers and books published and some reduction in attendance at church services.

Only a minority of Americans shared the affluence that made their country the economic wonder of the world. Nevertheless, this minority constituted a far larger proportion of the population than had emerged from poverty in any other nation, and that achievement gave millions of less fortunate Americans a sense of pride, along with more bitter feelings. Unfortunately, a battered Model T Ford or a radio did not appreciably improve the quality of life enjoyed

The excitement and variety of America's great cities—where almost everything was a five-cent subway ride away—is conveyed in *City Activities with Subways* by the American painter Thomas Hart Benton (born 1889).

The New School for Social Research

by a tenant farmer or a slum dweller. The only electrical appliance owned by a majority of American families in 1929 was an electric iron, and 1.3 million homes served by electricity lacked even that.

Probably the most significant aspect of the 1920's was not the pleasure disseminated by gadgets, spectacles, and the new morality, but the decade's broad and deep cultural changes. Americans of all classes found established ideas and values under attack and traditional social relationships disrupted. As a consequence, intense animosities ran strongly through the decade. Religious and ethnic groups all but entered into civil war as a result. Intellectuals who reminisced later about the joys of the postwar decade have left a record of their horror at the spiritual and economic poverty they saw when they viewed that American society at close range. An understanding of American civilization in the 1920's requires an especially sensitive awareness that pleasure and anxiety, optimism and despair, can coexist within individuals as well as within societies, among intellectuals and black migrants to Harlem, as well as among members of the Ku Klux Klan.

The "Excitement"

A peculiar excitement pervaded the United States after the armistice in November 1918. Contemporary journalists at first attributed the high feelings to a continuation of wartime fervor. However, as months passed and the intensity of popular agitation mounted, it became apparent that millions of Americans were deeply disturbed by events connected only peripherally to the war. Blessed with the prescience that magazine editors and politicians have been granted about the conclusions of unborn historians, the *Saturday Evening Post* proclaimed in November 1919: "History will see our present state of mind as one with that preceding the burning of witches, the children's crusade, the great tulip craze and other examples of softening of the world's brain." The *Post* editors referred not to the frenetic American Red Scare or to popular approval of Attorney General A. Mitchell Palmer's disregard for the Constitution as he commenced his efforts to round up all allegedly radical aliens. Rather it was the specter of expanding Bolshevism that aroused the editors' fears for their civilization's collective sanity.

Millions of especially susceptible Americans already were similarly perturbed by a series of postwar dislocations. These, combined with threats to the dominant culture antedating and accompanying World War I, created an atmosphere of anxiety and hatred among citizens who felt that the nation's integrity was seriously threatened. This atmosphere hung over much of the country until at least 1924–1925, but for more than a year during 1919–1920, these fears reached such an exaggerated state that they bordered on national madness.

The postwar "excitement" took a particularly virulent form in the United States, although all the former European combatants also suffered from acute dissatisfaction in 1919–1920, manifested in extreme form by revolutions and counterrevolutions in Eastern and Central Europe and by vigorous radical and nationalist movements in Western Europe. Despite the slight losses suffered by Americans during the war compared to the enormous casualties and destruction that embittered Europeans, and the relatively mild class antagonisms in America compared to those in most European nations, only in Germany, Russia, and Hungary did the postwar turmoil last so long and take more severe forms. These nations, however, were in the throes of armed revolution in 1919, afflicted with terrible wartime losses—and defeat—as well as with powerful extremist movements contending for political control of each country.

Sources of stress peculiar to the United States stimulated fears resembling those which afflicted nations actually undergoing armed insurrection. Millions of foreigners from races often considered interior in their new land had flooded most of America's greatest cities before 1914, and hundreds of thousands of black migrants crowded against the recent immigrants in these same northern cities during and after the war. The size of the migrations alone would have ensured a racist movement of some strength when the occupation of the cities became apparent.

These strains coincided, moreover, with other extraordinary events that left old-stock Americans disoriented and frightened. Prices skyrocketed, more than doubling between 1915 and 1920, often causing distress among unorganized white collar employees with their constricted mobility and fixed salaries. In most sectors of the economy industrial wages failed to keep pace with prices. Vital industries—coal, steel, and railroads—were first threatened and then paralyzed by strikes. Business suffered a postwar recession, including a brief but drastic stock market decline. Bitter arguments raged over continued American participation in volatile European affairs. Newspapers featured daily reports of revolutions abroad and threats of revolt at home. Intellectuals and artists, increasingly disillusioned as the horrifying nature of the war and the inadequacies of the peace settlement became clear, stepped up their prewar attack on traditional values and openly flouted conventional morality. They encouraged wider revolt against both with an unprecedented outpouring of books, stories, poems, essays, and other artistic productions. These intellectuals and artists posed an insidious threat to the system of ideas underpinning the established social order.

Furthermore, evidence of real danger to the national government existed in 1919. Membership in a secure nation provided the chief emotional support for millions of Americans, and these citizens, therefore, responded readily to charges by newspapers and government officials of a domestic radical menace. The Communist revolutions throughout Eastern and Central Europe—especially the Bolshevik triumph in Russia—made Americans look more anxiously at potential insurgents here. Domestic radicals encouraged these fears, boasting exuberantly in pamphlets and newspapers that the United States stood on the verge of revolution. The Industrial Workers of the World (IWW), openly rebellious even during the war, and the Socialist left wing, already preparing to ally itself with Moscow, compared favorably both in numbers and in volume of revolutionary rhetoric with the groups that had seized power in Europe, even with the Russian Bolsheviks.

Actually American radical organizations in 1919 were pathetically disorganized and poverty-stricken. The Socialist left was almost devoid of contact with American workers and not yet dominated or subsidized by Moscow. The IWW, shorn of its effective leaders by wartime arrests and internal strife, was distrusted by organized labor and generally declining in influence and power. Anarchist groups were isolated in a handful of tiny local organizations.

Hysteria in the United States reached epidemic proportions beginning in February 1919, when workers in Seattle tried to bring their wages into accord with runaway prices by staging a general strike. The mayor of that city, sensing an opportunity for national prominence, abandoned his role as a defender of labor and charged that the strike was the first step in a Bolshevik and IWW plan to paralyze the nation. A crude scheme to assassinate a number of prominent Americans was uncovered in April. A bomb blew up the front of Attorney General Palmer's home in June, and other bombs exploded almost simultaneously before several public buildings. The culprits completely eluded the police and the Justice Department's long investigation—probably because, as that investigation finally indicated, they were members of a small anarchist group that undertook no further violent action. In addition to an injured night watchman, the only casualties were the bomb thrower, who apparently slipped as he threw his missile against Palmer's home and blew himself and, judging from the limbs found in the neighborhood, an accomplice to bits.

Traditional May Day speeches and parades, sponsored by labor and radical organizations, suffered attack by ardent patriots in cities throughout the country, and these ceremonies disintegrated into a series of gigantic street brawls. Police, federal troops, state militia, and in one city even army tanks intervened to control the wild disorders. Newspaper reports of the riots almost invariably stressed provocative actions by the marchers and quoted officials who feared that the battles presaged a nationwide rebellion.

When radical Socialists formed the American Communist and Communist Labor Parties in August 1919, with the announced intention of promoting the proletarian revolution they pronounced near at hand, the more fearful citizens succumbed to complete panic. Millions of otherwise rational Americans, including reporters for liberal newspapers and almost every influential member of the Wilson administration, among them the President, the Vice-President, and the entire Cabinet, believed that these unarmed, disorganized, isolated parties threatened the national government.

The most dramatic official response to thunderous public demands for action against those who threatened American civilization emanated from the Justice Department. Palmer ordered a giant dragnet to gather in all alien Communists and anarchists. On January 2, 1920, federal agents and local police, organized by J. Edgar Hoover, the young head of the anti-radical division in the Justice Department's Bureau of Investigation, swooped down on Communist headquarters and other meeting places, including pool halls, social clubs, and private homes, arresting between six thousand and ten thousand persons over the next few days. Citizens as well as aliens were taken, almost all without proper warrants. They were held in overcrowded jails and other hastily chosen detention centers, in many cases for weeks and even months, without the traditional rights to bond and counsel. Almost all but the most radical newspapers and public officials applauded this evidence that the government intended to protect American institutions. The ordinarily liberal New York *World* took the opportunity to support drastic new sedition legislation to assist Palmer's defensive actions against Bolshevism, which it termed "a tyrannizer of mankind." Eventually, largely because of the intervention of Louis F. Post, assistant secretary of labor temporarily in charge of deportation proceedings, only 556 of those arrested were found to be both aliens and members of proscribed radical organizations and were deported.

Almost every state and many cities demonstrated their determination to prevent revolution. Among the most flagrant violations of civil liberties committed during this period was the New York state legislature's expulsion of five members guilty of election on the Socialist Party ticket. During a three-month period in 1919, the state of Washington convicted eighty-six men simply for membership in the IWW. In California, where Communists, European immigrants, and even blacks were scarce, political leaders of both major parties met demands for patriotic action by issuing a joint declaration in September 1919. Among Japanese-Americans, they proclaimed, "loyalty was first to Japan and second, if at all, to America"; because Japanese emigrated to the United States largely in pursuance of their government's plan to populate the Pacific coast of America, they constituted an economic, political, and social peril. A year later, California voters approved by a three-to-one margin an initiative measure forbidding the purchase of land in California by Japanese-Americans and their agents.

Hundreds of thousands of southern blacks, fleeing the boll weevil, poverty, and the southern caste system enforced sometimes by lynch mobs, caused almost as much consternation in northern cities as did the Communists. Among the results was a system of residential, occupational, and educational segregation imposed almost everywhere. More dramatic consequences began in the summer of 1919, referred to by black spokesmen as the "red summer," not because of the radical activities that frightened so many white Americans but because of blood that flowed during the long and terrible race wars that raged in northern cities. Those tragedies left hundreds dead, thousands seriously injured, and property damage, mostly in black ghettos, amounting to millions of dollars. These events, and the rapid growth of the twentieth-century Ku Klux Klan, stimulated the development of Marcus Garvey's huge United Negro Improvement Association and other black nationalist organizations, which further distressed those who feared for the future of the established cultural order.

The postwar ferment left a legal heritage. The most notorious victims were Nicola Sacco and Bartolomeo Vanzetti, Italian immigrants

Ben Shahn (1909–1969), America's best known painter of subjects with "social significance," helped keep alive the myth of Sacco and Vanzetti's martyrdom with a series of twenty-three paintings completed in 1932. Much of Shahn's effectiveness can be traced to his experience as a photographer; many of his paintings, including this one, were his impressions of photographs.

with anarchist beliefs, arrested in Brockton, Massachusetts, during the height of the Red Scare for a payroll robbery and murder. After their conviction on conflicting evidence before a hostile judge in 1921, a higher court upheld the decision. The judge sentenced Sacco and Vanzetti to death, and the governor denied clemency on the advice of a "blue ribbon" investigation board. The two were executed on August 22, 1927, despite pleas for mercy and justice from thousands of American lawyers and intellectuals and huge demonstrations before United States embassies throughout the world. Twenty people died in one of many huge Sacco-Vanzetti riots in Paris; Benito Mussolini protested angrily from Rome; and the two were supported by massive action throughout Latin America, including a general strike and a boycott of American products in Montevideo, Uruguay. The electrocution of Sacco and Vanzetti, and Vanzetti's alleged proud eloquence in the face of extinction ("If it had not been for this thing . . . I might have died unmarked, unknown, a failure. . . . Never in our life can we hope to do such work for tolerance, for justice, for man's understanding of man, as we do now by an accident"), provided radicals with the most potent symbols of bourgeois injustice since the Dreyfus case. For the first time, the United States was assigned the role of the most flagrant, or at least the best publicized, oppressor of individuals holding unpopular beliefs.

National and state legislation added to the Red Scare's legal residue. Several measures made it easier to deport radical aliens. A draconic sedition act, which would have made almost any criticism of the national government a serious crime, failed to pass in 1919–1920 only because Congressmen vied too long for the honor of sponsoring the final bill. The crucial session at the apex of the Red Scare adjourned before legislators could agree on whose measure to support.

The states, however, more than compensated for federal negligence in defending the country against the menace of revolution. Twenty-nine state red flag laws passed in 1919 alone. All provided for heavy penalties of up to twenty years in prison and $20,000 fines for flying a red flag, pennant, or any other sign identifiable with revolution. Almost every state adopted such acts during 1919–1920, but only one, Massachusetts, repealed its red flag law during the 1920's, and then only after someone tried to apply it to the crimson banner of Harvard. In California, six female camp counselors and a handyman were arrested as late as 1929 for conspiring to raise a small red flag at a summer camp for working-class children. The handyman, in ill health because he had been gassed in action during World War I, hanged himself in prison before trial rather than undergo further confinement. The female counselors were convicted and sentenced to terms ranging from six months to ten years in San Quentin state penitentiary, their sentences varying according to the degree of their contact with the offensive cloth. Thirty-two states had passed criminal syndicalist laws between 1917 and 1920 forbidding membership in organizations advocating revolution. Used mostly against the IWW, these measures, on top of the wartime federal persecution, practically destroyed the potential power of this militant collection of unions. The Supreme Court, most notably in two cases

decided in 1919—*Schenck* v. *U.S.* and *Abrams* v. *U.S.*—upheld restraints on free speech and freedom of the press when they posed
what the majority opinions termed "clear and present danger" or
encouraged "bad tendencies."

The immigration restriction bills of 1921 and 1924 constituted the
most consequential legislative result of the frenzied postwar nativism. They made a mockery of the Statue of Liberty with its inscription welcoming the poor and oppressed. These were the very people
that most native-born Protestant Americans and their representatives wished to bar from the country. The 1924 act passed despite
objections from the immigrant groups it insulted with implications
of their inferiority, and also despite opposition from the major industrial firms and business organizations, which objected that low-
cost labor already was in short supply. However, labor unions, most
of which represented skilled craftsmen, were delighted with the new
law. It reduced immigration—and thereby the entry of potential

Immigration of Mexicans into the United States, 1910-1930[a]

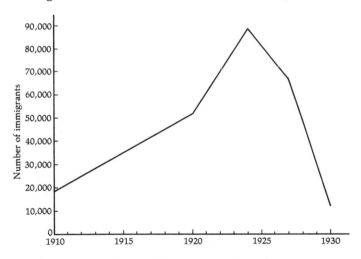

Source: *Historical Statistics of the United States, Colonial Times to 1957.*

[a]The apparent decrease in migration from Mexico after 1924—when immigration from
Europe was severely limited by quotas to which Mexicans were not subject—is traceable
to two factors. The Border Patrol was expanded greatly and given additional powers in
1924 and 1925. And the Mexican government, anxious to retain labor needed to rebuild
Mexico after the Revolution, raised visa and head tax rates in 1925. Mexican government
statistics for re-entries indicate that illegal immigration into the United States rose sharply
between 1925 and 1929.

competitors—from strife-torn and impoverished Eastern and Southern Europe to negligible quantities. The law all but excluded Orientals, while setting generous quotas for the "Nordics" of Northwestern Europe. Among the unforeseen consequences of the immigration acts, however, was an accelerated movement of southern blacks and then Mexicans and Puerto Ricans—exempt from the new quotas—into large northern and western cities to take over menial jobs that formerly had gone to European and Oriental immigrants. Such migrations eventually stirred nativistic responses as severe as those responsible for barring continuation of the "new immigration."

The Guardians

Americans anxious to halt assaults on the foundations of their traditional culture—attacks on accepted values, challenges from "inferior" social groups, and economic and political experimentation—won a resounding victory in the national election of 1920. Middle-class northern progressives, especially former followers of Theodore Roosevelt, deserted in large numbers the party castigated a generation earlier as the home of "Rum, Romanism, and Rebellion," depriving the Democrats of the precarious majority that had coalesced temporarily behind Woodrow Wilson in 1916. Even before the election, however, the Wilson administration, in a series of crucial postwar decisions concerning labor, radicals, natural resources, railroads, shipping, and anti-trust law enforcement, came down primarily on the side of conservative business interests, against the pleas of farm and consumer organizations and advanced progressives. Some historians argue that Wilson's illness (he suffered a severe stroke on October 2, 1919) and the exigencies created by the war and the postwar Red Scare account for the wilting of Wilsonian Progressivism. Others observe that Wilsonian democracy flowered primarily for the benefit of the middle class and that the administration's domestic policies were predictable when positions on vital issues polarized after the war. The Wilsonians do not seem to have surrendered willingly the votes of 100 percent Americans. In any case, the conservative policies of the Republican administration during the 1920's, and to a lesser extent Hoover's after 1929, frequently continued those adopted in 1919–1920 by Wilson and his Cabinet.

Nationwide strikes in the steel, coal, and railroad industries failed mostly because of force exercised by the Wilson administration. In

Election of 1920

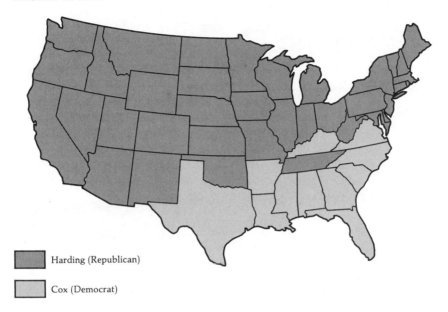

Harding (Republican)

Cox (Democrat)

each case, the strike occurred largely because wages failed to rise appreciably while prices soared. During the steel strike in the autumn of 1919, workers asking for wages commensurate with those in other industries, abolition of twenty-four-hour shifts, and institution of a six-day, forty-eight-hour week were labeled Communists and anarchists by industry leaders. Public support was requested by the industry in the name of "Americanism." Spokesmen for the steel companies fortuitously could point to the chief American Federation of Labor (AFL) organizer of their workers, William Z. Foster, a former syndicalist and later a Communist Party leader, as an example of the radicalism they were combating. Foster, temporarily convinced that Communist objectives in other countries could be obtained through established unions in the more industrially advanced United States, actually seems to have opposed stimulation of class antagonism during the walkout. When Attorney General Palmer ordered a Justice Department investigation, it failed to substantiate industry charges. Nevertheless, Palmer did not deny publicly that radical forces caused the strike until it was almost broken. Meanwhile federal troops under General Leonard Wood had been

Leaders of the nation's great steel companies charged in 1919 that striking workers in their industry—such as these men in Chicago—were dangerous Communists engaged in a gigantic plot against the country. Reasonably impartial investigations later demonstrated that these accusations were unfounded . . . but by then the strike had been defeated.

dispatched by the administration to help black strikebreakers imported from the South reopen the giant United States Steel plant in Gary, Indiana.

No one denied that wages of coal miners also had fallen behind rising living costs during the war. Mine workers district representatives put extreme pressure on their new union president, John L. Lewis, to obtain more satisfactory contracts. When mine operators refused to cooperate, the executive board of the United Mine Workers (UMW) voted to strike. Again the administration bowed to widespread public apprehension and business charges of radical influence and intervened to halt the walkout. With the assent of every Cabinet member except Secretary of Labor William B. Wilson, a former UMW official, Palmer obtained a temporary injunction forbidding union officials to participate in the strike. President Wilson,

Palmer announced, approved this action, although because of the President's illness no one but Palmer and perhaps Mrs. Wilson discussed the situation with him.

When union officials continued to defy the government, Palmer used wartime legislation—still technically in effect because of disputes over the peace treaty—to obtain a decisive injunction ordering the UMW to recall the original strike order. Swift and angry labor response followed. Even the usually placid AFL President Samuel Gompers, infuriated by the renewal of injunctions against labor's right to its most powerful weapon, the strike, called the executive committee of the AFL into special session. That ordinarily cautious body immediately agreed to take any action necessary in support of the coal strike. After the meeting, Gompers denounced the injunctions as a move "so autocratic as to stagger the human mind," and he urged all workers to aid the embattled miners. Nevertheless, faced with criminal charges for contempt and the threat that government power in various forms would be used against strikers, Lewis and William Green, secretary-treasurer of the UMW, capitulated. As Green explained to an angry convention of coal miner representatives, public opinion against the strikers had been inflamed to "such an acute stage that if they had taken the local officers and the leaders of your organization out against some stone wall and shot them to death the public would have applauded and said 'Amen.'"

The third nationwide labor disturbance of the period, a railroad workers' walkout that paralyzed the country's transportation system, occurred spontaneously in the spring of 1920. Talks between railroad brotherhoods and government negotiators broke down, and union members ignored threats from both sets of officials when they left their jobs. Promptly denounced as dangerous radicals by the government (which still controlled the rails) and by railroad executives, as well as by union officers, strike leaders demanded such revolutionary changes as overtime pay for Sunday and holiday work, twenty-minute lunch periods, and a minimum wage of $150 a month. Once more, Attorney General Palmer took responsibility for ending the crisis. First he charged that strike leaders were members of the IWW, provided with funds by Russian Communists. Then he informed a Cabinet meeting that his Bureau of Investigation had conclusive proof that the walkout was part of a worldwide Communist plan. Palmer's agents arrested strikers for interfering with the interstate movement of mail. Leaders were jailed for violation of the same wartime statutes used against the coal miners. Meanwhile, President Wilson, though trying to impress observers with the extent of his physical and mental recovery, gave no indication that he disapproved of the Justice Department's policies. Again a major strike failed, but labor leaders served notice that they did not entirely lack power to retaliate by publicly marking Palmer for political extinction.

Returning servicemen also suffered from the government's conservative stance. Rather than resort to comprehensive planning—including federal rehabilitation and industrial training, educational subsidies, and employment centers—the Wilson administration adopted a policy of releasing troops immediately into an economy already suffering from a high rate of unemployment. For a brief period, the United States Employment Service, established to help allocate manpower during the war, found jobs for released servicemen. However, the agency practically ceased this function when the President passively allowed Congress in January 1919 to reduce its appropriation by 80 percent.

The administration left farmers too to fend for themselves. Wartime government policies encouraged production of huge crops and livestock supplies. These started glutting peacetime markets late in 1919, sending prices into a terrible two-year decline, which accelerated beginning in the spring of 1920 when European production recovered. Prices of most major farm commodities dropped 50 percent or more in a little over a year. Again the Wilson administration resisted all suggestions that it help alleviate some of the suffering for which it was at least partially responsible.

Many large business interests, on the other hand, received the kind of sympathetic treatment that usually is associated with the Republican administrations of the 1920's. Sole rights to German-owned chemical patents, for example—some applied for as late as 1917—were turned over to an independent, nonprofit Chemical Foundation in the spring of 1919. This organization licensed American producers to use the patents at very low cost, effectively reducing foreign—especially German—competition, thus raising profits of United States chemical firms. During the war, the government had operated the nation's railroads, shipping and shipbuilding industries, and telegraph and telephone facilities. Despite improvement and expansion of these facilities with taxpayers' funds, all but the railroads simply were returned to their private owners soon after the war ended.

Leaders of labor and farm organizations demanded continued

government control of the railroads and received strong support from Congressmen, several Cabinet members, and other administration officials. During the war, the railroads had degenerated until the government took charge, integrated, and rehabilitated them. The railroad brotherhoods recommended nationalization, common in Europe, in the belief that a more efficient railroad system would provide higher wages and safer working conditions. President Wilson, however, dismissed plans for continued government direction of the lines and limited debate on the issue by informing Congress late in December 1919 that the roads would be returned to private management on March 1, 1920, under whatever terms legislators established by that date. Congress passed the Esch-Cummins Transportation Act a day before the President's deadline, handing the lines over to their former owners. This measure profited those who held securities of the few strong railroads but deprived most of the financially unstable American railroad system of benefits obtained during the period of wartime centralized control. Within ten years the weakest lines approached bankruptcy.

Businessmen who raised prices in the immediate postwar period were subjected only to mild pressure, in contrast to federal power exercised directly and even brutally against workers seeking higher wages. The Wilson administration allowed the Food Administration and War Industries Board to lapse, leaving the government without means of forcing compliance with its attempts to prevent runaway prices.

Furthermore, under Palmer, the Justice Department tended increasingly to settle anti-trust actions by consent decrees (compromise agreements between the government and the defendant), despite allegations that terms more favorable to consumers could have been won in court. In the most notorious case, the five largest meat packers agreed to divest themselves of related businesses—like stockyards and livestock information services—but no provision was made for enforcement, which remained negligible until years later when New Deal attorneys reopened the case.

Congressman Fiorello La Guardia of New York complained when the packers were permitted to control distribution of surplus canned meat originally purchased for use by the armed forces. Despite a severe meat shortage and consequent rising prices, they successfully prevented sale of the excess meat in the United States. The head of the Bureau of Surplus Supplies assured congressional interrogators that he expected to find a market for his agency's huge supplies of canned roast beef, corned beef, and bacon in Rumania, Bosnia, or Herzegovina. La Guardia, who had served in Italy during the war and earlier had represented the U.S. government in Hungary and acted as consul in Fiume, replied that the Balkan countries were not a promising market for the bureau's surplus: Hardly anyone in the area ate canned meat, and he doubted whether a can opener could be found in Rumania. He expressed surprise that the bacon had not been offered to synagogues.

There is some justification, however, for the view that the Republican national leadership of the 1920's moved even further than the Wilson regime in its final years toward a position as conservative defender of the traditional business civilization. The most spectacular, though not the most conclusive, evidence in support of this opinion was the corruption uncovered within the Harding administration. Even in the lax atmosphere of the 1920's, it seems remarkable that so many high government officials were guilty of illegal dealings with businessmen. Perhaps it is even more remarkable that so many went to prison for their crimes. Others escaped jail by suicide or because juries could not agree about their guilt. Charles R. Forbes, head of the Veterans Bureau under Harding, received a sentence of two years in Leavenworth penitentiary and a heavy fine for fraud and bribery connected with bureau contracts. Thomas W. Miller, alien property custodian, who accepted bribes for supporting false claims to valuable corporate property under his jurisdiction, was convicted and sent to prison. Jesse Smith, an intimate of Attorney General Harry M. Daugherty, accepted and distributed payoffs from large-scale violators of the prohibition and tax laws. He also dealt in pardons for convicted criminals. When the President ordered him back to Ohio, Smith committed suicide in the apartment he shared with the attorney general, but not before he had made many large deposits in the bank account he shared with Daugherty. Forbes' general counsel and chief confidant, Charles Cramer, also killed himself rather than face an imminent investigation. Attorney General Daugherty avoided trial until 1927, when he was charged with sharing bribes paid to Smith. Daugherty refused to testify, implying that he was protecting Harding's reputation, and with the chief witness against him dead, grand juries twice failed by narrow margins to indict him.

Secretary of the Interior Albert B. Fall was less fortunate. After leasing the valuable Teapot Dome oil field to Harry F. Sinclair and the Elk Hills oil field to Edward L. Doheny—in both cases by private negotiation—Fall, whose personal financial situation had been precarious, began to show evidence of astonishing prosperity. He paid his delinquent tax bills and other debts, restocked his New Mexico cattle ranch, and expanded his landholdings, producing a large number of hundred-dollar bills to complete the last transaction. Eventually, largely because of a persevering Senate committee investigation headed by Thomas J. Walsh of Montana, Fall was arrested and tried for conspiracy to defraud the government. Sentenced to the federal penitentiary in Santa Fe, New Mexico, Fall became the only Cabinet member in United States history to serve a jail term. Sinclair and Doheny, whose payments of hundreds of thousands of dollars were responsible for Fall's conviction, nevertheless were acquitted when brought to trial for conspiracy and bribery in 1926. Sinclair, however, spent a term in prison for attempting to tamper with the jury in his case. The two men earned profits of at least $8 million as a result of contracts negotiated with Fall. Most newspaper editors directed indignation at those who exposed the corruption in high places rather than at the thieves and probable thieves.

The well-publicized characteristics of the three Republican Presidents—including small-town Protestant origins in each case—gave confidence to those who feared that political as well as cultural dominance in the United States was slipping away from the Protestant middle class. These men stood as symbols of business-as-usual, though more efficient and profitable than ever. Even Herbert Hoover, though he distrusted Wall Street speculators, made businessmen feel that their interests rated high among his concerns. His activities on behalf of trade associations while he was secretary of commerce skirted so close to encouragement of illegal business combinations that he received a stiff warning from Attorney General Daugherty.

Harding had always felt sympathetic toward businessmen's needs. As a newspaper proprietor in Marion, Ohio, he had enjoyed warm friendships with local merchants. While President, Harding essentially turned formulation of the nation's financial policies over to Andrew Mellon, president of the Mellon National Bank and largest shareholder in the Aluminum Corporation of America. Washington insiders knew Harding as a man inordinately fond of poker games, whiskey, women other than his wife, and stock market speculations. He could easily have been a leading character in Sinclair Lewis' *Babbitt*, the most effective satire of American bourgeois culture.

Warren G. Harding had his front porch remodeled to resemble the porch from which William McKinley had successfully campaigned for the presidency in 1896 and 1900. Other Republican leaders agreed that Harding's best strategy after his nomination in 1920 was to receive delegations of loyal party members at his home in Marion, Ohio. "Keep Warren at home," the shrewd Senator from Pennsylvania, Boies Penrose, allegedly ordered. "Don't let him make any speeches. If he goes on a tour, somebody's sure to ask him questions, and Warren's just the sort of damn fool that'll try to answer them." Except for a few brief trips, Harding spoke from his porch, as he is doing here.

It was Calvin Coolidge, however, who declared during his annual message to Congress in January 1924 that "the business of America is business." Raised in Vermont, one of two states that gave its electoral votes to Taft in 1912 and to Alfred M. Landon in 1936, Coolidge fairly exuded the old American virtues so neglected in the large impersonal cities — honesty, sobriety, thrift, stability, and a Victorian primness. If he projected the reassuring impression of a

President who would not interfere with the proper activities of Americans, it was largely because he sincerely believed that the best president governed least. Coolidge's passive role was further ensured by his metabolic need for ten hours of sleep every night plus a lengthy nap following lunch. After 6 P.M. he seemed to run down, avoided work until he dined, and then retired for the night promptly at 10 P.M. After reading the newspapers every morning, giving some attention to his family, and attending to the President's customary ceremonial functions, Coolidge had very little time to interfere with Congress, business, or much of anything else. It has been estimated that he averaged four hours of work a day while he was chief executive.

Hoover, the most intelligent and creative of the three Republican chief executives, was the only really successful business executive among them. In fact, no other true representative of American business ever has occupied the White House. Born on an Iowa farm and raised in rural Oregon, Hoover made a fortune as an engineering consultant and mine operator on several continents. Service during the war as chairman of the Relief Commission for Belgium and as United States food administrator won Hoover wide popular acclaim for effective, fair administration. A member of the new breed of American corporation leaders who placed great faith in planning for efficiency and growth, Hoover, even more than his predecessors, seemed to represent the triumph of America's magnificent business civilization.

Among the policies promulgated by the Republican administrations, none cheered businessmen more than the tax revisions initiated by Secretary of the Treasury Andrew Mellon. Referred to as the only Treasury secretary served by three Presidents, the multimillionaire Mellon persistently urged the dismantling of the Wilsonian tax structure. During the 1920's, despite resistance from the progressive rear guard in Congress, he gradually approached achievement of his objectives. Arguing that low taxes on high incomes encouraged investment, which created new jobs, Mellon reduced surtaxes on the highest income bracket from 65 percent in 1920 to 20 percent in 1928. Inheritance tax levels fell by about the same proportion, and the federal gift tax disappeared altogether, as did the excess profits tax. Mellon's leniency in interpreting tax exemptions and earnings further reduced the law's effect on those with wealth or high earnings. The high tax rates and stringent regulation had been formulated as wartime legislation; nevertheless, progressives argued unsuccessfully

"Silent Cal" Coolidge, campaigning for the presidency in 1924, agreed to don a Sioux headdress at a western celebration. Coolidge was not an enthusiastic campaigner.

that the laws should be retained because the money would benefit the country most if used for federal programs like a proposed expansion of the Muscle Shoals hydroelectric project in the Tennessee Valley, for farm price supports, and for aid to the unemployed.

Meanwhile, taxes on imports that competed with American products were raised in the Fordney-McCumber Tariff Act of 1922, which imposed the highest duties in United States history. Through the Chemical Foundation and nearly prohibitive tariffs on most drugs and chemicals, the American people subsidized the development of a new giant industry. They also subsidized high profits for many established industries. The Republican Presidents did use a clause in the new tariff law enabling them to adjust tariff rates as foreign and domestic costs changed; more than 85 percent of these revisions were upward.

Farmers benefited only slightly from the new Republican tariff because the United States imported little that competed with products of the nation's farms, except sugar, flour, potatoes, and certain grades of wool. Crop prices dropped severely after World War I, bringing widespread economic distress to farm operators. However, when leaders of the farm bloc in Congress, led by Republicans Charles L. McNary in the Senate and Gilbert N. Haugen in the House, introduced measures for federal price supports, which would have provided protection for farmers comparable in effect to that already given industrial firms, their bills were killed by a succession of presidential vetoes. Farm representatives did obtain legislation that regulated speculation in grain futures, expanded agricultural credit, and tightened federal control over stockyards, but these acts did little to alleviate farmers' basic economic problems.

Workers also suffered because of a firm conviction within the Republican administrations that whatever helped business also benefited the country—and the Grand Old Party. Attorney General Daugherty surpassed his predecessor Palmer in denouncing radical influence as a cause of strikes and of attempts to organize workers. Judges appointed during the 1920's almost invariably handed down decisions unfavorable to labor. Federal regulatory boards that dealt with business and labor were stocked with former business executives and corporation lawyers. One of these agencies, the Railway Labor Board, ordered a reduction in wages that sent four hundred thousand railroad workers out on strike. When the walkout continued, despite the board's instructions that the railroads establish company unions to break the strike, Daugherty obtained a restraining order that forced union officials to call their men back to work. The court order forbade almost every conceivable activity in support of the strike—including telephone calls.

Soon after the war, American business firms and associations began an attack upon labor organizations. They concentrated on establishing the "open shop," in which theoretically all employees enjoyed freedom to join or reject any unions seeking to represent them. In practice this concept, which employer organizations persisted in calling the "American plan," usually meant that trade union members either were fired or denied employment, except for members of compliant company-run unions. Assaulted both by government policies and by this concerted, well-financed effort by industry to establish open shops wherever possible, unions suffered severe losses. Membership fell from over 5 million in 1920 to less than 3.5 million in 1929, even though the industrial work force increased in size. Every important attempt at organization failed during the decade. Even several once-powerful unions—the United Mine Workers, the Textile Workers, and the International Ladies Garment Workers—declined.

Herbert Hoover's efforts to encourage cooperation among business firms and between business and government, especially while he served as secretary of commerce from 1921 to 1929, generally are regarded as the most creative national policies of the decade. However, outside of some innovations in finding and analyzing foreign markets for American products, Hoover only put into practice wishes long expressed by industrial and financial leaders, as well as by political spokesmen for Theodore Roosevelt's New Nationalism. In most cases, these ideas already had been implemented during World War I by the War Industries Board and by the Commerce Department under Secretary William C. Redfield. During the decades before World War I, executives of America's largest corporations increasingly converted to the belief that production and prices should be determined cooperatively by industry representatives, rather than by what they considered inefficient competition. Wartime experience with such cooperation under government sponsorship and leadership won further support for this idea within both industry and government. Although direct government leadership or coordinated business activity ended temporarily with the demise of the War Industries Board, Franklin Roosevelt later adopted such a system as part of his program to revive business during the early New Deal. Many of those who had helped operate the board were chosen by Roosevelt to direct agencies established to relieve business and agriculture.

Hoover, a member of Wilson's team of wartime administrators, drew on that experience as well as on the ideas circulating among efficiency-minded business executives of his generation. Under Hoover, the Commerce Department engaged in an effective campaign to encourage cooperation among businessmen, without quite acting as a central planning agency. However, some of the department's literature and certain conferences held under its auspices barely avoided such supervision. Hoover and his assistants were constrained not by attachments to doctrines of laissez-faire but by warnings from the attorney general's office against taking part in possible conspiracies to violate the anti-trust laws and perhaps by their sense of the impropriety of such blatant interference in the economy. Hoover's business career as well as his speeches and writing won him a politically valuable reputation as a champion of individual economic activity—a reputation he did not care to lose in a suit implicating the Commerce Department in conspiracies to restrain competition illegally.

Under Hoover's direction, his department employed professional economists to prepare reports for the information of businessmen. The duties of the Bureau of Standards expanded until it became the recognized arbiter in many industries, not only for quality of product but also for efficiency in design and manufacture. The net result of these Commerce Department activities was increasing standardization within industries, both of product and of price. That objective was furthered by Hoover's attempts to invigorate trade associations, the official organizations of firms within a given industry. In most large industries, trade associations needed little stimulation. Through regular meetings and weekly issues of the industry's trade journal or journals, essential information about matters like technological improvements, legislation affecting members, the state of sales, inventories, and prices, and the development of new markets was disseminated throughout the industry. Under Hoover's active direction, the Commerce Department urged trade associations to institute uniform cost accounting procedures among members, thus reducing price competition. The department also arranged conferences for representatives from industries that had not already formed trade associations, usually because the companies involved were too small or scattered or too fiercely competitive. Department officials addressed these meetings, explaining the advantages of cooperation and the techniques for establishing effective organizations. Hundreds of new trade associations were established during the 1920's, most of them with Commerce Department encouragement and guidance.

The most visible defender of the dominant American culture, however, was not the federal government but the self-styled Invisible

Empire, the Ku Klux Klan. The Klan, which probably enrolled 4 million or 5 million white Protestant native-born male members during the 1920's, was described by an able contemporary journalist who studied the organization as "the most vigorous, active, and effective force in American life, outside business." Almost all the fears that gripped the susceptible among white Protestant Americans after World War I—anxiety about national racial mongrelization, moral degeneration, and above all, the dread (as old as the country's history) of a Catholic conspiracy—were distilled in the Klan's ideology.

The Klan of the 1920's originated in 1915 when William J. Simmons of Atlanta, a visionary who devoted much of his adult life to planning a resurgence of the post–Civil War hooded order, decided that the time was ripe. While he awaited the propitious moment, Simmons had eked out a living as a circuit rider for the Southern Methodist Episcopal Church and as an insurance salesman for the fraternal order Woodsmen of the World. He arranged his call for the formation of a new Klan to coincide with the appearance in Atlanta of the tremendously popular motion picture *The Birth of a Nation,* which depicted heroic Klansmen redeeming the South and its precious cultural heritage from the clutches of Radical Reconstruction. At the picture's climax, brave hooded warriors saved the fairest of southern women from ravage by a semi-barbaric black. As *The Birth of a Nation,* which already had been shown to wildly enthusiastic crowds in other southern cities, was about to open in Atlanta, Simmons gathered sixteen disciples on a nearby mountain. Before an American flag and a burning cross, all swore allegiance to the twentieth-century version of the Ku Klux Klan. Simmons took the title Imperial Wizard, or supreme leader.

Until the crisis of 1919–1920, the new order remained small, usually impoverished, and almost entirely southern. Even in Atlanta, a commentator doubted that the Klan could match the membership or influence of the Jewish organization B'nai B'rith. In the spring of 1920, however, two clever public relations experts, Edward Young Clarke and Mrs. Elizabeth Tyler, decided that the anxieties that produced the Red Scare, the race riots, prohibition, and the powerful movements for Americanization and immigration restriction could be exploited by the Klan. Simmons, an evangelist who was not averse to capitalistic success, agreed to turn recruitment over to Clarke and Tyler in exchange for a percentage of the proceeds.

The promoters quickly discovered that the largest potential source

Induction ceremonies of Ku Klux Klan chapters, such as this one held near Brunswick, Maryland, on June 28, 1922, sometimes attracted tens of thousands of spectators to watch thousands of Klansmen accept hundreds of new members. Many of these events resulted in bloody riots when meetings were attacked by armed opponents of the Klan.

of Klan dues lay not in the southern strongholds of Confederate and anti-black sentiment but in the growing towns and cities of the Midwest and Southwest. In places like Youngstown, Helena, Indianapolis, Muncie, Hammond, San Antonio, Shreveport, Oklahoma City, Santa Barbara, and Anaheim, citizens thronged to pay the $10 initiation fee, of which $4 went to the kleagle, or chapter organizer, $2.50 to Clarke and Tyler, $2 to Simmons, and $1.50 to the local grand goblin, or chapter head. Further payments of about $6 were obtained from members for the white cotton regalia supplied by the promoters, and an additional monthly tribute was extracted in the form of dues. An overabundance of fraternal orders was available to those who merely sought companionship or secret ritual, and many orders also proclaimed patriotic objectives; thus the Klan must have offered a powerful and unique cluster of inducements to people for whom the $16 for a card and some linen was frequently about half a week's salary.

The two hundred or more kleagles—professional Klan organizers—operated under instruction from the shrewd Atlanta sales managers to discover outstanding grievances of potential members immediately upon entering an area. Newspaper editors, clergymen, and small businessmen were considered prime sources of such marketing data. Then kleagles called meetings in local churches or in halls of other Christian organizations, arranged for advertisements, announcements, and interviews in local newspapers, all designed to exploit the fears and prejudices previously uncovered. Imperial Wizard Simmons, who seems to have assumed originally that blacks—supposedly mad for race amalgamation—would once again be the chief targets of Klan activity, adroitly changed his mind when the dues began rolling into Atlanta from the North and West. He announced in 1920: "Any real man, any native-born white American citizen, who is not affiliated with any foreign institution [that is, not a Catholic] and who loves his country and his flag may become a member of the Ku Klux Klan, whether he lives north, south, east, or west." Of course, he had to have a minimum of $10, preferably $16, available immediately.

Throughout the nation, happy kleagles discovered a deep well of fear of Catholics, Jews, blacks, and recent immigrants. They also found white Protestants worried about the erosion of moral standards and angry about widespread lawlessness, especially connected with violations of the prohibition laws. Frequently moral laxity was associated with urban ethnic minorities. Established government institutions seemed incapable of handling these elements. At first the Klan tended to resort to its predecessor's tradition of vigilante justice—beating and branding bootleggers, prostitutes, "uppity" blacks, drunks, wife beaters, and unmarried lovers—but adverse publicity, a congressional investigation, and unexpectedly strong counterattacks by the order's intended victims soon inhibited such action.

After the Klan practically abandoned its secret violence, kleagles enjoyed an even warmer welcome when they began organizing an area's "real Americans" for moral and political battle against threats to their civilization. One of the most effective pieces of Klan recruiting literature read: "Every criminal, every gambler, every thug, every libertine, every girl ruiner, every home wrecker, every wife beater, every dope peddler, every moonshiner, every white slaver, every Rome-controlled newspaper, every black spider—is fighting the Klan. Think it over, which side are you on?"

Local chapters took action against what they considered indecent motion pictures and books, attempting to remove them from circulation. This work was considered just as important as political efforts to destroy parochial school systems, to force Bible reading and end the teaching of evolution in classrooms, to enforce prohibition, and to defeat Catholic and Jewish candidates for public office. The Klan, then, became the primary organized defender of white Anglo-Saxon Victorian culture, which in practice included the continued supremacy of the white Protestant male. Although members of all social and economic classes joined the Klan, in the most cosmopolitan cities upper-class citizens who shared most of the Klan's values usually found other organizations more suitable — the National Civic Federation, the American Loyalty League, and the Sons of the American Revolution, for example. Workers throughout the country — especially in mining and steel manufacturing centers — divided bitterly after Klan chapters formed in their communities.

First in the great cities and then in large sections of the country as a whole, however, the hooded Invisible Empire discovered that the time had passed when an organization devoted to the supremacy of the old verities and the traditional cultural leadership could operate both successfully and safely. Because Klan members were concentrated so heavily in certain northern and western areas, the order won considerable political power in at least eight states — Indiana, Illinois, Ohio, Missouri, Arkansas, Oklahoma, Texas, and Oregon — and in large sections of about ten others. Even this political influence, though, proved ephemeral, lasting no longer than a few years at most. In some respects, the whole movement for 100 percent Americanism was an anachronism in the post–World War I era; the Klan, like those who still boasted that the sun never set on the British Empire, depended on a widespread but nevertheless nearly insane delusion that this was still the world of William McKinley and the young Rudyard Kipling. By the 1920's, realists ranging from Jan Smuts in South Africa and André Malraux in France, to Woodrow Wilson and Marcus Garvey in the United States, understood that the phrase "white man's burden" meant little more than hatreds already incurred — and higher taxes. Books like Lothrop Stoddard's *The Rising Tide of Color* (1920) and Madison Grant's *The Passing of the Great Race* (1916), written to arouse "Nordics" to defensive action, achieved that purpose, but they also revealed deep and perhaps insoluble reasons for long-term despair on the part of those who shared the authors' values.

Except during brief earlier periods of nativistic frenzy, Americans generally had expected — or at least accepted — a high degree of diversity within the population. The natural superiority of the democratic environment was relied upon to bring the foreigners to adopt the ways of their new country. Even if foreign-born parents were unable to make a full transition, the public schools were expected to help their children complete the transformation to reliable citizenship.

However, some of the most fearful patriotic groups, watching the strange "new immigrants" from Southern and Eastern Europe, lost faith in the institutions that had guaranteed an acceptable degree of ethnic unity in the past. Starting in the 1890's, the Daughters and the Sons of the American Revolution and a few kindred associations established informal programs of patriotic education to indoctrinate adult immigrants with the language and mores approved by the patriots. When World War I revealed a shocking absence of loyalty to the nation's military effort, especially among Americans of Irish, German, and Austrian ancestry, the general easy acceptance of diversity all but disappeared. Even moderate citizens who did not expect a postwar revolution supported vastly expanded and cleverly organized Americanization programs aimed at adults and children of foreign stock. Though less notorious than the Klan, this gigantic postwar Americanization effort perhaps protected dominant American values more effectively than did the Invisible Empire.

The 1920 census showed that 14 million of the 105 million United States inhabitants were foreign-born. Of these, 1.6 million had migrated from Italy, 1.4 million from Russia, and more than 1.1 million from Poland alone from 1890 to 1920. An even larger number were American-born children of these immigrants or members of ethnic groups that had migrated earlier, like the German and Irish, most of whom, the 100 percenters believed, clearly required further training. Throughout the 1920's, Americanizers debated how individuals with these origins, as well as blacks and even white citizens with an affinity for foreign ideologies, could be exposed to the reculturation programs.

Leaders of the Americanization project accepted Theodore Roosevelt's 1915 speech on that subject as the finest expression of their objectives. Roosevelt had declared that Americanism demanded: (1) a common language, (2) undivided loyalty from a citizenry "which acknowledges no flag except the flag of the United States and which emphatically repudiates all duality of intention or national loyalty," and (3) an understanding on the part of each of the nation's inhabitants "that unless he in good faith performs his duties he is not entitled to any rights at all." It should be noted that Roosevelt's dictums were not directed exclusively at the foreign-born. A few years earlier, E. P. Cubberly, one of the nation's foremost authorities on education, had outlined similar objectives: "Our task is to break up their groups or settlements, to assimilate and amalgamate these people as a part of our American race, to implant in their children the Anglo-Saxon conception of righteousness, law and order, and popular governmer.t, and to awaken in them reverence for our democratic institutions and for those things in our natural life which we as a people hold to be of abiding worth." The principles advocated by Roosevelt and Cubberly, and repeated by thousands of popular writers and speakers, became the basis of the postwar Americanization movement.

Behaviorist psychology provided the guiding principles for most of the Americanization programs. Edward L. Thorndike of Teachers College, Columbia University, probably exerted the greatest influence with advice that paraphrased the guiding principle of the great Russian physiologist Ivan Pavlov: "Reward desirable connections and make undesirable connections produce discomfort." Manuals for leaders of Americanization "classes" stressed the need for teachers to "know the past life of the student, his point of view, his interests, and his purposes." Modern psychology as well as history confirmed: "A state of mind cannot be compelled. To obtain the attitude we desire toward American society, American institutions, and the American heritage, we are obliged to win a real respect and sympathy, a genuine admiration, and upon this basis establish those habits and traits which are necessary for the making of a good American." This particular advice was written for schoolteachers and intended for implementation in the regular school curriculum.

Those who planned the massive reculturation programs applied modern public relations and sales techniques as well as recently systematized psychological concepts. Participants were recruited by a combination of advertising in newspapers, including foreign language papers, church publications, and moving picture theaters, notices given to schoolchildren or placed in pay envelopes and bankbooks, and personal pressure from clergymen, foremen, employers, and teachers, who not only spoke to their pupils but also visited their homes. Most of the Americanization "classes," or study groups, met in public schools during evening hours and weekends.

United Press International

An enthusiastic beginning for the "great experiment" — prohibition. These virtuous citizens are dumping beer into Lake Michigan.

Churches, labor organizations, business corporations, settlement and community houses, courts, and other public institutions also provided meeting places and sponsored "courses."

Americanization programs failed to achieve the measure of success expected for them, largely because of the democratic institutions they purported to protect. These permitted varieties of resistance to their expected passive reluctance to change. Ethnic minorities counter-attacked with Americanization courses of their own, actively encouraging the retention of "foreign" languages, traditions, and values. Catholic organizations opposed the original Americanization program almost as effectively as they did the Klan, and Jewish organizations enjoyed only slightly less success. Certain Protestant groups, including many Lutherans, contributed to the opposition.

One of the great religious revivals in American history took place during the 1920's. Throughout the country, the most popular evangelist preacher was Billy Sunday,
a former professional baseball player and a reformed alcoholic. Sunday preached
patriotism and abstinence from alcohol, as well as faith in the Lord.

Religious fundamentalists and prohibitionists also defended
elements of the dominant culture during the 1920's. Instituted to a
large degree as part of the white middle-class progressive crusade to
purify America, prohibition's continuation became an obsessive
goal of its proponents during the 1920's. Wherever possible prohibitionists attempted to obtain strict enforcement, but the more realistic

among them soon realized the impossibility of achieving this ideal. The contest over enforcement and retention of prohibition did not take place simply between urban and rural Americans (or their descendants), as some historians have implied, although a tendency toward such a division existed. Prohibition's most bitter opponents tended to live in large cities because the groups that constituted the adamant wets — the foreign-born, their children, Irish Catholics, and cosmopolitan intellectuals — formed a high proportion of the population in most of those cities. However, rural German-Americans also despised anti-liquor laws, though white Protestant city dwellers had voted to make large sections of major cities dry even before passage of the Eighteenth Amendment. In urban areas where white evangelical Protestants predominated, prohibition remained a sacred cause, and the Klan's enormous popularity in those districts can be attributed in part to its role as an instrument of liquor law enforcement. In the South, especially, cultural fears directed at blacks helped mobilize support for prohibition, but in some southern rural counties hard-drinking whites violated the Volstead Act, which implemented the prohibition amendment, with the same impunity as New Yorkers.

Although it is impossible to ascertain how many millions of Americans literally believed the doctrines espoused by the fundamentalist church organizations to which they belonged, there is abundant evidence that millions did believe fervently. Among the fundamentals to which they gave allegiance were the infallibility of the Bible, the imminence of the second coming, and the reality of heavenly salvation. Most prohibitionists and most Klansmen belonged to the fundamentalist religious sects whose members thronged to hear evangelical preachers like former big-league baseball player Billy Sunday. These sermons and the response they elicited indicate that most of the audiences shared the conservative moral and racial principles of the Klan. Sunday in particular welcomed Klan participation in some of his meetings, at which he denounced bootleggers and jazz along with evolutionists.

Urban newspapers and magazines throughout Europe as well as in the United States interpreted the trial of John Scopes in Dayton, Tennessee, as a triumph for the concept of biological evolution, modernized religion, and scientific knowledge in general. They exaggerated the extent of this triumph, although the publicity accompanying the trial revealed to fundamentalists the extent to which their opponents controlled the nation's newspapers and

A friendly moment is enjoyed by the chief antagonists—Clarence Darrow and William Jennings Bryan—at the trial of John Scopes, arrested for violating a Tennessee law forbidding the teaching of evolution. At the trial held in Dayton, Tennessee, in July 1925, Scopes was convicted; but Darrow made a fool of Bryan when the latter appeared as a witness for the state.

magazines and the depth of the scorn with which they were regarded by "enlightened" Americans.

Scopes, charged in 1925 with violating Tennessee legislation that forbade the teaching of "any theory that denies the story of the divine creation of man as taught in the Bible," was defended by a team of distinguished attorneys led by Clarence Darrow. William Jennings Bryan directed the prosecution. More than a hundred newspaper reporters and movie cameramen found themselves in the midst of one of the decade's most dramatic confrontations when Bryan agreed to take the witness stand as the prosecution's chief expert on the Bible. After Darrow completed his cross-examination, the former secretary of state and three-time Democratic candidate for President stood revealed before readers of the urban press as an opponent of modern science who believed literally that God had created Eve from Adam's rib, that the tale of Jonah and the whale was true, and that the Tower of Babel was responsible for humanity's diversity of languages. Yet the cities as well as rural areas of the

United States contained millions of fundamentalists who agreed completely with Bryan. The Great Commoner may have reached the height of his national popularity just as he was pilloried by the agnostics and religious modernists who wrote for urban periodicals. The Tennessee jury that listened to the arguments of Bryan and Darrow convicted Scopes of teaching the proscribed ideas in his high school classroom. No state repealed its anti-evolution laws as a result of the Tennessee trial; Mississippi's remained in force until 1970.

The Undermining of Victorian Culture

The desperate measures taken by those like Klan members who sought to protect the dominant American culture during the 1920's slowed, though they failed to halt, the serious threats to the culture's integrity. At a deep level, these threats were products of the same long-term technological changes responsible earlier for crucial aspects of Victorian culture itself. Few Americans grasped the inextricable relationship between the economic development they admired inordinately and the new social conditions this development brought in its wake. One group contained a higher proportion of those affected by the attacks on conventional ways and values than any other—white Protestant males, the group that had dominated the society since its origin.

Of the series of changes, potentially most damaging to the traditional culture was the movement of women out of the home. It would be nearly impossible to exaggerate the importance to most old-stock Americans as well as to immigrant groups of a stable, nurturing home, revolving around a woman who played the crucial role as wife and mother. At the war's end, more than 8 million women were serving in the labor force, and despite the temporary nature of most of those wartime jobs, over 10.5 million women worked outside their homes a decade later, constituting about one-fifth of the labor force. Meanwhile, the number of women who completed secondary education and entered college continued to rise swiftly, as did the proportion who continued on to professional careers. In 1870, fewer than 100,000 worked in the professions; in 1930 more than 1 million women occupied such positions according to the census definition. Almost half of all those enumerated by the 1930 census as professional or semi-professional workers were women, most of them teachers or nurses. Moreover, some 20,000 or about 15 percent of all college and university teachers were women, as were 48 percent of all musicians and music teachers, 38 percent of all artists and art teachers, and 27 percent of all authors, editors, and reporters.

The number of females over ten years of age doubled between 1900 and 1930, but the number of working women grew much more rapidly, concentrating in certain sectors of the economy. During that period the total of women engaged in personal services increased by only about one-half, and rapid growth in jobs for waitresses, hairdressers, and workers in cleaning establishments accounted for most of that rise. Manufacturing employed only about 27 percent more women in 1930 than in 1900. At the same time, the number of women in clerical positions multiplied tenfold and became the largest single category of female workers. By 1930, over 775,140 women served as stenographers and typists compared to 86,000 in 1900, and in addition 1.2 million females were employed as bookkeepers, cashiers, and as various kinds of office clerks. Another 700,000 worked as salesgirls in department stores. In 1870, 13.1 percent of females ten years of age and over were gainfully employed; in 1900, 18.8 percent; and in 1930—despite a decline in child labor—22 percent.

With the seemingly inexorable movement of women into the commercial world, once the preserve of men, came a concomitant insistence on the part of highly vocal feminist leaders that sexual roles be adjusted to reflect new technological conditions and that as a first step the law should guarantee equal pay and opportunities for female employees. The primary organ for such demands was the National Woman's Party, guided by Alice Paul, an intense (some said fanatical) idealist, completely devoted to the cause of women's rights. In the hope that women would use their voting privileges to insist on feminist objectives, she and the party she led had played a controversial but important role in forcing female suffrage upon reluctant or indifferent legislators. By 1923, the party had embarked on an ambitious nationwide campaign for equal rights legislation concentrating first on the states and then on obtaining an amendment to the Constitution. However, the goals of the National Woman's Party received practically no support from working-class females and little from middle-class married women, who tended to believe fervently that women's primary duty was to maintain the sanctity of the home and their families' well-being.

A number of careful studies by professional sociologists conducted during the peak of prosperity in the 1920's showed that few married

These girls are being arrested in 1922 for endangering Chicago's public morality by wearing the newest creations in bathing suits. Within a few years such suits were a common sight on the nation's beaches. Defenders of traditional morality nevertheless remained outraged.

women worked unless they had to, which meant that hardly any middle-class married women worked outside their homes. An analysis of a large sample of married working women in Philadelphia indicated that 89 percent worked solely because of economic necessity and that a high proportion of the rest were workers' wives anxious for middle-class luxuries, including a college education for their children. Robert and Helen Lynd discovered only one working wife among Middletown's business class, and she was considered rather odd by her friends. In the large cities, however, daughters in professional and business-class families often found employment before marriage. As early as 1920, one-third of all women in cities larger than 100,000 worked; less than 20 percent in smaller cities and towns were gainfully employed. At the same time almost half of the nation's black women worked outside their homes.

When Miss Paul, Alva Belmont, Crystal Eastman, and other radical feminists urged women to revolt for equality, they were politely ignored by the great majority of American females and were subjected to hostile criticism by the rest. The middle-class members of the National Women Suffrage Association disbanded their organization after obtaining the vote in 1920, and those who joined its successor, the League of Women Voters, seldom adopted a political stance except on issues affecting the protection of children. Working-class women and social workers tended to regard the National Woman's Party as the enemy, attempting to undo a generation of protective legislation written to defend members of their sex against the long working day and back-breaking labor to which men were assigned. Even when a wide range of women agreed on an issue — such as the welfare of pregnant women and infants — females were so divided on the method of implementation that the Sheppard-Towner Act embodying these objectives was allowed to lapse by Congress in 1929. Many middle-class women considered such legislation a step toward Socialism, if not Bolshevism, much as their husbands viewed suggestions for government programs offering unemployment compensation or subsidized medical care for the aged.

Women's role as a spiritual — almost angelic — repository within the home of society's highest moral values was severely impaired, nevertheless. The presence of alternative life styles, even for middle-class wives, and the example of large numbers of successful business and professional women considerably modified women's self-image. Most of the generation that came of age during the 1920's in urban areas practically discarded some crucial aspects of the old ideal. Home and children remained the goal, but meanwhile the vast majority apparently enjoyed many of what had been the pleasurable prerogatives of men: Drinking, smoking, and a degree of sexual experimentation seem to have become the rule. The proportion of women chaste at marriage decreased sharply during the 1920's according to several sociological and medical investigations, although about half still claimed to have maintained their virginity. Offices and speakeasies filled with women in short skirts did not bode well for the future of female purity, that cherished Victorian ideal, nor did the behavior of characters in the most popular movies of the decade — for example, the sex kittens portrayed by Clara Bow and the sophisticated lovers played by Gloria Swanson. Nudity and near-nudity on the screen finally evoked self-censorship, starting cautiously in 1922, but blatant love affairs, including a fair number

Clara Bow, the movies' "sex kitten" of the 1920's, seldom played the part of a virtuous young lady. But she did get married in the motion picture from which this photograph was taken: *Her Wedding Night.*

involving adultery, continued to be displayed. Ku Klux Klan journals repeatedly assaulted the decade's movies as part of a Jewish plot to undermine traditional values, although they acknowledged that Jews produced the movies because the American public, especially its younger members, paid to see them.

Despite the terrible poverty and the bigotry suffered by black, Mexican, Oriental, Jewish, and Irish inhabitants of the urban slums, the alleged dreariness of life for unemancipated women, and the disgust with American civilization expressed by some of the nation's leading artists and intellectuals, no group complained more piteously or continually about the conditions under which they were obliged to live than the 100 percent Americans. The Klan's objections represented those of millions of other white Protestant citizens. Not only was the home under siege but cultural enemies occupied the great cities: "From the murky waters of Europe, Asia, and Africa that flood our beautiful land from shore to shore," the Klan's grand dragon for the state of Colorado lamented to a convention of his fellow grand dragons in 1923, "a band of patriots have raised their heads and have seen that this country of ours is not a nation of Americans, but a conglomerate mass of aliens—aliens in thought and act. . . . The reason there is a Klan in America today is to make America safe for Americans." The unfortunate "band of patriots," it turned out, could not even make America safe for the Klan.

As the Klan spread from Atlanta, carried by the tide of nativism that swelled after World War I, violence attributable to it seemed almost to disappear, while the order itself mushroomed in size. No one has yet suggested that Klan members suddenly lost their taste for beating defenseless sinners. Klan leaders did, nevertheless, become aware that an unseemly image could damage recruiting and reduce income. Denying that members of their organization engaged in criminal activities, they accused other Americans of settling private grudges behind protective white hoods.

The emergence of a peaceful, law-abiding Klan, however, may be more closely connected to the discovery that potential victims were far from defenseless. Klan spokesmen left no doubt that their organization's chief target was the Catholic Church. Staid Catholic organizations replied with warnings that should have been taken very seriously. The editor of *The Catholic World*, published by the Paulist Fathers, addressed himself to the Klan early in 1923: "Catholics will not be driven to retaliation. But they may be driven to self-defense, even to the extent of bloodshed." This message was echoed by the National Catholic Welfare Council's *Bulletin:* "In this struggle for the supremacy of law and order over lawlessness and despotism, no quarter should be given those self-appointed patriots who distort and disgrace our Americanism and whose weapons are darkness, the mask, violence, intimidation and mob rule." Unfortunately for these "patriots," the paths out of poverty and powerlessness taken by many Catholics had led into politics and into municipal police forces with their traditional ties to local politicians.

Black organizations, led by the National Association for the Advancement of Colored People, were infuriated when their demands that the federal government take action against the Invisible Empire went unheeded. The most influential black radical order, the African Blood Brotherhood, proclaimed in its journal: "The nation-wide mobilization under the Christian cross and the Stars and Stripes of cracker America is plainly an act of war . . . , war of the cracker element of the white race against the whole Negro race." Privately, blacks prepared for race war. Especially in the North, black Americans mobilized to resist another round of intimidation by an organization bearing the hated name Ku Klux Klan. When the Klan elected a whole city government, including a mayor, in Youngstown, Ohio, the nation's second greatest steel-producing city, enormous numbers of identical oblong boxes began arriving at the Youngstown post office from a New York City mail order house. A suspicious postmaster, observing that all the packages were addressed to men in the city's black district, found an excuse to open a few. Inside each he found a German-made automatic pistol. He immediately warned city administrators that his office already had delivered more than a thousand of the packages. After publication of this information, no incidents were recorded of actions by the Klan against blacks in Youngstown.

Public statments about the Klan by Jewish spokesmen were restrained, though uniformly hostile. Private letters and editorials in the Yiddish press indicated a horror at the organization's growth and announced intention of combating the alleged Hebrew menace. During this period, Jews were reading daily of pogroms in Poland and Russia and an attempted Nazi revolution in Germany. Repeated references to the lynching of Leo Frank, which had taken place in Georgia in 1915 after a vicious anti-Semitic campaign, and the pronouncements of Klansmen and other advocates of immigration restriction served as reminders that violent crusades against Jews had occurred west of the Danube and could break out even in the United States. Jewish leaders throughout the country quietly cooperated in countermeasures against the hooded order.

Another enemy not to be underestimated emerged when the powerful New Jersey Klan, with more members per inhabitant than in any other state, publicly declared war on the bootleggers who had been making good use of the state's long, sparsely inhabited shoreline. *The New York Times* reported on January 15, 1924, that New Jersey bootleggers and rumrunners had met and formed defense councils, which openly announced their intention to "shoot to kill" anyone attempting to interfere with their trade without proper warrants. In Chicago also a strong Klan—the largest in any American city in 1922—heard Imperial Kleagle Edward Young Clarke announce at a mass meeting that the branch would soon be large enough to help enforce prohibition laws and otherwise reduce the alarming local crime rate. When a conglomeration of the city's civic associations started its own investigation of Chicago crime under the leadership of a prominent Protestant clergyman, however, the minister's body—riddled with bullets—was found in Cicero, not far from Al Capone's headquarters. Like almost every other gangland killing in Chicago during the 1920's, the murder remained unsolved, and after Clarke returned to the safety of Atlanta the Klan discreetly left law enforcement in Chicago to the authorized agencies, which were overwhelmed by the task.

Klansmen were correct, however, when they associated violation of the "noble experiment," prohibition, with the ethnic and religious minorities they already were committed to combating. In the cities dominated politically by these groups, enforcement simply was impossible. Politicians and policemen in those urban areas—themselves frequently members of ethnic groups that regarded drinking as anything but sinful, or at least as a delightful and indispensable sin—soon ceased enforcing the prohibition laws except under special circumstances. Among the results was a thriving and well-organized industry that supplied liquor to the defiant cities. Because this traffic was illegal, the industry soon fell into the hands of professional criminals, of whom Capone was only the most notorious. These gangsters expanded their operations into other commercial ventures, some of them legal, with high profits from the production and distribution of alcoholic beverages.

Irish (or German, Italian, or Polish) Catholic policemen could hardly be expected to act at the Klan's request, in any case, and Irish-Americans controlled the police force in many of America's largest cities. As a result, Klan members often were deprived of needed protection, and when police did intervene between the Klan and its enemies, they tended to treat the klansmen as criminals. As a consequence, the organization was obliged to enter politics in many areas primarily to gain control of law enforcement agencies.

The Klan's position was pitiful in cities like New York, Boston, Pittsburgh, Chicago, and San Francisco. In New York, the world's wealthiest city, the center of America's high culture, the home of more than a million white Protestant citizens, Klan members dared not meet in public. No sooner did kleagles enter the city in 1922 than Mayor John F. Hylan telegraphed his police commissioner: "I desire you to treat this group of racial and religious haters as you would the Reds and bomb throwers. Drive them out of our city." Klan spokesmen interpreted this order as an invitation to legal murder of their order's members. Actually, New York's police were comparatively generous—though rough—in their treatment of Communists, anarchists, and klansmen. However, the police refused to protect Klan marchers in outlying districts of the city against irate members of ethnic "minorities." During the largest such march, in Queens county on Memorial Day in 1927, most of those injured and almost all those arrested for initiating the inevitable riot were klansmen.

In Carnegie, Pennsylvania, outside Pittsburgh, a gigantic Klan rally addressed by Imperial Wizard Hiram Wesley Evans culminated in a parade that ended at a bridge defended by thousands of armed citizens. When a hail of rocks and bottles failed to halt the marchers, shotguns were fired, klansmen fell dead, scores of others were wounded, and Klan activity in that area also became a private matter. Even more typical than assaults on hooded marchers were night-riding attacks by motorized columns, which sent bricks and rocks through store windows and homes of known or suspected Klan members in many towns. Klan meeting places throughout the country were blown up by bombs or burned down by fires. In one three-week period late in 1924, the huge, new Ku Klux Klan Hall in Fort Worth, Texas, and Klan offices in San Antonio, Texas, and Terre Haute and Jeffersonville, Indiana, were completely destroyed.

Klan meetings often were interrupted in highly impolite fashion. In Perth Amboy, New Jersey, a Jewish resident organized a mob of six thousand people who besieged a meeting of the knights of the Invisible Empire, who had received a city permit from a Protestant mayor to induct new members at the local Odd Fellows Hall. Klan members refused orders from the Hebrew leader to disperse. During the ensuing riot police arrived and threw tear-gas bombs, not at the mob trying to enter the hall but through windows at the klansmen. Firemen arrived to help the police and loosed streams of water through the meeting hall. Police promised to lead the klansmen to safety and then turned them loose in the midst of the mob. Again, most of those arrested for initiating the riot were klansmen.

The most common style of attack on the Klan took place at the melodramatic outdoor initiation ceremonies. Typically, just as the darkness was broken by the lighting of an enormous fiery cross before thousands of proud klansmen and their awed friends and relatives, shotguns would be fired at the white-robed targets from every direction. A mob estimated by klansmen at fifteen hundred opened fire just as a huge wooden cross was ignited at New Castle, Delaware, for example. The klansmen, fleeing with more than fifty wounded, were ambushed again as they drove through a nearby black settlement where they were showered with rocks and bottles.

An editorial in the chief Klan periodical, the *Fiery Cross of Indiana,* complained in July 1923 of "the reign of terror, launched to intimidate Protestants." A year later, the paper charged that "the list of the outrages against Klansmen is so long that it would take weeks to compile even an incomplete list." Why, the editors asked poignantly, did not anyone "ever read about halls of Knights of Columbus being destroyed mysteriously"?

As an attempt to protect the traditional culture, the Klan experienced only partial success. The organization's greatest effect on American history may have been its role in mobilizing the opposition of huge minority ethnic and religious groups. Although no one knows whether the Klan garnered more support from Democratic or from Republican Party members, leaders in northern states who entered politics almost invariably ran for office as Republicans. Opposition coalesced within the Democratic Party. From California to West Virginia, Catholics, Jews, and blacks cooperated to oppose Klan-backed candidates for office.

When the Chicago City Council appointed a committee to recommend legislation concerning the Klan, the body chose a "representative" committee consisting of a Catholic, a Jew, and a black. Their report led to swift action by the council, which voted 56 to 2 for a measure forbidding city employees to join the Klan; offenders were to be fired immediately. The report, turned over to the Illinois legislature, resulted in a state law prohibiting the wearing of masks in public. New York's state legislature, responsive to pressure by Catholics and Jews and prodded by Governor Al Smith, passed a series of acts applying solely to the Klan. These obliged the order to file with the state its membership lists and all resolutions passed by New York chapters. The membership lists were to be made available to the public. One law forbade the Klan to take part in political activity; another denied it use of the mails for any purpose other than the sending of literature to members. Boston's Mayor James Michael Curley denounced the Klan as anti-Christian and un-American; he declared Klan meetings illegal in Boston, even in private homes. Not only Boston's Catholic and Jewish organizations but most members of the City Council expressed approval of this action.

Unintentionally, the Klan brought together Irish, Italian, Polish, and German Catholics; Russian and German Jews; middle-class blacks and black laborers newly arrived from the South. Thus it played a role—powerfully reinforced by the Depression and the New Deal—in forming the political coalition that would fatally erode the national political power of the heretofore dominant white Protestants.

A huge black migration to northern and western cities during the first three decades of the twentieth century threatened the established social, political, and economic order; mobilization of these blacks was another ominous development for the future of "Nordic" supremacy in the great northern cities. By 1920, 2 million of the nation's 11 million blacks lived in the North. At least 600,000 migrated from the South during the 1920's, and tens of thousands more came from the Caribbean islands. In New York City at least one-fourth of the migrants originated in the West Indies. Meanwhile, the movement of southern blacks from rural to urban areas within the South continued.

The societal dislocation that gave rise to the movement for 100 percent Americanism affected black Americans also. The shift from the rural and even the urban South to densely populated northern cities—most of them with inhospitable weather as well as people—left even reasonably adaptable migrants somewhat disoriented, despite the obvious compensations. Not only were familiar, loved friends and relatives left behind, but so were most southern customs, games, landmarks, and to some extent language. Difficulties in adjustment, added to the well-publicized Klan activity and the race riots, made black Americans susceptible to movements to revivify their culture. The most successful black nationalist organizations incorporated strong religious components in their rhetoric and provided imposing titles for all members, becoming increasingly magnificent as one rose in rank. In these respects, the black movements resembled not only familiar black fraternal orders but the Klan as well.

The most powerful black nationalist organization ever established in the United States—Marcus Garvey's Universal Negro Improvement Association—was founded in 1914, a year before the modern Klan. Like the leading organization for 100 percent Americans, the UNIA failed to attract converts in large numbers until the "excitement" of 1919–1920. Garvey himself, born in the West Indies far from the horror stories of the post–Civil War Klan on which American blacks

Marcus Garvey, head of the Universal Negro Improvement Association, stands at the right in full military regalia.

were raised, viewed members of the Invisible Empire less contemptuously than he did those whom he regarded as hypocritical white integrationists. So long as the Klan kept out of black districts, he seemed willing to coexist with it. Most of Garvey's followers did not share his expressed tolerance of the Klan, and it was used against him with telling effect by his black enemies.

Garvey's organization, like Noble Drew Ali's Moorish-Americans, the Abyssinian movement, and the African Black Brotherhood, among others, urged separatism from whites and implicitly if not explicitly encouraged violent retaliation to white provocation. Garvey's speeches and essays in his newspaper *Negro World* repeatedly stressed the superiority of black men. A black skin, he declared, was a badge of honor not of shame. It served to prove membership in a race with a glorious past and a powerful future. "I am the equal of any white man," Garvey proclaimed. He warned that blacks never again would fight the white man's wars: "The first dying that is done by the black man in the future will be to make himself free." Huge meetings and parades by uniformed Garveyites during UNIA conventions rivaled the assemblages of Klan members in Indiana. These words and events thrilled blacks, especially those from the South, who had been trained never to think such thoughts, let alone express them publicly, and who never had witnessed such evidence of black power.

This is not to suggest, as some historians have, that Garvey's appeal was limited solely or even largely to recent migrants from the South—the "black peasantry" as one historian termed them. Garvey's capitalistic economic program, which included UNIA ownership of a shipping line and light industry, attracted budding capitalists among the black middle class. His suggestions that blacks in America would gain in political influence when Africans won independence also struck sympathetic chords within middle-class blacks and among the younger generation of black intellectuals and politicians.

Like each of the other potentially strong black nationalist movements, Garvey's was struck down by a combination of outside black opposition, internal dissension, government attacks on the leadership, and the untimely death, imprisonment, or exile of the leaders. Garvey went to jail for mail fraud in 1925. He was deported to Jamaica in 1927, leaving his movement a shambles of warring factions. But his fiery speeches, marching legions, and jammed convention halls should have warned Americans of the changes taking place in a world in which "Nordics"—as immigration restrictions were pleased to call them—were vastly outnumbered.

The vital intellectual foundations of the traditional culture meanwhile were being undermined by professional writers, artists, and scholars. Most of the influential literary intellectuals who took part in this assault were old-stock white Protestants. An equally successful attack emanated from the universities, aimed at traditional religious beliefs, concepts of racial superiority, and the conventional view of the United States as a fluid democracy. This intellectual rebellion was well under way before World War I, as Henry May has demonstrated amply in *The End of American Innocence*. During the 1920's, however, several new groups of societal critics joined the damaging chorus, helping to constitute the most formidable body of social criticism—and perhaps the most extraordinary era of aesthetic production—in American history.

Some of these influential postwar authors responded directly to their wartime combat experience; for others the war verified their disgust with American society and in some cases with Western civilization. These authors poured out such a formidable collection of novels, stories, essays, and poems that some commentators have accepted them as representative of the postwar rebellion, and the war, therefore, has sometimes been given an importance far out of proportion to its actual influence on the intellectual revolt in America. This is not to suggest that the war's effect was negligible. Shortly after the United States entered World War I, Randolph Bourne, foremost spokesman for the young radical intellectuals, warned with admirable prescience that if the fighting and attendant wartime repression of dissent continued very long, "the work, so blithely undertaken for the defense of democracy, will have crushed out the only genuinely precious thing in a nation, the hope and ardent idealism of its youth."

Bourne's prophecy proved accurate, certainly for dozens of the literary intellectuals and the section of the population for whom they spoke and for those they influenced. Although it is difficult to demonstrate that Ernest Hemingway, William Faulkner, or E. E. Cummings held any appreciable patriotic idealism before their wartime experience, their postwar mood of disillusionment is unmistakable, suggesting that the war at least exaggerated prewar tendencies. Hemingway's *A Farewell to Arms*, Faulkner's *Soldier's Pay*, and Cummings' *The Enormous Room* are moving indictments of the horrors Western civilization perpetrated on itself. John Dos

Passos' *Three Soldiers* and *1919* (part of his *U.S.A.* trilogy), Willa Cather's *One of Ours,* Lawrence Stallings' *Plumes* and his more famous play written with Maxwell Anderson, *What Price Glory,* also are bitter accounts of the victims the war left in its wake. It was impossible to read any part of this literature without sharing to some degree the authors' disgust with the war's consequences and with America's role as an accomplice in causing them.

In evaluating the effects of World War I in the United States, even on these authors, it should be noted that Willa Cather's occasionally naive but in some respects exceptionally perspicacious account of a "war lover" was written by a middle-aged woman who never witnessed a battle and whose protagonist greatly resembled the victims of the Middle West's stifling emotional atmosphere whom she had written about before. Faulkner never left North America during the war, although he obtained a taste of violence when he crashed a plane while celebrating receipt of his flight wings in the Canadian air force. Cummings reached France but before he could see action was interned in a French concentration camp because of his haughty replies to interrogation by a French officer. Even Hemingway's novels and stories continue a concern with violence and death evident in his prewar writing. The war, nevertheless, did provide a terrible shock as well as corroboration for those already inclined toward dissatisfaction with their civilization.

During the 1920's, prewar rebels against the dominant culture like Theodore Dreiser, Van Wyck Brooks, Max Eastman, Floyd Dell, Ellen Glasgow, T. S. Eliot, Ezra Pound, H. L. Mencken, and Zona Gale (Bourne, unfortunately, died in the influenza epidemic of 1918) wrote some of their finest work just as a great variety of younger writers joined the revolt.

The ferocious critics of the war continued to produce magnificent novels, stories, and plays. In 1919 Sherwood Anderson in *Winesburg, Ohio,* and Sinclair Lewis with *Main Street* opened the harshest phase of the intellectual assault on the American village. Lewis' *Babbitt, Arrowsmith, Dodsworth,* and *Elmer Gantry* provide a devastating, though curiously sympathetic, portrait of the lives of middle-class Americans. Dreiser's great novel, the sprawling *An American Tragedy,* published in 1927, added further dimensions to the critique of America's value system. It also helped stabilize Dreiser's income at close to $100,000 a year, indicating the size of the audience available to this large and entertaining group of rebels.

A generation of writers who reached maturity during and just after the war took up many of the same and related themes. F. Scott Fitzgerald described flapper civilization and dissected the habits and mores of the very rich, most successfully in *The Great Gatsby*. Ring Lardner wrote deadly satire about America's sports heroes. Most aspects of the nation's culture that the literary rebels despised — Philistine disrespect for artistic creation, puritanical opposition to individual freedom (especially sexual freedom), overemphasis on materialistic goals, and the pervasive racism — came under scrutiny in a series of superb plays by Eugene O'Neill. A group of cynical and literate critics with elegant writing styles, including Joseph Wood Krutch and Ludwig Lewisohn, joined Mencken, Brooks, and others whose reputations were secure before the war in chastising American culture more than they criticized American literature.

The primary objectives of this postwar generation of literary intellectuals, however, frequently were not social but aesthetic, although intimate connections existed between these goals. Novelists like Hemingway, Faulkner, and Fitzgerald, and poets like Cummings, Pound, Eliot, Robert Frost, and Robinson Jeffers — all critical of American culture — were more concerned with developing thoughts, images, and emotions truthfully than with the effect of their social commentary, although they hoped that one would strengthen the other.

The authors who produced this monumental body of American literature appear to have agreed almost unanimously (although not with equal fervor) with critic-essayist Harold Stearn's contention that "the most moving and pathetic fact in the social life of America today is emotional and aesthetic starvation." Yet novelists like Faulkner, poets like Cummings, biographers and critics like Brooks and Krutch, and painters like Georgia O'Keefe, John Marin, and Joseph Stella developed original, effective styles, satisfactorily close to their objectives. So did expatriates Hemingway, Pound, and Eliot, and even their work continued in directions set in the United States. Somehow this vulgar, materialistic society, hostile to the artist and intellectual, gave birth to a great artistic and intellectual community. Actually, aspects of American society that encouraged artistic and intellectual development were more powerful than these critics could acknowledge — or understand.

A sizable group of black authors also appeared during this period, at least ten or fifteen of whom demonstrated mature literary talent. W. E. B. Du Bois, who for decades had been the most prominent black intellectual, declared in 1920: "We have today all too few

writers. . . . A renaissance of American Negro literature is due."
As if in response to this call, and indeed partly because of Du Bois'
aid and encouragement, by the mid-1920's scores of black authors
were publishing poems, short stories, essays, and novels, many of
which displayed artistic excellence. Though at first these appeared
mostly in the NAACP's journal *Crisis,* edited by Du Bois, and in
Opportunity: A Journal of Negro Life, published by the Urban League
and edited by the social scientist Charles S. Johnson, magazines
and publishing houses with predominantly white audiences soon
discovered a widespread curiosity among readers about black life.
In 1925, Alain Locke, like Du Bois a Harvard Ph.D., edited what he
called "the first fruits of the Negro Renaissance." Locke's volume,
entitled *The New Negro: An Interpretation,* contained selections by
black authors from recent editions of *Harper's Magazine, The Atlantic
Monthly, Survey Graphic, Foreign Affairs,* and *The Liberator,* as well
as from books published during the previous few years by Alfred
A. Knopf, Boni and Liveright, and Harcourt, Brace. The shocks of
the postwar years, Locke wrote in his foreword, "are making by
subtle processes of internal reorganization, a race out of its own
disunited and apathetic elements. We have, as the heralding sign,
an unusual outburst of creative expression. There is a renewed race
spirit that consciously and proudly sets itself apart." Locke might
have added the congregation of hundreds of thousands of blacks
in northern urban enclaves and the creation of a sizable educated
black middle class as factors contributing to the burst of creativity.

The young writers represented in Locke's collection included
novelist and poet Jean Toomer, playwright Willis Richardson,
scholar-essayists E. Franklin Frazier, Walter White, James Weldon

Three literary giants of the 1920's: W. E. B. Du Bois, Ernest Hemingway, and F. Scott Fitzgerald.
Du Bois (top left) was for over fifty years the nation's most formidable black intellectual. He
ended his career a dedicated black nationalist, a Communist, and an expatriate in Africa.
Hemingway (top right), here displaying the reward for a day's shooting in Sun Valley, Idaho,
with his wife Martha Gelhorn, became a symbol of tough disillusionment, violence, and
virility. His spare, direct prose style exercised great influence over generations of writers in
Europe and the United States. Fitzgerald (bottom) is shown here with his wife Zelda
and daughter Scottie during a Christmas celebration in Paris. The subjects
of his stories and his own fast-paced life typified the jazz age and fed the imaginations
of Americans who seemed to be fascinated with the idle rich.

Johnson, Kelly Miller, W. A. Domingo, and Du Bois, and a group of serious poets, four of whom earned places among the period's distinguished writers of verse. In addition to Jean Toomer, whose esoteric style is reminiscent of Eliot and Pound, yet with its own peculiar mystical component, they included the angry but lyrical Claude McKay, Countee Cullen, highly sensitive to the nuances and subtle psychological effects of American racism, and the inimitable Langston Hughes, possessed of a rare sense of humor, as well as remarkable poetic and story-telling abilities.

Locke's collection, several others appearing soon afterward, and most of the other novels, plays, short stories, and critical essays published by black intellectuals during the 1920's shared several tendencies. Most obvious was the search for an individual identity as both a black and an American. Frequently Africa was used as a symbol of American blacks' rebirth (or birth) as a people with a separate cultural identity, and often beauty was identified with black women.

Despite some obvious affinities between this literary and artistic renaissance and the more militant, black nationalist movements started in Harlem at about the same time, most black intellectuals and artists showed little sympathy for the popular movements, and militant black organizations and journals expressed deep suspicion if not hostility toward the middle-class, college-educated intellectuals. The intellectuals and artists enjoyed an illustrious if not a large audience among whites. Mabel Dodge, who never felt quite as comfortable with blacks as she did with equally emotionally expressive American Indians, nevertheless tried to make them feel welcome in her Greenwich Village salon, the favorite meeting place of New York's liberated intellectuals. Carl Van Vechten, who per-

Louis Armstrong (top left) and Bessie Smith (top right) were virtual symbols of the jazz that poured from the South over the whole United States during the 1920's. Armstrong, like twentieth-century jazz itself, started playing trumpet in New Orleans bordellos and in street parades accompanying funerals, visiting dignitaries, etc. (bottom). Born in 1900, Armstrong by the late 1920's was the standard against which other trumpeters were measured. Bessie Smith held a comparable position as a blues singer with a voice like a magnificent musical instrument and with an inimitable style that has influenced several recent singers, especially Janis Joplin and Aretha Franklin. Smith died tragically in the South when she required immediate hospitalization and all hospitals in the area accepted white patients only.

Culver Pictures

Culver Pictures
Lee Friedlander

haps felt a bit more comfortable with his black friends than their true attitudes toward him warranted, brought New York's cultural leaders to Harlem, where they became acquainted with some aspects of black life, as well as with black writers, artists, and musicians.

Derived partially from West African musical forms, incubated in the bordellos and saloons of New Orleans, jazz moved north with the black migrations of the early twentieth century through the cities of the Mississippi Valley. During the 1920's, jazz surfaced in the bars and dance halls of Harlem and Chicago and soon proved to be the most vital influence in the history of American music. Its effects were diluted somewhat when white composers, arrangers, and band leaders, such as Paul Whiteman and George M. Cohan, demonstrated that jazz could be expressed more profitably for white audiences in a softened, semi-symphonic style, with sentimental lyrics written in a stilted language that blacks seldom heard except on phonograph records. Nevertheless, the driving, syncopated rhythms and lusty but melancholy blues that had emerged from New Orleans survived, especially among blacks, but with considerable support from white audiences and musicians like Bix Beiderbecke and Jack Teagarten. Black jazz probably exercised a more powerful and lasting effect on American civilization than any other element in the renaissance.

The vogue of the New Negro turned out to be more fragile after 1929 than most of those involved had suspected. Langston Hughes, almost as suspicious as Du Bois of the apparently promising intellectual and artistic racial integration—though he made the best of the delightful situation while it lasted—later remarked caustically: "Some Harlemites . . . thought the race problem had been solved through Art. They were sure the New Negro would lead a new life from then on in green pastures of tolerance created by Countee Cullen, Ethel Waters, Claude McKay, Duke Ellington, Bojangles [Robinson] and Alain Locke. I don't know what made any Negroes think that—except that they were mostly intellectuals doing the thinking. The ordinary Negroes hadn't heard of the Negro Renaissance. And if they had, it hadn't raised their wages any." The Harlem renaissance, nevertheless, stimulated racial consciousness among educated blacks and provided white intellectuals with incontrovertible proof of the tremendous abilities their society previously had repressed among American blacks.

Meanwhile, in American universities, another high culture was developing rapidly, one that may have been even more effective than the literary intellectuals in hastening the disintegration of many traditional ideas and values. Despite decades of challenge by Darwinians, conventional old-stock white Americans still tended to cherish beliefs in evangelical religion and in the symbolic if not the literal truth of the Bible. They believed also in the unquestionable intellectual and moral superiority of the white race and in the existence of a fluid American society that made possible nearly unlimited success for any intelligent hard-working white Protestant and perhaps for any other industrious white man as well. As late as 1919–1920, influential social scientists subscribed to the idea of intrinsic white supremacy, a concept supported by the results of "scientifically" prepared and administered army intelligence tests. By the late 1920's, however, it was nearly impossible to spend four years at a major American university or to read the most important books published during the decade by American scholars and retain an unshaken belief in those former verities.

The destruction of these traditional convictions was led by anthropologists, but sociologists, psychologists, historians, and physical and biological scientists played important roles. Anthropologists at this time had at their disposal a fairly well developed theory of culture, which they used as their chief weapon against established myths. Starting with a relativistic view of cultures, they discovered case after case of supposedly primitive societies, which they joyfully presented as superior in various respects to American middle-class civilization. Most of these investigations owed their inspiration to Franz Boas, senior anthropologist at Columbia University, who directed the doctoral research of the majority of the finest young anthropologists during the first decades of the twentieth century.

Boas himself led a study that measured bodily characteristics, especially head forms, of almost 18,000 immigrants and their children. The wide changes he found between generations—descendants of immigrants tended progressively to resemble the rest of the American population—threw doubt on the concept of stable racial types. He later used data from measurements of blacks' skulls and brain cavities to help disprove the myth that low scores by blacks on intelligence tests were due to smaller and therefore naturally inferior brains. In a series of books and articles, beginning with *The Mind of Primitive Man* in 1911, Boas attempted to demonstrate that environment rather than heredity usually played the major role in determining the ability and performance of ethnic groups. Not until the 1920's, however, did Boas' theories gain wide acceptance among social scientists.

Boas' most famous early students included Alfred Kroeber of

Berkeley and Edward Sapir of Chicago and Yale, who found much to admire among North American Indians and a great deal to criticize about the white culture that had intruded upon them. In his essay "Culture, Genuine and Spurious," published in 1924, Sapir expressed the thesis that distinguished the Boas school of cultural anthropology, although Sapir stated his value judgments more frankly than did his associates, who preferred to hide them behind an appearance of relativistic impartiality. The American Indian tribes whose cultural integrity had not been destroyed by white intrusion, Sapir declared, usually remained "inherently harmonious, balanced, self-satisfactory . . . , the expression of a richly varied and yet somehow unified and consistent attitude toward life." He compared these cultures favorably to American civilization, with its spiritually meaningless work for most of the population, its education that all too often bore no relationship to the rest of life, its fragmented activities without inherent intelligibility or interest. "Part of the time we are dray horses," Sapir concluded, "the rest of the time we are listless consumers of goods which have received no least impress of our personality. In other words, our spiritual selves go hungry, for the most part, pretty much all of the time." Sapir's harsh indictment, published in the *American Journal of Sociology,* resounded through the academic world.

Other students of Boas supported Sapir's views, among them Melville Herskovits, Margaret Mead, and Ruth Benedict. Herskovits, the first professional anthropologist to apply the culture concept to American blacks, found advanced civilizations in West Africa whose members exhibited some cultural characteristics that seemed to him similar to those of blacks in the United States. The African civilizations, Herskovits suggested, had been affected adversely and in some cases destroyed by contact with Europeans. In *The American Negro: A Study in Racial Crossing* (1928) and *The Anthropometry of the American Negro* (1930), Herskovits opened serious scholarly consideration of the biological and cultural characteristics of blacks in the United States. Although he tended at first to emphasize the acculturation of American blacks (he found, for example, that wives in Harlem worked only when the husband's income was inadequate), Herskovits increasingly stressed distinctive black cultural traits. By the time he wrote *The Myth of the Negro Past* in the 1930's, Herskovits was arguing that there was an Afro-American culture with identifiable African cultural survivals.

Margaret Mead traveled to the southern Pacific in the mid-1920's

Young anthropologist Margaret Mead plays with children on a visit to the Admiralty Islands in
the South Pacific in 1928. Mead was already famous for her study
of Samoan youngsters, who seemed to reach maturity with much less emotional storm
and more happiness than did American adolescents.

and returned to write *Coming of Age in Samoa*. The well-known crises
of adolescence in Western civilization, she demonstrated, were cul-
turally determined and were all but absent among the more permissive Samoans. In addition, she maintained, marriage in Samoa
seemed happier and more stable as a result of this more casual
adolescence.

In a series of articles published between 1923 and 1929, Ruth
Benedict developed variations on the theory of cultural configura-
tions advanced also by other students of Boas, and she began applying her theory to Indian cultures in the Southwest. A few years
later, she published *Patterns of Culture*, probably the most influential
book written by a social scientist during the interwar period. Her
sympathies clearly lay with the allegedly uncompetitive, nonma-
terialistic, expressive Zuni tribe of Pueblo Indians. She described

also the Kwakiutl of Vancouver Island, a people highly concerned with the accumulation of wealth that could be translated directly into the power to humiliate one's opponents. The obsessive concern of the Kwakiutl with goods and prestige, as Benedict described it, frequently seemed an intentional parody of some of Western civilization's less lovely characteristics. In a third culture, the Dobu of northwestern Melanesia, suspicion, treachery, and almost unrestricted competition were carried to an extreme that illustrated the terrible results when these tendencies—evident in American society—were encouraged rather than checked. Other anthropologists—among them Robert Lowie, Robert Redfield, Clyde Kluckhohn, Ralph Linton, Leslie Spier, Elsie Parsons, Irving Hallowell, and Leslie White—contributed to the near-complete triumph of the relativistic view of culture during the 1920's and to the consensus among social scientists that culture rather than biology determined most of what had formerly been referred to as hereditary racial characteristics.

Social scientists in every discipline soon applied the culture concept and the relativistic approach to race within their specialties. Inspired, encouraged, and partly directed by Boas, social psychologist Otto Klineberg began in 1923 to study the effect of migration to northern cities on the intelligence test scores of blacks. As in Boas' earlier head-form research, Klineberg found that scores varied in correspondence with length of residence. Second-generation black migrants in the North scored higher as a group than poor white southerners. Low scores by blacks on wartime intelligence tests, administered under army auspices, thus were discredited as evidence of inherent black inferiority. The wartime scores had been used for a decade as conclusive evidence of this inferiority by otherwise skeptical and fair-minded sociologists and psychologists.

A group of sociologists at the University of Chicago, strongly influenced by anthropological studies and, in the case of William Fielding Ogburn, directly through long association with Boas at Columbia, began to apply the culture concept to American communities. Relations between sociologists and the Chicago anthropologists Fay Cooper Cole, Ralph Linton, Robert Redfield, and Edward Sapir remained close during the period; indeed the two groups were not separated into two departments until 1924. Sociologists William I. Thomas and Florian Znaniecki, in *The Polish Peasant in Europe and America,* published in five volumes beginning in 1918, not only treated their subjects as members of a distinct culture but traced cultural disintegration as a consequence of migration and described conditions that seemed conducive to cultural reintegration. Not only social scientists but social workers were influenced by this account, which leading sociologists, acting as a committee of the Social Science Research Council, named in 1937 as the most significant work in American sociology.

Led by Robert Park with the approval of department head Albion Small, Chicago sociologists Ogburn, Thomas, Louis Wirth, Robert Faris, and Ernest Burgess directed anthropological studies of neighborhood communities and various social groups within Chicago. Even undergraduates were directed into these projects. Among the most important discoveries was that each succeeding immigrant group, as it poured into slum areas, experienced the same severe disorganization. As the groups proceeded to prosper and migrate from the worst slums, the symptoms of disorganization, which earlier investigators had accepted as evidence of racial deficiency, declined. Again, theories of innate racial inferiority were discredited.

Another group of sociologists explored the myths conventionally supposed to distinguish American political, economic, and social democracy, while studying the effects of industrialization and urbanization on Americans. Robert and Helen Lynd titled their study of Muncie, Indiana, *Middletown: A Study in American Culture.* "Nothing can be more enlightening," they declared in their introduction, "than to gain that degree of objectivity and perspective with which we view 'savage' peoples." Readers of the book could be pardoned if they concluded that the Lynds, like many of the cultural anthropologists, perceived more to admire in the culture of "savage" peoples. Behind a sincere attempt at objectivity in weighing evidence and reaching conclusions, the use of quantitative evidence whenever possible, and an empathy with Middletown's citizens made possible by their own youth in the Middle West, the Lynds clearly found life in a typical midwestern city during the mid-1920's just as intolerable for intelligent, sensitive people as did the most critical contemporary novelists. Like Lewis and Dreiser, however, the Lynds seemed to have found what they set out to describe. Life in Middletown *may* have been nearly intolerable for most inhabitants, but it certainly was for the visiting intelligentsia.

In almost every important area of life, the Lynds described a wide gulf between conventional beliefs and practice. Political democracy was almost dormant. An elite and its representatives dominated the town. Education served mainly as social conditioning. It also kept children of the poor off the streets and eventually provided sons of the business class with the certification necessary for college entrance. Social and economic mobility remained a dream for most of the poor and their children. A great majority of workers existed on the edge of subsistence and in constant fear of layoffs. Workers over forty lived with the certainty that permanent dismissal from skilled or semi-skilled jobs lay not far in the future as their speed, strength, and accuracy gradually decreased in comparison to the efforts of young competitors with lower salaries. Older workers could look forward, at best, to slipping gradually down the economic ladder to positions as unskilled laborers. Family life suffered among workers when wives and children found it necessary to leave home and school for work; it suffered also from differences in values and moral standards between generations. Greater cohesion existed in most aspects of life among the business class, but they also suffered from the pressure for conformity and the spiritual poverty of this "typical" community. The Lynds quoted a "highly respected" citizen of "wide experience" who grew up in Middletown and reported upon his return from travel that the two things he felt most about the city were "its prejudice and superficiality. These people are all afraid of something," he asserted. "What is it?" Another substantial businessman who kept up an appearance of conformity and good humor confessed: "I'm just tired—tired in the legs—tired in the spirit. I know there are others as lonely as I am." Sinclair Lewis, Eugene O'Neill, Sherwood Anderson, or John Dos Passos could not have been more devastating.

The Lynds' book inspired hundreds of similar community studies during the next few decades, including the Lynds' return to Middletown during the Depression. In a project begun in 1930, W. Lloyd Warner found even greater distance between the myths of American life and the realities in a medium-sized New England city (Newburyport, Massachusetts, called Yankee City in the research reports). Warner, trained as an anthropologist at Berkeley and by the social anthropologist Edward Evans-Pritchard in Australia, also claimed to be applying insights obtained by anthropologists to an industrial community. His depiction of American life was even more dismal than that of the Lynds.

The literature produced during this period by social scientists so undermined traditional racial beliefs that when a representative sample was polled in 1929, only 4 percent of the social scientist respondents maintained that blacks were inherently inferior. Two decades later these new attitudes and the scholarly literature they inspired would help bring about a series of far-reaching social and legal changes—including the Supreme Court's 1954 decision on school segregation, which expressly cited the evidence collected by social scientists as a persuasive reason for the necessity of implementing new policies.

Physical and biological scientists contributed to the disorientation of those who shared conventional beliefs inherited from the nineteenth century. As evidence of biological evolution accumulated, added to archeological studies, belief in the literal truth of the Bible seemed increasingly incongruous. Scholars of religion, studying in theological seminaries attached to universities, attempted to modernize religion by reconciling belief with verifiable fact. Almost every Protestant denomination was torn with strife between modernists and fundamentalists, who counterattacked in defense of the traditional creed.

Modernists felt increasingly certain that religious dogma must be revised as new theories of genetics, relativity, and quantum mechanics implied that man could understand and interfere with the Creator's most magnificent achievements. Fundamentalists observed that influential laymen as well as clergymen who had attended secular colleges tended to side with the modernists. As the major universities were strengthened enormously during the 1920's by injections of money, expanded facilities, and the addition of talented scholars, they became almost impervious to demands that they retain their old function—conserving established doctrines. These universities trained—and indoctrinated—the teachers who staffed college faculties. Cognizant that an increasing proportion of college-age Americans were being exposed to skepticism in institutions of higher learning, the faithful became increasingly anxious that the society was headed for complete secularization—fears whose intensity were not fully appreciated by those who took this secularization for granted.

Fundamentalists frequently expressed awareness that the nation's intellectuals and the universities threatened the supremacy of traditional ideas and values. They pleaded pathetically for scholars to write texts defending the old beliefs. In desperation, Klan organizations attempted to purchase both Lanier University of Atlanta and Valparaiso University in Ohio in order to offer a 100 percent American education. "The radical tendencies of many of the finest educational institutions of the country," the Klan journal *The Dawn* pro-

High School Graduates, 1890–1930

	Number	As percentage of population aged 17 years
1890	43,731	3.5
1900	94,833	6.4
1910	156,429	8.8
1920	311,266	16.8
1930	666,904	29.0

Source: *Historical Statistics of the United States, Colonial Times to 1957.*

Institutions of Higher Education, 1890–1930

	Number of institutions	Number of faculty		Enrollment[a]	
		Male	Female	Undergraduate	Graduate
1890	998	12,704	3,105	154,000	2,000
1900	977	19,151	4,717	232,000	6,000
1910	951	29,132	7,348	346,000	9,000
1920	1,041	35,807	12,808	582,000	16,000
1930	1,409	60,017	22,369	1,054,000	47,000

Source: *Historical Statistics of the United States, Colonial Times to 1957.*
[a] Excluding junior college enrollment.

claimed in June 1923, "and the un-Godly atmosphere of others has created a necessity for a college such as the Ku Klux Klan college would necessarily be." These hopes were destroyed by the discovery that universities, although profitable in the terms that the Klan considered most valuable — production of ideas and influence over the values of the academic community, including students — were highly unprofitable financially, yet required huge initial capital expenditures.

Two major assaults were launched against the national political power of the entrenched social order. Both failed. The Republican candidates for President, Coolidge and Hoover, won by huge majorities in 1924 and 1928. Nevertheless, these attacks contributed to the realignment of political forces that became obvious during the 1930's.

By 1922, a number of political groups were moving toward creation of a third national party. Some of these apparently possessed formidable strength; others, potential influence over large segments of the electorate. The most encouraging sign of possible success for the developing enterprise emerged in Minnesota, where a Farmer-Labor Party, organized in 1918, shocked the established parties in 1922 and 1923 by electing both of Minnesota's United States Senators, a Congressman, twenty-four state senators, and forty-six state representatives. Almost immediately after electing its second United State Senator in a special election on June 6, 1923, the Minnesota organization announced that it planned to "form the nucleus of a national progressive party into which the producing classes and all progressives" could unite. The Minnesota Farmer-Labor Party itself demonstrated the possibilities of such a union, comprised as it was largely of members of the state farmers' Nonpartisan League and the Minnesota trade unions. The strong Wisconsin, North Dakota, and South Dakota Nonpartisan Leagues already had indicated their interest in a third party.

The Socialist Party also responded eagerly to the call for a new political union. Certainly in 1912, and to a lesser extent in 1920, the Socialists had appeared a promising alternative to the established parties. Despite an impressive vote for the imprisoned Socialist presidential candidate Eugene V. Debs in 1920, however, the Socialists were demoralized by wartime repression and divisions, conflict with the new Communist parties, and deficient leadership.

The railroad brotherhoods and the AFL at first withheld support from the developing political movement, partly because they hoped for the election of the leading Democratic candidate, William G. McAdoo, who had managed the nation's railroads during the war to the brotherhoods' satisfaction. However, when McAdoo acknowledged receipt of large legal fees from Edward L. Doheny, the notorious oil speculator deeply implicated in the Teapot Dome–Elk Hills scandal, both the brotherhoods and the AFL began to consider seriously the advisability of entering the expanding farmer-labor alliance. The brotherhoods, angered by the refusal of both major parties to adopt their plan for nationalization of the railroads in 1920, had organized a movement to back progressive candidates from both parties in 1922. With McAdoo apparently removed as a viable contestant, brotherhood leaders decided to support an alternative political organization.

Several other groups soon joined the developing coalition. Communists, reorganized into the Workers' Party, decided to participate in forming the new entry, although their full cooperation would require approval from the Communist International. Segments of the old Bull Moose Progressive movement, dissatisfied with the era's conservative politics, enthusiastically encouraged promotion of another progressive crusade. Members of disaffected minority ethnic groups, angered by political indignities like immigration restriction, prohibition, and the spreading power of the Klan, stood ready to join a party that expressed their views.

Radical movements in the United States present a long history of fatal internal dissension, invariably encouraged by conservatives. The 1924 Progressive campaign could serve as an archetype of this experience. Almost from the moment the movement was born its parents began throttling their offspring.

With a convention planned for June 17, 1924, the aged Samuel Gompers, who would die later in the year, called a meeting of labor leaders and political friends of labor. The AFL president, still doubtful about the efficacy of an independent labor political effort, despite the success of Britain's Labour Party, warned that Communist leaders William Z. Foster and Charles E. Ruthenberg exercised behind the scenes control over the developing third-party organization. The railroad brotherhood leaders also warned of Communist domination. Among those convinced that precautions had to be taken was Robert La Follette, the preferred candidate of every element in the movement. La Follette, in most respects an old-fashioned progressive, had been the candidate endorsed by insurgent Republicans in 1911 and early 1912, before Theodore Roosevelt entered that contest. La Follette's opposition in 1917 to United States intervention in World War I made him acceptable to radical Socialists, and in fact he was the only potential nominee upon whom the diverse elements brought together as Progressives in 1924 could agree without disruptive struggle. The Wisconsin Senator issued a public letter on May 29, 1924, repudiating Communist support and charging that the Communists aimed not at the triumph of progressive democracy but rather at "a soviet form of government and the dictatorship of the proletariat." Admitting them into the coalition would be a "fatal error" that would alienate farmers, workers, and all other progressives.

Meanwhile a disconsolate Foster, who had hoped to take part in a triumphant movement of America's plain people, was returning from Moscow with discouraging news for his fellow Communists. European radicals had denounced the effort at cooperation as reminiscent of the collaboration that almost ruined the international Socialist movement during World War I. The Comintern presidium in Moscow had voted unanimously against the proposal just as Gompers and La Follette were condemning it in America. Consequently, during the campaign, Communist candidates Foster and vice-presidential nominee Benjamin Gitlow, a former Socialist Party leader, devoted their speeches to vilification of La Follette and his "petty-bourgeois" reformers. La Follette, his running mate Senator Burton K. Wheeler of Montana, and even Eugene Debs, who also came under fire from the Communists, responded with attacks on those who were guided from Moscow.

The Republican candidates and press, however, in complete disregard of the real situation, campaigned against the threat of Bolshevism they claimed was presented by La Follette and his modern platform. That document called for support to farmers and for labor's right to organize, ratification of the child labor amendment, limitations on the powers of the Supreme Court, and government ownership of railroads and waterpower resources. All the other candidates virtually ignored the Democratic nominee, John W. Davis, a conservative Wall Street attorney who ran as a resident of West Virginia.

The AFL and brotherhood leaders gradually removed themselves and their union treasuries from the La Follette campaign, contributing very little in any respect. The Socialists, having merged with the Progressives in almost every state, allowed most of their state and local organizations to disintegrate. As a result, although La Follette won almost 5 million votes (more than 15 percent), an unprecedented total for a farmer-labor or Socialist party and potentially an auspicious beginning for a new party, the election actually marked the demise, at least for several decades, of the radical movement in American politics.

The radical coalition, so promising in the spring, had fragmented irrevocably by the fall of 1924. Nevertheless, several of its achievements during the election proved significant for the future of American politics. A price rise in farm commodities before the election blunted La Follette's appeal in agricultural districts. But his total vote in rural districts of Minnesota, Wisconsin, North Dakota, and South Dakota—where the Progressives maintained a semblance of political organization—demonstrated farmers' willingness to swing toward a party presenting new solutions for their long-term economic troubles. Despite the fact that only half of the eligible electorate bothered to vote in 1924, urban minority ethnic groups turned

Election of 1924

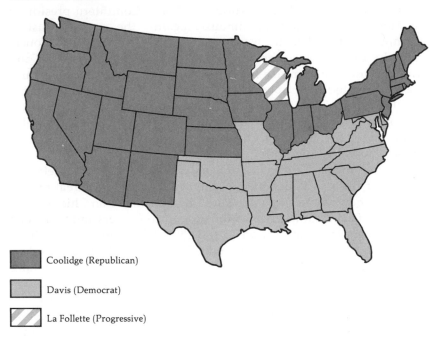

Coolidge (Republican)

Davis (Democrat)

La Follette (Progressive)

out in larger numbers than ever before. Irish, Italian, German, and Jewish citizens gave a significant vote to the third party. Approximately 20 percent of Boston's Italian voters, 18 percent of New York City's German voters, and 22 percent of New York's Jewish electorate, for example, evidently supported La Follette. Most of these voters shifted from the Republican Party. Black voters also showed evidence that their roots in the Republican Party were loosening. Although they failed to support the Progressives (who offered them little), 28 percent of New York's black voters supported the Democratic candidate; only 3 percent had voted for the Democrats in 1920. Even in Chicago, where blacks exercised considerable influence within the Republican organization, about 20 percent of the normal Republican vote in black districts went to the Democrats in 1924. Before long this variety of ethnic groups would control the great cities politically. Their stirrings were significant portents.

By 1928, the minority ethnic vote almost made a serious contender out of New York governor Al Smith, the Democratic presidential nominee. Hoover won easily, but Smith ran abnormally well compared to Democratic congressional candidates, especially in areas with a large foreign-born population. He actually ran a much stronger race in these areas than in predominantly Catholic districts with a high percentage of American-born citizens, although he took most of the latter districts also. Probably no Democratic presidential candidate could have done as well as the New York governor in 1928, with his unique appeal to self-conscious ethnic minorities. Smith had to compete not only against a well-publicized prosperity, for which the Republicans took full credit, but with the strongest possible Republican opponent, Herbert Hoover, whom the voters and many politicians of both parties had regarded as the most eligible candidate in the country after World War I. Hoover's record as commerce secretary during the Harding and Coolidge administrations had enhanced his reputation as a farsighted, competent, and fair-minded administrator.

Nevertheless, Smith came out fighting, denouncing prohibition and the Klan in an unmistakable Lower East Side New York accent. He publicly praised Tammany Hall and the virtues of urban civili-

Election of 1928

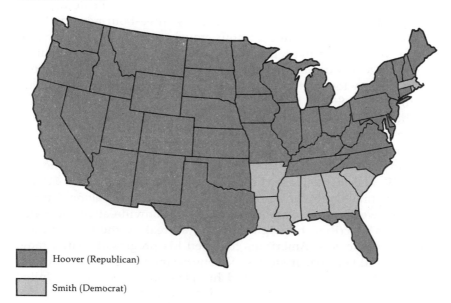

Hoover (Republican)

Smith (Democrat)

zation. An autographed picture of the Pope remained in the New York governor's mansion, but he did compromise by agreeing to cease drinking, or at least to cease drinking in public, during the campaign. He readily admitted that he enjoyed alcoholic beverages, despite federal laws against their shipment and sale. He lost, of course, having alienated westerners, frightened southerners, and contributed to a temporary resurgence of the Klan. In the large cities of the North and West, however, where the vote was disguised superficially by a shift of native-born Protestants — especially those with rural backgrounds — into the Republican Party, the ethnic minorities voted overwhelmingly for Smith. More than 40 percent of New York's blacks supported the Democrats, and well over 80 percent of Chicago's Polish electorate voted Democratic. Irish and Italian voters moved en masse into the Democratic Party, and for the first time the Jewish vote went decisively (apparently over 75 percent in New York and Chicago) to the Democrats. Thus, in defeat, the Democrats established the basis on which the remarkable and long-lasting New Deal coalition in the North would be built.

The "New Era"

The *Spirit of St. Louis*, a fragile monoplane, landed at Le Bourget Air Field, Paris, on May 21, 1927, after a thirty-three-hour nonstop flight from New York City. An enormous crowd greeted the pilot, a handsome, young stunt flyer. In the next few years, despite his apparent attempts to avoid the limelight, Charles A. Lindbergh would be one of the most widely admired men in the world and the foremost hero in the United States. Brave and unassuming, yet master of that most sophisticated and mysterious modern invention — the flying machine — Lindbergh seemed the epitome of virtuous American youth triumphing over enormous obstacles.

Many others had crossed the Atlantic in airplanes before, the first in 1919, and in one case the prize awarded was twice the $25,000 won by Lindbergh. However, Lindbergh had flown alone through adverse weather, after having attracted nationwide attention when reporters described his vigil awaiting a break in the rain and low clouds. Millions of Americans followed his progress through radio reports and newspaper stories. No one seemed to find it odd, therefore, that the young aviator and his plane returned to the United States on a navy cruiser dispatched by President Coolidge for that purpose. Lindbergh was greeted in Washington with one of the

President's longest and best speeches. The convoy following Lindbergh in his parade past a gigantic audience in Washington included a car filled with 55,000 telegrams of congratulations; one, from Minneapolis, was signed by 17,500 admirers.

In New York, the sanitation department estimated that eighteen hundred tons of shredded paper were showered upon the hero as a parade in his honor proceeded through the city. (Only 155 tons of paper had been picked up by the department after the wild march celebrating the armistice in November 1918.) As Lindbergh proceeded to western cities the enthusiasm of the crowds honoring him almost equaled the fantastic eastern welcomes. Never before had an American captured such fervent attention or held the public's interest for so long. However, never before had the radio and moving pictures, as well as newspapers and magazines, been available to promote a comparable idol. Lindbergh won additional respect by refusing $700,000 to appear in a film and millions for a sponsored trip around the world, but he did not object to the sizable fortune in consulting fees thrust upon him by aircraft manufacturers anxious to exploit his fame.

The same publicity techniques and media that maintained interest in Lindbergh were used to make household words out of Babe Ruth, Henry Ford, Rudolph Valentino, Red Grange, and Admiral Richard Byrd—and of Ivory soap, Buick, Listerine, Kodak cameras, G.E. light bulbs, RCA radios, Lucky Strike cigarettes, and hundreds of other manufactured products. Specialists in various aspects of advertising, brought together in large advertising agencies, combined modern psychological concepts with old-fashioned showmanship in the grand American tradition of P. T. Barnum. The guiding principle of the merchandising specialists was stated succinctly in 1903 by Walter D. Scott in an essay called "The Psychology of Advertising." How many advertisers, he asked, "describe a piano so vividly that the reader can hear it? How many food products are so described that the reader can taste the food? . . . How many can describe an undergarment so that the reader can feel the pleasant contact with his body?"

Few could answer Scott's queries affirmatively in 1903, when advertisers still depended largely on descriptions of their product, prices, and simple slogans ("The Beer That Made Milwaukee Famous"). By the 1920's, however, advertisers not only were implanting messages like those suggested by Scott deep in the psyches of their audiences, but they were also selling the fountain of youth and sexual ecstasy in various guises.

The "Lone Eagle," Charles Lindbergh, stands before his plane, the *Spirit of St. Louis,* shortly before his transatlantic flight. Lindbergh radiated modesty, integrity, and competence. His boyish good looks also contributed to his immense popularity.

Total advertising expenditures in the United States more than doubled between 1919 and 1929, as did the number of national advertisers, prime users of the new techniques and services of large agencies. An estimated $1,782,000,000 was spent on advertising in 1929, nearly as much as total national expenditures for all other forms of education. New media expanded the market for advertisements. The first commercial radio station was licensed in 1921, and about 100,000 rather primitive sets were manufactured in 1922. In 1929, 4.5 million sets were produced, many of them radio-phonograph combinations ("like having the Philadelphia Orchestra in the next room," one ad boasted), and more than 10 million families owned radios. Millions of listeners were bombarded daily with commercials that seemed almost unceasing. Intermissions between films at movie houses also were filled with projected sales messages. High-

"The Sultan of Swat," "The Babe"—Yankee Stadium was paid for by fans who came to see Babe Ruth do his act. A strike-out by Ruth aroused more excitement than anything in baseball, except one of his gargantuan home runs.

ways built to accommodate the millions of cars sold every year soon were lined with billboards.

Among the advertising industry's achievements was its role in convincing manufacturers that they could create demand for their products beyond the clear needs of consumers. In addition, purchasers were successfully persuaded that they could buy goods with the aid of credit before their savings made ownership possible.

The experience of Gerard Lambert, president of a small company that produced a harmless antiseptic called Listerine, is illustrative. Lambert, in the expansive spirit of the era, decided in 1922 that Listerine's sales should increase. He sent for his advertising manager:

At that time I knew absolutely nothing of advertising. We went into my brother Marion's office and I closed the door. I announced that we would not leave until we had an advertising idea for Listerine. . . . [Eventually] I asked him [advertising director Deacon] if Listerine was good for bad breath. He excused himself for a moment and came back with a big book of newspaper clippings.

"Here it is, Gerard. It says in this clipping from the British [medical journal] *Lancet* that in cases of halitosis . . ."

"What is halitosis?" I interrupted.

"Oh!" he said, "that is the medical term for bad breath." I bustled the dear old gentleman out of the room. "There," I said, "is something to hang our hat on."

Before the 1920's ended, everyone in the United States who was not illiterate *and* deaf would know about halitosis—and Listerine. The firm's advertising budget for its wondrous halitosis cure rose from $100,000 in 1922 to almost $5 million in 1928. Sales expanded proportionately.

Pleasures even more delightful than the lingering kisses hinted at in Listerine's advertising seemed available to purchasers of Red Cross shoes: "Just a few steps—a dozen perhaps in all—yet the vision of her as she crossed the Ritz will linger long in many memories. She was so gloriously graceful, so light of foot . . . so naturally lovely in every move she made. . . . Who can blame any man if his eyes grow a bit brighter, his heart a bit lighter at the sight of such buoyant beauty—free footed, unrestrained, the poetry of motion in every poised step." Any woman could achieve this seductive effect, but she needed the right shoes: "They must be Red Cross Shoes—or so I am told by women who wear them."

Advertisements for Lux soap promised at least the appearance of moderate wealth: "Need a woman's hands say 'I have no maid?'" an ad asked. "236 leading beauty shops answer: 'With all our experience, we are unable to distinguish between the hands of a woman who never washes dishes and those of a housewife who uses Lux in the dishpan.'"

Sex, beauty, the facade of wealth, even youth, came with the marvelous new products shown in magazines, newspapers, bill-

With an innovative scare campaign as skillfull as any ever mounted, Listerine multiplied its sales and profits during the 1920's. This advertisement remains a classic, and its theme still claims almost all of Listerine's huge advertising budget.

boards, and movie commercials. A lovely young girl and an older woman with obvious potentialities in her figure and hope in her eyes appeared in magazines over the caption "Modernizing Mother." After describing the modern young lady—healthy, graceful, unconventional—an ad for female sanitary napkins continued: "Millions of mothers whose girlhood was repressed are being trained by their daughters to be young again—to know freedom—to grasp the idea that drudgery and useless labor are a sinful waste of life. Modess is one of the many recent inventions which do away with drudgery and discomfort." Ads for washing machines, refrigerators, toasters, cosmetics, and vacuum cleaners made similar claims. None seemed to promise more than advertisements for luxurious, aesthetically stimulating, powerful automobiles, or for cigarettes, somehow liberating and sexy as well as delicious.

The success of such advertising campaigns was made possible not only by the new media, skillful agencies, and increased use of consumer credit. In addition, a steady rise in real wages and in the proportion of married women in working-class families employed outside the home vastly increased the number of families with income available for purchases beyond the necessities of life. The real annual income (income taking account of price changes) of employed wage earners increased by 22 percent between 1921 and 1928, according to economist Paul Douglas.

Still, at least half of farm and nonfarm workers earned barely enough for subsistence. Gross income figures obscure the fact that most of the increase went to skilled workers; income of laborers rose hardly at all. Also, unemployment lingered at a high level; inadequate statistics indicate that from 7 to 12 percent of nonagricultural wage earners were jobless at any given time during this "prosperous" decade. Between 1919 and 1924, because agricultural production continued to increase even while most farm prices fell, workers willing to remain on farms found jobs, but usually at wages so low that farm laborers' families remained almost completely outside the new consumer-oriented economy. Most other families dependent largely on a wage earner's pay required not only credit to enjoy goods like autos and radios but a second and perhaps a third and a fourth income also. In addition to the contribution of employed wives, children in working-class families usually left high school to earn money for their own needs as well as for their family's.

Most white collar workers found themselves in only slightly less straitened circumstances, although these families sent wives to work more reluctantly and in smaller proportions and they were even more loathe to allow their children to leave school completely without a high school diploma. A 1928 study in five cities of federal employees with what were then moderate incomes of $2500 or less disclosed that between 15 and 33 percent of the husbands worked at second jobs, 15 to 32 percent of the wives were employed, and in most cases children contributed to family income. The proportion of these "middle-class" families able to live on the husband's federal salary alone varied from 2 to 10 percent. In this fashion the majority of white Americans enjoyed the delights of the "new era."

The decade's celebrated prosperity almost completely eluded the overwhelming majority of nonwhite Americans. Despite the movement of nearly 2.5 million blacks to northern cities by the end of the 1920's, most black Americans continued to labor in the South as tenant farmers, sharecroppers, and farm workers. In 1930, about 3 million blacks—25 percent of the nation's total black population—lived in the three deep southern states of Georgia, Mississippi, and Alabama, and 80 percent of these existed in rural poverty. Even in the North, blacks justifiably claimed that they were the last hired, the first fired, and that few obtained employment as skilled workers, except temporarily as strikebreakers. Furthermore, in almost every industry they received lower wages than whites doing the same work. With few exceptions, labor unions contributed to this situation by consistently denying membership to black applicants. The Urban League estimated that only 81,658 blacks belonged to American unions during the period 1926–1928. Of these, the majority were members of independent black unions, the Longshoremen, the Hod Carriers, or the Railroad Maintenance of Way Employees. Most of the budding black middle class lived on the edge of the white world's standard of respectability as teachers in segregated schools and as small-scale entrepreneurs. Only a handful collected the capital necessary for larger businesses or obtained access to the training requisite for success as artists, writers, musicians, actors, or even in organized crime.

Americans of Mexican birth or descent, by far the largest minority group in the Southwest, suffered similar economic discrimination. Like blacks, they found it extremely difficult to rise above the dirtiest, most physically demanding, lowest paying work. In the area from Texas, New Mexico, and Colorado to California, Mexicans provided at least three-fourths of the labor that combined with irrigation to transform that section from brush and desert land into the nation's

Settlement and Population in the United States, 1900-1920

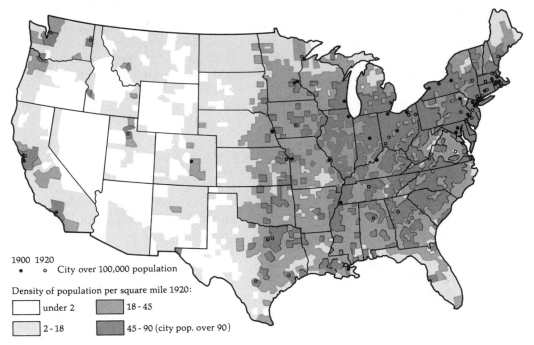

1900 1920
•   ○   City over 100,000 population

Density of population per square mile 1920:

under 2   18 - 45

2 - 18   45 - 90 (city pop. over 90)

Source: Copyright © 1966 by American Heritage Publishing Co., Inc. Reprinted by permission from *The American Heritage Pictorial Atlas of United States History*.

richest agricultural region. By 1925 the southwestern states produced 40 percent of the country's fruits and vegetables, almost all on farms developed during the twentieth century. Attempts by Mexican farm workers in the 1920's to raise their incredibly low wages by forming unions invariably were smashed by a combination of violence and deportations. Gradually, Mexican-Americans gravitated toward cities like San Antonio, El Paso, and especially Los Angeles, which promised a life of greater variety if not more economic opportunity than labor in the reclaimed deserts. In these cities, however, Mexicans were segregated by walls of prejudice, poverty, and language into *barrios* with inferior schools, sanitation, and housing facilities. Spanish-speaking parents sent inadequately prepared children to schools dominated by "Anglo" teachers and administrators, so that the parents' academic and economic handicaps frequently were handed down to the next generation. Nevertheless, urban Mexican-Americans demonstrated a surprising ability to collect capital, largely by sending almost the entire family to work—in nearby fields when factory jobs were scarce. Within about five years of their shift to the city, perhaps 15 percent of the Mexicans in the center of the Los Angeles *barrio* owned their own houses and were accumulating the goods that ordinarily accompanied home ownership.

To a lesser extent, other ethnic minorities—Irish, Italians, Eastern European Jews, and Poles—in cities throughout the country shared the handicaps of blacks and Mexicans, as did' the approximately 40,000 Puerto Ricans who moved to New York City after the restrictions of European immigration. Those among them who were raised in ghetto slums escaped only through tremendous exertion, and many lacked a desire to leave their familiar ethnic enclaves. However, unlike colored laborers, most members of white ethnic minorities enjoyed a fighting chance of moving into the consumer economy and even of rising to middle-class status.

At the other extreme from colored farm and factory laborers, 5 percent of the population received about one-third of the nation's personal income. While wages rose slowly, dividends from common stocks more than doubled during the 1920's, and stock prices increased even more. This top 5 percent—less than 2 million of the nation's 28.5 million families—comprised the prime audience for advertisers of expensive autos, elaborate home fixtures, and large appliances. Early in 1929 about 1,223,000 American homes had electric refrigerators, for example, according to the trade journal *Electrical World.* A larger proportion of Americans enjoyed basic and less expensive consumer goods. The maldistribution of income did not prevent the sale of about 4.5 million automobiles and more than 4 million radios in 1929. By that year, about 20 percent of American families owned electric toasters and 25 percent had vacuum cleaners. Over two-thirds of the population lived in dwellings with electric lighting, compared to 16 percent in 1912. Close to 3 million houses were constructed during the period 1925–1929 alone. These homes were sold despite the fact that banks were only beginning to experiment with credit arrangements common in the auto industry— scheduling monthly mortgage and interest payments over long periods. Bankers' conservatism in this area, in contrast to their aggressive use of funds in the stock market, probably prevented further expansion of the market for single-family homes after 1925, when a gradual slide in home sales began. Too many enticing goods competed for consumers' dollars, and the average worker could not accumulate the savings necessary for home ownership in the 1920's.

Nevertheless, good reasons for cautious optimism about the American economy existed in 1929, probably all too clearly for a society susceptible to speculative excess. Businessmen responded to the enlarged market with important innovations. The research laboratory became a well-established fixture in most major industries. As a result, an abundance of new products ranging from airconditioners (scores of large department stores installed this equipment during the late 1920's) to self-regulating ovens and talking motion pictures were introduced to enthusiastic consumers. The basic patents for television were obtained during the 1920's, and the development of a widely publicized new home entertainment industry seemed near at hand in 1929. Skillful techniques in market research and in advertising assisted the steady sale of goods pouring out of American factories. Over four-fifths of the increase in gross national product (total production of goods and services) between 1919 and 1929 was due to increased sales of consumer goods and services. Production costs were lowered by an upsurge in the installation of automatic machinery and by great improvements in material-handling equipment and techniques. The consequent higher profits were plowed back into the expansion of production facilities and more efficient machinery and were handed out as dividends to stockholders more often than they were distributed in the form of wage increases or lower prices. Hourly wages in manufacturing increased 8 percent between 1923 and 1929, but the average work week was reduced slightly and the manufacturing work force grew by only one-half of 1 percent. Meanwhile, manufacturing output increased 30 percent, profits 62 percent, and dividends 65 percent. Stock market prices responded to this favorable situation by rising 176 percent. Electricity became available to many agricultural areas during the decade, enabling the most prosperous farmers to use the host of electrical products—lighting, refrigeration, radios, washing machines—that were changing the life styles of city dwellers. A sympathetic federal government not only encouraged optimistic attitudes and actions among businessmen but in some cases gave important aid, such as Mellon's tax policies and Hoover's encouragement of standardization and trade agreements.

Few of the weaknesses that economists and historians later discovered in the 1929 economy were visible then, and the importance of several of these has been overestimated. Residential construction had been slipping since 1925, but commercial, industrial, and government building (especially for roads) took up the slack in the construction industry. Defects in the banking system's structure could be seen only in rural areas where banks holding mortgages on depreciated farm land folded by the hundreds between 1921 and 1927. However, rural banks began recovering along with the prices of farm land and products after 1925. Undoubtedly, many urban banks had invested too heavily in the stock market and in dubious foreign loans. Nevertheless, until the value of apparently sound assets — such as bonds, real estate mortgages, secured personal loans, and investments in flourishing foreign enterprises — suffered severe decreases after 1930, the banking system as a whole seemed strong and flexible. It remains difficult to determine the extent to which appearances were deceiving. Modern banking is based on the premise that much more money can be loaned out than is deposited, and a sudden decision by most depositors to demand their money still will bankrupt the most secure financial institution. Furthermore, American banks were extremely susceptible to unexpected financial catastrophe in other nations, which frequently could be traced to the Depression in America. Given the general economic conditions of the early 1930's, perhaps the pressure on the banks should be accented more and their weaknesses less than often has been the case, although fundamental weaknesses certainly existed, not only in individual banks, but in the impotence (some economists call it incompetence) of the Federal Reserve Board.

Although the highly unequal distribution of income set a limit on consumer spending, discretionary income was available to a higher proportion of Americans than ever before. Most Americans remained poor, but most always had lived on the edge of subsistence. The prosperity of the 1920's has been exaggerated frequently, but so have the effects of the continued uneven distribution of income and wealth. Many highly placed businessmen undoubtedly misused their firms' (and the public's) funds, and as always in American history, a colossal amount of unsuspected dishonesty was disclosed when losses had to be covered and depositors and other creditors called for their money. That American businessmen were more dishonest during the 1920's than usual is a dubious proposition at best, and one that has yet to be proved.

In three critical areas the United States economy was terribly susceptible to serious reverses in 1929: Faulty economic theory caused a lag to develop between modern practice and needed institutional changes. Partly for the same reason, and partly because of defects caused by World War I, a rickety international monetary structure stood ready to collapse under any strong pressure. An atmosphere that encouraged speculation caused expansion in some sectors—including the stock market—to take place at a rate more rapid than could be sustained.

Major changes in the economy had occurred since the beginning of the twentieth century. The days when a few great bankers could shore up the entire financial system were far behind, and attempts by alliances of the most important financiers to halt plunging stock values and to support threatened banks after the collapse began in 1929 fell pitifully short of success. Yet the economic ideas of leading businessmen and government officials remained appropriate to a bygone era. Bankers who for twenty years had stubbornly resisted proposals for federal deposit insurance, for instance, were obliged to watch their own and thousands of other banks fail for lack of that simple system. As the whole economy ground toward a halt in 1932, the platforms of both Democratic and Republican Parties, and Franklin D. Roosevelt as well as Herbert Hoover, insisted that the foremost remedy available to the government was a reduction in spending to balance the budget.

By the late 1920's, the United States not only produced most of the world's manufactured goods but was by far the world's leading creditor nation. Thus any disturbance in the American economy that reduced United States investments and purchases abroad would inevitably affect almost every nation dependent on American capital and markets, and the consequent financial difficulties in these nations would exacerbate American problems, not only in banking but throughout the economic system.

Perhaps most important, by 1929 too many Americans viewed their own economic prospects and the future of American business not with the cautious optimism that probably was justified but rather with an extravagant enthusiasm that approached ecstasy. Symptoms of this high enthusiasm included a use of consumer credit that increased far more rapidly than income. A series of speculative disasters—including a sharp stock market decline in 1920–1921 and a fantastic Florida real estate boom that collapsed in 1926—should have warned off those who sought effortless wealth through speculation, but they did not.

The best thermometer of the speculative fever that seized millions of Americans was the stock market. Encouraged by a steady increase in corporate profits and dividends, stock prices began rising rapidly in 1927, bounded ahead even more swiftly starting in March 1928,

Automobiles in Use in the United States, 1900-1970

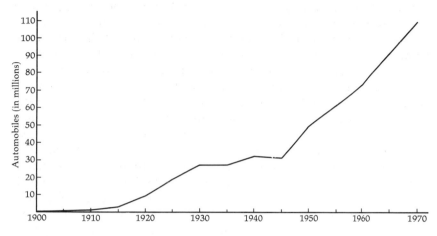

Source: *Statistical Abstract of the United States.*

and reached frenzied heights in August 1929, when one of the last obstacles on the way to economic paradise, the summer slump in consumer purchases and manufacturing production, seemed to be conquered. The ascent of prices was encouraged by low margins (actual cash required for stock purchases), which varied between 10 and 50 percent during 1929. Brokerage houses loaned customers the remainder of the price at high interest rates with money borrowed from banks, other financial institutions, and industrial corporations, as well as with funds from their own capital reserves.

A few crucial industries had been overproducing, partly for competitive reasons but also because of the speculative optimism that afflicted investors in their companies' stocks. Of these industries, the most important was automobiles, in which Chevrolet, the new Chrysler Corporation low-cost car, Plymouth, and the even newer Ford Model A vied for market leadership. Henry Ford had discontinued production of the simple but efficient Model T in 1927, when he finally realized that his plain black cars no longer could compete effectively against General Motors products stressing comfort, styling, and color. Even after introduction of the popular Model A, however, Ford was unable to reclaim clear leadership in the industry he had dominated for over a decade. During the manufacturers' battle, retailers were obliged to accept more autos than they could sell. Down payments were all but abolished, and credit terms were stretched to suit any potential customer. When it became plain late in the summer of 1929 that dealers could absorb no more cars, manufacturers finally cut back production severely, and at the same time reduced orders for steel, rubber, copper, glass, and other materials. Shifts in auto sales accounted for only a minute part of the economic catastrophe, but the industry's rapidly shifting fortunes did have a dramatic impact on businessmen's attitudes. As the situation in the auto industry became apparent and order backlogs of large suppliers like United States Steel suffered temporarily, the shrewdest and most nervous speculators began retreating from the market. In response, stock prices declined, and in September 1929 thousands of speculators, determined to get out of the game while they still were ahead, began unloading their holdings. The retreat then became a rout. Margins, which had added leverage to the market boom, gave impetus to the decline as brokerage houses protected their loans by selling the holdings of customers whose stock dropped in value close to or below the amount of their cash investment and who could not or would not produce more margin funds.

In mid-November 1929, the first great massacre of stock values ended. On November 13, *The New York Times* average of industrial stocks on the New York Stock Exchange stood at 224, down from 452 on September 3. This index included stocks of conservatively managed companies in stable industries such as food and clothing, which declined less than average. It did not include the smaller companies whose speculative stocks lost almost their entire value. The total loss in stock prices on the New York Stock Exchange alone between September and mid-November 1929 amounted to about $25 billion in a year when the gross national product was slightly over $100 billion. Losses on other exchanges, including those in unlisted securities, may well have approached the total erosion suffered by stocks listed on the Big Board. As prices rose again between November 1929 and March 1930, many of the wise investors who had sold in September took advantage of the "bargains" available. They were caught in the even more severe decline that followed.

Among those who understood the significance of the market catastrophe was President Hoover. Ignoring the advice of Treasury Secretary Mellon to allow liquidation to proceed unchecked until an equilibrium was reached, Hoover decided to act. Only a few stubborn supporters still maintain that he took the proper actions. A somewhat larger number of economists and historians claim that no

A mixture of curious and panic-stricken people mill around the New York Stock Exchange on "Black Friday," October 29, 1929. During most of this terrible day, almost every trader lost money, no buyers appeared for many stocks offered, thousands of portfolios held on margin were dumped by brokerage houses for whatever they would bring, and tens of thousands of confused investors saw their savings disappear in a few hours. Millions of dollars were lost during the panic, despite efforts late in the session by representatives of major banks and large investors to "stabilize" prices and to take advantage of "bargains."

one knew what actions to take, despite an abundance of bills introduced in Congress during 1930–1932 for vast public works programs, severe tax cuts of all kinds, federal government offices, unemployment insurance, direct relief to the unemployed, farm price supports, massive currency inflation, guaranteed annual wages, and investigation of conditions in the banking and securities industries. Almost all these bills either were killed or severely reduced in scope by conservative congressional leaders encouraged by the President.

Hoover met in the White House on November 21, 1929, with the

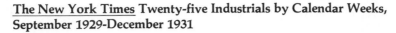

The New York Times Twenty-five Industrials by Calendar Weeks, September 1929-December 1931

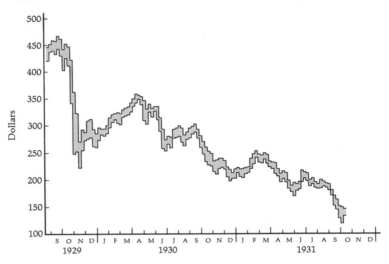

nation's leading industrialists. These included heads of the Ford Motor Company, General Motors, United States Steel, Standard Oil, General Electric, American Telephone and Telegraph, and DuPont. At that point, the Federal Reserve Board index of industrial production, which had reached its peak in June 1929, had declined only about 8 percent from that all-time high. Nevertheless, Hoover spoke gloomily about the strong possibility of a worldwide depression as a result of the crash, and he requested assistance from the giant industrial corporations, whose example others certainly would follow. At the conference's conclusion, Hoover announced that the country's largest employers of labor had promised not to reduce wages. Indeed, Henry Ford promptly announced a wage increase for all his employees. The industrialists pledged also to avoid layoffs if possible and to proceed with planned construction.

A series of similar White House meetings followed. Labor leaders, officials of farm organizations, heads of large construction companies, and public utilities magnates received approximately the same warnings and requests for cooperation. Promises to hold the line on wages, prices, and capital expenditures were extracted. The President's chief concern was that the market crash would trigger a wave of uncontrollable pessimism that would drag down all other economic values. He confided to the Washington, D.C., Gridiron Club on December 4, 1929: "Fear, alarm, pessimism, and hesitation swept through the country, which, if unchecked, would have precipitated absolute panic throughout the business world with untold misery in its wake. Its acute dangers were far greater than we are able to disclose." Hoover therefore sought and received expressions of confidence from the economic spokesmen who attended his conferences. After the November 21 meeting, financier Julius Rosenwald was so carried away that he expressed fear of an imminent severe shortage of labor. Farm leaders announced that agriculture's morale was higher than it had been for years. Secretary of Labor James J. Davis declared publicly early in 1930 that the country had recovered completely from the effects of the stock market's difficulties and that a sharp upturn had taken place in employment. Nevertheless, he took the precaution of choking off funds from the Bureau of Labor Statistics, whose energetic and honest head, Ethelbert Stewart, continued to announce figures that showed rising unemployment. Stewart was fired in 1932. To a friend Davis wrote in March 1930: "One doesn't improve the condition of a sick man by constantly telling him how ill he is."

Hoover also took more concrete steps. He announced a cut of one percentage point in income and corporation taxes. However, thanks to Mellon's successful efforts to lower taxes during the previous nine years, the income tax reductions amounted to only a few dollars a year for the average middle-class family. The President also agreed to a sharp rise in tariff rates, effectively protecting some American industries but exposing others to retaliation from nations that imported their products. He obtained funds from Congress for a public works program much more modest than most legislators wanted, claiming that a larger program would necessitate severe tax increases to maintain a balanced budget. When all other attempts to revive industry failed, Hoover agreed under great pressure in December 1931 to creation of the Reconstruction Finance Corporation (RFC), which began functioning in February 1932. This agency, intended to make emergency loans to business firms through banks and other financial institutions, gave most of its aid to favored big city banks and to railroads. Hoover vetoed a bill that would have made homeowners and other individual debtors eligible for RFC loans. He approved creation of agencies to purchase agricultural surpluses (the Cotton Stabilization Corporation and the Grain Stabilization Corporation were the largest of these), to halt the downward spiral in farm prices. Even more seriously undercapitalized for their purposes than the RFC, they soon found themselves swamped with commodities and depleted of funds. Prices continued to sink. The agencies terminated their purchasing programs in 1931, when they were needed more than ever. With the possible exception of the attempt to shore up confidence in American business, the farm price support program probably was the greatest single fiasco of the unfortunate Hoover administration. A Federal Home Loan Bank, authorized in 1932, proved as inadequate as the RFC and the commodity stabilization corporations.

In the fall of 1931, the failure of financial systems in Austria and Germany, Britain's melodramatic abandonment of the gold standard, and the international economic disorganization that followed placed an intolerable strain on America's already tottering banking and manufacturing. Industrial production, prices, and stock market values, which, after a few months of apparent recovery, had turned downward about two months before the European financial collapse, collapsed again. Bank suspensions in the United States reached epidemic proportions. A total of 2,294 closed in 1931, 522 in October alone. Industrial firms no longer even pretended to maintain prices, wages, employment, or capital spending.

Local relief funds, which Hoover had counted on to meet the needs of the unemployed, were exhausted in virtually every city and town in the United States. Still Hoover resisted attempts to found federal relief organizations. Such schemes, he warned, would undermine the "spirit of responsibility," which provided "the one safeguard against degeneration of that independence and initiative which are the very foundation of democracy."

To ward off congressional plans that he considered "socialistic," Hoover created the President's Organization on Unemployment Relief (POUR) under the direction of Walter S. Gifford, president of the American Telephone and Telegraph Company, to coordinate local, county, and state relief efforts. Although POUR did help local agencies raise funds, it accomplished little else except to ruin the public reputations of Gifford and the other businessmen associated with it. Called before a Senate subcommittee preparing federal relief bills in January 1932, Gifford testified that POUR's information indicated that such measures were unneeded. Asked how many people needed relief, or were receiving it, Gifford answered that he did not know. He possessed no knowledge whatever of needs in rural areas of the country. Asked specifically, "How many people in the

United States at this hour are on the verge of starvation?" Gifford replied, "I have no such information." Congress refused Hoover's request for funds to continue POUR's activities.

In 1932, as unemployment in manufacturing mounted toward 40 percent of the 1929 labor force, with 70 percent of coal miners and over 80 percent of building trade workers jobless and most of the other workers who remained employed in these industries on part time and sharply reduced wages, Hoover earned his reputation as the American equivalent of the Roman Emperor Nero. Nearly every time the President exultantly announced a turn for the better, newspapers published official government figures showing further deterioration. Democratic Party spokesmen made the most of these discrepancies.

Because of an apple surplus in 1930, the International Apple Shippers Association organized masses of unemployed workers—six thousand in New York City alone—consigned them crates of apples on credit, and set them to selling the shiny, red fruit at five cents apiece. Fortunately, Hoover did not state until later that "many persons left their jobs for the more profitable one of selling apples." However, this near-complete lack of empathy with the situation of the unemployed manifested itself in Hoover's use of army tanks in 1932 to disburse a ragged "bonus army" encamped outside Washington, hoping for early payment of a bonus already authorized to veterans of the Spanish-American War and World War I. It was communicated to the population sufficiently to help obtain spontaneous acceptance of the name "Hooverville" for the towns of shacks and huts that sprang up outside almost every American city. These, along with parks and caves, housed those among the unemployed unable to find ordinary shelter, despite a widespread willingness on the part of landlords to forgo rent from the jobless. Even successful attempts to evict the unemployed in working-class districts resulted only in empty housing. In some areas, almost everyone was either without work or on short wages. At the giant J. Edgar Thompson Works of United States Steel in Pennsylvania, for example, only 424 full-time workers were employed in March 1932, out of a 1929 work force of 5,235. In the city of Donora, Pennsylvania, 277 held jobs in a population of 13,900.

Under these circumstances, no possibility existed of Hoover's re-election in November 1932. Despite Al Smith's decision to renege on his pledge not to risk splitting the Democratic Party again by seeking renomination, Governor Franklin D. Roosevelt of New York

A booming new retail business developed in American cities — especially in New York — during the early 1930's: the sidewalk sale of apples. An apple surplus in Washington state and a shortage of jobs everywhere contributed to the rapid growth of this business.

Hundreds of shantytowns, thrown up by impoverished, unemployed Americans on the edges
of cities between 1930 and 1932, were called "Hooverville." This
Hooverville was built near the lower end of Central Park's reservoir in New York City.

took a commanding early lead in pledged delegates. Roosevelt, a
distant relative of Theodore Roosevelt, had served in Wilson's Cabinet as assistant secretary of the navy before receiving the Democratic
nomination for Vice-President in 1920, when he was thirty-eight
years of age. His promising career appeared to have been cut short
in 1921 by a serious polio attack, which paralyzed both of his legs.
While recuperating, however, he retained his contacts with Democratic politicians and with potential campaign contributors among
businessmen. At Al Smith's request, he ran for governor of New
York in 1928, winning election by 25,000 votes, while Smith lost the

state to Hoover by 100,000. As governor, he followed a moderately progressive course until 1931, when he decided that federal action to relieve the misery of the unemployed was insufficient. He then adopted policies indicating that as President he would take a much more positive attitude than Hoover's toward drastic measures designed to alleviate the nation's economic misery. Roosevelt obtained $20 million from the state legislature for an agency to provide unemployment relief through the nearly bankrupt cities and counties, and he named Harry Hopkins, a New York City social welfare administrator and a professional social worker, to be executive director of the new agency. More than 10 percent of the state's families received aid from Hopkins' organization, which served as a model for agencies in other industrial states.

Until the 1932 convention, Roosevelt shrewdly avoided controversial statements, while allowing his representatives to trade for the votes that he needed. The New York governor obtained a large majority on the first ballot but did not win the two-thirds then necessary for nomination until his advisers apparently promised the vice-presidential nomination to Speaker of the House John N. Garner of Texas. Roosevelt dramatically flew to the convention and accepted the nomination in person with a speech that promised a "new deal" for the American people.

A rather restrained campaign followed, considering the circumstances, enlivened by Hoover's warning that should the Democrats win and put their policies into effect, "grass will grow in streets of a hundred cities, a thousand towns; the weeds will overrun the fields of millions of farms." Roosevelt swept into office with 27,821,857 popular votes to Hoover's 15,761,841. The most surprising result was the small vote for the Socialist candidate, Norman Thomas (884,781), and the Communist, William Z. Foster (102,991). The urban ethnic minorities, not at all impressed with Hoover's attempt to protect their "character" and "moral integrity" by preserving them from federal relief funds and emergency jobs, presented the Democrats with enormous majorities. Disillusioned western farmers and the solid poverty-stricken South further swelled the Democratic vote. For the first time since the disintegration of the pre–Civil War Jacksonian coalition, the majority of America's voters thought of themselves as Democrats.

When Hoover left office on March 4, 1933, the nation hardly resembled that which he had assured confidently in 1929: "We in America today are nearer to the final triumph over poverty than ever

A strained Herbert Hoover greets two of his rapidly diminishing number of friends in June 1932: Mrs. Floyd Bennett, wife of the aviator, and Viola Gentry, the famous flier.

before in the history of any land." One-third of the wage and salary earners in the United States were out of work, and a high proportion of the rest toiled part time for starvation wages. In steel, textile, auto, rubber, and mining areas, whole towns were virtually without jobs. Charitable funds for relief, both public and private, were practically exhausted. No one could count the consequences of malnutrition, except in local hospitals that still accepted charity cases, where the results of surveys were horrifying. American industry as a whole was operating at a loss, as it had during 1932 also. As a consequence, corporate dividends and stock prices had fallen to small fractions of their 1929 values. Almost every bank in the country was closed; state laws and inadequate resources were about to shut down the

Election of 1932

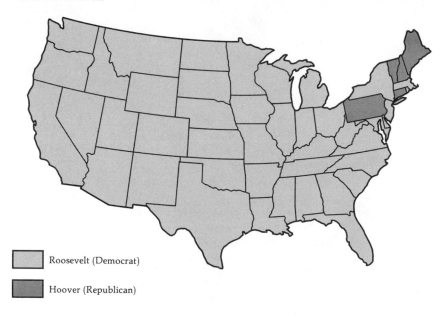

Roosevelt (Democrat)

Hoover (Republican)

rest even as Roosevelt took office. Nevertheless, in self-protection, financial institutions were foreclosing home and farm mortgages by the hundreds every day. Both marriages and births had dropped to the lowest recorded rates in American history, but the suicide rate had increased by one-fourth since 1929 to a new high. More people were emigrating from the country than were entering, despite depression almost everywhere in the world. For the first time, more Americans were moving to farms—where they could eat, at least—than were leaving farms for the city. Labor unions, seriously depleted during the 1920's, were devastated. Construction union membership stood 40 percent under 1929; the Oil Workers retained 300 members, fewer than the Long Beach, California, local membership in 1929. Probably at least a million vagrants, most of them young men and a lesser but increasing number of girls, roamed the country by train and highway, seeking work or at least a milder climate to compensate for their inability to purchase clothing and shelter. Most demoralizing of all, after years of cheerful predictions, no one dared prophesy convincingly that conditions would improve rather than deteriorate further.

SUGGESTED READINGS

A lively romp through the period is provided by Frederick Lewis Allen in *Only Yesterday* (1931). An equally readable but much more careful and thoughtful treatment can be found in William E. Leuchtenburg, *The Perils of Prosperity, 1914–1932* (1958).

The standard work on the postwar hysteria is Robert K. Murray, *The Red Scare* (1955), but the interpretations are of dubious validity and the book should be supplemented by the appropriate chapters in John Higham, *Strangers in the Land* (1954); Stanley Coben, *A. Mitchell Palmer, Politician* (1963, 1971); Coben, "A Study in Nativism: The American Red Scare of 1919–1920," *Political Science Quarterly*, 79 (March 1964), and Bobbs Merrill Reprint Series; and William Preston, *Aliens and Dissenters: Federal Suppression of Radicals, 1903–1933* (1963). On the most famous case arising out of the disturbances, see G. L. Joughin and E. M. Morgan, *The Legacy of Sacco and Vanzetti* (1948). Francis Russell reluctantly reaches the conclusion that the men may well have been guilty in *Tragedy in Dedham: The Story of the Sacco-Vanzetti Case* (1962).

On the breakup of the Wilsonian Democratic coalition, see David Burner, *The Politics of Provincialism: The Democratic Party in Transition, 1918–1932* (1968); and Wesley M. Bagby, *The Road to Normalcy: The Presidential Campaign and Election of 1920* (1962). The growing political alienation of organized labor can be followed in Coben, *A. Mitchell Palmer* (1963, 1971). Samuel H. Adams, *Incredible Era* (1939), and Karl Schiftgiesser, *This Was Normalcy* (1948), give the Harding administration scandals a thorough airing. Andrew Sinclair attempts, with slight success, to rehabilitate part of Harding's reputation in *The Available Man* (1965). Frances Russell is more successful, at least in creating sympathy for the unfortunate President, in *The Shadow of Blooming Grove* (1968). Donald R. McCoy, *Calvin Coolidge: The Quiet President*, is the standard biography of that surprisingly talkative man. Arthur M. Schlesinger, Jr., *The Crisis of the Old Order*, is a lucid account of the Republican dynasty and its downfall; also see John D. Hicks, *Republican Ascendency* (1960). Two of the major economic problems of the era are discussed in the relevant chapters of John D. Hicks and Theodore Saloutos, *Agricultural Discontent in the Middle West* (1951); George B. Tindall, *The Emergence of the New South, 1913–1945* (1967); and R. E. Paul, *Taxation in the United States* (1954). The travail of American labor, organized and unorganized, is described in Irving Bernstein, *The Lean Years* (1960). Herbert Hoover's attempts to rationalize business activity can be followed in Albert U. Romasco, *The Poverty of Abundance* (1965); and in the appropriate volumes of Hoover's *Memoirs* (1952).

On the Klan during the 1920's, see Kenneth T. Jackson, *The Ku Klux Klan in the Cities, 1915–1930* (1967); A. S. Rice, *The Ku Klux Klan in American Politics* (1962); Charles C. Alexander, *The Ku Klux Klan in the Southwest* (1965); and David M. Chalmers, *Hooded Americanism: The First Century of the Ku Klux Klan* (1965). The related battles for religious fundamentalism and prohibition can be studied in Norman F. Furniss, *The Fundamentalist Controversy, 1918–1931* (1954); Paul Carter, *The Decline and Revival of the Social Gospel* (1954); Andrew Sinclair, *Era of Excess* (1962); Herbert Asbury, *The*

Great Illusion (1950); and Lawrence W. Levine, *Defender of the Faith: William Jennings Bryan, The Last Decade, 1915–1925* (1965). The Americanization movement is described in Higham, *Strangers in the Land* (1954), and in Edward G. Hartmann, *The Movement to Americanize the Immigrant* (1948); it is analyzed in unique fashion by Horace M. Kallen in *Culture and Democracy in the United States* (1924).

William L. O'Neill, *Everyone Was Brave: The Rise and Fall of Feminism in America* (1969), and the later chapters of Andrew Sinclair, *The Emancipation of the American Woman* (1965), describe the changing role and status of women. Some accounts of counterattacks against the Klan can be found in Jackson, *Ku Klux Klan in the City* (1967). On the black migration, see Louise V. Kennedy, *The Negro Peasant Turns Cityward* (1930). The best study of Marcus Garvey is Theodore G. Vincent, *Black Power and the Garvey Movement* (1971); but Edmund D. Cronon, *Black Moses* (1955), remains useful. Black intellectuals and artists are discussed in Nathan I. Huggins, *Harlem Renaissance* (1971). For the broader literary currents of the period, Edmund Wilson, *The Shores of Light* (1952), and chapters in Alfred Kazin, *On Native Grounds* (1942), provide a good introduction. The better specialized studies include Mark Schorer, *Sinclair Lewis* (1961); C. Brooks, *William Faulkner: The Yoknapatawpha County* (1963); Carlos Baker, *Ernest Hemingway, a Life Story* (1969); Arthur Mizener, *The Far Side of Paradise: A Biography of F. Scott Fitzgerald* (1951); B. H. Clark, *Eugene O'Neill* (1947); Charles Norman, *Ezra Pound* (1960); Malcolm Cowley, *Exile's Return* (1934); and William Manchester, *Disturber of the Peace* (1951) on H. L. Mencken. The academic intellectuals are treated in Merle Curti, *The Social Ideas of American Educators* (1935); Morton G. White, *Social Thought in America: The Revolt Against Formalism* (1937); and Norman Welfel, *Molders of the American Mind* (1933). Biographies of academic leaders and monographs on the revolutionary changes within academic disciplines remain scarce, although a number are in various stages of preparation. For a sample of those available, see Robert E. L. Faris, *Chicago Sociology, 1920–1932* (1967); George Stocking *Race, Culture and Evolution, Essays in the History of Anthropology* (1968); Theodora Kroeber, *Alfred Kroeber* (1970); Irwin Edman, *John Dewey* (1955); and Nuel Pharr Davis, *Lawrence and Oppenheimer* (1968).

The political rebellion of 1924 is described from different perspectives by James Weinstein, *The Decline of Socialism in America, 1912–1925* (1967); Kenneth C. MacKay, *The Progressive Movement of 1924* (1947); and Russel B. Nye, *Midwestern Progressive Politics* (1951). On the 1928 campaign, see Roy Peel and Thomas Donnelly, *The 1928 Campaign* (1931); Edmund A. Moore, *A Catholic Runs for President* (1956); Ruth C. Silva, *Rum, Religion and Votes: 1928 Reexamined* (1962); Samuel Lubell, *The Future of American Politics* (1952); but compare the interpretations advanced by Silva and Lubell with Jerome Clubb and Howard Allen, "The Cities and the Election of 1928," *American Historical Review*, 74 (April 1969).

Provocative interpretations of the public response to Lindbergh and his flight can be found in John W. Ward "The Meaning of Lindbergh's Flight," *American Quarterly*, 10 (1958); and Kenneth S. Davis, *The Hero, Charles A. Lindbergh* (1959).

Thomas Wilson, *Fluctuations in Income and Employment* (1948), surveys the economy of the 1920's from a business cycle approach. M. Friedman and A. J. Schwartz, *The Great Contraction*, places a heavy emphasis on monetary factors. George Soule, *Prosperity Decade: From War to Depression, 1917–1929* (1947), is a superior economic history of the period. Business attitudes and practices are studied in J. W. Prothro, *The Dollar Decade: Business Ideas in the 1920's* (1954). Siegfried Giedion, *Mechanization Takes Command* (1948), is a stimulating interpretation of the growth of industrial technology. For a detailed account of the decade's most famous industrialist, see Allan Nevins and F. E. Hill, *Ford: The Times, the Man and the Company* (1954), and *Ford: Expansion and Challenge* (1957). Labor's plight during the 1920's receives sympathetic and skillful treatment in Bernstein, *The Lean Years* (1960).

Hoover's economic policies are ably defended by the former President himself in his *Memoirs: The Great Depression, 1929–1941* (1952); by R. L. Wilbur and A. M. Hyde, *The Hoover Policies* (1937); and by Harris G. Warren, *Herbert Hoover and the Great Depression* (1959). These volumes together, however, are hardly a match for the contrary views expressed with sparkling wit in John K. Galbraith, *The Great Crash* (1955).

In addition to Schlesinger's volume, mentioned above, good accounts of the campaign and election of 1932 can be found in Frank Freidel, *Franklin D. Roosevelt: The Triumph* (1956); James McGregor Burns, *Roosevelt: The Lion and the Fox* (1956); Rexford Tugwell, *The Democratic Roosevelt* (1957); James Farley, *Behind the Ballots* (1938); H. F. Gosnell, *Champion Campaigner: Franklin D. Roosevelt* (1952); R. V. Peel and T. C. Donnelly, *The 1932 Campaign* (1935); and Alfred B. Rollins, Jr., *Roosevelt and Howe* (1932).

Significant Statistics

	1900	1920	1932
Population	76,094,000	106,466,000	124,949,000
Percentage urban	39.7	51.2	NA
Percentage rural	60.3	48.8	NA
Percentage non-white	12.0	10.0	10.0
Life expectancy			
White	47.6	54.9	63.2
Nonwhite	33.0	45.3	53.7
Gross national product (current dollars)			
Total (billions of dollars)	17.3	88.9	58.5
Per capita (dollars)	231	835	468
Defense spending (millions of dollars)[a]	332	4,329	1,688
As percentage of GNP	1.9	5.0	3.0
Military personnel on active duty	125,923	343,302	244,902
Labor union membership	791,000	5,034,000	3,226,000
Birth rate (per 1,000 live births)	32.3	27.7	19.5
Advertising expenditures (millions of dollars)	542	2,935	1,627
Motor vehicle registrations	8,000	239,161	24,391,000
Persons lynched			
White	9	8	2
Nonwhite	106	53	6
High school graduates (as percentage of all persons over 16 years old)	6.4	16.8	NA

Sources: *Historical Statistics of the United States, Colonial Times to 1957; Statistical Abstract of the United States,* 1970; and *Digest of Educational Statistics,* 1970.

[a] Includes veterans spending; excludes interest.

4

Years of Crisis

**America in Depression
and War, 1933–1945**

OTIS L. GRAHAM, JR.

The end of 1932 brought the fourth and worst winter of the Depression. At least 13 million men could find no work. Their dependents, perhaps 30 million people, existed on private charity, meager public aid from city and state governments, vanishing savings. The economy, after a slight and deceptive rally in the fall, spiraled down to a 1932 national income of $42 billion. America produced in 1932 about half of what it had in 1929, when the national income had reached $88 billion. Debts contracted at the income levels of the 1920's could not be carried, and a chain of defaults clogged the channels of trade and banking. Families and corporations were absorbed in the nightmare of debt: How to pay out of shrunken incomes? How to collect from strained debtors? The cold months from November to March were paralleled by a frigid investment

climate. No new technologies, no new industries, lured capital from
its retreats. Nowhere was there any large-scale stimulus to expand,
to employ men and materials. Businessmen contracted payrolls and
plans, trying through individual acts of economy to last out the
baffling economic ice age that had begun in Hoover's first year.

Oddly, the general temper of the country was still one of hope-
lessness and defeat rather than of revolt. No one seemed to have
any new ideas or much faith in the old ones. Business leaders filed
before the hearings of the Senate Banking and Currency Committee
in January and February and grimly advised a return to thrift and
a balanced budget. Some offered even less. Jackson Reynolds, president of the First National City Bank of New York, replied, when
asked if he had any solution, "I have not, and I do not believe anybody else has." Congress went into session on December 5 and could
muster no majority for the few legislative proposals available —
organized labor's thirty-hour bill and a new and complicated agricultural measure. President Hoover's ideas had already been given
legislative form, and the outgoing President had nothing else to
recommend beyond international debt adjustment. There was an
absence not only of ideas but of concerted, applied energy. The
public was largely apathetic. Here and there signs of revolt appeared,
but they remained scattered. Farmers in the Midwest had swelled
the ranks of Milo Reno's Farm Holiday Association in the summer
of 1932, and their threat of a farmers' strike was given some substance by a few mob actions to prevent foreclosures. But most of
rural America endured the Depression without protest. The cities
were even less rebellious than the countryside. The bonus army of
veterans that encamped near the Capitol from May to July had been
interested in pensions, not in revolution, and when violence broke
out in late July it was initiated by the government, which decided
to clear the camp with troops under General Douglas MacArthur.
In the winter of 1932–1933 there were riots or mob actions by
hungry unemployed men in Seattle, Detroit, and Des Moines, but
all were brief and unconnected. The unemployed and transient
wandered or waited in a country stuffed with food in silos and bins,
its magnificent industrial plant half idle. Bread lines, as Norman
Thomas said, were knee deep in wheat. Yet such a revolting spectacle did not drive Americans to revolt. They voted out their President in November and voted in the other man, but nearly 16 million
voted to retain the leadership they had, and the Socialists and
Communists together polled only 984,000 votes. The country seemed

to be waiting—for an end to winter, for the inauguration of the new President in March, or, in many cases, for nothing at all.

In March, Franklin Roosevelt's "new deal" would shatter the quiet and fill the nation with a sense of action. To contemporaries who lived through the listless final days of the Hoover administration, this sudden political activism created a sharp sense of discontinuity. Such dynamism had not been expected. The Democratic Party was a conservative, states rights party, and its leading figures— John Nance Garner, Alfred E. Smith, Albert Ritchie, Newton D. Baker — had no broader conception of government functions than Hoover had. The new President, Franklin D. Roosevelt of New York, had appeared to many observers as a genial man of no striking personal or intellectual talents. Nothing in his background suggested the slightest radicalism. He was descended from an old, wealthy Hudson River family, educated at the best patrician schools (Groton, Harvard, and Columbia Law), and had been a moderate progressive in the New York state legislature (1911–1913). During two terms as governor of New York (1928–1932), Roosevelt had taken liberal positions on public power and unemployment relief, but the DuPont wing of his party was not alarmed. He believed in a balanced budget and was above all a loyal party man.

Certainly his campaign had been characterized more by breezy confidence than by clarity or new proposals. Hoover thought he detected the outlines of a radical program in Roosevelt's speeches at Oglethorpe University in April and at San Francisco's Commonwealth Club in September, but his intuition was not widely shared. Roosevelt appeared a mild progressive, using the words "planning" and "experimentation" more than some liked and endorsing the regulation of stock exchanges, publicly owned electric power projects, federal relief, and expanded public works. But he struck conservative notes in all his speeches, and in some, such as at Pittsburgh, he attacked Hoover's unbalanced budget and sounded like a candidate to the right of the current President. Informed people thought him open-minded, but without strong convictions—hence no source of innovation or reform. During the four months of the "interregnum" he surprised no one by confining his attention, so far as could be determined, to putting together a Cabinet rather evenly balanced between progressives and conservatives.* One well-mean-

---

* Progressive appointments included Secretary of the Interior Harold L. Ickes, Secretary of Labor Frances Perkins, and Secretary of Agriculture Henry A. Wallace. Secre-

This cartoon by Miguel Covarrubias of Roosevelt's first inauguration captures Hoover's resentful
mood exactly — the furrowed brow, the refusal to iron his trousers or wear
the traditional top hat (artist's imagination here). Roosevelt's jaunty confidence
comes through clearly. But the pastoral background and general serenity
misrepresent the actual occasion, which took place over a cold, wintry weekend in the
midst of a complete collapse of the nation's banking system.

ing politician had apparently replaced another. When the New Deal
burst upon the country, it was quickly learned that FDR had unsuspected strengths and a strong bent toward social reform. For the
next twelve years, one man seemed to make a breathtaking difference.

But one can see in retrospect that many forces converged to produce federal action in 1933, whoever the President or whatever the

tary of State Cordell Hull was a Wilsonian whose radicalism was far behind him.
The others, Secretary of the Treasury William Woodin, Secretary of War George Dern,
Secretary of the Navy Claude Swanson, Secretary of Commerce Dan Roper, Attorney
General Homer Cummings, and Postmaster General James Farley, were either known
to be conservatives or to have no political ideas beyond loyalty to the party.

party in power. Roosevelt shaped the New Deal in vital ways, but an expanded federal role was as inevitable in 1933 as anything in history can be. Since the 1880's there had been a trend toward federal intervention in American economic life, a trend accelerated during the Progressive era and World War I. In the 1920's many groups agitated for political solutions to their economic problems, and the Harding, Coolidge, and Hoover governments responded in some cases, extending or inaugurating federal subsidization and regulation in agriculture, the merchant marine, aviation, and railroads. These developments would surely have been extended into the 1930's in one form or another had Hoover been reelected. Naturally, the differences would have been important. The conservative Republican administrations of the 1920's, had they been retained in office during the succeeding decade, would probably have resisted pressures for government action in areas Roosevelt invaded, such as public power, labor relations, and exchange regulation. But the contrast between the 1920's and 1930's, between Hoover and Roosevelt, has become too sharp in our memories. Not only were there antecedents for New Deal activism, but historical accidents exaggerated the impact of the new regime. Constitutional arrangements forced a four-month interregnum in which there was no leadership. A snowballing of bank failures in February culminated in a national bank holiday on March 4, inauguration day, which heightened the end-of-an-era sensation. These circumstances, plus the striking contrast between the personalities of Hoover and Roosevelt, gave an impression of historical discontinuity that obscures the force and direction of fundamental social trends in America.

The Hundred Days

There is no denying that the spirit of the New Deal was exhilaratingly new, and after an initial period of conservatism, so was much of its substance. Roosevelt from the start seemed to enjoy innovation more than Hoover had and was markedly less restrained by fears that his actions might have doubtful historical or constitutional precedents. It is true that his response to the bank closing was to choose the conservative path of federal inspection, loans from the Reconstruction Finance Corporation (RFC), and the reopening of sound banks on March 9, when he might have nationalized the

banks. Although nationalization would have been technically difficult, given the personnel available, there would probably have been
little political resistance to it under the circumstances. Roosevelt
acted conservatively, but the manner of his action—extending the
bank holiday until March 10 and going ahead with reorganization
without waiting for Congress to reconvene, citing the dubious
authority of a 1917 law—revealed that the new President had a
broad view of his powers and responsibilities. On March 9 Congress
in just eight hours legalized what Roosevelt had done, and the only
complaints came from a few progressives who thought he had lost
an opportunity to bring greater discipline to banking. On the next
day Roosevelt asked Congress to cut the budget by some $500
million. Again the only voices of criticism were progressive voices,
and Roosevelt's momentum was irresistible. It was a curious inter-
lude. Change was in the air, yet the dynamic new President asked
only for conservative legislation.

Then, on March 16, Roosevelt decided to hold Congress in session
to enact an entirely new program. During the next three months

Bank Failures, 1929-1945

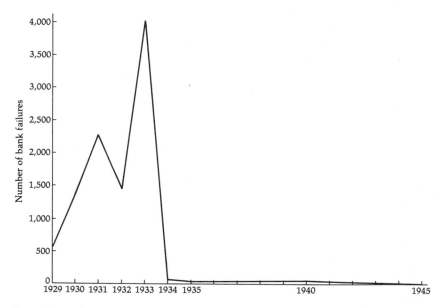

Source: *Historical Statistics of the United States, Colonial Times to 1957.*

Congress, in an atmosphere of crisis and urgency, enacted fifteen major laws. The period had revolutionary appearances to contemporaries. New agencies and programs were piled on one another, and the normally obstructive Congress yielded to the chief executive in a fashion that had no real American precedent. But most of the revolutionary appearance was in the pace, not the substance, of policy. And though Roosevelt gave the appearance of a man who had mastered events, the truth is that he and his advisers neither originated nor fully controlled much of what was done. The President was actually hard pressed to maintain control of countless groups whose patience with the old policies had run out. Yet even if the New Deal had little clear pattern, that we can discern any pattern at all testifies to Roosevelt's unexpected ability to become identified with and to guide the unprecedented pressures for social reform.

Amid the clamor, Roosevelt established certain priorities. Relief for the unemployed seemed to come first, after the banking crisis was met. From 1933 to 1935 the basic relief agency was the Federal Emergency Relief Authority (FERA), a flexible agency headed by the hard-driving social worker Harry Hopkins. FERA, through federal grants, stimulated states and cities to provide work for those with the requisite health and skills and "doles" to unemployables. Hopkins and the FERA staff disliked the delays and inequities of operating through local agencies, and in the winter of 1934–1935, with unemployment still over 10 million, Hopkins persuaded Roosevelt to underwrite an agency, the Civil Works Administration (CWA), to directly employ 4 million people without investigating their eligibility. Double that number wanted work. But the CWA effort was the largest yet by the federal government, and both its magnitude and its inventiveness in devising ways to channel money to millions out of work reflected the humanitarianism of its director. Journalist Ernie Pyle perhaps captured the reason for Hopkins' success as a relief administrator when he wrote: "Your neck is sort of skinny, like poor peoples' necks."

Yet the President soon became alarmed at the actual and potential expense of offering a federal job to all the unemployed. He terminated CWA in the spring of 1934, and in early 1935 announced his permanent relief program. The government would "quit the dole" (which Roosevelt, like Hoover, thought corrupting) and provide work relief for no more than 3.5 million people. The bulk of these jobs would be created by a new agency, the Works Progress Administration (WPA); young males might also find work in the

Civilian Conservation Corps (CCC), established in April 1933, administered by the army and involved chiefly in reforestation. The rest of the needy were assumed to be unemployable by reason of age, bad health, or dependency. Roosevelt, recalling that his hometown of Hyde Park, New York, had "taken care of" its eight relief families, decided that unemployables were a local responsibility. Through the Social Security Act, the federal government would aid local governments in assuming the "dole" burden through matching grants for aid to the disabled, orphaned, and aged.

The Congress agreed to the relief program in April 1935, and for the rest of the 1930's the WPA employed between 1.9 million (in September 1937) and 3.2 million (in February 1936) a month. The CCC enrolled on the average of 250,000 a month. This was the federal work-relief program after 1935. An able-bodied man might also be hired by the "heavy public works" agencies, the Tennessee Valley Authority (TVA) and the Public Works Authority (PWA). Or he might secure a job as one of the 350,000 government workers added as the number of people employed by the government grew from 600,000 in 1933 to about 950,000 in 1939. When the WPA was at its peak, the federal government employed as many as 4 million people.

By any absolute standard, this response to unemployment was disappointing. In the month Roosevelt proposed that the WPA assume responsibility for hiring 3.5 million men, there were 11 million or 12 million unemployed, most of them able to work. WPA wages were lower than necessary to avoid competition with private industry, but even with such economies the agency never hired more than 39 percent of the eligible unemployed, and the figure fell as low as 17 percent at one point. Those not hired by WPA or CCC were expected to find their way to private employers. Some surplus food might reach those who waited for jobs, either through the activities of the Commodities Surplus Corporation or, after 1939, the food stamp plan.

But if one uses a relative standard, remembering the past, the New Deal relief performance was superior. The government stepped in when local relief was drying up and for the first time provided money and food to many who could not work. The sudden availability of federal funds spurred local agencies and governments to establish and improve relief laws and procedures. Although New Deal work relief was never sufficient, it was offered in such a variety of forms that it retained the skills (and some of the self-respect) of many professional and skilled workers. The WPA em-

This photograph of idle men and boarded store fronts could have been taken as early as 1930, or as late as 1940. It is a Depression classic, capturing the dejection and resigned waiting of the unemployed. The scene is San Francisco in 1934, Roosevelt's second year.

ployed 40,000 artists and writers to decorate public buildings with murals and write local history; its 6,200 musicians played to 2.8 million people; its 158 theaters entertained 30 million. A division of WPA, the National Youth Administration (NYA), gave part-time work to 2 million students and 2.6 million youths not in school. In all, the range of activities was astonishing. Money appropriated to FERA, CCC, CWA, and WPA put people to work building schools, hospitals, parks, airports, auditoriums, and tennis courts, reforesting eroded farm land, teaching illiterate adults, repairing roads, exterminating rats, stuffing birds, filling teeth. The work was not always efficiently done or even necessary, but much of it was of great social value and would not have been accomplished at all without the willingness of the federal government to borrow and spend for this new purpose—federal work relief. More important perhaps than the tangible results, New Deal work relief restored both earning power and a sense of social usefulness to millions who could find no place in the private economy. "We aren't on relief anymore," one woman said. "My husband works for the government."

While relief had high priority in the early New Deal, reform of financial institutions was a pressing issue, especially in a Democratic administration where men remembered William Jennings Bryan and Woodrow Wilson. The President's decision to pursue recovery through cooperation with business gave corporations an initial period of freedom from anti-trust activity, but banks and the stock exchanges could not escape the reform impulse. There was little public sympathy for the institutions that collapsed in 1929 or for the bankers whose financial manipulations and tax evasions were exposed in Senate Banking and Currency Committee hearings in 1933. After perfunctory debate, Congress enacted laws requiring disclosure of essential information in connection with stock issuance (the Securities Act of 1933) and submitting the exchanges to the regulation of the new Securities Exchange Commission (the Securities Exchange Act of 1934). Speculation by banks on the market was made more difficult by the Banking Act of 1933, which divorced commercial banks from their investment affiliates. The reform energies of the early New Deal were satisfied with these controls on finance. Later, when cooperative policies had not produced recovery, the administration would seek reforms much closer to the heart of business power—anti-monopoly suits, regulation of wages and hours, protection of the right of labor to organize, stricter taxation of capital gains and profits.

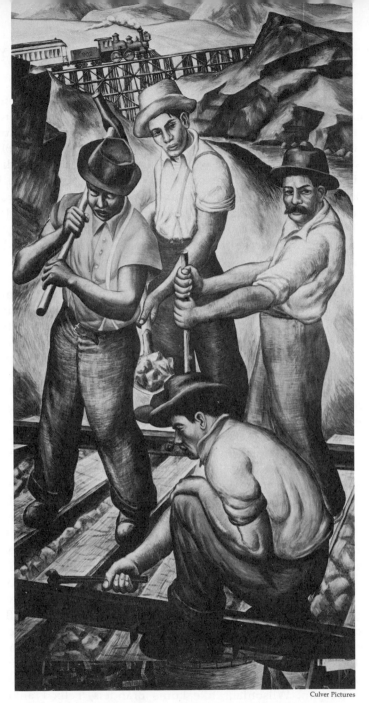

American art in the 1930's bore the mark of the Depression in its increased attention
to working-class themes. This WPA mural by Charles Davis depicts the joint
labors of black, Italian, perhaps Mexican-American,
and Chinese workers in building the nation's railroad system.

But such reforms are by their nature divisive and were deferred because they conflicted with Roosevelt's general strategy for recovery. Like most of his decisions, the choice of a recovery strategy was made haltingly and erratically, was dictated more by political pressures than by logic, and was not so firm as to bar contradictory policies. When Roosevelt arrived in Washington during the bank holiday, he found an almost wartime mood of national unity. This favored the strategy of national economic "planning" that had been urged on Roosevelt before and during the campaign by three of his "brain trust" advisers from Columbia University—Adolf Berle, Raymond Moley, and Rexford G. Tugwell. Because their idea of planning did not involve nationalization of industry, it could be carried out only if businessmen cooperated with the government's price, labor, and investment policies. The spirit of unity encouraged Roosevelt to think such an approach to expanded production a feasible one. The experience of World War I was also a strong influence; production miracles had been worked by government and industry planning in a capitalistic setting. Several leading businessmen urged the government in the spring of 1933 to legalize their search for economic stability through some sort of planning machinery. So Roosevelt decided to move toward a planned economy.

It is easy to see how this approach to recovery was chosen in 1933. The alternatives were in varying ways less attractive. Hoover was thought to have tried the classic route of waiting for confidence to revive, and any more of this sort of passive policy was unthinkable. The notion that the government, in a depression, should run up a large deficit through spending for public works or however it wished, thereby borrowing "idle" money and returning it to the spending stream, was an idea advanced by some American economists before John Maynard Keynes formulated it in *The General Theory of Employment, Interest, and Money* (1936). Most economists distrusted the idea, and it had no significant following among Congressmen, industrialists, or bank presidents. Monetary inflation was an old idea with a particularly strong foothold in the Democratic Party. Its agrarian political backing was so potent that Roosevelt was forced to attempt some of it. But both the President and the eastern wing of the party feared inflation and would not make it a major weapon. Wilsonians like Louis Brandeis, Felix Frankfurter, and Cordell Hull urged on Roosevelt the old Wilsonian policies of free trade and stern anti-trust measures to bring down prices, and the eclectic President would try these remedies too, especially later

on. But in 1933 he did not think them quick enough, distrusted their
negativism, regretted their divisiveness, and perhaps remembered
that a recession had followed Wilson's domestic reforms of 1913–
1914.

No, the most compelling idea was the one that recent experience
had most confirmed—economic planning through various forms of
government-industry-agriculture cooperation. This approach had
worked during the war, and it took advantage of the mood of unity
and harmony of interests that Roosevelt discovered in his first
months in office. This idea guided the major legislation of the
Hundred Days. The government would plan for industrial recovery
through the National Recovery Administration (NRA) and for
agricultural recovery through the Agricultural Adjustment Administration (AAA). In each case, those who owned the means of production were to combine with government officials in the planning
process. As it turned out, conflicts appeared between the goals of
officials responsible to the public and those who owned the factories
and fields. This was not adequately foreseen. The President trusted
to his resourcefulness to iron out any difficulties. Businessmen and
farmers had some doubts about allowing bureaucrats they did not
know to help them make decisions formerly made in the marketplace, but they were desperate. For all involved, it was clear that
the free, unplanned economy led to waste, vanished profits, suffering, radicalism. Were not coordination, rationality, harmony, and a
rising standard of living preferable to the selfish, undirected war
of competitive capitalism? In 1933, it was an attractive vision and,
because contemporaries had not yet lived through the New Deal,
a plausible one.

The centerpiece of New Deal planning was the NRA. This two-
year enterprise has long since vanished, and it is hard to recapture
its rationale, its magnitude, or the enthusiasm it briefly generated.
Actually, the fundamental idea behind NRA was not as preposterous
as the bureaucratic monster that finally emerged. Business profits
had been eradicated as supply swamped demand. Because businessmen were engaged in supply, they saw oversupply rather than
underdemand when they puzzled over their problems. Some corporation executives had come to feel that, if all competitors could
agree on shares of the market and an industry-wide price, the
fratricidal war for the dwindling market could be halted. At least
a small profit would return, if prices were set properly. Survival
would be assured. Perhaps later, expansion would come—from

somewhere. These arrangements were attractive, but they were also illegal. Yet why not set aside the anti-trust laws and allow industrialists, with the participation of government officials and union representatives, to reach agreements on quotas, prices, and wages? Labor agreed to planning if it could secure higher wages, which business seemed to accept if it could be sure of higher prices. Labor also received, in Section 7-a of the law, the right to organize and to bargain with employers (just to bargain; no one was obligated to agree). Relief from unrestrained competition, prices held at levels that returned a profit, an end to the brutal necessity to slash payrolls—all this the NRA would arrange and legalize.

How could this scheme possibly have brought general recovery? Businessmen saw it as a way to survive the downward spiral of prices and profits and to buy time while they waited for an upturn of vague origins. Their attachment to the idea was chiefly defensive. But the administration had more positive goals. The conservative planners, notably Raymond Moley and NRA administrator Hugh Johnson, hoped that such a haven for businessmen would restore their confidence and lead them to invest. Other New Dealers intended that the NRA codes and administrative machinery would force wages up but hold prices down, thereby squeezing from business the purchasing power necessary to stimulate recovery. (They were presumably to get the money to cover higher wage costs by borrowing or by dipping into some hoard of their own.) In this view, NRA was to act chiefly as a taxing device. This, of course, would require firm administration. To increase the chances of success, Title II of the act establishing NRA appropriated $3.3 billion for a public works program to "prime the pump." All this, along with the agricultural recovery expected under AAA, would restore the national economy to pre-1929 health.

To achieve recovery this way would require hard bargaining in code formation and administration and businessmen willing to have expansion squeezed out of their savings or credit. Pricing power was the key. Business must not be allowed to pass on higher labor costs to the consumer. But mere persuasion would not be enough to get businessmen to pay out more than they took in, certainly not for long. This would require power. Here NRA failed, perhaps inevitably. Had only a few codes been attempted, perhaps the President and his thinly manned staff could have mastered the economic details and focused public opinion to prevent prices from outstripping wages. Businessmen treated in this way would not have been in a mood to expand, but perhaps profits would have reappeared as volume increased. Roosevelt appointed as head of the NRA Hugh Johnson, a former executive of the Moline Plow Company and War Industries Board official in 1917–1919. Johnson, a man of titanic energies and colorful speech, had not underestimated the difficulties. "It will be red fire at first and dead cats afterward," he predicted for NRA: "This is just like mounting the guillotine on the infinitesimal gamble that the axe won't work." Yet, like the other New Dealers, Johnson's confidence was stronger than his misgivings. He arranged 557 codes in a summer of hectic activity, and they turned out to be more than the government could carefully administer. Johnson was forced to hire men from industry itself to serve as NRA officials. Labor organization was weak, and the consumer interest was almost totally unrepresented. In the end, business dominated the writing and administration of NRA codes, so that in most industries prices went up ahead of or parallel to wages, and no addition to consumer demand resulted.

This was the record of the regulatory commissions all over again. A public institution to force the "Public Interest" on America's mighty corporations could be set up, but the public soon looked the other way and the corporations turned the new agency to their own ends. Moreover, the public works side of NRA proved a slow way to spend money. Secretary of the Interior Harold Ickes, administrator of the agency (Public Works Administration) created to spend the $3.3 billion granted in Title II, moved with ponderous deliberation, hating waste and graft more than he understood the need for speed. Only $1.2 billion of the $3.3 billion was spent by the end of 1933. Neither business nor government, then, had allowed itself to be forced into a significant expansion of payrolls. The good will of all parties faded as NRA proved cumbersome, complex, and disappointing. Not even the giant nine-hour parade in New York in August or the effort to mobilize consumer power through the "Blue Eagle" sticker could be effectively brought to bear on businessmen who fought to keep the price-wage ratio favorable to themselves. By the winter of 1934 it was clear that the previous summer's economic spurt had been merely an effort to beat rising labor costs, not the beginning of recovery. NRA was snarled in internal conflict, bureaucratic detail, and the gigantic task of understanding the labyrinthine American economy. Even the leaders of large businesses were disgruntled with NRA, and economic individualists stepped up their attacks on its monopolistic features. When the

Supreme Court invalidated NRA on May 27, 1935, in the *Schechter* case, there were only scattered, minor regrets.

NRA was only half of Roosevelt's planning effort. The other half was a massive program of controlled production in agriculture. New Deal farm policy, like most of the New Deal, was a complicated, overlapping, even contradictory cluster of policies, and the word "planning" does not properly apply to much of it. The refinancing operations of the Farm Credit Association were essentially unrelated to planned production, as were the activities of the Resettlement Administration (1935–1937) and the Farm Security Administration (1937–1946) to convert tenants to landowners. But these were secondary. The basic policy involved controlled production, and the key agency was the AAA.

When FDR took office, the farm groups were badly split over the proper remedies. They all agreed on the need for broader federal support and a regulatory role, however, and the idea of controls on production was gaining strength as prices declined to disaster levels. The administration short-circuited all the disputes among contentious farm groups by supporting a law (the Agricultural Adjustment Act, signed in June 1933) empowering the secretary of agriculture to utilize any or all of the schemes then current in agricultural circles. He could pursue "parity" (a level of farm prices equal in purchasing power to the "good" years, 1909–1914) through benefit payments for crop reduction, crop buying and storage, marketing agreements between farmers and processors to limit production, export subsidies, and monetary inflation. Some of these steps were traditional. Federal purchase and storage of nonperishable crops had been commenced under Hoover, and export subsidies and inflation were old ideas. The new element in the AAA approach was restriction of supply, either through benefit payments for reduced acreage or through marketing agreements. With this step the New Deal brought central planning to agriculture, as the NRA had done for industry.

Cumbersome and philosophically alien as the program was in some respects, it was popular with farmers, for economic gains came early and were substantial. Crops were already in the ground for 1933 when the act passed, so the government paid cotton growers $160 million to plow under 10 million acres of cotton and spent $30 million to take 6 million sows and little pigs off the market. Bad weather helped cut the 1933 wheat crop, and prices for those three commodities were up by the end of summer. After that, prices fluctuated, but by 1936 a combination of direct payments, acreage reduction, and drought had helped remove price-depressing surpluses and had raised farm prices to 83 percent of parity (from a 1933 low of 56 percent). Cash income for farmers almost doubled, from the 1932 low of $4.3 billion to $7.6 billion in 1935, a considerable gain despite offsetting inflation. All this represented marked improvement to most farmers, even though the goal of parity with 1909–1914 was not reached until the war years.

But farmers did not share equally in the gains. Tenants, who constituted 55 percent of all farmers in 1930, rarely received their proportion of benefit payments mailed to landowners. Worse, the AAA was actually forcing tenants from the land. A study of cotton tenancy in 1935 estimated that from 500,000 to 1 million families (or from 2 million to 5 million people) had been displaced by the AAA, both from acreage restriction and the automation financed out of benefit payments. This was a massive human tragedy, because there were no jobs in the cities for these rural people; but it was largely an invisible tragedy until tenants in Arkansas attempted to organize in 1934–1935. Their meetings (often interracial) were disrupted by landowners and police. There were beatings and jailings for union activity. The sympathetic involvement of the Socialist Norman Thomas and of Eleanor Roosevelt, among others, brought press coverage, and the relation of AAA to tenants was painfully exposed. Both the President and his liberal secretary of agriculture, Henry A. Wallace, were disturbed by the uneven distribution of rewards and burdens under AAA. Yet to alter this outcome would have meant taking the side of the agricultural lower classes, which in the South included most blacks, against the politically powerful large landowners. The issue came to a head when a group of liberals within AAA (largely in Jerome Frank's legal division) insisted that AAA contracts protect tenants from displacement. Southern congressional leaders forced Roosevelt and Wallace to fire or reassign the reformers in AAA. New Deal farm policy continued to displace tenants throughout the 1930's at a rate of some 40,000 families a year. An effort was made to resettle tenants through the Resettlement Administration and the Farm Security Administration, but the scale of these projects was dwarfed by the problem. Economically, the solution to the "farm problem" was fewer farmers, but under the New Deal the industrial sector never expanded enough to absorb displaced rural people. Thus the New Deal achievement in agriculture may be characterized as substantial, though the benefits were largely channeled to the upper half of American farmers. Much of the cost was borne by the lower half.

With planned production in industry and agriculture the New

Deal expected to eliminate the "burden" of oversupply. Expansion
would then be possible, and it was hoped that the stimulus of PWA
and FERA spending would start the climb upward. While Congress
was in a pliant mood in the spring of 1933, Roosevelt asked for fifteen
major laws, and all were enacted in one form or another. In addition
to economic planning, banking reform, securities regulation, and
relief, there were steps toward debt refinancing and public power
projects. The crushing load of debt incurred at pre-Depression prices
had to be carried on Depression incomes, and mortgage foreclosures
and bankruptcy helped block economic revival. Debt forced 76 percent of all farm sales in 1933, for example, and urban foreclosures
were reported at a thousand a day. Debt refinancing and downward
revision became one of the New Deal's most uncontroversial and
successful programs. Farm lending programs were centralized in
the Farm Credit Administration, and by mid-decade about one-fifth
of America's farms had been refinanced with the agency's help.
For urban homeowners the Home Owners' Loan Corporation
(HOLC) was established, and it refinanced about 1 million homes
in the same period. These agencies worked quietly throughout the
1930's, along with the RFC, which lent some $12 billion to banks,
insurance companies, and railroads. Here the New Deal emerged
most clearly as a rescue operation for private property.

The lending agencies were conservative in concept and rested on
considerable precedent. Another successful agency, the Tennessee
Valley Authority, demonstrates the great range of the New Deal's
experimentation. The conception behind TVA had a revolutionary
potential. Roosevelt and TVA's legislative "parent," Senator George
Norris, building on a half-century of conservationist thought, conceived of the Tennessee River basin (a 40,000 square-mile area
touching seven southeastern states) as an organic physical, economic,
and social unit requiring unified regional planning. The TVA was
to engage in multi-purpose planning and development in the basin,
an interlocking assignment in flood control, navigational dredging,
soil conservation, reforestation, and the production and sale of electric power and fertilizers. The first chairman of TVA's board of
directors, Arthur E. Morgan, dreamed of social planning that would
transform the life of the region. In his view, TVA's main job was
not the production of electric power but the education of the people
in better land utilization and the encouragement of native crafts
and decentralized light industry. Morgan's ideas were not clearly
articulated, but to some they seemed to imply radical political

The Tennessee Valley Authority

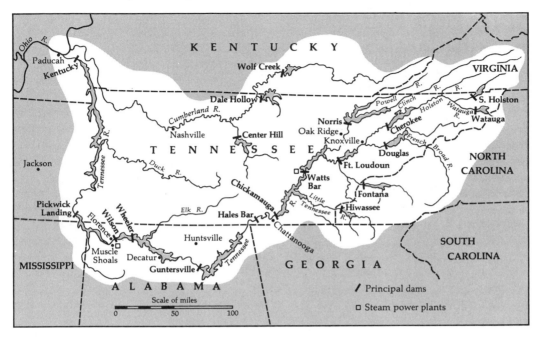

changes—on the one hand centralized regional decision-making, on the other an intellectually and economically independent local citizenry in place of the unorganized, politically apathetic farmers of southern Appalachia.

TVA did encourage economic diversification and carried on an extensive campaign to improve agricultural methods, but effective regional economic and ecological planning never really materialized. Such a departure seemed politically too risky to a vulnerable new agency. TVA decided instead to conduct educational work among rural people, working wherever possible through the conservative network of Farm Bureau county agents and the staffs of the land-grant colleges. Further, director David E. Lilienthal managed to steer the agency toward a primary emphasis on public electric power. To Lilienthal, TVA's most important task was the production and sale of electricity at low rates, providing a measure that would drive down private rates in the region and in the nation at large. In this TVA was successful, after long and acrimonious legal battles with private utilities ably led by Wendell Willkie, the president of Commonwealth and Southern Corporation. By the start of World War II, TVA was providing electricity to seventy-six municipalities and thirty-eight rural cooperatives, and everywhere in the region rates were down and the use of electricity was on the rise. Tupelo, Mississippi, for example, had tripled its consumption between 1929 and 1941, and rates had fallen from 7.4 to 1.7 cents a kilowatt hour. The low cost of TVA power drove private utility companies in the Southeast to reduce their own rates, but their sales also increased, confirming Lilienthal's faith that lower rates would dramatically expand the market for electricity. By 1942, the consumption of electricity in the area served by TVA was up 196 percent from 1932, as compared to 63 percent for the rest of the nation. The effect on people's lives was incalculable: Rural people could purchase electric lights, pumps, cream separators, refrigerators, freezers, washing machines.*

Although TVA was associated in the public mind with electricity, its other functions made their impact. By the mid-1940's, TVA managed twenty-one dams in the Tennessee basin, maintained a nine-foot channel over a 650-mile stretch of the river from Paducah, Kentucky, to Knoxville, and had protected the area from the great floods that had formerly terrorized low-lying communities. Traffic on the Tennessee River had increased tenfold over the level of the 1920's, and recreational lakes and parks enriched the leisure lives of millions. This was a splendid accomplishment and moderated the disappointment of those who had hoped that TVA might become the institution to bring multi-purpose planning to the squabbling and fragmented resource users along a river system. TVA was a dramatic success in demonstrating what could be done through a public developmental agency to invigorate the private economic sector. Roosevelt intended to repeat the experiment on other river systems, but the threat of public planning rallied many local economic groups to the side of private power interests in a common fight against the expansion of public power. The TVA idea did not spread to other parts of the country.

* Not only did the people of the Tennessee Valley benefit from Franklin Roosevelt's interest in public power. The New Deal built dams on the Columbia River at Bonneille and Grand Coulee that produced electric power, and the Rural Electrification Administration made low-cost loans to cooperatives to extend power lines into sparsely settled areas. By 1950, 80 percent of American farms were served by electricity; in 1932, the figure had been 11 percent.

The End of the Honeymoon

It took only three months to enact the New Deal—or what proved to be the first installment of it. Even though the country was not transformed, the capital certainly was. Washington was electric with activity and confidence. New agencies scrambled for office space, lights burned late into the night in the Federal Triangle as the new administration surged with the energy appropriate to a new party, new men, and new directions in American policy. At times it seemed that every bureaucrat in Washington was a "New Dealer"—young, liberal, aggressive, with a university or social work background rather than business experience. Rexford G. Tugwell, who came to symbolize the young liberals, said he was eager to "roll up my sleeves, make America over." Years later it would be clear that the New Dealers had been only a tiny fraction of the federal civil service, that their influence had never been so great as conservatives had feared. But for a few years the "boys with their hair ablaze," as an older party figure called the New Dealers, brought a new spirit of idealism, self-sacrifice, and dynamism into American government. Edmund Wilson commented:

For a graduate of the school of New York liberalism, it is Old Home Week today in Washington. Everywhere in the streets and offices you run into old acquaintances; the editors and writers of the liberal press, the "progressive" young instructors from the colleges, the intelligent foundation workers, the practical idealists of settlement houses, the radicals who . . . conceive that there may just be a chance of turning the old order inside out.

Congress adjourned in June 1933, and the summer was filled with the hectic activity of putting new agencies and programs into shape. Economic indexes climbed, and the President seemed popular with all classes and groups. Then, toward the end of August, came a sudden slump. As fall arrived, it was clear that the structural approach to recovery, in which crucial private economic decisions shifted in part to public institutions, was very slow. Roosevelt cast about for quicker remedies and, being a Democrat, proved vulnerable to the allure of manipulating the money supply. He was assisted toward this decision by a terrific clamor from agrarian groups and politicians when farm prices fell precipitously in September. Five midwestern governors in October demanded that the government guarantee farmers the cost of production. This was tantamount to declaring farming a public utility. Perhaps monetary experimentation would head off such drastic demands. Some inflationary steps had already been taken, such as the decision in April to go off the domestic gold standard. But as late as autumn FDR had not used any of the six methods of inflating the dollar that had been granted him in the so-called Thomas amendment to the Agricultural Adjustment Act. From among the various inflationary devices he chose the "gold buying" theory of Professor George Warren of Cornell. Beginning on October 25, the government bid up the price of gold on the international exchange, devaluing the dollar in the hope of stimulating sales of export crops and raising commodity prices generally. Prices refused to respond. Inflationist pressure continued unabated, and Roosevelt felt forced on December 21 to agree to purchase the entire domestic output of silver at a price nineteen cents above the market in an effort to raise price levels.* Neither goldbuying nor silver-buying had much inflationary effect. After these futile experiments, Roosevelt largely lost interest in monetary policy.

If recovery would not come by some quick monetary scheme, the President must wait for it to be produced by the slower operation of the economic planning agencies. In the meantime, he relieved the political pressures of the autumn by the show of action on gold and silver, by ordering the Commodity Credit Corporation to buy cotton at ten cents a pound (it had slipped to six cents by the autumn), and by allowing Hopkins to employ 4 million people for the winter of 1933–1934 in the hastily devised CWA. The farm agitation subsided, but Roosevelt's honeymoon was over. The New Deal was the status quo and would be held responsible for America's unsolved problems—in particular, for the continuing Depression.

The Impact of Continuing Depression

The Depression had not ended in 1933. After the first year of Roosevelt's presidency, unemployment had fallen from the 1933 high of 25 percent of the labor force to 22 percent; the national income in 1934 was $49 billion, up from the 1933 total of $40 billion but still far short of the 1929 level of $88 billion. Just as under Hoover, jobless men by the millions made the rounds of employment offices and factory gates and found the peremptory "No Help Wanted" signs. New Deal relief payments kept many families and individuals

---

* A side-effect unintended by FDR but definitely intended by the twelve silverbloc Senators was a $1.2 billion subsidy to the silver industry.

from outright starvation, and federal credit saved many homes and farms. But the Depression ran on through the 1930's, etching in the national memory a decade of poverty, of lowered standards of living, of deferred plans, of career frustrations.

Some groups were hit harder than others. Young people waited an average of two years after schooling before finding a job in the 1930's, and about 25 percent of them never found employment until the war. General unemployment in 1933 was 25 percent; for youths fifteen to nineteen years of age it was 50 percent, and for the group aged twenty to twenty-four it was 36 percent. Nor was it a good time to be over fifty. Older industrial and clerical workers were first to be fired, and many would not find reemployment even when the economy revived somewhat after 1933. Another zone of special misery was the export-crop sector, particularly the cotton South. Large cotton, wheat, tobacco, and corn farmers benefited somewhat from the higher prices and benefit payments under the AAA, but the small farmer and the tenant endured desperate poverty. Indeed, there had been a depression for farmers in export crops since the early 1920's; the 1930's were simply worse. For one group of farmers —rural blacks—fate arranged a special burden. They were at the intersection of the two lines of greatest economic disadvantage in American life—an agricultural occupation and colored skin. Three million blacks lived on annual family incomes of less than $500 ($300 in Arkansas, as low as $132 in Mississippi), and when the decision was made to reduce the acreage under cultivation, many were driven from the meager security of a wooden shack. In 1939, a group of black tenants displaced from farms in Missouri camped on the roads, drawing national attention to one of the unintended and painful effects of long-range agricultural trends and national policy. Only in one respect did the black farmer have an advantage: He had experience with a marginal economic existence. "The Negro was born in depression," a black farmer commented on the 1930's. "The best he could be is a janitor or a porter or shoeshine boy. It [the Depression] only became official when it hit the white man."

The continuing distress of a stagnant economy loosened many people from their geographical moorings and sent them searching for opportunities. The economist's model assumes that labor ought to act in this way, flowing readily from defunct enterprises and regions to more viable ones. Yet the human aspect of a mobile labor force in a period of economic stagnation was very unpleasant. Indeed, one of the striking features of the 1930's was the sight of so much misery in motion. The hobo armies that had become familiar

Dorothea Lange, The Oakland Museum Collection

No one knows exactly how many Midwestern and Southern rural people migrated westward in the 1930's, victims of the Depression, a severe cycle of droughts, and the acreage-reduction programs of the New Deal. The children of these "Okies" are very probably Californians now, and cannot remember the desperation in their father's eyes.

in the days of Hoover did not dissolve at the change of administration. They were in evidence until the very edge of the war, loitering in railroad switchyards, grouped around fires in vacant city lots or at remote water-stops along western railroads. Much of this transient population was made up of young people, boys and girls, but the bulk of it was men in their fifties and sixties, of all colors. "Black and white . . . everybody was poor," a jobless man who rode the rails in the late 1930's recalled of his anonymous companions. "They didn't have no home, they were dirty, they had overalls on, they didn't have no food, they didn't have anything."

The wandering of the hoboes was aimless. But there were some patterns in the human flight of the 1930's, the chief one being the trek westward to California. Historian Clarke Chambers estimates that 1.2 million people entered California between 1930 and 1940, many of them the "Okies" driven from Oklahoma, Arkansas, and even the deep South by drought and the collapse of agricultural prices. The threadbare, desperate poverty of these migrants has had its chroniclers, most notably the novelist John Steinbeck. No evocation of Depression rootlessness, however, surpasses the last lines in John Dos Passos' *U.S.A.*:

The young man waits on the side of the road; the plane has gone; thumb moves in a small arc when a car tears hissing past. Eyes seek the driver's eyes. A hundred miles down the road. Head swims, belly tightens, wants crawl over his skin like ants:

went to school, books said opportunity, ads promised speed, own your home, shine bigger than your neighbor, the radiocrooner whispered girls, ghosts of platinum girls coaxed from the screen, millions in winnings were chalked up on the boards in the offices, paychecks were for hands willing to work, the cleared desk of an executive with three telephones on it;

waits with swimming head, needs knot the belly, idle hands numb, beside the speeding traffic.

A hundred miles down the road.

The Rise of Radicalism

Observers of American life had predicted an upsurge of radical sentiment since the first winter of the Depression. Eventually it came, but as is often the case the growth of radicalism coincided with economic improvement. Beginning in 1934, a spirit of revolt animated many groups who had been quiescent at the trough of the cycle. They were stirred by the contrast between minimal or nonexistent economic gains and the expectations stirred by the rhetoric of a reform government. It may also be that the patience of the middle and lower classes would have run out after five years of economic stagnation, whatever the stimulus from the world of politics.

The distribution of the spirit of revolt was uneven. Young people were disproportionately injured by the unemployment of the 1930's, but they made only scattered efforts to unite for redress. The vast majority endured the long Depression without protest. "Ours was a bewilderment, not an anger," recalled one of the unemployed young men of the 1930's. "We weren't talking revolution, we were talking jobs." The Student League for Industrial Democracy, the

American Youth Congress, and the American Student Union exercised some influence on eastern college campuses, the last organization leading a student strike against future wars in 1935 and 1936. A group with more serious economic problems, the blacks, produced a small but significant increase in self-organization. A Black Cabinet of about forty black civil servants exerted pressure for greater representation of blacks within the federal bureaucracy. Blacks were prominent among the tenants in Arkansas, Mississippi, and Tennessee who formed the Southern Tenant Farmers' Union in 1934–1935. And, after 1935, the American Negro Congress met annually to press for an end to racial discrimination and a reformed economic order.

By far the most extensive protest came from the ranks of industrial labor. For over a decade, following the recession of 1920–1921, the labor movement had declined in membership and vitality, and the labor force in general exhibited few signs of a disposition to risk conflicts with employers. Then, toward the middle of 1933, the American blue collar worker began to change his mood. Workers were undoubtedly encouraged in a greater militancy by the improved political climate. After NRA's guarantee of collective bargaining (in Section 7-a), union organizers in 1933 had aggressively expanded union membership. Established unions such as the United Mine Workers jumped from 150,000 to 500,000 in a year, new unions were formed in steel and autos, and by the end of 1933 the AFL had recovered the 1.5 million members lost during the 1920's.

The year 1934 saw a wave of strikes and violence, as labor reached an unprecedented militancy and employers responded with hostility and preparations for armed conflict. Some employers and even some unionists forecast the eruption of open class warfare in America. In Minneapolis, when a businessmen's alliance refused to deal with the teamster's union, a strike commenced, uniting the city's working classes and bringing armed retaliation by employers and police. Violence broke out in both May and July, taking several lives and requiring Governor Floyd Olson to call the state's national guard. San Francisco longshoremen under Harry Bridges went out on strike in May 1934 and were joined by the teamsters. Open warfare between pickets and police-backed strikebreakers paralyzed the city. Horrified conservatives unsuccessfully appealed for armed intervention by federal authorities. Other cities were the scene of violence over labor disputes in 1934, among them Toledo, Ohio, and Kohler, Wisconsin. In 1934, strikes temporarily immobilized Minneapolis, Milwaukee, Philadelphia, Toledo, San Francisco, and other cities, shut down the east coast textile industry in August, and involved at least 1.5 million workers before the year was over.

Even migratory agricultural workers began to strike for higher wages and union recognition. This was a shock to large growers, especially in California, where Mexican-American laborers had been welcomed in the 1920's because of their presumed docility and willingness to do the "stoop labor" that whites would not do for the same wages (which averaged perhaps $12 a week, or from $300 to $500 a year). The labor unrest of the Depression now extended to workers in the fields and vineyards, who in fact had more grievances against the American system than low wages and long layoffs. Viable union organization was established in the Imperial Valley of California in 1927, and small strikes erupted in 1928, 1930, and 1931. In 1933 the Cannery and Agricultural Workers Industrial Union (CAWIU) began to exert aggressive pressure against the growers in the citrus groves of Orange County, in the celery fields near Los Angeles and Long Beach, and in the Salinas Valley. Employers met the CAWIU organizing effort with beatings, murder, and the deportation of as many as 20,000 Mexican-Americans, including many union leaders. The insurgent spirit ran deep among California's pickers, and the Imperial, San Joaquin, and Salinas valleys surged with class conflict through 1936. California was not the only site of agricultural strikes. They took place among cotton pickers in Arkansas, in the cranberry, onion, and citrus areas on the east coast, in the apple orchards of Washington, in the hops fields of Oregon. But in California the struggle was most bitter and protracted, possibly because of the racial dimension of the struggle to contain the aspirations of the Mexican-American work force. In the end, the growers, united as the Associated Farmers, suppressed union organization among migratory laborers with tactics more brutal than those used to break strikes in the Ford plants in Michigan or among tenant farmers in Arkansas.

Rising militancy in the work force was not merely a problem for employers. To the leadership of the AFL the great increase of spontaneous unionization presented interesting difficulties. Many of the new unionists were semi-skilled industrial workers rather than the elite of skilled craftsmen who had always dominated the AFL. Their leaders were younger and their spirit more aggressive than labor had known since the days of 1919. They demanded a labor movement broadened to include the mass of industrial workers whom craft unionism had ignored, and they wanted more from the New Deal than the NRA had produced.

The conservative leadership of the AFL, led by Gompers' hand-picked successor, William Green, responded defensively at first. To them, the AFL was a home for craft unionists. If a man was a pipe-fitter or a machinist, an AFL local welcomed him. Yet factories full of semi-skilled workers could be grouped only into industrial unions. The AFL leadership could not bring itself to spend much time and money organizing mass unions so alien to the AFL tradition. When the UMW's John L. Lewis, along with Sidney Hillman and David Dubinsky from the garment trades, were unable to force the 1935 AFL convention at Atlantic City to adopt a policy of support for industrial unionism, they broke with the leadership and formed the Committee for Industrial Organization (CIO).

The CIO consolidated its base among industrial unions unhappy with the AFL and then in 1936 commenced a vigorous drive to unionize the great nonunion industries — steel, automobiles, textiles. The workers were highly receptive, and in 1937 the CIO extracted a collective bargaining agreement from "Big Steel," one of the most intensely anti-union sectors of American industry. Often, even CIO leadership was not aggressive enough for the rank and file. The "sit-down" strikes of 1936–1937 that finally forced General Motors and Chrysler to recognize the United Auto Workers were à spontaneous but well-disciplined tactic that caught the CIO leadership largely by surprise. By the end of the 1930's, the CIO (its name changed in 1938 to Congress of Industrial Organizations) had organized autos, Big Steel, rubber, northeastern textiles, glass, lumber, electrical products, and the maritime industries. The AFL was strong in the building trades, food processing, machine tools, and trucking. The AFL actually ended the decade with a membership of 5.1 million, compared to the CIO's 2.6 million, but the older union's growth reflected its belated acceptance of the CIO principle of industrial unionism and the CIO's high level of class militancy.

Alternatives to the New Deal:
Coughlin, Townsend, Long

While organized labor began to erupt in protest against the continuing Depression and its own lack of power vis-à-vis capital, the meteoric rise of politicians of radical coloration revealed that millions of rural and small-town Americans were also deeply discontented. A California physician, Dr. Francis E. Townsend, set up his Old Age

Revolving Pensions organization in early 1934 to obtain pensions of $200 a month for citizens over sixty. By the end of the year he claimed twelve hundred clubs and was so strong that Congressmen were afraid to hazard a roll-call vote on the scheme, even though the economic details of the plan were known to be faulty. Through Townsend the administration learned of millions of discontented people untouched by any program yet enacted by the New Deal. In the Midwest, the dynamic Floyd Olson, governor of Minnesota, openly identified himself as a radical and threatened the rich with confiscation of property. From Royal Oak, Michigan, radio broadcasts on economic and social themes by the Catholic priest Charles E. Coughlin were reaching in 1934 a mass audience acknowledged

Father Charles E. Coughlin was one of the first public personalities created by the new medium, radio. Brilliantly effective over the wireless, he was only an average platform speaker and a very poor judge of political moods. Here he speaks for the Union Party on October 27, 1936, undoubtedly saying some of the un-Christian things about bankers, "international Jews," and Franklin D. Roosevelt that resulted in a reprimand by his church superiors. When the party gained no electoral votes, Coughlin announced his retirement from politics, but he continued to make pronouncements on social issues until World War II.

to be the largest in the world. Coughlin's message was a confusing mixture of monetary theories and social resentments (against bankers and eastern intellectuals), which some thought resembled the philosophies of rightist leaders in Italy and Germany. Still, the sixteen principles of his National Union for Social Justice included recommendations that marked Coughlin as in important respects a man of the left—jobs for all, progressive taxation, nationalization of key industries, and condemnation of the waste of competitive capitalism. When Coughlin broke with the New Deal in 1934 after a year of warm support, the move was interpreted by some as a sign that the minimum demands of much of America's working classes had not been met by Roosevelt.

The clearest sign that discontent in 1934 was primarily to the left of the New Deal was the dramatic emergence of Huey Long. After four years as governor of Louisiana, Long moved to the Senate in 1932, a provincial politician whose brilliance and drive were concealed in a pudgy frame and clownish manner. Long's appeal in Louisiana had been to the dispossessed, and during Hoover's last year his neo-Populist demands for progressive taxation met no national response. He supported FDR at first, becoming critical when tax reform was ignored. In early 1934 he founded the Share Our Wealth Society and emerged as a national figure. His program, like Coughlin's, was both vague and shifting ("Never explain, my boy, never explain," Huey told a newspaperman, "explanation is the mother of sectarianism."), but it always included heavy taxation of the rich and a minimum income, decent housing, and public education for all.* He reached out for a national following, claiming 7.5 million members in the Share Our Wealth Society, and drew huge and enthusiastic crowds in places as diverse as Des Moines and New York's Madison Square Garden. A poll requested by Roosevelt showed that 4 million voters might swing to Long if he ran on a third-party ticket in 1936.

Thus the year 1935 brought unprecedented political ferment as the

---

* The centrality of redistributive appeals marks both Long and Coughlin as men of the left in 1935. Yet many contemporaries, knowing of Long's dictatorial methods in Louisiana and the antipathy of both men to racial and ethnic minorities as well as to organized labor, saw these mass leaders as incipient fascists. Both rightist and leftist elements were present in their programs and their constituencies, as has often been the case in American politics. Yet Long, Coughlin, Upton Sinclair, Olson, and even Townsend were in varying ways leaders of the native American left, demanding immediate aid to the middle and lower classes whatever the cost in parliamentary niceties.

This photograph of Huey Long catches the Louisiana Senator's pudgy flamboyance, but it cannot convey the brilliance and wit of his public address. He is shown hitting hard at the New Deal in a nationwide speech on March 7, 1935, as Roosevelt drifted between the first and the second New Deals.

New Deal seemed to lose momentum. Roosevelt's personal popularity remained high; he received more mail than any former President by a wide margin and in most weeks more letters even than "the Radio Priest" Coughlin. The mid-term elections of November 1934 had strengthened the Democratic hold on both houses of Congress—an apparent endorsement of the New Deal—but Roosevelt knew that support for the New Deal was eroding. NRA had not worked as planned, and recovery remained elusive. The national income climbed only to $57 billion in 1935, and unemployment declined only to 10.6 million. This unsatisfying record seemed to embolden critics on all sides. If Roosevelt was alarmed by the rise of men like Long, he was angered by attacks from business. Conservatives, who had been frightened by the crisis of 1933, began to think in 1934–1935 that the system could function without New Deal–ish interference. Former President Hoover toured the country in 1934, denouncing the New Deal as socialism, and drew appreciative audiences. A superintendent of schools from Gary, Indiana, gained press coverage by charging that radical New Dealers were using FDR as a front while they communized the country. Wealthy industrialists such as Irenée DuPont and disgruntled conservative Democrats such as Al Smith of New York and Governor Albert Richie of Maryland formed the American Liberty League in August 1934 to rally anti–New Deal opinion.

So the signs in 1934–1935 were mixed. Roosevelt's original hope had been to avoid class division, to forge a program offering something to all classes without redistribution of power or wealth. Through 1934 and into 1935 evidence accumulated that such a program had not satisfied any major group and that FDR might have to choose between the owners and the workers, between more social reform and less. It could have been predicted that in such circumstances Franklin Roosevelt would move toward the dispossessed. Conservatives dominated the press and held crucial positions on the Supreme Court and on congressional committees, but much evidence indicated that the voting center of gravity had shifted to the left. In addition, Roosevelt had all his life inclined toward humanitarian politics. In this he was continually reinforced by his compassionate, resourceful wife, Eleanor, and by men like Harry Hopkins and Harold Ickes. Roosevelt was hardened against the comfortable classes by their attacks on his family and by their hostility to the modest reforms he had so far sponsored. If leadership was to be given to the millions who still lacked economic security, FDR was determined to give it.

New Directions for the New Deal

There took place in 1935 a discernible shift in New Deal policy. The pivotal issue was the administration's attitude toward "Big Business." If American industrialists would not cooperate in Roosevelt's all-class alliance, if they could not see the need to accept with good grace some modest reforms and some minimal attention to the needs of the unemployed in return for the government-industry planning they wished, then Roosevelt would make a virtue of their defection. He would shape his program henceforth to meet more of the needs of nonbusiness groups and cast the businessman as the antagonist rather than as the partner he had been in 1933–1934. Yet though a shift toward reform-oriented federal policy might be politically sound, what would be its strategy for recovery? Businessmen held the key to that, because they made the private investment decisions that meant jobs and expansion. This troublesome question, along with Roosevelt's personal indecisiveness (a quality most contemporaries underestimated), delayed the shift to the "second New Deal" for many months after the elections had revealed the mood of the country. And even after the shift, remnants of the old fondness for cooperative planning would continue to crop up.

The first evidence of a change came in the annual message of January 1935, when FDR spoke of unfinished business, including public works and a comprehensive social security program. In April, Congress agreed to spend $4.8 billion for a new relief and public works package in which the government would provide jobs for 3.5 million persons while turning unemployables back to the states. The sheer size of the appropriation suggested a strong commitment to the casualties of the Depression. Yet the relief bill did not satisfy social workers and liberals, who knew the states were being handed a greater burden than they were prepared to carry. If Roosevelt hoped to undercut the appeals of Long, Townsend, and the other militants of lower-class discontent, he had to do more than announce his plans for an expanded public works program. The administration in January submitted a social security bill containing old age insurance, unemployment compensation, and grants to states to assist them to shoulder the expense of extending minimum aid to the unemployables. Even so, the President showed no sense of urgency about its passage. Throughout the spring of 1935, he seemed undecided about his direction, and he even veered toward the conservatives. He vetoed the Patman bill for bonuses to veterans with a stern message on the need for fiscal responsibility, and he allowed southern pressure to force the pro-tenant faction out of the AAA. Then two events in May seem to have resolved his indecision. The Chamber of Commerce, which had been officially friendly, denounced the New Deal at its convention, and on May 27 the Supreme Court invalidated the NRA. The President was angered, and both emotionally and legally his ties were cut to the original cooperative strategy.

At once he threw his weight behind a bill he had shunned, the

This perceptive cartoon depicts an administration staffed by equal numbers of liberals and conservatives, steered by a slightly left-of-center President toward a crossroads where an ideological decision seems imperative. The only thing wrong with the cartoon, historically, is the crossroads. Roosevelt managed to find a third path between these two sharp alternatives.

Reprinted by permission of *The New York Post*

Wagner-Connery bill to require employers to bargain in good faith with the union that received a majority of the vote in an election conducted by the National Labor Relations Board (NLRB). In June, Roosevelt asked Congress to make substantial revisions in the revenue code, in particular to raise rates on corporations, inheritances, and individuals in higher income brackets. In his new mood the President also pressed for passage of the Social Security Act, an act to dissolve at least the top layer of public utility holding companies, and a banking law strengthening the influence of the Federal Reserve over bank credit. With the exception of the Social Security Act, none of these measures had greatly interested the administration prior to the summer. They were all passed by September, and the New Deal was clearly identified with progressive taxation, support for organized labor, anti-trust action, old age pensions, and unemployment insurance. The economic effect of these measures was less significant than either friends or enemies of the New Deal predicted, but the political effects were striking. The President had emerged as the undisputed leader of reform forces in America and in so doing had profoundly reshaped American politics.

Through 1936 he strengthened his image as the friend of those the business system had forgotten. He did this not with further legislation, of which there was little in 1936, but with speeches. He promised his Cabinet in November 1935 that "we are going to make it [the campaign of 1936] a crusade," and he boldly led off in his annual message. The acceptance speech at the Democratic convention in Philadelphia in June breathed fire against the wealthy, and through the ensuing campaign Roosevelt stressed the New Deal's reform, humanitarian, and redistributional accomplishments. Despite these speeches, the President acted conservatively in 1936. The only major requests of Congress were a replacement for the first AAA, invalidated in January 1936 in the *Butler* decision, and an undistributed profits tax on corporate earnings. Other legislative requests were on the liberal agenda and in the President's mind. In 1936 he deferred them—a reformed Supreme Court, reorganization of the executive branch, a federal minimum wage law, public housing, medical insurance, more TVAs. Throughout the year Roosevelt fought to balance the budget, forcing agencies like WPA and CCC to contract their spending.

His political instincts proved sure. The voters he hoped to bring into the new Democratic coalition did not look critically at the unfinished agenda or at restricted relief and public works spending in a year when 9 million were still out of work. They were impressed by the gains made since 1932—unemployment reduced by at least 4 million, labor organization spurred, a social security program enacted, farm income almost doubled. And even if the New Deal held its disappointments for the middle and lower classes, they had nowhere else to go. The New Deal was fortunate in its predecessors. In the eyes of lower-income groups, it was far better than earlier governments "frozen in the ice of their own indifference," as Roosevelt unkindly put it. The political behavior of blacks during the 1930's offers a ready example of the New Deal's ability to make strong political friends with relatively modest programs. The blacks were discriminated against in the New Deal relief and public works programs, and Roosevelt would not jeopardize his support among southerners in Congress by pressing for the NAACP's anti-lynching or anti–poll tax legislation. Yet CCC and WPA jobs did go to blacks, even if not in proportion to their needs. No other government had done so much; no other President had seemed so concerned about the poor of both races; no earlier President's wife had shared Eleanor Roosevelt's conspicuous commitment to racial justice. Negroes

Governor Alfred M. Landon waves the sign of his state at the Republican Party convention in June 1936, where he was nominated for the presidency. Landon was badly beaten because both his party's philosophy and his own personality were less attractive than the alternatives offered by the New Deal and Roosevelt. But historians are agreed that Landon was an unusually candid, honest, and able person. Roosevelt respected him highly, and invited him into the Cabinet in 1940.

Election of 1936

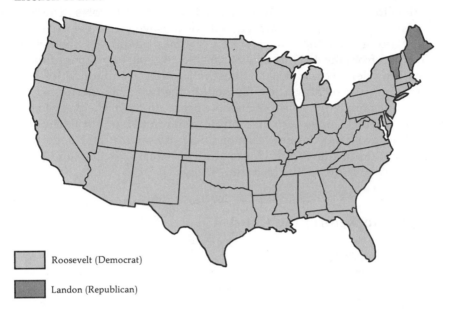

Roosevelt (Democrat)

Landon (Republican)

weighed the present against the past rather than against an ideal and switched dramatically from the party of Lincoln into the Democratic column in the election of 1936.

If there had ever been any doubt that FDR would attract the votes of the economic have-nots, they were resolved when his opponents to the left and right fielded their campaigns. The Republican Party, over the objections of progressives like Senator William E. Borah, accepted the class alignment shaped by FDR and took its position decidedly to the right. The GOP nominated a mildly progressive governor, Alfred M. Landon of Kansas, but the campaign tone was set by a conservative platform and by the speeches of former President Hoover and vice-presidential nominee Frank Knox. It was a tone of undisguised hostility to the use of the state to do for the unemployed, the farmers, the aged, and for the darkened valleys of the Tennessee basin what government had done in the 1920's for industry and banking. That political appeal in 1936 carried two states and netted 16 million popular and eight electoral votes.

On the left, the assassination of Huey Long in September 1935 created a vacuum of leadership. The new Union Party tried to unite the followers of Long, Coughlin, and Townsend, but its candidate,

William Lemke, could not provide a convincing or attractive alternative to the New Deal and received only 882,000 votes. The Socialists, whose support had eroded to Roosevelt, did even worse. They nominated the able Norman Thomas again, but their vote dropped from the 1932 total of 885,000 to 187,000. The Communists' Earl Browder received 80,000. Roosevelt polled 27 million votes and carried forty-six states. The alignment of the two major parties along class lines brought a defeat of massive proportions for the party identified with a business-oriented public policy and a political triumph for Roosevelt and the new Democratic Party so vast and deep that it kept him in the White House until his death in 1945 and gave his party majority status into the 1970's.

The Struggle to Reform the Court

In the year 1936, 9 million workers were unemployed, and the national income stood at $65 billion, well under the 1929 level of $88 billion. Despite a relatively successful farm program, unprecedented relief spending, public works, and the lending and refinancing efforts of RFC, HOLC, and FCA, recovery had been slow and incomplete. And the New Deal had done little in the areas of low-income housing, minimum wages and maximum hours (NRA wage and hour provisions were invalidated in 1935), and economic concentration outside of public utilities. Moreover, liberals believed that much the New Deal had done was greatly in need of improvement. The social security law was criticized for several weaknesses: The old age insurance program was financed by a joint employer-employee tax that turned out to be not only regressive (employers could usually shift it to consumers) but a drag on recovery. Both the retirement and the unemployment compensation provisions excluded groups such as farm workers and domestics, who needed help most, and the unemployment titles of the law lacked adequate national standards. The effort to resettle tenants, carried on in 1936 by the Resettlement Administration, was starved on the small sums that Roosevelt could divert from the relief appropriation. The TVA idea, public power advocates urged, should be extended to other river systems. Thus New Dealers saw much to be done in Roosevelt's second four years.

FDR chose to move first not toward any of these goals but against one of the two major institutional obstacles that had so hampered

President Roosevelt and his wife, Eleanor, attend a dinner at the Mayflower Hotel on March 4, 1937. Eleanor was a remarkable person in her own right and was an asset to her husband, both as a gadfly to his conscience and as a liaison with groups such as the NAACP and the Southern Tenant Farmers' Union who found it difficult to get a hearing through normal channels.

the New Deal in its first four years—the Supreme Court. (The other obstacle, the Democratic Party's conservative wing with its power base in the Congress, Roosevelt would confront in 1938.) Since the 1890's, a conservative majority on the Court had narrowed the limits within which the federal government might regulate interstate commerce and legislate for the general welfare. Major decisions limiting federal power, such as *Hammer* v. *Dagenhart* (1918) and *Adkins* v. *Children's Hospital* (1923), threatened any efforts to legislate for national recovery and economic reform. Yet it was hoped that the Court would appreciate the gravity of the emergency and lean toward a more permissive attitude, for which there were also legal precedents. In this hope the President and Congress had gone ahead in 1933 with legislation of doubtful constitutionality.

No New Deal laws were ruled upon in 1934. The Court validated a state debt moratorium and a price-fixing law and seemed, despite its conservative majority, to be cooperating with the government's efforts to cope with the Depression.* Beginning in 1935, the Court began to reject the New Deal. In a sixteen-month period in 1935–1936, the Court struck down twelve New Deal laws, including the National Industrial Recovery Act and the Agricultural Adjustment Act. Among major laws, only the Tennessee Valley Authority Act survived the Court's review, and that decision (*Ashwander* v. *TVA*) was inconclusive. The Social Security and National Labor Relations acts were unreviewed and obviously in danger.

Although Roosevelt had been urged to move against the Court as early as 1935, he chose to wait until after the anticipated landslide in November 1936. His options then were several, among them to ask Congress to narrow judicial review by statute and to request a constitutional amendment that would either restrict the range of the Court's jurisdiction or require a two-thirds vote to overrule economic legislation. Roosevelt decided that an amendment would be intolerably slow and that whatever wording Congress used, either in a statute or in an amendment, the Court itself would interpret. The present Court was the problem, and Roosevelt determined to ask Congress to enlarge its size, for which there was ample precedent. On February 5, 1937, FDR startled the country and most of his associates (he had said nothing about his plans in the campaign or in his inaugural address in January) by proposing that the court be enlarged by one justice for every justice who reached the age of seventy and declined to retire, to a maximum of fifteen justices. Roosevelt gave as his principal reason for the plan a desire to expedite the work of an overburdened Court—an inept subterfuge that did not enhance his reputation for candor.

What followed was not what Roosevelt had planned. Much of the public apparently supported the President, but a surprising volume of criticism arose, revealing that in laying hands on the Court the President had touched an institution that millions thought to be beyond politics. Further, his support was reduced by the evasiveness of the plan's presentation and by a timely shift toward more liberal constitutional ground by the Court itself. A series of decisions between March and June indicated that the Court had retreated from

* Four members were unwavering conservatives—Pierce Butler, James McReynolds, George Sutherland, Willis Van Devanter. Chief Justice Charles Evans Hughes and Justice Owen Roberts were conservative but unpredictable. Only Louis Brandeis, Benjamin Cardozo, and Harlan Fiske Stone stood consistently for broader federal powers in economic regulation.

The Richmond Times-Dispatch

This cartoon was not as hostile as most journalistic and editorial commentary to Roosevelt's Supreme Court reform plan. Indeed, it caught the essence of the situation—the legislative and executive branches understood the nature of the emergency and were making energetic efforts to end the Depression, while the more isolated third branch had not heard the appeal of the public for action.

its obstructionism. The key decisions were the validation of the Wagner Act in the *Jones and Laughlin Steel* case in April and the upholding of the Social Security Act in May. Justices Hughes and Roberts were voting with the three liberals, displaying a change of heart that FDR attributed to the impact of his proposal but that may have resulted from the astonishing electoral victory of November.

The new 5 to 4 majority was far from comfortable, but the timing of the Court's shift and Justice Van Devanter's announcement of his intention to retire reduced pressure for what was being called Roosevelt's Court-packing plan. By June, senatorial opposition to the plan was formidable, and the cost in time and political friendships was becoming great. Roosevelt pressed the issue stubbornly into the hot summer, then in August was forced to accept a face-saving measure embodying some minor administrative reforms of the federal judi-

ciary. The entire struggle had been a valuable experience for opponents of the New Deal. The President had squandered seven months
and much political capital and lost the momentum picked up from
his massive triumph at the polls. He showed that his political judgment was not infallible, that his popularity did not automatically
transfer to any program he approved. A conservative coalition of
southern Democrats and northern Republicans took shape in the
Congress and gained confidence from the defeat of the Court reform
bill. The conservatives, however, had paid a price for blunting the
momentum of the New Deal. The Court had withdrawn its constitutional objections to regulation of the national economy. Of the many
defenses of property, one had crumbled. The Court would henceforth ensure procedural fairness, but the right of the national government to subordinate property rights to other social goals was
established.

The Final Days of the New Deal:
Reform, Recession, Stalemate

The year 1937 saw less legislative advance toward the remaining
goals of the New Deal than the election results had forecast. In some
areas the President was successful. In his second inaugural in January he had spoken with unusual passion of unfinished business
ahead: "I see millions of families trying to live on incomes so meager
that the pall of family disaster hangs over them, day by day," he
had said. "I see millions denied education, recreation, and the opportunity to better their lot. . . . I see one-third of a nation ill-housed,
ill-clad, ill-nourished." Given Roosevelt's rural orientation, he doubt-
less had primarily in mind the tenant class of farmers, who constituted half of all southern farmers and one-third of those outside the
South. The agricultural program of the New Deal had not worked to
their benefit. AAA was a "big-farmers" agency, and the abortive
liberal revolt within AAA in 1935 demonstrated that it could not be
expected to care for the farmers whom its acreage reduction operations were displacing. In cold economic terms, the out-migration of
farmers made sense. Too many men worked the land, and the poor
farmers were the least likely to adopt proper soil conservation methods. In human terms, the cost was terrible. Poor farmers who clung
to the land were captured in their desperate suffering in the words
and pictures of books like James Agee and Walker Evans' *Let Us Now*

Praise Famous Men and Erskine Caldwell and Margaret Bourke-White's *You Have Seen Their Faces;* those who tried to escape westward with their threadbare belongings and their gaunt families had their story told in John Steinbeck's novel *The Grapes of Wrath.* Though the rural lower classes had little political power, they had the sympathy of liberals, and powerful politicians like Alabama's Senator John Bankhead responded to their situation out of loyalty to a symbol — the family farm. Given the climate established by Roosevelt's 1936 victory, these allies of the rural poor were able in 1937 to expand the New Deal's commitment.

Actually, the New Deal had been involved in aid to tenant farmers from the start. FERA's rural rehabilitation division moved some tenants from submarginal lands, and the Department of Interior's subsistence homesteads division established a few planned communities in rural areas where families could supplement farming with part-time factory work. All these forms of rural social work were combined in 1935 into the Resettlement Administration, under Tugwell. The agency, skimpily funded on money diverted from WPA, had managed to resettle only 4,441 families by 1937. The President's Committee on Farm Tenancy reported in February 1937 that 2.8 million tenant families had annual incomes of $500 or less, and the inadequacy of existing policies became glaringly apparent. The committee recommended a new agency to make loans to selected tenants for land and equipment purchase, to advise farmers on crop rotation, to set up camps for migrant workers, to establish medical clinics. Congress responded by creating the Farm Security Administration in 1937, an agency that for nine years (until 1946) pursued these goals, although on a less ambitious scale than friends of the tenant farmer had desired.

Another second-term success obscured by the furor over the Court plan was the Wagner-Steagall Housing Act, signed on September 1, 1937. Here again there was consolidation and expansion of efforts carried on earlier by other agencies. The PWA had built fifty-one public housing projects containing 21,000 units, and starting in 1934 the Federal Housing Administration had insured loans made by private lending institutions to middle-income homeowners for improvements or new construction. The FHA stimulated little new construction, and none that benefited the lower one-third that Roosevelt had mentioned in his 1937 inaugural address. The initiative for a stronger program came from New York's Senator Robert F. Wagner, and the administration belatedly offered its support. In August 1937,

Roosevelt signed the Wagner-Steagall Housing Law establishing the United States Housing Authority, empowered to lend the comparatively modest sum of $500 million to local housing authorities to erect low-income housing.

Despite these measures, the New Deal was losing momentum in 1937. Roosevelt called Congress into special session for November and December 1937 to enact a new farm bill, a wages and hours act, a reorganization of the executive branch, and "seven little TVAs." All four became snarled in disputes, and the session produced no legislation. The farm bill was enacted in the following spring, after the most powerful farm groups had resolved their differences. On all other programs Roosevelt faced mounting opposition. Congress was especially balky on tax reform. Treasury officials had discovered huge loopholes in the federal tax structure, and Roosevelt's disclosure of some blatant cases of tax evasion forced Congress to close minor holes with the Revenue Act of 1937 (signed in August). By 1938 Congress was in a more bellicose and conservative mood and sent the President a tax bill in April 1938 that virtually eliminated the undistributed profits tax of 1936 and reduced the capital gains tax. Roosevelt refused to sign the bill, and it became law without his signature. Congress finally approved the Fair Labor Standards Act (wages and hours) in June after eighteen months of dispute, seriously weakening it in the process. The act prohibited child labor but affected only 6 percent of working children; there were also many exemptions to its wage and hour requirements, and few of the workers covered received any immediate benefit. A million and a half workers found their hours slightly shortened by the law; only 750,000 had their wages raised. The minimum wage decided upon was forty cents an hour (a $16 weekly wage, assuming a forty-hour week). Congress decided to allow employers eight years to adjust to that level and started the minimum at twenty-five cents. Though Roosevelt was glad of the precedent, on which he hoped the government might build, he cannot have been happy with the feeble wages and hours legislation Congress sent him in June 1938.

The New Deal's loss of momentum resulted from several things. A chief cause was the manner in which Roosevelt managed the Court fight. His defeat changed his domestic opponents from November's routed minority to a determined, resourceful opposition. At least as important as the outcome of the Court issue was the economic recession of 1937–1938.

The administration's experience with the business cycle had been a mixture of success and frustration, and even when there was success there was bafflement. The initial decision to combine national planning with a reasonable degree of pump priming produced a few months of boom, then a disappointing slump followed by a slow climb from the 1933 national income of $40 billion to $57 billion in 1935. The administration abandoned industrial (not agricultural) planning after the 1935 *Schechter* decision, and though it replaced its political strategy of cooperation with business with a strategy of assistance to nonbusiness groups, it did not replace its recovery strategy with much of anything. Relief spending helped keep the budget out of balance, but the President never conceived of the deficit as an instrument of economic policy, merely as a temporary concession to humanitarian and political considerations. Without a real recovery policy, the administration in 1935 and 1936 was the pleased beneficiary of accelerating improvement in the economic picture. The index of employment climbed from 94 in 1935 (100 = 1923–1925) to 96 in 1936 and 112 in mid-1937, finally surpassing the number of jobs offered by the American economy in 1929. Yet, given the growth in population, as many as 8 million workers were still unemployed in 1937 (a drop of from 5 million to 7 million from the first year of the New Deal). Disposable per capita income in mid-1937 reached the level of 1929 (although prices were higher); the national income stood at $73 billion.

Unfortunately, Roosevelt and his advisers decided in 1937 that they were the masters of the situation and that, rather than drift any more, they had better adopt proper fiscal and monetary measures. They adopted new policies; these terminated the recovery. The fiscal policy Roosevelt decided on by 1937 was the one most educated men, ranging from Roosevelt through Herbert Hoover, assumed to be the correct one—a balanced budget. Roosevelt was no slave to the idea and often tried (without much enthusiasm) to explain to the public why he had not balanced the budget. But he had a stronger dislike for deficits than the record showed. In 1936 he tried hard to reach what was often called "solvency" (reflecting the tendency to think of government as a business), and only a veterans' bonus paid out over his veto helped produce a deficit of $3.5 billion. Throughout 1936 FDR forced agency heads, including Hopkins of WPA, to restrict spending, and with the improved revenues of 1937 he began to imagine an end to the deficits.

By 1937 Roosevelt thought his fiscal policy to be moving toward equilibrium, where he believed it belonged, with revenues matching expenditures. Actually, leaving aside the question of whether the state of the economy in the 1930's made a balanced budget a proper fiscal policy, the government's accounting system concealed the fact that what looked like a balanced budget was in fact deflationary. Social security accounts were segregated from other obligations and revenues on the books, but the economy responded to the cash flow, not to the government's accounts. When social security taxes went into effect on January 1, 1937, they took a heavy bite from workers' paychecks. By 1940, social security taxes were taking out of the income stream $1 billion more than the government paid out in benefits. Because state and local governments were turning to sales taxes and were reducing their own debts during the late 1930's, federal fiscal policy needed to be in a sizable deficit to make up for the heavy drag of its own social security taxes and those of other units of government. A balanced budget was an illusion; as the government brought expenditures and revenues into line, it was actually participating in the sizable fiscal drag exerted by all government units in the 1930's.

Monetary policy was equally misguided in 1937. After the active months of gold and silver buying in 1933–1934, monetary policy became essentially passive through 1936, though basically correct. Interest rates were low. There was not much else for monetary authorities to do. Banks had plenty of reserves, and credit was easy. Monetary authorities could not force industrialists to borrow for expansion or banks to lend; they could only keep credit cheap, make optimistic statements, and wait. But the chairman of the Federal Reserve Board, Marriner Eccles, was an activist. Fortunately, his reputation rests on his pioneering understanding of the need for an expansive fiscal policy in times of depression, an idea he derived from hard thinking rather than from reading Keynes. In 1937, as chairman of the "Fed," all he could do about fiscal policy was to write memos to a resistant President. But where monetary policy was concerned Eccles could act, and act he did in mid-1936 and twice in the spring of 1937, tightening bank credit by raising reserve requirements. The move had wide endorsement among economists and bankers, for large reserves seemed to hold a dangerous inflationary potential. But the pressure for inflation was imaginary. The real potential in the economic situation in 1936–1937 was toward collapse, as local governments and the Treasury increased their fiscal drag. Private investment was not ready to take up the slack. No new industries appeared to stimulate large capital issues; basic industries

John Maynard Keynes was a brilliant British economist whose book, *The General Theory
of Employment, Interest and Money* (1936), helped eventually to revolutionize
economic thinking. Keynes met Roosevelt once and wrote him several letters advising
him to pursue recovery by government spending financed by borrowing, but the
President did not grasp his theory and never consciously employed
it. Keynes was thought to be a radical, but it is now realized that to stabilize
capitalism by deficit spending is a very conservative notion.
Conservatives have absorbed Keynes, and economists have gone beyond him.

such as steel, automobiles, and construction were still depressed. The
monetary and fiscal contractions of the federal government in 1936–
1937, though not great, were deadly to the puny recovery managed
by a still sluggish, psychologically fearful private sector.

The collapse came in August 1937 with a severe market decline, a
drop in industrial production, and a rise in unemployment. By conservative estimates, joblessness mounted to 10.3 million during the
winter of 1937–1938 and was 9.4 million for 1939 and 8.1 million for
1940. The New Deal, which had seemed so close to bringing recovery
in early 1937, was forced to finish out two full terms without solving

the nation's economic problems.* In April 1938, after six months of indecision, Roosevelt let the "spenders" among his advisers convince him to resume large expenditures for relief and public works. Again the sum he requested ($3.75 billion) was about half of the figure that considerations of adequate relief or Keynesian economics would have indicated, and again FDR allowed spending to be undertaken slowly and with one eye on the budget. The spending brought some improvement; the level of it ensured that the improvement would be minor. While he switched back to what he (and most contemporaries) thought was heavy relief spending, Roosevelt accepted the argument of those who maintained that the monopolistic structure of American industry was responsible for the recession. In that view, "administered" prices in key industries diminished consumers' buying power and produced underconsumption. Government economists gave the argument an impressive statistical basis, and the appropriate remedy — vigorous anti-trust measures — suited Roosevelt's mood in 1938, after business had disappointed him once again. He named Thurman Arnold to head the anti-trust division of the Justice Department to invigorate the prosecution of monopolies, and he secured from Congress an appropriation for a Temporary National Economic Committee (TNEC) to investigate the extent and manner of market control in America. Unfortunately, these moves were too late for either recovery or reform. Even if administered prices prevented recovery, anti-trust action was a slow corrective. And businessmen argued that the damage it would do to the investment climate would more than offset the gains of flexible prices. Recovery could probably not be achieved until the government, having broken up the leading monopolies, had aban-

---

* Other nations experienced similar difficulties in fashioning successful recovery policies. Comparisons are misleading, but it is probably fair to say that, considering the severity of the Depression in the United States, American recovery (from the low of 1932–1933) was better than that of Canada and France, approximately as good as that of Britain and Sweden, and inferior to that of Germany and Japan. All things considered, American recovery was about average in comparative terms. The New Deal certainly excited much admiration in Europe, both for what Roosevelt did and for what he refused to do. British historian and philosopher Isaiah Berlin recalled in 1955: "As the skies of Europe grew darker . . . he [Roosevelt] seemed to the poor and unhappy in Europe a kind of benevolent demigod who alone could and would save them in the end. . . . He showed that it is possible to be politically effective and yet benevolent and civilized; that the fierce left and right wing propaganda of the thirties . . . was simply untrue. Mr. Roosevelt's example strengthened democracy everywhere — that is to say, the view that the promotion of social justice and individual liberty does not necessarily mean the end of all efficient government; that power and order are not identical with a strait jacket of doctrine."

doned anti-trust action and either fostered a favorable investment mood or established new government enterprises. But in 1938 the government was running out of time. The TNEC took three years to finish its work, and by then (1941) its report, supported by thirty-one volumes of testimony and forty-three monographs, suggested measures of economic decentralization that the war made impossible. So Hitler, not Roosevelt, provided the key to economic salvation. Recovery waited for huge orders for steel, heavy machinery, rubber, and chemicals to build the war machine and for a mood of cooperation between business and government that all Roosevelt's speeches, concessions, and threats had not been able to produce.

The failure to control the business cycle hurt the New Deal badly. It cost FDR the support of those who had gone along with the New Deal because it promised to revive production and consumption and who had always been cool to social reform. This wavering of support, along with alienations produced by the Court struggle, so strengthened the anti–New Deal forces that eighteen months after Roosevelt had carried forty-six states the New Deal could not move forward.

Contrary to some accounts, the New Deal did not "run out of ideas" in 1938. The administration in that year and in the next asked for expansions of the Fair Labor Standards Act and the Social Security Act, more TVAs, and a broader program of public works. The President commended to Congress the closing of tax loopholes, medical insurance, and federal aid to education. Agencies such as FSA and the NLRB were at the peak of their fervor, organizing and aiding the New Deal's lower-class constituents. There were energy and ideas left in the New Deal for more rearrangements of American society, and polls showed that the President's personal popularity remained awesome. Unfortunately for Roosevelt's plans, Congress had replaced the Court as a formidable barrier to social reform.

By party figures, Roosevelt after 1936 had an irresistible majority. The election propelled the Democrats to an incredible 331 to 89 edge in the House, 76 to 16 in the Senate. But the numbers were misleading. Roosevelt's majority contained many conservative Democrats, most of them from the South, who had been unhappy with the New Deal since 1935. As legislators they resented the recent presidential domination; as states-righters they objected to the centralization in Washington; as southerners from the successful classes they worried about the post-1935 friendliness for urban labor, tenants, and blacks.

In Roosevelt's second term the air of crisis abated, and these Democrats broke into revolt at the first opportunity—which for most of them was the Court fight. They formed a coalition of convenience with Republicans in both houses, and though the coalition was not large or cohesive enough to command a congressional majority for programs of its own, it could block the President on all but the most uncontroversial legislation. The result was stalemate in 1938 and after, with the New Deal arrested in a half-finished condition.

To Roosevelt this bind in the political machinery was intolerable. The New Deal was not complete, and he was sure the people were with him. When early 1938 primaries gave victories to two southern liberals, Roosevelt decided to take a hand in the forthcoming congressional elections to produce a more liberal party. This effort drew from conservatives the label "purge," a word with obvious international connotations to discredit the President's attempt to align the parties according to political belief. By campaigning for liberal Democrats against conservative Democrats, FDR was trying to drive conservatives out of his party, so that the voters would have the choice of clearly distinguishable programs and philosophies. The idea has attracted political scientists for years and a quarter-century later, in 1964, was endorsed by GOP presidential candidate Barry Goldwater. In 1938, deep-seated institutional and attitudinal forces resisted it, and Roosevelt was beaten. He made major efforts in four campaigns—against Senators George, Smith, and Tydings, and Congressman O'Connor—and his only victory was against O'Connor. The electorate seemed to rally to local candidates facing "outside" interference and resisted Roosevelt's urgings to vote for programs rather than for personalities. The President's attempt to strengthen the liberal wing of his party failed, and the Congress returned in 1938 was more conservative than its predecessor. Democratic conservatives ran strongly, liberals were beaten in a number of close races, and Republicans gained eight seats in the Senate and eighty in the House.

What historian James T. Patterson calls "the Great Aberration of 1933–1937" was over; the forces of movement were stalemated. On Capitol Hill, in fact, the New Deal in 1938 went on the defensive. The anti–New Deal coalition repealed the undistributed profits tax and ignored the President's disclosure of tax loopholes used by the rich. It passed the Executive Reorganization Act only after deleting its major proposals, cut WPA appropriations, and killed the Federal Theatre. It reduced spending on public housing, launched investigations of WPA's political activities and the NLRB's alleged pro-labor bias. Roosevelt fought back verbally on several occasions and defiantly sent several liberal appointments to the Hill. Some were refused confirmation, but the Court was liberalized by the appointments of Hugo Black (1937), Stanley Reed (1938), Felix Frankfurter (1939), William O. Douglas (1939), and Frank Murphy (1940)—appointments that helped account for the Court's post-1937 swing toward defense of civil liberties and civil rights. The appointment of James L. Fly (1939) as chairman of the Federal Communications Commission brought a reform spirit to that agency and threatened radio network monopolies. The Justice Department, under Frank Murphy (1939) and Robert H. Jackson (1940), intensified anti-monopoly prosecutions. The food stamp program was inaugurated in May 1939 and gave promise (before it was terminated in 1943) of replacing policies of enforced scarcity with efforts to route America's abundance to the poor.

The American Political Economy at the End of the 1930's

Whatever the outcome of the struggle for control of public policy at the end of the 1930's, no one doubted its importance. From the office of a New Deal bureaucrat it must have seemed that all eyes were fixed on Washington, where Congressmen and administrators were daily debating and deciding domestic and foreign questions touching every life. After eight years of the New Deal, the federal government exercised vast powers over the lives of American citizens. About 14 percent of the population relieved their poverty with some type of federal support (exclusive of social security benefits). The federal presence was felt in labor-management disputes; federal law set wages and hours in many industries. The income of farmers of basic crops was virtually decided in Washington. The government regulated stock margins and the exchanges, rates on interstate buses, trucks, air passenger flights, and interstate telephone calls, built low-income housing, supplied funds to rural electric co-ops, and, beginning in 1940, drafted males for military service. None of these contacts with the government had existed in 1932. One should add to these new powers conferred during Roosevelt's first two terms those already vested in the central government by 1932—preponderant influence over the supply and cost of money, taxation of incomes,

regulation of the fares of railroads and steamships and of the label-
ing and contents of food and drugs, management of vast forestry
reserves, assignment of radio frequencies, approval or veto of corporate mergers, agricultural instruction for farmers. One might be
excused for thinking that after the New Deal the lives of Americans
were for all intents and purposes shaped in the national capital by
the decisions of elected political leaders.

The expansion of the sway of public authority, a development
often termed collectivism, is the primary historical significance of
the New Deal. Although there was little consistency in the methods
or the beneficiaries of government action, there was consistency in
the central drive—to expand the realm of "public" control over private, uncoordinated activities. Few Americans excelled Roosevelt in
his commitment to the ideal of democratic collectivism. Beginning
with the campaign of 1932, he established what was to be the New
Deal's distinguishing rhetoric: He spoke of the end of individualism,
of the extinction of the self-sufficient man, of the interconnection of
lives in a modern industrial world, of the need to put an end to hap-
hazardness and waste through the coordinating, planning, adjusting
interventions of democratic government.

This analysis (in which Roosevelt was tutored by Tugwell, Berle,
and others) foretold a great expansion of the managerial functions
of the national state. American progress, Roosevelt assumed, would
no longer take care of itself. It had to be planned and administered.
"Today," he said in 1935, "we can no longer escape into virgin territory; we must master our environment." Roosevelt's speeches
often specified the areas where interdependence was most advanced
and least recognized, hence areas most in need of the coordinating
power of government. His favorite examples were four—the mutual
dependence of agricultural and industrial sectors of the economy,
something industrialists had ignored as farm income declined in the
1920's; the degree to which "private" banking and stock exchange
institutions had become so crucial to the national economy that they
required comprehensive public regulation; the dependence of profits
on the purchasing power of labor, a discovery requiring public intervention in the relation between wages and prices; and the necessity to see the resources of the continent as a whole, which must
not and could not be exploited in uncoordinated ways.

The last was probably Roosevelt's most sustained preoccupation
and often served him as the best example of modern interdependence. From the beginning, Americans had treated their continent

Dust storms like this one which hit Clayton, New Mexico, on May 21, 1937, were analogous to the Depression in many ways. They were sudden and unexpected, inexplicable to the average citizen, and although usually not fatal, they were a terribly unpleasant experience. The New Deal made a start toward preventing dust storms through the Soil Conservation Service and the shelterbelt tree plantings, but a series of wet years were chiefly responsible for ending the storms of the 1930's.

as a mosaic of private possessions. Individuals cut timber if it happened to be "their property," strip-mined if the minerals were "theirs," farmed in any way the "owner" of the land wished, fished and trapped and shot "their" animals, dumped waste into "their" nearby creek. The first two or three decades of the conservation movement made no significant dent in this heritage of the private disposition of pieces of the common natural environment. The great floods of 1926–1927 forced some people to see the futility of the piecemeal treatment of river systems, of cities downstream expending millions building levees or dredging while men upstream continued to send down an avalanche of mud (400 million tons annually down the Mississippi alone) because of their tilling and lumbering practices. In November 1933 came the first of the dust storms that continued through the 1930's, bringing what the ecologist Paul Sears called "a sea of powdered earth, miles high," to blacken the air and lungs and the very snow of cities a thousand miles from the stricken

Great Plains. Roosevelt saw the parallel between these natural disasters and the Depression. Americans had let individualism go too far, he pointed out; the time for exploitation was over, the era of social management had come.

So the federal government was strengthened in order that it might coordinate and rationalize more of American life. Conservatives, observing the increase of federal employees from 605,000 in 1932 to 1,042,000 in 1940, and seeing the new vigor of the executive branch under Franklin Roosevelt, lamented the arrival of what they perceived as an all-powerful government in full control of all the instruments of tyranny. The truth was quite different—indeed, almost the reverse. First, there remained great zones of American life where the national government exercised little or no influence at all. The American people, 135 million of them, pursued their hopes across 3 million square miles of geography, and the vast web of their lives was too intricate for the close direction of any government. Most citizens dealt with the Depression for ten years without receiving any direct federal help—money, food, or employment. Americans made many vital decisions free of any visible bureaucratic coercion. Most never voted or knew their Senators' names, or communicated with any public official. No government effectively controlled or even kept track of their basic interactions. Most American institutions remained beyond reach of any governmental influence—religion, scientific research, technological and entrepreneurial innovation, outdoor and indoor recreation, medicine, family planning. Others, such as education, marriage, and divorce, were loosely regulated by local governments and enjoyed complete and traditional freedom from centralized, national control.

Not even that most collectivistic of the New Dealers, the bête noir of the conservatives, Tugwell, and certainly not Roosevelt, had ever seriously proposed extensions of public authority that would have truly socialized decision-making in the society. At the end of the 1930's, Roosevelt had requested an enlarged public role in medical care, scientific research, and electric power and was disappointed that Congress would not grant the authority. Even these steps, added to those already taken by the New Deal, would have left America a place where most areas of life were private, most decisions made without reference to centralized public direction. More frustrating to liberals than finding the government blocked from taking on additional responsibilities was the realization that even in the areas where the federal government attempted to perform a regulatory role its performance left much to be desired. The state had undertaken to manage the economy, and it entered its task with a vitality, idealism, and youthful energy not seen since World War I. Yet government proved chasteningly inept, unable to muster the power or knowledge to accomplish its larger economic ends. At the beginning of the 1940's, 9 million people were still unemployed, one-third of the nation still lived in poverty, and the market power of large corporations was if anything more concentrated than it had been ten years before. Success at matters of detail, such as social insurance, wage and hour legislation, and collective bargaining, could not ease the disappointment of a failure to achieve the government's larger goals.

In addition to an unexpected ineffectiveness at its relatively new tasks of macroeconomic management, the state further distressed liberals by the tendency of its branches to serve private rather than national interests. The New Deal had assumed that an extension of federal power was per se an extension of the national interest. In practice, entire agencies and programs were captured by private groups and subordinated to private ends. Woodrow Wilson had warned of this tendency in 1912, when he forecast that any regulatory apparatus would be dominated by the interests it was designed to regulate. Experience had largely confirmed his fears. The constituency of the regulatory agencies was in theory the broad public, but in practice the facts of private power and public apathy brought most of the agencies to adopt the regulated industries as their clientele and to operate virtually as a branch of public power under private control. Roosevelt had hoped, through new appointments and a new sense of purpose, to restore the regulatory agencies—the Federal Trade Commission, the Interstate Commerce Commission, the Federal Reserve Board, and the Pure Food and Drug Administration —to a greater independence. He experienced limited success with the FTC and the Federal Reserve, but he had many battles to fight, and the tendency of these semi-autonomous agencies to adopt the viewpoint of their sector of American capitalism was powerful. Indeed, the New Deal proliferated regulatory agencies, making the prospects for a unified national policy even more remote. At times the expansion of federal regulation was opposed by the affected portions of the business community, as with the Securities Exchange Commission (1934), the strengthening of the Federal Reserve in the Banking Act of 1935, and the establishment of the National Labor Relations Board (1935). But the private sector also understood, despite pronounced anti-government rhetoric, that government could be an agent of friendly regulation, promotion, and subsidy when falling demand was throwing entire industries into suicidal competitive wars. For this reason, much of the expansion of federal regulation in the 1930's originated in the business community and, though signed into law by the President, was not properly part of his New Deal at all. Some of the pressure for the NRA originated with large corporations, and other legislation came almost entirely because of business pressure — the two Guffey Coal Acts, in 1935 and 1937 (supported also by the United Mine Workers), the Connally "Hot Oil" Act of 1935, the Emergency Railroad Transportation Act of 1933, the Motor Carrier Act of 1935, the Merchant Marine Act of 1936, the Air Mail Act of 1934, the Civil Aeronautics Act of 1938, the Robinson-Patman (1936) and Miller-Tydings (1937) "fair trade" laws. In each instance, hard-pressed commercial interests sought the haven of public utility status, accepting the regulation of rates and other conditions of business in exchange for stability and security. This was piecemeal regulation, and the establishment of so many protected zones actually made the task of overall economic management more difficult. The federal government was getting in its own way.

The New Dealers saw this happening, and the "planners" among them deplored the fragmentation of public policy. They were disappointed that the government emerging out of the scramble of the 1930's was not the unified, powerful state envisioned by Theodore Roosevelt, Tugwell, and FDR in his planning moods, a government that firmly subordinated private to public interests. And certainly the planners were right that the American political economy at the end of the 1930's was a halfway house between national planning and an unfettered "free enterprise" market economy. But many observers, especially after 1935, argued that a centralized, planned economy had been neither possible nor desirable. The American character and tradition were individualistic and suspicious of political authority, and the political system itself, especially in Congress, offered procedural and constitutional barriers to comprehensive federal supervision of economic affairs. Many of these barriers might be the selfish defenses of groups with narrow perspectives, but to reduce them to obedience would require unprecedented and perhaps even extra-legal methods, which Roosevelt and most of those he brought into government instinctively shrank from. As the 1930's went on, Americans gradually lost an early fascination with European planned economies. Russian communism had attracted many, and even Mussolini's Italy had its admirers. But a series of events, including Stalin's political purges and suppression of the kulaks, Hitler's anti-Semitism and denial of civil liberties, and Mussolini's imperialistic adventure in Ethiopia, dampened the enthusiasm for governments that overrode the delays of political democracy in the name of economic efficiency and national advancement. Perhaps an American middle way was possible, combining the advantages of strong government with the vigorous participation of a multitude of private interest groups.

Out of this line of thinking came the description of the post–New Deal political economy as a "broker state," a phrase first given wide publicity in John Chamberlain's *The American Stakes* (1940) and explored most systematically in John Kenneth Galbraith's *American Capitalism* (1952). Chamberlain and Galbraith saw the broker state as a distinct improvement over the government of the 1920's and thought it should be seen as reformist, not conservative. In place of the "one-interest" government of the 1920's, where all subsidies and assistance went to large and aggressive corporations, the New Deal had created a more pluralistic state, where the interests of labor, small farmers, small business, cattle ranchers, even the unemployed, were sheltered by some form of federal intervention. The government may have continued, under the New Deal, to lend its power to business interests, but it was also trying to build up what Galbraith termed "countervailing power" among groups that would keep business in check. As these theorists saw it, broker-state liberalism removed social decisions from the economic arena, where the large corporations had overwhelming strength, to the political arena, where all groups were roughly matched.

The new broker state perhaps had all the merits claimed for it. Certainly the major alternative, a government strong enough to rise above interest groups, proved more than Americans, with their instinctive and not unreasonable fears of centralized government, would accept. The post–New Deal broker state was increasingly referred to as a welfare state by liberals, to call attention to the benefits directed toward the underprivileged. Perhaps the total of federal interventions in 1940 did favor the economic and social underclasses more than groups above them, though this was arguable. But the passage of time saw control over public policy shift back to the economic elites who had always held economic power in America. Powerful groups, which now included organized labor, became more expert at manipulating public policy, and the unorganized interests the New Dealers had tried to foster remained underorganized and outmaneuvered. For a generation after the New Deal, the broker state deployed its new powers more to enhance the welfare of large business, large agriculture, upper middle class suburbanites, and military contractors, than to aid Roosevelt's "forgotten men"—the unemployed, the transient, the center-city worker and small businessman, the rural poor.

Perhaps this outcome was inevitable no matter what model of government action the New Deal selected—the "national planning" model that seemed dominant from 1933 to 1935, or the "broker state" model that emerged after 1935. We can never be certain, for neither was ever given a clear trial. The planning approach, never more than tentative, was abandoned in 1935; and the general strategy of the mature New Deal, a broker government arranging compromises be-

Republican presidential nominee Wendell Willkie receives the cheers of his party's national convention in 1940. Willkie had never run for elective office before, and was actually listed by *Who's Who* in 1940 as a Democrat, but his battles against the New Deal as president of Commonwealth and Southern Corporation gave Willkie national prominence, and he was by far the most attractive, energetic, and flexible contender for the third GOP campaign against Franklin D. Roosevelt. Willkie ran strongly (22 million votes to Roosevelt's 27), and until his death in 1944 led the GOP toward an acceptance of the New Deal and collective security.

Max P. Haas from European

Election of 1940

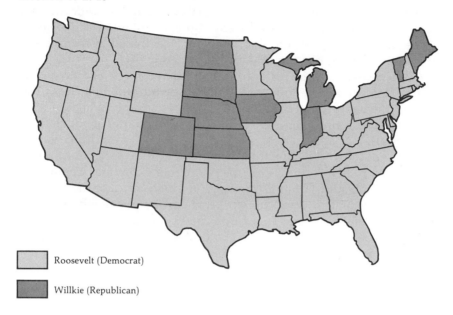

Roosevelt (Democrat)

Willkie (Republican)

tween carefully watched capitalists and new "countervailing" worker and consumer groups, was soon rudely interrupted. A world war intervened, and in mobilizing to fight the war, America was so changed that we shall never know what might have become of the New Deal experiment.

The Social Consequences of the Great Depression

War-related spending, first by the Allies and then by the American government, brought an end to the Great Depression in 1941. The effect of the preceding twelve years of economic slump on American life is difficult to estimate, for many other shaping factors were operative, among them New Deal policy as it worked against the Depression. To contemporaries, the Depression was the overriding fact of life in the 1930's, and they generally agreed that its impact was not only pervasive but almost exclusively harmful. From our own vantage we see that the Depression as a social force joined powerful long-range tendencies at work in American life and that its impact was therefore neither simple nor invariably deplorable. Indeed, such was the stability—some would say rigidity—of American institutions, that the Depression, like the New Deal, failed in many areas to make anything like the impact one would expect.

Contemporaries were justified, of course, in considering a crippled national economy an influence both powerful and injurious. The cost to the nation in goods alone has been estimated as high as $325 billion—a sum one might envision as a mountain of food, clothes, automobiles, hospitals, schoolbooks, the things Americans would have produced and enjoyed had the growth of the 1920's continued. In testimony before the Temporary National Economic Committee in 1938, Dr. Isador Lubin estimated conservatively that the Depression had cost every American worker the fruits of one year and two months of employment. This huge cut in the national standard of living was not distributed evenly. Some Americans prospered, building huge fortunes or thriving businesses. William Randolph Hearst made $500,000 in 1936, Mae West reported $480,000, Marlene Dietrich $368,000; Joseph P. Kennedy, Norton Simon, and J. Paul Getty built fortunes without interruption; Adolph Lewisohn continued to enjoy his four estates; and Mrs. Henry Seligman pruned her budget by laying off a footman. The comfort of the very rich was of course exceptional, but there were broad social groups whose standard of living did not decline perceptibly during the Depression—college professors, airline pilots, military officers, some skilled laborers.

For most other groups, the Depression brought painful retrenchment. Public school teachers went unpaid, architects saw their business decline to one-fifth of the level of 1928, millions of small businessmen fell into bankruptcy, farmers especially in the staple crops suffered intensely. The Depression drove into poverty and idleness those who had labored in marginal areas most sensitive to the business cycle—barbers and beauticians, recreational staff, musicians, travel agents, landscape gardeners. The American Indian, existing on the sale of handicrafts and the tilling of infertile land, saw his per capita income drop from $200 to $81 a year in four years after the crash. For all of these, the Depression meant hunger, malnutrition, overcrowding, poor health, the disruption of plans and hopes, a descent to the drab conditions of survival living.

Because America was a place where self-worth was tied closely to earning capacity, the psychological cost of having no place in the

Dorothea Lange, The Oakland Museum Collection

Economists tell us that there were too many people in farming in the 1930's, given a collapsed world
market and long-range trends toward large, mechanized farms.
The marketplace then operated according to its relentless logic, forcing part of the rural
population to relocate. Here an Oklahoma family "responds to the marketplace,"
a euphemistic phrase that, translated into human terms, meant a desperate, painful, futile
wandering by uncomprehending rural people along roads that had no end.

economy was also severe. Those to whom fate handed out these consequences of the Depression were not a cross-section of the public.
Employers, facing a labor surplus, naturally released first the citizens
whom the society at large felt to be of inferior social value—the
middle-aged and the old, the colored, the Jewish, and, where they
had penetrated high-status executive, managerial, and technical
fields, women. For such citizens, the Depression terminated the
useful period of life and ushered in a time of dependency and
anguish.

Nevertheless, some aspects of American life seemed relatively un-
touched by the Depression, and in others its impact was either slight
or oblique. One sees little evidence of a social cataclysm in statistics

on the national birth rate, life expectancy, and the long-term shift
of population from rural to urban areas. The birth rate had been falling since the middle of the nineteenth century, and it dropped every
decade thereafter, reaching thirty per thousand in 1910, twenty-
seven in 1920, twenty-one in 1930, nineteen in 1940, and then climbing back to twenty-five. One discerns World War II behind these
figures, but the Depression did not warp long-term trends. Life
expectancy, which had been mounting steadily as modern industrial-
urban life massed its medical and public health resources, continued
to climb through the 1930's, reaching fifty-nine (at birth) in 1930,
sixty-three in 1940, sixty-six in 1950. Other trends in modern American society show the same momentum—the data on concentration
of economic power, the steady decline in the number and variety
of American newspapers, or the equally steady rise in the size of
the average farm. Consolidation had the master hand in modern
America, and if anything the Depression accelerated this tendency
by driving marginal economic enterprises to the wall.

These long-run developments appeared to ignore the economic
cycle and changes in Presidents and public policy. However, many
social institutions and indicators did show the impact of a decade
of hard times. It was widely predicted that churches would gain
many converts as a result of the rude collapse of temporal hopes.
Figures on church attendance and membership, however, show a
slower rate of growth than in the 1920's. Upper-class churches, such
as the Episcopalian, Presbyterian, Unitarian, and Methodist, lost
ground to the evangelical sects, although the shift was not striking.
Greater social and political radicalism was observed among urban
ministers from the larger churches, but economic and social questions apparently did not make an appreciable entry into the sermons
of rank-and-file clergy. Both the marriage and the divorce rates declined sharply at the onset of Depression, but both had recovered
to the level of the 1920's by about 1935. Economic stringency forced
many couples to defer both mating and unmating, to the undoubted
discomfort of people in both categories; it was not long, however,
before pre-Depression trends and patterns reasserted themselves.
Much the same was true of recreation; the years 1930–1935 show a
marked decline in purchases of sporting goods and attendance at
athletic events. New lines of interest opened up in parlor games—
dominoes, chess, Monopoly, bridge. Then about mid-decade attendance at baseball and football games reached the levels of the
1920's, and the long-range trend toward a more active recreational

life reasserted itself in dramatic increases in visits to national parks, skiing vacations, and cycling.

If population growth during the 1930's aligned itself with long-term trends, migration reflected more clearly the special hardships of a depression decade. For more than 100,000 Puerto Ricans, life in New York City was more attractive than in hard-hit Puerto Rico, and they came to the mainland. For the Mexican migrant, the situation was reversed: one-half million Mexicans left Texas, New Mexico, Arizona, and California for Mexico between 1929 and 1935, many of them forcibly repatriated when city relief officials and agricultural employers found themselves faced with a mass of unemployed workers. The Depression sent 350,000 white families to the Pacific Coast, slowed the historic drift of population to the cities, and in one year (1933) reversed it.

The economic slump of the 1930's lowered the level of social investment in human capital, just as it had with physical capital. Communities and states (although not the federal government after 1933) as well as families and individuals reduced their expenditures on education and medical care. It is a tribute to the American commitment to public health and education that the cuts were modest. Hospital bed capacity grew more slowly in the 1930's than in the previous decade, but it increased every year nonetheless. Total spending on education declined only from $3.234 billion in 1930 to $3.200 billion in 1940, and college enrollments regained their pre-Depression levels in 1935 and continued upward. However, there was much distress in education, especially at the grade-school level, where teachers experienced salary cuts and moratoria; new construction was halted; and some twenty-six hundred schools were closed at the trough of the Depression. When the war came, Selective Service examiners rejected 50 percent of the recruits in 1940–1941 on medical (and dental) and educational grounds, revealing, as in 1917–1918, the social cost of poverty. The Depression, of course, did not introduce the practice of human neglect. It simply widened the orbit of poverty that had long engulfed from one-third to one-half of the population, perpetuating underinvestment in the maintenance and improvement of America's human capital.

In ethnic relations the impact of national economic hardship is particularly difficult to assess. Judging by the figures on lynching, hard times may have engendered a feeling of greater human solidarity and compassion. Lynchings ranged from fifty-two to ninety-seven annually in the decade prior to World War I, dropped below twenty for five of the years between the armistice and the crash, reached eight in 1932, and after a brief rise settled below ten annually from 1936 onward. The second half of the 1930's were the least barbaric years for which we have statistics, if the crime of lynching is the measure. There continued to be incidents of racial violence, and it is difficult to judge whether the broad patterns of white hostility to blacks moderated during the Depression. Certainly the cele-

Attorney Samuel Leibowitz consults in a cramped cell in Decatur, Alabama, with the chief defendant, Haywood Patterson, and the rest of the "Scottsboro boys." In 1931–1932, on the false testimony of two white prostitutes (one of whom recanted in court), the youths were charged with and convicted of rape. Four of them were released in 1937, the others individually paroled from 1943 to 1950, when the last Scottsboro boy, Andrew Wright, went free of Alabama justice at age thirty-nine. "I am just like a rabbit in a strange wood," Wright wrote, "and the dogs is after him and no place to hide."

Brown Brothers

brated trial and conviction of eight black youths in Scottsboro, Alabama, in 1931–1932 for the alleged rape of two white prostitutes brought out familiar southern racial hatreds in all their ugliness. A portent of changed attitudes appeared in the vigorous and successful defense effort waged by the Communist-led International Labor Defense Fund and the NAACP. Relations between blacks and whites in the 1930's were full of crosscurrents, and we cannot be sure whether there was a slight drift toward greater tolerance, let alone what causal role the sustained economic crisis may have played. In one area of ethnic relations there is reasonably good evidence that the Depression heightened racial tensions. Studies report a sharp increase in anti-Semitism beginning about 1933 and running into the war years. A leading scholar estimated that a dozen anti-Semitic groups were founded annually during the 1930's, the total reaching 121. Father Charles E. Coughlin became increasingly vocal and critical of the role of "Jewish bankers and internationalists" and along with William Dudley Pelley stirred fears among Jews and civil libertarians of a major fascist, anti-Semitic movement in America in the late 1930's. The sources of anti-Semitism are complex, but it appears that the economic and status dislocations of the Depression contributed significantly to the undoubted rise of anti-Semitism just before the war.

Were there no benefits in the decade or more of economic depression? Those who proclaimed that a little adversity was good for individuals and nations were tragically mistaken, but few human experiences, even unpleasant ones, are without any redeeming feature or side effect. Perhaps, as some economists argue, the first year of the Depression was useful in checking an inflationary psychology and in correcting abuses in banking and finance. As for the rest of the Depression, one might at least assign to its credit the many reforms extending public regulation and economic security—in a word, the best parts of the New Deal. In this sense, the Depression, which intensified many American social problems, put in motion an unprecedented attack on these problems through the agencies of democratic government.

At least one other social advance is clearly a by-product of the economic adversity of the 1930's—an upsurge of social introspection and realism, an intense interest in the lives of the poor, those Michael Harrington would call thirty years later "the Other Americans." Such interest was long overdue. Very little was known about the economically unsuccessful—sharecroppers, migratory farm workers, the

Workers stage a "sit-down strike" at the Fisher Body Plant in Flint, Michigan, in early 1937. This scene was tranquil enough, but there was violence later on when employers and police attempted to dislodge the strikers. The "sit-down" tactic successfully organized much of the auto industry, but it alarmed the public and cut heavily into labor's support.

hill people of Appalachia, ghetto blacks, families without a working parent, the white male industrial laborer himself. In 1932, government officials admitted that they did not know how many were unemployed. By the end of the 1930's, much more was known about American life than had been known ten years earlier—in particular, about the lives of those Roosevelt called the "forgotten men" or the "bottom one-third." Frederick Lewis Allen, author of two brilliant books about American society in the interwar years, wrote that the secondary sources for his history of the 1920's, *Only Yesterday* (1931), filled only one shelf. When the time came to begin research for the history of the 1930's, *Since Yesterday* (1939), the secondary literature filled a library of its own and was beyond his capacity to digest. The government made several revealing inquiries and collected a solid body of fact about previously uncharted zones of American existence. The AAA's troubles in Arkansas publicized the plight of the landless farmer and led in 1937 to the report of the President's Committee on Farm Tenancy. The hearings of Senator Robert M. La Follette, Jr.'s Civil Liberties Committee (1936–1940) exposed the violence and intimidation often inflicted on workers attempting to unionize and along with Congressman John H. Tolan's Committee on Defense Migration unearthed some of the shocking facts of the working and living conditions of migratory agricultural laborers. Throughout the New Deal men and women were eager to expose the suffering of groups formerly ignored. WPA artists decorated post offices with murals depicting the hardship of working-class life; WPA funds helped produce both Caldwell and Bourke-White's *You Have Seen Their Faces* and Agee and Evans' *Let Us Now Praise Famous Men*. And one should not forget the influence of Roosevelt, who on many occasions reminded the nation of its poor.

The New Dealers had no monopoly on this new interest in the poor. The decade was rich in the production of published studies of marginal economic groups.* Howard Odum's *Southern Regions of the United States* (1936) and Arthur F. Raper's *Preface to Peasantry* (1936) were impressive socioeconomic studies of southern rural poverty, and in 1939 came Carey McWilliams' almost unique study of migratory farm labor, *Factories in the Field*. The same proletarian interests ran strongly in fiction. Much of this writing, such as Robert Cantwell's *Land of Plenty* (1934), Albert Halper's *The Foundry* (1934), Grace Lumpkin's *To Make My Bread* (1935), and Fielding Burke's *Call Home the Heart* (1935), is worth rereading less for its literary merit than as evidence of the penetration of class-consciousness into American thought in the 1930's. But novelists of skill and timeless insight also turned for inspiration to the largely unexplored realms of lower-class life. The period produced John Dos Passos' magnificent *U.S.A.* trilogy (1930–1936), with its impressionistic recapturing of the plebeian side of interwar culture; Erskine Caldwell's *Tobacco Road* (1932), a story of Georgia sharecroppers; James T. Farrell's *Studs Lonigan* trilogy (1932–1935), a powerful evocation of the physical and psychological costs of lower middle class urban life; Paul Green's *This Body the Earth* (1935), a novel of chain gangs and southern penal life; Richard Wright's *Native Son* (1940), a black author's narrative of the life of a young black in an urban ghetto;

---

*Proving again that history is untidy, at least one of the classic investigations of injustice and poverty in America was commenced and completed in the prosperous 1920's. This was the 1928 Meriam Report on the life and culture of American Indians under federal policy.

William Faulkner's *As I Lay Dying* (1930) and *Light in August* (1932), two unforgettable novels set in rural Mississippi, where the Depression had started with Reconstruction; and John Steinbeck's best seller, *The Grapes of Wrath* (1939), a novel of tenant farmers in flight from the Oklahoma dust bowl to California.

Although the stage and screen were wary of the commercial risks involved in the realistic treatment of poverty, class conflict, and war, they too reflected the sobering impact of economic and social crisis. Many successful plays were built around themes of exploitation and economic conflict, such as the Broadway adaptation of Erskine Caldwell's *Tobacco Road* (1934), Marc Blitzstein's *The Cradle Will Rock* (1937), the WPA Children's Theatre production of *The Revolt of the Beavers* (1936), Clifford Odets' *Waiting for Lefty* (1935), and *Awake and Sing* (1935). The musical *Pins and Needles* (1937) was suffused with a pro-labor orientation and bequeathed a catchy song symbolizing the new element in Depression-era entertainment—"Sing Me a Song of Social Significance." The Hollywood film industry ventured a number of movies in the realistic mold, among them Warner Brothers' *Black Legion* (1937), a frank evocation of racial tensions and violence, and *I Am a Fugitive from a Chain Gang* (1935), which conveyed sympathy for the victims of an old and barbaric American institution. One of the best movies of the decade was Charlie Chaplin's *Modern Times* (1936), a tragi-comic indictment of industrialism.

Thus the Depression left its mark on the culture of the 1930's by stimulating inquiries into the darker corners of American life. One is led to categorize this realism as a gain, not only on the grounds that all increases in self-knowledge are desirable but because factual and artistic probings of the society's economic and ethical failures help to stimulate remedial action. When the New Deal undertook social welfare programs, when the poor began to emerge from apathy and disorganization, the changed political climate was only one reason. Another was a changed moral climate, the product of a vast, uncoordinated, spontaneous educational effort carried on by artists, government committees, and scholars as they reported what they found in the formerly invisible, uninteresting world of the poor. "We have turned over the American board," said Harry Hopkins, "and seen how many people live like slugs beneath its plenty." Without the Depression, this board would have remained in place.

The Depression years, then, were a time when social realism and activism reached an intensity and scale surpassing the days of progressive muckraking and reform. "It was a decade of involvement,"

Charlie Chaplin's great films were mostly products of the 1930's. There was much hilarious comedy in *Modern Times* (1936), but, as this still from the movie reveals, its background was quite serious: the relentless, impersonal, industrial society in which anonymous men found themselves caught.

wrote Saul Alinsky. "It's a cold world now. It was a hot world then." Yet it is important to specify the extent of the penetration of social issues into the culture. The desire to unveil the sectors of American life screened from view for so long was almost a monopoly of the better-educated urban classes. The popular culture was far from suffused with critical introspection. Louis Adamic traveled around the country in 1938 and reported that "the proletariat did not read proletarian literature. Probably it did not want to work in factories in the daytime and behold factories and mines at night in the theatre." For the average American, the absorbing developments of the era were not primarily economic and political trends, changes in labor or race relations, or historic shifts in public policy—at least if one judges by space allocation in the daily press. The big stories of the 1930's were the kidnapping of the son of Mr. and Mrs. Charles A. Lindbergh and the trial of the abductor; the birth of the Dionne quintuplets in Canada; the abdication of Edward VIII of England in order to marry an American divorcée; the killing of gangster John Dillinger; the "swing" rhythms of Benny Goodman's band. Popular tastes in reading showed no shift toward the hard facts of the social struggle. The best sellers were not the novels of protest or the readable economic studies of Stuart Chase and George Soule but books that allowed the citizen to escape contemporary reality. The largest best seller of the 1930's was by far and away Margaret Mitchell's *Gone with the Wind* (1936), a novel offering not only a love story but apparently a comforting picture of relations between blacks and whites in the Civil War and Reconstruction South. Not far behind were other romanticized historical novels, such as Hervey Allen's *Anthony Adverse* (1933) and Kenneth Roberts' *Northwest Passage* (1937).

In journalism, tabloid newspapers, simple in format and message and preoccupied with the eccentric behavior of entertainers and crimes of violence, tripled their circulation. Comic strips expanded in number and attracted a large and loyal readership. Women's magazines, claiming 13 million subscribers, offered an almost unrelieved diet of maudlin love stories, travel accounts, and housekeeping hints. The most popular journal of the decade was the *Reader's Digest,* full of pleasant stories of business, personal, and marital successes and appropriately mailed to its 7 million or 8 million readers from Pleasantville, New York. Pulp magazines flourished, expanding their monthly sales from 8 million in 1928 to 14 million by 1938. Because their income came almost entirely from newsstand sales rather than from advertising, the pulps probably reflected the taste of their readership better than did the daily press, polite fiction, films, or even the occasional public opinion poll. And the pulp magazines were jammed with stories of crime, gangsters, G-men, and death. Robert Cantwell, in a study of journalism in the 1930's, said of the pulp magazines that "the mixture of insipidity, superstition, and violence found in them gives an appalling picture of working-class culture. The best of them . . . are characterized by a complete remoteness from the problems of the class they reach; the worst have a morbid and nightmarish quality of frenzy." To Cantwell, the only connection made by the vast world of popular journalism with the contemporary Depression was that the women's magazines, pulps, comics, and newspapers were depressing: "They are depressing because of their extreme aloofness from everything that has been going on; the country has been shaken from top to bottom with panics and riots, and they have kept right on doing business at the same old stand, with the same symbols, with the same cast of characters."

The 1930's was a golden decade for radio. News analysis expanded, and series such as "Town Meeting of the Air" discussed difficult contemporary issues. But the public loved best the comedians Jack Benny and Fred Allen, the ventriloquist Edgar Bergen with his friend Charlie McCarthy, the Lone Ranger with his inarticulate but loyal Indian companion Tonto, and the happy, trivial escapades of two "black" (the men behind the microphones were white) comics, Amos 'n' Andy. At the movies, an average of 54 million people each week saw some fictionalized treatments of unemployment or racial troubles but for the most part enjoyed historical romances such as *Mutiny on the Bounty* (1936), the western *Stagecoach* (1939), *Gone with the Wind* (1939), Walt Disney's fantasy *Snow White and the Seven Dwarfs* (1937). A director commented on American film tastes in the 1930's: "The American public—the American public with the mind of a twelve-year old child, you see—it must have life as it ain't."

Thus wherever one looks in popular magazines, newspapers, moving pictures, fiction, the pulpit, the speaker's lectern at Rotary Club luncheons or meetings of women's literary clubs, even the themes of advertising, one finds these sources of the popular culture continuing through the Depression to offer to the American public reassurance and diversion. Social realism penetrated American culture, but critical social perspectives, then as now, were uncongenial to the public. It may be, as some observers have argued, that the collapse of the economy for so long a time had an impact on the popular mind that movies, popular fiction, and other sources do not reveal. There is some evidence that people in all walks of life experienced a loss of faith in formerly unquestioned assumptions, in particular the superiority of American economic arrangements and the inevitability of American progress. Perhaps W. H. Auden expressed a disquiet and pessimism that had spread even beyond the intellectuals when he wrote in 1940:

> Tonight a scrambling decade ends,
> and strangers, enemies and friends
> stand once more puzzled underneath
> the signpost on the barren heath
> where the rough mountain track divides

to silent valleys on all sides
endeavoring to decipher what
is written on it but cannot
nor guess in what direction lies
the overhanging precipice.

World War II and Economic Mobilization

The Japanese attack at Pearl Harbor put an end to the paralyzing
foreign and domestic policy disputes of 1938–1941 and appeared to
give Roosevelt a climate of national unity within which to manage
the home front. Yet while the American public remained more united
about this war than about any other in our history (save perhaps
the short war of 1898), the war years brought political and social conflicts as divisive as those of the 1930's. It could hardly have been
otherwise. Ethnic and racial conflicts were predictably heightened as
the public sought scapegoats in the frustrations of early military
defeat and as accelerated social changes strained the social fabric.
Even more predictable were the fierce political battles of the wartime period, for the enormous expansion of the powers of government made the prize more valuable than ever before. Given the personality of the President and his identification with the New Deal,
wartime political struggles, for all their complexity, developed a
simple outline: Would policy have a New Deal cast, or would it shift
to favor the large industrial capitalists on whom America relied for
war-winning production? The former would mean mobilization
tightly controlled by public officials rather than by industrialists, a
tax system bearing heavily on the rich, a squeeze on profit margins
rather than on wages, an expansion of security programs for the work
force, a general sympathy for the underdog, which would probably
include racial and ethnic minorities. The business community, despite its divisions, wished policy in the hands of businessmen and
hoped for a tight reign on labor, no impairment of the profit motive
by heavy taxation, no government ownership of production facilities. The position of the President on these issues was equivocal.
Like war leaders everywhere and in every time he instinctively
reached for domestic policies that would be socially neutral, allowing a wartime government to retain the broadest consensus and
unity. But federal policy could not be neutral. Every policy decision
redistributed income, shifted current and postwar economic advantages, rearranged political strongholds, allocated life and death it-

self. As choices had to be made, Roosevelt's emotions inclined him to steer, as he put it in a press conference in 1940, "a little left of center."

The duties of government on the home front were to organize war production, finance it without disastrous inflation, and maximize unity of purpose. The first, mobilization for war production, was ultimately so successful, measured by the avalanche of supplies and firepower that buried the Axis, that we forget the stupendous complexities and snarls of the effort. The New Dealers who had talked glibly of economic planning had been humbled by the NRA experience, and yet the problems of planning for war production far exceeded the problems of planning in peacetime. Roosevelt's first step was to appoint a committee to study the problem of conversion — the War Resources Board — in August 1939. In view of divided public opinion on mobilization, FDR shelved the committee's report. In May 1940, stunned by the fall of France, the President asked Congress for funds to build 50,000 planes a year and set up the Advisory Commission to the Council of National Defense to begin construction of defense production facilities. (He was improvising again. The council no longer existed, though the Advisory Commission did.)

As odd as it may seem to today's generation, businessmen hung back from accepting federal contracts or discussing conversion with purchasing agents from the armed services. They were unsure of the profits in defense work and not eager to tie up their facilities and allow their competitors to capture the booming consumer goods market. To entice big business to cooperate, the administration offered cost-plus contracts and generous tax advantages and constructed some facilities through the Reconstruction Finance Corporation. In addition, Roosevelt built confidence among businessmen by bringing conservatives into his Cabinet and businessmen into positions in the mobilization machinery: In 1940, Henry L. Stimson and Frank Knox (both Republicans) became secretary of war and secretary of the navy, respectively. The President named United States Steel's Edward R. Stettinius, Jr., to head the War Resources Board and gave General Motors' William Knudsen the job of co-chairman, along with the CIO's Sidney Hillman, of the Advisory Commission. Expenditures for defense (in 1940, $1.6 million) jumped in 1941 to $6.2 million. Measured by the need, however, the actual production of planes, tanks, and ships was lagging, with bottlenecks and shortages plaguing orderly expansion. Just as FDR had reached a point

This airplane factory in Stratford, Connecticut, produced over 6,000 "Corsair" fighter planes for wartime service on aircraft carriers. In factories such as this,
where with marvelous efficiency the American people fashioned tools of destruction,
the Depression generation finally found full employment.

of diplomatic drift in the summer of 1941, with the nation hesitant
and divided around him, so in preparedness he refused to strike
decisively for all-out conversion. Bernard Baruch was foremost
among those who urged a "czar" with adequate powers to override
all conflicts in production. Roosevelt preferred to multiply agencies
and channel decisions through himself, rather than to establish a
superagency under a director whose authority might rival the President's. In January 1941, Roosevelt replaced the Advisory Commission
with the Office of Production Management (OPM) under Knudsen
and Hillman, and set up a separate agency, the Office of Price Administration and Civilian Supply (OPA) under Leon Henderson in
April to control price distortions. In August he responded to rising
criticism of the disorderly and inefficient conversion by creating the
Supplies Priorities and Allocation Board (SPAB), with Sears, Roe-

buck's Donald Nelson as head. The Washington mobilization machinery mirrored the nation's confusion in the fall of 1941.

Pearl Harbor and the opening of a two-front war required drastically revised production goals and new mobilization machinery. In his January state of the union address FDR asked for 60,000 planes in 1942, 25,000 tanks, 6 million tons of shipping. In that same week, he replaced SPAB with the War Production Board, retaining Nelson as head. Nelson encountered stiffening criticism through 1942, both for indecisiveness and failure to assert civilian control over military procurement. In May 1943 Roosevelt made his sixth major adjustment of the planning apparatus. He named the capable and conservative James F. Byrnes, former Supreme Court justice, to head the Office of War Mobilization (OWM). More personnel changes and agency reorganization lay ahead, but in Byrnes and OWM the President had finally found the combination of man and agency with just enough power to manage the war production tangle and not enough to remove essential national powers from the President.

FDR's planning machinery has been widely criticized, even in the Bureau of the Budget's official history, *The United States at War*. Oddly enough, the President who was so often charged with a love of regimentation refused to create planning and coordinating institutions with adequate power and instead muddled through with dozens of overlapping agencies too weak for their tasks. But only a small part of the confusion of the mobilization may be attributed to Roosevelt's relatively loose administrative habits. The government in wartime was forced to set aside the price system, and only then did the bureaucrats, intellectuals, and politicians glimpse the magnitude of the daily job done by the marketplace—allocating resources among users, bringing men to jobs and providing services for their maintenance, balancing the supply of items against the demand for them, maintaining incentives, rewarding effort. In wartime this mechanism is fundamentally disrupted, and bureaucrats must do the monumental work of the price system. If the government wishes tanks, planes, and ships, it appropriates money and orders them. Then a scramble begins for the copper, vanadium, steel, rubber, optical glass, machine tools, electricity, even expert labor, necessary to produce them, and the government cannot allow the highest bidder to carry off limited resources. If contractors for the navy move first and bid highest on supplies of copper for ships (they will have a tendency to overpurchase, hoarding against shortages), there will not be copper for the valves of the oil refineries or

oil pipelines on which the ships eventually depend. Orderly production required enforced priorities overruling prices. Public officials had to estimate the amount of copper each vital industry needed
(and Washington had no such data), allocate it, and make certain not
to forget some minor industry producing vital parts. Then these
priorities had to be defended against not only the multiple and competing purchasing agencies of army, navy, lend-lease, the Allies
(buying through the Munitions Assignment Board), the Office of
Civilian Defense, and the coast guard, but also against the refrigerator industry and the tractor industry, which were screaming that they
too were a vital part of the war effort.

Labor was even more difficult to allocate than material. Fifteen
million Americans ultimately passed through the armed services,
and these new "jobs," combined with industrial expansion, erased
the labor surpluses of the Depression. Suddenly there were more jobs
than workers, and bureaucrats had to intervene against market
forces to decide whether optometrists and machinists and experienced farmers would be sent to France, left in Kansas, or allowed to
follow the lure of wages to Detroit's defense plants. When men with
no appropriate experience and little data began to shoulder the work
of the price system, operating from dozens of agencies with overlapping responsibilities, the result was shortages, surpluses, delays,
waste, and short tempers. Everybody in Washington knew the story
of the New York banker who joined the Bureau of Economic Welfare,
received a letter six months later rejecting his own application for
the job, and noticed the letter was signed by himself, or the story
of the Japanese spy who advised his government not to bother
bombing any building in Washington because the Americans had
another building just like it filled with people doing the same thing.

In the end, we remember not the waste, delays, and confusions of
the mobilization but the stupendous output of the implements of
war. American factories doubled the production of the Axis by 1944,
turning out 299,000 aircraft, 59.9 million tons of merchant and naval
shipping, warehouses full of bayonets, tents, canned food, bomb-
sights, mosquito nets, a mountain of military supplies ultimately
reaching a value of $183.1 billion. At the same time the partnership
of the government, industry, and the universities accelerated scientific research and development, producing electronic navigational
and guidance systems, radar, sonar, combat rockets, DDT, penicillin.
The largest scientific effort was also the most significant for the future: At a cost of $2 billion and the man-hours of the finest physicists

**United States Munitions Production, July 1940-August 1945
(in standard 1945 munitions dollars)**

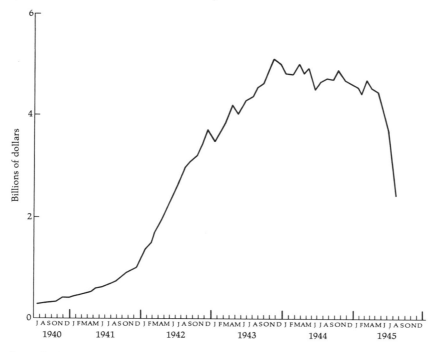

Source: Civilian Production Administration, *Industrial Mobilization for War*, vol. I, 1947.

in the Anglo-American camp, the Manhattan Project under General Leslie Groves controlled nuclear fission and created the atomic bomb. The scale and quality of the nation's scientific and production effort surprised even American industrialists, astonished the world at large, and justified Churchill's confidence that American intervention would tip the balance against the apparently irresistible war machine of the Axis.

Taxing, Borrowing, Rationing, and Inflating: The Financing of the War

In addition to the job of converting or building new defense production facilities and allocating materials and labor in the complex, interlocking effort of supply, the government faced a formidable job in the matter of war finance. More than anything else, the question of who was to pay for the war embittered America's wartime politics. In four years, 1941 through 1945, the government spent $321 billion, a sum twice as large as the expenses of government from 1789 to Pearl Harbor and ten times as great as the cost of World War I. The government determined exactly who was to bear this burden, allocating sacrifices among various groups of citizens. Understandably, given the immediacy of the foreign threat, Congress first authorized spending for defense and only later turned to the question of providing the money. No Congress likes to raise taxes, and the Congress that voted to spend $34 billion in 1942 voted to raise only $12 billion of this in taxes. In 1943, Congress approved "the greatest tax bill in history" and still took in only $22 billion while spending $79 billion. The balance was raised by borrowing. This pushed the national debt from $49 billion in 1941 to $259 billion in 1945.

No intelligent person worried about the debt, for the nation could

National Debt, 1900-1945

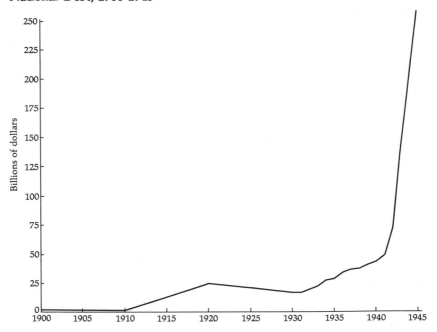

Source: *Historical Statistics of the United States, Colonial Times to 1957* and *Statistical Abstract of the United States, 1970.*

easily carry the interest charges on such a sum. However, financing through borrowing did have a serious drawback. The expenditure of huge sums by government is not inflationary if private bidding for goods and services is reduced by exactly as much as the government spends. Taxation accomplishes this. But if a government decides it must borrow rather than tax, inflation is inevitable. Inflation may be deferred for a few years if the debt is sold to citizens, depriving them at least for a time of the funds they would otherwise use to bid up prices. If sums are borrowed from banks, this creates additional reserves and is immediately inflationary. Roosevelt, recognizing that heavy borrowing would cause inflation, asked Congress in April 1942 for a seven-point program of inflation control, including heavy and steeply graduated taxation, price, wage, and credit controls, and rationing. For the rest of the war a bitter struggle was carried on over this program, and it was a struggle to determine which citizens would sacrifice most in order to divert American resources to the destructive purposes of war.

The battle over taxation was bitter, and Congress compiled the worst record. Roosevelt asked for $14 billion in new taxes in early 1942, on a steeply graduated schedule (he suggested that no citizen be allowed to retain more than $25,000 annually), but Congress would not act. Only a threatened use of the President's emergency powers in October brought passage of a law raising $7 billion in new revenue. In 1943 Roosevelt asked for $16 billion in new taxes, and Congress one full year later agreed to an increase of $2.2 billion. In the end, only $131 billion of the $321 billion was raised by taxes; the rest was borrowed. Wartime taxes did make the federal tax schedules more progressive, with individual rates going as high as 94 percent and corporate income taxes going to 50 percent. But only a modest redistribution of income resulted. The graduation of the tax system was much less than the administration had asked, and the schedules contained many loopholes for those able to employ tax lawyers. The top 5 percent of income earners, it is true, saw their share of the national income drop from 26 percent to 16 percent, but their share was absorbed by the upper middle and middle classes, not by the poor. At the end of the war, the top 20 percent of earners had lost only 2.8 percent of their share (from 48.8 percent to 46 percent of the national income), and the bottom 20 percent had gained only 1 percent (from 4 percent to 5 percent). This degree of redistribution hardly constituted a revolution. At least as significant as the slight redistribution of income accomplished by wartime taxation was the extension of the income tax system to include the lower classes. Only 4 million families were subject to federal income taxes in 1939, but by 1944 the tax net reached out to drain the funds of 42.4 million families.

With Congress unwilling to raise more than 40 percent of the war expenses by taxation,* the Treasury was forced into inflationary borrowing. The $100 billion in bonds sold to the public had the same immediate effect as taxes, draining away purchasing power. But the $87 billion sold to the banking system expanded the money supply and fed inflationary pressures. The OPA imposed a general price and wage ceiling in April 1942, but the farm bloc had largely exempted agricultural prices from OPA authority, and prices rose an average of nearly 2 percent a month through the summer. This inflation created resentment among urban workers, and FDR pleaded with Congress for power to control food prices and for higher taxes. The threat of presidential emergency action brought a comprehensive anti-inflation law, including a tax increase in October. For the rest of the war, OPA, with adequate legal authority but inadequate staff, struggled to contain prices and rents and to enforce the rationing system against a public with more cash than at any time since the 1920's. During four years of war, prices were held to a 30 percent increase, most of that coming in 1941–1942. Yet congressional unwillingness to tax the public's buying power into manageable proportions led to consumer demand that no controls could contain. Though wartime inflation on paper may have been held to 30 percent, considerable inflation was hidden in the deterioration of quality in consumer goods and in the operations of the black market, where prices reached their natural levels. And in the twelve months after the war the pent-up buying power of the public pushed inflation from 30 percent to 50 percent, a delayed wartime inflation that should be charged to the Congress, not to OPA.

It is hard to estimate the relative gains and losses of various groups in the struggle to distribute the burdens of war among Americans left at home. Farmers clearly used their political power to good advantage, forcing Congress to allow food prices to reach 110 percent of parity. This triumph in Washington helped bring farm income from the 1940 level of $2.3 billion to $9.5 billion in 1945. Inflation, the farmers learned, was a happy condition if one could arrange to have more of it in one's sales than in one's costs. Labor's experience

---

* The figure for World War I was 33 percent, an even poorer record.

was less happy. Union leaders had agreed to a "no strike" pledge just weeks after the attack on Pearl Harbor, and the War Labor Board (WLB) was set up to adjudicate wage disputes. When the government did not control inflation in 1942, labor unrest was expressed in wildcat strikes and increasing pressure on the WLB. The board groped for guidelines that would make labor neither the victim nor the beneficiary (or cause) of inflation, and in July adopted the "little steel" formula, which allowed wage hikes of 15 percent to compensate for increases in the cost of living since 1941. Continuing inflation soon made the little steel formula appear as a lid on wages rather than as a fair settlement. The WLB, understaffed and bound by the anti-inflation law of October to adhere to the 15 percent formula, held the line on wages, allowing only a few upward adjustments in unusual cases. Labor felt itself victimized by the wage-price relationship the government arranged. The average weekly wage in manufacturing went up from $29.58 to $44.39 over the course of the war; inflation and taxes cut into the figure, however, and it was earned by longer hours and at an increased tempo. Yet a sense of patriotism and gratitude for full employment after years of Depression reconciled American workers to the government's apportionment of rewards and burdens. Strikes were actually rather infrequent during the war, idling fewer workers in 1942 and 1944 than in any New Deal year and costing one-tenth of 1 percent of all working time in industry, or one day per worker for the four years of war. Only a few unions were angry and bold enough to strike and defy federal seizure of facilities. When this happened, as with John L. Lewis' mine workers in the summer of 1943 and with railway workers in the fall, favorable settlements for the workers involved were offset by intensified anti-labor sentiment in the public at large, which did not share labor's feeling that nonfarm working people were carrying more than their share of the sacrifices of war.

Loyalty and Disloyalty: The Government as Manager of Opinion

As important as were full production and noninflationary financing, mass warfare made the manipulation of public opinion a crucial task of government during World War II. Here, too, the Roosevelt administration compiled a mixed record, comparing unfavorably with what some contemporaries thought possible but favorably with the record of Wilson in World War I. Successful prosecution of the conflict required that the public be both united and strongly committed to the war, and there were both positive and negative approaches to that goal. Like all wartime governments, the Roosevelt administration understood that divisive ideas and ideologies could not be allowed the freedom of expression permitted in peacetime and must be repressed. It also understood that the mere absence of dissent was not enough, that it must take the lead in providing war aims attractive enough to mobilize the invaluable energies of America's 135 million people. In the suppression of dissent the government followed a moderate course, largely because the attack on Pearl Harbor had silenced most pro-Nazis, pacifists, and isolationists. Potentially disloyal groups, such as the seventeen hundred Nazi bundists, were quickly rounded up by the FBI, but the government brought only a handful of leaders to trial, releasing the rest. Neither Roosevelt nor Attorney General Francis Biddle, a strong civil libertarian, felt the need for mass sedition trials, and the Supreme Court encouraged such restraint by placing a heavy burden of proof on the government. There was little anti-German hysteria in the country, and the government made no effort to stimulate hatred of the enemy as it had during World War I. Censorship of the press was imposed, but with the cooperation of American publishers it was largely voluntary and did not attempt to preclude the expression of criticism of the administration. Some 43,000 conscientious objectors were registered by the Selective Service, and 6,086 of these were imprisoned for refusing to participate in the war in any way. The practice of alternative service was developed for less rigorous objectors. The Civilian Public Service enrolled 12,000 as volunteers in medical research or outdoor conservation work, and the rest were willing to serve in noncombatant roles in the army.

The major exception to this record of restraint in the control of sedition was the removal and incarceration of the Japanese living on the west coast. This episode revealed American society and its government at their worst. A wave of rumors of Japanese invasion and sabotage swept the west coast after the attack on Pearl Harbor, and the army, under General John DeWitt, prepared to transport Japanese away from the vicinity of coastal military installations. Panic, feeding upon a deep racial prejudice against Orientals, mounted in January and February into a campaign for the evacuation of all Japanese from the three coastal states. Local and state political leaders, journalists, and prominent citizens questioned the loyalty of all 120,000

Japanese-Americans on the coast, most of whom were citizens, and demanded their exportation to the interior. Only Attorney General Biddle and Secretary of War Stimson expressed doubts about the necessity of wholesale evacuation. The military insisted that none of the Japanese could be trusted, and few voices were raised against the assignment of guilt to the Japanese on racial grounds even though German-Americans and Italian-Americans were dealt with individually. Although Nisei spokesmen correctly pointed out that there had been no sabotage, west coast Americans, actuated by racial dislike and in some cases by a desire to acquire the landholdings of Japanese-Americans, demanded total removal. On March 21, 1942, President Roosevelt, after assuring himself that the military thought the move necessary, signed Executive Order 9066 authorizing evacuation. Some 112,000 Japanese-Americans were uprooted and moved to eleven camps in the interior (located from Wyoming to Arkansas),

Japanese-Americans salute the American flag at morning ceremonies in a Wyoming internment camp. Despite the hardships of their wartime confinement, the overwhelming majority of these West Coast citizens remained loyal to the United States.

Hansel Meith. LIFE Magazine. © 1972 Time Inc.

at a cost of property losses estimated at $400 million and a degree
of personal humiliation impossible to quantify. Despite the laudable
efforts of the War Relocation Authority to ensure as much comfort
and community self-determination as conditions permitted, life in
the American concentration camps was bleak. "Truthfully," wrote
a Nisei assigned to the camp at Poston, Arizona, "I must say this
scorching Hell is a place beyond description and beyond tears." In
December 1944, the Supreme Court, in *Korematsu* v. *U.S.*, agreed that
this evacuation of American citizens was constitutional under the
emergency circumstances cited by the army. Despite the injustice
of the removal, the vast majority of the Japanese held stubbornly
to their American loyalties. Though 4,000 renounced their citizenship, 14,000 eventually served in the armed forces, many of them in
the celebrated 442nd Combat Team, which performed heroically at
Anzio and elsewhere.

With this major exception, the government's handling of "subversive" ideas and groups during the war was commendably calm
and effective. But a population untroubled by treasonous ideas or
agitation was not adequate for the efforts of total war. There had to
be energetic commitment and dedication by the entire people. The
government might ask the public to sacrifice for military victory over
attackers, but this appeal was of declining effectiveness during a
long war and did not generate a really intense determination to defeat Germany. (A poll in the summer of 1942 showed that one-third
of the public was ready to negotiate peace with Germany and concentrate on Japan.) Roosevelt understood that modern war required
an ideological basis for the maximum public effort, especially when
the fighting was not to take place on one's own soil. So the government gave considerable attention to providing a powerful rationale
for the sacrifices of global warfare. As was his custom, Roosevelt
established several propaganda agencies with overlapping duties
and jurisdictions. The Office of War Information (OWI) under the
journalist Elmer Davis was the basic information agency, but there
were also Nelson Rockefeller's Inter-American Affairs Office, propaganda agencies for each branch of the service, and the speeches of
the President and members of his Cabinet. Their joint efforts appear
to have been successful. The American public from 1941 to 1945
exhibited a remarkable unity behind the war effort. Voluntary en-
listments were high, there was little draft evasion and few deser-
tions, tax avoidance was never a problem, rationing was broadly
accepted (although a lively black market developed toward the end

of the war), and man-hours lost to strikes fell below the level of the 1930's in every year but 1943.

The administration, nonetheless, was criticized for its performance in mobilizing the intellectual and moral energies of the American people. Critics argued that the public support for the war enjoyed by the government was the result not of the administration's educational leadership but of the attack on Pearl Harbor and the barbarism of the Nazi regime. With national unity virtually assured, they thought, the President should have stressed the ideological meaning of the war much more resolutely than he did. The struggle, critics hold, should have been clearly and continuously depicted as one between the worldwide status quo and the cause of progressive social reform. Fascism should have been described not only as political tyranny but as elitist economic rule and open racism. Because this was not adequately accomplished, the New Deal coalition was weakened, and both domestic and foreign policy veered to the right in the course of the war. The work of reform was set back, and American foreign policy took on a conservative tinge that rendered it less flexible and less successful in dealing with a world in social revolution.

These views, in the form of premonitions, reached Roosevelt early in the war, and he seems to have agreed that the war had an ideological meaning that the American people had to be led to see. Yet the President's ideological leadership was intermittent, and the propaganda agencies he established transmitted an ambiguous message. Most of the official discussion of the aims of the war, as expressed in pamphlets, films, advertising, and radio, made the Axis armies and totalitarian politics the enemy and military victory the appropriate remedy. Radio, press, and movies generally reinforced this simple, military focus of the war effort. Actor Brian Donlevy, in the movie *Wake Island,* said that the Japanese at Pearl Harbor had shown themselves to be "sheer destruction," and "we've got to destroy destruction. That's our job."

On the other hand, some writers in the OWI produced pamphlets and films linking the war to internal social reform, urging respect for the rights of racial minorities, extolling the contributions of labor, identifying the President clearly as the founder of the New Deal. Roosevelt's own efforts to clarify war aims were equally inconsistent. There were occasions when he struck out boldly to associate the war in the public mind with the libertarian and democratic values of the New Deal. He joined with Churchill on August 12, 1941, to issue the

Atlantic Charter, pledging postwar independence to all nationalities
then in colonial status. In his state of the union address in January
1941, FDR stressed the American commitment to the "four freedoms," of which the third, "freedom from want," recalled the New
Deal's drive toward economic security for the lower classes. Then
when the congressional elections of 1942 arrived, Roosevelt called
for "an end to politics" and took virtually no interest in the selection of this crucial wartime Congress. As a result, the normal mid-
term swing away from the administration, intensified in 1942 by
military reverses and inflation, ran unchecked by presidential influence. Democrats stayed away from the polls in unusual numbers,
conservatives ran well in both parties, and the Republicans gained
nine Senate and forty-four House seats. In a press conference in
December 1943, the President went so far as to announce that "Dr.
New Deal" had been replaced by "Dr. Win the War," clearly divorc-
ing the war from political goals. Then came another reversal. In his
state of the union address two weeks later, Roosevelt made his most
radical speech, adding to the political rights already accepted as
essential to freedom an "economic bill of rights" — the right to a job,
food, clothing, recreation, a home, medical care, education.

This sporadic educational effort was not enough to revive the New
Deal majority and to maintain liberal control over domestic policy.
Perhaps no amount of presidential talk could have averted the drift
to the right. The reform coalition contained many internal tensions,
such as those between urban and rural elements, between northern
and southern Democrats, between blacks and whites. Roosevelt
seems also to have been inhibited from taking the path of strong
ideological leadership because to do so might have increased political divisiveness in the midst of war and would certainly have
alienated the conservative industrialists whose cooperation was
vital to defense production. In addition, Roosevelt was burdened
with military and diplomatic decisions and was in increasingly ill
health. In the view of some, these considerations would have prevented any President from asserting powerful ideological leadership during the war; according to others, the reform coalition was
there to be led and Roosevelt demonstrated again, as he had in the
1930's, his characteristic vacillation.

Whatever the President's personal responsibility for the course of
events, the goals and constituent interests associated with the New
Deal suffered a number of important setbacks during the war. Congress, more conservative after 1942 than it had been since the 1920's,

abolished New Deal agencies thought to be making no direct contribution to the war effort, such as CCC, WPA, and NYA. It eliminated the National Resources Planning Board because of its penchant for social research and planning, harassed the FSA (ending it in 1946), and curbed OWI's issuance of pamphlets expressing sympathy for social reform. On the vital matter of taxation, Congress forced Roosevelt and Secretary of the Treasury Morgenthau to accept less revenue and a more regressive tax structure than either thought desirable. Roosevelt fought back occasionally, as when he vetoed the tax bill of 1944 because it lowered rates on corporations and high-income individuals, but for the most part he avoided energy-consuming struggles with a conservative Congress. The heart of the New Deal, after all, was not threatened. There was no significant opposition to a broad planning role for government in the postwar period, no attack on the social security system, no objections to federal subsidies for agriculture or to the right of labor to organize and bargain collectively with employers. Because these fundamentals were not at stake, Roosevelt usually avoided conflict with conservatives. He allowed them their minor victories against the New Deal so long as they did not seek major ones. Just before the Democratic convention in 1944, the President allowed conservatives in his own party to force Vice-President Henry Wallace from the ticket, but he was cool to the southerners' candidate James Byrnes, and finally accepted a border-state moderate who had always supported the New Deal, Harry S. Truman from Missouri.

Roosevelt took with apparent calm the defeats inflicted by a conservative Congress, and he did not respond to liberal critics who claimed that presidential leadership could have restored the momentum of reform. There is evidence that he intended to resume the work of the New Deal when the war was over. But even if Roosevelt had lived, he would have found it difficult to move public policy again to the left. The war left the country structurally and ideologically more conservative than in 1938. The political and economic position of businessmen, along with their reputation in the nation at large, had improved enormously since the end of the 1930's. The war buried the anti-trust drive launched by Thurman Arnold and the TNEC, and despite the activities of Senator Truman's Special Committee to Investigate the National Defense Program, war contracts went principally to the large corporations, encouraging tendencies toward economic concentration, which the New Deal had hoped to reverse.

Election of 1944

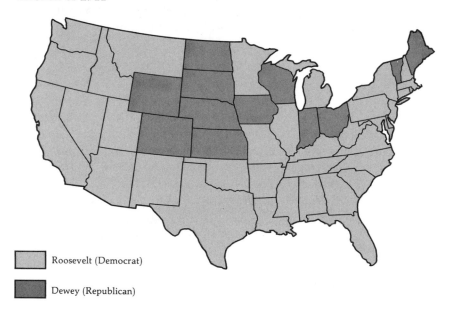

Roosevelt (Democrat)

Dewey (Republican)

After the war, the labor movement was numerically stronger (10 million in 1941, 14 million in 1945) but had irretrievably lost its public approval. Perhaps most important, the personnel staffing the government had changed significantly in social background. Businessmen, often working for only a dollar a year, had come to Washington to help with the mobilization of industry, had regained the prestige lost in the Depression, and had become a force to be reckoned with inside as well as outside the government. Experience in Washington had lessened their doctrinaire fear of an active government, and they were prepared to accept the essentials of the welfare state — deficit spending, social security, collective bargaining, agricultural supports — in order to retain the regulatory apparatus that ensured stability. Two successive Republican presidential nominees, Wendell Willkie (1940) and Thomas E. Dewey (1944), expressed this acceptance of the framework of the welfare state, which by the end of the war was widespread among leading figures in the industrial and financial community. In this new frame of mind, businessmen like James A. Forrestal, Edward Stettinius, William Batt, William Clayton, and thousands of others serving in government would be much more effective shapers of policy than the alienated, angry business spokesmen of 1934–1940. For all these reasons, the American government, with its massive intervening powers, was a more conservative force at the end of World War II than it had been at the beginning.

Life on the Home Front

World War II squandered human life and treasure on a stupendous scale. The costs of the war to America were not great compared to the costs to nations that experienced fighting on their own soil, but they were staggering by any other standard. Some 322,000 Americans were killed, 800,000 wounded or missing in action; $288 billion was spent on the war by 1945, and the eventual costs have been estimated by the government at $664 billion. An incalculable treasure in resources—scarce metals, oil, coal, chemicals, forest reserves, soil fertility—lay scattered across Europe and at the bottom of the seas. Because of these costs, and an uncertain future in which military defeat was a distinct possibility, the American wartime mood took on elements of melancholy and anxiety reminiscent of 1932. Americans intended to win the war, but they had little of the utopian hopes, the elation, the boisterous confidence of 1917–1918. Although the danger of enemy attack on the homeland receded after the coastal alarms of early 1942, much had to be endured at home that was unpleasant. Rationing commenced in 1942, with sugar, then coffee, then meat, canned goods, and shoes becoming luxuries. Rubber and gasoline were rationed in 1943, forcing people to largely forgo a prime source of pleasure and diversion—the evening or Sunday drive in the automobile. With 12 million men ultimately drawn away from home into the armed services, young couples were separated and lovers forced to defer marriage. War disrupted family life not only through death and long separations for overseas service but also by drawing mothers into the work force, often in the crowded, alien surroundings of new centers of defense industry such as Mobile, Norfolk, San Diego, and Detroit. One noticed preschool children idling away the hours, often in the movies, while mothers worked. Juvenile delinquency began a steady increase. The popular culture reflected these strains. Songwriters created snappy, optimistic songs, hoping to strike the response given to George M. Cohan's "Over There" in World War I, but jaunty songs were rarely commercial successes. A stronger response was accorded the songs of melancholy and loneliness—Irving

Berlin's "When the Lights Go On Again All Over the World" and "White Christmas." Songs that made a lasting impact were often those reflecting the war-enforced separation of lovers—"I'll Walk Alone," "Don't Get Around Much Anymore," "Long Ago and Far Away," "Laura," "I'll Be Seeing You."

On occasion the burdens of wartime living, real and psychological, intensified American racial and ethnic animosities and produced violence. In the best of times, most whites disliked the red, brown, yellow, and black minorities with whom they shared citizenship. When the war came, the least tolerant of the native whites, the "hillbillies" from Appalachia, poured into cities such as Detroit, Akron, Mobile, Chicago, and Los Angeles and found themselves suddenly in close contact with ethnic minorities who were also in search of employment. Competition for jobs, housing, even recreational space, kept tempers short, and rumors of race wars swept many cities. There were brief riots in Mobile and Beaumont; then in June 1943, a vicious interracial conflict in Detroit took the lives of twenty-five blacks and

Rationing of gasoline and rubber was necessary to divert these scarce materials from civilian to military use, and perhaps no other economic measure brought the war home to the American people with more immediacy. Here cars line up in 1943 in Brooklyn, New York, while one pump delivers a recent shipment of rationed gasoline.

United Press International

nine whites. Two months later, in August, a riot in Harlem killed six and caused $5 million in property damage. Blacks were not the only targets of urban, large-scale violence. In Los Angeles the antagonism felt by white sailors for the young Mexican-American "zoot-suiters" led to riots in 1943. The epidemic of racial violence in 1943 consisted of a total of 242 racial outbreaks in 47 cities, according to a study done at Fisk University.

Yet American society is never without cultural complexity. The anxious, somber mood appropriate to a time of danger and sacrifice was offest by a new dynamism as all the energies of the nation, stifled since 1929 by the mysterious forces of the Depression, were enlisted in a great national effort. Suddenly there were jobs again, jobs not just for young men, but earning opportunities for older people, for blacks, for women, for the blind, even for ex-convicts. Seven million unemployed people, as well as nearly 4 million young people who had never worked, found jobs in war industry. The word of economic opportunity went out across the country, reaching remote rural and mountainous areas. People began to move, 27 million of them in four years, catching trains and buses in search of steady work. Thirty-five states lost population during the war, while thirteen experienced unplanned, disorderly, tumultuous growth. Mobile staggered under a 65 percent increase; 220,000 people flowed into Detroit–Willow Run, 440,000 into Los Angeles. Weekly wages in industry went up 70 percent, more than keeping ahead of inflation; farmers experienced the best years since 1918–1919, with net annual farm income jumping from $2.3 billion to $9.4 billion over the war, a 300 percent increase.

Thus the war brought jobs to people desperate for a chance to work and actually produced a higher standard of living than in the 1930's, despite the diversion of resources to military purposes. Economically, America was a thriving, dynamic place in the years after Pearl Harbor, and although the improved picture in jobs and profits could not entirely overcome the melancholy mood induced by casualty lists and imminent national peril, it did project into the maelstrom of wartime culture a certain optimistic, buoyant influence. The war years, after all, saw the production of the musicals *Oklahoma, Carousel,* and *Bloomer Girl,* saw the nightclub business break records, saw horse racing attract $1.4 billion and 17 million people in 1945. It was a serious time for America and a time of expanding horizons and zest. Despite the grim presence of military peril, the war years are probably remembered more pleasurably by the American people than are the lean years of the Depression.

The Social Consequences of War

In view of the wartime drift of public policy to the right, some have said that World War II brought a turning point in modern American history. The New Deal, with its leveling tendencies and its determination to master the corporation, had given way by 1945 to a government filled with men sympathetic to corporations. The Depression-era commitment to a greater share of the national income for those who owned and sold only their labor, it has been said, was lost in the rising prosperity of full production and employment. As important as this shift in mood and policy may have been, the war experience should be seen less as a time of the interruption of prewar trends than as a continuation, even an acceleration, of the fundamental social changes operating through the 1930's and before. Both public policy and social changes beyond the reach of government contributed to the progressive collectivization of American life.

In a thousand ways, American life during the war became more interrelated and interdependent, fewer areas remaining free of the pressures of standardization and nationalization. A prime agent of this transformation was the corporation. The large corporations came out of the war even larger and more confident of the future than at any time since the 1920's, determined to expand their operations into what publisher Henry Luce called the "American Century" ahead. The growth of the large corporation relative to the rural and small business sectors expanded the zones of regularity in American society, extending planning and control to the marketplace and to the occupational lives of growing numbers of Americans. Other pressures toward an interrelated, mass society came from the media, whose influence and reach grew steadily. Radio stations during the war expanded their number and more than doubled their income, joined millions of citizens in common experiences as jejune as the comedy of Fibber McGee and Jack Benny, as educational as the broadcasts of H. V. Kaltenborn and Edward R. Murrow. Of a population of 135 million, 54 million attended movies weekly, 70 million faithfully read cartoons each day; book sales increased. Thus the influence of national media steadily widened, its content mostly innocuous and escapist, its effect a growing force for a homogenized culture conscious of its common values and common nationality. The increased geographical mobility of the war period had a similar effect. Whereas some 15 million people had moved out of their county of residence during the 1930's, the war moved 27 million Americans to new surroundings, either through military travel or in search of jobs. The effect, whether through the exposure of rural people to urban and cosmopolitan life or through regional migration, was to break down parochialisms and immerse increasing millions in an urban, industrial milieu. The dispersal of war plants to the South and to the West Coast stimulated industrial development and reduced the economic uniqueness of both regions.

Possibly the most striking examples of the trend toward a more uniform national culture were the advances of women and blacks toward economic opportunities hitherto reserved to white males. More than 6 million women entered the work force during the war, raising the total number of women in the work force to more than 18 million. In late 1943, four-fifths of new factory workers were women, and the male proportion of the labor force had dropped to 70 percent. The shortage of labor led reluctant employers to use women not only as clerical workers but as machinists, riveters, truck drivers, meteorologists, and electrical engineers. By 1944, women constituted 12 percent of the work force in shipbuilding and 40 percent in aircraft plants, and their creditable performance in tasks formerly thought too dangerous or strenuous for females was not lost on them or on their employers. Many of these jobs did not survive the war, but old attitudes about the capacities of women were permanently altered, and two-thirds of the women employed during the war remained in the work force after 1945. A War Labor Board order that women receive "equal pay for equal work" was widely ignored, and women's wages continued to be 40 percent lower than those for men. But as firm as wage inequalities appeared to be, they rested on social attitudes, which had begun to shift. The physical and occupational mobility of the war period seem to have altered the horizons of women so much as to make the period the seedtime of the "liberation" movement of the 1960's and after.

For another group with separate and inferior status in America, the blacks, World War II was also the beginning of a historic change in mood, expectations, and self-conception. The signs of the change came early. When a pattern of job discrimination against blacks emerged from the early mobilization efforts, A. Philip Randolph of the Sleeping Car Porters' Union and Walter White of the NAACP pressed Roosevelt for federal guarantees of nondiscriminatory hiring. When the President stalled, a march on Washington was scheduled for July 4, 1941, with predictions of from 50,000 to 100,000 black

Every welder working on this section of a heavy bomber is a woman. This was the year 1943, when women began a major breakthrough into wartime industry. Most returned to domestic roles after the war, but the experience of wartime employment permanently altered American ideas about the capacities of females.

marchers. On June 25 Roosevelt gave in and issued Executive Order 8802, establishing a Fair Employment Practices Commission (FEPC) to investigate and arbitrate charges of racial bias in war production. The FEPC was not given legal authority to enforce its rulings, and Roosevelt, alarmed by the political implications of anti-black riots in Birmingham shipyards and rumors of high tension elsewhere, did not urge a reluctant Congress to give the agency stronger legal and financial underpinnings. The establishment of FEPC was an important precedent, but little more. The 1 million new jobs secured by blacks during the war would have come with or without the agency, and FEPC could force no real change in the American pattern of utilizing black labor in menial and unskilled jobs.

But the pressure exerted by Randolph's March-on-Washington organization was a portent of changed attitudes in the black commu-

In the 1930's Leroy "Satchel" Paige, like all black baseball players regardless of their skill, was forced to perform in the Negro leagues where there was little money and less publicity. Yet white players like Dizzy Dean who faced him in pre-season exhibition games judged him one of the greatest pitchers in baseball. After Jackie Robinson broke the color barrier in 1947, Paige was hired by the Cleveland Indians. The forty-year-old Paige, well past his prime, won six games while losing only one, helping the Indians to a pennant. He was elected to the Baseball Hall of Fame in 1971.

nity. One could see an important difference in blacks' conception of their obligations in World War I as contrasted with their feelings about World War II. The black press during World War I had reflected the desire to serve the country found in white media. During World War II, the NAACP's *Crisis* and black newspapers such as the *Chicago Defender* and the Pittsburgh *Courier*, though not opposing the war, made it clear that the war made sense to black people only if it encompassed an attack on inequality everywhere in the world, including at home. The national emergency had stimulated thought about the place of blacks in white society, and as defense jobs opened up the new militancy expressed itself not solely in the March-on-Washington movement but in a wartime increase in NAACP membership from 50,000 to 450,000 and in the organization of the Congress for Racial Equality in 1943. More than 1 million black males served in the armed services, some with conspicuous bravery. Yet many expressed a newly critical outlook toward their own country. One black soldier told Swedish sociologist Gunnar Myrdal: "Just carve on my tombstone, here lies a black man killed fighting a yellow man for the protection of a white man." Before the end of the war, a half-million blacks had moved out of the South to northern and western cities, where their mental horizons expanded much faster than their actual economic and social opportunities. Magazines such as *Negro Digest* and *Ebony*, founded in wartime, expressed new self-consciousness and heightened group pride.

The changes that had come to the black community should not be exaggerated. In the practical details of life, blacks still found no way but to acquiesce in their employment as menials and unskilled laborers, in segregated housing and public accommodations, in the slights and threats and paternalism that were a part of having a black skin in America. There was no real revolution for blacks in income or occupational mobility or educational opportunities during the war, and the spirit of revolt touched mostly the younger blacks. The biracial system nonetheless was fatally wounded by the decision to fight in World War II—a result no southern politician who voted for war ever imagined. The mental attitudes and horizons of blacks had decisively and irrevocably begun to shift, and even among whites there was a stirring of guilt and questioning of racial relations, expressed in the publication of books like Lillian Smith's *Strange Fruit* (1943) and in the reception of Gunnar Myrdal's *An American Dilemma* (1945). To some observers the war-stimulated escalation of black expectations was an unwelcome source of social conflict; others would describe it as the beginning of liberation. It was both. Yet its fundamental importance lies in its place in a broader pattern of collectivization that the war propelled, in which the great variations in outlook and life style and life opportunities among Americans were being smoothed and graded out by the inexorable advance of modernism.

The pressures toward a standardized national culture were the inevitable concomitants of global war and could not have been prevented by any policies adopted in Washington. Public policy, naturally enough, reflected in its own way this historical evolution of America toward a society whose parts were less different and independent, more and more meshed into a self-conscious whole. In the war years the government continued its work of the 1930's — reaching out to control and coordinate ever-growing areas of American economic and intellectual life. Indeed, under the peculiar circumstances of war, government went far beyond what society would normally have tolerated in the way of intervention, ultimately gaining control of prices, wages, rents, commanding labor and the entire production process, shaping opinion, subsidizing and subordinating to its purposes even university education and scientific research. After the war the ideological enemies of national coordination (called "conservatives") appeared strong enough to throw off not only the wartime controls but some of those of the 1930's. In 1945 and 1946 they were able to eliminate wartime price, wage, and rent controls, shrink the federal budget, end the federal influence on science and higher education, and terminate the federal involvement in racial relations. Despite these steps back from the high-water mark of 1945, the intervening role of government remained enlarged far beyond that of 1939. Too many powerful groups preferred the assistance of federal management to the uncertainties of an unregulated economy, and the public at large seemed accustomed to thinking of the society as requiring constant management by public officials. Prewar regulation of industries such as transportation, communications, oil and gas, coal, agriculture, shipping, home financing, and banking remained, along with regulation of labor relations and resource use. The responsibility for overall economic performance was codified in the Employment Act of 1946. Under the pressure of cold war, the government would soon reenter education, research, medicine, racial relations, even patronage of the arts. The struggles of the postwar years, despite the rhetoric of unreconciled individualists, would revolve not around the penetration of government's coordinating role into every area of the national life but around the distribution, among classes and groups, of the burdens and favors of federal management. Postwar American society was not what the New Dealers had in mind, for federal control was not comprehensive or entirely rational or altogether successful at attaining social justice. But even though the steps toward collectivization had satisfied neither rugged individualists nor social reformers, they seemed permanent, and the future held more of the same. For better or worse, the future of American society would be shaped decisively in the public sector.

The End of the Age of Roosevelt

On April 12, 1945, Franklin Roosevelt slumped over his desk in Warm Springs, Georgia, with a fatal cerebral hemorrhage. An immense outpouring of national grief accompanied his funeral train up the east coast to Washington, then to Hyde Park for burial. The millions of silent people who lined the tracks, weeping and casting flowers, served even more than Roosevelt's repeated electoral victories to remind contemporaries that they had lived under the most popular President of modern times. His days in power would be called "The Age of Roosevelt." He welcomed the power that label implies and would not have shunned any fair accounting of his service. Historians agree that he did not merit the hatred of conservatives. He was a decent, Christian man, instinctively democratic, reluctant to hurt. Today he would find a consensus among scholars on these essentials. But there is also a sizable library of thoughtful criticism, most of it arguing that the circumstances of his day both demanded and permitted bolder measures of internal reform than he would risk. His leadership, it is true, was not entirely satisfactory. He had led an attack on many problems, but few of them had been solved when he died. In the end, a public figure must be judged by his actions, not merely by his promises. But words also are a form of action, especially when uttered by men of power. Roosevelt's critics remember him as the author of bland assurances and superficial rhetoric, rarely penetrating to the core of America's difficulties. Others prefer to recall him on the occasions when he uttered truths that other public men feared to voice. On one of these moments, in 1935, he expressed the humanitarianism and displayed the unstudied candor that made him the most beloved man of his times, when he said to an audience of young people:

A man of my generation comes to the councils of the younger warriors in a very different spirit from that in which the older men addressed the youth of my time. Party or professional leaders who talked to us twenty-five or thirty years ago almost inevitably spoke in a mood of achievement and of exultation. They addressed us with the air of those who had won the secret of success for themselves and of permanence of achievement for their country. . . . While my elders were talking to me about the perfection of America, I did not know then of the lack of opportunity, the lack of education, the lack of many of the essential needs of civilization which existed among millions of our people who lived not alone . . . in the forgotten corners of . . . America but even under the very noses of those who had the advantages and the power of Government of those days. I say from my heart that no man of my generation has any business to address youth unless he comes to that task not in a spirit of exultation, but in a spirit of humility. . . . We may not have failed you in good intentions, but we have certainly not been adequate in results. Your task, therefore, is not only to maintain the best in your heritage, but to labor to lift from the shoulders of the American people some of the burdens that the mistakes of a past generation have placed there.

SUGGESTED READINGS

Surveys of the New Deal period are legion, but the indispensable ones are William E. Leuchtenburg, *Franklin D. Roosevelt and the New Deal: 1932–1940* (1963); Arthur M. Schlesinger, Jr., *The Crisis of The Old Order* (1957), *The Coming of the New Deal* (1959), and *The Politics of Upheaval* (1960). The conservative view is well represented by E. E. Robinson, *The Roosevelt Leadership: 1932–1945* (1955). Criticism from the left came from Benjamin Stolberg and Warren J. Vinton, *The Economic Consequences of the New Deal* (1935); Howard Zinn's, "Introduction" to *New Deal Thought* (1966); Barton J. Bernstein, "The New Deal: The Conservative Achievements of Liberal Reform," in Bernstein, ed., *Towards a New Past* (1968); and Paul Conkin, *The New Deal* (1967). On Roosevelt himself, see James M. Burns, *Roosevelt: The Lion and the Fox* (1956). Leading memoirs of the period include Raymond Moley's critical study, *After Seven Years* (1939); and Rexford G. Tugwell's memoir-history, *The Brains Trust* (1968). The best biographies of important contemporaries are J. Joseph Huthmacher, *Senator Robert F. Wagner and the Rise of Urban Liberalism* (1969); T. Harry Williams, *Huey Long* (1969); and Donald McCoy, *Landon of Kansas* (1966).

Many aspects of the New Deal have by now been given monographic treatment. On agricultural policy, the basic study is Edwin Nourse, Joseph Davis, and John D. Black, *Three Years of the Agricultural Adjustment Administration* (1937). Effects of New Deal policies (and the Depression) on the poorer farmers are illuminated in David E. Conrad, *The Forgotten Farmers* (1966). New Deal labor policies are appraised in Irving Bernstein's *Turbulent Years: A History of the American Worker, 1933–1941* (1970). On NRA, see Ellis Hawley's indispensable study, *The New Deal and the Problem of Monopoly* (1966). The passage of the Social Security Act is treated in Edwin E. Witte's memoir, *The Development of the Social Security Act* (1963). New Deal relief programs are given extended coverage in the National Resources Planning Board's *Security, Work and Relief Policies* (1942).

The New Deal experiment in the Tennessee Valley is studied in C. Herman Pritchett, *The Tennessee Valley Authority* (1943). The story of the Court Plan is told in William E. Leuchtenburg's "The Constitutional Revolution of 1937," in Victor Hoar, ed., *The Great Depression* (1969). New Deal tax policies are surveyed in Randolph Paul, *Taxation in the United States* (1954); and the extent of income redistribution that occurred over the 1930's and war years is estimated in Gabriel Kolko, *Wealth and Power in America* (1962). On the New Deal and the Negro, see Bernard Sternsher's useful anthology of essays, *The Negro in Depression and War* (1969); and Raymond Wolters, *Negroes and the Great Depression: The Problem of Economic Recovery* (1970).

Although no good study of the entire Congress in the 1930's has yet been made, much may be learned from James T. Patterson, *Congressional Conservatism and the New Deal* (1967). The left is the subject of Donald McCoy, *Angry Voices* (1958). For the conservative opposition, consult George Wolfskill and John Hudson, *All but the People* (1969). Samuel Lubell's *The Future of American Politics* (1952) remains an unsurpassed survey of the New Deal's political effects. For the New Deal impact on state and local politics, see James T. Patterson, *The New Deal and the States* (1969). Otis L. Graham, Jr., *An Encore for Reform* (1967), studies the political ideas and contributions of surviving progressives in the 1930's. The best social history of the 1930's remains Dixon Wecter, *The Age of the Great Depression, 1929–1941* (1948). A very provocative short intellectual history is Charles C. Alexander, *Nationalism in American Thought, 1930–1945* (1969).

The literature on the American economy in the 1930's is disappointingly inconclusive. The results of the Temporary National Economic Committee investigations (1937–1941) are summarized in David Lynch, *The Concentration of Economic Power* (1946). Fiscal policy is surveyed in E. Cary Brown, "Fiscal Policy in the Thirties: A Reappraisal," *American Economic Review,* 46 (December 1956). Robert Lekachman examines the impact of the ideas of John Maynard Keynes in *The Age of Keynes* (1966). Murray N. Rothbard, *America's Great Depression* (1963), and Herbert Stein, *The Fiscal Revolution in America, 1931–1962* (1969) are critical.

The "broker state" theory and its application in the 1930's is appreciatively described in John Chamberlain, *The American Stakes* (1940), and in John Kenneth Galbraith, *American Capitalism* (1952). Recent writers have been more critical: see Henry Kariel, *The Decline of American Pluralism* (1961); Grant McConnell, *Private Power and American Democracy* (1966); and Theodore Lowi, *The End of Liberalism* (1969).

The best general account of wartime mobilization is the Bureau of the Budget, *The United States at War* (1946). It may be supplemented by Bruce Catton's *War Lords of Washington* (1948); I. F. Stone's critical study, *Business as Usual* (1942); and Eliot Janeway, *The Struggle for Survival* (1951). The special problem of economic stabilization is the subject of Lester V. Chandler and Donald H. Wallace (eds.), *Economic Mobilization and Stabilization* (1951). Walter Wilcox, *The Farmer in the Second World War* (1947), and Joel Seidman, *American Labor from Defense to Reconversion* (1953), are useful monographs.

The government's record on civil liberties is examined in American Civil

Liberties Union, *Liberty on the Home Front* (1945); and its propaganda effort is examined in Sidney Weinberg, "What to Tell America: The Writers' Quarrel in the Office of War Information," *Journal of American History*, 55 (June 1968). Lawrence S. Wittner, *Rebels Against War: The American Peace Movement, 1941–1960* (1969), is sympathetic to conscientious objectors and pacifists. The removal of the Japanese-Americans is discussed in Jacobus ten Broek et al., *Prejudice, War and the Constitution* (1954), and with much illuminating detail drawn from interviews in Audrie Girdner and Anne Loftis, *The Great Betrayal* (1969). For the wartime history of black Americans, see Roi Ottley, *"New World A-Coming"* (1943), Richard M. Dalfiume, *Desegregation of the U.S. Armed Forces, 1939–1953* (1969); and Neil A. Wynn, "The Impact of the Second World War on the American Negro," *Journal of Contemporary History*, 6 (1971). On the major race riots, see Harvard Sitkoff, "The Detroit Race Riot of 1943," *Michigan History*, 53 (Fall 1969); and Fritz Redl, "Zoot Suits: An Interpretation," *Survey Midmonthly*, 79 (October 1943). Further illumination of the wartime experience of Mexican-Americans may be found in Carey McWilliams, *North from Mexico* (1949).

James M. Burns, *Roosevelt: Soldier of Freedom* (1970), is a brilliant portrait both of Roosevelt and of wartime America. Roosevelt's chief political opponent is the subject of Ellsworth Barnard, *Wendell Willkie* (1966). Also useful on national politics are Roland Young, *Congressional Politics in the Second World War* (1956); Donald R. McCoy, "Republican Opposition in Wartime, 1941–1945," *Mid-America*, 49 (July 1967); and Leon Friedman, "Election of 1944," in A. M. Schlesinger, Jr., ed., *History of American Presidential Elections* (1971). The social history of the war is engagingly told in Richard Lingeman, *Don't You Know There's a War On?* (1970); and Jack Goodman (ed.), *While You Were Gone* (1946). More analytical accounts of the social impact of war are Jesse D. Clarkson and Thomas C. Cochran, eds., *War as a Social Institution* (1941); Francis E. Merrill, *Social Problems on the Home Front* (1948); and William F. Ogburn, ed., *American Society in Wartime*. The important population movements of the period are analyzed in Henry Shryock, "Redistribution of Population, 1940 to 1950," *Journal of the American Statistical Association*, 46 (December 1951). On the problems of working women, see Women's Bureau of the Labor Department, *Women's Wartime Hours of Work* (1947).

Significant Statistics

	1900	1920	1932	1945
Population	76,094,000	106,466,000	124,949,000	**139,928,000**
Percentage urban	39.7	51.2	NA	**58.6**
Percentage rural	60.3	48.8	NA	**41.4**
Percentage non-white	12.0	10.0	10.0	**10.0**
Life expectancy				
White	47.6	54.9	63.2	**66.8**
Nonwhite	33.0	45.3	53.7	**57.7**
Gross national product (current dollars)				
Total (billions of dollars)	17.3	88.9	58.5	**213.6**
Per capita (dollars)	231	835	468	**1,526**
Defense spending (millions of dollars)[a]	332	4,329	1,688	**84,311**
As percentage of GNP	1.9	5.0	3.0	**40.0**
Military personnel on active duty	125,923	343,302	244,902	**12,123,455**
Labor union membership	791,000	5,034,000	3,226,000	**14,796,000**
Birth rate (per 1,000 live births)	32.3	27.7	19.5	**20.4**
Advertising expenditures (millions of dollars)	542	2,935	1,627	**2,874**
Motor vehicle registrations	8,000	239,161	24,391,000	**31,035,420**
Persons lynched				
White	9	8	2	**0**
Nonwhite	106	53	6	**1**
High school graduates (as percentage of all persons over 16 years old)	6.4	16.8	NA	**NA**

Sources: *Historical Statistics of the United States, Colonial Times to 1957; Statistical Abstract of the United States,* 1970; and *Digest of Educational Statistics,* 1970.
   [a] Includes veterans spending; excludes interest.

5

The Price of Isolation
American Diplomacy, 1921–1945

ROBERT H. FERRELL

For the people of the United States after 1918 the full meaning of the world war was impossible to discern, and it proved difficult to measure for many years thereafter. In our own time, with more than a half-century of retrospect, World War I has come to appear a catastrophic event separating the nineteenth century from the twentieth. The latter century, numerically speaking, commenced in 1900 or 1901 (there was some argument about that point), but the war marked the end of an era and the beginning of another. The world war separated an age of innocence from an age of confusion, an era of economic concerns from an era characterized in its largest outlines by political initiatives. In the nineteenth century there had been a continuing trust in rationality. The twentieth saw increasing cer-

tainty that men acted out of impulses above or below rationality. Individuals in the nineteenth century believed they controlled their destinies. In the twentieth people looked to the power of the state. Marx, a nineteenth-century theorist, envisioned the state as withering away. In the twentieth century no state withered away.

At the beginning of the postwar years Americans failed to grasp the importance of the world war, to sense its position in history. President Woodrow Wilson, a historian by profession rather than a politician, in some respects saw more clearly than his countrymen and in other ways did not. He believed that whatever the mistakes of Americans in 1914 in estimating the ramifications of the war, by the time they entered the conflict in 1917 they knew what they were about. His war message in April 1917 expressed the convictions about neutral rights, democracy, and the moral superiority of Americans that he took to the Paris Peace Conference. Neither he nor his fellow citizens understood the deeper nature of the war, the fact that it not merely broke up the empires of Germany, Austria-Hungary, Russia, and Turkey but fragmented the economy of Europe and undermined the foundations of European society. The war went on too long, its hatreds burned themselves into the minds of tens of millions of people. The solutions proposed at Paris in 1919 had to be only a beginning and not the end of an effort led by the world's greatest power, the United States, to ensure peace.

With a limited understanding Wilson had labored at the Paris Conference, and while he was in the French capital a surge of nationalism overwhelmed his countrymen, nationalism born of impatience with the peacemaking, of distrust of the delegation at Paris, of weariness with the war's rhetoric (not least that of the President), of desire to return to the old ways. The country moved back to the principles of the administrations of George Washington, Thomas Jefferson, and James Monroe. Former Secretary of State Philander C. Knox, one of the bitter-enders against the Treaty of Versailles, wrote George Harvey in 1920, "I cannot accept the illusion that we are living in a new world or in a new era. Such claims have been made following every world convulsion." Senator William E. Borah, who would become chairman of the Committee on Foreign Relations in 1924 upon the death of Henry Cabot Lodge, could comment in similar vein: "I believe that we can be of tremendous service to the cause of peace without surrendering any of our traditional policies or entangling ourselves in the political affairs of Europe."

To no avail did Europeans attempt to point out that Americans might sometime find Europeans helpful, that there might even be a community of interest between the New World and the Old. Georges Clemenceau in his *Grandeur and Misery of Victory,* published at the end of the 1920's, remarked:

You are still in the bloom and heyday of a young civilization. You make us act the part of those greybeards that are the laughing-stocks of the stage but who had their great days—without which you would never have been what you are. Do not despise Europe. Your judgments might prove double-edged. Do not treat us too badly. No one knows what fate history has in store for you. A weaker brother is often useful in time of need.

These were eloquent words, but they meant little to Americans of the time. The problems of Europe after 1918 seemed only the problems of Europe. Two million fresh American troops in the Allied lines in France in the autumn of 1918 had broken the German army, and Americans believed they thereby had paid their debt to Lafayette. Clemenceau had known an America that had not been so sure of itself; he had been a reporter during the Civil War and the first years of Reconstruction. By the end of the world war the veterans of 1861–1865 were old men like Clemenceau, no longer important in their country's reckonings.

It is possible that the Wilson administration could have halted the drift back to isolation if upon the President's return to the United States he had compromised with the opposition to the Treaty of Versailles. Still, a more sensible stand toward reservations to the Covenant of the League of Nations might not have made much difference. The wonder was that the country had supported European intervention as long as it did, given the rooted nature of the policy of isolation; it was almost inevitable that the country would go back to the old ways. Whatever the chance of a new policy, it disappeared with the virtual collapse of the administration in its last year and a half, while its leader lived out the remaining part of his term as an invalid in the White House. For months before his stroke in October 1919, Wilson's hold on the opinions of his countrymen had been slipping. After he was struck down, there was almost no national leadership. For the last months of his presidency, from July 1920 to March 1921, the American public, except for certain eastern journals, lost interest in Wilson. Although President of the United States, he was almost forgotten. The country thought of him only to dislike what he had stood for—participation in the world war. The vote for Senator Warren G. Harding in November 1920 was in fair part a vote against Wilson and what was known as Wilsonism. A few years later a group of Wilson's friends established the Woodrow Wilson

Former President Wilson on his sixty-fifth birthday, in moody retirement, stands in the doorway of his house on S Street, N.W., in Washington. From 1921 until his death early in
1924, he mulled over his triumphs in the presidency and his abysmal defeat over the issue of
the League of Nations. His stroke in 1919 had made him an invalid, and his
physical condition gradually deteriorated. He briefly considered running for the Senate in
1922, but decided against it because of the presence of "that old Lodge" in the Upper House.

Foundation, but contributions from men of wealth plus campaigns
in more than a hundred colleges yielded barely one-third of the
funds the foundation sought.

World War I admittedly had taught some lessons. American foreign relations after the war often showed the sensitivity of the Senate
to its prerogatives, its unwillingness again to come under presidential domination as it had during the war. In the years after the world

war it was evident that Presidents would have to be careful with the Senate. Not without reason did the three Republican Presidents of the 1920's take precautions, often consulting senatorial committees or putting Senators on diplomatic delegations.

Another lesson of the war appeared to be the importance of public opinion, newly aroused by the war's issues. American foreign affairs would not be the same again. The war produced an enormous interest in public opinion, and Walter Lippmann published a book on it in the early 1920's. Not merely in the United States but abroad the hope arose that the force of public opinion would prevent a second world war. The British statesman Lord Robert Cecil remarked that "by far the strongest weapon we have is the weapon of public opinion." And again, "What we rely upon is public opinion . . . and if we are wrong about it, then the whole thing is wrong." There was much talk about the moral force of public opinion. It was believed that if, say, the people of the United States acting together could offer their advice on world problems, there would be a peaceful solution through the sheer morality of the American position, which consisted of the united opinions of the people. To many individuals in the United States, and to some in Europe, it appeared as if the will of a nation's people, or of the world's people, could not be opposed by any government that hoped to last.

A third lesson of the war was that peace was preferable to fighting. There was a peace system, Americans believed, and a war system; the latter had characterized the politics of prewar Europe and, if the Europeans had half a chance, would afflict postwar Europe. Never was there such a popular desire for peace as appeared in the United States after the armistice of 1918. Protestant ministers laced their sermons with talk of peace, pointing out how in a single day on the western front the war system expended the equivalent of countless churches, universities, hospitals, orphanages. Something close to pacifism gripped many American minds after the world war, and its force lasted through the 1930's, down to the attack on Pearl Harbor. Even if leaders of the American government did not usually share this belief, they had to reckon with it.

The larger lessons of the war, however, were lost. In some respects they were lost even upon European governments and peoples. The German situation, for example, should have engaged the most careful attention of Americans and Europeans interested in world peace. The problem of world peace in the interwar years was German power, the existence of a hundred million hard-working, nationalistic Germans in the center of the Continent, their dislike for the

Versailles Treaty and the Treaty of St. Germain with Austria, their willingness to break those treaties if opportunity presented. The task of peace-keeping (to use a latter-day phrase) in Europe was to restrain the Germans. The French governments of the interwar period believed that force was the best means to hold the Germans down. British governments, having had less experience with German aggression, the British Isles being separated from the Continent by the Channel, trusted to German promises rather than to coercion. A subtle but highly important rivalry went on between France and Britain over policy toward Germany and in the resultant confusion between the former Allies the German government eventually was able to find numerous openings. In the 1920's, especially in the early part of the decade, the French government dominated the League of Nations through the votes of its European allies — Belgium, Poland, the Little Entente (Czechoslovakia, Rumania, Yugoslavia) — and the League tended to support a French policy of forcefulness. The Americans should have gotten into the League and upheld this point of view.

The subtleties of European politics in the interwar years were mysteries to American statesmen, who considered the Continent's concern for the balance of power to be one more indication of a mistaken reliance on force, a continuation of the age-old European concern for boundaries, for national advantage. All the prewar Presidents except Theodore Roosevelt had chosen to ignore European power factors and often Asian power factors, and the postwar Presidents and their advisers believed the balance of power to be part of the Old Diplomacy, outmoded before 1914 and bankrupt thereafter.

A secondary task of American foreign policy should have been to right and keep right the international economy. If politically the war produced more democracies and hence from American measurement had a good result, economically it was almost wholly destructive. It smashed the prewar organization of Central Europe, and the breakdown of peace occurred in that area during the 1930's. In his polemic of 1919, *The Economic Consequences of the Peace*, John Maynard Keynes was at least partly correct in his opinion that the most serious problems "were not political or territorial but financial and economic." The European nations and the government of the United States should have cooperated not merely politically but they should have taken steps to ensure the freer flow of trade in Europe and elsewhere in order to make viable the small states of Central Europe, and even large states such as Germany, during the 1920's. After the

Depression commenced in 1929, Arnold Toynbee soon was writing that the key to British greatness in the late nineteenth century was that the British world order had been economic, unlike the Roman world order of ancient times, which had been predominantly political. By 1931, when he wrote this judgment, he felt that preoccupation with politics during the 1920's had been a mistake.

Americans did not give economic problems the attention they deserved, and almost in total default the opportunity passed. If the American nation in 1919 and 1920 had realized that the world's peace, including the peace of the United States, still was in hazard and that the cost of postwar economic and political measures would be minuscule compared to the cost of participation in a second world war and in the necessary combinations for peace thereafter, the United States could have struck out boldly in support of a true world economy during the 1920's when it became the leading creditor nation. Unfortunately, foreign trade was no large part of the American economy. William E. Leuchtenburg has written, "It was the misfortune of the world and, ironically, a curse for the United States that the American economy was too well balanced to let the nation play the role of creditor." When necessary, the government patched the pattern of war debts and reparations created by the Treaty of Versailles and the other peace treaties, but beyond these relatively small operations neither public nor private imagination seemed able to go. Leaders of government and of business during the 1920's were not slow to extol the virtues of trade, but national legislation belied their words, the Fordney-McCumber tariff of 1922 and in particular the Hawley-Smoot tariff of 1930 raising schedules to the highest levels in American history.

When the Depression dramatically called attention to economic affairs, there was a flurry of concern, but before it could produce anything serious the problem of world peace turned almost entirely political, becoming a problem of stopping aggressors by political—which eventually meant military—means. World peace has been mostly a political problem ever since.

A Great Secretary of State

When the Wilson administration came to its inglorious end and the handsome Harding took over the government, Harding's appointee as secretary of state, Charles Evans Hughes, seemed a remarkably shrewd choice. The bearded, imposing New Yorker looked like a secretary of state, and there soon was considerable evidence that he was a good one. Hughes' four years in office during the presidencies of Harding and the latter's successor Calvin Coolidge appeared as a highly organized, careful era because of the secretary's methodical, logical manner. It was true that as a lawyer, former governor of his state, former justice of the Supreme Court, he had utterly no experience in foreign affairs and had not enjoyed much opportunity to read or think about them. In 1893 he served briefly as an instructor in international law at Cornell University. As a presidential candidate against Wilson in 1916, he had talked about some of the issues presented to the country by the world war. To his contemporaries after the war it appeared that he had the essential qualifications for

The unflappable Charles Evans Hughes perhaps carries an evening's reading under his arm. He was said to have possessed an almost photographic mind. Much as Theodore Roosevelt was accustomed to perusing pages almost with a glance, so Hughes could move through a thicket of words and—observers testified—repeat the contents almost verbatim.

Culver Pictures

his post in the Harding administration—namely, intelligence and integrity. Well before the convening of the Washington Naval Conference, where he made a considerable show of his qualities of leadership, Hughes became known as one of the nation's better holders of the secretaryship. After the Washington Conference his reputation rose to a remarkable height, and reporters and magazine writers began to announce him as one of the country's great secretaries.

People in the early 1920's must have sensed that Hughes' chief, Harding, a denizen of small-town Ohio, would need advice from a great secretary of state. The President after taking office apparently told a reporter: "I don't know anything about this European stuff. You and Jud [Judson Welliver, his personal secretary] get together and he can tell me later; he handles these matters for me." Harding acutely felt the need to refer foreign matters to the secretary of state. When reporters asked him about his foreign policy, his standard reply was, "You must see Mr. Hughes about that." According to Harding's recent biographer, Robert K. Murray, the President was not afraid of Hughes, as some people believed at the time, but sensed where he could get good advice and was always willing to take it.

The contemporary appraisal of Hughes' abilities, including the judgment of the President, may have been somewhat in error, for in the retrospect of a half-century Hughes appears to have been too much of a legalist, a constitutionalist. Justice Brandeis said Hughes had the most enlightened mind of the eighteenth century, and another contemporary said Hughes had a fatal habit of oversimplification. It may be that his unwillingness to depart from traditional ways derived from experience in politics, where he had discovered that few large arrangements were constructed out of beautiful theories or derived from novel approaches. "Foreign policies are not built upon abstractions," he once wrote. "They are the result of practical conceptions of national interest . . . standing out vividly in historical perspective." He favored conferences over treaties. To be sure, seventy-one treaties were ratified during his administration of the State Department, more than in any administration since the time of Theodore Roosevelt and Elihu Root. But he preferred voluntary conferences rather than "hard and fast engagements."

At the outset Hughes recognized that the American government could not maintain a state of war with the former enemy nations, that the failure of the Senate to consent to the treaties of peace negotiated at Paris had led to an absurd situation that could not continue.

One of his first tasks was to negotiate separate treaties with the former enemies, ending the state of war. Each of these instruments lifted verbatim from the pertinent Paris treaty all the sections dealing with rights due the United States.

The return to a judicial state of peace did not mean that the secretary was going to urge that the United States join the League of Nations, for Hughes took no major moves in regard to the world organization domiciled in Geneva. On no subject of diplomacy was his carefulness more evident. Although he had been a member of a group of thirty-one Republicans who, prior to the presidential election, had signed a public statement saying that they believed that Harding if elected would support the League, Hughes never had favored Article 10 of the Versailles Treaty, by which League members undertook to respect and to preserve against external aggression each other's territorial integrity and existing political independence. He knew also that the irreconcilables were too strong in the Senate. A story broke in *The New York Times* in July 1921 revealing that the Department of State had not been answering letters received from the League. After discovering that a subordinate had been pigeon-holing League communications, Hughes began to answer Geneva's inquiries. At the outset of his secretaryship he believed there was a need to end controversy. With the war officially ended and the League recognized at least as a mailing address, he refused for a while to go any further. "I accepted office to do the best that I could for the country," he explained, "and I have remained in office for the same reason." Under his leadership the State Department named a delegation to represent the United States at the League's Second Opium Conference in 1924. This initiative began a cautious policy of sending United States delegates to the League's nonpolitical conferences, and by the close of the decade Americans had taken part in more than forty League meetings, all presumably nonpolitical.

Hughes' principal work as secretary of state concerned the Washington Naval Conference, which assembled on the day after the entombment in Arlington of the Unknown Soldier, on November 12, 1921, and lasted into February of the following year. By the time the conference met, the issue of limiting armaments, sometimes loosely described as disarmament, had become compelling for the American government and for other major governments. The three naval powers of the years after World War I, the United States and Great Britain and Japan, were all finding themselves in financial trouble because of the cost of their navies. The presumption of the publics in the three nations was that with destruction of the German navy it no longer was necessary to maintain huge battle fleets. The Senate was openly refusing to pass appropriations for the Naval Act of 1916, which had looked forward to a navy as large as or larger than the British fleet. The British government, in financial straits because of its huge war debts, was embarrassed because it owed money to the United States and could not easily compete with the American navy unless at the same time it paid off its war debt. The Japanese government in 1921 was spending a third of the national budget on its navy, and a building program then being proposed would have taken much more.

Public opinion in Britain and the United States, and some popular feeling even in Japan, favored the limitation of armaments, if only because of what seemed the lesson of the world war. Publicists were writing that war had come in 1914 not necessarily because any one nation had wanted it but because all the nations were prepared for it. The wartime foreign secretary of Britain, Lord Grey, wrote in his memoirs, published in the middle of the 1920's: "The enormous growth of armaments in Europe, the sense of insecurity and fear caused by them—it was these that made war inevitable. This, it seems to me, is the truest reading of history, and the lesson that the present should be learning from the past in the interest of future peace, the warning to be handed on to those who come after us."

Secretary Hughes wanted to get these feelings, public and official, under his own management and supervision, and so after a few preliminaries he proposed the Washington Naval Conference. He decided to invite not merely the major naval powers but the two lesser naval powers, France and Italy. Because he thought it would be advantageous to discuss Far Eastern political arrangements, he also included China and three European nations with Far Eastern interests—the Netherlands (interest in the East Indies), Belgium (interest in Chinese railways and a concession at Tientsin), and Portugal (interest in Macao).

Of the three leading agreements made during the conference, naval limitation proved the most difficult and time-consuming, partly because there was so much technical discussion and partly because the American plan of limitation made it necessary to eliminate some vessels either under construction or virtually commissioned. The Japanese proved exceedingly unhappy about the ratio chosen for them, a ratio set out by an enterprising newspaperman as 5 : 5 : 3, quickly translated by the Japanese into Rolls Royce : Rolls Royce : Ford. The numbers stood roughly for tonnage of battleships—525,000 : 525,000 :

OUR GREATEST NAVAL VICTORY

Nothing succeeds like total destruction, which seems to be the message of this cartoon. There may be some symbolism in the airplane, for the idea was rising in the early 1920's that planes could sink ships.

Harding, *Brooklyn Eagle*

272,000. The Japanese government at the Washington Conference expected to obtain naval superiority in the Far Pacific, and for this purpose the 5 : 5 : 3 ratio was not quite enough; it was necessary for Japan to have 3.5. The reasoning was theoretical in the extreme. According to a principle known to the Japanese as "nonmenace and nonaggression," a 3.5 ratio would give the American fleet, possessing a ratio of 5, only a 43 percent margin of superiority. Naval experts thought that an invading force needed to be 50 percent stronger than a defending force, so with 3.5 opposed to 5, Japan was safe. With a ratio of 3, the Japanese were unsafe, for the Americans would have a 67 percent edge. All sorts of problems were present in this kind of reasoning. The American fleet probably would not have come together in one huge group for the purpose of attacking the Japanese. Vessels surely would have been left on the Atlantic coast, and in any case putting every American vessel into an attacking force was not feasible because the navy was not organized to do that. Moreover, as World War II showed, it was highly advantageous for Japan to possess the League-mandated islands—the Marianas and Carolines and Marshalls—to serve as unsinkable aircraft carriers. Another weakness in the ratio arguments at Washington was that the ratios applied only to battleships and carriers (there was a smaller tonnage for carriers, to prevent conversion of battleship hulls into carriers) and did not limit cruisers, destroyers, and submarines. The intensity of the contentions over battleship limitation is in retrospect difficult to understand, but it shows how fine points could affect negotiation long before the atomic age, when limitation of armaments became truly difficult because of the enormous technicalities.

Secretary Hughes sensed the danger of allowing the conference to take its own course in complicated arguments over disarmament. For this reason and also because public opinion was pressing him to get an agreement, he forced the whole issue in his opening speech to the conference on November 12. The secretary of state had begun his remarks, supposedly a perfunctory address of welcome, with a few calculated banalities. Even when he remarked about naval competition, just before advancing his proposals, that "there is only one adequate way out and that is to end it now," no one quite understood the moment for what it was. Hughes not merely presented the American plan for limitation but named the ships that the other leading naval powers should scrap. His speech was a sensation. Years later, in 1946, William Allen White considered his address "the most intensely dramatic moment I have ever witnessed." Carried forward by a tide of popular approval, the conference managed an arrangement that, however inadequate over a long span of years, lasted into the early 1930's. Hughes froze over the Pacific, people said. This was no mean achievement. Although his legalistic outlook prevented him from going beyond naval limitation in the direction of world peace, one must admire how he gathered together the loose strands of thought and opinion on one subject in the early 1920's and took a negotiation to an acceptable conclusion. The Japanese moved away from this arrangement in the early 1930's because the Depression had inspired them to separate Manchuria from China and other opportunities for aggression were beckoning. A new naval negotiation, backed by a threat of force and by other diplomatic incentives, might then have succeeded. Unfortunately such a negotiation was not tried.

In addition to the naval agreement (the Five-Power Treaty), the

Washington Conference arranged two other treaties of importance, both looking to peace in the Far East. The Four-Power Treaty engaged the United States, Britain, Japan, and France to respect peace in the Pacific, called for consultation in the event of a threat to peace, and served to replace the Anglo-Japanese Alliance of 1902, which had worried some American planners because it might be aimed at the United States and had worried the American public much more. The Nine-Power Treaty, which included as signatories all the nations present at Washington, affirmed the principles of the Open Door, the first such affirmation in treaty form, and thereby constituted a long-delayed victory for John Hay, who a generation before had begun to urge these principles upon the leading nations of the world.

The importance of the Washington Conference probably lay not so much in its treaty engagements as in its effect on future American diplomacy. In this sense it was a profoundly important meeting. It gave diplomatic approval to Japan's control over the Far Pacific. The Washington-approved size of the Japanese fleet meant that Japan was supreme in its own sphere. Other facts were militating toward that end, such as the agreement in the Five-Power Treaty that Britain and the United States would not further fortify Hong Kong, the Philippines, and Guam. The League of Nations, confirming a secret treaty of the war, had awarded Japan the mandated island groups. The Washington Conference confirmed the Japanese government in a position that the United States would change by force years later.

The Washington meetings gave great popularity to the conference method of resolving or at least camouflaging international problems. The 1920's and 1930's were to see many meetings. To be sure, as time passed the conferences became less formal and were made to appear only conversations, nor did they resemble the latter-day summit conferences. Yet the feeling that an assemblage of leading statesmen might solve difficulties was common to all the sessions, however nominally organized.

Another and more immediate result of the Washington Conference was to encourage the American people to conclude that, having organized naval armaments and Far Eastern affairs, they had done enough for world peace and that future negotiation was up to the nations meeting in the Salle de la Réformation at Geneva. Almost a smug attitude developed after 1922. The Republican Party did its best to take credit for Hughes' achievement, and in 1924 its platform called the Five-Power Treaty "the greatest peace document ever drawn." A Senator, employing the exaggeration permissible to a

**Immigration into the
United States, 1920–1945**

	All countries	Japan
1920	430,001	9,432
1925	294,314	723
1930	241,700	837
1935	34,956	88
1940	70,756	102
1945	38,119	1

Source: *Historical Statistics of the United
States, Colonial Times to 1957.*

member of America's senior legislative body, said that "the very
angels in heaven sang at the work of that conference." These passages of nonsense aside, the American people took too much pride
in what Hughes had done.

In addition to the conference of 1921–1922 the State Department
under Hughes concerned itself with three special problems—the
exclusion of Japanese immigration to the United States, policy toward Latin America, and the issue of the war debts and its connection with German reparations to the Allies.

Postwar nationalism had inspired the provisional immigration act
of 1921, which established quotas for immigration from all countries. During the next four years there was much agitation to make
the act permanent. Meanwhile, fourteen states passed laws, similar
to prewar statutes in California, forbidding aliens (read: Japanese)
to hold lands. The Wilson administration recalled the ambassador to
Japan, Roland Morris, who together with the Japanese ambassador
to the United States, Baron Kijuro Shidehara, had drawn up a formula, in model treaty form, that would have nullified the state laws
on land ownership. When it reached the Senate Committee on Foreign Relations, Hiram Johnson of California pigeonholed it. At the
Washington Conference, Hughes had refused to bring up this problem and its accompanying, indeed fundamental, issue of immigration. He evidently trusted to time to solve this problem, but though
time solves many problems it only exacerbated this one. When the
Senate began to consider a permanent immigration law, there was
talk of exclusion. According to one account, the critical development
came when a State Department official drafted a formal statement of

protest against exclusion, which Hughes persuaded the Japanese ambassador to sign and give to him for presentation to the Senate. The letter contained the ill-advised expression that exclusion would bring "grave consequences." Senator Lodge, in his last months of life, perhaps feeling that he needed some issue to revive his flagging senatorial reputation, seized upon this expression. The Senate obliged him by denying Japan a quota in the immigration act of 1924; thus no Japanese subject could enter the United States for the purpose of becoming a citizen. The consequences of this unfriendly action were to be dire, for within Japan exclusion became a major barrier to good relations between the two countries. For two decades the interests of the United States and Japan had been rapidly diverging, and the real parting of the ways would not occur until Japanese aggression in Manchuria and China during the 1930's; nevertheless, the exclusion act was surely a milestone along the way toward war.

Hughes' Latin American policy was mainly a holding action prior to the Good Neighbor Policy. The protectorates of the Roosevelt, Taft, and Wilson years continued during Hughes' time, though he showed a new sensitivity to the need for cooperation among all the American states rather than leadership by the United States. Hughes helped with a boundary dispute between Panama and Costa Rica in 1921, presided over a convention in Washington in the next year during which the five Central American states renounced (temporarily, it turned out) the right of intervention in one another's affairs, arranged ratification of a treaty giving Colombia $25 million for the loss of the Canal Zone and the province of Panama in 1903, avoided intervention in Cuba under the Platt Amendment in 1923 when the Havana government was on the verge of collapse, took the marines out of the Dominican Republic in 1924, and arranged a détente with Mexico over American subsoil oil rights. The centennial of the Monroe Doctrine occurred during his secretaryship, and it could have afforded an occasion for him to multilateralize the principles of Monroe, as many Latin American statesmen would have liked him to do. He refused, saying without a smile that every nation of the hemisphere could have its own Monroe Doctrine. At this time he began to speak of the word "interposition"—rather than intervention—the word he was to use at the Havana Conference in 1928, where before all the Latin American delegations and in an extempore speech he held the line against the suggestion that the United States renounce the right of intervention in their countries' affairs. Hughes, in fact, was so sensitive to any subtraction from the rights of the United States under the Monroe Doctrine that he prevented League of Nations observers from attending the 1923 Pan-American Conference and viewed the abortive Geneva Protocol of 1924—an innocent effort to strengthen the League—as a possible reincarnation of the Holy Alliance of Czar Alexander I, which had called forth the Monroe Doctrine.

War debts totaled about $10 billion, $7 billion of which had been advanced to the European Allies by the United States Treasury during the world war and the remaining billions lent to the Allies immediately after the war for reconstruction. Collection of these debts was one of Hughes' tasks. In this work he, like his countrymen, showed no large imagination. The European nations could not have paid the debts in specie, for doing so would have reduced the gold cover of their currencies, a cover already too thin for comfort. Nor could they earn money to meet their obligations by selling goods to the United States, because the high American tariff walls kept their products out.

The war debt problem quickly involved the United States government in the collection of reparations from Germany. The debtors in 1922, according to a statement by British Foreign Secretary Lord Balfour, resolved only to send to the United States the funds they could obtain through reparation payments from former enemies, particularly Germany. The United States government had forsworn reparations, except for a small amount necessary to maintain its troops in the Rhineland during the first months after the war, and carefully refrained in subsequent years from officially connecting reparations to the war debts. And with good reason, for why should America have loomed before the world as not merely the collector of debts from the Allies but of reparations from the Germans? Yet, practically speaking, the Americans had to take interest in reparations, if only to get the war debts paid. Two American bankers, Charles G. Dawes in 1924 and Owen D. Young in 1929, gave their names to nominally private but actually official negotiations with the German government. Hughes was in London during the talks on the Dawes Plan. (The American Bar Association, of which he was president, held joint meetings with the British bar that year.) Secretary of State Frank B. Kellogg was not in London in 1929 but took equal interest in the work of his unofficial envoy Young. The Dawes Plan and the Young Plan looked forward to an orderly payment of reparations, the former by systematizing reparations payments, the latter by scaling down German reparations from $33 billion set by

an Allied commission in 1921 to $9 billion plus interest. The Young
Plan anticipated payments over a period of fifty-nine years, to the
year 1988, at an interest rate of 5.5 percent.

A critic said Secretary Hughes was a whiskered Wilson, but by
the end of his service at the Department of State, with the inaugural
of Coolidge for a full presidential term on March 4, 1925, few individuals would have agreed. Hughes' legalism had not permitted him
to follow the Wilsonian ideas about world organization, and he had
been inhibited by his cautious desire for achievable results.

Keeping Cool with Coolidge

In the late 1920's the attention of the American people turned largely
to domestic concerns — Coolidge prosperity and the great bull market.
In Europe, too, after several years of desultory postwar economic
activity, the various business indicators began to show remarkable
rises. If there was any time in Europe when most of the problems
raised by World War I disappeared from view, it was the period from
1925 until 1929, from the Locarno Pact (a French, British, and Italian
guarantee against German aggression) until the market crash, when
the tides of prosperity seemed to have washed away the rancors of
war.

During this interval the tasks of American foreign policy became
less urgent than they had been under Secretary Hughes, and of
Hughes' successor, Frank B. Kellogg, there was little initial observation except that Coolidge had chosen an elderly man who would do
nothing drastic. Kellogg, a contemporary of Theodore Roosevelt, had
achieved a reputation as a trustbuster through his successful prosecution of the Standard Oil Corporation. In 1911 he had become president of the American Bar Association. After a Senate term during
which he had shown good judgment on the Versailles Treaty (he
was a mild reservationist and sought to rally his fellow Senators for
a League with reservations), he had lost his seat in the election of
1922, gone to London as ambassador in 1923, and returned to head
the Department of State when Hughes resigned.

The issue of the world court came to a vote during Kellogg's secretaryship, in 1926, although the question of whether the United States
should join the League-sponsored court had arisen at the end of the
Wilson administration. In 1920, Elihu Root had joined an international committee of lawyers to draw up rules for the court — its pow-

ers, functioning, membership. The jurists envisioned the new body as an appellate group of judges to which nations might bring claims only with the consent of the parties, unless the parties in advance adhered to the so-called optional clause of the court's constitution, which provided in specified cases for mandatory jurisdiction. The court was to take its decisions according to the rules of international law and presumably set precedents with a resultant strengthening of the law of nations. Countries not members of the League could join the court. President Harding and Secretary Hughes both had been firmly in favor of United States membership (though not of adherence to the optional clause), and the country seemed to have little to lose by joining. The world court's name, Permanent Court of International Justice, implied the introduction of order to international affairs, and the new body seemed a logical institution to carry on the work of the Hague peace conferences of 1899 and 1907. A court of arbitration established in 1900 at The Hague had been an ad hoc arrangement, consisting of a panel of jurists from which disputing nations might draw arbiters. Creation of a court sitting for regular sessions had much attraction. The two almost equal parts of international law, the laws of peace and the laws of war, needed codification. They also required more international recognition, for international law applies only to the nations that recognize it. A court sitting year after year could accumulate a body of precedent that might find the approval of most of the nations of the world instead of reposing uncertainly in the books of the writers of international law.

Despite administration support, the treaty establishing American membership in the world court went down to defeat. The Senate after the Wilson war years was in no mood to grant away any of its powers, and in particular it was unwilling to agree to any arrangement that looked even obliquely toward participation in the work of the League of Nations. The treaty came to a vote twice in the Senate, in 1926 and 1935, and each time the ghosts of the League fight of 1919–1920 appeared. The Senate in 1926 put a series of reservations on the treaty that proved so onerous that obtaining the consent of the forty-four member nations would have taken years. There were five reservations in 1926, the most important of which was the last: "nor shall it [the world court] without the consent of the United States, entertain any request for an advisory opinion touching any dispute or question in which the United States has or claims an interest." After Root at the age of eighty-four went to Geneva in 1929

MARRIED AGAIN

Fifteen nations were original signatories of the Kellogg-Briand Pact
in Paris in 1928. The incongruity of the
marriage is apparent.

Ireland, *The Columbus Dispatch*

and revised the treaty, President Hoover resubmitted it to the Senate,
where it languished until 1935. In that year a sudden campaign of
opposition led by William Randolph Hearst and the Detroit "radio
priest," Charles E. Coughlin, produced its final defeat by vote of
fifty-two in favor to thirty-six opposed, seven short of the required
two-thirds. In truth little was at issue, for the court proved an inconsequential organization. The importance of the question of the
League court was the time it subtracted from more important matters. It was unfortunate that so much public and official attention
went to the world court during the interwar years.

The most striking negotiation of the late 1920's was the effort to
outlaw war, which came to fruition in the Kellogg-Briand Pact of
1928. Sixty-four nations signed or agreed to adhere to this grand
treaty to outlaw and renounce war. Only three states of any importance—Argentina, Bolivia, and Uruguay—failed to go along
with it.

The history of this curious treaty reached back into the early part
of the 1920's, when many United States citizens were privately seeking a formula for American participation in world affairs. They fav-

ored peace but could not readily agree on a program, differing among themselves on the value of the League of Nations. Few found the Washington Naval Conference or the prospect of additional naval conferences (a conference of the three major naval powers over limitation of cruisers failed at Geneva in 1927) ambitious enough to ensure world peace. They took interest in United States membership in the world court but realized that the court could not possibly solve what they liked to describe as the war problem. The administration of President Coolidge gave no evidence of doing anything more for peace than sending observers to some of the nonpolitical commissions of the League of Nations in Geneva and taking part in enterprises such as the League-sponsored opium conferences. The peace movement found the peace policies of the American government far too insignificant and wanted a dramatic program.

The origin of the Kellogg-Briand Pact lay in the peace sentiment of the American public and in the design of French Foreign Minister Aristide Briand, who was obsessed by fear of the revival of German power and thought he saw a chance to line up the United States against the Germans. With other French statesmen Briand had made the League as much of an anti-German organization as he could. In addition the French in the 1920's maintained the largest army in Europe, and they had arranged a set of military alliances, which unfortunately were all with small powers (Belgium, Poland, Czechoslovakia, Rumania, Yugoslavia). Communist Russia had canceled the old prewar alliance with France, and the British government was wary of postwar ties to any nation — and to France in particular. The British, believing the Weimar Republic was a far more peaceful regime than the Second Empire of Bismarck and Kaiser William II, advised French statesmen to live peaceably with the new Germany. They thought it was possible to use moral force on the Germans, even as the Americans were seeking to exert it on Europe and the rest of the world. The French, not put off by moral force from any quarter, devoted their attention to keeping the Germans in their place. Out of this devotion came Briand's scheme — extraordinary in its apparent simplicity — to enlist the innocent American government in supporting the security of France in Europe.

At the request of Nicholas Murray Butler, president of Columbia University, and James T. Shotwell, also of Columbia (both were officers of the Carnegie Endowment for International Peace), Briand on April 6, 1927, the tenth anniversary of America's entrance into World War I, released a personal message to the American press asking for a treaty between France and the United States that would outlaw and renounce war forever between the two nations and bind them to settle all disputes by peaceful means. In careful language, the parlance of peace in the use of which he was a master, he was proposing nothing less than a negative military alliance—a promise by the American government not to go to war against France if on some future occasion the French went to war against Germany. This meant that in case of a German war the French could act as arbitrarily as they wished against American neutral rights, and the Americans could only acquiesce. In the meantime, the French government could boast, perhaps to the Germans, that it had concluded a treaty with the United States, and the Germans could start to worry about whether the treaty contained a secret military clause providing for more Franco-American cooperation than appeared on the surface.

Briand knew that Secretary of State Kellogg would divine his purposes, but he trusted that American public opinion, led by the peace organizations, would find his proposal so enticing that Kellogg would be unable to turn it down. If Kellogg was so rude as to ask Briand whether the French proposition was a negative military alliance, Briand would deny that it was.

The French foreign minister did not count on the ingenuity of the State Department. After waiting until December 1927, hoping that public enthusiasm for the French proposal would die down, the department suggested as an alternative that the French extend their treaty to all the nations of the world. The department knew that leaders of the peace movement understood neither the difference between a bilateral and multilateral treaty renouncing war nor that the best way to make so specific a treaty meaningless was to generalize it. Briand tried to forestall this novel American idea, but Kellogg pressed him and began to solicit the approval of other nations.

At last Kellogg relented, qualified his proposal enough to obtain Briand's approval, and carried it through to signature. Kellogg arranged the anti-war pledge so that it would not apply to wars fought in self-defense, a large exception to the pact's promises. At the request of the British government he excluded "certain regions of the world," unspecified but presumably Egypt and India, which were in danger of civil disturbances. The pact thereupon seemed safe for most nations; it contained loopholes for all occasions. With what grace he could muster, Briand gave in and signed the treaty with Kellogg and representatives of the leading nations at Paris on August 27, 1928. For this gesture toward peace, an "international kiss" one Senator called it, Secretary Kellogg received the Nobel Peace Prize.

In subsequent years the only discernible diplomatic result of the pact was the tendency of the signatories to engage in undeclared wars. At the Nuremberg and Tokyo war crimes trials after World War II, the victors of that conflict made a strange application of the pact to individuals rather than to nations, an eventuality that had never crossed the minds of Briand and Kellogg during their discussions.

Much of the modest diplomacy elsewhere during Kellogg's years as secretary of state centered in Latin America, especially on problems in the little republic of Nicaragua, where the withdrawal of the marines in 1925, after an occupation that had begun in 1912, led quickly to a revolution and the marines' reappearance. The Nicaraguan revolution of 1925–1928, in which the United States became deeply involved, was hardly a contest worthy of the attention of a great power, but it showed the blundering way in which Americans in the 1920's still were participating in the politics of the small Latin American countries. The revolution in this minuscule republic of 700,000 people was in essence an argument over the presidency, an office that apparently changed hands in 1926 for the sum of $30,000, paid to President Carlos Solórzano by the strong man of Nicaraguan politics, General Emiliano Chamorro. The latter became President of Nicaragua for a few months, until he had emptied the national treasury. Under Chamorro's successor, President Adolfo Díaz, a revolution broke out. Díaz invited United States marines to neutralize areas of the country containing American nationals or investments, and soon several thousand marines were in Nicaragua. So egregious an example of American imperialism outraged President Coolidge's critics, including Senator Borah, who called Coolidge's attention to the fact that President Díaz had once worked for an American concession in Nicaragua. Díaz's opponent, General José Moncada, began to win against the supposed American puppet Díaz, and Coolidge in 1927 sent down Henry L. Stimson to mediate the dispute. Stimson arranged the Peace of Tipitapa. In 1928 in a relatively free election supervised by the marines—the most honest election in the country's history—the Nicaraguans elected Moncada. The marines reorganized the Nicaraguan constabulary, and after the Americans departed in 1933 the leader of the constabulary became President and inaugurated the dictatorship that has continued in his family to the present.

In Mexico in the late 1920's, despite an executive agreement negotiated by Hughes, there was a continuing dispute over the extent of American oil holdings, for the Mexican government wished to conduct itself in accord with the constitution of 1917, an article of which declared that all subsoil mineral deposits belonged to the Mexican government and people. American oil companies, which had received grants of these deposits from preceding Mexican governments, considered that provision of the 1917 constitution confiscatory. The Department of State supported the oil companies with edgy statements about Mexican behavior, and Undersecretary of State Robert E. Olds in 1927 remarked publicly that the Mexican government was under the domination of Bolsheviks. In that same year, however, President Coolidge seems to have decided that peace in Latin America was more important than a few property rights. After sending Stimson to Nicaragua, he appointed the New York banker Dwight W. Morrow as ambassador to Mexico and gave him the task of making a settlement. Morrow negotiated a modus vivendi between the oil companies and the Mexican government; it lasted until 1938, when the Mexicans virtually confiscated $200 million worth of oil property.

The Depression's First Years

The Depression brought the comparatively quiet decade of the 1920's to an end. From that point onward the nations of the world, including the United States, were to advance from trouble to trouble until it would seem as if international affairs had never been without argument and dissension, revolution and counterrevolution, conflict and war. The Depression, which commenced with the stock market crash in New York in October 1929, marked the beginning of a long downturn in the American and world economies. It had several causes but surely was in part a result of dislocations caused by World War I. The four years of fighting in Europe had disarranged the livelihood of the Continent, and though national arrangements were patched together during the 1920's, it did not take much of a disturbance to threaten trouble. Many economic problems of course had been accumulating for decades, not simply for a few years. When in the late nineteenth century the United States and Germany began to challenge Great Britain's position as the workshop of the world and the industrial revolution was spreading to other nations, not merely to the countries of Europe, the world's economy required adjustments. The British did not respond easily to competition, refusing to modernize their industrial plant. They relied on their prestige and sales to the empire, lending money to customers who needed the money to buy. Nor did the Americans and Germans and other peoples affected by the industrial revolution ever stop to question whether the world's economy could cope with the planless development of national economies. World War I fostered a hothouse growth of industrial plant without much regard to what would happen to it after the war. When the war was over, the nations protected their "infant industries" by tariffs and quotas, rather than by allowing them to adjust to the world economy. All through the 1920's the national economies creaked along with the application of expedients, and in the United States and to only a lesser extent in Germany speculators took control of banks and great industries and proceeded to erect edifices of stocks and bonds that were even more artificial than the growths of the world war. The war had concentrated and focused the developing problems of preceding decades, and ten years after the Paris Peace Conference came the day of reckoning when the New York stock market tumbled.

The almost immediate result was a turning inward of the national psyche. Americans found themselves perplexed by the onset of the Depression, and as the great economic descent gained momentum, until it reached the bottom in late 1932 and early 1933, they felt that they had been betrayed by the irresponsible acts of European nations and by participation in the war, which had brought the contagion to American shores. President Herbert Hoover was sure that in 1929 the American economy was fundamentally sound and that troubles were a result in part of poor banking practices in New York but much more of misbehavior, public and private, in Europe. In the latter category he included the causes, costs, and consequences of the war of 1914–1918. The problem, then, was primarily European, not American, and it seemed certain that whatever the United States sought to do for Europe would either be superfluous or harmful until the citizens of the Old World could, by their own restorative efforts, put their house in order.

Given this outlook, it was impossible for American leaders to understand that their own country, the world's leading creditor nation, had to bear responsibility for at least some of Europe's troubles. The American people and their leaders could not comprehend the need to take measures to assist major trading nations

**Exports and Imports, 1920–1945
(in millions of dollars)**

	Exports	Imports	Excess of exports (+) or imports (−)
1920	8,664	5,784	+2,880
1925	5,272	4,419	+ 852
1930	4,013	3,500	+ 514
1935	2,304	4,143	−1,839
1940	4,030	7,433	−3,403
1945	10,097	4,280	+5,816

Source: *Historical Statistics of the United States, Colonial Times to 1957.*

such as Great Britain and Japan, and economic policy continued after 1929 to be narrowly national in outlook. The statistics of exports and imports were obvious: America had become a great creditor nation after World War I. It was utterly necessary for Americans to invest abroad to enable Europeans to pay off their debts; yet the figures for investment went up with almost agonizing slowness. Only with the onset of the cold war and the Marshall Plan did investment begin to move in the direction it should have taken years earlier. (By 1950, American investments abroad were up to $32.8 billion and five years later had reached $44.9 billion.) Meanwhile, all through the 1920's and 1930's tariff rates had been going ever higher. The Fordney-McCumber tariff of 1922 set an average ad valorem rate on dutiable imports of 25 percent. The Hawley-Smoot tariff of 1930, vociferously opposed by almost all the professional economists in the United States before Congress enacted its high schedules, established an average rate of 50 percent.

Although the Depression almost paralyzed American diplomacy, what with public and official attention elsewhere, at least one accomplishment in foreign policy can be credited to the economic distress: It stopped the charade of war debts and reparations—the desire of the American government to obtain principal and interest regardless of any discomfort caused the debtors in paying up, the refusal to admit that practically speaking the collection of debts was tied to collection of reparations. President Hoover in 1931 arranged a year's moratorium on the payment of both debts and of reparations, at last virtually admitting that one was connected with the other. He found his hand forced by American bankers who in the late 1920's had lent large sums to European banks, municipalities, and provincial government agencies. The funds the bankers lent privately more than equaled the annual reparations payments of the German government, so that indirectly the American investor was financing the reparations and thereby the war debts. The Depression ended this circular exercise—with a double loss, to the American investor and to the American taxpayer. In June 1932, the European debtors met at Lausanne and lowered reparations to a mere $714 million, contingent on a sacrifice of the debts by the United States. The Americans failed to respond, and when the Allies could get no more money from the Germans, they defaulted on the debts. In June 1933, Britain, Czechoslovakia, Italy, Rumania, Lithuania, and Latvia made token debt payments, their last. Only Finland continued to meet the obligations in full. President Franklin D. Roosevelt shunted the debt problem to Congress, which on April 13, 1934, passed the Johnson Act stipulating that there could be no public loans to any government defaulting on its war debt.

In the first years of the Depression, during the Hoover administration, the government of the United States undertook only two important diplomatic initiatives—in disarmament and in what Hoover's secretary of state, Henry L. Stimson, later described as the Far Eastern crisis. The disarmament initiative was an extension of the interest that had developed over the Washington Naval Conference. The London Naval Conference of 1930 attempted to limit the tonnage of vessels other than battleships and aircraft carriers—the fleet auxiliaries, namely, cruisers, destroyers, and submarines. A covert rivalry had gotten under way after the Washington Conference. The British, Japanese, and Americans all sought to build the largest cruisers permitted under the Washington Naval Treaty, which had defined a battleship as any vessel displacing more than 10,000 tons and armed with more than 8-inch guns. The Washington definition of a cruiser's maximum tonnage and gun caliber became an architectural ideal, and naval officers tried ingeniously to discover the best arrangements of armor and propulsion possible within the Washington limits. The London Naval Treaty of April 1930, drawn up after many pourparlers and strenuous negotiation, limited large cruisers roughly to the Washington 5:5:3 ratio, although the Japanese were allowed to build their cruisers more rapidly than the Americans and thereby obtained a head start in what, after the failure of the second London Naval Conference in 1935–1936, became a new competition in all categories. The treaty of 1930 gave the Japanese a ratio of 3.5 in small cruisers and destroyers and parity in submarines.

The depths of the Depression saw a series of meetings in Geneva, in 1932–1934, devoted to general problems of disarmament, land as well as naval. After almost interminable speeches and after proposals by the leading naval powers nothing came from the discussions. At one point President Hoover suggested a one-third cut in all arms. But he soon understood that that would do nothing for peace, for it would only push the major powers toward the low arms levels of Germany and Soviet Russia. The American government took almost no interest in land armaments; at this time both manpower and equipment in the United States army were at extraordinarily low levels. Americans believed that land disarmament was the task of the Europeans, especially the French, who, after proving dilatory throughout the 1920's in negotiating terms for repayment of their war debt, were continuing to maintain the largest army in Europe. The discussions at Geneva, at what was called the World Disarmament Conference, cast reflections of a critical sort on French armaments and put the armament desires of the Germans in an ever more favorable light. When the German government withdrew from the conference in 1934, that body adjourned *sine die,* never to assemble again.

Thus the idea of disarmament, like that of economic cooperation, unfortunately brought forth a doctrinaire—that is, unthinking—policy by the government of the United States. Having negotiated a limitation of heavy ships in 1921–1922, the Americans felt that a policy that befitted a conference held just after the world war could carry over at London to other categories of vessels. The Washington Conference had been accompanied by political agreements, behind which was an implicit threat by the Americans and British that the Japanese would get into trouble, perhaps war, if they did not sign the naval treaty. Such a situation was absent in 1930. It was similarly missing in regard to German land armaments during the meeting in Geneva. Moreover, all the disarmament discussions reflected more serious problems. The limitation of armaments could not ensure world peace.

The success of naval disarmament was mainly up to Japan. In the Hoover era the Japanese commenced the aggressions that heralded World War II. Japan's actions were in large part caused by the economic troubles after 1929. As a result of the Depression, the market for silk in the United States collapsed. The market for cotton goods in China weakened, and what remained was under constant threat of a nationalistic Chinese boycott; the Chinese in the 1920's

THE OPEN DOOR

The helplessness of the Kellogg-Briand Pact, and the old Hay pronouncements about the Open Door that had been written into the Nine-Power Treaty of Washington, appears in this contemporary cartoon. The unpleasant smile on the face of the soldier evidences the feeling of Americans during the 1930's that the Japanese were insincere and all looked obnoxiously alike.

Cesare, *Outlook*

and 1930's occasionally boycotted the trade of all nations that maintained extraterritorial privileges in China. Japanese merchants began to yearn for an area in the Far East where they could trade without fear of tariffs or boycotts. On September 18, 1931, the Japanese army, already concerned by what it considered the corruption of domestic politics, the inattention to Japan's "place in the sun" given by the civil governments of the 1920's, took the arrangement of trade into its own hands by attacking the Chinese in Manchuria. It was an easy task, for troops had been stationed along the right-of-way of the Japanese-owned South Manchuria Railway ever since the construction of that line in the years before World War I. The army had only to concoct an incident and move against the Chinese from prepared positions. There was hardly a battle and almost no bloodshed. Chinese resistance collapsed. After nearly two years the Japanese and

Chinese governments in May 1933 signed a truce, the effect of which was to place the three northeastern provinces of China, a most fertile and relatively unsettled area of the country, in Japanese hands. In 1932, the Japanese had established the former Manchu boy emperor of China as emperor of a new state named Manchukuo, previously Manchuria.

America's response to the events in the Far East proved entirely ineffective. At the outset the United States sought to work with the League of Nations, which in December 1931 established a committee of investigation, the Lytton Commission. Its report, published in October 1932, condemned the Japanese. Exasperated by the League's slowness, Secretary of State Stimson announced on January 7, 1932, that his government would not recognize any treaty concluded by the belligerents or situation de facto arranged by the Japanese that would endanger Chinese sovereignty. In February 1932, after a Japanese admiral at Shanghai opened a large-scale effort against the Chinese to take that great city, Stimson released a letter to Senator Borah, the chairman of the Foreign Relations Committee, reiterating American rights under the Nine-Power Treaty of Washington and the Kellogg-Briand Pact and threatening delicately to abrogate the agreement not to construct additional fortifications on Guam and the Philippines, which was part of the Five-Power Treaty of 1922. A noble statement of American purposes, the sort of legal pronouncement that diplomats of the United States for many years have found useful to summarize their positions, the letter to Borah marked the end of Stimson's active diplomacy.

By 1932, President Hoover's mind was almost constantly on the economy; there was little time for foreign policy. When Stimson went to the White House to ask the President about diplomatic problems, he would find Hoover upstairs in the Lincoln study, hard at work, late into the night, feeling "blue" from some novel downturn in business and finance. Such likewise was the concern of the country. It was an impossible time for anything more than admonitions in the Far East.

One must ask whether the failure of the Western democracies to halt Japanese aggression in Manchuria encouraged the subsequent ventures of Hitler and of the Italian dictator Benito Mussolini. Publicists in the 1930's and some historians later lamented that the road to Poland lay through Mukden. Aggression in the Far East resembled that in Europe because it too was caused by the dislocations of the Depression. The Japanese in the 1930's never hesitated to take advantage of the preoccupation of the Western powers with the disintegration of peace in Europe. But the metaphor does seem misplaced. If the road to Pearl Harbor lay through Mukden, that is as far as the metaphor will go. The moves of Hitler developed out of the failures of the European democracies and of the United States to support democracy on the Continent, together with the Nazi leader's own uncanny sense of timing and his ability to organize the German nation for his purposes. The Nazis never concerted their military actions with the Japanese, or vice versa. The two parts of the world existed almost as if a wall divided them.

No New Deal in Foreign Affairs

In the history of the interwar era, 1933 like 1929 has a meaning of its own and stands out from the years that surround it. It was the year that Franklin D. Roosevelt became President of the United States, but even more important was the fact that Hitler became Chancellor of Germany on January 30, 1933. Although his government was to last only twelve years, instead of the thousand he anticipated, it was perhaps the most important twelve-year regime in the history of the world, surely in the history of modern times. The advent of this premier adventurer of the modern age may be compared to the great catastrophes of earlier history—the fall of Rome in the fifth century A.D., the fall of Constantinople in 1453. The accession of Hitler to office was a somber, tragic event that in consequences ran beyond all the occurrences of its time. Years after the death of Hitler his legacy of expediency, of the state's purposes being higher than those of individuals, seems ineradicable from the conduct of international affairs, and the more dangerous because of those relations' being conducted in an age of dreadful weapons.

The appearance of a twentieth-century Attila was altogether unexpected in 1933—and unbelievable. Much of Hitler's early success in foreign policy is traceable to the incredulity with which civilized, mannered, intelligent leaders of the Western democracies faced up to this man who looked like and often talked as if he were a reasonable person but in whose disordered mind were the darkest thoughts and purposes. The ambassador of the United States to Weimar Germany in the late 1920's, a former president of Cornell University, Jacob G. Schurman, had seen not the slightest likelihood that the best-educated country of Europe would succumb to evil leadership.

German President Paul von Hindenburg and newly appointed Chancellor Adolf Hitler, pictured on May 1, 1933, pose an interesting juxtaposition of the old and the new: the hero of Germany's World War I battles against the Russians, and the man whose military adventuring would bring Russia perhaps permanently into the heart of Western Europe. When Hindenburg died in 1934, Hitler made no effort to obtain the post of president, but instead designated himself as the Führer, or leader, of his country.

"If you read in the newspapers that something radical is proposed in Germany," he had said in 1928, "you may be sure that it can never amount to anything." Hitler posed as a conservative and nicely hoodwinked the conservatives of Germany as at the outset he did those of other countries. The middle class in Germany tended to support him because he stood for law and order, which had been breaking down in the last years of the Weimar Republic mostly because of the deterioration of the German economy in the Depression. Some of the Socialists noted wistfully that the name of Hitler's party was the National Socialist Party and put their trust in words. The Communists considered his appearance only as a step in the inevitable breakdown of German capitalism: *Nach Hitler kommen wir* ("We will come after Hitler"). Hence, Hitler did not have to make a frontal assault on the citadel of power, as had Lenin in Russia. He captured the citadel from within, with the complicity of part of the garrison. Once in office he could use the machinery of government, which he had obtained intact, to revolutionize all sectors of German society and then to undertake the conquest of Europe and perhaps the world. The Reichstag placed absolute power in Hitler's hands on March 5, 1933, one day after Roosevelt became President of the United States.

In Roosevelt's first term both the new administration and Americans generally were overwhelmingly concerned with getting out of the Depression; the administration in this period did little of a concrete nature to contain Hitler. There was no New Deal in foreign affairs. The old policies of the 1920's continued—careful behavior toward the League of Nations (Roosevelt had said during the campaign in 1932 that the United States should not connect itself with the League), an enduring interest in disarmament, a belief that economic solutions of a large sort would avail nothing for the world economy. Unlike Hoover, Roosevelt did not see the Depression as a hurricane from abroad; he found its primary cause in the weaknesses of the American economy, especially in the inability of purchasing power to keep pace with production. But his principal concern was to raise domestic purchasing power. The foreign trade of the United States seemed too insignificant a part of the national economy, and if any international measures were likely to hurt recovery, the new President wanted nothing to do with them.

This point of view appeared clearly in Roosevelt's behavior toward the London Economic Conference, which assembled shortly after he took office. Secretary of State Cordell Hull, an old congressional Wilsonian who because of his following in the South was awarded the administration's first Cabinet post, was enamored of economic approaches to problems of world peace. He believed that something important might come out of the London Conference and that Roosevelt perhaps would allow him to offer tariff reciprocity to the foreign representatives there. The conference began to consider the stabilization of currencies and looked to pegging the dollar. The President sent over Assistant Secretary of State Raymond Moley, whose prior diplomatic experience had consisted largely of being a member of Roosevelt's brain trust. Moley gave the appearance of being about to negotiate stabilization. Then to the bewilderment of almost everyone the President sent the delegation, including its chief Hull, a message that promptly was released, refusing stabilization and describing it as "an old fetish of international bankers."

How could one justify such an act? There was of course some reason to refuse to tie the American economy to the world economy. Keynes thought the President right in avoiding tariff reciprocity and monetary stabilization. One could argue that Roosevelt faced enough troubles in attempting to obtain domestic recovery and did not need to take on more, such as the troubled economies of Europe. Still, he had misled his secretary of state, sending Hull to London to negotiate and giving him nothing to offer. Hull thought of threatening to resign but failed to do so. Hence within the first months of what eventually would be the longest tenure in the Department of State of any secretary, nearly twelve years (Hull resigned in November 1944), Hull placed himself in a position of weakness. It was commonly said of the Roosevelt era that the President was his own secretary of state.

A year later, in 1934, the President proved willing to negotiate reciprocal trade treaties, but they were small forward steps during a time that required large steps. The instruments gave the President the right to lower tariffs as much as 50 percent in exchange for some kind of concession by the other treaty signatory. They got rid of a few trade discriminations and won a little goodwill. The small benefits they obtained came at the cost of Secretary Hull's excessive concern with negotiation of these instruments. Hull was no favorite of his fellow Cabinet member Harold Ickes, and Ickes it was who once characterized Hull privately as an individual who went about "looking like an early Christian martyr." But it was Ickes who said that the treaties "might have led to something in ordinary times when peace was the principal preoccupation of the nations of the world, but as I remarked to the President on one occasion, with the world in a turmoil they were like hunting an elephant in the jungle with a fly swatter."

Unlike some of his predecessors in the White House, Roosevelt was not doctrinaire about international affairs, and he quickly decided that America's relations with the Soviet Union needed to be normal, which was to say that the United States should recognize officially the government of Bolshevik Russia. To do this required changing the policies of his four predecessors in the presidency; nonrecognition had been instituted by Wilson and followed by the Republican Presidents of the 1920's. Wilson had conceived a hearty distrust for the Soviets, who had signed a separate peace with Imperial Germany at Brest-Litovsk in March 1918 and thereby gave the Germans a chance to concentrate on the western front before the American Expeditionary Force could get fully into action, an advantage the German high command failed to exploit. Moreover, the Bolsheviks had shocked Americans by their slaughter of domestic opponents within Russia, including the last czar and his entire family, and by their hostility to religion. The Soviets had refused to acknowledge the validity of debts previous Russian regimes had incurred abroad, including sums lent by the United States government. The Wilson administration found alarming the Bolsheviks' willingness to support revolutions abroad, an attitude that had first became apparent during the Paris Peace Conference when for a while it looked as if Bolshevism would spread to Western Europe. For such reasons Wilson's last secretary of state, Bainbridge Colby, had announced a policy of nonrecognition of the Soviet regime, which looked so shaky in its first years that caution in its recognition was surely in order. *The New York Times* announced ninety-one times within two years that the overthrow of the proletarian dictatorship was about to occur. By 1933 it was not likely to, and Roosevelt decided to recognize the Soviet government.

The principal reason for the President's decision probably was the regime's longevity. Businessmen during the Depression found recognition attractive, for they hoped commerce between the two countries might increase. Actually it decreased (exports to the Soviet Union usually constituted between 1 and 2 percent of total United States exports). There was some talk in 1933 that recognition would help the American diplomatic position toward Japan, which had been impaired with the establishment of Manchukuo, by encouraging talk of a Russian-American entente to contain Japan. The principal United States negotiators, other than the President, believed, however, that Japan's role did not figure prominently in the decision to recognize.

Whatever the reasoning, the Roosevelt-Litvinoff accord of November 16, 1933, concluded by the President with Foreign Commissar Maxim Litvinoff, recorded Russian promises to (1) abstain from propaganda in the United States, (2) extend religious freedom to American citizens in the Soviet Union and negotiate an agreement to guarantee fair trial to Americans accused of crime in Russia, and (3) reopen the question of outstanding claims of both governments (the Soviets had been claiming indemnity for losses caused, they said, by American occupation troops in Siberia and at Murmansk in 1918–1920). The first United States ambassador to Moscow was the sympathetic William C. Bullitt, who did his best to improve relations, going to the length of equipping some Russian citizens with baseballs, bats, and gloves. As early as 1936, Bullitt's sympathies had turned to hostility, and Roosevelt replaced him with a more pro-Soviet ambassador, Joseph E. Davies.

The most successful foreign move in the first Roosevelt term came in the heartening improvement in relations toward Latin America. The new President built upon a foundation laid by his predecessor Hoover who, rather than Roosevelt, was the real author of the Good Neighbor Policy. Hoover's first move toward Latin America had taken place even before his inauguration, when he had made a good-will tour of ten nations south of the Rio Grande. His pronouncements en route had seemed to one Argentine observer to be wind blowing across the pampas, but they were in earnest, and Hoover on several occasions had used the phrase "good neighbor." His secretary of state, Stimson, in 1930 abandoned the Wilsonian policy of nonrecognition of revolutionary Latin American governments unless those regimes showed respect for democratic procedures. In the same year President Hoover permitted publication of a long memorandum drawn up in 1928 by Undersecretary of State J. Reuben Clark, which after an exhaustive exegesis of 236 pages showed that the Roosevelt Corollary of 1904 (asserting a United States right to intervene in Latin America) should not have been attached to the Monroe Doctrine. The subsequent Roosevelt administration refused to recognize the validity of the so-called Clark Memorandum, but publicists and Latin American officials quickly did so, and by virtue of such recognition it obtained its own force, the Department of State finding that it was difficult to disavow what had been released.

Hoover and Roosevelt both carried out what was nothing less than a policy of United States withdrawal from involvement in the internal politics and affairs of the Latin American countries. As Hoover had taken the marines out of Nicaragua in 1932, so Roosevelt abandoned the Platt Amendment for Cuba in a Cuban-American Treaty of 1934 and in the same year pulled the marines out of Haiti. The United States in 1940 gave up the protectorate over the Dominican Republic. And in two inter-American conferences, at Montevideo in 1933 and a special meeting at Buenos Aires in 1936, the United States forswore the right of intervention in Latin American affairs. According to the Convention on the Rights and Duties of States, adopted at Montevideo, "No state has the right to intervene in the internal or external affairs of another." Secretary Hull, present at Montevideo, added a reservation mentioning "the law of nations as generally recognized and accepted," a considerable hole in the pledge, in view of the fact that international law was full of holes. Seeking to close the gap, the Latin states arranged another conference at Buenos Aires and obtained the signature of the United States government on a Declaration of Principles of Inter-American Solidarity and Cooperation, in which the signatories "proclaim their absolute juridical sovereignty, their unqualified respect for their respective sovereignties and the existence of a common democracy throughout America." Sophisticated observers of international affairs understood that the pledge of 1936, which appeared to be absolute, was in the form of a declaration, not a treaty, and thus did not bind the signatories in any serious way. Yet it was not to be taken lightly by the United States. If after the pledges of 1933 and 1936 the Monroe Doctrine still seemed to exist somewhere in the lexicon of the principles of the American government, there was not much more talk about it, and even on so dire an occasion as the Cuban missile crisis of a generation later no responsible Washington official mentioned the Monroe Doctrine by name. Nonintervention, though not entirely subscribed to by the United States, was the going policy for most hemispheric occasions. Cooperation was to take the place of dominance, which during the administration of Theodore Roosevelt had been so obvious an American principle.

The local results of withdrawal proved disheartening. In almost every case where the United States had intervened in a prolonged way — notably in Nicaragua, Haiti, the Dominican Republic, and Cuba — oppressive dictatorships followed the American occupations. In Nicaragua it was the Somoza family, in Haiti the Duvaliers, in the Dominican Republic Trujillo, and in Cuba Machado, Batista, and Castro. Trujillo ardently admired the Good Neighbor Policy, and after he was assassinated the statue of Cordell Hull was one of the first to be pulled down. All this seems to argue either for less intervention or for more. Americans of the 1970's, with Vietnam in mind, would not have to think much about such a choice.

All the while, during the exit of United States marines from the Caribbean and Central America, the rearrangement of treaties, and the offering of hemispheric pledges, a remarkable peace sentiment was rising within the United States, and this time — unlike the 1920's — it was a feeling that was not going to attach itself to a useless Kellogg-Briand Pact. The peace movement of the 1930's shared with the Good Neighbor Policy a common principle — a diminished role for the United States in world affairs.

In the 1920's, partly in response to the failure of the United States to join the League, partly in support of the Washington Naval Conference and subsequent diplomatic efforts to limit naval and land armaments, small groups of Americans had formed themselves into peace organizations. The most conservative and largest were domiciled in New York—the Carnegie Endowment for International Peace (founded in 1910), the League of Nations Association, the Woodrow Wilson Foundation. Boston was the home of the World Peace Foundation (established in 1910). Other organizations, such as the National Council for the Prevention of War and the Women's International League for Peace and Freedom, were more radical, wishing to rid the world of war through the abolition (not limitation) of armaments and other such measures. All these groups united in hope that the United States could avoid a second world war; they bore in mind the world war of 1914–1918 with its often senseless loss of life; they mused over the failure of the United States to obtain any clear advantages from participation in that war. In some considerable measure because of the activity of the peace movement—although the climate of American opinion had not been created by this peace movement—there emerged the most solidly based public desire for isolation in the twentieth century.

The isolationist opinion of the country was everywhere in evidence during the first Roosevelt term, and it appeared even in eastern citadels such as the Ivy League colleges. In 1935 a practical joke among a group of upper-classmen in a Princeton eating club led to creation of the Veterans of Future Wars, and chapters soon appeared in three hundred colleges. The Veterans proposed to enjoy privileges while they, the future veterans, were able to—a $1000 bonus for each prospective fighter, due June 1, 1965, but to be paid in 1935 with retroactive 3 percent interest compounded semi-annually for thirty years back to June 1, 1935. In 1936, while the VFW chapters were still agitating not very seriously for their bonuses, a student strike was held on college campuses across the country, and the strike day, April 2, 1936, brought an estimated half-million to three-quarters of a million students out of classrooms to parade for peace. At Harvard a Committee for the Recognition of Classroom Generals distributed toy medals to unsympathetic professors. Students wearing gas masks picketed the classroom of one such professor.

The peace organizations mounted a serious campaign through Congress. The Nye Committee investigation of 1934–1936 was begun at the request and encouragement of the Women's International

League for Peace and Freedom, whose Washington lobbyist, Dorothy Detzer, persuaded Senator George W. Norris of Nebraska to sponsor hearings on munitions makers and American entrance into World War I. She and Senator Norris picked a relatively unknown Senator, Gerald P. Nye of North Dakota, to head the investigation.

The committee galvanized the public opinion of its day, which already had been moved toward agreement by an article in *Fortune* magazine in 1934 concerning the so-called merchants of death and by a best-selling book of that title by two journalists, Helmuth C. Engelbrecht and Frank C. Hanighen. Nye collected a small staff of assistants headed by an assistant professor of economics at Dartmouth College, Stephen Raushenbush (the son of the leader of the social gospel movement of another day, Walter Rauschenbusch, Stephen had taken the *c*'s out of his name). By investigating the files of munitions companies and by interrogating masters of international finance such as J. P. Morgan, Jr., and Thomas W. Lamont, the Nye Committee arrived at what should have been a foregone conclusion, namely, that American industry and finance had profited from the country's participation in World War I. The committee went a step farther by examining hitherto unopened State Department files and showing that the Wilson administration at the outset of the war in 1914 had refused to allow New York financiers to arrange the flotation of Allied bonds in the United States but under pressure from the bankers had given in. The presumption of the committee's investigation, though its report carefully refrained from judgment, was that from 1914 until 1917 the country had become financially too involved with the fate of the Allies and that in early 1917, with the credit of the British government stretched to the breaking point, it became necessary for the American government to enter the war to give the British access to the American Treasury—thus protecting the pocketbooks of its investing citizens.

The thesis that emerged from the Nye investigation made sense to a generation obsessed by economic concerns, and Americans who believed otherwise could hardly obtain a hearing. When some critics of Nye sought to argue that the submarine issue, not munitions, had forced American entrance into the war, the researches of Nye's staff in the Department of State records suggested that President Wilson deliberately provoked the submarine issue by insisting on the right of Americans to travel aboard belligerent ships. That Wilson in 1914–1917 had chosen a latitudinarian interpretation of neutral rights because he believed in the widest possible rights for

Americans, and that he could not easily have anticipated the involvement of the country's citizens in a series of submarine sinkings of merchant and passenger vessels because that sort of thing never had occurred before, did not seem plausible to individuals who believed that the President wanted to push the country into the war. That Wilson's public utterances gave no support for such an allegation, and that his papers, available to his biographer Ray Stannard Baker in the 1930's, offered no evidence of any scheming, seemed to isolationists proof of scheming. Wilson in 1914–1918 had talked about a balance of moral power, the opposition of right to might, the need for America to defend the right, but these concerns had come to count for little with a generation interested mainly in making a living. As for the possibility that because Americans and Britishers spoke the same language and had the same great cultural heritage they had joined in opposition to Imperial Germany, Americans preferred to think of themselves separated rather than joined by a common language.

People preferred to believe that war resulted from the machinations of evil conspirators, the merchants of death. According to a piece of doggerel published at the time:

> Munitions men, bowed down with care,
> And worries here and everywhere,
> Each nite must breathe this little prayer—
>
> Now I lay me down to snore,
> I hope tomorrow there'll be war—
> Before another day shall pass
> I hope we sell some mustard gas;
> Bless the Germans, bless the Japs,
> Bless the Russians, too, perhaps—
> Bless the French! let their suspicions
> Show the need for more munitions!
> Now I lay me down to snooze;
> Let the morrow bring bad news!

The American nation vowed that it would never be tricked into going to war again. Philip C. Jessup (the biographer of Elihu Root), who was to have an important diplomatic career in the 1940's and 1950's, was writing in the 1930's:

The United States will not now enter into any treaty, pact, covenant, agreement or understanding, which binds it in advance to use its military, air, or naval forces as a means of bringing pressure on a state which threatens to resort to war or actually begins hostilities. There is no realistic advantage from the American standpoint in discussing such an arrangement at this time. Further, it may be asserted that the United States is also unwilling to bind itself in advance to apply economic or financial sanctions.

President Roosevelt in a talk with the Prime Minister of Australia was saying in 1935 that not again would the country be drawn into a European war, regardless of circumstances. Early in the year Roosevelt met with the Nye Committee and, ignoring a memorandum in which Secretary Hull urged the President not to encourage the committee in any way, incautiously told the Senators that he had come around entirely to the ideas of Mr. Bryan about prohibiting American ships from transporting munitions and American citizens from traveling on belligerent vessels in time of war, and Roosevelt asked the committee to consider the neutrality issue with a view to introducing legislation in Congress.

The series of neutrality acts that passed Congress beginning in the mid-1930's accurately reflected the isolationist feeling of the country. A law of August 31, 1935, hurried through just before the Italian attack on Ethiopia, gave the President little leeway after the outbreak of a war: Upon proclaiming a state of war, he had to prohibit all arms shipments to belligerents and could forbid American citizens to travel on belligerent vessels except at their own risk. The President had gotten more than he had asked for; he had lost a considerable amount of the freedom of action that an effective chief executive needs, especially to deal with frequently changing situations in foreign affairs. He signed the legislation reluctantly and said it was calculated to "drag us into war instead of keeping us out." This same act placed a six-month limit on the arms embargo and was followed by a law of February 29, 1936, continuing the embargo and also forbidding loans to belligerents. Almost a year later, on January 6, 1937, a joint resolution embargoed shipments to the opposing forces in the Spanish Civil War; the acts of 1935 and 1936 had applied only to war between nations, not to civil conflicts. An act of May 1, 1937, brought together the provisions of the preceding legislation and added some new features. Travel on belligerent vessels was forbidden, rather than allowed at the risk of the traveler. The President was authorized to enumerate commodities other than munitions that belligerents might purchase in the United States and transport abroad in their own ships (this "cash-and-carry" provision was limited to two years and expired on May 1, 1939, exactly four months before World War II broke out). The act of 1937 had a single redeeming feature in its proviso that the President had to "find" a war before proclaiming it ("Whenever the President shall find that there exists a war . . ."). When an undeclared Sino-Japanese war broke out in July 1937, an effort by the Japanese to take over broad sections of China including the important coastal areas, the President chose not to "find" it and thus was able to allow, under the neutrality rules, American ships to transport munitions to the Chinese.

Beginning in 1937 the war in Asia and in the next year a crisis in Europe sounded the knell for world peace, and the policy of no New Deal in foreign affairs came to an end, although the President, who took alarm earlier than his countrymen, was unable to move the country to other policies until virtually the fall of France in June 1940. In the meantime the aggressions of the Japanese and especially those of Hitler in Europe went unchecked by American power. The containment of Hitler was left by American officials to the faltering hands of the leaders of Britain and France. America's delay in instituting a collaboration with the Western democracies almost gave success to the Germans.

Europe's Descent into War

If there had been any doubt about whose initiatives and whose will was controlling the destinies of the continent of Europe, that doubt began to evaporate in 1936, and by the summer and autumn of 1938 there could not be the slightest question of Hitler's power. Late in the 1930's events came with such rapidity that Americans, still absorbed by the Depression, could not understand why every few weeks newsboys were coming through the residential sections of cities, sometimes in the morning, sometimes in the afternoon, crying out their extras concerning some new move by the Chancellor of Germany, who after the death of President Paul von Hindenburg in 1934 had become known as the country's leader or Führer. Actually, the most important Nazi move, strategically speaking, had occurred in March 1936, when the German army occupied the area on the west bank of the Rhine River, which the Treaty of Versailles had declared permanently demilitarized. The reoccupation of the Rhineland, as it was called, allowed the Germans to fortify a defensible line against France and also split off France's eastern allies, the nations of the Little Entente — Czechoslovakia, Rumania,

Yugoslavia. Before 1936 the French army was able to threaten a march into the heart of Germany in the event German troops chose to invade, say, Czechoslovakia. After the reoccupation of the Rhineland, this tactic, essential to the maintenance of France's alliances in Eastern Europe, was no longer possible.

In the late 1930's the Germans were active everywhere in Europe. In 1936, the year of the Rhineland reoccupation, the Spanish Civil War broke out, and soon German forces, in the guise of volunteers, were involved on the side of the conservative General Francisco Franco. Not to be outdone, the nearby Italians also sent in troops for Franco. Despite Soviet Russian aid to the Loyalist government in Madrid, it gradually became evident that Franco would triumph. The fact that his victory required three years (1936 to 1939), the bombing of open cities by German planes, and the exhaustion of his countrymen showed the depth of native Spanish resistance to fascism, but with Germany on Franco's side it was not enough. The democratic countries, Britain and France, did little for the Madrid regime. In the United States the slow demise of the legitimate government of Spain became a cause of anguish among a small minority of Americans concerned about European and world affairs, and some of them joined the International Brigade and put their lives where their ideals were. The United States government showed a restrained sympathy for the Loyalists.

In March 1938, Hitler ordered the military occupation of Austria on the theory that the government in Vienna, which had sought a plebiscite to determine Austrian feeling for union, or *Anschluss*, was hostile to the purposes and future of the Third Reich. Even if the majority of Austrians perhaps did favor *Anschluss*, the dictator was taking no chances.

The Führer next eyed Czechoslovakia. The Munich crisis of September and October 1938 followed. The German leader, after meetings with Premier Mussolini of Italy, his ally since 1936, and with Premier Edouard Daladier of France and Prime Minister Neville Chamberlain of Britain, arranged to take the German-speaking area of Czechoslovakia, the Sudetenland. Having promised Chamberlain that this was his last territorial demand, leading the Prime Minister to tell joyful Britons that it was "peace for our time," the German leader in March 1939 went back on his promise by taking the rest of Czechoslovakia.

Soon Hitler was agitating the issue of Danzig, the German-speaking port city for the Polish Corridor, a strip of land through what

The leader of Great Britain, Neville Chamberlain, leaves the Hotel Dreesen at Godesberg after conversing with the German Führer, Adolf Hitler, during the Czech crisis of September 1938. Behind him, second from left, is Germany's foreign minister, Joachim von Ribbentrop, later executed at Nuremberg. Here, indeed, was a processional into war.

had been East Prussia that had been given to Poland by the Paris Peace Conference so that the Poles might have access to the Baltic. But the seizure of the already truncated Czechoslovakia in the spring of 1939 had sent alarm throughout Europe, and the British government, at last realizing that its position of "appeasement" at Munich had been a mistake, offered alliances to any state threatened by Hitler. The Polish government, which had been so shortsighted as to have participated in the dismemberment of Czechoslovakia in 1938 by seizing a strip of Czechoslovak land containing Polish-speaking localities, hastily accepted an alliance from London. Hitler carefully moved to protect his flank against Soviet Russia by the Nazi-Soviet Pact of August 26, 1939, and then challenged the British guarantee to the Poles, with some feeling that the British government and its ally France would not declare war and that even if the two democratic nations did it would not matter much because Poland meanwhile would be lost to the Anglo-French side.

The game was for very high stakes, nothing less than the complete mastery of Europe, and a historical question of considerable proportion is how long it took President Roosevelt to sense what was going on in Europe and what the American government ought to do about it. On this point there has been some scholarly debate. Arthur M. Schlesinger, Jr., one of the President's notable biographers, is certain that Roosevelt at an early point knew what he was doing and sought to lead the country toward involvement in the anti-Hitler coalition. Schlesinger has written, "There can be no serious doubt that Roosevelt had a basic and steady purpose, revealed first in the 'quarantine' speech in Chicago in 1937." Yet if one takes a close look at the quarantine speech of October 5, 1937, at what the President said at the time and in the weeks afterward, it seems doubtful that FDR had a basic and steady purpose, at least in 1937, already a year late for an effective policy to stop Hitler.

In the speech at Chicago the President said that aggressors should be quarantined like diseased individuals. On the next day the League of Nations called a conference of countries concerned with the aggression of Japan in China, a call that resulted in the Brussels Conference of the signatories of the Nine-Power Treaty of 1922. The quarantine speech and its sequel looked like parts of a policy, and commentators remarked that Roosevelt was hitching his country's wagon to the League. In the last line of the speech the President had asserted that America "actively engages in the search for peace." Public reaction was at the outset quite favorable, and a turning point in the policy of neutrality seemed to have been reached, a new era to have opened.

But the next day the President in an off-the-record press conference dashed the hopes of his supporters, revealing that he had nothing specific in mind and was perhaps just "throwing out" a suggestion to see the response. Part of the press conference interchange went in this way:

President: . . . the lead is in the last line, "America actively engages in the search for peace." I can't tell you what the methods will be. We are looking for some way to peace. . . .

Question: Foreign papers put it as an attitude without a program.

P: It is an attitude and it does not outline a program; but it says we are looking for a program.

Some of the papers raised alarm immediately, and Roosevelt continued to give little or no evidence of specifically what he had in mind. If he had anything in mind, it certainly was not in sight at the Brussels Conference in November 1937—as sorry an international conference as the United States government ever sent a delegation to. At that meeting the Americans were authorized to do nothing in concert with the other Nine-Power Treaty signatories against the aggression of Japan.

During the winter of 1937–1938 the country seemed as strongly isolationist as in the past Depression years and, despite a flurry of interest over the sinking of the United States navy gunboat *Panay* in the Yangtze River by Japanese planes, an act quickly disavowed by the government in Tokyo, showed little desire to stand up to the Japanese or to anyone else. In the House of Representatives that winter Louis Ludlow of Indiana managed to bring to a vote his proposed amendment to the Constitution, which would have required a national referendum before a declaration of war. Such a proposition would have made any Washington administration powerless in the face of a sudden attack, for before doing anything it would have to count the ballots for and against. Despite the strongest pressure by the President and his assistants, the amendment failed on January 10, 1938, by a vote too close for comfort, 209 votes against to 188 in favor. The vote exposed the administration's lack of support for an active foreign policy.

The President in 1937–1938 was also having trouble with domestic policy. The economic recession of 1937 exposed FDR to the serious charge that the New Deal had not availed against the Depression. Earlier in 1937, Roosevelt made his only major political miscalculation during his long presidency by seeking to liberalize the Supreme Court. As a consequence of his defeat on the Court bill, he intervened unsuccessfully in 1938 in Democratic primaries in some of the southern states to purge his party of conservative Senators.

Domestic trouble, coupled with the deeply isolationist sentiment evident in the *Panay* affair and the close vote over the Ludlow Amendment, must have seemed good reason to be careful in foreign affairs, and the historian can only lament that in 1938, when such a foreign policy was most inappropriate for the potentially strongest power in the world, the President did almost nothing. When Austria

Culver Pictures

The sinking in December 1937 of the U.S.S. *Panay*, a nearly harmless river gunboat, brought a quick apology from the civil government in Tokyo. The time was not right for challenging the United States.

ceased to exist as an independent nation, no strong initiatives came from Washington. The Munich crisis found the President writing Hitler of America's hope for peace. Upon hearing of Chamberlain's surrender, he sent the Prime Minister a two-word cable containing a well-understood British expression: "Good man."

In the spring and summer of 1939 as Europe moved visibly toward war, American policy was more adventurous than in 1938, but not to much avail. The President found himself in some embarrassment because of the Neutrality Act of May 1937. The cash-and-carry provision of that act had expired after its two-year limit, in May 1939. Roosevelt sought to get Congress to enact a new neutrality statute that would continue the cash-and-carry proviso and would also reflect the country's increasing sympathies with the British and French against the aggressions of Nazi Germany. Congress in the spring and summer of 1939 was leery of tinkering with the Neutrality Act of 1937, and leadership virtually was held by isolationists such as Senator Borah. When a meeting convened in the White House in July 1939, with Borah present as ranking minority member of the Foreign Relations Committee, Roosevelt canvassed the chances of a new neutrality act only to hear Borah say at a crucial juncture that there would be no European war and that he, Borah, had his own private sources for this information. The White House meeting broke up in an atmosphere close to consternation. Years later, long after events had proved the Idaho Senator completely wrong, Borah's papers in the Library of Congress revealed that the Senator had subscribed to a British newsletter published by a private Londoner who had had a hunch there would be no war. Borah had reported the hunch as fact. As late as the summer of 1939, American policy could hinge on such surmises.

Meanwhile the letter-writing had continued. The President in March 1939, after Hitler took Czechoslovakia, sent the dictator a letter containing a long list of European and Middle Eastern countries that he asked the German government not to attack. Hitler with a straight face went before a raucous session of the Reichstag and read the list, raising his voice until he began to shout, moving down the list faster and faster until he came to the countries of the Middle East. He produced a great burst of laughter as he almost shrieked out the name of Palestine.

The war came in Europe with the United States standing by as an observer. One State Department official wrote in his diary during the period after the Nazi-Soviet Pact: "These last two days have given me a feeling of sitting in a house where somebody is dying upstairs. There is relatively little to do and yet the suspense continues unabated." Twenty years of American foreign policy thus had failed. The initiatives of Secretaries of State Lansing, Colby, Hughes, Kellogg, Stimson, Hull, of Presidents Wilson, Harding, Coolidge, Hoover, Roosevelt, had in essence failed. Europe was entering a second world war, which in due time would draw in the United States. It was ironic in the extreme that on the morning of September 1, 1939, while German troops were pouring across the German-Polish border, officials of the League of Nations assembled in Geneva to dedicate a huge bronze sphere, emplaced on the terrace in front of the League's Peace Palace. Beneath it was a tablet with the inscription,

"To the Memory of Woodrow Wilson, President of the United States, Founder of the League of Nations."

The Undeclared War

It is a melancholy spectacle, the enactment of tragedy, to observe a great nation moving into a world war. The American people wanted no more part in the second world war than they had in the first, but in each case the time came when national interest and the interest of humanity forced the country's entrance. The tradition of the Republic's early years, abstention from "the ordinary vicissitudes . . . or the ordinary combinations and collisions" of the European powers could not hold when, as President Washington had predicted in 1796, "extraordinary emergencies" arose.

As had happened at the outbreak of World War I in 1914, so in September 1939 President Roosevelt duly announced the nation's neutrality in a proclamation, but from that point onward the events that forced American intervention in December 1941 proved quite different from those that had taken the nation to war in 1917. For one thing there was no argument between the Roosevelt administration and the European countries about neutral rights. The entrance of the United States into World War II was not to come because of any contentions with belligerents over the rules of neutrality. After the war began, the administration brought up a new proposed neutrality bill, which Congress enacted in November, allowing cash-and-carry exports of stipulated raw materials and finished products. The act permitted the President to define combat zones, into which American ships and citizens could not go. On November 4 he defined an area including the Baltic and the Atlantic from southern Norway to the northern coast of Spain. The German government would have no problem with American merchant vessels as in 1914–1917 or with United States citizens traveling on British liners.

The opening months of World War II saw little serious fighting, and it did not seem as if the United States would have to exert itself unduly to assist the Allies. German forces quickly defeated the Polish troops, and in exchange for neutrality during the Polish conquest the Soviet Union received half of Poland together with the Baltic countries — Latvia, Lithuania, and Estonia. On the western front there was a quick stabilization, what became known as the *Sitzkrieg*. The Western Allies, Britain and France, apparently secure behind the Maginot line and with superior naval power, had little idea of what was in store for them, no large sense of how dire their situation was. Their purchasing missions in the United States sought to save supplies of dollars and concentrated on building up production at home through buying American machine tools. Gradually the British began to sense that their limited home production would not suffice. In April 1940, only a month before the German invasion of the Low Countries, two months before the fall of France, they started actively to arrange for acquisition of finished war goods in the United States. French purchasers in America followed the British lead, and because France's military position was in fact far more exposed than Britain's, they were subsequently to feel even more remorse for the lost months of September to April.

American policy during the first months proved virtually irrelevant to the crisis of Europe and, as events were to prove, of the world. The government in Washington was fascinated by the possibility of German penetration of Latin America. It sent increased numbers of military representatives to the embassies there, hastily offered armaments on liberal terms, and took steps to obtain control of civil airlines in the Latin American countries, having discovered that one local airline owned by a German was flying planes within three hundred miles of the Panama Canal. The Americans also demonstrated their fear that the new European war might retrace the moves and countermoves toward neutral commerce that had involved the United States in the war of 1914–1918. Secretary of State Hull doughtily sought to arrange an Organization of Neutrals, the constitution of which he was composing early in 1940. At about the same time, the State Department, with an unerring sense of irrelevance, organized a special committee to study questions of peace terms and postwar reconstruction for Europe.

The war admittedly seemed to be widening a little, for at the end of November 1939 the Russians attacked Finland, having attempted futilely to get the Finns to cede territory without a fight. The Winter War lasted until March and created embarrassment for the American government as well as for the Finns. The embattled citizens of the faraway Baltic country sought to obtain military supplies in the United States, perhaps even a government loan, and there was a good deal of sympathy for Finland, attacked by a huge neighbor. As the only country to continue payment on their debt from World War I, Finland had a reservoir of goodwill. But the State Department avoided too ostentatious a friendship for the Finns, and the end of the fighting soon made any American aid valueless.

The American government embarked on two missions of observation, one semi-permanent and the other a quick tour. The President in November 1939 carefully designated the industrialist Myron C. Taylor as a personal representative to the Vatican, in hope of obtaining information and of indicating the moral support of American Catholics for the Church's faithful in fascist Italy and other fascist-dominated places. In February 1940, the President announced that Undersecretary of State Sumner Welles was going on a mission to the major European capitals — Rome, Berlin, Paris, London — to ascertain bases for peace. The undersecretary carried no special mandate and indeed could offer "no proposals or commitments in the name of the United States Government." He was to listen and learn. In Berlin he found much food for thought, provided by the German financier, Hjalmar Schacht, who had lost favor with Hitler a year before. Meeting Welles privately at the house of the American chargé d'affaires, he informed the American of a movement among German officers to remove Hitler and supplant the regime. He described the Führer as the "greatest liar of all time" and said Hitler was an abominable mixture, "a genius, amoral and criminal." To Welles such sentiments seemed extreme. The undersecretary refused to allow himself to become involved in an intrigue and after his return to the United States in March ignored subsequent communications from Schacht.

So the weeks and months passed, and from April to June 1940 the *Sitzkrieg* turned to *Blitzkrieg*. The German offensive had been long in preparation and struck with the full fury of planning and purpose. First came the occupation of Denmark and the conquest of Norway. Then, as in 1914 but with less resistance, German troops pushed through the Netherlands, Belgium, and Luxembourg. By sending the main body of troops through the supposedly impassible Ardennes forest, the Germans crossed the Maginot line, which hardly existed at that alleged barrier. Soon there was a race between the outflanked and retreating British Expeditionary Force and the German tank units to see who would reach the Channel first. By June 4, 1940, 338,226 troops, mostly British, had got across to England. The French government, after departing Paris, which it declared an open city, removed to the south of France. After some acrimony with the British, who it complained had pulled out rather than continue to fight, the French government signed an armistice with Hitler in the railroad car in the forest of Compiègne used by the Allies and Germans in November 1918.

The catastrophe of the British withdrawal from the Continent and of the fall of France, the brilliant victory of Hitler's *Panzer* or tank troops, the success of *Blitzkrieg,* at long last brought the American government to a full realization of what was going on in Europe. The Western democracies had been reduced to a single democracy. Hitler, like Napoleon nearly a century and a half earlier, controlled the Continent except for the Soviet Union. Russia in 1812–1814 had forced Napoleon's downfall; things in 1940 seemed immeasurably bad because the two dictatorships were allies. This time it appeared as if nothing could prevent the invasion and defeat of Britain. The Germans were collecting hundreds of ships and thousands of barges in the ports, large and small, on their side of the Channel, and fighter planes of the German air force began to engage the Royal Air Force by day as Nazi bombers fire-bombed British cities, especially London, by night. Leading American officials including the American ambassador in London, Joseph P. Kennedy, gave the British no chance of standing up to Hitler. In discussion with Canadian officials Roosevelt broached the possibility of the British fleet's withdrawing to the Dominions in the event of a successful invasion; according to this plan, fanciful though it now seems, the king was to reside in Bermuda.

The question in June 1940 became what Hitler could do against Britain and what the United States might do to support Britain. In the next months the Roosevelt administration extended help of a minor sort that in itself was not too important but held promise of more. This was enough encouragement to keep up British morale. The American army was not much of a military organization as late as the summer of 1940, and it seemed necessary to keep at home the stocks of munitions and equipment that existed. The President nevertheless had munitions shipped immediately to the British Isles, though not without objections from Secretary of War Harry Woodring, who would not assume responsibility and resigned. Assistant Secretary Louis Johnson, as acting secretary of war, approved the necessary orders and said later that the only authority he had was a "chit" from the President promising a pardon if he, Johnson, should go to jail for the action. Over $43 million worth of ammunition and small arms went across the Atlantic in June 1940.

The problem of the British navy, whether it might surrender to Hitler rather than be sent to the New World, obsessed Roosevelt in the summer of 1940. At last he hit upon a temporary solution — reinforcing the Royal Navy with ships of the United States fleet, a plan so audacious that he had some doubts he could carry it off. The new

St. Paul's Cathedral is surrounded by smoke and flames during the London blitz in 1940. When
the German bombs leveled buildings surrounding the cathedral
an unforeseen result was to display the great church (which the bombs only
slightly damaged) in all its symmetry.

British Prime Minister, Winston Churchill, was imploring him for a
loan of fifty World War I destroyers, old "four-stackers" that had
been reposing at anchor for years and could assist the British navy
in convoy and patrol activities. But the President could not lease
them to the British, for that would have been a grossly unneutral
procedure contrary to international law. And according to the Walsh
Act of June 1940, military equipment could be made available for
sale only if the navy certified it to be without value for defense, and
naval officials had recently testified to the value of the destroyers because Congress had wanted to scrap them. If Roosevelt went to Congress for special enabling legislation, the isolationists in that body
probably would defeat it. What to do? The British ambassador in

Washington, Philip Kerr, had been trying to trade British territorial possessions in the New World, in particular some of the Atlantic and Caribbean islands, for American military equipment. Roosevelt had refused to take the islands. "See here, Philip," he said at one juncture, "you may as well get this straight once and for all: I'm not purchasing any headaches for the United States. We don't want your colonies." Then the idea of acquiring leases to bases in British possessions came to mind, and from this inspiration emerged the destroyers-bases deal announced on September 2. It provided an exchange of fifty destroyers for ninety-nine-year leases on naval and air bases in Newfoundland, Bermuda, the Bahamas, Jamaica, St. Lucia, Trinidad, Antigua, and British Guiana. The President made this swap as an executive agreement and carefully informed Congress on the next day, September 3, 1940, that it was the most important territorial arrangement concluded by a President since the Louisiana Purchase. He had, of course, been uneasy about going to Congress for consent to such an agreement and had said some days before he arranged it that "Congress is going to raise hell about this." Still, something had to be done, and his attorney general, Robert H. Jackson, told him that presidential action was possible under a statute of 1917. FDR acted, for he believed that "even another day's delay may mean the end of civilization . . . if Britain is to survive, we must act."

Years later a historian was to publish a volume about the agreement of September 1940 under the title *Fifty Ships That Saved the World,* but in truth the importance of the old four-stackers did not prove large, and many of them were in such poor condition that they could barely get to sea. Nor were the New World bases essential to American security. The exchange was a symbol that at long last the two English-speaking countries had a common cause. Churchill told the House of Commons:

Undoubtedly this process means that these two great organizations of the English-speaking democracies, the British Empire and the United States, will have to be somewhat mixed up together in some of their affairs for mutual and general advantage. For my own part, looking out upon the future, I do not view the process with any misgivings. I could not stop it if I wished; no one can stop it. Like the Mississippi, it just keeps rolling along. Let it roll. Let it roll on—full flood, inexorable, irresistible, benignant, to broader lands and better days.

Fortunately for Britain and the United States, the German air attack on the British Isles, designed to neutralize the Royal Air Force as a prelude to invasion, failed during the weeks before and after the destroyers-bases deal. The Battle of Britain began on August 13 and ended on October 12, when Hitler postponed Operation Sea Lion, the invasion of England.

On September 16, 1940, the United States adopted the first peace-time compulsory military-training program in the nation's history. The enabling legislation was for one year. The leaders of the United States army had opposed a draft; the army's chief of staff, General George C. Marshall, believed it would force him to break up seasoned units to train draftees. Roosevelt hesitated to back a peacetime draft during an election year. A group of east coast private citizens who twenty-five years before had trained for World War I at a camp in Plattsburg, New York, took matters into their own hands, managed to get a bill introduced in both houses of Congress, and discovered that as the summer wore on, with Britain in peril, support for it mounted. Roosevelt and Marshall accepted it, and the first men were drafted in late October.

According to the Constitution of the United States, a presidential election was to be held in November 1940, and the most serious military situation in Europe in modern history, the largest threat to the country's security since 1776, found politics moving along as usual. The campaign of 1940 of course reflected the agonizing situation in Europe. The cliché that politics should stop at the water's edge applied to using foreign affairs for domestic purposes, not to the discussion of foreign matters in campaigns. But in retrospect it does seem extraordinary that while the power balance in Europe was drastically changing, while the threat to American neutrality was becoming ever more urgent, the political parties were putting up candidates and fighting each other for the presidency and for seats in Congress and for state and local offices.

Typically, Americans sought to organize committees to deal with foreign policy on a nonpartisan basis, and the two notable groups of 1940 were the America First Committee and the Committee to Defend America by Aiding the Allies. The former, largely Midwest-based, the creation of a Yale law student, R. Douglas Stuart, Jr., whose father was a vice-president of the Quaker Oats Company, enlisted figures such as General Robert Wood of Sears, Roebuck, and Jay Hormel, the meat packer. By the time of the attack on Pearl Harbor, America First boasted approximately 450 chapters and subchapters. Its membership was impossible to calculate, though estimates ran from 800,000 to 850,000 (presumably such figures repre-

The speakers at an America First meeting—John L. Lewis of the United Mine Workers, Senator Burton K. Wheeler, and Dr. Francis E. Townsend, who was championing an old-age pension plan. These men, and their followers, much preferred what the historian Charles A. Beard described as "the open door at home" rather than a national policy of intervention abroad.

sented people who had shown interest). Nearly two-thirds of the membership apparently was located within a three-hundred-mile radius of Chicago. A notable non-Chicagoan was Charles A. Lindbergh, the hero of 1927, who, after a conducted tour of the German air force, came to believe that the Germans were bound to dominate the Continent, with or without American intervention, and that their hegemony should be allowed even if they defeated Great Britain. The Committee to Defend America by Aiding the Allies, chaired by the aging Kansas journalist William Allen White, by November 1940 had organized 750 chapters throughout the country, with about ten thousand active members. Its strength lay along the eastern seaboard, especially in New York City. Its membership comprised in part "the old League of Nations crowd," people who had supported the League in the 1920's and 1930's, such as Clark Eichelberger, director of the League of Nations Association, and Nicholas Murray Butler, president of Columbia University. Not an interventionist group but a gathering of individuals who wished to do precisely what the committee's name promised, White's committee found itself constantly embarrassed by members who wanted to go farther (like the Century Group, which met at the New York club of that name and urged an immediate declaration of war). The Roosevelt administration in 1940–1941 sought to use White's committee for trial balloons and general support. As the months passed, the committee moved closer to the goal of the Century Group.

Roosevelt himself, easily sensing the country's hesitation in 1940 to enter the European war, seems to have tried to arrange a non-partisan military establishment in advance of the November election. He offered the secretaryship of war to the Republican presidential nominee of 1936, Alf Landon, and the secretaryship of the navy to Frank Knox, Landon's running mate. Knox accepted, but Landon, seeing a plot, refused; FDR then chose Stimson, Hoover's secretary of state. This was a shrewd political move, and the choices bolstered his Cabinet.

But whatever the purpose of this preliminary activity, the campaign proved difficult. The President faced the most serious Republican challenger of his four campaigns for the presidency. Wendell Willkie, the Indiana-born utilities lawyer, the barefoot boy from Wall Street as Harold Ickes described him, had a popular appeal not possessed by Hoover, Landon, or FDR's opponent in 1944, Thomas E. Dewey. The result was that Roosevelt ran hard in 1940 and in the last days of the campaign made a promise about foreign policy that he should not have given. At Boston on October 30, after Willkie had said, "If you elect me president I will never send an American boy to fight in any European war," the President himself remarked: "I have said this before, but I shall say it again and again and again: Your boys are not going to be sent into any foreign wars." At Buffalo on November 2 he said, "Your President says this country is not going to war." Willkie later testified before Congress that some of his remarks in 1940 had just been campaign oratory. Roosevelt explained to advisers after the Boston speech that he had spoken not of wars but of foreign wars and that a war for the defense of the United States was no foreign war—a distinction without a difference, perhaps. In any event the campaign had inspired promises by both contestants and, more seriously, on the part of Roosevelt who was President and knew better, an indication of how strong the forces of isolation were.

With assurance of four more years of authority, the administration showed a new confidence, and in a fireside chat on December 29, 1940, the President declared that the nation would become the "great arsenal of democracy." In his state of the union address of January 6, 1941, he championed four freedoms — freedom of speech and expression, freedom of worship, freedom from want, freedom from fear. And in this same speech the President proposed what was to be the single most important move by the government of the United States in the entire period of neutrality from 1939 until December 1941 — "lend-lease."

The time had arrived for a large American policy in support of Britain and perhaps other anti-Hitler nations, and lend-lease was to be that policy. Roosevelt had not simply "hit on" the formula for lend-lease. As Warren F. Kimball has written, it was "the culmination of months of thought and the heavy pressure of events. . . . Lend-Lease was developed rather than invented." On November 23, 1940, Ambassador Kerr had returned from London and provided the catalyst that forced the Roosevelt administration to face up publicly to the question of the British dollar shortage. As he left his plane at La Guardia Airport in New York, he held an impromptu press conference and casually and without excess of words stated, "Well boys, Britain's broke; it's your money we want." The administration had known that some sort of request was coming and had been oscillating in indecision, fearing the need to go to Congress for a repeal of the Johnson Act of 1934, which prohibited a loan because Britain had been among the nations defaulting on their war debts, but fearing too what might happen to the world if the former mother country, bankrupt, closed its books and gave up. Roosevelt and some of his advisers maintained that the British had more money than they professed, that in 1917 when Britain had claimed a financial shortage there was no such crisis. As Kimball has written, the President believed in the myth of British opulence and thought that for some time to come Britain could continue to pay, somehow. At last Roosevelt in January 1941 proposed to Congress a bill, numbered H.R. 1776 in the House of Representatives, according to which the President could "lease, lend, or otherwise dispose of" to any country whose defense was vital to the United States, arms and other equipment and suplies to an extent of an initial appropriation of $7 billion. Fiscally the

Lend-Lease Act, passed on March 11, 1941, made history, for it was the largest single appropriation to pass Congress until the inflationary era after World War II.

Lend-lease did not get through Congress without a great deal of debate, which showed that isolationism was alive if not well. The debate was marked by bitterness, for the act's foes realized that once such an enormous appropriation passed there would be no turning back and the country would have to enter the war. Another reason for the intense opposition to lend-lease was a concern that the President, so recently elected to an unprecedented third term, might make himself a dictator. The vote when it came in March was sufficient for the President's purposes—62 for to 33 against in the Senate, 317 for to 71 against in the House. Senator Arthur H. Vandenberg wrote in his diary after the Senate vote, with the flamboyance that was his senatorial habit but also marked his transparent sincerity,

If America "cracks up" you can put your finger on this precise moment as the time when the crime was committed. . . . I doubt if *all* those who supported it realized its implications. I hope I am wholly wrong when I say I fear they will live to regret their votes beyond anything else they ever did. I had the feeling, as the result of the ballot was announced, that I was witnessing the suicide of the Republic.

Under the Lend-Lease Act and its subsequent appropriations approximately $54 billion was extended to Britain and the other Allies. About $4 billion was returned in what was called "reverse lend-lease," payments in the form of goods and food to American forces abroad, mainly in Britain. The total of American largesse thus exceeded the war and postwar loans of 1917–1919 by four times. The Soviet Union might have collapsed had it not been for lend-lease, extended a few days after the German attack on June 22, 1941. Shipments to the Soviet Union up to September 1945 amounted to $11.047 billion, about one-fifth of all material exported under the program. In addition to explosives, petroleum products, food, and steel, assistance to Russia included 14,700 planes, 7,000 tanks, 52,000 jeeps, 376,000 trucks, 35,000 motorcycles, 2,000 locomotives, 11,000 freight cars, 3.8 million tires, and over 15 million army boots. This enormous contribution to Russian mobility should have convinced the Soviet leaders of America's goodwill. No ally in history had ever furnished assistance on this scale, to one nation or to any group of nations.

Once the Lend-Lease Act had become the law of the land, the administration engaged in two other efforts to show its sympathies,

Lend Lease, 1941–1945

	Millions of dollars
American Republics	493
Belgium	156
British Empire	31,610
China	1,602
Denmark	4
Egypt	2
Ethiopia	5
France and possessions	3,269
Greece	81
Iceland	4
Iran	8
Italy	186
Liberia	19
Netherlands and possessions	246
Norway	47
Poland	12
Saudi Arabia	22
Turkey	42
U.S.S.R.	11,047
Yugoslavia	32
Total	$50,208,400,948.09

Source: *Forty-Fourth Report to Congress on Lend-Lease Operations for the Period Ending December 31, 1962, 1963,* Appendix 1.

one of them a statement of principles, the other a virtual declaration of war. In mid-August 1941, the American President met the Prime Minister of Great Britain in a secret rendezvous in Placentia Bay off Newfoundland, and on August 14 the two leaders agreed to a press release—it was no treaty, not even a signed document—which became known as the Atlantic Charter. They pledged their countries and, as it turned out, their allies—including the Russians, who signed a pledge of adherence to the charter's principles in Washington on January 1, 1942—to seek no aggrandizement, territorial or other; to support "no territorial changes that do not accord with the freely expressed wishes of the peoples concerned"; to ensure the right of all peoples to choose their own form of government; to provide "access, on equal terms, to the trade and to the raw materials of the world"; to assist economic collaboration among nations; to work for freedom from fear and want; to enable the ships of all nations "to traverse the high seas and oceans without hindrance"; and to disarm aggressors and limit the arms of peace-loving peoples. Churchill later told Roosevelt at Yalta that he considered the charter not a law but a star. Russian adherence to the charter in the United Nations Declaration of January 1, 1942, was hedged, but the American President and people took the charter seriously, and other leaders and their peoples thus had to reckon with it during the years of World War II and the peace that followed.

The second act of the American government in the last months of 1941 amounted to a declaration of war on the German submarines then operating in the Atlantic. It often has been said that President Roosevelt was at his best when moving with the support of public opinion and in pursuit of a great cause. When he was direct, he was wonderful. But when he was unsure of support and moving by indirection, he could be so sideways as to be deceptive, and this was the case in regard to convoying, the necessary sequel to the Lend-Lease Act. What good was producing great quantities of war materials to send to Britain and Russia, if German submarines sank the goods in the Atlantic crossing? At the time of debate over lend-lease there had been questions in Congress, questions in private discussions at the White House, questions by reporters, and the President had avoided them. In Congress his supporters led opponents off into irrelevancies. At the White House in private meetings the President waved aside queries from Secretary Stimson as being anticipatory and theoretical. In press conferences he said that the difference between what he had instructed the navy to institute in the Atlantic, a patrol, was—as compared to a convoy—the difference between a cow and a horse. After these preliminaries the President waited for a naval war to break out in the Atlantic, for the German submarines to attack, because when they did (so he seems privately to have told Churchill during the Atlantic Charter meeting) he would have an incident and be able to make something out of it.

Three incidents involving American destroyers occurred. The President had arranged an agreement on April 9 with the Danish minister in Washington to include Greenland in "our sphere of cooperative hemispheric defense." On July 7 came a similar understanding with Iceland. Under both arrangements the United States received convenient bases for convoying British and American merchant ships as far as Iceland. On September 4 the destroyer *Greer* was attacked as it was following a German submarine. The President in a deceptive radio address said that the vessel was carrying mail to Iceland and had been assaulted without warning, though the destroyer had in fact been broadcasting the submarine's position to a nearby British plane before the submarine fired two torpedoes and received in return a pattern of depth charges. On September 11 the President issued a sink-on-sight order to the navy, and five days later the navy announced convoying in the Atlantic as far as Iceland. The destroyer *Kearny*, attacking German submarines, was torpedoed on October 17, with severe damage and the loss of eleven American lives. The *Reuben James* was hit on the night of October 30, with the loss of ninety-six men.

The Hitler government had reason to declare war on the United States, and President Roosevelt would not have objected, but German leaders did not then want to embroil themselves in a war with America when the fighting in Russia was moving to a climactic stage. The Germans waited, and the United States government waited, and then, suddenly, the American navy reeled from a blow struck on the other side of the world.

Pearl Harbor

In analyzing why the United States went to war with Japan, why the Japanese attacked Pearl Harbor, and thereby how the United States got into World War II, not merely in the Far East but in Europe, it is necessary to examine five prime factors in Japanese-American relations. One of them is racism. Ever since 1924 the American government had refused to admit Japanese to the United States for the purpose of becoming American citizens. It was extremely difficult to conduct diplomacy with a country whose people were not wanted as permanent residents. There were other aspects to Americans' racism, such as a tendency to poke fun at "cheap Japanese goods" and believe that the Japanese could not make manufactured items as well as the Western nations could and were essentially imitators.

A second factor in the outbreak of war in 1941 was the weakness of America's Far Eastern policy. In 1898, when the United States took the Philippines and Guam and annexed Hawaii, the responsibility of governing the new territories seemed separate from the duty of protecting them. Not until most of the American navy was shifted to the Pacific after World War I could anyone have felt confident of the safety of Hawaii in case of a Japanese attack. Planners in the War and Navy Departments almost from the outset had written off the

Philippines as indefensible; President Theodore Roosevelt in 1907 had admitted that it would take an army as large as the German army and a navy as large as the British navy to protect them. The State Department proved sensitive to the exposed position of the United States empire in the Pacific, especially the remote Philippines, sixty-two hundred miles from San Francisco. They were so close to Japan that most visitors to the islands passed through the Japanese islands en route. The department knew the Philippines were virtually a hostage to Japan for American good behavior in the Far Pacific. Unfortunately, the American people never quite realized this and not merely took the defense of the Philippines for granted but were willing to acquire even more responsibilities in the Orient. When the government of China threatened to collapse at the end of the nineteenth century, and subsequently a series of weak regimes made the "cutting of the Chinese melon" attractive to the Japanese, the American people were happy to have the Department of State stand up to Japan with a series of admonitions—the Open Door Notes of 1899 and 1900, a proposal to participate in management of Chinese and Manchurian railroads during the Taft administration, a warning to the Japanese in 1915 against dismembering China, a stronger warning by Secretary Stimson in 1932. In the developing antagonism between the United States and Japan over China there was never any continuing effort by the Americans to back up their diplomacy with force; the Japanese by the 1930's had discovered that American protests led to nothing but diplomatic notes.

Racism and an inadequate Far Eastern policy were accompanied by naval rivalry, a third factor in the deterioration of Japanese-American relations. One of the pilots who attacked Pearl Harbor wrote years afterward, "By the time I entered the Naval Academy in 1921, the Navy was already indoctrinating its future officers with the idea that 'the potential enemy is America.'" Although some elements in Tokyo thought a showdown with Russia or Britain more likely than a conflict with the United States, over the entire interwar period there hovered the possibility of a Japanese-American naval war. The American government in 1921–1922 had forced the Japanese into a naval ratio that was unacceptable to young officers in the Imperial Navy, and once the occupation of Manchuria began in 1931 the navy commenced planning for superiority against the Americans. By 1941 the Japanese navy was a good deal more powerful than the combined forces the Westerners could marshal against it.

The size of the American navy increased during this period, but not fast enough. President Roosevelt, a friend of the navy, knowing that labor costs were 84 percent of the total cost of shipbuilding, had authorized $238 million for construction on June 16, 1933. The Vinson-Trammel Act of 1934 permitted advances in tonnage up to the Washington and London treaty limits, and Congress appropriated funds in 1935 and 1937. In 1938 the fleet was permitted to exceed treaty tonnages by 20 percent. Early in 1940 there was another rise, of 11 percent. After Hitler invaded the Low Countries, Congress passed a 70 percent supplementary increase, which at least in theory brought into existence a two-ocean navy. Unfortunately, the construction authorized from 1933 to 1940 called for only three aircraft carriers, as compared to eight battleships. The American navy's strategic planning in the 1930's looked to Jutland rather than to Midway. The construction of the decade came too late to be of much use by December 1941 but probably just soon enough to be provocative. American naval strength in the Pacific in 1941 was far below what it needed to be to allow for defense of the Philippines, and as events turned out even the Hawaiian Islands were in danger. The Asiatic Fleet, the flotilla based on the Philippines, was almost as weak in the late 1930's as in the time of Commodore Dewey. It was little more than a token flotilla of one cruiser, a few destroyers and submarines, and some river gunboats such as the *Panay.* In January 1937, General Douglas MacArthur, then field marshal of the Philippine army, wanted President Manuel Quezon to use the cruiser *Augusta* for a trip to the United States. The commander of the Asiatic Fleet, Admiral Harry E. Yarnell, was furious over this request, for the *Augusta* was his only sizable modern warship. No coordination occurred between the ambitious goals of American Far Eastern policy, which involved possession of the Philippines and the protection of China, and the military force maintained to ensure those goals. The navy feared correctly that its strength vis-à-vis the Japanese was weakening. Moreover, the navy was endangered not merely because of Japanese construction and the slowness of its own construction, for the possibility loomed of some sort of diplomatic initiative for disarmament. Norman Davis, Roosevelt's ambassador-at-large in the early and middle 1930's, was constantly talking about disarmament, though perhaps had Europe in mind more than the Far East. In any arrangement he might have made the navy sensed that a desire for agreement would be more important than strategic calculation.

The joint strategic plans of the American army and navy, based on almost no diplomatic advice, looked narrowly to the past, to the nineteenth century, ignoring the experience of World War I, which had been fought by a coalition, and the possibility—even probability—that any new conflict involving the United States would also be a coalition war. Throughout the interwar era the military services and the Department of State each worked out arrangements largely by itself and failed to benefit from its own experiences. Officers of the army and navy put together war plans designated by a color code name for each country involved—Red for Great Britain (the planners thought such a war might be possible), Black for Germany, Green for Mexico, Orange for Japan. It was exhilarating to think of an Orange War, a Red War, a Green War. Only in 1939 did a new series of war plans, five in all, appropriately labeled "Rainbow," attempt to meet the probability of various coalitions. Rainbow Five was invoked in December 1941.

The fourth and fifth factors in bringing on hostilities between the Japanese and Americans appeared only in the last years before war. The fourth factor was the ferocity of the Japanese attack on China, which commenced in July 1937. The effort to take the coastal cities of China and as much of the hinterland as the Japanese army could easily hold began with a series of unexampled excesses. In the sack of Nanking the butchering of Chinese troops and civilians ran to perhaps 100,000 killings. Unlike the actions of the Nazi government, much of whose wanton behavior was away from public view and whose worst excesses had not yet begun in 1937, the Japanese excesses were out in the open, observed by American missionaries and businessmen and newspapermen who wrote home horrified accounts. The uncivilized behavior of some of the Japanese troops in China became common knowledge in the United States, passed about from church to church in the letters of the missionaries. Nothing like it had been read before, and American opinion hardened.

The final factor producing war was increasing diplomatic pressure by the Japanese on British and other colonial possessions in the Far East. The American government and people came to believe that it was useless to try to shore up the British government in Europe when the Japanese were threatening to knock the props out from under the empire in the Orient. Something had to be done, and as the Japanese acted the United States reacted. Tokyo in 1940 took full advantage of the disintegration of French power in Europe and the weakness of Britain and on September 22 concluded an arrangement with Vichy France for air and land bases in Indochina. On

September 27, at a very low point in the European war, the Japanese signed in Berlin a three-power pact with Germany and Italy providing for a ten-year military and economic alliance. By this pact Japan became a member of the Axis, each of the signatories pledging mutual assistance in event of war with a nation not then a belligerent (Russia? the United States?). The American government considered this Tripartite Pact a most unfriendly action. In that same event-ridden month President Roosevelt proclaimed an embargo, effective shortly thereafter, on exports of scrap iron and steel to all countries (that is, Japan) outside the Western Hemisphere except Britain. The Japanese ambassador in the United States pronounced this move an unfriendly act.

One event followed another in the developing enmity. In the spring of 1941, and contrary to the desire of the Germans, Japanese Foreign Minister Yosuke Matsuoka signed a nonaggression pact with the Soviet Union, in the course of which negotiation Matsuoka and Stalin embraced and the Russian dictator said they were both Asiatics. The pact of April 13 appeared to ensure Russia's eastern border against Japanese attack and thus was convenient to the Russians in case Germany moved against Russia in the west (which happened two months later). But it gave a green light to what some Japanese had been describing as a possible southward advance, into the Far Eastern possessions of France, the Netherlands, and Britain, perhaps into the Philippine Islands. The American government took alarm. In the summer of 1941, on July 24, the Japanese occupied French Indochina. Two days later President Roosevelt froze Japanese assets in the United States, cutting off all exports including the commodity the Japanese most needed—oil for the Imperial Navy and for civilian use. On that same day FDR nationalized the armed forces of the Philippines and placed them under General Douglas MacArthur, whom he named commander-in-chief of forces in the Far East.

By midsummer 1941, with no more American oil, strategists of the Japanese navy began to support a logic that led straight into war. For a long time they had considered taking the oil of the Dutch East Indies, and it now became highly attractive. Seizing the Indies would probably mean war with the United States. The Japanese navy since January 1941 had pondered an attack on Pearl Harbor, and plans began to take shape. If the navy could knock out America's Pacific Fleet, it would eliminate the only military force of size in the Pacific. Japan then could fortify the surrounding island chains reaching out for hundreds, even thousands, of miles from the home islands, constructing such an impregnable military position that when the United States eventually recovered from the blow, and meanwhile had become involved in the war in Europe, the Americans would have lost their desire to fight in the Far East and in return for a treaty of peace with Japan would grant the Tokyo government hegemony over the entire Pacific region. This was a brilliant piece of reasoning. But it ignored the two nations' grossly unequal war potential.

The basic diplomatic miscalculation of the Japanese in the era before Pearl Harbor was to refuse to meet the American demand that they disentangle themselves from China. During the years after World War II it became evident that China was not necessary for Japan's economy, that the Japanese could prosper beyond any prewar dream by trading with other nations, even with the United States.

It has been argued also that just as it was a mistake for Japan to have refused to back down over China, so it was a mistake for the United States to be so stiff-necked about the Chinese. For the Americans, the result was a two-ocean war, and China was later lost anyway, to the Communists in 1949. Still, given the dreams of a democratic China and of a China market, even of a Christian China, that had accompanied the developing antagonism toward Japan, no accommodation could have been made in 1941. Only an entirely hypothetical rearrangement of the factors that brought war would have allowed the different policy sometimes talked about by historians and political scientists in the 1960's and 1970's.

In view of what had gone before, there was an inevitability to the Japanese attack on Pearl Harbor that was almost overwhelming. The samurai tradition, the militarization of the country during the 1930's when the army was getting ever deeper into China, the lack of democracy throughout the body politic, the peculiarly balanced nature of the government—a balance in which military and civil components conducted their operations side by side in a sort of compartmentalized arrangement—these forces were inspiring the Tokyo government to take a huge risk. For years, relations between Japan and the United States had been deteriorating. When the war in Europe began to engage American attention, the "opportunity of a thousand years" arose—the conquest of European imperial possessions and of American possessions too.

But before turning to military force, Japan sought to negotiate. The regular ambassador in the United States, Admiral Kichisaburo

Nomura, tried to make an arrangement with the American government at the expense of China (the United States was to recognize
Japan's dominant interests in China and cease support of the
regime of Chiang Kai-shek) and engaged in dozens of talks with
Secretary Hull. In mid-November, after the Cabinet of Prime Minister Prince Fumimaro Konoye had fallen and the new Prime Minister,
General Hideki Tojo, gave a deadline to the negotiations, a second
ambassador, Saburo Kurusu, joined in the Washington talks. The
American government wavered, under pressure from the army and
navy for more time to reinforce the Philippines, but the talks proved
unavailing. When word got out to the Chinese there was a protest.
Meanwhile, through the cracking of the Japanese code, President
Roosevelt and the other high officers of the government were
reading of Japanese intransigence, and Roosevelt on November 26
learned of a great convoy in the South China Sea en route apparently
to Siam, present-day Thailand. He advised Hull to give up any
thought of a modus vivendi and restate the American demand that
the Japanese get out of China. This Hull did that very day. As it
happened, on the preceding day the Pearl Harbor attack force of six
carriers, two battleships, and a full complement of cruisers, destroyers, and submarines sailed from a fog-shrouded harbor in
northern Japan.

On Sunday morning, December 7, 1941, the fleet of the United
States lay peacefully at its anchorage in Pearl Harbor, battleships
moored singly or in pairs along the quays of Ford Island, smaller
vessels distributed elsewhere, some in dry dock. The fleet's two
carriers were at sea, returning from ferrying planes to the marines
stationed at Guam and Wake Island. Of the seventy combat ships
and twenty-four auxiliaries in harbor, only one, a destroyer, was
under way. Planes were on the ground at the nearby air stations,
lined up wing to wing along the runways in accord with a sabotage
alert that applied to all forces on the island of Oahu. The sky in the
early morning, at 7:55, was beautifully clear, and nearby hillocks
and mountains with their lush vegetation stood out in great detail.
A few civilian planes were in the air, Piper Cubs droning quietly
over Honolulu and outskirts. Many of the fleet's sailors had been in
the city the night before, Saturday night, and the ships were not fully
manned. The men were preparing for their morning routines when
with a roar the first Japanese planes came over. The initial reaction
was incredulity, belief that the attack was a crazy maneuver by a
war-games-minded admiral, until bombs started to drop, torpedoes

The destroyer U.S.S. *Shaw* explodes during the Japanese raid on Pearl Harbor, December 7, 1941. When the first planes swooped down over Pearl Harbor it was not clear whether they were attacking or, perhaps, some crazy American admiral had conjured up a new sort of war game and disguised American planes with the Japanese "meatball" insignia. The nature of the attack soon became apparent as the sheets of flame leaped skyward.

crisscrossed the anchorage, the boom of exploding ammunition split the air, sheets of orange flame raced skyward. Then came the spreading clouds of smoke, sure signs of disaster, especially with the hoarse klaxons sounding along battleship row where the attack clearly was centering. One battleship, the U.S.S. *Nevada,* got up steam and managed to move into mid-channel, serene in the face of the carnage; a lieutenant commander was taking the proud ship out; but bombing hits so disabled the big vessel that it had to be beached before reaching the mouth of the channel. On came the waves of enemy bombers and torpedo bombers. Within a half-hour the damage had been done—sunk and listing vessels scattered like trash about the harbor, planes in the nearby airfields masses of charred wreckage, the greatest American military base in the Pacific a shambles. All eight battleships were disabled, four of them capsized. The death toll was 2,403, including 68 civilians.

Americans on and after December 7, 1941, wondered what step or steps might have saved the battleship fleet disabled or sunk by the Japanese on that Sunday morning, and opinions will perhaps always differ on this point of naval tactics. The "Magic" intercepts, the broken code, might have helped if Admiral Husband E. Kimmel at Pearl Harbor had obtained a code machine and could have watched for intercepts bearing on his command. Four machines had been constructed. One was given the British, two remained in Washington, and one went to MacArthur's command in the Philippines. Kimmel thus failed to benefit from the broken code and did not even know it was broken. In subsequent years the commander of the Pacific Fleet—he lived until 1968—contended that he did not possess enough planes to keep up a search of all the surrounding seas. His critics retorted that he did not need to send out planes on a 360-degree arc, that he should have known the direction an enemy force would be coming from, that in exercises of the American navy in 1932 and 1938 carrier task forces had "attacked" Pearl Harbor from the stormy northwest quadrant and on both occasions had "destroyed" the fleet. Kimmel said that when, just a few days before the Japanese assault, his carriers were sent out on missions to Wake and Guam, their absence together with the weakness of shore batteries virtually forced him to keep his battleships in harbor. Critics countered that in 1940 the British navy in an attack on Italian vessels in Taranto had shown the feasibility of torpedoing ships anchored in shoal water and that Kimmel should have placed anti-torpedo baffles alongside his big ships. Kimmel said that if he had possessed a code machine he could have anticipated the Japanese attack, taken his fleet to sea, met the Japanese force coming down from the northwest, and annihilated it. Yet if he had gotten his ships out of harbor, the exodus would have revealed to the Japanese that the United States had cracked their code. They would have changed the code, as the Germans had been urging them to do, and as a result the Americans would have been denied what proved to be one of the primary weapons of United States strategy throughout the war (the Battle of Midway in 1942 was largely an intelligence victory, for the American navy knew the positions and strength of the approaching

Japanese fleet). Moreover, as the historian Samuel Eliot Morison pointed out some years ago, if Kimmel had taken his battleships to sea, they might have been sunk by Japanese submarines waiting outside—sunk in deep water, rather than in the shallow harbor where they came to rest and from which most of them were salvaged.

The Roosevelt administration chose to sack both Kimmel and the army commander in Hawaii, Lieutenant General Walter R. Short. This treatment, which could be described as ungenerous, differed notably from that meted out to General MacArthur, who was not enjoying his finest moment at the time of Pearl Harbor. The Philippine commander's B-17 planes were caught lined up on the ground at Clark Field despite the fact that MacArthur's officers, because of time differences (when word of the Pearl Harbor bombing and torpedoing arrived, it was 2:30 A.M. in the Philippines) and because of a delay in the Japanese attack, had ten hours in which to arrange the islands' defenses. Was MacArthur treated differently because he was a former army chief of staff, a well-known military man with an ability to defend himself verbally, and the Roosevelt administration was afraid of him? Against this kind of contention it is possible to argue from a military point of view that the commander of a base or force is responsible for a disaster and from a political point of view that the Pearl Harbor disaster was so large that it demanded a scapegoat.

The personal tragedies of careers ruined were less important than the tragedies of the military and civilian deaths at Pearl Harbor, the fact of surprise less important than the loss of the fleet battleships. The latter destruction was far less important than it initially seemed, for battleships were little used in the naval actions of World War II. Beyond all these calculations was the fact that the Japanese had brought war to the United States, declared formally by Congress on Monday, December 8. Three days later the German and Italian governments declared hostilities, apparently in the belief that American intervention in Europe could not be of importance before the probable defeat of Russia in 1942 and that it was necessary to observe the form of helpfulness to the Japanese even if Tokyo had not bothered to tell the European Axis powers about the planned attack against Pearl Harbor.

In the years immediately after World War II publicists and a few historians suggested that FDR might have pushed the nation into war through the Japanese "back door" when the Germans refused to open the front door and that he had deliberately exposed the fleet at Pearl Harbor to achieve his ends. The late Charles A. Beard ominously described what he called "appearances and realities" in a book published in 1948 entitled *President Roosevelt and the Coming of the War.* No proof of so extraordinary a scheme has ever appeared, though supporters of this theory could cite considerable circumstantial evidence. It was of course almost an incredible fact that, after the code intercepts pointed to a crisis somewhere around 1:00 P.M., Washington time (shortly after dawn, Pearl Harbor time), a warning had gone out from the army chief of staff, General Marshall, to the Hawaiian command an hour or so before the attack but by mistake was sent by Western Union rather than by navy wireless, took ten hours and thirty-eight minutes to reach Hawaii, and was delivered by a messenger boy on a motorcycle.

The Grand Alliance

From the outset of American entrance into World War II, the purpose of the war was clear—defeat of the Axis in Europe and Asia. The Western Allies—Britain and the United States—had to draw a ring around the Japanese, help the Russians ring the Germans, and manage to hold these rings while they marshaled their resources, in the main the resources of the United States, for the ultimate defeat of the foe.

The British and Americans had no question about which theater of war was more important. Their leaders, Churchill and Roosevelt, meeting in the White House at Christmas 1941, affirmed their belief that it was advisable to defeat Hitler first. Hitler threatened Britain; Russia was fighting German forces on a vast European front. The German enemy was the more dangerous in immediate military power and, perhaps, in future scientific capability (on December 6, 1941, the American government had begun to organize its atomic program). But the problem in the winter of 1941–1942 was to prevent a debacle in Asia. In the first six months after Pearl Harbor, the army and navy shoved everything they could into the Pacific to stop the Japanese. It was a tremendous job, for the Pacific war opened with a series of Allied defeats.

The Japanese navy followed up its smashing success at Pearl Harbor by attacking off the Malay peninsula a British battle cruiser, the *Repulse,* and the brand-new battleship *Prince of Wales* and in a few hours of sorties by planes sank them both on December 10. Jap-

The Pacific Theater of War

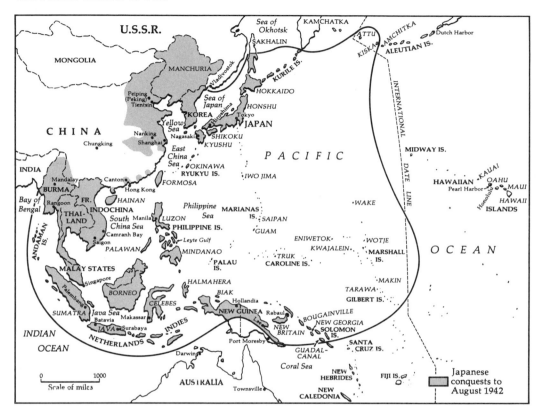

anese troops landed on the peninsula and moved down through jungle to the great British naval base of Singapore. On February 15, 1942, the base surrendered. Especially galling was the fact that 60,000 Japanese had beaten 140,000 British and imperial troops; the fall of Singapore was a crushing military defeat, despite brave words by Churchill about the fighting qualities shown by the defenders. The Singapore collapse opened the way to Burma, which the Japanese occupied in a few weeks. The American General Joseph W. Stilwell, on the scene in Burma, refused to gloss over what had happened there, after he and a small group of Allied personnel walked back to India. "I claim we got a hell of a beating," Stilwell told a press conference in the presence of red-faced Britishers who wished he would not be so blunt. "We got run out of Burma and it is humiliating as hell." At that time, the early summer of 1942, all India was in danger.

One after one, the Allied holdings fell. The American defenders of Guam gave up on December 13, 1941, and the marines on Wake surrendered a week later. The Dutch East Indies succumbed with almost no resistance. Japanese forces made landings in the Gilbert and Solomon Islands, and as the way was opening to India so it opened to another great imperial possession, Australia.

A particularly hard blow to Americans was loss of the Philippines. In the two and one-half weeks after Pearl Harbor day General MacArthur had failed to round up food and medical supplies. When the Japanese landed along Lingayen Gulf and American and Filipino troops fell back to positions on Bataan peninsula and on the island fortress of Corregidor, they had to go to half-rations almost immediately. Soon the islands' situation was hopeless, as military experts had been predicting it would be for nearly forty years. In an effort to galvanize the government in Washington—not to offer a serious proposal—President Quezon of the Philippine Common-wealth (the islands were scheduled to become independent in 1946) in a cable to President Roosevelt proposed the neutralization of the archipelago and withdrawal of both Japanese and American forces. Authorities in Washington were shocked, the more so because Mac-Arthur had forwarded Quezon's morale-destroying proposal and seemed to concur with it. In an answering cable Roosevelt explained the impossibility of neutralization, how it would adversely affect United States morale and perhaps the entire course of the war. The project died, though the shock of its reception lingered for weeks. Not long afterward Quezon and MacArthur were ferried out of the islands by torpedo boat and submarine. Quezon went to the United States, where he remained until his death from tuberculosis in 1944, and MacArthur went to Australia to become commander of Allied forces in the South Pacific. Bataan fell on April 9, and the Japanese mercilessly marched 72,000 of their 74,000 prisoners—half-fed, sick, wounded—fifty-five miles on their way to prisoner-of-war camps. From 7,000 to 10,000 died during the Bataan death march, including 2,330 Americans. Corregidor surrendered on May 6. The fall of the Philippines was the greatest military defeat in American history, involving the capture of nearly 140,000 American and Filipino forces.

The Japanese next sought to take Port Moresby in southern New Guinea, for possession of this little locality would cut American communications with Australia and constitute a virtual bridgehead for invasion. MacArthur knew the importance of holding Moresby, and the United States navy pulled together a scratch fleet of American and Allied units, under the command of Rear Admiral Frank Fletcher, which on May 7 and 8, 1942, successfully engaged an opposing and more powerful Japanese fleet. The Battle of the Coral Sea proved the first of the Pacific engagements in which attacking fleets never saw each other's units. Fighting was done by carrier planes, with the major purpose of sinking the opposing fleet's carriers. Coral Sea turned back the Japanese, who lost a carrier, but the Japanese sank the carrier *Lexington*. Such a loss at that time was serious, for it left only three American carriers in all of the Pacific (*Yorktown, Hornet, Enterprise*).

A thinning line of American and Filipino prisoners approaches the end of the Bataan death march at Camp O'Donnell on Luzon. Improvised stretchers were used to carry injured comrades. How many of these men—sick and well—survived until August 1945?

Brown Brothers

The climactic naval battle of the year and of the entire Pacific war came at Midway, where from June 3 to June 6 American carrier-based and land-based planes attacked and defeated a major Japanese fleet. The Japanese badly wanted the Midway base, for possession of it would place Japan's planes 1,135 miles northwest of Pearl Harbor. The Pacific Fleet's base would have become untenable. A huge enemy fleet of eleven battleships, ten carriers, twenty-three cruisers, sixty-five destroyers, and twenty-one submarines moved majestically toward Midway. This grand armada might have taken the island from the much smaller American defending force under Rear Admiral Raymond A. Spruance had the American commander not known Japanese fleet dispositions because of possession of the enemy's code. Spruance arranged his forces accordingly, and on June 4 his planes managed to catch the Japanese carriers in their most vulnerable position. The enemy planes had landed and were refueling. Japanese sailors carelessly had arranged their fuel stores so that any hit on a carrier's deck would likely set off a train of explosions that would move below decks directly toward the carrier's magazines. Within a few minutes, between 10:22 A.M. and 10:28, Spruance's navy fliers set three carriers on fire, and later in the day they got a fourth. Defeat of the Japanese fleet in four days of sorties marked the farthest western advance of the Japanese navy, as Coral Sea had marked its farthest southern advance. The main cost to the United States navy was the carrier *Yorktown.* By the summer of 1942 the Americans with some British help, mostly that of Australians and New Zealanders, had managed to draw a ring around the Japanese in the Pacific, but it had been anxious work.

After the Battle of Midway the Chicago *Tribune,* a long-time isolationist and anti-Roosevelt paper, published a story reporting the Japanese order of battle—naming ships and thus threatening to reveal that United States code breakers knew the Japanese code. The Federal Bureau of Investigation and the Office of Naval Intelligence converged on Chicago, a special grand jury was summoned, the attorney general flew to Chicago. But after a short time the case was dropped. The Japanese, it turned out, had not noticed all the activity. It was a close call, the most flagrant violation of security of the entire war.

Meanwhile the European theater seemed to be going from bad to worse. In early 1942 the German position in Europe appeared almost impregnable. The Nazi government and its Italian partner controlled the entire Continent, with the exception of a small part of European

During the Battle of Midway, a Japanese heavy cruiser burns after attack by United States planes on June 5, 1942. Naval experts had not anticipated the destruction that planes might wreak on ships, and World War II demonstrated not merely the dominant role of aircraft carriers but also the extreme vulnerability of vessels that did not bristle with anti-aircraft guns.

Russia. The Swedes and the Spanish, the two largest neutrals, could be conquered whenever it suited the Führer's convenience, but he deemed their conquest unnecessary so long as he could exploit their economies. About 400 million people were within his jurisdiction, from the Arctic Circle to the Mediterranean and Aegean seas, and eastward to the Caucasus, where German armies had driven in the campaign of 1941. They were about to resume their thrust, perhaps moving south after taking the rich Russian oil regions and linking with German and Italian forces under Lieutenant General Erwin Rommel that were in North Africa and about to open an offensive against the hard-pressed British defenders of Egypt and Libya. In the Atlantic, German submarines were beginning to operate almost without interference, and in 1942 sinkings steadily increased until in November submarines sank 1 million tons of Allied shipping. In the first eleven months of 1942 they sank a total of 8 million tons.

Faced with so bleak a scene in Europe and crisis in the Pacific, American military planners found themselves pushed almost to the point of despair. In this period the decision was taken that Secretary of War Stimson later wrote was to delay the second front in France for an entire year and that would be regarded as one of the prime reasons for the cold war. The difficulty centered on when and where a second front (in addition to the "first" front in Russia) should be created. On May 8, 1942, MacArthur cabled General Marshall that "the necessity for a second front is self-evident. That front should be in the Pacific theater. Nowhere else can it be so successfully launched and nowhere else will it so assist the Russians." This reasoning found no favor with Marshall, whose planners were working on a proposal to invade France via the British Isles in late 1942; Sledgehammer would presumably involve only a few divisions and be both a toehold and a diversion, giving support to the hard-pressed Russians by drawing off some German troops that otherwise would have found employment in Russia. Sledgehammer was to be followed in 1943 by Roundup, a full-scale invasion via the bridgehead opened up in the preceding year. President Roosevelt breezily told Foreign Minister Molotov in May 1942 that there would be a second front that very year.

Churchill was hesitant about committing British troops in strength on the Continent. The traditional British military approach to Europe had been to attack the Continent's periphery. On the sole occasion when British commanders had done otherwise, during World War I, when their troops eventually outnumbered the divisions of their French ally, the cost had been nearly a million British deaths in a series of dreadful and largely futile offensives. Churchill in 1914–1915 had advocated a counterstrategy, an invasion of Turkey at the Dardanelles and Bosporus, that if successful might have opened a supply route to Russia and turned the entire course of the war. He wished to try a similar strategy during World War II. Moreover, British troops had been thrown off the Continent at Dunkerque, and the high command was in no hurry to return.

In the summer of 1942 setbacks in North Africa offered an occasion for the Prime Minister to force a change in American plans. Rommel sent British forces on a pell-mell retreat back into Egypt to a place called El Alamein, which was only seventy miles from Egypt's second

This is one of the last pictures of Dunkerque to be taken before the Allied withdrawal. Two beached ships, the air filled with black smoke and the small, clustered bursts of anti-aircraft fire—a dismal scene that marked the triumph of the German army.

city, Alexandria, a British naval base virtually next door to the Suez Canal. On June 21 the fortress of Tobruk in Libya, with a garrison of 40,000 men, surrendered to Rommel's forces with hardly a fight. The crushing defeat in North Africa stiffened Churchill against any new front in France that year—and the next year if he could help it. In meetings at Hyde Park and Washington the Prime Minister stood up to President Roosevelt on this point. The British possessed the only battle-trained troops among the Western Allies, so there was not much for Roosevelt to do but give in. Churchill magnanimously agreed to go to Moscow and explain the decision personally to Stalin, which he did in August.

During the discussions with Churchill, Roosevelt had broached the possibility of, and obtained the enthusiastic support of his British friend for, an invasion of North Africa by an Anglo-American force in November 1942, an operation that when mounted became known in American military parlance as Torch. It was cleverly designed, for by putting forces into the western part of North Africa and sending supplies and men around the Cape of Good Hope and up the Red Sea to strengthen the British Eighth Army in Egypt, the Allies would be able to catch Rommel's army in a nut-cracker. And this is just what happened. The Eighth Army jumped off against Rommel in the Battle of El Alamein, which began on October 23. The main American force meanwhile had sailed from Hampton Roads, Virginia, under the command of Major General George S. Patton, and joined troop transports coming down from the British Isles. Troops went into Morocco and Algiers against minor opposition from local French forces, and soon the Allied commander, General Dwight D. Eisenhower, had a half-million men to pit against the Germans. By May 13, 1943, Rommel's mixed German and Italian force of 350,000 men was virtually all in Allied prisoner-of-war cages —at an Allied casualty cost of about 70,000 killed and missing.

On July 10, 1943, the Allied veterans of the North African campaign invaded Sicily and on September 3 crossed into Italy. Shortly after the Sicily invasion, the government of Mussolini collapsed, the Duce being deposed by his Cabinet colleagues on July 25 and placed under house arrest. The ensuing government under Marshal Pietro Badoglio surrendered to the Allies on the day that troops crossed the Straits of Messina. But surrender of the Italian government did not ensure the end of the war in Italy, which dragged on into the spring of 1945. German paratroops rescued Mussolini and established him in a puppet regime in northern Italy, where he ruled until its collapse in the last days of the war and his death at the hands of partisans. The Allied advance up the Italian peninsula proved agonizingly slow. As the American General Mark W. Clark wrote afterward, it was "a rough road all the way." The Allies opened a bridgehead at Salerno on September 9, 1943, and managed to take Naples on October 1. They opened another bridgehead at Anzio on January 22, 1944, but barely held it for several months until their main forces could move northward and join with the bridgehead's defenders. Not until June 4, 1944, two days before the Normandy invasion, did Rome fall to the Allies.

Americans such as Stimson and Marshall sharply questioned the Torch strategy because they were perturbed by its consequences.

The United States army's planning in World War I had proved enormously successful. Two million fresh troops from the New World had turned the balance against Imperial Germany. Stimson had been a colonel of field artillery during the earlier conflict and Marshall a colonel on the staff of General Pershing, and both men had been deeply impressed by the direct strategy of 1917–1918. In World War II, with a different plan, North Africa had led to Sicily and the hard road up the boot of Italy. They feared that once American troops were moving freely about the Mediterranean, Prime Minister Churchill might hoodwink Roosevelt and compel the American military command to sponsor excursions into what Churchill in a piece of sheer rhetoric was wont to describe as Europe's soft underbelly. The American military leaders knew that the area was anything but soft, that the terrain of Yugoslavia was mountainous. By the autumn of 1943, because of the increasing output of their economy and the multiplying numbers of magnificently armed American troops, they were able to demand that when a second front came it would not be a contest for Belgrade and Budapest. In late 1943 the Americans at last obtained British support for a front in France, but by then it was impossible to mount such a front until late in the spring of the next year, 1944.

Is it likely that Churchill's tactics delayed the invasion of France by at least a year and maybe by two? It is hard to say. In the autumn of 1942 the Western Allies did not possess many battle-hardened troops. At that time the Germans had large forces in France, and considering that in June 1944 the chance presence of a German division at one of the beaches chosen by the Americans for their landings almost brought that particular operation to a tragic conclusion, one can only wonder what might have happened if the Allies had mounted Sledgehammer and had been thrown back into the sea. In the summer of 1942 the British had sent a small force, about six thousand troops, against German defenses at Dieppe along the Channel coast, and the Germans had killed or captured half of the attackers in what was a small catastrophe. Suppose there had been a large one a few months later. Suppose that in an effort to help the Russians the Anglo-Americans were gravely defeated. If recriminations came from the Russian ally in 1942 and 1943 because of postponement of the second front in France until 1944, one can envision what the Russians would have said if after a failure in 1942 the second front had to be postponed to 1945 or 1946.

Still, there is a good deal more to the issue of a second front than the question of delay. The uneasy aspect of the second front question is not what it seems to have become a quarter-century and more after the war—a historical exercise in the origins of the cold war— but rather how many lives, Jewish and gypsy and other, might have been saved from the death camps if the Americans and British had moved more quickly. Several million lives were lost in the death camps as those places got into operation in 1943 and 1944. If the Western Allies had thrown in their troops, admittedly green, in Russian tactics whereby losses were not deemed important so long as territory was taken, the front might have held and might even have drawn German troops from the eastern front, ending the war earlier than it did end. But this is a fanciful redrawing of the past. It is highly improbable that American public opinion, never likely to take high battle casualties with Russian stoicism, would have stood for a human assault on Hitler's *Festung Europa,* even if (which was not the case in 1943–1944) Americans had known fully what was going on in the death camps.

The invasion of 1944 proved none too soon in one respect, for the Germans were attempting to win the war with novel weapons and the emplacement of some of those arms in Belgium and the Netherlands threatened the safety of England. The Allies captured the launching platforms for the German V-1 rockets and the much more dangerous V-2 ballistic missiles in the nick of time, before those weapons had begun to pound the British into submission.

Whatever the reasoning and the cost for the moment and the future, history went the way it did; there can be no rewriting. While the English and Americans were elaborating their strategy, the Germans and Russians fought it out on the steppes and in the Caucasus. The German summer offensive of 1942 came up against increasing behind-the-lines resistance, a stiffening foe, the almost illimitable stretching of Russian territory out to the east, and then at last another Russian winter that turned roads into quagmires of mud and seas of ice and snow. In the winter of 1942–1943, while the Western Allies were closing the net on Rommel's forces, the Russians surrounded an entire German army at Stalingrad and captured it on February 2, 1943, remnants of twenty-two divisions, with a galaxy of German generals including a field marshal. The Battle of Stalingrad was another turning point, evidence that the critical era was coming to an end and the years—or perhaps months—of victory beginning.

When the course of the war was becoming more favorable, the Western Allies in a diplomatic initiative demonstrated to the

Russians that whatever the delay in the much-desired second front the spirit and purpose of the Westerners looked to victory and not to compromise or defeat. For eleven days in January 1943 Roosevelt and Churchill met at Casablanca on the Atlantic coast of French Morocco and elaborated the doctrine of unconditional surrender, announced by the President to a group of newspapermen. Roosevelt afterward requested that the Casablanca meeting be called the Unconditional Surrender Conference.

No single policy of the Western Allies came in for so much criticism, then or later. The doctrine made no distinction among Germans and Italians and Japanese, assuming that the three Axis nations were equally culpable of aggression, their regimes impossible to treat with in any way. It was of course transparently untrue that the United States government could not deal with tainted regimes or leaders, for the Americans had maintained diplomatic relations with the government of Vichy France. During the occupation of North Africa, General Eisenhower's headquarters had negotiated with Admiral Jean Darlan, a well-known Hitler sympathizer who happened to be in Algiers when American troops landed. Darlan was the number-two man in the Vichy regime, able to command the loyalty of French troops in North Africa and persuade them not to attack the invading Americans. In the invasion of Italy, several months after the announcement of the unconditional surrender doctrine, the Western Allies not merely offered terms to the government of Marshal Badoglio but accepted that regime as an ally when it declared war on Germany. The doctrine of unconditional surrender, ignored in the cases of North Africa and Italy, offered the Nazi government incentive to fight on. The diary of Joseph Goebbels, discovered in the wreckage of Berlin after the war, showed the elation of the German propaganda minister over the principle announced at Casablanca. The new Allied doctrine demonstrated to the German people, so Goebbels calculated, that the Allies would not try to separate the people from their government, as they had during World War I. Germans had no recourse but to fight on to the bitter end, and that is what they did.

Even so, there was much to recommend the principle set forth at Casablanca. The opportunity to separate the German government from its people that had obtained in World War I was not present in World War II. The Nazi leadership was in control of the instruments of terror, and the German people could not have escaped, no matter what terms the Allies held out. Unconditional surrender had

Josef Stalin, Franklin D. Roosevelt, and Winston Churchill pose on the portico of the Russian Embassy in Teheran, Iran, during the conference in 1943. The Soviets invited Roosevelt to stay at the embassy, which he did—to the disgust of Churchill, who sensed problems of both security and proximity.

a special advantage that made the doctrine worthwhile. It was in reality an implicit promise to the Russians, who were annoyed because of postponement of the second front. By promising to fight until the unconditional surrender of their foes, the British and Americans virtually were offering the Russians a treaty of alliance, an essential of which must always be a promise of no separate peace. At this time the Russians were calling for the extermination of

Hitlerites and fascists, and the English and Americans were sub-
scribing to the Soviet program. To be sure, some leaders among the
Western Allies feared that the Russians might offer Hitler a separate
peace out of the belief that the Westerners were waiting to see the
two antagonists on the eastern front bleed themselves white. After
all, the Russians had made an arrangement with Hitler once before.
The doctrine of unconditional surrender obliquely sought to counter
such a diplomatic tactic by the Russians. Criticized by the un-
imaginative, it offered far more than it seemed to.

The first two years of American participation in the war closed
with a meeting of the Big Three—Churchill, Roosevelt, Stalin—at
Teheran, the capital of Iran, from November 28 to December 1, 1943.
In the surroundings of tiled mosques and brightly colored buildings
the Allied triumvirate got personally acquainted. The English and
Americans promised a second front in France in May or June 1944
and agreed to show their resolve by designating a commander, who
proved to be General Eisenhower. The three Allies decided to give
assistance to Marshal Tito in Yugoslavia and to withdraw aid from
General Draga Michailovitch, a Serb whom Tito executed after the
war. At Teheran there was tentative agreement on the division of
Germany into zones of occupation and on the need to impose
reparations on Germany. Most important, the Russians for the
third time pledged to enter the war in the Pacific after the defeat of
Germany. (During a conference of foreign ministers in Moscow in
October preceding the Teheran meeting, Stalin told Secretary Hull
that the Soviets would do so. Molotov subsequently gave similar
assurance to Ambassador Averell Harriman.) Stalin at Teheran on
November 28 promised again: "Our forces now in the East are more
or less satisfactory for defense. However, they must be increased
about threefold for purposes of offensive operations. This condition
will not take place until Germany has been forced to capitulate.
Then by our common front we shall win."

Victory

Beginning in 1943 almost everything that happened in the West
constituted a preparation for the opening of a second front, and one
of the most important developments was victory in the Battle of the
Atlantic. At the height of the so-called wolf-pack attacks by submarines, U-boats tore through the convoys at night, firing torpedoes

right and left, almost without danger to themselves. The ratio of merchant ships sunk to submarines destroyed was an appalling 40 to 1. In a single attack a Russia-bound convoy in mid-1942 lost twenty-two out of thirty-four ships. Early in 1943, ninety-six ships went down in twenty days. Then the tide turned, almost abruptly. In forty-four months of war up to May 1943, the Allies had sunk 192 U-boats; in three months — May, June, and July 1943 — they sank 100. The ratio of ships sunk to subs destroyed was reduced to less than 1 to 1.

This dramatic improvement in Allied anti-submarine warfare was, quite simply, a triumph of science, much of it American. Centimeter radar, developed at the Massachusetts Institute of Technology, used very short wavelengths and thus gave great detail, making an aircraft a powerful enemy of the U-boat. Scientists designed so-called sonobuoys, dropped by plane to listen for submarine noises and broadcast what they heard, so that a destroyer could pick up a sub on its sonar and then keep in contact. They developed sonar to give distance as well as direction, and soon a destroyer could distinguish a moving sub from stationary decoys planted by the hunted sub. They invented sheaths for depth charges, to make the charges sink more rapidly than conventional canisters, and they produced forward-thrown depth charges named Mousetrap and Hedgehog. They designed anti-submarine rockets, a terrifying weapon, so that a plane could come in at treetop height, zoom up a bit, dive a bit, and as it pulled out with a roar release at a target six rockets, which would take a long shallow underwater trajectory and go clear through a submarine. The Mark X mine, a self-propelled target-seeking torpedo, when dropped into the swirl where a U-boat had just submerged would listen for its quarry, and, as the American scientist Vannevar Bush later wrote, "steer itself to run into the submarine with fatal results." With such infernal devices the sinkings of 1941 and especially of 1942 became memories.

To prepare for the invasion, too, the Continent was being "softened up," as the Anglo-Americans liked to describe their tactics, by air power. The Royal Air Force had been making sorties of several hundred planes even in 1942, but early in 1943 the RAF began to send a thousand bombers at a time over Germany and occupied Europe. The American Eighth Air Force, stationed in England, received the fighter planes of the Ninth Air Force in 1943. The Ninth had started in India, gone to North Africa, and with the close of the African campaign had gone to England. American planes attacked the German city of Hamburg in July 1943 in a series of raids that killed over 60,000 people and leveled large sections of the city. Then in October the Eighth Air Force in a daylight raid on ball-bearing plants in Schweinfurt, a locality in southern Germany, sent in 228 planes without fighter escort. That was a large mistake, for the Germans shot down 62, causing the deaths of 599 airmen. The Eighth Air Force went over to night raiding until the spring of the next year, when longer-range fighter aircraft became available. By the end of the war the planes of the Americans and British numbered more than 28,000, and the tonnage of bombs dropped on occupied Europe and Germany was more than 2.5 million.

The softening up of Europe was not as helpful as the Allies believed, for German military production continued to rise throughout most of 1944. There admittedly was a loss in effectiveness of the

Hamburg, Germany, was reduced to a plain of rubble by Allied bombing in July 1943. Destruction of cities (known to military men as "built-up areas") reached a level never seen before in warfare, and this by conventional bombing.

United Press International

German labor force because of nights spent in air raid shelters and, presumably, because of worry about what might happen to housing from night to night. Still, much Allied bombing proved ineffective, in particular the bombing of railroad marshaling yards. The Germans were able to rearrange tracks almost as rapidly as the bombers disarranged them. Two target systems that paid dividends were German oil production and associated chemical industries and German internal transportation. The Allies attacked both systems late in the war, the latter almost at the very end. But the military historian Bernard Brodie has written, in a summary of the postwar Strategic Bombing Survey sponsored by the American air force, that evidence for the effectiveness of bombing was "on the whole fairly equivocal." This experience, and a similar result in Japan, did not stop United States strategists even in the 1970's from thinking that bombing raids could soften up an enemy and lead to surrender.

Finally, after the softening up, after defeat of the U-boats in the Atlantic, the invasion jumped off on June 6, 1944. What a stupendous operation it was! Paratroopers with blackened faces had dropped into Normandy during the night. Long before daybreak the invading armada had sailed from English ports, to loom up before the German defenders in France as an incredible forest of masts and superstructures standing out to sea for miles. Rippling flashes from battleship guns, followed by the boom and hiss of the shells, raised up an infernal sound, the very noise of death. The first assault troops came ashore in small craft, the Americans at beaches known as Omaha and Utah, the British somewhat to the north. At Omaha Beach the Germans put up savage resistance against all the firepower the Americans could assemble, with grave danger of a collapse of the landing, until by sheer bravery United States troops worked their way to the beach's heights and pushed far enough inland to permit the landing of reinforcements. All the while Allied planes were in the air over the attacking armada, the beaches, the harassed German troops; the invasion was protected by the most spectacular air power ever seen. By the end of "the longest day," as a later writer would entitle his account of the landing, 120,000 men had made it into France.

By July 25, a month and a half after D-Day, 1 million men were on the Continent, a huge force to have landed, with equipment, in so short a time. Two million were across by the end of the summer.

July 25 was the day the Allies broke out of the Normandy bridgehead, out of the narrow fields with their hedgerows, which so often

Signal Corps

The invasion of southern France, August 15, 1944. Invasions by sea were huge, complicated affairs, and must have been awesome to the German defenders—who from their prepared positions would behold a forest of superstructures stretching for miles out to sea.

provided natural defensive points for the beleaguered German troops, out into the open country that gave space for tanks to maneuver. Tank columns began to lace through France, cutting first to the south of the Normandy peninsula and swinging broadly up toward Paris and beyond. By the end of the summer the Americans had secured France and Luxembourg and the British were in Belgium. Meanwhile, on August 15, an American army landed in southern France and within a month had swept north to connect with the other Allied forces, a spectacular contribution to clearing German troops from France.

The occupation of France gave opportunity for the forces of the

Free French under General Charles de Gaulle to take Paris. French forces purposely were sent into the city ahead of the Americans to receive the German surrender, only to find the boulevards largely in the hands of the populace, which had revolted when Allied entrance had become imminent. The appearance of De Gaulle in Paris was a sign for a great public outburst of emotion, and because elections were momentarily out of the question and De Gaulle was the most charismatic Frenchman available for heading up a provisional government, the Americans and British found themselves with an ally who on many occasions was an embarrassment rather than a help. Churchill had quipped during an early period of trial that the greatest cross he had to bear was the cross of Lorraine. Roosevelt liked De Gaulle only slightly more than Churchill did. The general seemed to have it in for people who spoke English. His touchy amour propre was often in evidence. Yet there was not much to do with Le Grand Charlie other than to ensconce him in office.

A plot to kill Hitler produced an abortive coup in Germany on July 20, 1944, a tragic affair both because it did not succeed and because of the terrible vengeance that the German leader took upon the conspirators, their families, and individuals even remotely — and sometimes not even remotely — connected with the attempt. The plan was for one of the conspirators, Colonel Count Claus von Stauffenberg, to deposit a briefcase containing a bomb alongside Hitler's chair in the meeting room in east Germany where the Führer was accustomed to hold staff conferences. The plot failed when one of the officers present at the conference inadvertently kicked the briefcase so that it slid behind the heavy wooden leg of the briefing table. This chance rearrangement saved Hitler's life when the bomb went off. It was a close call. Upon receiving word that the bomb had gone off, not knowing it had proved ineffective and only wrenched Hitler's arm, members of the conspiracy in Berlin sought to organize army headquarters there; but word eventually came that the Führer was safe and the conspiracy collapsed. The result was a long series of trials, tortures, and executions, the most important of which Hitler witnessed by means of film flown to his headquarters. The Allies tended to play down the attempted coup of July 20, and in many ways it was an amateur undertaking, but it showed that honor and uprightness still had a place in German military and civil life.

Not long afterward the Western Allies reached the German border, troops penetrating into Germany near Prüm on September 11, but the offensive in the west slowly came to a halt in a grand line that went from Belgium through Luxembourg down to the Swiss border. Despite heroic efforts it had proved impossible to supply the huge Anglo-American army from Normandy and other Channel ports. What the Allies needed was the port of Antwerp, but although British troops had taken the city, they failed to dislodge German units controlling the long and tortuous approaches to the great Belgian port via the Scheldt River. The inability to open Antwerp meant that the Western offensive would stall through the winter.

The stabilization of the western front encouraged the German high command and especially Hitler to believe that a lightning offensive in the west might break the Anglo-American lines. Early in December 1944, when the skies were overcast and the Allies' vast air power lay immobile on the airfields of England and France, the Germans sent tank units and accompanying infantry in strength into the weakly held area between the British and American forces in Luxembourg and Belgium and in days managed to push a great bulge into the Allied lines. The Battle of the Bulge brought consternation to Eisenhower's headquarters, by this time established at Versailles outside Paris. The attack was altogether unexpected, and the collapse of the lines, held by a few green American divisions, created the possibility that the front might turn into a swirling chaos before air power could come to the Allies' rescue. The high tide of the German advance was reached on the day after Christmas, December 26, when German advance units nearly drove to the Meuse at the Belgian town of Dinant. But then Allied reserves began to stiffen the lines. A special scientific breakthrough, the proximity fuse for artillery shells, by chance was going into use just at the time of the Bulge, and it caught German divisions in the open, for the weather was bad and they felt secure against timed fire. General Patton later said the proximity fuse saved Liège. Then the skies lifted, and the combination of counterattack, increased effectiveness of artillery, and air power blunted and forced back the German troops, although it took until February 1945 for the Allies to push in the bulge. The cost of this offensive was heavy, 8,000 Americans killed and 21,000 captured or missing. Coming just two months before the assembling of a three-power Allied meeting at Yalta in the Crimea, it cast doubt on the West's military abilities and did not ease the task of Roosevelt and Churchill in standing up to Stalin, determined to demand a high price for Russian entrance into the Far Eastern war.

Diplomacy in the last two years of World War II never was as

The Big Three at Yalta. Russian wartime banquets often were bacchanalian feasts, and signs of Bacchus appear on the table. United States Secretary of State Edward Stettinius seems to be proposing a toast to the dour Soviet Foreign Commissar V. M. Molotov (to the right of Churchill), while Roosevelt looks on quizzically and Stalin and Churchill look elsewhere.

important as military events. Wherever the troops of either the West or the Soviets were victorious, the diplomatic arguments became frosting on the military cake. Yet the course of the parleys among the Big Three well showed the strengths and limits of their hopes and ambitions and thereby the shape of the postwar world—and, in a sense not then much thought about, the origins of the cold war. The Teheran Conference in November and December 1943 anticipated the Yalta Conference of February 1945. At Teheran the Western Allies obtained a Russian promise of entrance into the Far Eastern war, and there was detailed discussion of the division of Germany into zones of occupation and talk of German reparations. In October 1944, Churchill and Roosevelt met at Quebec and momentarily considered the German question, initiating a curious plan advanced by Secretary of the Treasury Henry Morgenthau, which, in Churchill's word, provided for the "pastoralization" of Germany, the reduction of Germany to a country primarily agricultural. Churchill seems to have assented to this proposal largely because it came from an American Cabinet member from whom, as Churchill afterward recalled, "we had much to ask" (that is, a postwar loan). Not long afterward the Anglo-American leaders quietly scrapped the Morgenthau Plan because of its impracticality: To turn Germany into pasture land would be to reduce drastically the entire industrial plant of the continent of Europe.

The Yalta Conference lasted from February 6 through 12, 1945, and was the final meeting of the wartime Big Three, for President Roosevelt died on April 12. At Yalta there was talk of $20 billion in reparations, half of which was to go to Russia because of the devastation wrought by the German armies in the Soviet Union, but no one discussed pastoralization. The Big Three held conversations on the division of Germany and discussed political structures and boundaries of Eastern Europe, a declaration of human and political rights for the latter area, and the United Nations Organization. They also considered the price of Russian entry into the Far Eastern war. In the eyes of some Americans the Yalta meeting afterward came to appear not the triumph Roosevelt believed it to be—the Americans and British had left the Crimea in a mood close to exaltation—but an inglorious surrender to Russian demands. In the postwar years the word "Yalta" seemed to carry all the weight of compromise and incaution that had, so the critics of Yalta said, brought on the cold war by allowing Russian power to expand over Eastern Europe. In truth it was a huge mirror held up to the military situation of the moment, which neither confirmed nor changed that situation but recognized it.

The division of Germany into occupation zones proved no difficult problem, for the Allies took the areas that their troops either had entered or soon would enter. The British obtained the Ruhr and the area up to Denmark; the Americans took southern Germany including Bavaria; the Russians occupied the eastern part including East Prussia. The Americans were to receive from the British the port of Bremerhaven and the city of Hamburg, to supply the troops in the south. The French, later admitted to the governance of Germany after a show of reluctance by the Russians, obtained a zone carved out of the Anglo-American zones.

The Occupation Zones in Germany and Austria

The main point of discussion at Yalta turned out to be Eastern Europe, in particular the government and boundaries of postwar Poland. This was a sore subject to the British, for the British and French had gone to war against Germany in 1939 in defense of Poland. President Roosevelt was sensitive about Poland, too, because of the large numbers—6 million or 7 million—of Americans of Polish descent, most of whom had been voting Democratic. However, the governing fact in 1945, unfortunately, was not British sensitivity or American domestic politics but that Poland was in the possession of the Red Army. The Soviets had entered Poland in 1944. In the baggage of their troops they had brought a group of Polish Communists, many of them long resident in Moscow, who announced the formation of a Polish government while situated in Lublin. Stalin told Roosevelt and Churchill that the Lublin Committee had to be the basis of any government for postwar Poland. The English and Americans had been maintaining recognition of the London-based government, the group of exiled Poles who were successors to the Warsaw government of 1939. The government-in-exile had antagonized the Russians in 1943 by accusing them, rightly as we now know, of complicity in the execution of thousands of captured Polish officers in the forest of Katyn. At Yalta the result was an uneasy compromise, the supposed amalgamation of the two Polish governments into a Polish Provisional Government of National Unity, soon dominated by the Lublin Communists.

The Big Three tentatively put Poland's eastern boundary with Russia along a line drawn by the British foreign secretary of 1920, Lord Curzon, a roughly ethnic boundary 150 miles to the west of the pre-1939 Polish border. In return the Poles were to have compensation in the west—German territory in East Prussia and in the neighborhood of Breslau. The Western Allies proved unwilling to recognize this western Polish border, but in 1946 the Russians made a treaty with the Poles recognizing it. Years later, in 1970, the West German government signed a treaty with the Polish government recognizing this western border, the so-called Oder-Neisse line, and ratified the treaty in 1972, virtually legitimizing the line.

At Yalta the State Department presented a Declaration on Liberated Europe, and the Soviets accepted it, binding them to free elections and maintenance of elementary human and political rights as set out in the American Declaration of Independence. Less than two weeks after the Yalta Conference, the Russian occupation authorities violated the declaration. Soviet Deputy Foreign Minister Andrei Vishinsky gave a two-and-one-half-hour ultimatum to King Michael of Rumania, demanding a new Cabinet headed by the Soviet-sponsored leader Petru Groza. An American report on this ultimatum testified that Vishinsky, upon leaving the King's presence, slammed the door of the royal antechamber so hard that he cracked the plaster. The Yalta Declaration later seemed to have been a visionary document, given the military situation of the moment, with Russian armies occupying all Eastern Europe save Czechoslovakia. Still, it was a convenient statement of American and British hopes. Years later, in 1953, when the United States Congress had a Republican majority and there was talk of abrogating the Yalta agreements, it was tardily realized that the Yalta Declaration was the only promise of Russia's good intentions the Western powers possessed, and nothing more was heard of abrogating it. Short of an American military occupation of Eastern Europe, which would have forced a war with the Russians, all the United States and Britain could do at Yalta was bind the Soviets to good behavior through a verbal promise, and this they did.

The Big Three set the date, April 25, 1945, for a conference to open in San Francisco to draw up a constitution for the United Nations Organization. At Yalta the Soviets obtained a promise of three seats in the future United Nations Assembly, to offset the seats to be given to members of the British Commonwealth. The United States also was to have three Assembly seats, but when word of this Yalta arrangement got out, a few weeks before the conference at San Francisco began, the American representatives hastily gave up their claim. It had been directed against America's closest ally, and its secrecy made it doubly embarrassing.

The price of Russian entry into the Far Eastern war had been talked about ever since the autumn of 1943, and the Yalta Conference made Russia's demands into a formal agreement. The Soviets wished to return the territorial situation in the Far East to where it had been before the Russo-Japanese War of 1904–1905, which meant that Russia obtained railroad concessions in Manchuria and use of Port Arthur as a naval base. The huge Japanese-developed port of Dairen was to be internationalized (that is, subject to Russian wishes). The Soviets obtained the southern half of Sakhalin Island and also the Kurile Islands, the chain that falls to the south of the Kamchatka peninsula, an island group not previously in Russian possession. In exchange for these territories the Soviets promised to enter the Far Eastern war two or three months after the end of the conflict in Europe, and as it turned out they entered three months to the day.

If the Western Allies had foreseen the quick end of the European and Asian wars, they perhaps would not have brought the Soviets into the Far Eastern conflict. From hindsight this result of the Yalta Conference now stands out as a debatable decision. The European war wound up rapidly after Yalta. On March 7 at Remagen the Americans seized a railroad bridge over the Rhine that the Germans had failed to destroy, and an entire army corps got across before the span collapsed. By mid-April the Ruhr had been encircled, bringing the capture of 1,325,000 German troops. The British took Bremen and Hamburg. Two American armies were racing into Czechoslovakia. East and west, 10 million men were converging on Nazi Germany, and the odds for Hitler were hopeless. On April 11, American units reached the Elbe, about fifty miles from Berlin, and on April 25, American and Russian troops shook hands at Torgau, seventy-five miles south of Germany's capital. At that moment the Americans

The Conquest of Germany, 1945

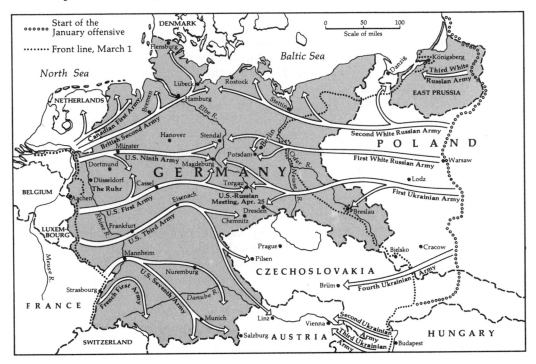

had only about 50,000 troops available to send toward Berlin, but their dispatch was quite unnecessary, for the Russians had moved 1,250,000 men within reach of Berlin and by the end of April this force had fought its way into the city. With shells falling on the Reich chancellery, Hitler on April 30 committed suicide in his bunker headquarters. The city surrendered on May 2. German resistance in Italy ceased on May 5. On May 7, two German generals appeared at Anglo-American headquarters in Reims to sign an armistice, which went into effect at midnight, May 8–9.

Japanese resistance was not to be what the leaders of the United States and Britain had envisioned in February 1945, and Russian help in the defeat of Japan proved unnecessary. The withdrawal of Japanese forces from Guadalcanal in the Solomon Islands in January and February 1943 marked a turning point of the Pacific war. From that date onward the Japanese faced ever larger American forces, and one by one the strong points protecting the Japanese islands were reduced as United States troops and planes and naval power moved north from Australia and west from Pearl Harbor. The Americans took the Gilbert and Marshall Islands in 1943 in a series of bloody marine encounters epitomized by the capture of Tarawa in the Gilberts in November. Thereafter the Pacific war moved into its final battles and the defeat of Japan.

In the reconquering of the Pacific the most important single event was the taking of the Mariana Islands—Saipan, Guam, and Tinian being the largest of the Marianas—in the summer of 1944. Saipan, only fifteen hundred miles to the south of Tokyo, at once became a base for the large new American bombers, the B-29's. The Japanese realized what the fall of Saipan meant, and the Cabinet of Premier Tojo collapsed and was replaced by a Cabinet headed by General Kuniaki Koiso.

In a conference at Pearl Harbor the leading American commanders in the Pacific, MacArthur and Admiral Chester C. Nimitz, argued before President Roosevelt the merits of moving next upon Formosa or the Philippines. Nimitz, fresh from observing the successes of the navy's new carrier and marine attacks on Japanese-held islands, believed that the Philippines could be bypassed and that the navy should take American power directly to Formosa and thence to the home islands. The American navy had just won the Battle of the Philippine Sea of June 19 and 20, 1944, when Japanese naval forces had sortied in an effort to prevent the capture of the Marianas. This engagement between carrier-based aircraft—the standard fleet engagement of the Pacific theater—had begun with the Great Marianas Turkey Shoot of June 19 in which Japanese planes, outmaneuvered by new American aircraft, fell like turkeys, the Americans shooting down 315 with loss of only 23. The Japanese navy also lost three carriers.

After listening to the arguments of the two commanders, Roosevelt decided in favor of MacArthur, who displayed an understandable fondness for retaking the Philippines; upon leaving the islands in the desperate spring of 1942 he had said, "I shall return." The Philippines were secured in the next few months. MacArthur's forces first attacked Leyte, the large southern island, and moved on to Mindanao and Manila, taking the capital in February 1945 after bitter Japanese resistance that left the city a shambles.

In the course of the fighting for the Philippines the Japanese navy came out in strength, for the last time, in the Battle of Leyte Gulf, losing three battleships, four carriers, and ten cruisers. Control of the entire Pacific rested indisputably with the serried ranks of United States carriers and their vast flotillas of supporting vessels, a fleet the like of which had never been seen before, vessels mostly constructed after the outbreak of the war with Japan.

By the beginning of the summer of 1945, American leaders were feeling that the Soviets might not be necessary for victory. The United States air force was laying waste vast sections of Japanese cities and was bombing Tokyo according to the advice of fire insurance tables obtained from the Library of Congress, dropping bombs on sections of Tokyo with the highest insurance rates and hence with the most combustible buildings. The American navy was so hard pressed for targets that its submarines were moving unopposed in the shallows between the home islands, sinking ferry boats and almost anything else that floated. United States battleships were sailing within sight of the home islands and sending salvos of high-explosive shells into industrial and other targets. General Koiso had resigned as Premier in April, upon the fall of Okinawa, and the new Premier, Baron Kantaro Suzuki, was permitting some discussion of peace terms by Japanese envoys in neutral capitals of Europe, in Switzerland and Sweden.

Still, no one could be sure what would move the Japanese government to surrender. The desperateness of resistance on the tiny island of Iwo Jima, two and one-half miles wide by four and two-thirds miles long (invaded in February 1945 with loss of 4,189 Americans killed, 21,000 Japanese deaths), and on Okinawa (taken in April, with 11,260 Americans killed, 110,000 Japanese deaths) seemed to say that the Japanese would fight to the end, that even after United States forces got to the home islands there would be massive resistance by troops and populace alike. The Japanese had used *kamikaze*—suicide plane—tactics at Okinawa, where attacks sank 38 American ships and damaged 368 others. In view of such experiences the American chiefs of staff had asked President Roosevelt at Yalta to obtain Russian help.

The Japanese gave every evidence of fighting to the end. Records that became available to the Americans after the war showed that the Tokyo government in July 1945 was beginning to think about surrender, but United States military leaders could not have counted on such a result. Experience in World War I and during the American Civil War taught that the way to defeat an enemy was not to negotiate a surrender but to force it. The American military in the early

Flame-tipped rockets from a United States navy landing ship (behind the ship in the fore-
ground) streak toward Japanese installations
on Okinawa—a prelude to a campaign against tenacious defenders.

summer of 1945 remembered poignantly the Battle of the Bulge and
could not be sure what surprises the Japanese might have in store.
The United States chiefs of staff reasoned that 2.5 million troops
were on the home islands. They went ahead with their plan to seize
the Japanese northern islands, beginning on November 1, with a
final attack on Honshu, the island containing Tokyo, in March
1946. Intelligence reports indicated that Japanese troops in Manchuria, numbering more than a million, would have to be contained by a Russian invasion from Siberia, or the American flank

would be exposed in any attack on the home islands. Moreover, arrangements had been made at Yalta to bring in the Russians, and the Soviets were shifting troops according to their promise.

In late July 1945, the third and as it turned out the last Big Three meeting (with a new American President, Harry S. Truman, and a new British Prime Minister, Clement Attlee, who replaced Churchill in the middle of the conference) assembled at Potsdam, near the rubble of wartime Berlin, and contemplated the occupation of Germany and warned of the swift destruction of Japan. The Allies were then in their German zones, and the Potsdam Conference established machinery by which they could coordinate their German policies. It arranged for periodic meetings of the Allied foreign ministers, including a representative of the newly constituted French government, to take up problems of European and world peace. For the Far East there could be no public announcement from Russia during the Potsdam Conference, for the Soviets were still at peace with Japan even though they had denounced the nonaggression treaty of 1941. Hence the Russians did not sign the Potsdam Declaration of July 26, 1945, which called on Japan to surrender and in a veiled way threatened a dire penalty ("prompt and utter destruction") if the Japanese turned down the declaration.

Behind the Potsdam Declaration was the atomic bomb. A test device had been exploded on July 16, the day before the conference opened. All through the war, American scientists had been working feverishly to make an atomic bomb, and with expenditure of about $2 billion the quest at last proved successful. At the outset it was necessary to draw upon the experiments of two German scientists who in their Berlin laboratory in 1938 had managed to split uranium atoms. This feat, for which the Germans later received the Nobel Prize, was but a beginning for scientists on the bomb project. They had to produce a nuclear chain reaction, which they achieved on December 2, 1942. The task thereafter became one of obtaining "bomb stuff," uranium in the proper form (U-235) or plutonium. For this purpose the so-called Manhattan Project was created, under the direction of Brigadier General Leslie R. Groves, with the scientific assistance of a galaxy of American, British, Canadian, and émigré scientists including several Nobel laureates. United States army engineers constructed two huge bomb-stuff plants at Oak Ridge, Tennessee (U-235), and Hanford, Washington. In the end, both plants produced enough material for bombs. A laboratory in Los Alamos, New Mexico, under the direction of J. Robert Oppenheimer designed

Two hours after the atomic blast in Hiroshima, this street two miles from ground zero was filled with the dead and dying. One wonders whether the living among this human flotsam survived a day, two, three. The nameless photographer died after he took this photograph.

bombs with both elements. When the test device (known because of its shape as the Fat Man) exploded in spectacular fashion at the Alamogordo proving grounds in New Mexico, it used plutonium, as did the Nagasaki bomb. The Hiroshima bomb (the Thin Man) employed U-235, and scientists were so certain it would go off that they did not bother to test it.

The events of early August 1945 are easy to describe but analyzing their relative importance is not so easy. What events and factors persuaded the Japanese government to end the fighting? On August 6 the American air force dropped the uranium bomb on Hiroshima, causing enormous destruction and killing about 60,000 Japanese. On August 8, Russian troops crossed the Siberian border and attacked the Japanese army in Manchuria. On August 9 came the plutonium bombing of Nagasaki, causing about 40,000 more deaths. On August 10 the Japanese Cabinet decided to surrender and did so on August 14. A formal surrender ceremony took place some weeks later, on September 2, 1945, in Tokyo Bay aboard the battleship *Missouri.*

What was the relation of event to event? It is impossible to be sure; at least no historian has managed to set out a case in a believable manner. It is clear that Russian entry into the war on August 8 did not change the military picture in two days. Even after the surrender on August 14, Japanese troops in Manchuria were fighting the Russians. It must have been the shock effect of Russian entry that influenced—if it did—the Tokyo decision. As for the atomic bombs, detailed news of Hiroshima arrived in Tokyo at about the same time as word of Nagasaki. The presumption must be that the crush of events brought surrender. Which events? When one adds weight upon weight, which weight crushes the object underneath?

Some later speculations are worth mentioning, though they can be nothing more than speculations. Would a single atomic bomb, not two, have brought the same result? Could there have been a warning, perhaps a bomb detonated over Tokyo Bay early in the evening when its effect would have been the most dramatic? Could the United States air force with conventional bombing, or the navy with a blockade, have forced the Japanese, admittedly after the elapse of some time, to surrender?

Whether the United States should have used atomic bombs on Japan is essentially a postwar question. During the war a psychology prevailed in both Pacific and European theaters that whatever means were necessary for defeat of the Japanese and German foes should be used. The discovery of the Nazi death camps containing their pitiful human remnants of the 6 million Jews and perhaps 2 million more prisoners and other *Untermenschen* killed by the Germans had mingled with memory of the Bataan death march and other Japanese inhumanities, so that it was easy to consider dropping atomic bombs. Their explosive power was less lethal than conventional air attacks by a thousand or more bombers. Eighty-three thousand Japanese had died in one night during the fire-bombing of Tokyo in March 1945. An attack on Dresden early in 1945 had cost

135,000 lives. Nor could any contrary view be aired, because the secrecy of the Manhattan Project made public discussion impossible. Two government committees, the so-called Interim Committee composed of high officials and a Scientific Panel of five atomic physicists, had considered the issue, and both committees recommended dropping the bomb. The very high, unexpectedly high, yield of the Alamogordo test device (most scientists had anticipated the TNT equivalent of several hundred tons, not twenty thousand) made a reconsideration of the use of the bomb highly advisable, but by that time the leading officials of the Truman administration were in Germany and no reconsideration was attempted.

As for the contention, heard twenty years after the end of the war, that the American government had undertaken the atomic bombing not to end the war so much as to impress the Russians with American power, the contention that the atomic bombings were a power-political move in the cold war, suffice it to say that the American government knew the Russians were going to enter the Far Eastern war within a week or two of the time they actually did enter and that the timing of the dropping of the bombs had been left to the Pacific air force commanders, Generals Carl Spaatz and Curtis E. LeMay. The bombings came off according to their arrangements, not those of the civil government — the leaders of which were in mid-Atlantic, returning from the Potsdam Conference. Moreover, no American official during this period made even an oblique effort to threaten the Russians with the nation's new atomic weapons.

The war ended in misery as it had begun, but at least with the preservation of American and British democratic traditions instead of the inhumanity of the Japanese and especially the Germans. The cost to the American government and people was 322,188 Americans killed and hundreds of billions of dollars expended (the cost continues to the present in veterans' benefits and hence is incalculable). The war's end found the Soviet government in possession of Europe to the very center of Germany, but the English and Americans could have done nothing to change that.

In retrospect one has the uneasy feeling that in the Pacific theater the Americans might have considered the possibility of occupying China before going into Japan. With the nuclear and missile power of Communist China looming as the most important unsettling aspect of the second half of the twentieth century, one wonders what might have happened on the mainland if the Americans had gone into China as the Western Allies had gone into France in 1944–1945.

In the latter case it was possible to organize a pro-Western government under the protective power of Anglo-American occupying troops. Could the same result have been secured through occupation of China during the same years? Would the fading power of Chiang Kai-shek have given way to a more representative group of the Chinese middle, leaders with democratic intentions, instead of what befell Chinese politics in the years after 1945 — the polarization of politics into the reactionary regime of Chiang and the revolutionary regime of Mao Tse-tung? The answer will never be known. Plans to occupy China as a step in the strategy of defeating Japan were scrapped when the military discovered in 1943 and 1944 that the weapons and manpower were becoming available for island-hopping of a sort unimaginable in 1941 and 1942, and the occupation of China was unnecessary. A major political possibility was lost in American technological progress. Yet one must add hurriedly that the postwar military development of Communist China exceeded the wildest dreams of American leaders during World War II. China had been in economic and political disarray for a century and more, and the expectation was for more of the same.

In final retrospect, looking behind the events and possibilities of World War II, the historian must return his gaze to the war of 1914–1918, the event that opened the historical twentieth century. If the government and people of the United States in the years after 1918 could have been led to understand what another world war would mean for their security, if the world war of 1914–1918 had been followed not merely by an ardent but by an intelligent American effort to maintain peace by preventing the revival of German power, the history of the recent past and of our own time might have unfolded in a vastly different way.

SUGGESTED READINGS

A comprehensive account of American diplomacy between the wars appears in Selig Adler's *The Uncertain Giant: 1921–1941* (1965), a volume in the American Diplomatic History series; and for coverage of a somewhat smaller period see L. Ethan Ellis, *Republican Foreign Policy: 1921–1933* (1968). Akira Iriye, *After Imperialism: The Search for a New Order in the Far East, 1921–1931* (1965), is best for its special subject. Merlo J. Pusey's Pulitzer-prize-winning *Charles Evans Hughes* (2 vols., 1951) is probably definitive, although adulatory and based too much on the papers of Hughes. For the leading senator of the time, the Lion of Idaho, there is Marian C. McKenna, *Borah* (1961). Thomas H. Buckley analyzed *The United States and the Washington Confer-*

ence (1970). See also J. Chalmers Vinson, *The Parchment Peace* (1956). Three books by Robert H. Ferrell bear on this essay: *Frank B. Kellogg and Henry L. Stimson* (1962), vol. 11 in The American Secretaries of State and Their Diplomacy series; *Peace in Their Time* (1952), on the Kellogg-Briand Pact; and *American Diplomacy in the Great Depression: Hoover-Stimson Foreign Policy, 1929–1933* (1957). Stimson's *On Active Service in Peace and War* (1948), done with the collaboration of McGeorge Bundy, is an excellent memoir. It can be supplemented by Elting E. Morison, *Turmoil and Tradition: A Study of the Life and Times of Henry L. Stimson* (1960); and Richard N. Current, *Secretary Stimson: A Study in Statecraft* (1954). *The Memoirs of Herbert Hoover: The Cabinet and the Presidency, 1920–1933* (1952) relates the President's concern for foreign policy. Raymond G. O'Connor, *Perilous Equilibrium: The United States and the London Naval Conference of 1930* (1962) states its theme in its title.

Diplomacy during the 1930's is in John E. Wiltz's *From Isolation to War: 1931–1941* (1968). The secretary of state during most of the period, Cordell Hull, published excruciatingly dull memoirs (2 vols., 1948), although some light gleams through the pages, as when the secretary tells readers about the virtues of croquet. Much easier to read is Julius W. Pratt's authoritative *Cordell Hull* (2 vols., 1964), vols. 12 and 13 in the American Secretaries series. The diplomacy of the President of the era is in Dexter Perkins' *The New Age of Franklin Roosevelt* (1956), a volume in the Chicago History of American Civilization series. Multivolume biographies are in progress, by Frank Freidel (1952–) and Arthur M. Schlesinger, Jr. (1957–). James M. Burns has finished his account: *Roosevelt: The Lion and the Fox* (1956); and *Roosevelt: Soldier of Freedom* (1970), a Pulitzer prize winner. Roosevelt sought to better American-Russian relations, and Beatrice Farnsworth's *William C. Bullitt and the Soviet Union* (1967) describes recognition and Bullitt's subsequent two years as ambassador to the U.S.S.R. An important part of Rooseveltian foreign policy appears in Lloyd C. Gardner, *Economic Aspects of New Deal Diplomacy* (1964). The title of Arnold Offner's *American Appeasement* (1969) epitomizes much of the European diplomacy of FDR's first years in office. John E. Wiltz, *In Search of Peace: The Senate Munitions Inquiry, 1934–1936* (1963), and Richard P. Traina, *American Diplomacy and the Spanish Civil War* (1968) are best for their subjects. See also Robert Dallek, *Democrat and Diplomat: The Life of William E. Dodd* (1968), American ambassador to Berlin in the mid-1930's.

Entrance into war, and the fighting of 1941–1945, are vastly complex subjects. For the former see William L. Langer and S. Everett Gleason, *The Challenge to Isolation: 1937–1940* (1952) and *The Undeclared War: 1940–1941* (1953). Theodore A. Wilson looks at the 1941 Atlantic Charter Conference in *The First Summit* (1969). Far Eastern affairs are in Dorothy Borg, *The United States and the Far Eastern Crisis of 1933–1938* (1964); Waldo H. Heinrichs, *American Ambassador: Joseph C. Grew . . .* (1966); Samuel Eliot Morison, *The Rising Sun in the Pacific: 1931–April 1942* (1948), a volume in Morison's History of United States Naval Operations in World War II; and Robert J. C. Butow, *Tojo and the Coming of the War* (1961). Pearl Harbor still seems a tragically unnecessary catastrophe: see Walter Lord, *Day of Infamy* (1957), one of the books of a genre popular in the 1960's, about "the day when . . ."; and Charles A. Beard, *President Roosevelt and the Coming of the War, 1941* (1948), concerning the "back door" to American entrance into World War II. For the era of participation there is Gaddis Smith, *American Diplomacy during the Second World War: 1941–1945* (1965); A. Russell Buchanan, *The United States and World War II* (2 vols., 1964), volumes in the New American Nation series; Herbert Feis' five-volume history of American diplomacy during World War II; and the grandest of the participants' accounts, Winston Churchill's *The Second World War* (6 vols., 1948–1953). An interesting diplomatic principle is traced in Raymond G. O'Connor, *Diplomacy for Victory: FDR and Unconditional Surrender* (1971). The war's most important diplomatic conference inspired John L. Snell, ed., *The Meaning of Yalta* (1956), and Diane Shaver Clemens, *Yalta* (1970). China's problems pass in review in Tang Tsou, *America's Failure in China: 1941–1950* (1963), and in Barbara W. Tuchman's Pulitzer volume, *Stilwell and the American Experience in China* (1971). Japan's difficulties stand out in John Toland's *The Rising Sun* (1970). Robert J. C. Butow authoritatively investigates *Japan's Decision to Surrender* (1954). For the most important scientific development of the war see Richard G. Hewlett and Oscar E. Anderson, Jr., *The New World: 1939–1946* (1962), the first volume of the official History of the United States Atomic Energy Commission.

Significant Statistics

	1900	1920	1945
Foreign trade (millions of dollars)			
Exports			
Americas	227	2,553	**2,564**
Europe	1,040	4,466	**5,515**
Asia	68	872	**849**
Australia and Oceania	41	172	**354**
Africa	19	166	**524**
Total	1,499	8,664	**10,097**
Percentage of GNP	8.6	9.3	**4.9**
Imports			
Americas	224	2,424	**2,874**
Europe	441	1,228	**409**
Asia	146	1,397	**407**
Australia and Oceania	29	80	**171**
Africa	11	150	**297**
Total	930	5,784	**4,280**
Percentage of GNP	5.3	5.9	**1.9**
Balance	+570	+2,880	**+5,816**
Investment (billions of dollars)			
U.S. investments abroad	0.7[a]	7.0[b]	**16.8**
Foreign investments in the U.S.	3.4[a]	3.3[b]	**17.6**
Net investment position	2.7[a]	+3.7[b]	**−0.8**
Department of State budget (millions of dollars)	3.3	13.5	**50.1**
Diplomatic missions	42	47	**56**
Alliances in force	0	0	**0**
Overseas travel (travelers in thousands)	120	157	**175**

Sources: *Statistical Abstract of the United States; Historical Statistics of the United States, Colonial Times to 1957;* and *Treaties and Other International Agreements of the United States of America, 1776–1949.*
[a] Data for 1897.
[b] Data for 1919.

6

The Imperial Republic

America in World Politics, 1945 to the Present

DAVID F. TRASK

Very shortly after World War II came to its end, the United States and the Soviet Union entered the cold war. This confrontation deeply affected the entire world because, between them, the two countries dominated international politics. All the other great powers had either been weakened or destroyed during the Armageddon just past. The onset of the cold war revived conflicts that had existed ever since the Bolshevik Revolution of 1917. Americans presented themselves to the world as prime exemplars of peaceful representative government and of dynamic material growth under the aegis of private enterprise. Russian leaders insisted that Yankee democracy really meant domination by great corporations and that capitalism, far from benefiting mankind, actually allowed the imperialists to

oppress the weak at home and abroad. The Soviet Union claimed leadership of a worldwide socialist movement designed to frustrate the exploitative designs of the bourgeois nations, but American critics, for their part, alleged that Russian concern for the downtrodden disguised an international conspiracy to dominate the world. However exaggerated, these distinctions enhanced political tensions, so that deep emotion permeated power struggles after 1945.

American historians soon began to explain the causes of the cold war. The first wave of scholars, writing in the 1950's, blamed its onset on the Soviet Union, holding that Communist expansionism in Europe had forced the United States to defend the "free world." Somewhat later, during the 1960's, a small group of "revisionist" scholars, many of them associated with the New Left, argued that the United States had brought on the cold war by launching a counterrevolutionary campaign to choke off the Soviet experiment and other social revolutions throughout the world. These conflicting views have something in common. Both assume a plot on the part of one power to dominate the world and a natural defensive reaction by the other power leading to a great political struggle. Nowadays most historians offer more complicated analyses, interesting themselves less in assessing blame than in understanding more clearly why the cold war began and how it has evolved.

The immediate origins of the cold war reside in the course and outcome of World War II. At its end two massive vacuums of power appeared in the territories where the conflict had been waged — at either extremity of the great Eurasian landmass. Germany, Italy, and France lay prostrate in Europe, and Britain was close to exhaustion. In Asia, Japanese military power had been destroyed, and Nationalist China did not control most of its territory. The cold war turned initially on conflicts over the future of the countries within these power vacuums.

At the same time, because World War II dealt a devastating blow to the imperial powers of Europe, particularly Britain and France, colonial possessions in Africa and Asia proved able to establish themselves as nations. The rise of the "third world" after 1945 may turn out to be a much more imposing historical development than the cold war itself. Given the importance of anti-colonial movements, it is not surprising that both Russia and America should have become deeply involved with them. The two rivals offered different models of economic and political development — one democratic and capitalist, the other totalitarian and socialist. For this reason the histories of the cold war and of the third world since 1945 have been so intertwined that scholars encounter difficulty trying to separate the two.

America's development of nuclear weapons greatly complicated world politics and threatened the very existence of mankind. When an American aircraft dropped what now would be considered a small atomic bomb on Hiroshima in August 1945, much of the city simply dissolved, killing tens of thousands of people and condemning many others to eventual death from radiation. Human beings everywhere recognized that all-out warfare no longer constituted a rational means of coping with international dilemmas, if in fact it ever had. Both superpowers soon developed thermonuclear weapon systems of inconceivably destructive strength. These "nuclear deterrents," as they would be called, may perhaps have helped prevent a hot war, but no one could guarantee that they would not be used at some future point in time. This realization stimulated a continuing search for nuclear arms control and also general disarmament.

Such circumstances indicate why an account of American foreign relations after 1945 must emphasize dangerous encounters with the

One of the most important developments of the period after World War II was the rapid appearance of many unprecedented and extraordinarily complex problems, a point emphasized by this *New Yorker* cartoon.

Copyright © 1948 James Thurber. Originally printed in *The New Yorker*.

"Do you remember, Crosby, when the only thing to fear was fear itself?"

Soviet Union as well as tumultuous relations with the new nations of Asia and Africa, all under the threat of a nuclear holocaust.

Containment in Europe, 1945–1950

In April 1945, the United States launched its campaign to shape the postwar world when a conference of nations met at San Francisco to draft a charter for a global security agency—the United Nations. President Harry S. Truman's opening remarks sounded a note of high seriousness: "You . . . are to be the architects of a better world. In your hands rests our future." Decisions made in San Francisco would reveal whether "suffering humanity is to achieve a just and lasting peace." To fulfill this charge the American delegation proposed a system of collective security, an approach intended to stabilize world politics and foster international progress. Hopeful of creating an "open world" devoid of imperial domains and huge military organizations, the United States helped form many institutions to accomplish the goals of the security organization. To protect against threats to peace, the conference founded a Security Council composed of five permanent members—the United States, the Soviet Union, Great Britain, France, and China—and four temporary members elected for terms of one year. Permanent members received the right of veto on substantive issues, establishing the requirement of unanimity to reach decisions. A second central institution, the General Assembly, represented all member nations, each with one vote. Designed to encourage all manner of activity that would foster international reconstruction and development, it provided a forum for debate on important questions and a center to coordinate commissions, councils, and committees such as the Economic and Social Council and the Food and Agriculture Organization, some of them carried over from the defunct League of Nations. Although difficulties arose during the negotiations in San Francisco, largely over Russian actions in Eastern Europe and American aims in Latin America, they were resolved, and both superpowers along with their allies soon ratified the United Nations Charter. Having set up the United Nations, Americans hoped to resume "business as usual," leaving to the new organization the task of rehabilitating the world and managing a peaceful era of prosperity.

The United States had emerged from the war as the strongest political and economic power in the world and therefore had a vested

The United Nations building looks out over the East River in New York City. Erected on land
donated by the Rockefellers, this building serves as the permanent home
of the United Nations secretariat. Some critics argue that the United Nations should
leave the United States for a more neutral country such as
Switzerland or that the headquarters should move from time to time.

interest in preventing great unsettling changes that might adversely
affect its power position. The traditional progressivism of the country encouraged its leaders to concern themselves with the well-being
of others. Americans were attracted to the United Nations because
it promised to inhibit conflict while at the same time managing international development along democratic and capitalist lines. Assuming as they did that victory over the Axis Powers had saved the world
for democracy and capitalism, all too many Americans failed to recognize that the collective-security blueprint might appear threatening to other nations. The people of many nations viewed stability

as a threat to their futures; they believed that democracy and capitalism American-style would perpetuate United States dominance in world politics while restraining other countries in subordinate positions and even prolonging colonialism.

The United Nations might serve American interests, but from the perspective of the Kremlin, nothing about the organization seemed to guarantee the future of the Soviet Union. Russian leaders feared that talk of "stability" represented "imperialist" efforts to undermine Soviet security. They suspected that America's purpose was to keep Moscow from assuming its proper role in world politics. At war's end Premier Stalin interested himself in efforts to consolidate the Soviet regime, rebuild the national economy, and discourage future incursions on Russian territory. If the Kremlin had in mind a "grand design" for the postwar world comparable to the American plan to foster global stability and progress through democracy and capitalism, it was its traditional sponsorship of social revolution in the domains of the bourgeois nations, but this endeavor ranked lower in priority than safeguarding the homeland.

Europe, immediately after World War II, appeared unstable; in this volatile situation each superpower accused the other of scheming to control the continent. North America in the past had become involved in European crises only when some great power—Spain, France, or Germany—threatened to conquer the western regions of Eurasia. For over 150 years Americans had benefited from a politically divided Europe—one that would not pose strategic or economic challenges to the Western Hemisphere. At the heart of the confrontation with the Soviet Union lay the nagging suspicion that Stalin might seek hegemony not only in the east but across Europe to the Atlantic. Such an empire would pose unprecedented danger to the United States. Russia had suffered untold damage from invasions out of Central Europe in 1812, 1914, and 1941. American initiatives that seemed to present a comparable strategic challenge to the Russian heartland were bound to arouse a vigorous response. Defensive considerations on both sides often proved more influential in stimulating foreign policy initiatives during the cold war than did grand designs such as the American campaign for an "open world" or Russian sponsorship of universal social revolution.

Soviet-American disputations revived in 1945–1946. American statesmen began to argue publicly that the Soviet Union was violating solemn engagements. Russian leaders insisted that their policies were corollaries of victory or were essential to national security. From such positions it was a short step to the traditional American view that freedom was indivisible — that tyranny anywhere ultimately endangered democratic societies everywhere — or to the Marxist dogma that the capitalist powers must ultimately undertake to crush the socialist nations. As early as February 1946, Stalin commented publicly on the impossibility of peaceful coexistence with the bourgeois powers, and Churchill in March made his iron curtain speech at Fulton, Missouri, bitterly denouncing Russian policies in Europe.

More than any other event a tragic struggle over Poland contributed to the outbreak of the cold war. World War II had begun when Germany invaded Poland in September 1939, and restoration of Polish sovereignty seemed especially important to the West. Poland could serve as a buffer state between Germany and Russia. After the Red Army overran Poland in 1944, the Russians gradually brought to power in Warsaw a "friendly" regime that outmaneuvered the government-in-exile based in London. The Soviet Union believed that cooperative governments along its western border constituted a vital component in its defense. No Russian could forget that this boundary had been violated twice within a generation by the German army. But to Americans, who assumed that the United Nations would guarantee all borders against future aggressors, Moscow's policy seemed unwarranted. Stalin's failure to honor a promise made at Yalta to allow "free and unfettered elections" in Poland angered the United States. In October 1945, President Truman publicly criticized Russian policy: "We believe that all peoples who are prepared for self-government should be permitted to choose their own form of government by their own freely expressed choice, without interference from any foreign source."

At the same time the superpowers engaged in another inflammatory controversy, this one over Germany. The conquered Third Reich had been temporarily partitioned into four zones of occupation. An eastern portion fell to the Russians; western Germany was divided into French, British, and American districts. Berlin, well within the Russian zone, was subject to four-power control. Moscow had secured an inter-Allied promise of massive reparations from Germany, but it had agreed to allow reasonable and joint economic reconstruction of the defeated enemy. Soon, however, arrangements for cooperative management of the German economy fell apart. Russia extracted huge quantities of materials from its zone and received shipments from the others; the Western powers subsidized recovery in their territories at great expense to themselves. In May 1946, after

"BASIS FOR AGREEMENT"

Illingworth in *The London Daily Mail*. Culver Pictures.

This cartoon, typical of many drawn shortly after World War II, shows how the danger of atomic warfare was a preeminent consideration in world politics. Here the foreign ministers of the great powers are discussing the postwar peace settlements in Paris while the fuse of an enormous atomic bomb burns toward its end. Just under the sign sits Russian Foreign Minister Vyacheslav Molotov, and to his right is Secretary of State James F. Byrnes of the United States.

the wartime allies had failed to negotiate a German peace treaty, the United States stopped transfers of reparations from its zone to Russia. During September, Secretary of State James F. Byrnes delivered a speech in Stuttgart that publicly charted a new course— one that led eventually to "two Germanys." It contemplated steps to assist western Germany, which proved largely unacceptable to Moscow, and demonstrated that the United States had no intention of abandoning Europe. "We have learned," said Byrnes, "whether we like it or not, that we live in one world, from which world we

Former British Prime Minister Winston Churchill makes his "iron curtain" address at Fulton, Missouri, on March 5, 1946. "I am convinced," he shouted, "that there is nothing they admire so much as strength and nothing for which they have less respect than for military weakness." This attitude toward the Russians became commonplace during the peak of the cold war.

cannot isolate ourselves." American leaders operated from mixed motives. They realized that Germany had to contribute to the economy of Europe. They assumed that German recovery would tend to impose restraints on Russian expansion.

Russian-American relations deteriorated further in 1946 when the United Nations failed to reach agreement on international control of atomic energy. Despite misgiving in the United States, the elder statesman Bernard Baruch presented to the United Nations a plan for transferring atomic information and control of future atomic development to a special international agency. He also proposed suspension of the great-power veto in atomic decisions. If these arrangements were made, the United States would destroy its stockpile of atomic bombs. Baruch dramatically delineated the alternatives open to the world. "We are here," he said, "to make a choice between the quick and the dead. . . . If we fail, then we have damned every man to be the slave of fear." Given the situation, the proposal was unrealistic; it quickly encountered intransigent opposition. Moscow claimed to believe that the Baruch plan would allow the United States to retain knowledge of atomic technology and hence control development of nuclear energy, circumstances that would make the Soviet Union a permanent second-class power. The Russian delegate to the United Nations offered a counterproposal that outlawed atomic weapons, retained the veto on atomic matters, and required the United States to destroy its atomic bombs. Extensive negotiations did not produce a compromise between these alternatives. Some relaxation of political tensions must usually precede arms control or measures of disarmament. In 1946 tensions were on the rise.

The United Nations provided the backdrop for another Russian-American controversy in 1946, this one over Soviet movements in the Middle East. In late 1945 Moscow supported an attempt by local Communists to subvert the northern province of Azerbaijan in Iran, adjacent to the Soviet Union. Prior to World War II the United States had shown little interest in Middle Eastern questions, but the diminution of British and French influence in the Arab world that occurred after 1939 and Russian pressure on the region forced Washington into activity. It could no longer ignore either the strategic importance of the Middle East, a crossroads of three continents, or the stores of oil located in the region. When Anglo-American support for Iran was expressed in the Security Council, Russian pressures on Azerbaijan came to nothing, but the episode showed that the United States had to develop foreign policies for many regions of the world that never before had attracted much attention.

Lesser disputes helped precipitate a decline in Russian-American relations during 1945 and 1946. The Kremlin reacted angrily when the United States, while protesting Russian takeovers in Eastern Europe, refused to allow it a major role in the occupation of Italy and Japan. Recriminations flowed from the refusal of the United States to subsidize the postwar reconstruction of Russia by extending loans, a policy that began when President Truman abruptly ended lend-lease assistance to the eastern front after V-E Day. For its part Washington became deeply concerned when the Yugoslavs and Russians lent aid and comfort to Greek guerrillas seeking to overthrow a conservative government in Athens and when Moscow applied pressure on Turkey to revise in its favor the international agreements governing passage of shipping through the straits area.

President Truman gradually became convinced that only firmness in the face of Russian initiatives would serve American interests and those of what came to be called the "free world" — that is, the non-Communist portions of the globe. (This term all too easily ignored the fact that democratic freedoms did not flourish in many places where the Kremlin exercised no influence, such as in Franco's Spain and Chiang Kai-shek's China.)

In September 1946, Secretary of Commerce Henry A. Wallace, the most prestigious of the old New Dealers remaining in government after Roosevelt's death, voiced the discontent of many liberals who opposed the drift toward a break with the Soviet Union and advocated patient conciliation. "We should recognize," he argued, "that we have no more business in the *political* affairs of Eastern Europe than Russia has in the *political* affairs of Latin America. . . . Under friendly peaceful competition the Russian world and the American world will gradually become more alike." In the stress of the occasion, Wallace cut from his prepared text the statement: "We must be certain that Russia is not carrying on territorial expansion or world domination through native communists faithfully following every twist and turn in the Moscow party line." Secretary Byrnes, then in Paris, objected strenuously. "If it is not clear in your own mind," he teletyped to Truman, "that Mr. Wallace should be asked to refrain from criticizing the foreign policy of the United States while he is a member of your Cabinet, I must ask you to accept my resignation immediately." The President brusquely discharged Wallace. "The people of the United States," the President said, "may disagree freely and publicly on any question, including that of foreign policy, but the Government of the United States must stand as a unit in its relations with the rest of the world." Wallace later

claimed that the President had gone over the speech with him page
by page prior to its delivery. W. Averell Harriman, a former ambassador to Moscow who had early advocated a "tough" reaction to
Soviet challenges, took Wallace's place in the Cabinet.

To provide a more effective military foundation for American
diplomacy, Truman in 1947 placed control of the army, navy, and
air force within a single executive department under a secretary of
defense. He created the Joint Chiefs of Staff, the National Security
Council, and the Central Intelligence Agency, all deemed necessary
to ensure coordination of the nation's military and foreign policies.
Reorganization strengthened military influence in the making of
foreign policy, although leading soldiers such as Generals George C.
Marshall and Dwight D. Eisenhower continued to champion civil
control of the military. Thereafter, Pentagon views often bulked
larger during international crises than those of the State Department.
At the same time the change established the concept that later became known as "deterrence." One of the recommendations that led
to unification of the armed forces articulated this principle succinctly: Americans must be prepared not only to defend against
attack but "through all available . . . means to forestall any such
attack. The knowledge that we are so prepared and alert will in itself
be a great influence for world peace." Growing fear of Russian motives forced the Truman administration to maintain a huge military
establishment, by far the largest in the American peacetime experience.

In early 1947 events took place that precipitated full-scale cold
war. Great Britain, traditionally the protector of the eastern Mediterranean against Russian inroads, confessed to Washington that it
could no longer continue support of Greece and Turkey and asked
the United States to assume this responsibility. Here was a truly
dramatic moment in world history. Stricken Britain proposed to
turn over the reins of empire to its former colony. President Truman
and his new secretary of state, General Marshall, decided to grant
the British request. To help overcome opposition at home, they
gained the assistance of a powerful Republican Senator, Arthur
Vandenberg of Michigan, who helped build what he, Vandenberg,
described as broad bipartisan support for the administration's foreign policies. Vandenberg advised the President to go before the
Congress to dramatize the critical state of affairs—as he put it, to
"scare hell out of the country."

Truman later recalled his thoughts as he challenged the powerful
tradition of no entangling alliances. "Inaction, withdrawal, 'Fortress

America' notions could only result in handing to the Russians vast areas of the globe now denied them," he wrote. "This was the time to align the United States of America clearly on the side, and [at] the head, of the free world." What about the isolationists? "I knew," he continued, "that George Washington's spirit would be invoked against me, and Henry Clay's, and all the other patron saints of the isolationists." He went ahead, convinced that "the policy I was about to proclaim was indeed as much required by the conditions of my day as was Washington's by the situation in his era and Monroe's doctrine by the circumstances which he then faced."

The President, on March 12, 1947, outlined to Congress a proposal that became known as the Truman Doctrine. After drawing a distinction between democracy and totalitarianism, he enunciated his principle: "It must be the policy of the United States to support free peoples who are resisting armed subjugation by armed minorities or outside pressures." After describing the consequences of failing to rescue Greece and Turkey, the President requested an appropriation of $400 million. Truman thus broke from Roosevelt's policy of "friendly persuasion." Henry Wallace could attract only slight support for his view that "a great part of our conflict with Russia is the normal conflict between two strong and sovereign nations and can be resolved in normal ways."

When Congress complied with the President's request in May, the United States committed itself to combat Communist aggression not only in Europe but everywhere else where it might occur. Very soon this stance became known as "containment." The Truman Doctrine confirmed the trend toward worldwide commitments that would characterize future American policy. The President thought himself bereft of other options. Only the United States could act to prevent what he deemed a well-organized and thoroughly cynical Russian conspiracy to obtain Europe and whatever other areas might be brought under Communist control. In this critical moment Truman bypassed the United Nations, a deed that aroused considerable criticism at the time. In doing so, the President recognized that the Security Council could act only when there was great-power unanimity. Truman wanted action, not talk.

Aid to Greece and Turkey presaged much more extensive help for friendly powers in Western Europe in order to frustrate Communist inroads. By 1947 the economies of Britain, France, Germany, and Italy had virtually collapsed. More than half of Britain's industrial plants were idle, lacking fuel to permit production. Adding to the chaos was one of the most severe winters in memory. Efforts to stimulate exports had failed, depriving Britain of capital with which to purchase foodstuffs and raw materials. Just after the war the United States had extended a loan of $3,750,000,000 to Britain, but despite the Labour government's austerity policies the island kingdom faced disaster. One observer summarized the danger in apocalyptic terms: "The biggest crash since the fall of Constantinople— the collapse of the heart of an Empire—impends." In Germany an almost unimaginable state of affairs had developed. Most of the defeated enemy's urban centers had been destroyed and along with them an imposing industrial plant. By the beginning of 1947 production amounted to only 31 percent of the levels for 1936. Cigarettes and candy bars had replaced currency as mediums of exchange. France, too, was overwhelmed, faced with the task of rebuilding its shattered industries and subsidizing a growing colonial war in Indochina to reestablish its prewar ascendancy in that troubled region. The historian Robert R. Palmer viewed Europe in 1947 as "A kind of huge continental city, cut off from the trading area with which it had exchanged . . . a former world capital in danger of becoming a slum."

To be sure, the United States had anticipated postwar economic problems, remembering the severe dislocations after World War I that had culminated in the Depression. Roosevelt had successfully avoided a war debt problem by adopting lend-lease. Well before the war ended, the government had helped found the International Monetary Fund to stabilize currencies and the International Bank for Reconstruction and Development to make loans. In 1945 it provided the capital for the short-lived United Nations Relief and Rehabilitation Administration (UNRRA), charged with the task of distributing foodstuffs and other emergency relief in many parts of the world. Unfortunately, neither the fund nor the bank could cope with the unprecedented costs of recovery in Europe, and the Congress ended contributions to UNRRA in 1947 because of widespread belief that Communists in Eastern Europe and elsewhere benefited from it.

In June 1947, the United States took action. Convinced like Woodrow Wilson before him that anti-democratic regimes grew principally "in the evil soil of poverty and strife," President Truman authorized a massive program of economic assistance that became known as the Marshall Plan. Secretary of State Marshall gave a commencement address at Harvard University in which he announced that the United States would supply struggling European nations with capital to bring about a thorough reconstruction of their econ-

Foreign Assistance, 1946-1954

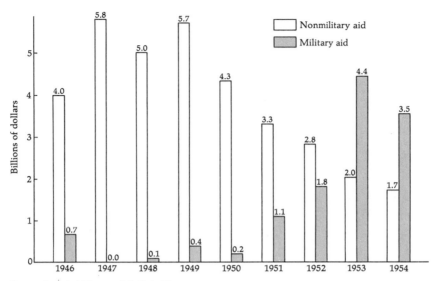

Source: *Statistical Abstract of the United States.*

omies. He asked, however, that interested countries prepare a proposal, after which Congress would be asked to make the necessary appropriation: "It would be neither fitting nor efficacious for this Government to undertake to draw up unilaterally a program designed to place Europe on its feet economically. This is the business of Europe. The initiative . . . must come from Europe." The offer encompassed the iron curtain countries as well as America's associates, but Marshall did not believe that the Russians would take part, and he was soon proved correct. After energetic consultations, a Committee on European Economic Cooperation organized in Europe presented a request for $22.4 billion in support funds. Truman scaled down this figure to $17 billion and presented the proposal to Congress in December 1947. A long delay ensued, despite the dedicated support of Senator Vandenberg and other internationalists in the Republican Party. From the political left, opponents such as Henry Wallace called it a Martial Plan that would sharpen international antagonisms, while conservative critics like Senator Robert A. Taft of Ohio maintained that the Marshall "give-away program" would bankrupt America. Meanwhile, the situation in Europe continued to deteriorate. Britain and the Continent suffered through another particularly cold winter; hungry children and disillusioned adults were everywhere, begging for food. Strong Communist parties in France and Italy seemed on the verge of sweeping electoral triumphs.

It took a dramatic event in Central Europe, the absorption of Czechoslovakia into the Russian satellite system, to force a congressional decision. President Eduard Benes had managed to avoid complete Russian domination by steering a middle course between the contending power blocs. During February 1948, the Kremlin, reacting against the American economic proposals, helped the local Communist leader, Klement Gottwald, to seize power from Benes. In March, the pro-Western foreign minister Jan Masaryk supposedly committed suicide by leaping out of a window in a tall building. Many people believed he had been pushed. This tragic event aroused a great wave of sympathy throughout the non-Communist world, for the victim was the son of the revered Thomas Masaryk, founder of modern Czech democracy. Convinced that the coup foreshadowed similar deeds elsewhere, Congress finally passed the Economic Cooperation Act in early April.

The most imposing program of international assistance ever undertaken, the Marshall Plan proved remarkably successful. Massive infusions of capital rapidly restored the European economy. Some $13.3 billion was ultimately invested. By 1951 industrial production in the Marshall Plan countries had achieved levels about 40 percent higher than before the war, and agricultural output had surpassed prewar standards by about 10 percent. Washington's practice of enlightened self-interest brought striking political and humanitarian benefits. Moscow had to be content with consolidating its position in the satellite countries rather than gaining control to the west of the iron curtain. The economic basis for an effective challenge to Russian pretensions in Western Europe had been put together, and at no dangerous cost to the United States, which experienced unprecedented prosperity at the same time. Those who had feared bankruptcy failed to take into account the stimulus to investment, production, and employment at home that stemmed from the aid program.

As the Marshall Plan began to take effect, a dangerous international crisis materialized over Germany and led eventually to the Berlin blockade of 1948–1949. Beginning in April 1948, Red Army forces sealed off highways leading to West Berlin, which lay 110 miles within the Soviet zone of occupation. As it happened, the Western powers had neglected to write clear arrangements for land access to Berlin into the four-power occupation agreement of 1945. On June 24 the Russians turned this harassment into a full-fledged confrontation by halting all surface transportation into West Berlin for an indefinite time, an act that deprived some 2.5 million people of food, fuel, and other necessities.

This dramatic initiative followed Anglo-American efforts to stimulate the economy of the Western zones and to create West Germany. After fusing the American, British, and French areas into a complex known as "Trizonia," the Western powers planned to initiate a currency reform there that would include West Berlin, in order to curb the runaway inflation that had inhibited recovery. This policy would threaten the less developed economy of the Soviet zone. The short-range goal of halting inflation reflected hopes of setting up an independent and anti-Communist German government. History had demonstrated that a strong German state in the heart of Europe constituted an imposing bulwark against Russian expansion. In early June 1948, Britain, the United States, and an unenthusiastic France agreed to establish West Germany and to introduce a new currency. The ensuing Berlin blockade represented Russia's response to these actions.

The blockade was maintained for about a year, but it failed to accomplish its purposes, thanks to the tenacity of the West Berliners and the improvisations of General Lucius D. Clay, the American commander in Germany. Clay conceived a massive airlift into West Berlin that supplied the city throughout the blockade. Operation Vittles provided 2.3 million tons of support. Month after month, despite all manner of harassment, American pilots flew their over-worked aircraft into crowded Tempelhof Airport, Gatow in the British sector, and a new field in the French sector, Tigel, while courageous Berliners remained steadfast under almost insupportable pressure. The airlift finally forced the Russians to relax the blockade; it was lifted in May 1949 in return for a promise to discuss a definitive settlement. The Soviet Union did not reimpose the blockade, even though a conference of foreign ministers failed to reach agreement. On May 23, 1949, the West German Federal Republic came into existence, and a few months later Moscow set up the rival German Democratic Republic.

Despite the desire of the German people on both sides of the iron curtain to live under one government, the two Germanys became an

An American transport aircraft makes its approach to a landing at Tempelhof airport in West Berlin, bringing in supplies as part of "Operation Vittles." This remarkable operation demonstrated the willingness of the United States to defend Western Europe against possible Russian aggression.

accomplished fact only four years after the conclusion of World War II. Ironically, the split contributed to the political restabilization of Europe, for it divided Germany and limited its ability to commit future acts of aggression. Although rearmament in both of the new countries later caused tension, the division of Germany lessened the probability of any attack on the Soviet Union and its satellites and precluded undue German influence in European politics, a development welcomed by most other nations.

The Marshall Plan, together with the Korean War boom, led to economic recovery in Europe, but it did not provide an effective military shield against Russian aggression. The North Atlantic Treaty Organization (NATO) sought to accomplish this purpose. Finally jettisoning the historic policy of "no entangling alliances," the United States, along with eleven other nations (Britain, France, Canada, Italy, the Benelux countries, Ireland, Denmark, Norway, and Portugal), on April 4, 1949, adhered to a multilateral treaty that set up NATO. Accepting the principle that an attack against "one or more of the member nations shall be considered an attack against

Secretary of State Dean G. Acheson signs the North Atlantic Treaty in Washington on April 4, 1949, while President Truman looks on with Vice-President Alben Barkley. A powerful supporter of containment, Acheson fully accepted the principle that the free world must solidify its defenses as a basis for negotiations with the Soviet Union.

them all," the United States agreed to aid any signatory power that came under attack by an aggressor. Obviously aimed at the Soviet Union and its satellites, supposedly linked together into a world-wide conspiracy, this collective-defense arrangement became the most important link in a chain of agreements that eventually stretched around the world. Theoretically compatible with the Charter of the United Nations, which at American insistence had specifically authorized regional defense understandings in its Article 51, NATO reflected further disenchantment with the Security Council, immobilized in many important crises by Russian vetoes. After the beginning of the Korean War, General Eisenhower agreed to become the first supreme commander of NATO. Its formations eventually included about twenty-five combat divisions along with naval and air components, though these forces never reached the levels planned at the outset. The treaty helped stimulate the movement toward European unity that culminated in cooperative associations such as the European Coal and Steel Community and EURATOM, the latter a program for sharing nuclear energy. Europe's defense also required extensive financial support. The Mutual Defense Assistance Act of 1949 provided over $1.3 billion for military aid to America's allies, the beginning of grants that extended into the 1970's.

Although energetic actions by the United States and its allies prevented further Communist inroads in Western Europe, the Kremlin intensified its domination of the satellites. Poland, Bulgaria, Hungary, Czechoslovakia, and East Germany became almost completely subservient to the Soviet Union, and Rumania and Albania also felt Russian influence. The Soviet Union tied the economy of the satellites to its own domestic requirements, exploiting neighbors to hasten recovery at home as rapidly as possible. It maintained troops in sufficient force throughout Eastern Europe to preserve friendly regimes in power. An exception to the satellite pattern was Yugoslavia, which managed to develop as an independent socialist state. If President Tito was a convinced Communist who had been trained in Moscow, he was also a dedicated Yugoslav nationalist who successfully defied Stalin's attempts to dominate his country.

By 1950, after five years of intense conflict, European politics had been stabilized in many important respects, even if the outcome disappointed many. The protagonists in the postwar struggle for Europe—Russia and America—remained influential where their armies had conquered during the war years. No peace treaties had been negotiated for Germany and Austria, and the status of Berlin remained unsettled, but dangerous crises had been eased without recourse to war. Neither Russia nor America resorted to violence, both sides exercising restraint at critical moments when threats and posturing might have sparked another holocaust. While the Americans enjoyed a monopoly of atomic weapons until 1949, they proved unwilling to use them either as diplomatic counters or as military ordnance. They found themselves at a disadvantage because the Russians maintained larger conventional forces. This rough balance of military power helped preserve an uneasy peace.

Events from 1945 to 1950 in Europe encouraged a consensus on foreign policy within the United States that most American decision makers, whether Republicans or Democrats, followed for two more decades. In 1947, a distinguished member of the foreign service, George F. Kennan, provided a striking rationale for what came to be called "containment." In an article published in *Foreign Affairs* under the pseudonym "X," he analyzed Russian attitudes toward world politics. The Kremlin was convinced, he argued, that "innate antagonism" separated capitalism and socialism. Soviet leaders believed that history was on their side and that in the long run they could anticipate a decisive victory against the bourgeois democracies. Kennan concluded that "the main element of any United States policy toward the Soviet Union must be that of a long-term patient but firm and vigilant containment of Russian expansive tendencies." The Russians could be frustrated by "adroit and vigilant application of counter-force at a series of constantly shifting geographical and political points, corresponding to the shifts and maneuvers of Soviet policy." Containment would be required for a long time to come, but Kennan believed that, if the opponents of communism persevered, desirable changes within the Soviet Union would help bring about a much more stable international situation. Somewhat later, Secretary of State Dean Acheson described the new attitude pointedly: "The only way to deal with the Soviet Union, we have found from hard experience, is to create situations of strength. Wherever the Soviet detects weakness or disunity—and it is quick to detect them—it exploits them to the full." World conditions were not hopeless, but only "unity and determination on the part of the free nations" would lead to acceptable settlements.

Adoption of the containment policy had important effects on American decision-making; for better or worse, the United States had taken on political and military responsibilities as a "world policeman" far beyond any ever before contemplated by the American people. Given the presumption that the nation faced an intransigent enemy, it was difficult to place much faith in diplomatic negotiations. The concept of "innate antagonism" emphasized deterrence of the Soviet Union and minimized political discussion. For the first time in the national experience, the United States had committed itself to a huge peacetime military establishment with its accompaniments — massive military budget and unprecedented military participation in national policy. Few Americans denied the existence of a Russian threat in Europe; even fewer realized the alarms that tough talk perhaps caused in the Kremlin. Soviet leaders apparently decided that Washington intended not only to prevent Communist triumphs in Western Europe but to threaten Communist power in Eastern Europe and in the Soviet Union. America's preoccupation with "situations of strength" may have inhibited rather than encouraged peaceful negotiation. In any event, the cold war promised to endure, the protagonists in the struggle having adopted "hard lines" that stressed military power rather than diplomatic settlement.

The Korean War, 1950–1953

While the United States and the Soviet Union concentrated on Europe, a crisis gradually built up in East Asia. The defeat of Japan and China's debility left another power vacuum, which America moved quickly to fill. After Japan surrendered in 1945, General Douglas MacArthur assumed direction of the American occupation. As vigorous in his proconsular role as in his wartime leadership, the autocratic MacArthur set about to demilitarize and democratize Japan, and in these endeavors he achieved considerable success. Under his tutelage the Japanese people developed a constitution that provided for permanent disarmament and Western parliamentary government. Trade unions were founded to improve the lot of urban workers, and land reform wrought improvements in country life. Energetic activity in Japan revealed that the United States did not intend to withdraw from East Asia, as did the policy of retaining strategic islands in the Pacific seized during the war. Friendly relations with disarmed Japan became a cardinal component of the nation's Asian policy, particularly after the Chinese Communists rose to power in Peking. Japan, of course, benefited from the onset of the cold war and American patronage; it received both protection and economic assistance in good measure. As in the case of Germany, the United States recognized that vengeance was both unsatisfying and dangerous.

The Soviet Union had entered the Far Eastern war during its last days, but the United States prevented its participation in the postwar occupation of Japan, just as the Kremlin excluded Washington from Eastern Europe after 1945. On the other hand, the Russians capitalized on the Yalta pledges, which permitted them to recover the territory they had lost to Japan in 1905, including their old sphere of influence in Manchuria and Outer Mongolia. They also occupied Korea north of the thirty-eighth parallel. Honoring his engagements at Yalta, Stalin established friendly relations with Nationalist China despite a powerful Chinese Communist movement.

President Roosevelt had sponsored the Nationalist government of Chiang Kai-shek as an eventual replacement for Japan in the Asian balance of political forces, but this project never came to fruition. Chiang received extensive diplomatic and economic support from the United States, but mismanagement, corruption, and lack of popular support laid Nationalist China open to conquest by the Communist armies of Mao Tse-tung. After World War II, President Truman sent General Marshall to China to facilitate negotiations between Chiang and Mao, but his good offices came to nothing. Neither side was prepared to bargain in good faith because each believed that it could destroy the other. Marshall's failure precipitated Washington's decision to let events take their course. Nothing short of initiatives such as those being developed in Europe appeared likely to influence the outcome in China, but the Truman administration assumed, correctly, that the American people at the time were unwilling to subsidize Asian projects comparable to the Marshall Plan and NATO. Like the United States, the Soviet Union concentrated on European questions, so that Chinese realities rather than outside influences largely determined the outcome of the struggle between the Nationalists and the Communists. Acheson in 1949 summarized the denouement accurately, asserting that the Communist victory was "the product of internal Chinese forces, forces which this country tried to influence but could not."

When Mao's armies forced Chiang to flee from the mainland to Formosa in 1949, the American people reacted in shock. Chiang's fall came at about the same time that the Soviet Union exploded its first atomic device. Both events aroused anger and fear in the United States, contributing to a raging Red Scare after disclosures of espionage that had conveyed information about the atomic bomb to the Soviet Union. Trading on this concatenation of events, members of the United States Congress and other opportunists soon began to advance the spurious thesis that high government officials had betrayed the United States from within. No exponent of this view made more capital out of it than Senator Joseph R. McCarthy, Republican of Wisconsin, who gave his name to the practice of issuing unsupported allegations of disloyalty against government officials and others who supposedly had sold out China to the "Reds." He reserved his greatest scorn for the State Department, which, he stoutly maintained, was "thoroughly infested with Communists."

Meanwhile a crisis was building in the small country of Korea, traditionally an outlying part of the Chinese empire but since 1910 a Japanese colony. When World War II ended, Korea was divided at the thirty-eighth parallel into Russian and American zones of occupation, pending elections designed to choose a government for the entire country. Unhappily for the Koreans, the cold war intervened. After the United Nations failed in an attempt to arrange elections, separate regimes appeared in the two zones. Voters to the south placed the conservative Korean nationalist Syngman Rhee at the head of the Republic of Korea. As in Germany, the Soviet Union sponsored a Communist nation in North Korea—the Democratic People's Republic. Russia energetically built up North Korea, particularly its armed forces, but the United States, attempting to minimize its involvement, had withdrawn its combat troops from South Korea by late 1949. Some economic help went to Rhee, but no extensive arrangements were made to protect South Korea against possible invasion from the north. During 1949 General MacArthur specifically excluded Korea as well as Formosa from the perimeter of American defenses in East Asia; he defined the line of demarcation as running from the Philippines through the Ryukyu Islands to Japan and thence to Alaska. Secretary Acheson may have conveyed the false impression that the United States might not defend Korea when in January 1950 he reiterated MacArthur's description of the perimeter and stated that in the event of aggression in the region "initial reliance must be on the people attacked to resist it and upon the commitments of the entire civilized world under the Charter of the United Nations."

Six months later, on June 24 (local time), 1950, North Korean troops swept across the thirty-eighth parallel into South Korea. Insufficient evidence exists to explain the reasons for the invasion, but appar-

The Korean War, 1950-1953

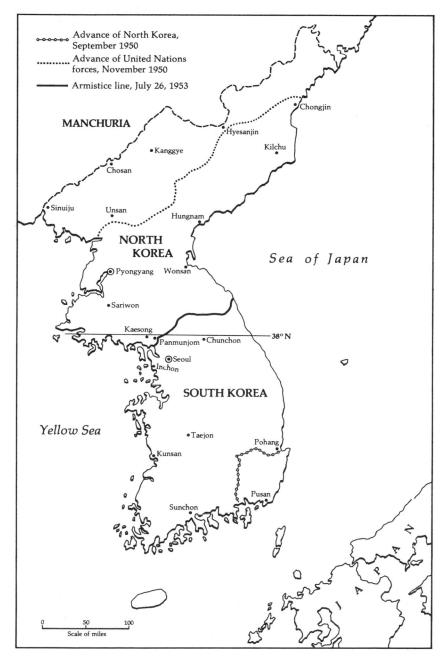

Advance of North Korea, September 1950

Advance of United Nations forces, November 1950

Armistice line, July 26, 1953

MANCHURIA

Chongjin

Hyesanjin

Kanggye

Kilchu

Chosan

Sinuiju

Unsan

Hungnam

NORTH KOREA

Sea of Japan

Pyongyang

Wonsan

Sariwon

Kaesong

Panmunjom • Chunchon

38° N

Seoul
Inchon

SOUTH KOREA

Yellow Sea

Taejon

Pohang

Kunsan

Pusan

Sunchon

JAPAN

0   50   100
Scale of miles

ently Stalin masterminded it, assuming that the United States would not use force and that the well-armed North Koreans could triumph easily. A conquest would recoup at least some of the prestige the Soviet Union had lost because of setbacks in Europe. Miscalculations of this nature, on both sides, have occurred all too frequently during the cold war.

Despite its earlier vagueness, the United States acted with remarkable energy; the Korean War became a test of containment in East Asia. President Truman arranged an emergency meeting of the Security Council, which passed a resolution branding the North Korean action "a breach of peace." (The Soviet delegate was not present to cast a veto; he was boycotting the Security Council because after Mao's victory the United States had refused to seat Communist China in place of Nationalist China.) The President instructed General MacArthur to provide naval and air support to South Korea and ordered the Seventh Fleet into the Straits of Formosa to prevent the Chinese Nationalists and Communists from attacking each other. After this decisive step, the United States sought sanction for its actions from the United Nations. When on June 27 the Security Council approved a proposal to resist the North Korean aggression, the United Nations accepted sponsorship of military operations to be conducted primarily by the armed forces of the United States and South Korea, acting as policemen for the world organization—hence the term "police action" as a description of the conflict. MacArthur soon recommended deployment of American ground, air, and naval units. The President ordered them into action on June 30.

In his memoirs Truman described his thoughts when he made the decision to resist the North Korean invasion, citing a historical analogy almost invariably invoked during other cold war crises: "In my generation, this was not the first occasion when the strong had attacked the weak. I recalled some earlier instances: Manchuria, Ethiopia, Austria. I remembered how each time that the democracies failed to act it had encouraged the aggressors to keep going ahead." What would happen if the United States failed to act? "I felt certain that if South Korea was allowed to fall Communist leaders would be emboldened to override nations closer to our own shores." Failure to control Communist aggression in Asia would lead to a third world war, just as appeasement in Europe had led to World War II. "It was also clear to me," the President wrote, "that the foundations and the principles of the United Nations were at stake unless this unprovoked attack on Korea could be stopped."

America's intervention frustrated an early North Korean success, but the conflict at first went badly for the United Nations command. By September, General MacArthur's forces had been corralled within a perimeter around Pusan on the extreme southeastern coast. Fortunately, reinforcements finally arrived, permitting a remarkable recovery. Brilliant landing operations near the thirty-eighth parallel at Inchon on the west coast of Korea in October, coordinated with a breakout at Pusan, virtually destroyed the North Korean forces. The aggressor had been contained. This victory raised difficult questions. Should the United Nations force stand at the thirty-eighth parallel? Or should it invade North Korea in order to reunify the peninsula by force of arms? Fatefully, the United States decided to support a move northward, a step that led to vast "escalation" of the war. The General Assembly of the United Nations approved a somewhat ambiguous resolution that was taken as authority to unify Korea by force. On October 11 President Truman conferred on Wake Island with his field commander. MacArthur, ignoring indications that the Chinese Communists might intervene in the struggle if his troops approached the Korean-Manchurian border, talked of victory by Thanksgiving. He told the President that the Red Army was not likely to act, but, "if the Chinese tried to get down to Pyongyang [North Korea's capital], there would be the greatest slaughter."

Despite the general's confident appraisal, his attacks to the north of the thirty-eighth parallel, some of which approached the Yalu River flowing between North Korea and the Chinese province of Manchuria, provoked an all-out intervention by Communist China. On November 26, the American Eighth Army began a precipitate retreat after it encountered a huge Chinese force. Almost immediately, MacArthur appealed for massive reinforcements, admitting that "the situation here must be viewed on the basis of an entirely new war against an entirely new power of great military strength and under entirely new conditions." By January 1951, the Eighth Army managed to establish a defensible position well below the thirty-eighth parallel.

These developments led to a serious conflict, long in the making, between General MacArthur and his superiors in Washington. The humiliated theater commander called for total victory, a stance that implied use of nuclear weapons. He also wanted to deploy Formosan forces against the Chinese Communist army. After tasting defeat, the general seemed to forget his earlier opposition to extensive land warfare in Asia. Truman and the Joint Chiefs of Staff proved much

General Douglas MacArthur, here wearing his famous campaign hat, was a master of public relations. He gained widespread popularity at home, and his prestige extended even to Japan, where he presided over the American occupation.

more cautious, favoring a limited war for limited objectives. General Omar Bradley later described MacArthur's strategy as "the wrong war, at the wrong place, at the wrong time, with the wrong enemy." This view precluded the use of nuclear weapons against the Chinese and also air raids against enemy bases on the Manchurian side of the Yalu River. MacArthur called these locations "privileged sanctuaries." When the administration refused to accept MacArthur's recommendations, the general became insubordinate. He failed to support the President's desire to seek a negotiated end of the war as the Eighth Army gradually regained control of South Korea to the thirty-eighth parallel. On April 5, 1951, a Congressman read to the House of Representatives a letter from MacArthur that bluntly criticized the policy of limited war. Truman, who had decided to act earlier, used this occasion to remove the general summarily from his duties. The discomfited commander returned to the United States amid a tumultuous public welcome. In New York huge crowds turned out for a parade in his honor.

MacArthur touched off a "great debate" when he presented his views to a joint session of Congress on April 19, 1951. Asia, he thought, should not have been placed second to Europe in American planning: "You cannot appease or otherwise surrender to Communism in Asia without simultaneously undermining our efforts to halt its advance in Europe." He had approved the decision to defend South Korea, but when the Chinese intervened he had assumed that new strategic departures were called for. Besides authority to bomb the enemy's "privileged sanctuaries" in Manchuria, he advocated more effective means of inhibiting the Chinese economy, improved naval blockade of the China coast, extensive air reconnaissance over China and Manchuria, and military operations against the Chinese mainland by Chiang Kai-shek's forces. Denying that he was a warmonger, MacArthur implied that the President's refusal to accept his counsel represented appeasement. Those who disagreed with him were "blind to history's clear lesson, for history teaches, with unmistakable emphasis, that appeasement but begets new and bloodier war." He closed his address with a sentimental reference that brought tears to the eyes of some legislators. He remembered an old barracks ballad that proclaimed: "'Old soldiers never die; they just fade away.' And like the old soldier of that ballad, I now close my military career and just fade away, an old soldier who tried to do his duty as God gave him the light to see that duty. Good-by."

Spokesmen for the administration replied vigorously before congressional investigators. General Bradley maintained that MacArthur vastly underestimated the likelihood that expanding the limited war in Korea would lead to global conflict. Local commanders often make such errors, but the Joint Chiefs of Staff had to consider each theater in relation to all others. Bradley maintained that "a policy of patience and determination without provoking world war, while we improve our military power, is one we believe we must continue to follow." Any other approach would play into the hands of the Russians, the real enemy, because it would "tie down additional forces . . . while the Soviet Union would not be obliged to put a single man into the conflict."

By the time that Congress concluded its extended discussion of the war, public opinion had rallied behind the policies of the administration. Although the American people admired MacArthur, they did not accept his call for a wider war, however much they disliked the idea of limited struggle. The necessity to avoid total victory proved a hard pill to swallow. It was difficult to endure the frustrations of not using all the power at the command of the nation, including, of course, the nuclear arsenal.

In American mythology, when conflict occurs between "good" and "evil," the solution, so often depicted in western films, is a shoot-out at high noon, producing a clear decision—for virtue. The western is a kind of American passion play, summarizing the approved national method for dealing with scoundrels. Truman's decision to pursue limited warfare precluded a triumph for virtue. It flew in the face of attitudes that found expression in General MacArthur's statement before Congress: "Once war is forced upon us, there is no other alternative than to apply every available means to bring it to a swift end. War's very object is victory—not prolonged indecision. In war, indeed, there can be no substitute for victory. . . . Why, my soldiers asked of me, surrender military advantages to an enemy in the field? I could not answer." MacArthur's emotional appeal derived largely from his portrayal of the international situation as a confrontation between good and evil, an approach that most Americans found congenial. Prudence dictated adherence to President Truman's middle course in Korea, but Washington's defense of limited warfare did not satisfy the people.

Widespread disillusion expressed itself in a burst of public antipathy toward Truman, Acheson, and other representatives of a party that had been in power since 1933. Senator McCarthy, hopeful of public support for his anti-Communist crusade, seized upon the occasion to elaborate the thesis that the Democratic Party had committed twenty years of treason. Senator Robert Taft of Ohio, widely accepted as Mr. Republican by his supporters because of his ascendancy in the conservative wing of the GOP, lent prestige to this notion when he stated, "The Korean War and the problems which

President-elect Dwight D. Eisenhower, redeeming his campaign promise to "go to Korea,"
tours the Korean front with Major General James C. Fry, commander
of the 2nd Infantry Division, in December 1952. The President succeeded in ending
the war seven months after taking office.

arise from it are the final result of the continuous sympathy toward communism which inspired American policy." Much of this partisan onslaught, of course, reflected efforts to profit during the approaching presidential election from disturbing domestic developments. Frustrations abroad combined with internal dissatisfactions to discredit the administration.

During June 1951, the United Nations indicated its willingness to accept an armistice in Korea based on a territorial division between the contending forces roughly following the thirty-eighth parallel. The Chinese had good reason to negotiate because by this time many thousands of their troops were being chewed up in General Matthew B. Ridgway's "meat-grinder offensive." China and North Korea responded favorably to the proposal, and truce talks began on July 7. Hopes for an early settlement disappeared when the conferees bogged down over several controversial questions, of which the most ticklish were procedures for prisoner exchange and Syngman Rhee's insistence on a settlement that would unify Korea under his leadership. When negotiators failed to announce an early armistice, public opposition to the conflict intensified further in the United States, particularly in response to casualty lists resulting from bloody positional warfare at so-called Heartbreak Hill and other parts of the front.

The American electorate in 1952 chose the Republican Party's candidate for the presidency, General Eisenhower, shortly after "Ike" promised to "go to Korea." He did just that, but his assessment of the situation confirmed that of the leaders he had been chosen to displace. Deciding against military action to unify the Korean peninsula under one government, Eisenhower instead hinted that the United States might use nuclear weapons if the armistice negotiations failed to produce a settlement. This tactic must have impressed the Chinese. Another event, the death of Stalin in March 1953, may have had some influence. The new Russian leaders appeared willing to lessen international tensions while making domestic adjustments required by Stalin's demise. In any event, a Korean armistice was finally agreed upon, taking effect on July 27, 1953, establishing a buffer zone close to the thirty-eighth parallel. Both sides developed fortifications adjacent to this demilitarized area, pending a permanent political settlement. No peace conference materialized, and antagonistic governments continued to function in North and South Korea. In subsequent years the United States maintained about 50,000 troops near the demilitarized zone along with important naval and air contingents, and Russia and China underwrote a buildup of North Korean forces.

The Korean War of 1950–1953 stimulated a series of initiatives that institutionalized containment in East Asia. This process began in 1951, when the United States and the other nations that had fought in the Far East during World War II, excluding the Soviet Union and India, signed a treaty with Japan. The United States also arranged a bilateral defense agreement with the former enemy. During the same period Washington made arrangements with Australia and New Zealand (ANZUS) to protect the southwestern Pacific and worked out a military accord with the Philippines. A comparable pact was negotiated with South Korea in October 1953. The chain of alliances in East Asia became complete when a bilateral treaty was negotiated in 1954 with Chiang Kai-shek's Republic of China on Formosa. These extraordinary departures, sounding as they did the death knell of "no entangling alliances," committed the United States to a political-military role in the western Pacific that was without national precedent. The conviction that expansive communism in the Orient constituted overwhelming dangers to national security had entered the American consciousness between 1950 and 1954, and this belief controlled Washington's Asian policy for many years to come.

The Korean War became a turning point in the history of American foreign relations because it raised the question of what role the nation would play outside the Atlantic region. Its settlement helped bring about a short-lived détente with the Soviet Union, but the rise of Mao's China posed the gloomy prospect of continuing conflict with another Communist opponent in world politics. Washington persisted in refusal to extend diplomatic recognition to the People's Republic of China or to support Peking's admission into the United Nations, maintaining that the Communists refused to accept obligations under the United Nations Charter appropriate to a peace-loving nation, particularly those that forbade aggression against neighbors. In regions of the Pacific where the United States had conquered during World War II, American power had been asserted. Similarly, the Soviet Union consolidated control of Asian regions turned over by the Yalta agreement. In mainland China, where neither of the superpowers had intervened, Mao's successful revolution against the Nationalists determined the future. As in Europe, political tensions caused occasional crises along the line from Japan to the Philippines, but the barrier that separated the American sphere of influence in East Asia from that of the Sino-Soviet bloc had been defined. Contentions in the region soon shifted to Southeast Asia, where anti-colonial warfare, particularly in French Indochina, threatened the status quo.

America's experience in Korea reinforced attitudes toward the cold war and the means of waging it, even if the conditions that had produced the conflict had altered. Most important, events both in Europe and in East Asia had largely eliminated the power vacuums over which Russia and America had contended for eight years. Classical containment dogma assumed a globe divided into two camps —free world and Communist bloc—but new centers of power exerted influence on international politics. The bipolarity of 1945 was a thing of the past by 1953. Innovations in policy seemed necessary in order to cope with the changing situation.

At this juncture, new leaders took office in both the Soviet Union

Principal United States Treaty Engagements Since 1945

1. Rio Treaty, September 2, 1947
   Purpose: Collective defense of the Western Hemisphere.
   Signatories:

Argentina	Dominican Republic	Nicaragua
Bolivia	Ecuador	Panama
Brazil	El Salvador	Paraguay
Chile	Guatemala	Peru
Colombia	Haiti	Uruguay
Costa Rica	Honduras	United States
Cuba (suspended 1962)	Mexico	Venezuela

2. North Atlantic Treaty, April 4, 1949
   Purpose: Collective defense of Western Europe and North America.
   Signatories:

Belgium	France	Luxembourg
Canada	Great Britain	Netherlands
Denmark	Greece (1951)	Norway
Federal Republic	Iceland	Portugal
of Germany (1954)	Italy	Turkey (1951)

3. Philippine Treaty, August 30, 1951 (bilateral)
   Purpose: Containment in East Asia.
   Signatories:

Philippine Republic	United States

4. Anzus Treaty, September 1, 1951
   Purpose: Collective defense of the western Pacific.
   Signatories:

Australia	New Zealand	United States

5. Republic of Korea Treaty, October 1, 1953 (bilateral)
   Purpose: Containment in East Asia.
   Signatories:

Republic of Korea	United States

6. Southeast Asia Treaty, September 8, 1954
   Purpose: Collective defense of Southeast Asia.
   Signatories:

Australia	New Zealand	Thailand
France	Pakistan	United States
Great Britain	Philippine Republic	

7. Republic of China Treaty, December 2, 1954 (bilateral)
   Purpose: Containment in East Asia.
   Signatories:

Republic of China	United States

8. Japanese Treaty, January 19, 1960 (bilateral; first negotiated 1951)
   Purpose: Containment in East Asia.
   Signatories:

Japan	United States

and the United States. President Eisenhower and Secretary of State John Foster Dulles assumed power in Washington, and a "collective leadership" took control in Moscow after the death of Stalin. These new men encountered many problems for which there were no easy solutions, as if tensions that remained from the earlier period were not sufficient to tax their abilities. Steeped in the wisdom accumulated during the earlier years of the cold war, the new statesmen too often pursued policies that worked against a stable and equitable world order. When criticizing, however, it is well to remember, as Arthur M. Schlesinger, Jr., has reminded us: "Man generally is entangled in insoluble problems; history is consequently a tragedy in which we are all involved, whose keynote is anxiety and frustration, not progress and fulfillment."

The Eisenhower Interlude, 1953–1961

Eisenhower's election to the presidency demonstrated the desire of many Americans for at least some surcease from the continual tensions of international politics. Cold war crises immediately after World War II denied to them the peaceful world they thought they had guaranteed when Germany and Japan surrendered abjectly. The unhappy course of the Korean War strengthened the nation's wish for a season of calm, and the Republican Party took advantage of this mood during the campaign of 1952. Unfortunately, global events permitted no vacation from responsibility, but foreign policy during the two Republican administrations from 1953 to 1961 suffered from the gap between the requirement of action and the impulse to quiescence.

President Eisenhower and Secretary Dulles presented a study in contrasts. The new chief executive espoused a modest conception of his role, deferring as much as possible to the desires of Congress and advocating decentralization of responsibility to state and local governments. Despite his military background, Eisenhower possessed remarkably pacific instincts; he never lost interest in means of lessening international tensions. "Against the dark background of the atomic bomb," he said to the United Nations Assembly in December 1953, "the United States does not wish merely to present strength, but also the desire and the hope for peace." Secretary Dulles, a vigorous and unusually self-assured activist, lacked the penchant for conciliation that marked his chief. A well-known

President Dwight D. Eisenhower is shown here with Secretary of State John Foster Dulles and Secretary-General of the United Nations Dag Hammarskjold during a visit to Geneva. Eisenhower showed much more interest in the United Nations than did Dulles, particularly in his advocacy of "atoms for peace." Hammarskjold died in an airplane crash in the Congo during 1961 while seeking to end the fighting there.

Presbyterian churchman, Dulles viewed the cold war as a classic conflict between rectitude and sin, an outlook that worked against accommodation with unfriendly governments. "[A] policy which only aims at containing Russia where it now is," he said just before he took charge of the State Department, "is in itself an unsound policy, but it is a policy which is bound to fail because a purely defensive policy never wins against an aggressive policy." Although he had broad prior experience in diplomacy, including the Japanese treaty negotiations of 1951, Dulles failed to recognize the extent to which world realities had altered after the initial postwar adjustments in Europe and East Asia. Problems in other parts of Asia, Africa, and Latin America—often unrelated to the cold war—required unprecedented attention, a development for which the new administration, in common with the country it led, had far too little preparation.

One of the premises of foreign policy during the Eisenhower years was that the United States must have a credible military deterrent—one strong enough to command the respect of potential enemies. This concept, of course, had provided much of the rationale for NATO. Unfortunately, credible deterrents were expensive, and the Republican Party was committed to balanced budgets. The solution to this dilemma was the "new look" military policy. In the future the United States would concentrate on developing its nuclear capability so that, if necessary, the free world could launch "massive retaliation" against an aggressor nation. America's allies would provide sufficient "conventional forces" to use on occasions when massive retaliation was inappropriate. The United States would extend funds through a military assistance program to finance its allies' operations. It would cost far less to support, say, a Pakistani infantry regiment than an equivalent American unit. This concept accounted for the growth of military assistance to America's friends overseas instead of economic aid. The "new look" had a weakness, which soon became apparent; it left the United States without sufficient conventional forces to act unilaterally. Pursued to its logical conclusion, this military policy would eliminate all options in confrontations except nuclear warfare or capitulation. A second premise of foreign policy in vogue after 1953 held that political-military alliances offered the most efficacious means of halting Communist expansion. When a new threat endangered the interests of the non-Communist nations, Secretary Dulles usually contemplated a multilateral treaty. Unkind critics called this response "pactomania." Yet in one sense this strategy represented a concession. During the campaign of 1952, Dulles had advanced the "roll-back" idea—that the free world should not merely seek to contain the tide of communism but should release captive peoples from bondage. In January 1953 he said: "It is only by keeping alive the hope of liberation, by taking advantage of whatever opportunity arises, that we will end this terrible peril which dominates the world, which imposes upon us such terrible sacrifices and so great fears for the future." Dulles soon abandoned such vagaries, but many other Americans did not.

The abortive plan to roll back the iron curtain created unrealizable expectations; a credibility gap between rhetoric and reality tested public confidence in the administration.

Despite Eisenhower's campaign promise to launch the nation upon a new course, his actions while in office represented a modified continuation of the Truman-Acheson approach to world politics. Like his predecessor, the new chief executive relied on containment to protect the nation from the spread of the "international Communist conspiracy." His coadjutor, Dulles, assumed as had Acheson that sound policies for Europe would largely determine the outcome of affairs elsewhere. This persistent "Europocentrism" tended to obscure the fact that problems in the so-called third world were becoming increasingly important. Dulles never seemed to consider the possibility that crises in Africa and Asia might require a shift away from the older emphasis on containment. The new administration could not ignore non-European problems because such difficulties recurred with increasing frequency, but it did not recognize the extent to which historical forces in Asia and Africa other than communism had to be taken into account, particularly the universal desire for economic development.

The Truman administration had recognized that the United States had to make grants and loans to the developing nations if they were to achieve their goals. After the experience of the Marshall Plan, the nation moved by stages toward a comprehensive program of foreign assistance that shifted from Europe toward the third world. In his inaugural address in January 1949, the President had included a proposal that the United States provide technical assistance to many countries around the world that lacked know-how to organize economic growth. This Point Four Program, administered through the Act for International Development (1950), proved popular, particularly in Latin America. Two years later Congress passed the Mutual Security Act, which combined overseas aid programs under one administrative umbrella. Between 1945 and 1960 total expenditures under this umbrella amounted to the staggering sum of $84 billion, of which about $57 billion was economic assistance and the rest military aid. After the Marshall Plan ended, most of this outlay went to Asian countries, particularly South Korea, Taiwan, India, and Japan. With each passing year after the beginning of the Korean War, military aid tended to absorb an increasing percentage of the total funds appropriated by Congress. New aid programs were established to satisfy needs not met through established institutions, among them a Development Loan Fund for long-range projects and "special assistance" grants to finance operations such as the United Nations Emergency Force, which helped keep peace in the Middle East.

Many problems afflicted the aid programs. Some of the funds, unavoidably, were misused by recipients; red tape and even corruption marred the administrative record; aid gravitated largely to areas where American security was most directly at issue, tending to avoid regions like Africa and Latin America. The United States encountered a serious balance-of-payments problem because the aid program as well as trade transactions forced transfers of gold to other countries to pay international monetary obligations. Criticism of the aid programs led to declining appropriations, particularly during the 1960's, but accomplishments throughout the world were plainly visible to the most casual observers. The persons who led the outcry against foreign aid often ignored its contributions to the domestic economy. Because the funds awarded to other countries were for the most part actually expended in the United States, they raised the level of production and therefore income. In the early 1970's, Congress emphasized multilateral programs through institutions such as the Inter-American Development Bank and the Asian Development Bank, a departure that permitted more flexible benefits to recipients. Despite the huge treasure expended, most students of the international economy continue to argue that the developed nations must expand their aid programs greatly, if they are to meet the needs of developing countries.

Secretary Dulles' preoccupation with Europe found expression most clearly in sponsorship of European integration and of West Germany. He believed that a unified Europe in which West Germany had an important part would ensure the containment of Russia behind the iron curtain. Unfortunately for Dulles, the very success of endeavors to rebuild Europe during the Truman era undermined interest in integration. Its earlier popularity in Europe had derived largely from immediate postwar fears of Soviet expansion, which had dimmed by 1953. American attempts to rearm West Germany aroused old fears of that nation among the NATO powers as well as in the Soviet Union. When France ultimately blocked Dulles' plan to incorporate German troops into a European Defense Community, German rearmament and European integration suffered setbacks. West Germany in 1955 finally regained full sovereignty and entered the NATO alliance, but this development worked against reunification, a central political object of Chancellor Konrad Adenauer. To bring reunification Dulles advocated free elections in which both German states would select a common government, but this approach found no favor either in East Germany or in Moscow. Voters in West Germany would dominate any such election, for there were three of them to every one in East Germany. During the Eisenhower era relations between Washington and Bonn were most cordial, but this association did little for either European integration or German reunification.

Dulles showed little desire for direct negotiations with the Soviet Union, a pattern established earlier, but President Eisenhower believed that a meeting of heads of governments might make progress toward resolving international tensions. If leaders could meet "at the summit," as during World War II, it might be possible to negotiate a German settlement and make progress toward one of Eisenhower's aspirations—international arms control, particularly of nuclear weapons. Dulles believed such gatherings might create public expectations that could not be fulfilled without sound diplomatic preparation; summit conferences should occur only after careful negotiation at lower levels clearly revealed the likelihood of a constructive result.

After some indication of a changing attitude in the Kremlin, particularly Russian cooperation in arriving at an Austrian peace treaty in May 1955, objections such as those of Dulles were overridden and the great powers agreed to meet at Geneva in July. Eisenhower joined Premier Nikolai Bulganin and Chairman Nikita Khrushchev of the Soviet Union at the summit along with the leaders of Britain and France. Negotiations produced little except the temporary manifestation of good feelings known as "the spirit of Geneva." The conferees discussed German reunification, disarmament initiatives, and removal of barriers to communication between the Russian and American blocs, but no substantive agreements were reached. Eisenhower's dramatic suggestion that the nations agree to aerial inspection as a means of enforcing an arms control agreement, the "open skies proposal," caused a flurry of excitement, but the Soviet leaders did not accept it. Neither side was prepared to make sufficient concessions to permit settlement of difficult matters. A little over a year after the Geneva summit conference, a combination of events in the Middle East and in Eastern Europe ended this period of relative calm in Russo-American relations.

In dealings with the third world the United States encountered a

John P. Taylor from Rapho-Guillumette

The titans gather at Geneva, July 1955. The leading participants in the Geneva Conference were, left to right, Soviet Premier Nikolai A. Bulganin, United States President Dwight D. Eisenhower, French Premier Edgar Faure, and British Prime Minister Anthony Eden. Nikita Khrushchev, chairman of the Russian Communist Party, also attended.

problem that it faced elsewhere as well — the difficulty of developing friendly relations with ex-colonial nations while at the same time aligning itself in world politics with the ex-imperial powers, particularly Britain and France. During the war President Roosevelt had supported anti-colonial aspirations in Asia and Africa, much to the annoyance of Churchill and De Gaulle, but after the conflict, when the United States sought to build European solidarity against the Soviet Union, it seemed impolitic to pursue this policy. American leaders frequently attempted to arrange compromises between the ex-imperial and ex-colonial nations to maintain the friendship of both groups, but all too often Washington's attempts to negotiate accommodations alienated both sides.

The emergence of Israel as a sovereign state in 1948 greatly muddled the complicated political problems of the Middle East. After World War II, Zionists moved eagerly to realize their goal of a Jewish national state in Palestine, despite opposition from Arab countries.

In 1947, the United Nations attempted to settle the problem when the General Assembly adopted a plan, to take effect on August 1, 1948, that ended the old British mandate and partitioned Palestine into two commonwealths, one Jewish and the other Arab. The decision aroused clamorous Arab objections. When Jewish leaders proclaimed the founding of Israel on May 15, President Truman eleven minutes later announced de facto recognition of the new state. He had overruled objections raised by the State Department, which feared that a pro-Israel policy might alienate Arab governments in control of enormous oil deposits. A loose coalition of anti-Israeli states, the Arab League, attempted to destroy Israel by force of arms, but the Jews proved easily able to defend themselves. An American official of the United Nations, Dr. Ralph Bunche, led a mission that managed to end the fighting in 1949. During May 1950, Britain, France, and the United States issued a Tripartite Declaration pledging themselves to support the arms status quo in the Middle East. But Arab defeat had an ironic outcome; it tended to unify otherwise quarrelsome Arab governments, which could rally around the idea of a holy war to destroy Israel.

Something of a Middle Eastern challenge to Western interests had occurred in 1951 when the Prime Minister of Iran, Mohammed Mossadegh, nationalized British oil holdings in his country. London retaliated by halting oil production, and a long struggle began. Dean Acheson later described the conflict succinctly: "It upset relations with the oil-producing states and opened rare opportunities for Communist propaganda; Britain might drive Iran to a Communist *coup d'état,* or Iran might drive Britain out of the country. Either would be a major disaster." Averell Harriman and others failed to arrange a satisfactory settlement. Finally, in 1953, the Shah of Iran, helped considerably by Washington, engineered a plot against his Prime Minister. American oil companies then joined a consortium set up to extract and sell Iranian oil. This settlement seemed eminently reasonable in the State Department, but enemies abroad insisted that the consortium represented the old economic imperialism in a new guise. Thereafter the United States assumed Britain's role as protector of Iran, expanding its international obligations in general and Middle Eastern involvement in particular.

Meanwhile other more fateful developments in the Middle East turned on the meteoric rise of Lieutenant Colonel Gamal Abdel Nasser in Egypt. In 1952 a group of army officers overthrew the venal King Farouk and launched an ambitious program of economic and social reconstruction under the banner of Arab nationalism. Their leader, Nasser, became an exponent of what came to be known as "neutralism." Rising nationalist governments in Africa and Asia wished to preserve general peace because it was necessary to rapid internal development. They desired outside assistance, especially from the United States and the Soviet Union, to subsidize economic growth. The cold war presented both dangers and opportunities for the new nations of the third world. Russia and America competed for the allegiance of these countries, but alignment with one or the other might create local imbalances of power leading to war. Choosing sides would preclude economic support from whichever bloc

A neutralist meets his people. General Gamal Abdel Nasser revitalized Egyptian nationalism in the service of social revolution. He failed, however, to realize his dream of uniting the Arab world under Egyptian leadership by leading a holy war against Israel.

Black Star

the rising nations decided to oppose. One way out of these dangers was to avoid alignment and seek aid from both sides. Nasser proved himself an energetic practitioner of this neutralist strategy.

Secretary Dulles in 1955 had mounted a strong challenge to Nasser's Arab leadership when he constructed a multilateral pact to forestall Russian encroachments in the Middle East. Along with Britain he had pushed the so-called northern tier of Arab nations — Turkey, Iraq, Iran, and Pakistan — into a Middle Eastern Treaty Organization (METO), otherwise known as the Baghdad Pact. The alliance alarmed the Israelis because it tended to unify usually undisciplined Arab opponents; Moscow predictably denounced METO as a vicious plot against the Soviet Union. Nasser objected to it because the alliance placed Iraq rather than Egypt at the center of Arab politics. He labeled the Baghdad Pact a return to the old imperialism, a claim that had some justification because the alliance represented an effort to reassert Western political leadership. Although Nasser had accepted considerable economic help from the United States, he now arranged an arms purchase in an iron curtain country, Czechoslovakia, playing both ends against the middle in the conventional neutralist fashion. At first Dulles tried to bargain with Nasser, offering aid to build a massive hydroelectric project, the Aswan high dam, an installation designed to increase Egypt's supply of electricity and arable land. When Nasser virtually demanded American support for the dam, meanwhile having mortgaged his country's cotton crop to obtain Czechoslovak arms, Dulles lost patience and abruptly withdrew the American offer.

When Nasser then nationalized the Suez Canal Company, he inaugurated a chain of events that led to a Middle Eastern war. As usual the United States attempted to mediate the dispute, but when these efforts came to nothing, Britain combined with France and Israel in a clandestine plot to overthrow Nasser by force of arms. Paris, seeking to halt Nasser's encouragement of nationalist revolutionaries in French North Africa, joined the anti-Egyptian coalition. No word of this secret Anglo-French-Israeli arrangement was conveyed to Washington. On October 29, 1956, the Israeli army attacked Egypt without warning and quickly smashed Nasser's forces in the Gaza Strip and the Sinai Desert. Britain and France then intervened, using the transparent excuse that they had to protect the Suez Canal from incursions by the belligerents. In actual fact the British had to enter the fight because they had promised to "take out" the Egyptian air force and thereby protect Israel's cities. Washington was shocked.

James Reston reported that when the President first heard of the Anglo-French action, "the White House crackled with barrack-room language the like of which had not been heard since the days of General Grant." Eisenhower and Dulles felt compelled to condemn the Anglo-French-Israeli aggression. The allies had defied both world opinion and the Charter of the United Nations and had given the Soviet Union an opportunity to strengthen its influence in the Middle East by posing as the champion of Arab sovereignty against "Western imperialism." The Russians took the same position as the Americans, a source of deep embarrassment in Washington. Russian-American pressure exerted at the United Nations eventually forced the invaders to withdraw their forces from Egypt. Nasser's defenses had been decimated, but he "won the peace," emerging from the crisis with new popularity not only in the Middle East but elsewhere in the third world. Moscow perhaps gained the most; by supporting Cairo, it gained favor in Arab capitals.

The Kremlin profited in another important respect; the Suez crisis helped it weather a severe challenge to its authority in Eastern Europe that had crystallized in the Hungarian revolution of 1956, which was at its height when the Suez war was raging.

Some months before the Middle Eastern affair the collective leadership of the Soviet Union surprised the world by launching a "de-Stalinization campaign." This enterprise included denunciations of the old dictator's deeds, removal of his supporters from power, and sponsorship of reforms at home. Nikita Khrushchev's secret speech to the Twentieth Congress of the Communist Party in February 1956 had set out Stalin's crimes in lurid detail. Unfortunately for Moscow, de-Stalinization created turmoil in the satellite countries because it robbed unpopular Stalinist leaders of their legitimacy. Some nations tried to increase their independence of Russia, although their allegiance to communism remained firm. Poland and Hungary seized the opportunity to remove Stalinists and eliminate the most irksome restraints on their freedom of action. During October 1956, a reformist government in Poland achieved considerable autonomy, although it stopped short of a definitive break with the Soviet Union. In Hungary, however, Imre Nagy and his followers pressed their anti-Soviet measures so extensively that the Russians sent in troops to overthrow the new government. The invasion took place on November 1, just two days after the Israeli incursion into Egypt. Russia crushed the revolt, employing armor against Hungarian "freedom fighters" who had little but "Molotov cocktails" and stones with which to

Gillhausen from Black Star

Dissident Hungarians and Soviet troops engage in a street battle in Budapest during the Hungarian revolution of 1956. The dissidents had no modern weapons and could not resist the power of Soviet armor. Despite much loose talk in the West about redeeming the captive nations, the United States and its allies proved unable to support the "freedom fighters."

fight back. A compliant local Communist, Janos Kadar, was placed in power. These actions caused an outcry outside the iron curtain. The General Assembly of the United Nations condemned Russia's actions by a vote of fifty-five to eight on December 12. But Moscow did not waver. Only armed intervention in Hungary could have altered the outcome, but few Western leaders were prepared to advocate military measures that probably would have precipitated a general war. After the Hungarian tragedy, loose talk about "liberating the captive nations" was heard no more.

In order to recover prestige in the Middle East, Dulles invented the Eisenhower Doctrine, a promise of assistance to any country in that region threatened by Communist aggression. Congress endorsed this concept by joint resolution early in March 1957, offering $200 million to friendly Middle Eastern regimes. A month later, the United States intervened in the affairs of Jordan when King Hussein rid himself of a Cabinet that strongly favored Egypt. Eisenhower reinforced the navy in the eastern Mediterranean, a show of strength that helped Hussein survive. During the summer of 1958 a much more dangerous episode occurred when pro-Nasser elements attempted to unseat a moderate regime in Lebanon that had taken American money and was seeking unconstitutionally to preserve itself in power. Syrian support of the Lebanese dissidents created concern in Washington, and fear of a setback grew when a revolution took place in Iraq. If that country reversed its traditional policy of opposition to Egypt, the balance of power in the Middle East might come apart. Eisenhower decided to send troops into Lebanon after receiving an appeal from the beleaguered government in Beirut. On July 15 a contingent of marines went ashore, the vanguard of an American force that ultimately included almost 15,000 troops. Britain sent 3,000 troops into Jordan to stiffen Hussein. Both Nasser and Khrushchev fulminated against these steps, but they did not make good their threats to meet force with force. Diplomacy at the United Nations and internal developments in Lebanon lessened tension sufficiently to permit American withdrawal from Lebanon by late October.

Eisenhower's activities in the Middle East failed to counter the rising influence of Nasser or to lessen instability in the region. His doctrine provided no antidote to subversion, a far more likely Communist strategy in the Middle East than aggression, nor did it come to grips with the continuing problem of Arab-Israeli relations. In 1959, Dulles reorganized the Baghdad Pact into the Central Treaty Organization (CENTO), but this last manifestation of "pactomania" soon became moribund. Despite energetic measures, anti-Americanism and instability were more common in the Middle East when Eisenhower left office than at the outset of his presidency.

In East Asia, the Eisenhower administration likewise encountered growing difficulties. Policies during the Korean War had represented an initial reaction to the Chinese Communists, but adjustments soon became necessary. Secretary Dulles placed every possible barrier in the way of Communist China's efforts to establish itself as a great power. He hoped that Washington's refusal to recognize the new regime or permit its entrance into the United Nations would force it to adopt more cooperative attitudes. Support of Chiang Kai-shek accompanied the administration's hostility to Peking.

Patronage of Formosa greatly angered Communist China. Mao insisted that the island was part of his domain, but Dulles reiterated determination to protect the Nationalists when he negotiated a mutual defense pact with Taipei in 1954 that covered Formosa and the adjacent Pescadore Islands. This treaty did not mention other small islands under Nationalist control that lay just off the Chinese mainland, the Quemoy and Matsu groups, to which the Communists also laid claim. Mao decided to test American resolve in the Straits of Formosa by harassing some of these islands. Artillery batteries on the mainland began to shell them in September 1954. Early in 1955 President Eisenhower obtained a joint resolution from Congress authorizing him to protect the Nationalists, but the resolution mentioned only Formosa and the Pescadores, avoiding reference to the offshore islands by using the term "closely related localities." Although some critics maintained that the offshore islands possessed insufficient significance to warrant hostilities, Congress voted overwhelmingly for the resolution. Dulles later held up American policy in this crisis as an example of successful "brinkmanship," the term journalists devised to describe the secretary's practice of approaching the brink of war to force concessions from opponents. The Communist batteries ultimately ceased firing; for the moment calm returned to the Straits.

Some three years later, in August 1958, the shelling resumed, and there ensued another contest of wills. Washington at first reacted truculently, despite Khrushchev's support of Peking. To demonstrate its commitment the United States permitted installation of eight-inch howitzers on Quemoy, a weapon capable of firing a nuclear shell. Public opinion did not react as favorably as in 1955; some critics asked whether the offshore islands were worth risking a third world war. Dulles retreated from his most advanced pro-Formosan position when he spoke against any attempt by Chiang Kai-shek to reconquer the mainland. Eventually the bombardment stopped; once again war had been avoided, but Eisenhower had made no constructive progress toward an accommodation with Peking. Critics of the administration's China policy pointed to its negative qualities, often with adjectives such as sterile and bankrupt. The nonrecognition strategy ignored the fact that Mao was in control of the mainland and that his revolutionary government exercised an important influence on world politics. Many experts on Chinese affairs urged a "two Chinas" policy, whereby the United States would recognize both the Peking and the Taipei governments and support both for membership in the United Nations. To such suggestions the State Department turned a deaf ear but offered no alternatives that reflected political realities.

Tragic events in French Indochina had greater long-run significance than the jousts with Peking over Formosa. Ever since 1940, when Japan began to displace the French overlords, Indochinese nationalists had fought to eliminate foreign control. When the French returned to Indochina in 1945, local anti-colonial elements launched a bloody war for independence. An experienced Indochinese patriot with a long Communist background, Ho Chi Minh, became the principal anti-colonial leader. After Mao came to power in China, Ho received the blessing of Peking. During 1950, in a little-known reversal of America's traditional anti-colonialism, President Truman had extended aid to French forces in Indochina. This minor exercise in containment seemed inconsequential. It was authorized as much to placate France as to halt communism, but Secretary Acheson advocated assistance in terms that later became familiar. "The choice confronting the U.S.A.," he had insisted, "is to support the legal governments in Indochina or to face the extension of communism over the remainder of the continental area of Southeast Asia and possibly westward." The sums sent Indochina grew considerably as the French army proved unable to mount anti-guerrilla operations. From 1950 to 1954 the total amounted to $1.2 billion. By 1954, when France appeared likely to suffer defeat at the hands of Ho's forces, some Americans began to fear that Indochina might soon be absorbed by Communist China, and President Eisenhower strengthened this concern when he advanced his famous "domino theory," arguing that if one country in Southeast Asia fell to the Communists the others would topple into their clutches: "You have a row of dominoes set up, you knock over the first one, and what will happen to the last one is the certainty that it will go over very quickly."

The French government in March 1954 officially requested American intervention in order to rescue its forces trapped in northwestern Vietnam at Dien Bien Phu. Admiral Arthur W. Radford, chairman of the Joint Chiefs of Staff, advocated air strikes from American carriers against the Indochinese revolutionaries, a proposal that received support from Secretary Dulles and Vice-President Nixon. The army chief of staff, General Ridgway, disagreed with Radford. Congressional leaders failed to support the plan, and agitation for intervention collapsed when Britain refused support.

The French forces at Dien Bien Phu surrendered on May 7, 1954, an extraordinarily humiliating defeat for France. This event led first to the installation of a new government in Paris desirous of ending the war. Meanwhile a conference in Switzerland arrived at the so-

East and Southeast Asia

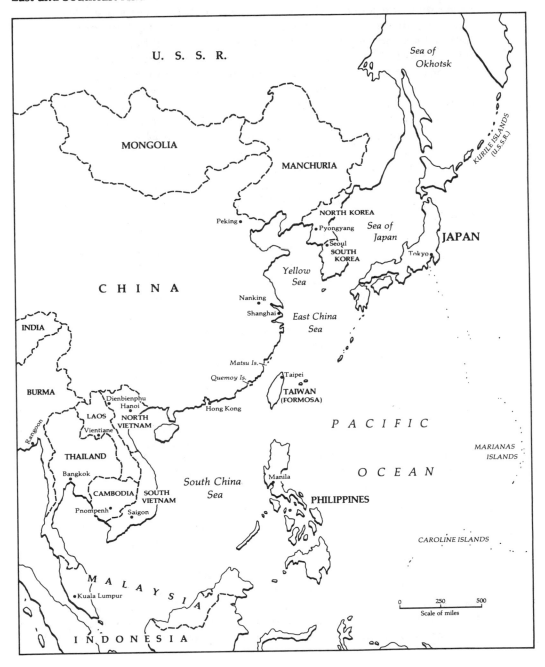

called Geneva Accords of July 20. Two of the three Indochinese states — Laos and Cambodia — were neutralized; Vietnam was partitioned temporarily at the seventeenth parallel. Ho Chi Minh would control North Vietnam, and France would remain in the south until elections scheduled for 1956 chose a government to preside over a reunified Vietnam. The United States refused to sign the Geneva Accords but decided not to prevent a settlement.

Eisenhower and Dulles did not reconcile themselves to this outcome; instead they made energetic attempts to set up a mutual defense arrangement for Southeast Asia. On September 8, 1954, the United States joined seven other countries meeting at Manila to create the Southeast Asia Treaty Organization (SEATO). Only three Asian nations subscribed — the Philippines, Thailand, and Pakistan — all American clients. Other signatories included Britain, France, New Zealand, and Australia. Indonesia and India, the two most important states in the region, failed to join, opting for neutralism, as did Ceylon and Burma. The signatories agreed that an attack on any member state would endanger all and that each would then take action in accord with "constitutional practices." In addition, members were to consult immediately in the event of subversion or indirect aggression in order to decide common measures. A special protocol extended the pact's coverage to the Indochinese states that could not join the alliance because the Geneva Accords prohibited such associations.

Far less potent than NATO, for it was essentially a consultative pact rather than a collective-security system, SEATO was intended to symbolize American commitment to the defense of Southeast Asia rather than to organize extensive forces such as those in Europe. Dulles disliked the term SEATO because it suggested that the alliance was similar to NATO, but the O was euphonically necessary. He would have preferred the acronym MANDAC (Manila Defense Accord). SEATO never established itself as an efficient means for dealing with crises in Southeast Asia. Instead of working through it, Washington drifted into entangling unilateral activity in Indochina.

When France pulled rapidly out of South Vietnam after accepting the Geneva Accords, the United States moved in. An anti-colonial politician, Ngo Dinh Diem, gained Washington's confidence. He decided to prevent elections scheduled for 1956 that were to unify the northern and southern parts of Vietnam. Diem knew perfectly well that Ho Chi Minh would easily win such elections, a view shared by President Eisenhower. The United States did not protest South

Vietnam's refusal to honor a solemn international understanding. Diem justified his actions on the ground that his country, like the United States, had not signed the Geneva Accords. Of course, it was apparent that no really free elections could take place on either side of the seventeenth parallel. Despite much brave talk Diem failed to bring about extensive social change and eventually encountered widespread domestic opposition. Saigon's inability to stimulate land reform and to stop rapacious bureaucratic exploitation of South Vietnam's poor people converted many potential supporters into actual revolutionaries. Resistance crystallized in 1960 under the banner of a National Liberation Front, the political arm of guerrilla forces popularly known as the Vietcong, which had begun to attack the government as early as 1957. The United States tried to enhance the combat efficiency of the South Vietnamese army by quietly dispatching assistance in the form of funds and advisers, but guerrilla tactics by the Vietcong nullified much of this activity. Eisenhower left office without managing any real progress in Vietnam.

Meanwhile, trouble had developed in another Indochinese state — the small and disorganized country of Laos. Washington had become interested in Laos because of its strategic location, sandwiched between Communist China to the north and Cambodia and Thailand to the south. After the departure of the French, a neutralist leader, Souvanna Phouma, headed an unstable government in Vientiane opposed by a pro-Communist movement, the Pathet Lao. In 1960 the United States, attempting to stabilize the country, lent support to a right-wing government, but this initiative only aroused the Pathet Lao, which received aid from Peking and Hanoi. The growing confusion in Laos exposed the limitations of SEATO; the alliance did not really affect the course of events there, even in 1961 when the Pathet Lao came close to taking over the country.

The Eisenhower administration experienced setbacks in its attempt to define sound policy for the Middle East and Southeast Asia, and it proved no more successful in dealing with Latin America. After World War II, Washington had given a low priority to problems in the hemisphere. The Truman administration had sponsored the Rio Pact (1947), which created a system of multilateral inter-American defense, and also the Organization of American States (1948), which championed hemispheric cooperation, but the United States stopped short of extending economic assistance comparable to the Marshall Plan for Western Europe. What little aid went to Latin America almost always strengthened local military establishments and landowning elites engaged in exploiting their people.

Only when the cold war threatened to spread to Latin America did the United States begin to take seriously relations with its neglected good neighbors. In 1954 Secretary Dulles reacted strongly against a left-wing government in Guatemala headed by Jacobo Arbenz, because he believed it might lead to Communist control in that small Central American country. The Central Intelligence Agency supported a group of Guatemalan dissidents who succeeded in overthrowing the Arbenz regime. United States leaders advertised this coup broadly as a notable victory for freedom, and Latin American leaders probably were glad to see Arbenz decamp to Czechoslovakia, although publicly they denounced the intervention as a violation of understandings made during the 1930's and after at inter-American conferences. *Norteamericanos* began to realize the extent of Yankee-phobia in Latin America when, in 1958, Vice-President Nixon made a goodwill visit to several countries and encountered anti-American demonstrations. In Caracas, the capital of Venezuela, a mob attacked Nixon's limousine and threatened his life. When he returned to the United States, the Vice-President called publicly for important changes in policy. President Eisenhower then advanced a program of expanded assistance to Latin America that included membership in the Inter-American Development Bank (1959), set up to supply loans, and support for the Act of Bogotá (1960), which envisioned long-term economic aid to the hemisphere beginning with an appropriation of $500 million by the United States.

This change in Washington's approach to Latin American affairs also reflected a serious crisis in relations with Cuba. At the beginning of 1959 Fidel Castro succeeded in overthrowing the hated authoritarian government of Fulgencio Batista, an event that many people in the United States welcomed as a victory for democracy. Very soon, however, Castro condoned drumhead trials of his opponents in public places before huge crowds and, much worse, executed hundreds of them. This flouting of basic human rights deeply alienated many of his early supporters in the United States. He did nothing to recover his declining popularity when he set up a leftist authoritarian government.

However much North Americans might hope for the growth of democratic capitalism in Latin America as well as in Africa and Asia, hard realities almost always dictated a different result. Local revolutionary leaders such as Castro had to establish powerful central governments to counter internal or external challenges to their authority. They opted for socialism because public management of the national economy seemed more likely than private enterprise to induce rapid

The Cuban revolutionary Fidel Castro took Cuba out of the inter-American system, depending instead on support from the Soviet Union and Communist China to bring about a massive social revolution.

economic growth and make possible equitable distribution of income. As Castro repudiated Washington's model for national regeneration, he turned to the Soviet Union and other nations in the Communist bloc for economic and political support. Nationalization of United States companies operating in Cuba completed the alienation of the Eisenhower administration. The United States demanded hemispheric action against Cuba through the Organization of American States and sought to undermine the Cuban economy by ending trade relations. In January 1961, Eisenhower broke diplomatic relations with Castro. Already the Central Intelligence Agency had begun to assist anti-Castro elements in preparations to overthrow the Havana regime, a violation of inter-American treaties to which the United States was a party. This activity demonstrated once again the limited value of United States promises not to intervene in the domestic affairs of Latin American states.

Although the United States had to give attention to third-world questions during Eisenhower's second term, relations with Europe and particularly with the Soviet Union continued to occupy first place on Washington's foreign policy agenda. Secretary Dulles had set about doggedly to repair the Atlantic alliance after it sustained the dual shocks of the Suez crisis and the Hungarian revolution. He gradually improved relations with Britain, but the return of General Charles de Gaulle to power in France during 1958 posed new problems. The French leader openly criticized NATO, the basis of containment in Europe and of continuing attempts to further European political integration. De Gaulle insisted that Europe must diminish its reliance on the United States because Americans could not be depended on to protect European interests when their own security was not at stake. In October 1957, the Soviet Union successfully orbited *Sputnik I,* the first earth satellite, an exploit that seemed to prove it had caught up with the United States in technological sophistication. The launch portended a frightening shift in the world balance of military power, for it demonstrated that the Soviets could employ an intercontinental ballistic missile (ICBM) capable of reaching all points in the United States.

Nikita Khrushchev, dominant in the Kremlin, took advantage of disarray within the NATO alliance and the psychological edge gained from Russian successes in space to seek a solution of the perennial German question. In November 1958, he called upon the Western powers to remove their troops from Berlin and went a step further in January 1959, threatening to make a separate peace with East Germany if the Allies refused to negotiate distinct treaties for both Germanys. The NATO powers opposed this initiative because it would require them to abandon hope of German reunification. Diplomatic recognition of East Germany would compromise the legal basis for Western access to Berlin, authorized by agreements between the occupying powers that would mean little if Russia ceded its rights to East Germany. Despite divided counsels, the NATO leaders refused to meet the Russian demands. After the foreign ministers of the Big Four held a conference that failed to settle the question, Khrushchev decided not to execute his threat.

President Eisenhower then began to contemplate another summit conference, hoping to break the diplomatic impasse in Europe. As a beginning he invited Premier Khrushchev to the United States

President Dwight D. Eisenhower with Soviet Premier Nikita Khrushchev during the latter's visit to the United States in 1959. At the left is Vice-President Richard Nixon and in the rear, left to right, are Henry Cabot Lodge, Jr., the American ambassador to the United Nations, and Secretary of State Christian A. Herter.

in 1959, planning to visit the Soviet Union himself at a later date. The Russian leader's sojourn in America stimulated the short-lived "spirit of Camp David," a brief relaxation in tensions that stemmed from friendly conversations at the presidential retreat in Maryland, but no substantive progress was made on the two primary issues — reunification of Germany and arms control. Although prior agreements had not been reached, a summit conference was scheduled for Paris during May 1960.

Just before the leaders gathered, the Soviet Union shot down an American airplane deep within its territory, an occurrence that gave Khrushchev an opportunity to undo the conference. For four years the United States had secretly conducted high-altitude photo-reconnaissance overflights of the Soviet Union, employing an aircraft called the U-2. On May 1, 1960, the Russians unexpectedly brought down a U-2 near Sverdlovsk, the Soviet Pittsburgh. The United States at first denied responsibility, but after the Soviet Union revealed that the pilot had been taken prisoner, Eisenhower admitted sponsorship of the flight. When the President arrived in Paris for the summit meeting, an abusive Khrushchev, bellowing that Eisenhower was "a thief caught red-handed in his theft," demanded that the United States suspend overflights and apologize for its past actions. Eisenhower agreed to the first requirement but not the second, prompting Khrushchev's return to Moscow. The Russian leader added insult to injury by canceling the President's invitation to visit the Soviet Union. Presumably Khrushchev used the U-2 incident as an excuse to extricate himself from negotiations that seemed unlikely to produce results desired in Moscow. Eisenhower's last great attempt to arrange a broad political settlement had ended ignominiously.

The President had planned to visit Japan in June, after touring the Soviet Union, to witness the renewal of the Japanese-American security treaty signed in 1951. He decided to proceed with the trip to Tokyo even though Khrushchev had vetoed his visit to Russia. Unfortunately, a serious controversy developed in Japan. Domestic dissidents had been protesting their government's close alignment with the United States. They became angry when Tokyo accepted a ten-year renewal of the security treaty in return for more American commitments to defend Japan and increased participation in decisions concerning deployment of American troops in the area. Serious riots took place. While Eisenhower was receiving a great public welcome in the Philippines, the Japanese Cabinet, fearful for his safety, asked him to delay his visit. The treaty survived the crisis, but the Premier who negotiated it was forced to resign, and the United States suffered a propaganda defeat as humiliating as it was damaging. As Eisenhower proceeded homeward on the *St. Paul* through the Straits of Formosa, Communist batteries once again opened up on Quemoy. Newspapermen on the ship joked, "Ike's the only Chief of State who ever got an eighty-thousand-gun salute."

When President Eisenhower left office in January 1961, the international situation looked bleak. The vaunted NATO alliance had fallen into disarray, and other treaty systems such as SEATO and CENTO had virtually failed. Germany remained divided, and no progress had been made toward arms control, not to speak of disarmament. The crisis in Indochina had not been resolved, and the

Middle East seemed likely to erupt in violence at any time. The retiring chief executive could justly claim credit for ending the Korean conflict and avoiding entanglement in other shooting wars. Despite the energy of the late Secretary Dulles, who had died in May 1959, Eisenhower's foreign policy reflected the tendency of the country to seek a respite from world politics. His administration remained largely committed to the doctrines of the late 1940's, although numerous critics raised objections. Even George Kennan, closely identified with containment, had become critical of this concept, claiming years later in an autobiography that his ideas had been grievously distorted to make them a rationale for policies he opposed. The problem was that "our government, finding it difficult to understand a political threat as such and to deal with it in other than military terms . . . failed to take advantage of the opportunities for peaceful political discussion when, in later years, such opportunities began to open up, and exerted itself, in its military preoccupations, to seal and to perpetuate the very division of Europe which it should have been concerned to remove." In his memoirs he would stress that containment had "lost much of its rationale with the death of Stalin and with the development of the Soviet-Chinese conflict" and that the nation must not "invoke that doctrine today in situations to which it has, and can have, no proper relevance." During the Eisenhower years he advanced as an alternative the idea of "disengagement," a neutral zone in Central Europe between the blocs to lessen tensions and break the stalemate. Such suggestions found no favor in Washington. It remained for leaders of the 1960's to offer new solutions for foreign policy problems that looked quite different from those of the immediate postwar years.

The Kennedy Years, 1961–1963

The new President who took office on January 20, 1961, John F. Kennedy of Massachusetts, had been elected by the narrowest margin of any successful candidate during the twentieth century, after waging an electoral campaign in which foreign policy had a considerable part. Kennedy's opponent Nixon had to defend Eisenhower's initiatives. In a series of television debates, Kennedy dwelt on a presumed missile gap between the United States and the Soviet Union, arguing that the Russians had surpassed the Americans in nuclear weaponry. He stressed the notable decline in America's international prestige and strongly criticized Eisenhower's Cuban policy but avoided commitments on these matters and most others. In his inaugural address he called for discussion among the contending powers: "Let us never negotiate out of fear. But let us never fear to negotiate." Of all international questions he stressed the danger of nuclear armaments. Reiterating the dogma that the United States must maintain an effective deterrent, he outlined the consequences of the arms race: "Both sides overburdened by the cost of modern weapons, both rightly alarmed by the steady spread of the deadly atom, yet both racing to alter that uncertain balance of terror that stays the hand of mankind's final war." Rather than the threat of Communist expansion, Kennedy emphasized what he called "the common enemies of man: Tyranny, poverty, disease and war itself."

The most appealing of Kennedy's many efforts to cope with "the common enemies of mankind" was the Peace Corps. Early in his administration, on March 1, 1961, he announced its formation. It was to be, he said, "a pool of trained American men and women sent overseas by the United States Government or through private organizations and institutions to help foreign countries meet their urgent needs for skilled manpower." Although the organization was open to Americans of all ages, most of the thousands who took part were young people of college age, idealists who sacrificed two years or more to work with Nigerian villagers, Filipino schoolchildren, Peruvian tin miners, and any number of other poor people throughout the developing world. Benefits accrued at home as well. Kennedy accurately predicted the future when he claimed that the individuals who served would "return better able to assume the responsibilities of American citizenship and with greater understanding of our global responsibilities."

Despite the openhanded attitude of the young chief executive toward international settlements, he and most of his associates, veterans of cold war encounters, shared the national commitment to the principles and practice of containment. Secretary of State Dean Rusk, presidential adviser McGeorge Bundy, Secretary of Defense Robert McNamara, and Attorney General Robert Kennedy accepted the thesis that the Soviet Union and its supporters continued to present profound dangers to peace and freedom in the world and that the task of frustrating Communist expansion should remain the primary object of American foreign policy. Europe-centered diplomatists paid too little attention to the rupture that had developed between Moscow and Peking during the late 1950's when Mao

Gail Egan was one of the best veterinarians in town (Portales, N.M.-pop. 10,529).

Now she's one of the best veterinarians in the country (Kenya-pop. 10,506,000).

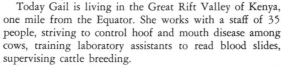

Ever since Gail Egan was old enough to ride a horse, she knew she wanted to work with animals. When she graduated from Colorado State University as a Doctor of Veterinary Medicine, a well-paid career as a veterinarian was open to her.

But Gail Egan wanted more than that. She wanted to aid people who really needed help with their animals. People, for example, whose very lives were dependent on their cattle. So she became a Peace Corps Volunteer.

Today Gail is living in the Great Rift Valley of Kenya, one mile from the Equator. She works with a staff of 35 people, striving to control hoof and mouth disease among cows, training laboratory assistants to read blood slides, supervising cattle breeding.

"The people here want someone who can help them with their herds," says Gail. "They know that since I am here, some of their cattle are doing better."

The Peace Corps today is open to every American of ability who wants to share that ability with people who need it. Among the thousands of Peace Corps Volunteers now serving in 60 countries are girls of 22 and grandmothers of 55; recent college graduates and self-taught master mechanics; single people and people with families; blacks and whites.

Like to know more?
Write to: Peace Corps, Washington, D.C. 20525.

The Peace Corps
You can be proud of it. You can be part of it.

This advertisement is typical of the appeals made by the Peace Corps for volunteers to serve in the many countries where it conducted its operations, almost all of them on a "people to people" basis.

had begun to challenge Russian leadership of the Communist bloc. Few agreed with Chester Bowles, Kennedy's undersecretary of state for a few months, who argued that the difficulties of the former colonial nations had become the most likely source of international instability.

The globalism of the Truman and Eisenhower years—a tendency to react to every international crisis indiscriminately without making an estimate of the nation's capacity to achieve its objectives—continued in somewhat altered form into the 1960's. All too few leaders appreciated the limits within which the United States could take action, even if the new President warned against overestimating the power of the United States. "We must face the fact," he said, "that the United States is neither omnipotent nor omniscient—that we are only 6 percent of the world's population—that we cannot impose our will upon the other 94 per cent—that we cannot right every wrong or reverse each adversity—and that therefore there cannot be an American solution to every world problem." Kennedy realized that neither the United States nor the Soviet Union possessed the freedom of action in world affairs that had been theirs during the first decade after 1945, but many of his countrymen did not agree. With their President they came to know the truth of the historian Schlesinger's observation that "the exercise of power is necessary to fulfill purpose, yet the world of power dooms many purposes to frustration."

Kennedy greatly altered the defense posture of the United States. Rejecting Eisenhower's "new look" program, with its stress on nuclear weaponry as against other armaments, the new administration emphasized "balanced forces"—a large number of capabilities—in order to ensure "flexible response"—that is, options to cope with many kinds of challenges. The indefatigable McNamara, an expert on modern managerial techniques, showed willingness to use the power inherent in his office as secretary of defense, something that his predecessors had not done. He diversified and enlarged the defense establishment, hoping by innovation to reduce tensions associated with the nuclear balance. One of his policies created difficulties with Europe. He believed that nuclear forces should be much more tightly controlled, to reduce the possibility of accidental war, and this view led him to oppose proliferation of nuclear arsenals within the NATO alliance. "Limited nuclear capabilities," he said in June 1962, "operating independently, are dangerous, expensive, prone to obsolescence, and lacking in credibility as a deterrent."

Acting on these opinions, the administration canceled plans to provide Britain with a nuclear air-to-ground missile called *Skybolt*. In Paris, De Gaulle took this action as further indication that the United States might not allow Europe to use nuclear weapons in some future crisis.

Much to the dismay of the new administration, its first venture in foreign policy turned into an unmitigated disaster. During April 1961, the United States supported an invasion of Cuba by anti-Castro irregulars, an operation planned during the last months of the Eisenhower administration. Kennedy decided to let it proceed, although he refused to authorize American air power as cover for the invading forces. The Central Intelligence Agency had anticipated local uprisings against Castro in support of the invaders, but none occurred. Within three days Castro's army destroyed the fourteen-hundred-man force that went ashore at the Bay of Pigs. Kennedy forthrightly accepted responsibility for the fiasco. "There's an old saying," he said afterward, "that victory has a hundred fathers and defeat is an orphan . . . . I am the responsible officer of the government and that is quite obvious." Nevertheless, the United States had suffered a truly damaging blow to its prestige. Continuing unilateral interventions in Latin American politics lessened the effect of America's protests against Communist aggressions elsewhere in the world.

Despite this beginning, President Kennedy ultimately achieved enormous popularity in Latin America, perhaps more than had any of his predecessors, largely because of his personal charm and his championship of the Alliance for Progress. Building on earlier plans developed by the Eisenhower administration, the United States advanced a program of economic aid, endorsed by the Latin American republics at Punta del Este, Uruguay, in August 1961, that contemplated the expenditure of $100 billion during the coming decade. The United States was to supply half of the $20 billion to be obtained outside of Latin America. Proponents of the alliance hoped that aid would penetrate beyond capital cities into local communities and the lives of ordinary people, avoiding one of the central weaknesses of earlier projects, which had frequently strengthened dictators at the expense of the poor. Kennedy followed his commitment to the Alliance for Progress with several highly successful visits to Latin America. He showed considerable distaste for right-wing governments to the south dominated by military men, believing that the United States should reserve enthusiasm for democratic regimes. In one respect Kennedy proved inflexible; he stubbornly opposed all proposals to seek accommodation with Castro's Cuba. The United States supported Cuba's expulsion from the Organization of American States and maintained a tight economic boycott. Castro's response was to proclaim his allegiance to communism and to align Cuba with the Soviet bloc.

While these events took place, the United States found itself for the first time directly engaged in the affairs of Africa below the Sahara. Nationalist movements in every European colony sought independence after 1945. Too weakened to prevent this trend, the European powers reluctantly acquiesced in the establishment of free countries. Ill prepared for self-government, the new nations in Africa all too often experienced instability. By and large the United States remained aloof from these developments, deferring to its European allies, particularly Britain and France. This course engendered suspicion in Africa; Washington often was criticized for encouraging attempts by the old imperialists to recover their former influence.

Of the new African nations, none proved more unstable than the Congo. After Belgium suddenly granted the Congo its independence in 1960, a struggle for power between factions turned into a bloody civil war. The Belgians had trained few Congolese for high-level leadership. Tribal loyalties proved more compelling than allegiance to the central government at Leopoldville (Kinshasa). By the time Kennedy took office there were two factions—one supported by Belgium, the other by the Soviet Union. Recognizing that no course would prove entirely satisfactory, Kennedy supported military efforts by the United Nations to suppress opponents of the central government. After many vicissitudes, United Nations forces operating in the Congo managed to reunite the country. Efforts by the Soviet Union to exploit the crisis for its own purposes came to nothing, as did endeavors by outside industrial interests to foster division of the country. The result was a qualified victory for the United Nations and for the United States, but problems remained in the Congo and elsewhere in Africa. American aid grew during the 1960's, in part as a function of pressure on the government generated by black Americans, but only a beginning was made toward creating a mature policy for the region.

Crises occurred regularly in Latin America and Africa, but civil conflict in Southeast Asia received even more attention in Washington. Kennedy showed particular concern about the situation in Laos.

The Pathet Lao, helped by Russia and North Vietnam, continued to menace the ineffectual central government at Vientiane, which received support from the United States. After weighing policies — among them withdrawal, intervention, and partition — Washington decided to press for a neutral coalition. The neutralization concept required the United States to discuss the issue with Peking and permit Communist participation in the Laotian government, but it also promised to preclude a Pathet Lao victory and allow Washington to minimize its involvement. In his second state of the union address, the President had Laos in mind when he argued that "no one nation has the power or the wisdom to solve all the problems of the world or manage its revolutionary tides; that extending our commitments does not always increase our security . . . that nuclear weapons cannot prevent subversion; and that no free peoples can be kept free without will and energy of their own." Negotiators in Geneva during 1961 and 1962, including Harriman for the United States, arrived at a new accord for Laos that avoided partition and left the country unaligned. American and Russian aid to the contending Laotian factions was supposed to end, although North Vietnam sustained its support for the Pathet Lao and kept open the so-called Ho Chi Minh trail, which allowed the North Vietnamese to supply the Vietcong in South Vietnam. This Laotian settlement was tentative but prevented an armed confrontation in Southeast Asia between the United States and the Soviet Union or Communist China. The Pathet Lao soon bolted the coalition and resumed a civil war, which continues against Souvanna Phouma's neutralist government.

Neutralization in Laos was part of a decision to base the American defense of Southeast Asia on South Vietnam, a dubious choice indeed because Diem, despite support from Washington, had failed to unite the country. Determined to foreclose domestic dissent, Saigon ruthlessly persecuted not only Communist opposition but any other criticism. This policy played into the hands of the guerrillas. By 1961 the Vietcong, aided by people in the countryside who were either enticed or terrorized into providing food, cover, and information, threatened the very existence of the Saigon regime. After Kennedy sent Vice-President Lyndon B. Johnson to investigate the situation, the Vice-President reported ominously, "We must decide whether to help these countries to the best of our ability or throw in the towel in the area and pull back our defenses to San Francisco and a 'Fortress America' concept." Johnson proposed an increase in American assistance. Later the presidential adviser Walt Rostow and General Maxwell Taylor visited Saigon and returned with specific recommendations on which the government based its future policy. The administration opted for a military solution and in so doing greatly expanded its commitment. American supplies and troops began to move across the Pacific. When Kennedy took office, about two thousand American "advisers" were in Vietnam. The number had increased to sixteen thousand by the end of 1963, but the President refused to throw American troops into battle. His policy was to sustain a limited but growing program of military aid for Saigon, emphasizing "counterinsurgency"—an attempt to use guerrilla tactics against the Vietcong. At first the administration assumed an optimistic attitude, basing its public statements on reports from Diem that indicated progress against the Vietcong. Actually, however, the situation worsened as Diem refused to liberalize his regime. In 1963, he reacted against criticism from the large Buddhist group in his country by attempting to suppress it, an initiative that destroyed what little confidence Washington still had in him. On November 1, a military conspiracy overthrew the government and murdered Diem. Although American officials in Saigon had been in contact with the plotters, the United States did not participate in planning or executing the coup. When Diem appealed for help, Ambassador Henry Cabot Lodge, Jr., would only express concern for his safety. For some time to come, the world witnessed a parade of military leaders in Saigon who proved no more successful than Diem in stabilizing the country.

Even though Kennedy faced crisis after crisis in the third world, he continued, like his predecessors since 1945, to give most of his attention to relations with the Soviet Union because of various challenges posed by Nikita Khrushchev. The Russian Premier made much of his concept of "peaceful coexistence" with the capitalist world, but belligerent statements such as the stray remark that communism would eventually "bury" capitalism negated the effect of his more pacific pronouncements. Much of Khrushchev's behavior reflected conflicts within the Kremlin. His enemies criticized weaknesses in the domestic economy, particularly the agricultural sector, but of even greater importance was the charge that he had not dealt effectively with Communist China. Tension between Moscow and Peking had grown rapidly during the 1950's; ideology failed to override conflicts of interest. Mao's aspiration to independent leadership within the Communist bloc proved unacceptable in Russia. Clashes along the Russo-Chinese border revived ancient struggles for control of Central Asia. Khrushchev appears to have opted for adventurous foreign policies in order to strengthen himself at home against those who opposed his domestic policies and his tough attitude toward China.

In 1961 the world experienced still another crisis over Berlin. President Kennedy traveled to Vienna in June to probe with Khrushchev the prospects for settling the German question and reaching accord on arms control. The experience proved sobering indeed. Khrushchev was unbending; nothing of value was accomplished. Once again the Russian leader established a deadline—December 1961—for a German peace treaty. Otherwise he intended to sign a separate pact with the East Germans, allowing them to control access to Berlin. When Khrushchev announced an increase in his military budget, Kennedy responded with a similar statement and mobilized some reserve units. "West Berlin," he said, "has now become the great testing place of Western courage and will, a focal point where our solemn commitments . . . and Soviet ambitions now meet in basic confrontation." The United States stood ready to negotiate, but it would also "be ready to resist with force, if force is used upon us. . . . We seek peace, but we shall not surrender." Thus the situation approached a climax; across the country some anxious Americans built bomb shelters to provide protection against nuclear weapons.

During the middle of August, the crisis intensified when the East Germans suddenly threw up a traffic barrier between East and West Berlin in order to seal off escape routes. Since 1945 some 3.5 million East Germans had fled westward, seeking to escape the tyranny that prevailed behind the iron curtain and to benefit from the thriving economy of West Germany. When the United States failed to react, the barrier became a barbed wire fence and finally a wall. Later on, the East Germans built a barricade along their entire western border. At one point Russian and American tanks faced each other across the boundary between East and West Berlin, dramatizing as never before the possibility of an all-out war over that city. Slowly the crisis disappeared, though not without anxious moments. Khrushchev's December deadline passed without incident. But the Berlin conflict inhibited prospects for a Russian-American détente. On June 26, 1963, when President Kennedy visited Berlin, he received a tumultuous welcome, and he made one of his most memorable pronouncements, insisting once again on the importance of Berlin as a symbol of freedom. "All free men," he concluded, "wherever they may live, are citizens of Berlin, and therefore, as a free man,

I take pride in the words *'Ich bin ein Berliner.'"* The statement demonstrated that the cold war was still far from ended and that divided Berlin remained a symbol of conflict.

Meanwhile had come the most dangerous of all cold war confrontations—the Cuban missile crisis of 1962. After the fiasco at the Bay of Pigs, the Soviet Union augmented its support of Castro. In the summer of 1962, Khrushchev secretly decided to emplace a large number of ballistic missiles in Cuba capable of attacking targets as far as twenty-two hundred miles away. Why did the Soviet Premier decide on such a provocative course, despite warning from Kennedy that the United States would not tolerate any attempt to arm Cuba with nuclear weapons? Perhaps he underestimated the President's courage. Evidently he sought an enormous alteration in the strategic balance, one that would vastly strengthen his hand at the bargaining table. Favorable settlements of international controversies, such as the German question, would restore his fading prestige within the

President John F. Kennedy, West Berlin Mayor Willy Brandt, and West German Chancellor Konrad Adenauer parade through an enthusiastic crowd and are showered with confetti during Kennedy's visit to West Berlin in June 1963. The President's trip to West Germany confirmed America's intention to stand firm in its defense of Berlin and of Western Europe, despite the doubts expressed at the time by General Charles de Gaulle of France.

United Press International

Kremlin and throughout the Communist bloc. Unfortunately for Khrushchev, he failed to achieve strategic surprise; U-2 overflights of Cuba disclosed clandestine construction of several missile launching sites. In an atmosphere of utmost tension, Kennedy convened secret meetings of his closest advisers. His brother Robert wrote feelingly of the setting. The group was asked "to make a recommendation which would affect the future of all mankind, a recommendation which, if wrong and if accepted, could mean the destruction of the human race. That kind of pressure does strange things to a human being, even to brilliant, self-confident, mature, experienced men." What could be done? Theodore Sorensen, one of Kennedy's closest advisers who participated in the discussions, listed several possibilities, including (1) doing nothing, (2) bringing diplomatic pressures to bear, (3) making a secret approach to Castro, (4) initiating a blockade, (5) conducting an air strike, and (6) launching an invasion. All but two were eventually eliminated. One group strongly urged a surprise air strike; another pressed for a blockade. The blockade won out when problems of the air strike became apparent, among them the fact that it would, as Robert Kennedy pointed out, constitute "a Pearl Harbor in reverse."

On Monday, October 22, President Kennedy made a television speech in which he revealed the Soviet tactic in Cuba. "The 1930's," he said, "taught us a clear lesson: aggressive conduct, if allowed to go unchecked and unchallenged, ultimately leads to war." America would not "unnecessarily risk the costs of worldwide nuclear war in which even the fruits of victory would be ashes in our mouth, but neither will we shrink from that risk at any time it must be faced." He announced that the navy would establish a "quarantine" of Cuba in order to prevent the arrival of additional missiles. The term "quarantine" was, of course, a euphemism for blockade, which in international law is construed as an act of war. Then came a solemn warning: "It shall be the policy of this nation to regard any nuclear missile launched from Cuba against any nation in the Western Hemisphere as an attack by the Soviet Union on the United States, requiring a full retaliatory response upon the Soviet Union." Kennedy asked, finally, that Khrushchev take out the missiles already in Cuba.

This speech put the two superpowers into an "eyeball to eyeball" confrontation. There ensued two of the most anxious days in the world's history. What would happen when Russian merchant vessels carrying missiles to Cuba approached the American block-

The Caribbean Nations

ade? The answer came on Wednesday, October 24, when sixteen ships stopped dead in the water short of the blockade and soon started their voyage back to Russian ports. Khrushchev had begun his retreat. On Friday, October 26, he sent a message to Kennedy that broached an acceptable settlement. The missiles would be withdrawn if the United States ended its blockade and pledged not to invade Cuba. The very next day, however, a contradictory message came, proposing a far less satisfactory arrangement. Robert Kennedy suggested that the President ignore the second message and respond to the first. This expedient proved successful. Khrushchev on Sunday agreed to withdraw the missiles, and the crisis ended as suddenly as it had begun.

The relaxation of tensions that followed the end of the missile crisis stimulated modest but real progress toward arms limitation, a national objective that had been frustrated regularly since the failure of the proposals of 1946 at the United Nations for control of atomic energy. Kennedy had placed arms control and disarmament high on his agenda, concentrating on stopping proliferation of nuclear weapons rather than on reduction of existing stocks. His hopes were set back disastrously when the Soviet Union broke a voluntary ban on nuclear testing in 1961. Shortly thereafter Kennedy advanced an ambitious program for "general and complete disarmament under effective international control." "Never," he argued, "have the nations of the world had so much to lose—or so much to gain. Together we shall save our planet, or together we shall perish in its flames." When this initiative failed, the United States resumed its testing program, although the administration continued to plan means of reducing nuclear tensions, working through the Arms Control and Disarmament Agency that it set up for this purpose.

Nothing inhibited arms control more than the attitudes of Communist China and France. Mao, of course, coveted nuclear weapons in order to strengthen his position vis-à-vis Moscow as well as capitalist countries. In Paris, De Gaulle once again emphasized Europe's independence and its need to rely on separate national defenses rather than on the NATO shield. America, he believed, could not be trusted in a real crisis.

During the summer of 1963, after the Cuban affair had passed, the Soviet Union agreed to consider a limited test-ban treaty. On June 10, in a speech at American University, Kennedy announced that serious discussions would soon begin in Moscow. Given developments since 1945, how could the President justify talking with the Russians? How could we "make the world safe for diversity"? His answer was simple and direct. "Our most basic common link is that we all inhabit this small planet. We all breathe the same air. We all cherish our children's future. And we are all mortal." On this basis, Averell Harriman skillfully negotiated a treaty that stopped nuclear testing in the atmosphere, on land, and on the seas. It did not provide for on-site inspection, long an American demand, nor did it limit production of nuclear weapons, but it took steps toward further accomplishments. Kennedy properly stressed the tentative character of the understanding. "This treaty is not the millennium," he said. "But it is an important first step—a step toward peace, a step toward reason, a step away from war." Neither

France nor China chose to ratify the test-ban treaty, and their resistance reemphasized for the rest of the world the dangers of proliferation.

During his thousand days of power, Kennedy had moved well beyond the relatively conventional view of the cold war and of world politics that he had espoused when he assumed the presidency. Always hopeful of détente with the Soviet Union, he had guided the country through the most dangerous of all cold war crises and helped to set both nations on the path of competitive peaceful coexistence. Far less progress had been made on another prime objective, constructive policies for the third world, but Kennedy's support of the Alliance for Progress, his actions during the Congo crisis, and his effort to limit hostilities in Southeast Asia remain as evidence of his desire to recast American attitudes and policies.

President Johnson and the War in Vietnam, 1963–1969

Whatever hope there might have been in 1963 for a definite end to the cold war or for an effective contribution to the needs of the third world soon faded away as the United States mired itself in a disastrous conflict in Southeast Asia — the Vietnam War. Fortune placed in the White House a man who said in 1964, "I am not going to be the President who saw South Vietnam go the way China went." By 1965, Lyndon Baines Johnson had concluded that the United States must either expand its armed forces in Vietnam and commit them to battle or else accept forcible unification of that country under the auspices of Ho Chi Minh. During the previous year he had obtained a mandate from Congress "to take all necessary measures" after North Vietnamese torpedo boats attacked American destroyers in the Gulf of Tonkin that had been reporting intelligence information to the South Vietnamese. Secretary McNamara denied allegations that the destroyers, as a means of provoking retaliation, had assisted operations conducted in the area by South Vietnamese commandos. The administration based its later actions on the authority granted by the Tonkin Resolution.

In February 1965, after the Vietcong killed nine American advisers during an attack on a compound at Pleiku, United States aircraft began to bomb North Vietnam, an act that led directly to further escalation. The bombing campaign, Operation Rolling Thunder, was

The inscription "LBJ'S HIRED GUN" on the jacket of this American soldier in South Vietnam reflects the broad unpopularity of the Vietnam War, even among the fighting men.

intended to break the enemy's will, but it seemed only to strengthen Hanoi's determination to sustain the war. It also alienated public opinion throughout the world.

Two months later, President Johnson decided to commit American forces on the ground. Recognizing the import of this step, he justified it in considerable detail. South Vietnam, he insisted, was under intense attack from North Vietnam, whose object was "total conquest." Behind Hanoi and all Asia brooded "the deepening shadow of Communist China. . . . The contest in Vietnam is part of a wider pattern of aggressive purpose." Johnson planned to fight in Vietnam "to strengthen world order"; people who depended on the United States all around the world would lose confidence if the nation retreated from Southeast Asia. And finally, Americans were in Vietnam because "there are great stakes in the balance. Let no one think that retreat from Vietnam would bring an end to conflict. The battle would be renewed in one country and then another. The central lesson of our time is that the appetite of aggression is never satisfied." In 1967 the President put his reasons more succinctly. "I am convinced," he maintained, "that by seeing this struggle through we are greatly reducing the chance of a much larger war — perhaps a nuclear war."

Washington stubbornly minimized and ignored the view of many that the struggle in Vietnam was at bottom a civil war in which outside forces had become engaged. The State Department published a "white paper" in February 1965, which documented North Vietnamese activity south of the seventeenth parallel. "The record," it claimed, "is conclusive. It establishes beyond question that North Vietnam is carrying out a carefully conceived plan of aggression against the South." The State Department dismissed the notion that the Vietcong was an indigenous revolutionary movement: "The [National] Liberation Front is Hanoi's creation; it is neither independent nor Southern, and what it seeks is not liberation but subjugation of the South." Those Americans who supported increased participation in the war (the "hawks") advanced the administration's arguments in various forms throughout the controversy that developed at home as the war dragged on and on. Within the government, the most notable opponent of intervention was Undersecretary of State George Ball, who recommended strict limits on American involvement in Southeast Asia. "The alternative," he wrote, "is almost certainly a protracted war involving an open-ended commitment of U.S. forces, mounting U.S. casualties, no assurance of a satisfactory solution, and a serious danger of escalation at the end of the road."

President Johnson's decision to enlarge the conflict revealed that neither he nor most of his advisers had detected important alterations in world politics since the immediate postwar era. They continued to believe that a monolithic bloc of hostile Communist nations led by the Soviet Union posed the primary danger to international stability and progress. Because they thought that the Communists still contemplated expansion as a prelude to domination of the world, it seemed that the only effective answer was to meet force with force. This viewpoint downgraded the importance of changes that had taken place throughout the world. In Europe the non-Communist countries had been restored to health. The Soviet Union had lost much of its influence over China, and it had been forced to liberalize its policies in the satellite region. A former member of the Johnson administration, Assistant Secretary of Defense Townsend Hoopes, has argued that the new configuration of nations represented "a proliferation of large and small power centers characterized by rather transient relationships. The world was no longer neatly divided between Free World and Communist bloc." He did not believe that these new realities lessened the danger inherent in the times, but he thought that they "strongly suggested the need for new analysis and new responses."

Secretary of Defense McNamara and others confidently predicted early victory, but events proved them entirely wrong. The administration correctly assumed that Communist China would not intervene as it had in Korea, provided that North Vietnam was not invaded, but it underestimated the difficulties of waging war in Southeast Asia. The air force bombed North Vietnam heavily but failed either to break the enemy's morale or to stop the flow of supplies to the Vietcong from points above the seventeenth parallel. The Pentagon itself acknowledged the reasons for the ineffectiveness of the air strikes. Strategic bombing assumed a highly developed industrial economy, but North Vietnam was "an agricultural country with rudimentary transportation systems and little industry of any kind." General William Westmoreland, the American ground commander, adopted a strategy as unsuited to local conditions as the bombing campaign. He sent "search and destroy" missions periodically through sections of the Vietnamese countryside in order to keep enemy troops off balance while a "pacification campaign" took place. "Pacification" consisted of measures to gain the loyalty of

The Vietnam War Since 1964

people living in the countryside. Neither the military operations nor the pacification procedures achieved their goals. Enemy forces habitually melted away in the face of search and destroy sweeps, only to return and reestablish control when American and South

Vietnamese forces withdrew. Henry Kissinger, a leading scholar of defense matters, correctly noted that guerrillas did not need to defeat the enemy to triumph; they had only to avoid defeat. Extensive efforts to create an effective South Vietnamese army encountered frustration. Early in 1968 the Vietcong and "volunteers" from North Vietnam managed to launch powerful raids on a number of southern cities formerly thought secure from enemy assaults, including Saigon. The dramatic success of this "Tet offensive" showed once again that victory was far from in sight. The most that could be claimed for the American intervention was that it had forced a stalemate.

Criticism of the war grew by leaps and bounds as the country became more deeply involved in the struggle without visible results. In July 1965, about 75,000 American troops were deployed in South Vietnam. The number grew to 200,000 by the end of 1966 and to over 500,000 in 1968. Among the arguments opponents of the war (the "doves") most frequently expressed was that it represented a highly dangerous new phase in American "globalism." Some asked how the war could further democracy if the United States cooperated with the repressive Saigon regime. Others held that control of Southeast Asia was really not vital to the defense of the free world and that the United States could not act in other parts of the world more important to national security because American power was tied down in Vietnam. Intervention in Vietnam alienated many of America's friends and further alarmed nonaligned countries, weakening the security of the nation in world politics. Certain opponents of the administration's policy conceded that the United States should sustain a military presence in the region as a bulwark against future aggression by China, but they asserted that this objective could be accomplished by concentrating air and sea power in easily defended insular locations such as the Philippines and Formosa. Some of this criticism reflected a resurgence of isolationist sentiment akin to that of the years just before World War II, but most of those who opposed President Johnson's war did not call for withdrawal to Fortress America. They asked for rational uses of American power to pursue attainable international goals.

Much of the leadership for dissent came from the United States Senate, many of whose members became concerned that legislative prerogatives, particularly the right to declare war, had been ignored by the executive branch. For many years liberals had championed a strong executive, but the Vietnam War stimulated new interest in the old doctrines of the separation of powers and checks and balances as a means of preventing arbitrary presidential decisions. J. William Fulbright, chairman of the Foreign Relations Committee, emerged as the most influential senatorial critic of Johnson's policies. Most of the "doves" in the halls of Congress belonged to the President's own political party, although they received support from a growing number of Republicans. One of the leading dissenters among the Democrats, Senator Eugene McCarthy, eventually challenged the party leadership during the presidential campaign of 1968 in order to force a change in national policy.

More extreme criticism came from both the left and the right. Radical war protesters advanced the thesis that the United States, in pursuit of its own selfish interests, had applied to Vietnam a counterrevolutionary policy that would ultimately be used against other third-world movements seeking to free themselves from the "imperialists." Domestic opponents of this approach, it was held, would also experience repression. Writing in the left-Socialist journal *Monthly Review,* Paul Sweezy and Harry Magdoff argued that "for an imperialist ruling class the unfettered freedom to make war is absolutely vital to its continued existence. Anything which interferes with that freedom will be considered on a par with a direct threat to the system itself to be dealt with by the full panoply of counter-revolutionary weapons, up to and including the scrapping of bourgeois democracy and the imposition of a fascist dictatorship." Other radicals such as Noam Chomsky and Staughton Lynd stressed moral and legal arguments against the war. On their part, right-wing elements maintained that the United States should have deployed all the power necessary, including nuclear weapons, to achieve a crushing military victory, regardless of the consequences at home and abroad. Southeast Asia was the place, they believed, to demonstrate that wars of national liberation would not prove ways to accomplish Communist expansion, even if military operations ran the risk of triggering a third world war.

Despite the extraordinary depth of his commitment to victory in Vietnam, Johnson finally heeded those who argued that division at home, the difficulties of warfare in Vietnam, and the untoward effects of the struggle on other aspects of American foreign policy dictated abandonment of the search for a decisive triumph. After relieving General Westmoreland of his command in late February 1968, the President made a television address on March 31, during which he disclosed that he would not run for reelection and an-

Participants in antiwar marches, such as this one in Washington, D.C., in May 1970, used imaginative means to express their moral outrage over the war in Vietnam. Public demonstrations of this nature played an important role in mobilizing public opinion against continuation of the struggle in South Vietnam.

President Lyndon Baines Johnson addresses troops at Cam Ranh Bay, South Vietnam, in October 1966. To the President's left, in order, are General William Westmoreland, United States commander in Vietnam; South Vietnamese President Major General Nguyen Van Thieu; South Vietnamese Premier Nguyen Cao Ky; and Secretary of State Dean Rusk. Johnson's frequent consultations with South Vietnamese leaders underlined his stubborn commitment to a decisive military victory over the Vietcong and North Vietnamese.

nounced several actions designed to prepare the way for peace negotiations. The United States would cease air attacks on all but the most southerly districts of North Vietnam, and the South Vietnamese army would gradually take over responsibilities from American units in order to permit large troop withdrawals. Shortly thereafter, Harriman went to Paris in order to inaugurate discussions with representatives of the National Liberation Front and North Vietnam. Thus began a frustrating effort to liquidate the ill-fated adventure in Vietnam, a task that soon fell to Johnson's successor, President Nixon.

The war largely obscured problems of policy elsewhere in the world, which was not the least of its devastating consequences. Some movement occurred in the all-important area of arms control, but certain nations, unwilling to place their destinies in the hands of the nuclear powers, continued to develop independent nuclear arsenals in defiance of the most solemn warnings against proliferation. In Europe the NATO alliance continued to lose cohesiveness as members adopted courses of action that often ran counter to desires in Washington. Whatever goodwill had been built up in Latin America was dissipated when the Alliance for Progress failed to produce results and Washington reverted to a policy of unilateral intervention. No real progress was made toward resolving the extraordinarily dangerous conflict in the Middle East.

Instability in many parts of the world impeded arms control. The United States and the Soviet Union agreed to a nonproliferation treaty in 1968 that was ratified in 1969, although neither France nor China subscribed to it. This breakthrough led to broad-ranging negotiations on arms control between the Russians and Americans, the Strategic Arms Limitation Talks (SALT), beginning in late 1969 at Helsinki. After two years the negotiators had made some gains, but difficult problems remained. The United States insisted on a comprehensive treaty that placed restraints on both offensive and defensive weapons, but the Soviet Union raised the possibility of selective agreements on particular kinds of weaponry, such as anti-ballistic missile systems. Many observers hoped that, despite these difficulties, the discussions would produce the most important arms control agreement since the onset of the nuclear age. The development of submarines capable of firing from beneath the sea (*Polaris*) and the invention of the MIRV (multiple independently targetable reentry vehicle), a warhead from which a large number of nuclear weapons could be launched against separate targets in the ground, drew attention once more to the supreme folly of the nuclear armament race. However, some relaxation of political tensions, particularly in Southeast Asia and the Middle East, appeared to be requisite for dramatic progress toward disarmament.

Johnson's European policies centered on completion of projects inaugurated during the Kennedy administration, particularly ambitious plans to improve defense and trade relations within the Atlantic community, but he achieved only small success. To head off European, and particularly French, desires for a separate nuclear capability, President Kennedy had proposed a "multilateral nuclear force" (MLF) as part of the NATO deterrent. MLF would have engaged NATO members in decisions concerning employment of America's nuclear arsenal as compensation for not developing their own weapons systems. General de Gaulle ultimately blocked MLF, insisting as usual that Europe could not depend on American support in all situations of danger. He eventually took French forces out of NATO and forced the transfer of NATO headquarters from Paris to a Brussels suburb.

The French President proved equally opposed to American plans for trade development. In 1962 Kennedy had obtained legislation from Congress that permitted easier access for European goods to American markets in return for tariff concessions. This Trade Expansion Act constituted an American reaction to the establishment of the European Common Market in 1958, which joined the Benelux countries with France, West Germany, and Italy, a relatively unified and powerful economic bloc. The United States originally approved of the Common Market because it promised to strengthen Europe against Russian aggression. American planning assumed that Britain would eventually enter the Common Market, but France blocked British membership. Tariff negotiations designed to lower existing customs, called the "Kennedy Round," fell far short of objectives. These developments prevented the emergence of a vast trading area reaching from West Germany to Japan within which goods and services could have been exchanged much more freely than before. As the war in Vietnam expanded, Washington devoted less and less energy to European questions. One result was a great slowdown of European integration, to which the United States earlier had given extensive support.

President Johnson paid little attention to Latin America. He gave no leadership when Congress lagged in appropriating the amounts the United States had promised to the Alliance for Progress, nor did he sponsor improvements when weakness became manifest. This neglect hurt the strategy of underpinning liberal political regimes with extensive programs of economic aid, although Latin American governments failed to take all the actions necessary to bring about important improvements. In addition, Johnson was quick to intervene when he believed that Castro-like governments might assume power in strategic countries. Washington lent considerable support to a right-wing military dictatorship that overthrew a leftist government in Brazil in 1964. The military government made some progress in halting the inflation that continued to poison life in Brazil, but at the expense of civil liberties and domestic reform. Washington in 1965 used force in the Dominican Republic to prevent what it thought were Castro-like revolutionaries from seizing control of the country. A government that favored a former President of democratic convictions, Juan Bosch, had encountered opposition from a conservative military faction. The latter group managed to convince President Johnson to send in marines, ostensibly to protect American lives and property but also to prevent radicals from seizing power. Johnson justified intervention on anti-Communist grounds. "What began as a popular democratic revolution that was committed to democracy and social justice moved into the hands of a band of Communist conspirators," he claimed. His action stimulated outraged protests both from those who favored nonintervention in the domestic affairs of the Latin American republics and those who believed that the United States should do all it could to support democratic regimes.

The rise of military dictatorships in many Latin countries since 1965 raised barriers both to stability and to progress in Latin America. During 1969, Governor Nelson Rockefeller of New York headed a wide-ranging commission that submitted a set of recommendations for the future, including devices to expand the trade of Latin America, but little has been done to put these proposals into practice. The Rockefeller report called attention to a prime source of discontent in Latin America: "Throughout the hemisphere, although people are constantly moving out of poverty and degradation in varying numbers, the gap between the advantaged and the disadvantaged, within nations as well as between nations, is ever stronger and ever more difficult to endure." In 1970 "Yankee-go-home" manifestations occurred in Bolivia, and the Chilean electorate chose an anti-American Marxist as President.

Middle Eastern politics remained volatile during the Johnson years and after. In 1967 Israel once again resorted to preventive war, devastating its Arab neighbors—Egypt, Syria, and Jordan—in a lightning offensive that required only six days. Israeli troops occupied the Sinai peninsula to the eastern bank of the Suez Canal, expelled Jordan from Jerusalem, and established a defensible boundary with Syria. Defeat forced the Arabs to align themselves more closely with the Soviet Union, providing Moscow with an opportunity to develop more influence in the Middle East. Arms again flowed to Egypt and other countries, and Russian ships entered the eastern Mediterranean to counter the American Sixth Fleet. A new element complicated the situation after the 1967 war; bands of Palestinian irregulars recruited out of communities of Arab refugees expelled from Israel in 1948–1949 engaged in guerrilla warfare against the Jews. As in other situations, the involvement of the United States in Southeast Asia minimized American contributions to the search for

An Arab passes two Jews in the rubble of Jerusalem caused by fighting during the 1967 Arab-Israeli war. Israel fought a preventive war to secure more defensible borders against its Arab enemies, particularly Egypt, Jordan, and Syria, but the victory failed to bring about stability in the Middle East.

stability in the Middle East. In recent years, the United States has attempted to maintain a military balance of power in the region while pressing for a peace conference between the Israelis and Arabs, but ethnic rivalries and oil politics seemed likely to prevent a comprehensive settlement at an early date.

For some years economic assistance sent from the United States to the third-world nations has been in decline. Foreign-aid appropriations fell regularly during the first years of the 1970's. Western European countries refused to participate fully in aid projects, in part at least because the United States did not offer effective leadership. If both stability and progress were to prevail in the third world,

economic growth had to occur, and new income derived from it had
to be distributed much more equitably among the population than
in the past. Unfortunately, economic failures often worked against
free governments. Throughout Africa, Asia, and Latin America,
military coups destroyed civilian regimes, and the new rulers rarely
fostered programs of development to help their suffering people.
The provision of massive economic assistance to the third world,
preferably through an independent international agency, ranked
with arms control negotiations among the important long-range
projects on the agenda of world politics during the 1970's. Otherwise, in many countries, huge population increases would continue
to outstrip improvements of gross national product.

The Nixon Years Since 1969

During the presidential campaign of 1968, the Republican candidate,
Richard M. Nixon, profited greatly from extensive national division
over the war in Vietnam. His main opponent, Vice-President Hubert
H. Humphrey, felt compelled to endorse Johnson's unpopular
policies, a course that alienated Democrats who had broken with the
retiring President. Nixon avoided detailed commitments, concentrating on pledges of his intention to make changes. He did state
that he had in mind a way to bring about an honorable and expeditious end to the Asian war, intimating that his administration would
expedite withdrawal more effectively than the Democratic incumbents.

After his election, President Nixon named William P. Rogers as
secretary of state and began a frustrating endeavor to liquidate the
American involvement in Southeast Asia. Henry Cabot Lodge, Jr.,
formerly ambassador at the United Nations and also to Saigon, replaced Harriman in Paris, but the talks dragged on with no sign of
progress. Lodge eventually returned to the United States, and the
President waited many months before appointing a replacement.
Peace negotiations failed because the parties were too far apart to
find a basis for accommodation. The United States maintained that
all outside forces should be withdrawn from South Vietnam and that
supervised elections should be held to decide the future of the
country. Hanoi called for an unconditional withdrawal of American
forces, making no mention of its own troops, and the replacement of
the Saigon regime by a coalition government, one-third of which

Phillip Jones Griffiths, Magnum

An American soldier in Vietnam appears guarded even while he is at rest. Many blacks served in
South Vietnam. Young white men in the affluent middle class,
particularly college students, often found ways of avoiding military service.

would be composed of NLF members. North Vietnam hoped for
total victory; for its part, the United States showed no disposition
to repudiate Saigon.

Seeking another way out of the war, Nixon turned to the strategy
of "Vietnamization." The United States would undertake a phased
withdrawal of its armed forces while South Vietnam strengthened
its army to the point of being able to continue the struggle. Administration officials, however, refused to specify a timetable for the
departure of American manpower, although they occasionally indicated interim figures. Since the pace seemed slower than expected
and the goal of victory remained, antiwar spokesmen charged that
"Vietnamization" was a sham. President Nixon cited statistics to

refute this claim. Battle deaths had fallen from 278 per week when he took office to 51 per week during the six months prior to February 1971. The ratio of South Vietnamese troops to American troops had changed from 2 to 1 to 3.5 to 1 after withdrawal of over 265,000 United States fighting men. The annual cost of the war had declined by about 50 percent from a high of around $22 billion.

Nixon's "credibility gap" widened when, in April 1970, American units joined South Vietnamese troops in an attack on Vietcong and North Vietnamese sanctuaries in supposedly neutral Cambodia. The President argued that the Cambodian invasion would help sustain the rate of withdrawal and increase Hanoi's interest in a settlement, but opponents castigated the step as an escalation that would interfere with "Vietnamization" and the talks in Paris. Nixon's inflammatory rhetoric at points during his speech announcing the Cambodian operations seemed inconsistent with the claim that his administration was "determined to put an end to this war." One tragic consequence soon became apparent; a civil war broke out between the American-backed regime in Phnom Penh and partisans of Prince Sihanouk, a former ruler, who received help from Vietcong and North Vietnamese soldiers. As Nixon had promised, American troops were soon withdrawn from Cambodia, but in 1971 they supported a short-lived incursion into Laos.

The President reduced troop strength in Vietnam dramatically, although his critics continued to label Vietnamization a sham and a delusion. By September 1972, force levels had fallen from a high of about 550,000 to less than 40,000. Almost all ground combat troops had been withdrawn, leaving only air and naval units in the field. Opponents in Congress continued to question the President's policy, and they came close to passing a resolution that would have placed a terminal date on military expenditures in Vietnam. Casualty figures declined, but the war between the Vietnamese continued wearily on. In April 1972, North Vietnam launched a major offensive in several areas of South Vietnam, hoping by this strategy to deliver a final blow to the Saigon government. President Nixon responded militantly, ordering resumption of air strikes against North Vietnam and mining of the enemy's harbors, including the important seaport of Haiphong. Hanoi thus attempted to end the war by military means, while the United States sustained its support for the faltering regime of President Thieu. Despite many efforts to bring about serious negotiations in Paris, no one could predict confidently when the fighting would end.

At the beginning of his administration, President Nixon had named Henry Kissinger, a well-known expert on international affairs, to his White House staff in order to direct the activities of the National Security Council and to counsel the administration on foreign policy questions. In February 1970, Kissinger produced a broad-ranging statement called "U.S. Foreign Policy for the 1970's: A New Strategy for Peace." It was presented as the first "state of the world" message by the President, paralleling the state of the union address. This document was without precedent in American history; it offered a plan for the new decade, to provide "a new approach to foreign policy, to match a new era of international relations." The President believed that "the whole pattern of international politics was changing. The challenge was to understand that change, to define America's goals for the next period, and to set in motion policies to achieve them." The report mentioned at the outset that the initial postwar period of international relations had ended, because (1) the ravages of World War II had been overcome; (2) the nations rising in the early postwar years had established themselves; (3) the monolithic Communist world of yore had been shattered, "its solidarity . . . broken by the powerful forces of nationalism"; (4) the United States no longer possessed a nuclear monopoly; and, finally, (5) the traditional ideologies had lost their force.

Nixon's message advanced three principles upon which to build a foreign policy for the 1970's. He called the first of these the Nixon Doctrine: "Peace requires *partnership*." America would no longer act alone in international politics but in association with other nations. A second principle held that "peace requires *strength*." The United States must maintain adequate military force but must nevertheless "place high priority on enhancing our security through cooperative arms control." The third principle maintained, "Peace requires a *willingness to negotiate*." Although the country must protect important national interests, "The most fundamental interest of all nations lies in building the structure of peace. . . . We will seek those areas in which we can agree . . . to accommodate conflicts and overcome rivalries." If these principles were followed, it would be possible to achieve international stability and above all "a durable peace" in order to give "full opportunity to the powerful forces driving toward economic change and social justice." These ideas were hardly new, but they had not been adopted as policy before. Certainly they contrasted sharply with views that Nixon had advanced before he became President.

However committed to these principles, the Nixon administration at first made slow progress in putting them into practice. After two years of Republican rule, *The New York Times* summarized the most common view of dissenters: "President Nixon has labored to protect and to perfect the foreign-affairs concepts of the last two decades against the widespread disenchantment with Vietnam and against the allure of insular doctrines." It seemed unlikely that the detailed plans contained in the Kissinger document could be acted upon fully until the United States extricated itself from the tragic war in Southeast Asia. President Nixon had rejected the extensive "globalism" of the early postwar period, but it remained to be seen whether the American Republic would indeed respond to the requirements of the 1970's and beyond.

The most dramatic demonstration of the President's intention to apply the principles he espoused in 1970 was his sudden break with established policies toward Communist China. In July 1971, the State Department announced that it would no longer oppose Peking's entry into the United Nations, an event that soon took place, and Nixon made known his intention to visit mainland China. The Chinese apparently decided to receive him because he had shown that he was sincere in his efforts to liquidate the American involvement in Vietnam and because some degree of association with the United States would help them achieve certain of their international goals. James Reston, writing in *The New York Times,* summarized the goals neatly. Peking wanted to regain Taiwan, to relieve both Russian and American pressure on its borders, to obtain "assurances against the rise of Japanese economic and military power in the Pacific basin," and to occupy a seat on the Security Council of the United Nations. The President's much-publicized visit to Peking took place in February 1972. While little of a substantive nature was accomplished, the visit marked a striking turn toward normalization of United States–Chinese relations and acceptance of full membership in the international community for Communist China.

During August and September 1971, an important breakthrough on the nagging German question took place. The new Chancellor of Germany, the Social Democrat Willy Brandt, had inaugurated a strenuous effort to normalize West German relations with the iron curtain countries. This *Ostpolitik* envisioned political accords with the Soviet Union, Poland, and even East Germany, along with efforts to improve trade relations. Of course, the old problem of divided Berlin placed serious obstacles in the way of *Ostpolitik.* Some improvement in the Berlin situation was needed. For over a year the ambassadors of the four occupying powers—Britain, France, the Soviet Union, and the United States—discussed an agreement designed to ease tensions over Berlin. Finally, the negotiators agreed on a proposal to clarify movement in and out of Berlin and to permit freer visitation between the two sectors of the city. Perhaps even more important was that all the occupying powers in effect recognized East Germany as an independent and sovereign state. The new accord on Berlin, ratified in June 1972, raised hopes that the long postwar struggle over Germany might soon come to an end.

In May 1972, President Nixon visited Moscow, part of his continuing effort to reorder the foreign relations of the United States to accord with Kissinger's three principles. His discussions with the Soviet leadership were businesslike; both sides made a strong effort to avoid divisive or inflammatory rhetoric. One encouraging outcome was recorded. The two powers signed two agreements that stemmed from the SALT negotiations. Although these documents did not bring about any significant disarmament, they had the effect of freezing the arms balance and depriving each side of foolproof defenses against nuclear attack, an arrangement that hopefully would deter each side from launching a preemptive strike against the other. Nixon did not succeed in efforts to negotiate a comprehensive trade agreement, but the two powers set up a joint commission to discuss this question in detail. Premier Kosygin expressed the feelings of most observers when he called the arms accords "a victory for all peace-loving people, because security and peace is the common goal." Despite improving Soviet-American relations, agreement still seemed far away on the settlement of the war in Southeast Asia and the continuing Arab-Israeli conflict in the Middle East.

President Nixon insisted that his administration would follow liberal international trade policies. "We recognize," he said in 1971, "that our preponderant size in the world economy gives us an international responsibility to continue on this path just as we have an international responsibility to manage our domestic economy well. I am convinced that liberal trade is in both our domestic economic interest and our foreign policy interest." Despite these brave words, the country encountered an adverse balance of trade for the first time in many years during 1971. This unexpected event worsened the adverse balance-of-payments condition that had plagued the country since the late 1950's. The balance of international payments includes the value of trade in services and capital as well as in goods. The adverse balance of payments resulted from a situation that produced a larger total value of imported goods, services, and capital items than the total value of exported goods, services, and capital items. Among the influences creating this imbalance were the foreign-aid expenditures of the United States, the costs of the war in Vietnam, and particularly domestic inflation, which raised the cost of American goods to foreign buyers. Among other things, the balance-of-payments deficit caused a flight of gold from the country; it also weakened the dollar in relation to certain foreign currencies, notably the West German mark and the Japanese yen.

To improve the nation's position in trade, President Nixon suddenly announced in August 1971 that the United States would impose a "temporary" tax on imports. He also said that the dollar would be allowed to "float" in international money markets; the Treasury would no longer guarantee payment of a fixed amount in dollars for an ounce of gold ($35) but would let market transactions determine the value of American currency. This procedure would in effect devalue the dollar, hopefully stabilizing its purchasing power in relation to other currencies at a realistic level. Devaluation presumably would encourage enlarged foreign purchases in the United States, for a mark or a pound would exchange for more dollars than before—if the United States succeeded in keeping domestic price levels from rising by means of controls. In 1971, however, the trade deficit reached $2 billion, and all indications pointed to an even greater gap in 1972. The administration insisted that it did not intend to abandon the liberal policies it had espoused, but the new departures of 1971 proved once again that protectionism, always in the past a powerful influence on American trade policies, might affect decisions during the coming years. If so, levels of foreign trade might ultimately be depressed.

Some historians, notably William Appleman Williams and his students, have advanced the thesis that efforts to bring about trade expansion have dominated American foreign policy throughout the country's history. This argument fails to consider the tremendous influence that protectionists have had on trade policy. It also ignores the fact that both international trade and overseas investments together have never represented more than a small percentage of gross national product. The total combined value of American exports and imports in 1948 amounted to only about 8 percent of gross national product for that year. In 1968 the figures stood at a little more than 10 percent. Total private investments by Americans in Latin America in 1957 accounted for $8.8 billion (about 35 percent of United States private investments overseas), a minuscule amount compared with investments in the domestic economy. This does not mean that the country's foreign trade and investments do not play a large part in the international economy, but it does suggest that careless generalizations about the importance of trade expansion as a determinant of American foreign policy should be treated skeptically. Economic pressures obviously enter into decisions in manifold ways along with a broad range of other considerations. In addition American decisions based on strategic or political considerations often produced economic changes that had considerable effect overseas. One of the most important tasks on the agenda of scholars interested in the history of American foreign relations is a more thorough and responsible investigation of economic foreign policy.

Nixon entered the presidential campaign of 1972 confident of victory. His visits to Moscow and Peking, all the more dramatic because of his reputation as an anti-Communist, caught the public imagination. The Democrats nominated Senator George McGovern of South Dakota after a divisive primary campaign, hoping that the Midwestern liberal could unite his shattered party and forge a new coalition of voters in support of drastic changes in national policy. McGovern made criticism of the war in Vietnam the most important issue in his campaign, a course that failed to sway the electorate, especially after Henry Kissinger, completing a long and tortuous series of secret negotiations with representatives of North Vietnam and the NLF, was able to announce just before election day that peace was "at hand." McGovern called for a "new internationalism" that in many ways paralleled the design expounded by Kissinger, although his idealism stood in sharp contrast to the realism of the presidential adviser. McGovern insisted that foreign policy had to rest on strength at home. "How we live in the neighborhoods and communities of America," he argued, "will determine how we live with our international neighbors, and in the broader world community." Clearly McGovern's views would have led to considerable retrenchment overseas, although he did not contemplate a reversion to the isolationism of an earlier age. Nixon's overwhelming triumph constituted a strong endorsement of his foreign policy, much to the discomfiture of his opposition, which had assumed that the unpopularity of the war in Vietnam would assure them the presidency.

As the United States entered the 1970's, some historians continued to advance the thesis that the ruling classes had adopted exploitative and repressive policies at home and abroad in order to preserve their power. Those who became disillusioned with the Vietnam War found this viewpoint particularly attractive. Intellectuals speculated frequently that widespread social discontent and disorganization would soon materialize at home because of the failure of the country to cope with the changing times.

Moderate critics of national policies rejected the view that the problems of the day were natural and unavoidable consequences of history, but they insisted that the United States, for both ethical and political reasons, must reorder its priorities to help improve the conditions of the poor throughout the world. Their profound opposition to the war in Southeast Asia flowed from the conviction that it represented a quixotic attempt to apply cold war doctrines where they had no proper place. Containment had had its uses immediately after World War II, when Russia and America were at loggerheads over power vacuums in Europe and East Asia, but it provided no guidance for dealings with Communist China or struggling new nations throughout the third world.

Senator Fulbright insisted throughout the 1960's that Americans must abandon what he called "old myths" and recognize "new realities." He asserted that "the master myth of the cold war is that the Communist bloc is a monolith composed of governments which are not really governments at all but organized conspiracies . . . all equally resolute and implacable in their determination to destroy the free world." The reality, he claimed, was that the Communist world was seriously divided and that if recognized this condition could be used to advantage. The American right and the American left both entertained their own myths, "that we can either win the cold war or end it immediately and completely. . . . We must disabuse ourselves of them and come to terms, at last, with the realities of a world in which neither good nor evil is absolute and in which those who move events and make history are those who have understood not how much but how little is within our power to change."

No one could foretell whether comfortable America, enjoying by far the highest standard of living in all the earth, could make the sacrifices needed to support economic development throughout the third world. Nor could anyone predict that the nation would recognize the dangers in sustaining the cold war beyond reasonable length. Foreign policy begins at home, at least in the sense that it is associated with domestic perceptions of national interest. Very different views of what was in the national interest divided the American people at the beginning of the 1970's. The future depended to a considerable extent on the degree to which there grew up a new national consensus on foreign policy to replace containment.

SUGGESTED READINGS

The materials listed here constitute only a small sampling of the vast literature available on American foreign relations since 1945. The bibliographies
in the general books cited in the following paragraph are most helpful for
additional references.

Historians' analyses of the cold war fall into three broad classifications.
The first generally accepted view is that Russian imperialism was the root
cause of the cold war. Examples of this outlook are Norman A. Graebner,
Cold War Diplomacy: American Foreign Policy, 1945–1960 (1962); John Spanier,
American Foreign Policy Since 1954 (2nd ed. rev., 1965); and Herbert Feis, *From
Trust to Terror: The Onset of the Cold War, 1945–1950* (1970). Another group
of historians, mostly writing in recent years, lays most of the blame at the
door of the United States, claiming that its foreign policy reflects a desire
to maintain the status quo against the desires of social revolutionary societies elsewhere in the world. The most effective revisionist analysis is
Walter LaFeber, *America, Russia, and the Cold War, 1945–1971* (1972), for
which the author provides two useful documentary collections, *The Origins
of the Cold War, 1941–1947* (1971), and *America in the Cold War: Twenty
Years of Revolution and Response, 1947–1967* (1969). The most voluble and
extreme revisionist is Gabriel Kolko, whose views may be examined in *The
Politics of War: The World and United States Foreign Policy, 1943–1945* (1965),
The Roots of American Foreign Policy: An Analysis of Power and Purpose (1969),
and *The Limits of Power* (1971). Other revisionist works include D. F. Fleming,
The Cold War and Its Origins (2 vols., 1951); David Horowitz, *The Free World
Colossus: A Critique of American Foreign Policy in the Cold War* (rev. ed., 1971);
Ronald Steel, *Pax Americana* (1967); and Thomas G. Paterson, ed., *The Cold
War Critics* (1971). A third group tends to account for the cold war as a natural
consequence of power imbalances created by World War II. The best ex-
amples of this view are Louis Halle, *The Cold War as History* (1967); and
Adam Ulam, *The Rivals* (1971). The historiographical dispute is illustrated
well in Lloyd C. Gardner, Arthur M. Schlesinger, Jr., and Hans Morgenthau,
The Origins of the Cold War (1970). Other general works of interest are Seyom
Brown, *The Faces of Power: Constancy and Change in United States Foreign
Policy from Truman to Johnson* (1968); John Lukacs, *A New History of the Cold
War* (1966); Stephen Ambrose, *Rise to Globalism: American Foreign Policy
Since 1938* (1971); and David Rees, *The Age of Containment: The Cold War
1945–1965* (1967). A magisterial European treatment is Andre Fontaine, *His-
tory of the Cold War* (2 vols., 1970). For documents and other important information consult the annual volumes produced by the Council on Foreign
Relations entitled *The United States in World Affairs* and *Documents on American Foreign Relations*. The official pronouncements of all the Presidents since
1945 appear in *Public Papers of Presidents of the United States*.

On the Truman era, the chief actor himself wrote an important autobio-
graphical account, his *Memoirs* (2 vols., 1956). The best general history is
Cabell B. Phillips, *The Truman Presidency* (1966). For documents consult
Barton J. Bernstein and Allen J. Matusow, *The Truman Administration: A
Documentary History* (1966). There is also Herbert Druks, *Harry S. Truman
and the Russians, 1945–1953* (1967). Works that give information on Truman's

various secretaries of state include James F. Byrnes, *Speaking Frankly* (1947); George Curry, *James F. Byrnes* (1965); Robert H. Ferrell, *George C. Marshall* (1966); Dean Acheson, *Present at the Creation* (1969); Gaddis Smith, *Dean Acheson* (1972); and McGeorge Bundy, ed., *The Pattern of Responsibility* (1952), a collection of Acheson's utterances. Lloyd C. Gardner has published a revisionist analysis covering this period entitled *Architects of Illusion: Men and Ideas in American Foreign Policy, 1941–1949* (1970). The thesis that the United States dropped the atomic bomb on Japan to frighten Russia appears in Gar Alperovitz, *Atomic Diplomacy: Hiroshima and Potsdam* (1965); but it is ably refuted by Herbert Feis in *The Atomic Bomb and the End of World War II* (1966). Books by or about important participants in statecraft include George Kennan, *Memoirs, 1925–1950* (1967); Arthur H. Vandenberg, *Private Papers* (1952); Robert Murphy, *Diplomat Among Warriors* (1964), a book that covers later presidents through Kennedy as well; and Walter Millis, ed., *The Forrestal Diaries* (1951), the output of Truman's first secretary of defense. Works dealing with the development of the containment policy in Europe include John L. Snell, *Wartime Origins of the East-West Dilemma Over Germany* (1959); Joseph C. Jones, *The Fifteen Weeks* (1955), on the origins of the Marshall Plan; Harry B. Price, *The Marshall Plan and Its Meaning* (1955); Lucius D. Clay, *Decision in Germany* (1950), by the commander of the airlift into Berlin at the time of the blockade; W. P. Davison, *The Berlin Blockade: A Study in Cold War Politics* (1958); Eugene Davidson, *The Death and Life of Germany: An Account of the American Occupation* (1959); Robert Osgood, *NATO: Entangling Alliance* (1962); and H. Bradford Westerfield, *Foreign Policy and Party Politics* (1955). Clark Eichelberger recounts the early activities of the United Nations as well as later developments in *UN: The First Twenty-Five Years* (1970). For another important subject see James M. Boyd, *United Nations Peace-Keeping Operations: A Military and Political Appraisal* (1971). For information on the debacle in China and the beginning of containment in East Asia see Tang Tsou, *America's Failure in China, 1941–1950* (1963), and the famous "white paper" on China published by the Department of State, *United States Relations with China, with Special Reference to the Period, 1944–1949* (1949). A good history of the Korean War is David Rees, *Korea: The Limited War* (1964). For additional information about the war and the Truman-MacArthur controversy, consult Allen S. Whiting, *China Crosses the Yalu* (1960); Ronald J. Caridi, *The Korean War and American Politics: The Republican Party as a Case Study* (1968); Trumbull Higgins, *Korea and the Fall of MacArthur* (1960); General Douglas MacArthur's *Reminiscences* (1964); and the report of the "great debate" precipitated in the Congress by MacArthur's resignation, "Military Situation in the Far East," *Hearings* before the Committee on Armed Services and Foreign Relations, U.S. Senate, 82 Cong., 1 Sess. (5 vols., 1951).

President Eisenhower published his own account of his leadership during the Eisenhower era entitled *The White House Years* (2 vols., 1963–1965); and Vice-President Richard Nixon contributed *Six Crises* (1962). The activities of Eisenhower's secretaries of state are treated in Richard Goold-Adams, *The Time of Power* (1962), about John Foster Dulles; Louis Gerson, *John Foster Dulles* (1967); and George B. Noble, *Christian A. Herter* (1970). Two interesting works on the debate over strategy and defense that began in the Eisenhower years and continued into the 1960's are Henry Kissinger, *The Necessity for Choice* (1961), and Herman Kahn, *On Thermonuclear War* (1961). Affairs in the Middle East are covered in the account of then British Prime

Minister Anthony Eden entitled *Full Circle* (1960), and in Nadav Safran, *From War to War, The Arab-Israeli Confrontation, 1948–1967* (1969). The President's brother, Milton Eisenhower, surveyed the troubled state of Latin America in *The Wine Is Bitter: The United States and Latin America* (1963). Norman Graebner criticized the course of events in *The New Isolationism* (1956); but for a favorable view consult the inside account by a close adviser, Sherman Adams, *Firsthand Report* (1961).

The policies of President Kennedy are well analyzed in a series of books by close advisers, including Arthur M. Schlesinger, Jr., *A Thousand Days: John F. Kennedy in the White House* (1965); Theodore Sorensen, *Kennedy* (1965); and Roger Hilsman, *To Move a Nation* (1967). A root-and-branch critique appears in Louise FitzSimons, *The Kennedy Doctrine* (1972), which popularizes revisionist interpretations. Robert Kennedy, the President's brother, wrote a striking short account of the missile crisis of 1962, *Thirteen Days* (1969). Other books on Cuban questions include Theodore Draper, *Castro's Revolution* (1962); William Appleman Williams, *The United States, Cuba, and Castro* (1962); Ramon Eduardo Ruiz, *Cuba, The Making of a Revolution* (1968); and Elie Abel, *The Missile Crisis* (1966). For the Kennedy outlook on defense matters see Robert S. McNamara, *The Essence of Security: Reflections in Office* (1968), and Maxwell D. Taylor, *Responsibility and Response* (1967). Two books on the Alliance for Progress are William D. Rogers, *Alliance for Progress* (1967), and Jerome Levinson and Juan de Onís, *The Alliance That Lost Its Way: A Critical Report on the Alliance for Progress* (1970).

President Johnson's remembrances of office are in *The Vantage Point: Perspectives of the Presidency, 1963–1969* (1971). The most sensitive account, by a White House adviser, is Eric F. Goldman, *The Tragedy of Lyndon Johnson* (1968). Most of the literature for this period concentrates on the course of the Vietnam War. See for background information Joseph Buttinger, *Vietnam: A Dragon Embattled* (2 vols., 1967); Bernard Fall, *The Two Viet Nams* (2nd rev. ed., 1967); Robert Shaplen, *Road From War: Vietnam 1965–1970* (1970); *The Pentagon Papers* (1971), which reprints many classified government documents published originally in *The New York Times;* Edwin O. Reischauer, *Beyond Vietnam: The United States and Asia* (1967); Marvin E. Gettleman, ed., *Vietnam: History, Documents, and Opinions* (1970); George M. Kahin and J. W. Lewis, *The United States in Vietnam* (1967); and Arthur M. Schlesinger, Jr., *The Bitter Heritage* (1966). For two interesting memoirs, see Townsend Hoopes, *The Limits of Intervention* (1969), which recounts the decision to seek a way out of Vietnam made in 1968; and John Bartlow Martin, *Overtaken by Events: The Dominican Crisis from the Fall of Trujillo to the Civil War* (1966). Two arresting essays by a leading critic of the Vietnam War, Senator William Fulbright, are *Old Myths and New Realities* (1964) and *The Arrogance of Power* (1966). For information on the vital question of arms control see Bernard G. Bechhoefer, *Postwar Negotiations for Arms Control* (1961) and William B. Bader, *The United States and the Spread of Nuclear Weapons* (1968). No serious works have yet appeared on Nixon's foreign policy. For his positions see his first "State of the World" address printed as "U.S. Foreign Policy for the 1970's: A New Strategy for Peace," *The Department of State Bulletin,* 62 (March 9, 1970). Two succeeding such messages for 1971 and 1972, "U.S. Foreign Policy for the 1970's: Building for Peace" (1971) and "U.S. Foreign Policy for the 1970's: The Emerging Structure of Peace" (1972), were issued by the White House as reports to the Congress.

Significant Statistics

	1900	1920	1945	1970
Foreign trade (millions of dollars)				
Exports				
Americas	227	2,553	2,564	**15,611**
Europe	1,040	4,466	5,515	**14,817**
Asia	68	872	849	**10,027**
Australia and Oceania	41	172	354	**1,189**
Africa	19	166	524	**1,580**
Total	1,499	8,664	10,097	**43,224**
Percentage of GNP	8.6	9.3	4.9	**4.4**
Imports				
Americas	224	2,424	2,874	**16,928**
Europe	441	1,228	409	**11,395**
Asia	146	1,397	407	**9,621**
Australia and Oceania	29	80	171	**871**
Africa	11	150	297	**1,113**
Total	930	5,784	4,280	**39,952**
Percentage of GNP	5.3	5.9	1.9	**4.0**
Balance	+570	+2,880	+5,816	**+3,272**
Investment (billions of dollars)				
U.S. investments abroad	0.7[a]	7.0[b]	16.8	**166.6[c]**
Foreign investments in the U.S.	3.4[a]	3.3[b]	17.6	**97.5[c]**
Net investment position	−2.7[a]	+3.7[b]	−0.8	**+69.1[c]**
Department of State budget (millions of dollars)	3.3	13.5	50.1	**225.5**
Diplomatic missions	42	47	56	**116**
Alliances in force	0	0	0	**42**
Overseas travel (travelers in thousands)	120	157	175	**5,260**

Sources: *Statistical Abstract of the United States; Historical Statistics of the United States, Colonial Times to 1957; Treaties and Other International Agreements of the United States of America, 1776–1949;* and *United States Treaties and Other International Agreements.*

  [a] Data for 1897.
  [b] Data for 1919.
  [c] Preliminary.

7

Consumer Culture and Cold War

American Society, 1945–1960

WILLIAM E. LEUCHTENBURG

In the summer of 1945 United States troop ships, carrying thousands of homeward-bound GI's from farflung battle fronts, steamed past the Statue of Liberty and up the Hudson River to be nudged into their berths on the New York waterfront. Aboard vessels like the majestic *Queen Mary*, jubilant soldiers and sailors howled with delight when they discerned the familiar tracery of the Manhattan skyline, and in the river fireboats sent geysers of water into the air as a signal of welcome. For some, the future seemed bright with promise. New York gave the triumphant commander, Dwight Eisenhower, arms raised above his head in a victory salute, a more tumultuous reception than had greeted Charles Lindbergh after his solo flight across the Atlantic in 1927, and the whole town of Farmersville,

Texas (pop. 2,206), turned out in 98-degree heat to hail the bashful Lieutenant Audie Murphy, the infantry's most-decorated combat officer. But others were advised painfully of the nation's short-comings. The window of a gas station in McFarland, California, greeted returning servicemen with a crudely lettered sign: "Colored Trade Not Solisited at Fountain," and in other west coast towns Japanese-American veterans, who had fought with conspicuous bravery in Italy, were assaulted, denied jobs, often unable to recover property which had been seized during the period of mass evacuation and internment. Congressional Medal of Honor winner Charles "Commando" Kelly came back to a Pittsburgh slum that lacked both plumbing and lights, a grim reminder of how recently the scourge of the Great Depression had ended.

As the veterans and their families tried to take the measure of the future, they riveted their attention on the interwar years, little real-izing that much of that recollection would be irrelevant to the post-war world. Often their questions went back to the 1920's, and they wondered whether the country would regress to an era like that of Harding and Coolidge, which had followed the first world war. Of much greater immediacy were the issues surrounding the age of Franklin D. Roosevelt. There were widespread forebodings that hard times would soon return, for many doubted that the economy would be able to absorb the 10 million war workers and the 12 million men in the armed services. The experience of the 1930's also determined post-1945 political alignments. Some hoped that the aggrandizement of the presidency and the government intervention associated with the New Deal would be halted; others looked forward to an extension of liberal legislation or even a radical reordering of social institutions. For years to come political debate would continue to revolve around the quarrels of 1935, and the lineaments of the Roosevelt coalition could still be seen in election returns in the 1970's.

Yet, however persistent, traditions of the Great Depression proved less pertinent to the quarter-century following the war's end than two other developments, the force of which was only dimly per-ceived in 1945 — the diffusion of affluence and the consumer culture and the impact of the cold war in the shadow of the nuclear bomb.

Of all the influences on postwar America, none exceeded that exerted by dramatic economic changes. Buoyed by consumer spend-ing and bloated military budgets, the economy expanded in so ex-plosive a fashion that the sociologist Seymour Martin Lipset could claim, "The fundamental problems of the industrial revolution have been solved." When the Harvard economist John Kenneth Galbraith

It's over! In New York's Times Square on V-J Day a sailor exploits the mood of celebration at the ending of World War II and the birth of the postwar era. The photograph is the work of Alfred Eisenstaedt, who came to the United States from Hitler Germany in 1935 and the following year pioneered the candid camera technique for the new magazine *Life*.

published *The Affluent Society* in 1958, he gave a name to a phenomenon that had been captivating writers on the United States for more than a decade. Never in the long annals of mankind had so many people in any nation enjoyed so high a level of prosperity, even though the impoverished continued to be numbered in the millions.

In the flush times of the postwar era, every standard by which Americans had measured material progress fell. Through the grim years of the Depression the country had yearned to reach once more the high plateau of 1929. But in 1956, the income of the average American was more than 50 percent greater than in 1929, even when allowance was made for increases in prices and taxes. By 1960, per capita income was 35 percent higher than in the war boom year of 1945. "The remarkable capacity of the United States economy in 1960," concluded the economic historian Harold G. Vatter, "represents the crossing of a great divide in the history of humanity."

This economic performance made possible the elaboration and diffusion of the consumer culture. With the nation at close to full employment, millions were freed from the anxieties about subsistence that had engrossed them in the 1930's, and manufacturers and advertising agencies encouraged the sovereign consumer to indulge his preoccupation with marginal differentiation of products. Much as life in medieval society centered around the religious observances of a cathedral town, postwar America became absorbed in the acquisition of goods and evolved a variety of institutions —from suburban supermarkets to gourmet food stores—that ministered to the shopper. Moreover, the consumer culture penetrated far beyond the shopping mall. Foreign countries that had earlier borrowed such American innovations as the assembly line and the skyscraper erected "Beba Coca Cola" signs, listened to Muzak, bought Colonel Sanders' Kentucky Fried Chicken, and became accustomed to wheeling carts laden with Campbell's soup and Quaker Oats through the aisles of the *supermarche* or *supermercado* or *supermarked*. Within the United States the consumer culture left its imprint on styles of travel and on modern art, on popular music and on presidential elections, even on the cold war.

America's role as the preeminent great power molded the United States in these years no less than did affluence and the consumer culture. In the midst of prosperity, there was always awareness of a dreadful apparition at the feast—the threat of nuclear holocaust. Secretary of War Henry Stimson predicted in 1945 that the Promethean feat of unlocking the secret of the atom would have "more effect on human affairs than the theory of Copernicus and the law of gravity," and some took pride in this latest of American technological achievements. But for many more the knowledge of Hiroshima meant that victory in World War II was, *Time* observed, "as charged with sorrow and doubt as with joy and gratitude." Man had bitten the

The cold war intrudes on the consumer society in Alan Dunn's cartoon from a 1947 issue of *The New Yorker*. While the periodical poked fun at cold war America, its advertisements were offering alluring images of the consumer culture.

"Oh, dear, I'd really be enjoying all this if it weren't for Russia."

Drawing by Alan Dunn. Copyright © 1947 The New Yorker Magazine, Inc.

forbidden fruit, had found "the ultimate stuff of the universe," and was troubled by his own temerity.

The post-Hiroshima generation felt a special awareness of impermanence and premonition of doom. Infants imbibed Strontium 90 with their morning milk, and pupils hunched under their desks as air raid sirens wailed during drills. Years later students at San Francisco State reported that nuclear bombs had exploded in their dreams, and young children expressed Doomsday anxieties. In the 1960's the "post-Hiroshima" people would make a jukebox favorite of P. F. Sloan's unsettling "Eve of Destruction":

> Don't you understand what I'm try'n' to say?
> Can't you feel the fear that I'm feelin' today?
> If the button is pushed there's no running away.

> There'll be no one to save with the world in a grave.
> Take a look around you boy,
> It's bound to scare you boy. . . .

Yet, curiously, the cold war, for all its hideous menace, would serve to foster more benign developments—prosperity, social advances, and, most unexpectedly, the movement for greater equality. Although the "military-industrial complex" raised justifiable alarm, armaments expenditures provided the biggest impetus for the boom in the 1950's that lifted many above the poverty line. Economists spoke of the "Soviet effect," meaning the way in which compulsive American countermoves to Russian actions came to justify everything from increased spending on research and development to the construction of the St. Lawrence seaway to the breakthrough in federal aid to education. Most important, at a time when the United States vied with Soviet Russia for the allegiance of the peoples of Africa and Asia, American racial and religious mores came under close scrutiny.

Despite the rumblings of change during the Great Depression and in World War II, the United States in 1945 remained a country dominated by WASPs. Jews confronted covert discrimination in the professions and, when they sought to buy homes, blatant rejection through restrictive covenants in which Gentile home owners contracted to sell only to their own kind. Radio showed the man of color how the white world preferred him—the faithful, obedient servant of the Lone Ranger's Tonto and the Green Hornet's Kato, or a jovial retainer like Jack Benny's Rochester. In the South, Negroes rode in the back of the bus, most were disfranchised, and none went to school with whites. Apartheid prevailed in much of the North too. Even Topeka in John Brown's Kansas segregated schoolchildren by race. The greatest democracy on earth recruited a Jim Crow army, and as late as 1945 in the downtown section of the nation's capital Negroes could not stay at a hotel, eat at a drugstore lunch counter, or attend a movie.

These patterns of prejudice proved an intolerable burden for the United States in international affairs. World War II brought America face to face with the inconsistency between fighting a war for democracy against Hitler's master race state and condoning discrimination at home. During the war *Fortune* pointed out that "a fracas in Detroit has an echo in Aden," and in what Richard Dalfiume has called "the forgotten years" of the Negro revolution Gunnar Myrdal made the country aware of "the American dilemma." In the cold war era Washington would take pains to highlight racial advances. After the Supreme Court handed down a desegregation decision, the Voice of America broadcast the news in thirty-four languages all day and night and through the following day. The iron curtain countries in turn exploited evidence of persisting racial discrimination in the land of their cold war rival. When a United Nations committee voiced disapproval of the Russian invasion of Hungary, a Budapest newspaper invited the committee "to make a study trip up the Arkansas River." Signs of "a new world acoming" were increasingly evident even in 1945. That year Bess Myerson became the first Jewish Miss America, and Branch Rickey of the Brooklyn Dodgers signed up the sensational black shortstop of the Kansas City Monarchs, Jackie Robinson.

The cold war and the consumer culture also defined the parameters of American politics. Both sustained a politics of the center. Though the rivalry with Soviet Russia provided an occasion for ideologues of the Right who wanted to launch a crusade to exterminate the heretics, the peril of nuclear devastation motivated most of the Right to advocate a less extreme course. At the same time the actions of the U.S.S.R. in Poland, in Berlin, and in Hungary diminished the appeal of the fatherland of socialism to all but a small fringe on the Left. The cold war drove a wedge through the liberal movement, with one wing organized by the avowedly noncommunist Americans for Democratic Action in 1947 and a more leftist sector mobilized under Henry Wallace. Beginning in 1950, liberal influence was diminished by a frustrating limited war that spawned phenomena like McCarthyism and focused attention not on present needs but on bygone encounters with alleged subversives. Assertion of the superior claim of the national interest in the cold war militated against demands for costly social welfare legislation and subdued the ardor of the union movement. The consumer culture generated a politics of inflation that plagued the Democrats in the aftermath of World War II and during the Korean conflict. In 1946 the Republicans would win their only emphatic victory in congressional elections over a period of four decades in a contest affected by the irritation of housewives about the price of hamburger. More significantly, rising income and the enticements of the consumer culture kindled a sense of contentment that encouraged a politics of moderation.

Both of the first postwar Presidents, Harry Truman and Dwight Eisenhower, operated within the boundaries fixed by the consumer culture and the cold war. If in his first term Truman was disconcerted by ill-humored consumers, in his second term he was troubled by the imperatives of the cold war. In the 1948 election

Truman narrowly missed defeat because of the challenge from a third party born of the cold war, and in 1952 the strains of limited war would terminate the Democrats' twenty-year reign. The circumstances under which he functioned explain in part why Truman was associated with, in Samuel Grafton's words, a "new centrism" —"a strange combination of conservatism without animus and liberalism without glow." From necessity and conviction his successor, General Eisenhower, did not stray far from the middle of the road. "Never has a popular figure who dominated so completely the national political scene affected so negligibly the essential historic processes of his time," observed the historian Norman Graebner. Yet Eisenhower appeared to suit millions of Americans, for he was credited with thawing the cold war and with a piping prosperity that brought the consumer culture to fruition. His opponents readily adapted to the temperate environment. In 1956, Adlai Stevenson said, "I agree that it is time for catching our breath; I agree that moderation is the spirit of the times." Four years later, John F. Kennedy concentrated his presidential campaign on suburban shopping centers, and when Norman Mailer decided to support him, he entitled his essay, "Superman Comes to the Supermarket."

In this "post-industrial society," Americans turned away from public issues to take up more personal matters—fitting together the pieces of marriages sundered by the war, nest-building, nurturing the psyche, enjoying the fruits of prosperity after the grinding years of the Depression. At a time when Leonard Bernstein was scoring a musical based on *Candide,* they heeded Voltaire's advice to cultivate their own gardens. Though critics found this society depressingly homogenized, there was more diversity and creativity than they conceded, in art and in the theater, in popular culture and in the university, even in life styles. As early as 1948, with the publication of Dr. Alfred C. Kinsey's *Sexual Behavior in the Human Male,* the nation was made keenly aware of divergent standards of behavior. Furthermore, reformers could point to a number of accomplishments—Truman's Fair Deal, Eisenhower's acceptance of a good part of the New Deal, the dedicated leadership of Adlai Stevenson, and, most particularly, the passive resistance movement of Martin Luther King and the pathbreaking decisions of the Supreme Court under the new Chief Justice, Earl Warren. But, overall, it was not a period hospitable to agitation for fundamental change. Having known more than fifteen years of crisis in depression and war, the nation rejected the politics of intensity much as it had in the 1920's. By the close of the Eisenhower era, Adlai Stevenson was stating that "for the first time in history the engine of social progress has run out of the fuel of discontent," and Walter Lippmann commented, "We talk about ourselves these days as if we were a completed society, one which has no further great business to transact."

The Man from Missouri

The death of Franklin D. Roosevelt on April 12, 1945, catapulted into the White House a man of very different background and temperament. In contrast to Roosevelt's patrician upbringing as the young squire of Hyde Park destined for Groton and Harvard, Harry

The first postwar President, Harry S. Truman, is caught with a characteristic grin. He attracted admirers by his openness and geniality as well as by his courage. In 1948 he made the transcontinental train part of American political folklore in his cross-country campaign against the Republicans.

United Press International

Truman's youth was spent in a small Missouri town where his father was a mule swapper. Shriner, Moose, Elk, Lion, Eagle, deacon of the Second Baptist Church, Truman traveled in circles far removed from FDR's *haut monde*. Roosevelt first won national attention as a foe of Tammany Hall. Truman—World War I artillery captain, consumer culture failure as haberdasher, courthouse politician—made his way under the tutelage of the notorious Kansas City boss Tom Pendergast. In 1934, Pendergast decided to send Truman to the United States Senate, where he became an obscure back-bencher. Even after he had won respect as the head of a watchdog committee in World War II and was elected Vice-President in 1944, he remained outside the main councils of government, and not until after he assumed the presidency was he briefed about the atomic bomb. To this man fell the awesome responsibility of persuading the country, and the world, that he could cope with the demands of the office that FDR had held for more than twelve years.

Truman brought to this task a mixed assortment of talents, sentiments, and personal qualities. None doubted his grit. He made bold decisions quickly and executed them briskly. However, he also was generally unreflective, sometimes cocky and brash. Determined to carry on the New Deal tradition, he sent Congress a twenty-one-point program that included liberal reforms just four days after the Japanese surrender. Yet he lacked the grand vision necessary to inspire a nation, and he appointed to office lackluster plodders who suffered by comparison with the New Deal luminaries. "It is more important to have a connection with Battery D, 129th Field Artillery, than with Felix Frankfurter," remarked one commentator. To FDR loyalists Truman never measured up. Each time he acted they would ask, "What would Roosevelt have done if he were alive?" (At the outset of his tenure, Truman himself consulted his predecessor's widow, observed Joseph and Stewart Alsop, "as he might have consulted a medium.") As late as January 1947, Fiorello La Guardia, the former New York mayor, said of Roosevelt: "How we miss him. Hardly a domestic problem or an international situation today but what we say 'Oh, if F.D.R. were only here.'"

Throughout his presidency, Truman lived in Roosevelt's shadow, but those who compared him to Roosevelt often did him less than justice. Truman benefited from the legacy the New Deal left him— an ideology of sorts, a legislative agenda, a corps of experienced administrators, an expansive view of the executive office, an effective electoral coalition of low-income voters in the great cities. But

FDR's admirers sometimes forgot that their leader had been fought to a standstill by the conservatives in Congress in recent years. Truman inherited the same opponents and had to work in an atmosphere that was not conducive to reform. His main assignment was to adapt the liberalism of the Great Depression to an age of economic growth and to make way for the newer emphases of the consumer culture, the cold war, and the civil rights revolution. In carrying out this task, he often met with setbacks. Still, a poll of historians would subsequently put him in the "near great" category of Presidents, for reasons best stated by Elmer Davis: "There are two Trumans—the White House Truman and the courthouse Truman. He does the big things right, and the little things wrong."

Hardly more than four months after Truman took office, the war ended, and the new President confronted the first of the "big things"—reconversion from a war to a peace economy. The job had been bungled after World War I, and many thought it would be again. Since the New Deal, government had become more humane, and measures like the GI Bill of Rights spared veterans the travail of the aftermath to 1918. But there was a more pertinent worry—that the economy, denied the artificial stimulus of war, would rapidly return to the massive unemployment of the Great Depression. Within a week after V-J Day, the Springfield Arsenal fired every employee, and across the country a million workers drew their final paychecks. Abruptly, contracts worth $35 billion were canceled. The mobilization director foresaw 8 million jobless by spring. However, the economy swiftly absorbed the millions of returning servicemen, and in a remarkably short time the reconversion had been achieved, although not until 1950 did real GNP reach its wartime high. This accomplishment owed a good deal to the fact that the American consumer came out of the war with a bulging wallet and a frustrated yen for goods that had too long been unavailable.

Yet this same consumer demand threatened to undermine these feats by creating a runaway inflation, and when Truman attempted to limit price rises, he precipitated a keen debate over the role of government in the postwar world. Businessmen, after more than a decade of regulation, wanted to lift the wartime controls, and they won backing from consumers weary of ration coupons and shortages. On the other hand, New Deal liberals saw need of more intervention from Washington and feared that a premature ending of controls would injure unorganized groups.

As the debate raged, every interest sought to protect itself, but the press focused the greatest attention on action by labor unions. In April 1945, when Truman took office, strikes devoured 1.5 million man-days; in September, 4 million; by February 1946, 23 million. Unions, smarting under the cut in take-home pay resulting from the ending of war industry overtime, insisted that wage increases were necessary to maintain real income. Their critics countered that wage boosts were driving prices up. Each group — business, labor, farm — demanded that the President clamp a bit on the others while giving it free rein.

Truman now confronted a problem that Roosevelt had not had to take on in the New Deal years. The historian Barton J. Bernstein has written, "Whereas the politics of depression generally allowed the Roosevelt Administration, by bestowing benefits, to court interest groups and contribute to an economic upturn, the politics of inflation required a responsible government like Truman's to curb wages, prices, and profits and to deny the growing expectations of rival groups." Roosevelt had faced this difficulty in World War II, but he could appeal to patriotism for sacrifices in the common cause. With V-J Day, these compunctions ended, and Truman was put in the unhappy position of trying to restrain not only businessmen, most of whom were in the Republican camp, but the farmer and labor elements in his own Democratic coalition. The President's troubles reached a climax in May 1946 when he asked Congress for authority to draft rail strikers into the army. Nothing came of this, but while failing to appease conservatives, his action served to hasten the defection of liberals and unionists from the administration. A CIO conference denounced Truman as the country's "No. 1 Strike-breaker."

By the time the first postwar elections were held in November 1946, Truman had been victimized by the politics of the pressure group state. When Congress in the summer of 1946 refused to grant him adequate price control powers, he found himself in a tiger's cage equipped with a cap pistol. Housewives blamed him when there was no meat on the butcher's counter and again when it appeared but at astronomical prices. A New York *Daily News* headline read:

PRICES SOAR, BUYERS SORE
STEERS JUMP OVER THE MOON.

During the campaign, Republicans derided "Horsemeat Harry" and jeered, "To err is Truman," and in Massachusetts Joe Martin, destined to become Speaker of the House, promised consumers that he would "take the meddling hands of political despots out of the kitchens of America." On election day, the GOP won decisive control of the House, as well as a narrow margin in the Senate. Democrats like J. William Fulbright of Arkansas recommended that Truman, having lost a vote of confidence, resign from office immediately and give way to a Republican. Henceforth, Truman referred to him as "Senator Halfbright."

The Eightieth Congress, that much disparaged progeny of the 1946 election, pushed aside Truman's recommendations for new social legislation and set out to repeal the New Deal. Since 1938 a bipartisan conservative coalition had blocked liberal endeavors. Now its ranks were swelled by Republican newcomers such as Joseph R. McCarthy of Wisconsin in the Senate and Richard M. Nixon of California in the House. The Eightieth Congress voted a "soak-the-poor" tax proposal, cut funds for rural electrification and crop storage, and enacted a displaced persons measure discriminating against Catholics and Jews. Under Robert Taft, the brilliant but often parochial captain of the Senate Republicans, Congress adopted a law, over Truman's veto, that made the first serious modification of the 1935 Wagner Act, the law that had put the weight of government behind efforts at unionization. The Taft-Hartley Act prohibited secondary boycotts, jurisdictional walkouts, and the closed shop; it increased the legal responsibility of unions and authorized the President to seek injunctions to delay strikes for eighty days. The cold war made its presence felt in the requirement that union officials file affidavits that they were not Communist Party officials or affiliated with any subversive organization. Hardly the "slave labor law" union leaders branded it, the statute did impede organizing drives for new recruits. In the same year, the Eightieth Congress approved the Twenty-second Amendment (ratified in 1951), which limited the President to two terms, "a belated act of vengeance" against FDR's Long Presidency.

Truman grappled with the Eightieth Congress not just over the legacy of the New Deal but about a new concern that had not found a place on Roosevelt's "must" list—civil rights for the Negro. In December 1946, following an outcry over vicious racial murders in the South, he appointed a President's Committee on Civil Rights, which on October 29, 1947, issued a magisterial report, "To Secure These Rights." On February 2, 1948, Truman sent a message to Congress calling for the implementation of the committee's precepts through measures such as a Fair Employment Practices Act. These propositions failed to win substantial Republican support, and southern Democrats were outraged. "Not since the first gun was fired on Fort Sumter, resulting as it did in the greatest fratricidal strife in the history of the world, has any message of any President of these glorious United States . . . resulted in the driving of a schism in the ranks of our people, as did President Truman's so-called civil rights message," protested Representative William M. Colmer of Mississippi. "No President, either Democrat or Republican, has ever seen fit heretofore to make such recommendations."

The controversy over the President's civil rights message appeared to remove any lingering doubt that Truman would go down to defeat in the 1948 elections. Truman's contingent of liberal advisers headed by Clark Clifford stressed the importance of appealing to black voters and claimed that the President could do this without risk because the South, "safely Democratic," could be "safely ignored." But it soon became clear that politicians in the Deep South were bitterly disaffected. Scared by the prospect of a rupture in Democratic ranks, the administration sought to moderate its stand on civil rights. At the nominating convention in Philadelphia, however, a liberal element organized by Americans for Democratic Action and supported by urban bosses upset these plans. Under the leadership of the young mayor of Minneapolis, Hubert H. Humphrey, they drove through a strong civil rights plank. Waving the battle flag of the Confederacy, Mississippi and Alabama delegates marched out in protest. Three days later a convention of States Rights Democrats, meeting in Birmingham, chose Governor J. Strom Thurmond of South Carolina as the presidential nominee of the bolting "Dixiecrats." Truman's hold on the "Solid South" was in peril.

While the civil rights dispute was cutting off a segment of the Democratic Party's right wing, the cold war was threatening to split off the left wing of the Democrats. In September 1946, Truman had fired his secretary of commerce, Henry A. Wallace, widely regarded as the main legatee of the Roosevelt tradition and more recently a critic of the administration's "get-tough-with-Russia" policy, in so inept a manner that *Time* accused the President of "a clumsy lie." At the end of 1947, Wallace announced he was taking leave of the Democrats. "There is no real fight between a Truman and a Republican," Wallace said. "Both stand for a policy which opens the door to war in our lifetime and makes war certain for our children." Seven months later, his supporters formed the Progressive Party and selected him their standard-bearer. Wallace's campaign of opposition to the cold war and advocacy of social reform, featuring rousing rallies at which singers like Paul Robeson and Pete Seeger performed, appealed especially to the big-city voters who believed that Truman was betraying FDR's ideals. Early polls showed that Wallace had put in jeopardy Truman's chances of holding the large bloc of states in which the big-city vote was pivotal. Given the defection of both wings of the Democrats, the Republican nominee, New York's Governor Thomas E. Dewey, was so certain of victory that he leaked his Cabinet choices to reporters. And the reporters, the columnists, the experts, "everyone," knew that Dewey would win in a canter.

Everyone but Truman and his liberal advisers. The Clifford circle argued that the President could beat Dewey by stressing his adherence to the New Deal tradition and by concentrating his campaign on the metropolitan areas that had given Roosevelt success. Truman agreed. He took off on a transcontinental give-'em-hell-Harry jaunt in which he blasted the do-nothing, good-for-nothing Eightieth Congress and told farmers and workers they would be ingrates if they did not vote Democratic. "If you send another Republican Congress to Washington," he would tell his audience, "you're a bigger bunch of suckers than I think you are." And the crowd would yell back, "Pour it on, Harry!" Dewey, in deliberate contrast, ran a restrained campaign, "with the humorless calculation of a Certified Public Accountant in pursuit of the Holy Grail." Nonetheless, George Gallup, Elmo Roper, and the other pollsters all agreed that Dewey could not lose.

On election day, Truman scored the biggest upset victory in American history, rolling up 24.1 million votes (49.5 percent) to Dewey's 22 million (45.1 percent) and a more emphatic 303 to 189 in the Electoral College; Thurmond's 1.2 million total gained him 39 of Dixie's electoral votes, all but one of them from four Deep South states in which he captured the Democratic Party's symbol. As V. O. Key, Jr., has shown, Thurmond ran best in counties of high black concentration (and high black disfranchisement), the area that had been fire-eating secessionist in 1861 but had stayed loyal to the Democrats in 1928 when parts of the upper South bolted. Wallace, with the same popular tally as Thurmond, did not break into the electoral column. He was embarrassed by the Communist coterie in the party and by the Soviet coup in Czechoslovakia and was undercut by Truman's liberal deeds. The President's party scored well in other races, too. Elected to the Senate in 1948 for the first time were Democrats Humphrey of Minnesota, Estes Kefauver of Tennessee, and, by eighty-seven votes, "Landslide Lyndon" B.

Election of 1948

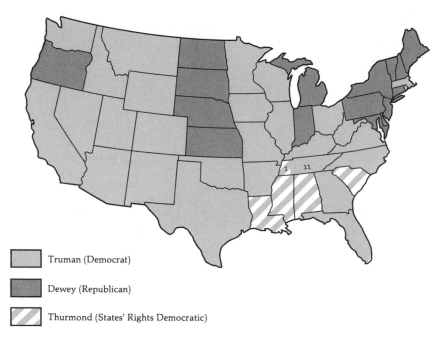

Truman (Democrat)

Dewey (Republican)

Thurmond (States' Rights Democratic)

Johnson of Texas; to the House from the St. Paul district came Eugene McCarthy; new governors included Adlai Stevenson in Illinois and Chester Bowles in Connecticut. Stunned by the surprising outcome, Gallup, said an election night reporter, looked "like an animal eating its young." In Chicago an elderly lady, disillusioned with the polls, was heard to tell her companion on a bus, "Now I don't know whether to believe even the Kinsey report."

The results were a tribute to Truman's spunk, but they demonstrated even more the tenacity of New Deal alignments. The 1948 contest was, in the terminology of the Survey Research Center at the University of Michigan, a "maintaining election" in which "the pattern of partisan attachments prevailing in the preceding period persists, and the majority party wins the Presidency." In a match marked by low turnout and sharp class cleavage, Truman won by mustering enough of the old Roosevelt following in Negro and labor precincts in industrial cities as well as by winning farmers angry at the performance of the Eightieth Congress. Truman ran particularly well, Richard Kirkendall has written, among those who "had recently joined a new, blue-collar middle class" and "were grateful to the Democrats for their prosperity and looked to them for the preservation of it." Although new preoccupations—the cold war and the civil rights revolution—had begun to make their way, memories of the Depression continued to dominate American politics.

President for the first time in his own right, Truman told the new Congress that "every segment of our population and every individual has a right to expect from his government a fair deal." To some observers, the Fair Deal seemed little more than a warmed-over version of the New Deal, with the same reliance on federal action to aid the identical elements who had benefited before, and Truman's tenure was categorized as "Roosevelt's Fifth Term." The Eighty-first Congress adopted more progressive legislation than any Congress since 1938, but, save for a rare exception like the legislation creating the National Science Foundation, the new acts were chiefly extensions of New Deal statutes—expansion of social security and minimum wage provisions, conservation and public power ventures, and a big low-cost housing and slum clearance program. The Fair Deal differed from the New Deal chiefly in the fact that it concerned itself with an economy of abundance rather than depression and that it embraced proposals the New Deal had not included or had given only minor attention. Among these were civil rights legislation, national health insurance, federal aid to education, and the "Brannan Plan" of Secretary of Agriculture Charles F. Brannan for a system of crop subsidies that would serve both the family farmer and the urban consumer. But on all these more novel Fair Deal measures, the President met defeat.

Truman's experience proved characteristic of this whole period, for in the quarter-century after 1938, Congress enacted almost no innovative legislation. It might amplify New Deal statutes, as by raising the minimum wage a few cents, but essentially it was living off the heritage of the 1930's. Occasionally a new principle would win limited approval—maximum employment in the badly gutted Employment Act of 1946, some modest civil rights legislation in the late 1950's—but that happened only rarely. Both conservatives and liberals were frustrated by this "politics of dead center." The strength of liberal Democrats, especially in the Senate, impeded most efforts by the right to repeal the New Deal. Neither could the liberals make headway against the pivotal bipartisan conservative coalition and the formidable obstacle course in Congress—malapportioned representation that overweighted rural areas opposed to spending for the urban masses, arbitrary committee chairmen, the filibuster, seniority rule, and the balky Rules Committee.

The stalemate owed something, too, to changes in the liberal persuasion. The revelation of human depravity at Belsen and Buchenwald, the mass deaths in Soviet Russia, the incineration of Dresden and Hiroshima, all shook faith in the onward march of progress. These events sensitized people to the complicity in evil of men of goodwill. The power of TVA's Norris Dam, wrote the poet Selden Rodman, stoked "the atomic ovens at Oak Ridge," and Buchenwald "lay in the beech forest where Goethe walked." Reformers found the old liberal texts less relevant than the "tough-minded" theology of moral ambiguity of Reinhold Niebuhr or the tortured novels and stories of Franz Kafka. Because collectivism in Soviet Russia had become associated with the barbarities of the secret police and because nationalization in Britain was not bringing a new Jerusalem, liberals became less certain that extending the power of the State was the answer to every social problem, but they were puzzled about where else to turn. The international situation also had a chastening effect, both because progressives shared a number of cold war assumptions and because the recognition that one hyped-up ideologue could blow the world to bits added to their distrust of thoroughgoing solutions. This set of influences helped persuade them to temper their criticism of the American system. Reflecting on the common sense of a people who understood the wisdom of pragmatic responses to problems, Daniel Boorstin, who in the 1930's had been a radical, lauded *The Genius of American Politics,* a politics of accommodation rather than doctrinal excess. Although still wistful for the era of Franklin Roosevelt, they became more appreciative of battlers like Harry Truman, whose struggle with Congress was waged against uneven odds but who managed nonetheless to chalk up small gains that expanded "the vital center."

Despite their uneasiness about unbridled governmental authority, liberals continued to believe in a potent presidency, and they admired the use Truman made of his executive powers, especially in civil rights. He was first to appoint a Negro to the federal bench, and he strengthened the civil rights division of the Department of Justice. His attorney general filed briefs *amici curiae* in support of endeavors by the National Association for the Advancement of Colored People to end segregation in the schools (an undertaking that would bear fruit after Truman left office) and to wipe out judicial enforcement of restrictive covenants, an action that led to a notable victory in the Supreme Court in 1948. Above all, he put the cold war to advantage by stepping up the pace of desegregation of the armed forces.

The executive office expanded significantly in the Truman years, even during the Eightieth Congress, in part as a consequence of the cold war. By January 1947 the President was sending Congress three separate messages—state of the union, budget, and economic report—the last of these as a result of the Employment Act of 1946, which also created a three-man Council of Economic Advisers charged with keeping a weather eye on the economy. Congress unified the armed forces under the newly established post of secretary of defense, set up an Atomic Energy Commission with civilian control, and, ironically, added to the President's authority over industrial relations by enacting the Taft-Hartley law. Truman took full advantage of these new grants of power and in addition reorganized some parts of the executive branch along lines suggested by a commission headed by Herbert Hoover. He stoutly resisted encroachments by Congress on his prerogatives and vetoed more bills than any two-term predecessor. "I mean to pass this office on to my successor unimpaired," Truman said.

Yet it was an assertion of presidential power that greatly eroded Truman's authority in his last years in office. By resolving to intervene in Korea in June 1950, he appropriated from Congress the right to declare war and in doing so opened up a hornets' nest. When North Korean and Red Chinese soldiers were killing young Americans in Asian rice paddies, those who warned of the Communist menace at home found a more attentive audience, and the news media shifted their focus from the White House to the klieg-lighted committee rooms on Capitol Hill. The accusation that the Truman administration, despite its willingness to fight in Korea, had been "soft on communism" served the Republicans as a bludgeon in the 1950 campaign. When the returns were in, the Democrats had sustained enough losses to end hopes for the passage of Fair Deal legislation, quite apart from the fact that the costs of the war served as a convenient excuse for not embarking on expensive new programs. Moreover, the war fueled an inflationary boom that irritated consumers. When Truman tried to halt a price rise in the critical steel sector by seizing the mills in the midst of a labor dispute, the Supreme Court, in the *Youngstown Sheet and Tube* case, invalidated his edict as presidential lawmaking, a decision that former FDR brain-truster Rexford G. Tugwell called "perhaps the most serious setback the presidency has ever suffered."

The "police action" in Korea provided the occasion, too, on April 11, 1951, for Truman's firing of General of the Army Douglas MacArthur as supreme commander of United Nations forces. After the general, who opposed the strategy of limited war and claimed "there is no substitute for victory," politicked with Republican leaders in Congress, the President concluded that he could "no longer tolerate his insubordination." Liberals believed that Truman had made a necessary move in defense of the presidency against one whose flamboyant manner sometimes gave the impression that he fancied himself as a man on horseback. The liberal editor Freda Kirchwey wrote that the dismissal had "ended a very present threat of Bonapartism." However, the "Asiafirsters," who had long been convinced that the United States should force a showdown in the Far East, and those who would brook no compromise in the struggle with the Communist world were outraged. Senator McCarthy called the President a "son of a bitch" and blamed the deed on a White House cabal stoned on "bourbon and benzedrine." Communications to the executive office ran 20 to 1 against Truman, and from Cape Cod to California flags flew at half-mast. After a congressional hearing revealed that all three chiefs of staff disputed MacArthur's contention that it was preferable to have a wider conflict, the controversy simmered down. But it had cost the President valuable political capital and placed in greater danger his party's twenty-year tenure.

History has been kinder to Harry Truman than his contemporaries ever were. No aftermath of a great war is ever easy. In retrospect, though, it was acknowledged that this "highly successful Andrew Johnson," to use Clinton Rossiter's phrase, had kept the reform tradition intact and even strengthened it. Truman encountered many reverses, but he at least raised new public issues that two decades later would still form part of the agenda of Lyndon Johnson's Great Society. Yet Truman left office in ill repute, his legislative proposals stalemated, his administration embroiled in rancorous disputes, his country bogged down in a land war in Asia. The revelation that an applicant for a government loan had helped the wife of a loan examiner acquire a fur coat and that the President's military aide had accepted a deep-freeze unit enabled Republicans to talk about "the mess in Washington" and made household words of "mink coat" and "deep freeze," early artifacts of the effect of the consumer culture on politics. In the spring of 1952, Truman's popularity rating in the polls plunged to the all-time low of 26 percent. No longer did the President have the stature to unify the nation.

Truman would be the first twentieth-century President, unhappily not the last, to learn the cost of fighting a limited war.

The Cold War in America

The cold war and America's role as an imperial nation affected the country in a multitude of ways. The economy was stimulated, and warped, by munitions spending; political currents were rechanneled by the perception that the Democrats were the "war party"; Senator McCarthy exploited cold war anxieties about national security; and the peacetime draft became an accepted feature of American life. The civil rights movement enjoyed the not inconsiderable benefit of the argument that the United States, as the leader of the free world, could not tolerate the blot of racial discrimination on its escutcheon. The Point Four program of United States aid to underdeveloped nations gave literature a new kind of protagonist in *The Ugly American* of Eugene Burdick and William J. Lederer and *The Quiet American* of the British novelist Graham Greene. In 1950 the country whistled the number 3 hit, the "Third Man Theme." And when sports writers matched the U.S.A. bag of gold medals against the U.S.S.R. total, Olympic games served as surrogate battlefields.

The United States rapidly assumed a more imperial style, as befit a republic that was, in Robinson Jeffers' phrase, "heavily thickening into empire." Even the symbol of discharge from the armed services was modeled on a bas-relief from Trajan's Forum in Rome. "As far as the Free World was concerned," the British historian H. G. Nicholas later wrote of the United States, "her shoulders held the sky suspended." In the prewar era, "empire" often suggested little more than a concern about the Caribbean, but in his report on the Potsdam Conference, President Truman discussed the Kiel Canal and the Far East, the Danube and the Dardanelles. United States proconsuls took up their stations in occupied Germany and Japan, and to house the envoys of the world's greatest power appropriately, architects such as Edward Stone in the 1950's designed embassies like the magnificent edifice in New Delhi, a work that asserted the mission of a society of untold wealth.

The country's move away from isolationism was accompanied too by a more cosmopolitan sensibility. World War II had uprooted millions of Americans and brought them in intimate contact with the culture of alien societies—New Guinea, the Aleutians, Tunisia,

In *Echo,* a 1951 work, Jackson Pollock swirls black paint across raw canvas, in what one critic described as "violently interwoven movement," to induce a sense of perpetual motion and limitless possibilities, qualities that foreign critics judged typically American. "If Pollock were a Frenchman," wrote Clement Greenberg after viewing the show in which *Echo* appeared, "people would already be calling him *'maître.'*" Born on a ranch in Cody, Wyoming, in 1912, Pollock died in an automobile crash at East Hampton, Long Island, in 1956.

Lombardy—and the postwar world bore the mark of this experience. The representative theme of the American novel of the late 1940's was the Young Man from the Provinces trying to adapt to Old World ways; the spread of Zen Buddhism in the 1950's reflected, in part, the acculturation of occupation forces in Japan; and a critic observed less "aggressive nativeness" in American poetry after the war. When a reporter toured the country in 1947, he found that hundreds of people to whom he spoke agreed with the wife of a trolley repairman in a small Indiana town who said, "I believe that talk about Europe is in every household now."

As the capital of the art world moved from Paris to New York, American painters turned their backs on the "corn belt academy" of Thomas Hart Benton, Grant Wood, and John Steuart Curry, who had won favor during the Depression by exploring indigenous subjects. Like their counterparts among poets, notably W. S. Merwin and Richard Wilbur, artists such as Mark Rothko evinced more interest in themes from mythology having a universal significance. Benton's student, Jackson Pollock, who was deeply affected by the migration to the United States of European surrealists, protested: "The idea of an isolated American painting, so popular in this country during the thirties, seems absurd to me just as the idea of creating a purely American mathematics or physics would seem absurd." Benton himself realized that the struggle had been lost. "Wood, Curry, and I found the bottom knocked out from under us," he wrote. "In a day when the problems of America were mainly exterior, our interior images lost public significance."

The cold war had its most direct and far-reaching effect on America in the enormous increase in military spending and the rise of "the military-industrial complex." After V-J Day, the yearning to go back to peacetime pursuits was so intense that troops at Pacific bases rioted and thousands of GI's marched down the Champs Elysées crying, "We wanna go home." Within a year an army of 8 million had been reduced to 1.5 million. Some even hoped that the United States could return to the situation of the 1930's when the air corps flew less than a thousand planes and the American army, with fewer than 135,000 soldiers, including Philippine Scouts, ranked seventeenth in the world. However, with the onset of the cold war, as well as of the costs of occupation, defense expenditures in 1947 were already up to nearly $14 billion a year. Still, Truman was scolded for putting a ceiling on such spending of "only" one-third of the government's budget. With the outbreak of the Korean War, the country quickly pushed through the ceiling to $44 billion (67 percent) in 1952. Although the outlays diminished after a truce was negotiated in Korea, they continued at a high level.

The United States by the mid-1950's nurtured 40,000 "prime" defense contractors and hundreds of thousands of lesser ones. A company like AC Spark Plug, once innocent of military affairs, turned out the internal power system for the *Thor* missile, and concerns that made goods not usually thought of as martial hardware—cloth and shovels—came to regard the Department of Defense as an important customer. During the 1960's, half of the government's money would go to military purposes, and by 1970 the Department of Defense had greater assets than the nation's seventy-five largest industrial corporations, employed nearly as many people as the top thirty firms, and was spending more than did the entire national government before the Depression.

Many communities and even whole regions of the country depended on the boon of the weapons industry. California thrived on Lockheed, Seattle on the contracts let to Boeing; in Georgia the payroll of one aircraft factory amounted to half of the value of the state's cotton crop. The Pentagon found that if it decided to cancel a defense contract or close down an unneeded base, the plan was met with howls of indignation from the citizens of the community. Congressmen made their reputations by securing juicy military contracts as once they had by gaining appropriations for rivers and harbors. Henry Jackson from the state of Washington was known as the "Senator from Boeing," and Richard B. Russell and Carl Vinson teamed up to cram twenty military installations into Georgia. But none matched the South Carolinian who would become chairman of the House Armed Services Committee, Lucius Mendel Rivers. That ardent defender of the Pentagon and advocate of hot war saw to it that his district housed an army depot, an air force base, a marine corps training center, a coast guard mine-warfare operation, and a navy shipyard, supply center, and weapons station, as well as defense plants with hundreds of millions of dollars in contracts. His predecessor as chairman of the committee, Carl Vinson, warned him, "You put anything else down there in your district, Mendel, it's gonna sink."

Radical critics perceived these arrangements not as a response to the challenge to security posed by the Communist powers but rather as evidence of the sickness of the capitalist system. In an article in *Politics* in 1944, Walter Oakes had predicted that the United States would develop a "permanent war economy," because capitalists preferred military public works to the perils of mass unemployment, and in 1961 Fred J. Cook delineated the creation of the "Warfare State." Arthur Selwyn Miller expressed concern over "the Techno-Corporate State" and H. L. Nieburg about the "contract state," which he characterized as "a fundamentally new economic system which at once resembles traditional private enterprise and the

The "Warfare State." At its Renton plant outside of Seattle, Washington, Boeing Aircraft sprawls over several acres. Builder of the 707, 727, 737, and 747 jets to meet the needs of the consumer culture, Boeing thrived on military orders to sustain the cold war. From World War II through the early 1960's, the firm turned out 744 B-52 bombers.

corporate state of fascism." Such critics noted the nexus between military expenditures and prosperity. One analyst stated flatly: "So long as relations between the U.S.S.R. and the U.S. are bad, military electronics will be a good business"; he added that a sudden thaw "would hit the industry very hard." During the Korean War, the gross national product soared; after military spending was cut back abruptly, a recession ensued.

When President Eisenhower left the White House in January 1961 he unexpectedly lent his great prestige to the argument that the United States was imperiled by these new developments. In his farewell address, he warned of "the conjunction of an immense military establishment and a large arms industry," a new phenomenon whose "total influence is felt in every city." He cautioned, "We must guard against the acquisition of unwarranted influence by the military-industrial complex."

If there was reason enough for grave concern about the military-industrial complex, those who pictured the United States as a "warfare state" painted with too broad a brush. Even in 1969 during the Vietnam War, 91 percent of the GNP went to nonmilitary spending. The rearmament program owed more to anxiety about Russian warheads and hydrogen bombs than it did to the frailty of the capitalist economy. In 1950, the United States had one tank division, the U.S.S.R. thirty, and the Russian army had four times more soldiers than the American army. By 1949 the Soviet Union had the A-bomb, by 1953 the H-bomb, and in October 1961 it exploded a nuclear device almost three thousand times as powerful as the Hiroshima bomb. Under these circumstances, no American President could have maintained popular support if he did not endeavor to match the Russians. While many undoubtedly thrived on the arms race, swollen military budgets represented less the machinations of malevolent men than the obsessions of ideological conflict, the tragic incapacity of nation-states to develop institutions of accommodation, and the headlong pace of technology that made costly weapons systems obsolete before they left the factory. Unhappily, each escalation of the arms race served to raise the level of terror and to make genuine world security still less attainable.

The cold war also gave the United States a new, and for many unwelcome, departure—the permanent peacetime draft. The draft card would become a young American's proof of identity and even of manhood, the palpable evidence that he had advanced beyond puberty and, in New York at least, was aged enough to buy a can of beer. Adopted briefly in 1946, the draft expired a year later, only to be reintroduced again in 1948 after the Communist coup in Prague. At first controversial, selective service legislation became so accepted that in 1963 the Senate devoted only ten minutes of debate to it before voting to renew authorization. Lewis B. Hershey, the general who headed what was ostensibly a civilian operation, even represented the draft to be an essential step in acquiring a sense of nationality. "Outside the income tax," he observed, "there aren't many things to make the male citizen feel much responsibility to his government any more. Selective Service is one of them." In truth, the draft did serve as a nationalizing force, pulling young men out of towns across the land and fitting them in olive drab at camps from Dix to Ord, speeding the desegregation of American life by throwing together boys from Tennessee farms and Chicago's black ghetto.

The cold war had one of its most venomous influences on American society in a phenomenon named for the junior Senator from Wisconsin—McCarthyism. In fact, the alarm over Communist subversion preceded the 1950 Lincoln's birthday speech in Wheeling that first brought Joe McCarthy to prominence. What Robert Griffith has called "the anti-Communist persuasion," the mindless conviction that all social change is the result of alien radical conspiracies, had a history as old as the republic. In the twentieth century, a "Red Scare" had sent tremors through the country during the aftermath of World War I and again, though in a much more muted form, in the Depression. Well before McCarthy seized upon the Communist issue, it had served the purposes of foes of reform, particularly the Republicans. Ever since its establishment in 1938, the House Committee on Un-American Activities had been a sounding board for the imputation that the New Deal had taken a long step on the road to Moscow. In the postwar period the cold war added plausibility to the view that the United States faced a serious threat from subversives within the government who were in league with Communist powers and movements abroad. When the State Department announced in 1949 both that Soviet Russia had the "secret" of the A-bomb and that China had "fallen," Republicans charged that traitorous architects of America's Far Eastern policy were to blame.

Furthermore, a series of shocking disclosures gave at least a semblance of credibility to some of these charges. Concern mounted from 1945 when a huge cache of purloined diplomatic documents was discovered in the offices of the magazine *Amerasia* to the announcement early in 1950 that the British physicist Klaus Fuchs, who had worked at Los Alamos, had confessed passing information on the atomic bomb to the Russians. For their part in this conspiracy, two Americans, Julius and Ethel Rosenberg, would subsequently be executed. Arthur Miller's drama *The Crucible,* about the Salem "witches," was understood to be a parable for the persecution of the innocent in modern America, and unhappily "witch hunt" was an apt metaphor for much that took place in the 1940's and 1950's. But it is sometimes forgotten that while the witches in seventeenth-century New England are presumed to have been illusory, McCarthyism thrived on the fact that there were real Communist plotters in the United States, though their menace was fearfully exaggerated.

The most consequential episode began in August 1948 when Whittaker Chambers, *Time* magazine's senior editor, told the House Committee on Un-American Activities that Alger Hiss, the president of the Carnegie Endowment for International Peace and a former State Department official, had been a member of the Communist Party. Since the unprepossessing Chambers produced little to back up these charges, and since the committee had often served as a forum for false accusations, President Truman seemed right to dismiss the allegation, brought out by the California Congressman Richard Nixon, as a "red herring" designed to distract attention from the shortcomings of the Eightieth Congress. But on a December night a month after the 1948 elections, Chambers led investigators at his Maryland farm to a hollowed-out pumpkin from which he extracted microfilms of classified government documents. Chambers declared that they had been given to him by a spy ring of which Hiss had been a member. On January 25, 1950, after two trials, Hiss was sentenced to five years in prison for perjury, the statute of limitations on treason having run out. Hiss could hardly have served the purposes of anti-Communist Republicans better, for he had been a New Deal official, had served as director of special political affairs in the State Department, had helped arrange the San Francisco Conference which gave birth to the United Nations, and had been present at Yalta. Truman's "red herring" remark appeared to indicate that the administration was indifferent to subversion, and troubles were compounded when Secretary of State Dean Acheson said, "I do not intend to turn my back on Alger Hiss." Acheson's statement did him credit as a man (he would base his conduct, he explained, on Matthew 25:34 — he who turned his back on one in trouble turned his back on Him), but it was politically maladroit because it could easily be misconstrued and came at an awkward time. In December 1949, Chiang Kai-shek's Nationalists had fled to Formosa; in late January 1950, Hiss was convicted and Acheson made his ill-advised comment; on February 3, Klaus Fuchs was arrested. Thus was the stage set for McCarthy's arrival in Wheeling on February 12, 1950.

The Wisconsin Senator's address to the Republican Women's Club rocketed him from obscurity to notoriety. Elected to the Senate in 1946 as one of the "meat shortage boys," he had made little mark save as a bully who continually flouted Senate rules and showed no inhibitions about making vicious verbal assaults. When he came to West Virginia, he was a little-known Senator, and the speech he gave on that occasion was a quiltwork of snatches taken from Nixon and others. But McCarthy had a genius for publicity, a shrewd understanding of the tactical advantages in talking not about treachery but about traitors, and a ruthlessness that others lacked. His exact words in Wheeling remain in dispute. He appears to have said: "I have here in my hand a list of 205 — a list of names that were made known to the Secretary of State as being members of the Communist Party and who nevertheless are still working and shaping policy in the State Department." By the time he had reached the airport to change planes for his next speaking engagement, he was besieged by reporters asking to see the list. There was no "list," but McCarthy was making headlines. Scarcely a month after the Wheeling speech, *The Washington Post*'s Herbert Block, who signed his political cartoons "Herblock," was searching for an expression to capture the new phenomenon of defamation of character. In that day's cartoon, on a drawing of a barrel of mud he lettered a word hitherto unknown in the national lexicon — "McCarthyism."

For a period of nearly five years McCarthyism besmirched American politics, and the issue of subversion left its mark on the pulpit and the Hollywood movie lot, the campus and the union hall. Critics of redbaiting sometimes exaggerated the extent of its reach. Some thought they were witnessing a parallel to the closing days of the Weimar Republic, and the theater critic Brooks Atkinson even blamed McCarthyism for a mediocre Broadway season. But there was genuine occasion for alarm, not only because the latterday Red Scare did claim victims who were ousted from their positions, within government and without, but because McCarthyism created an atmosphere which suffocated serious consideration of critical public issues.

Truman tried to free himself of the albatross of the Communist subversion issue, but with little success. In 1947 he established a program to screen government employees for disloyalty, and in 1951 he augmented the authority of the Loyalty Review Board. The Justice Department in 1948 secured an indictment of eleven top Communist Party leaders for violating the Smith Act of 1940, which outlawed conspiracies that advocated the violent overthrow of any government in the United States. In 1951, in the *Dennis* case, the Supreme Court under Chief Justice Fred M. Vinson affirmed the convictions of the Communists and upheld the constitutionality of the Smith Act, although the law proscribed the mere advocacy of revolutionary doctrines. The administration's actions horrified liberals but failed to appease Congress, which enacted legislation sponsored by Senator

Pat McCarran requiring Communist organizations to register with the attorney general and submit lists of their members, barring the admission of Communists from abroad, and even providing for concentration camps in the event of war. Truman vetoed these measures ("In a free country, we punish men for the crimes they commit, but never for the opinions they have"), but Congress passed each bill over his veto. The overwhelming support for these proposals demonstrated that "McCarthyism" had a solid base in Congress, among Democrats like McCarran as well as among the Wisconsin Senator's more numerous followers in his own party.

Contemporary analysts diagnosed McCarthyism as a disease of class mobility and the consumer culture. Seymour Martin Lipset asserted that the Senator "directed his appeal to the status resentments occasioned by prosperity." Another sociologist, Daniel Bell, explained that "the central idea of the status politics conception is that groups that are advancing in wealth and social position are often as anxious and politically feverish as groups that have become *déclassé*." Hence, McCarthy's legions numbered both WASPs on the decline, including "a thin stratum of soured patricians," and social groups on the rise, ranging from Texas oil wildcatters to upwardly mobile ethnics eager to affirm their Americanism. Certain "authoritarian personality" types, of the sort studied by T. W. Adorno and Hannah Arendt, were believed to be especially prone to exhibit these characteristics.

Subsequent investigation has raised doubt about these hypotheses and has advanced new ones. It has been pointed out that affluence and mobility were conditions of American society before McCarthy's rise and after his decline and that anti-communism was more an elite than a mass phenomenon. In particular, McCarthyism has been seen as an expression of the frustrations of desperate middle west and mountain state Republican officials, conservative and nationalist in persuasion, who had seen certain victory snatched from them in 1948. Yet if the protagonists of McCarthyism came from the leadership, his following derived disproportionately from the less educated, from manual workers and other lower socioeconomic groups, and from Catholics identifying with an Irish coreligionist who stuck pins in the establishment.

Although McCarthy was regarded as the lay cleric of a creed of conformity, he won a good deal of his following precisely because he flouted convention. Richard Rovere, who characterized him as "inner-directed," "closer to the hipster than to the Organization Man," wrote: "He seemed to understand, as no other politician of his stature

The Grand Inquisitor, Senator Joseph R. McCarthy of Wisconsin, cocks an ear at one of the hearings that made his name a household word. To his right stands his aide Roy Cohn, whose effort to secure special treatment in the army for his buddy, G. David Schine, led to the army-McCarthy hearings that brought about McCarthy's downfall.

ever has, the perverse appeal of the bum, the mucker, the Dead End kid, the James Jones–Nelson Algren–Jack Kerouac hero to a nation uneasy in its growing order and stability and not altogether happy about the vast leveling process in which everyone appeared to be sliding, from one direction or another, into middle-class commonplaceness and respectability." McCarthy, Rovere added, "didn't want the world to think of him as respectable. He encouraged photographers to take pictures of him sleeping, disheveled, on an office couch, like a bum on a park bench, coming out of a shower with a towel wrapped around his torso like Rocky Marciano." A boxer in his college days at Marquette, McCarthy attracted a segment of his supporters because he seemed to be a "guts fighter." Some of McCarthy's backers found his brutishness disturbing; others, as a New London, Connecticut, study learned, admired him because he was "not afraid to 'get tough.'"

McCarthy appealed to a deep-seated distrust of eastern seaboard patricians by his tirades against striped-pants diplomats and "State Department perverts." Those who had been "selling the Nation out," he asserted, were "the bright young men who are born with silver spoons in their mouth." McCarthy found a ready-made target for such abuse in Truman's secretary of state. Leslie Fiedler observed:

Acheson is the projection of all the hostilities of the Midwestern mind at bay: his waxed mustache, his mincing accent, his personal loyalty to a traitor who also belonged to the Harvard Club; one is never quite sure that he was not invented by a pro-McCarthy cartoonist.

With something like genius, McCarthy touched up the villain he had half-found, half-composed, adding the connotations of wealth and effete culture to treachery, and topping all off with the suggestion of homosexuality.

McCarthy intimidated opponents who had an exaggerated notion of his political power. In 1950, one of his aides doctored a photograph to make it appear that Senator Millard E. Tydings of Maryland was collaborating with the leader of the Communist Party, and Tydings went down to defeat. Other Democrats trembled at the prospect that they might be next on Joe's list if they incurred his wrath. On the other hand, conservative Republicans like Taft concluded that McCarthy's fulminations against "Commiecrats" were giving the Republicans the same sort of advantage, as one of the Wisconsin Senator's lieutenants claimed, that the Democrats had enjoyed with the "Hoover apple." In 1952 Richard Nixon made uninhibited use of McCarthyite invective by denouncing "Adlai the appeaser" who "carries a Ph.D from Dean Acheson's cowardly college of Communist containment" and saying he would rather have a "khaki-clad President than one clothed in State Department pinks." When the GOP triumphed in 1952, after a campaign of K_1C_2 (Korea, Communism, Corruption), McCarthy was credited with a share in the national victory as well as with eliminating critics such as Senator William Benton of Connecticut. In truth, concern about communism had little influence on the 1952 outcome, and as late as the summer of 1953 most of those polled disapproved of McCarthy. Even in 1954, when the Senator reached his all-time high of 50 percent support

HERBLOCK
©1954 THE WASHINGTON POST CO.

This "Herblock" drawing is one of many depicting McCarthy as an unshaven Neanderthal. Herbert Block, political cartoonist of *The Washington Post*, played no favorites in the cold war. He won his second Pulitzer prize in 1954 for his sketch on the occasion of Stalin's demise, in which Death says, "You were always a great friend of mine, Joseph."

"Have A Care, Sir"
From *Herblock's Here and Now* (Simon and Schuster, 1955).

(with 29 percent unfavorable), the proportion of Americans who stated they were worried about the Communist peril was under 1 percent.

Eisenhower drew some of his backing in 1952 from those who believed that only a man of his stature could curb the Wisconsin Senator, but the general actually abetted McCarthy. When Eisenhower came to Wisconsin in 1952, he even deleted from a speech a paragraph praising General George Catlett Marshall, Ike's mentor in the army, whom McCarthy had damned as part of "a conspiracy so immense and an infamy so black as to dwarf any such previous venture in the history of man." Eisenhower's victory propelled McCarthy for the first time to chairmanship of the Senate Committee on Government Operations, and "the Grand Inquisitor" used his new power to rampage through the foreign affairs agencies of the

Republican administration. But the President refused to grapple with him ("I will not get in the gutter with *that* guy," he confided), and Secretary of State John Foster Dulles not only abandoned his subordinates but sent a directive excluding books and works of art of "any Communists, fellow travellers, et cetera" from United States information centers abroad. Some books were actually burned, a grim suggestion of the Nazis' *Walpurgisnachten* and of Ray Bradbury's *Fahrenheit 451*. While Dulles' edict reached out to the creations of "et ceteras," Eisenhower issued an executive order expanding the category of ineligibility for federal employment from disloyalty to "security risk," and Republicans and Democrats carried on an unseemly debate over which administration had fired the greater number of its civil servants. In December 1953, the Atomic Energy Commission shocked the scientific community by withdrawing the security clearance of the "father of the atomic bomb," J. Robert Oppenheimer.

However, when McCarthy chose to assault the military establishment, he overstepped himself, for he reckoned neither on the nation's tender concern for the army in the cold war nor on the peering lenses of the new medium of television. The televised portions of the army-McCarthy hearings, which lasted from April 22 to June 17, 1954, gave many Americans their first close glimpse of McCarthy — his bullying, his rasping intrusions, his unshaven face like that of a Hollywood "heavy." If there was a single point in time when McCarthy's house tumbled down around him, it came when the army's sweet-natured counsel Joseph Welch, outraged by a wanton accusation against a young associate, cried out, "Until this moment, Senator, I think I never really gauged your cruelty or your recklessness. . . . If it were in my power to forgive you for your reckless cruelty, I would do so. I like to think I am a gentle man, but your forgiveness will have to come from someone other than me. . . . Have you no sense of decency, sir, at long last?"

Thereafter McCarthy went rapidly downhill, carrying this latter-day "Red Scare" with him. The Democratic victory in November deprived him of his chairmanship at the same time that some of his fellow Republicans had become miffed at his badmouthing of GOP colleagues. It was a bit much to say of Senator Ralph Flanders of Vermont, "Senile — I think they should get a man with a net and take him to a good quiet place," and even more offensive to call Senator Robert C. Hendrickson of New Jersey "a living miracle in that he is without question the only man who has lived so long with neither brains nor guts." On December 2, 1954, the Senate voted, 67 to 22 (with no negative Democratic votes and the Republicans dividing evenly), to "condemn" McCarthy for various affronts to the dignity of the Senate. Shortly afterward a professional lecturer in San Francisco removed the Communist menace from his offerings because it no longer sold. Three years later, McCarthy died at the age of forty-eight. In his place, the voters of Wisconsin chose a Democrat who had married into the eastern seaboard aristocracy and, still worse, held degrees from both Yale and Harvard.

As a self-advertised gladiator against communism, McCarthy proved to be a charlatan. He first gained the limelight by piecing together a set of fabrications and innuendos. When a Senate subcommittee investigated his charges, it concluded that McCarthy was waging "the most nefarious campaign of half-truths and untruth in the history of the Republic." Curiously, even when McCarthy achieved immense power as chairman of a Senate committee, he did nothing to rid the government of alleged subversives. "Like Gogol's Chichikov, McCarthy is a dealer in dead souls," observed Dwight Macdonald. "His targets are not actual, living breathing Communists but rather people who once were or may have been but were not but may be made to appear to have possibly once been Communists or sympathizers or at any rate suspiciously 'soft' on the question." The astonishing fact about McCarthy is that he never once exposed a Communist in high places; his biggest catch was a "pink dentist" in the signal corps. Ironically, his inflated reputation owed much to his enemies, who insisted that because of him a reign of terror gripped American campuses and portrayed him as the leader of an incipient totalitarian movement. But, as the political scientist Earl Latham has written, "the sick forebodings of some liberals of the time did not materialize," and McCarthy, a man with neither an ideology nor a serious purpose, showed no inclination to exploit cold war anxieties to become America's first Führer.

Affluent America

Because of both cold war expenditures and unfaltering consumer purchases, the depression fears of 1945 proved groundless. The American economy pulled through the postwar reconversion and in the 1950's took off into the wild blue yonder of skyhigh prosperity. By the middle of the decade, the country, with only 6 percent of the earth's people, was producing and consuming over one-third of the

Gross National Product in Constant Dollars, 1929-1960

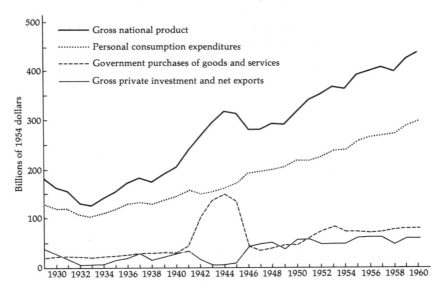

Source: Board of Governors of the Federal Reserve System, *Historical Supplement to Federal Reserve Chart Book*, 1961, p. 74.

world's goods and services. Economists were troubled that the average gain in gross national product (in dollars of the same purchasing power) ran only 2.9 percent in the 1950's, well below the 4.7 percent increment for the 1920's. Yet the economy still showed a rise in real GNP of 51 percent between 1949 and 1960. Since the standard of living in 1949 was already very high compared to that of other nations, the level in 1960 gave America an abundance that made concentration on the modest annual growth rate misleading. The real GNP increased from $206 billion in 1940 to above $500 billion in 1960, and the big leap of the 'sixties still lay ahead. The United States would close that decade with the world's first trillion-dollar economy (albeit measured in inflated money).

The cold war and the consumer culture contributed to this growth in several different ways. In the postwar period the United States moved into what W. W. Rostow called the "high mass-consumption" stage, and spending in the private sector played an important part in setting in motion a vigorous upswing in 1949. But it was the stimulus of the swollen military budget in the Korean conflict that accounted for the mightiest boom of the 1950's. By the third quarter of 1951 "national security expenditures" totaled more than all private domestic investment, and in just three years aluminum production doubled. The Pentagon provided the main market for new "glamour" industries like electronics, placed multi-billion-dollar orders with west coast aircraft plants, and financed experimentation in research and development. When military disbursements fell off after the Korean ceasefire, consumer purchases took up the slack, though output rose at only half the rate of the first part of the decade. Millions of suburban home owners took advantage of installment credit to purchase "consumer durables" and provided the motivation for the construction of imposing shopping centers. In the 1950's consumer use of electricity nearly tripled because of the evolution of household appliances, and advertising outlays more than doubled. The twin force of the cold war and the consumer culture, both dependent on a responsive government, emboldened corporations to adopt technological innovations like the computer and to step up investment at home and abroad.

The consumer culture thrived on a rapidly augmented home market. As the shrunken ambitions of the 1930's gave way to the great expectations of the postwar era, the two-child family came to seem inappropriate to the more expansive life style of the middle class, just as the confining coupé gave way to the station wagon. A Harvard senior who said his aim was six children explained that it was "a minimum production goal." Economists even suggested "that babies are viewed as a consumer durable good expected to yield a stream of psychic income through time." The burgeoning population, a source of grief in pre-industrial nations, guaranteed steadily growing demand, most immediately for diaper services and supermarket items like baby food.

The American people multiplied their numbers in these years at a pace that upset the predictions of population experts. The lowering horizons of the Great Depression had led demographers to forecast that in another generation the United States would enter a period of long-term decline. Even the spurt during World War II, which the Census Bureau soberly attributed in part to "occasional furloughs," was dismissed as a temporary phenomenon. But, to the chagrin of the prognosticators, the returning GI's (and their brides) proved intent on making up for lost time. In the 1940's, the population grew by 19 million, more than twice the increase in the previous decade, and the phenomenal gain of 29 million in the 1950's moved

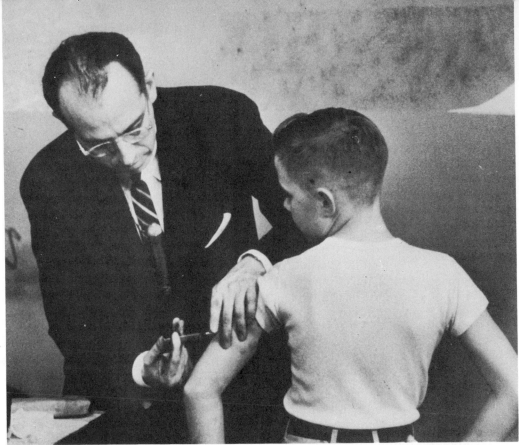

The benevolent needle. On March 28, 1953, Dr. Jonas Salk of the University of Pittsburgh announced the development of a vaccine for poliomyelitis (infantile paralysis), the dreaded crippler. Two years later, on April 13, 1955, Salk inoculated ten-year-old Randy Bazilausakas, the first person to receive the vaccine after its approval by the National Institutes of Health.

at the same pace as that of teeming India. "No decrease is in sight this century," announced a Census Bureau official in 1955. "We have come to consider it routine to report new all-time-high records."

Demographers ascribed the increments chiefly to the rising birth rate but also to decline in the death rate. Births, at below 19 per 1,000 people before the war, soared to above 25 in the mid-1950's, and only slowly fell thereafter. "It seems to me," wrote a British visitor in 1958, "that every other young house-wife I see is pregnant." To a lesser extent, the growth resulted from medical achievements (among others, streptomycin in 1945 and aureomycin in 1948) that lengthened lives, especially those of the young. A new-born child in 1900 could expect to live forty-six years; in 1940, sixty years; and by the early 1960's, seventy years, the biblical three score and ten.

The tides of population surged through the Southwest and the West, swelling the size of cities such as Houston, which became the nation's space capital, desert oases like Tucson, and, above all, the metropolises of California. By the time some got to Phoenix (which jumped from 65,000 in 1940 to 439,000 in 1960), others knew the way to San Jose (which tripled in the same period). Like forty-niners following the Oregon Trail, the Athletics, once the pride of Connie Mack's Philadelphia on the eastern littoral, stopped briefly in Kansas City, then pulled up stakes again and settled in Oakland. In 1958, the unthinkable happened. The Brooklyn Dodgers took French leave

Settlement and Population in the United States, 1940-1960

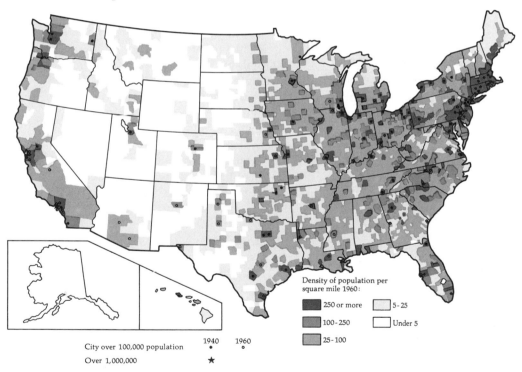

Density of population per square mile 1960:

250 or more
100-250
25-100
5-25
Under 5

City over 100,000 population   1940 •   1960 ○
Over 1,000,000   ★

from Ebbets Field and moved to Los Angeles, and the New York Giants departed the antiquated Polo Grounds for windy Candlestick Park in San Francisco. Duke Snider, whose home runs had once bounced into Bedford Avenue, felt lost in the vastness of the Los Angeles Colosseum, and Willie Mays, who had delighted Bronx youngsters by turning up unannounced for stickball games, played before strangers from Sausalito and Menlo Park. A year later, Old Glory added two more stars when Hawaii and Alaska entered the union. No longer a continental nation of contiguous states, the United States had admitted to equal status the outposts of empire.

While the country's population increased 33 percent between 1940 and 1960, statistics for the Pacific states climbed an astonishing 110 percent. By 1960 half of the native citizens of the Far West were living in a different state from the one in which they were born. In the 1950's, one-fifth of the nation's population expansion was accounted for by the single state of California, which had become, as the British historian Arnold J. Toynbee said, the New World's New World, and in the 1960's Orange County, with the Anaheim of Disneyland and the California Angels, sustained a stupendous 102 percent growth to reach a 1,420,000 total. By 1963 California had moved past New York to be the number 1 state in population.

Other sections prospered too. Agreement to complete construction of the St. Lawrence seaway, which would make ocean ports of Chicago and Duluth, quickened expectations throughout the Midwest. After the army moved Wernher von Braun and his German rocket specialists to Huntsville, Alabama, that town of 30,000 in 1950 reached 115,000 in 1963. Huntsville tore down its Confederate monument and put up nineteen shopping centers. Space became the third-ranking industry in Florida, following tourism and citrus fruits. From 1950 to 1961 the personal income of Floridians rose a fantastic 187 percent, and in metropolitan Atlanta manufacturing employment in the 1950's increased 64 percent. French visitors, expecting to find "a Scarlett O'Hara land of cotton plantations" in the South, were surprised to see instead "oil, natural gas, helium, steel, magnesium, atomic energy and chemical plants." In the Houston–Beaumont–Port Arthur complex, there arose a huge petrochemical industry, and in the 1950's in Texas natural gas more than tripled in value to pass the half-billion-dollar mark. But despite all these regional gains, the performance of the Pacific coast remained the most impressive. The westering migrants, one eye on the main chance, the other on the high style of life in the sun country, pro-

News that statehood has been achieved is hawked before Iolani Palace, Honolulu. Statehood legislation for Hawaii was approved on August 21, 1959, eight months after Alaska became the forty-ninth state on January 3, 1959.

vided both a mobile work force for new industries and a seemingly insatiable demand for the products of those industries.

These multitudes with their augmented incomes made the cash registers chatter even more noisily because of the ready availability of credit. From 1946 to 1958 short-term consumer credit, particularly for buying Fords and Chevvies on the installment plan, rose from $8.4 billion to almost $45 billion. So easy did credit become that scores of pawnshops were driven out of business. In 1950 Diners' Club introduced the credit card; within fifteen years, it had more than a million card-carrying members, as did American Express.

Largely in response to consumer demand, capitalists risked billions of dollars in new investment. Even when government spending fell from $83 billion to $31 billion from 1945 to 1946, the economy did not collapse because corporation ventures and high consumption sustained it. Cured of the depression "psychosis" by the shock therapy of World War II, the private sector proved much more resilient than New Deal economists had anticipated. From 1946 to 1958, industrialists put an average of $10 billion a year into new plant and machinery, three times the pace set in the "golden twenties." The phenomenal rise in output per man-hour (35 to 40 percent a decade) was made possible by investment in mechanization and in the application of power. In the two decades after 1940, the generation of electric energy increased 340 percent.

Application of power did less to increase productivity than a dramatic new step in scientific management—automation. A term apparently first coined in 1946, "automation" originally signified the automatic handling of parts between successive stages of manufacturing but soon came to refer more particularly to the use of self-regulating electronic mechanisms to run complex operations, even immense strip mills in the steel industry. Automation made its greatest advance with the evolution of the computer, erected at Harvard and the University of Pennsylvania during World War II and first marketed in 1950, after the development in 1948 by Bell Telephone Laboratories of an indispensable component, the transistor. So great was the demand for computers that IBM, the industry's leader, could not turn them out fast enough. The twenty computers of 1954 had multiplied to more than 1,250 in 1957 and over 35,000 a decade later. When instructed, computers could remember, select, and give orders; they could write beatnik poetry, compose an avant-garde suite, and even devise original strategy at checkers to beat the human who had taught them the game. The computer, declared Dr. Herbert A. Simon of Carnegie Tech, represented "an advance in man's thinking processes as radical as the invention of writing." Computers were utilized to speed airline reservations, process bank check hieroglyphics, forecast election returns, advise sausage makers which meats to select in concocting salami, and figure out for Billy Graham the rate of "decisions for Christ" at his revival meetings. They were even able to increase inefficiency in college registration. Electronic data-processing machines, whose factory sales jumped from $25 million in 1953 to $1 billion in 1960, transformed the modern business office by performing the mundane but invaluable function of coping with the mountains of paper that were threatening to strangle the businessman like the snakes encoiled around Laocöon.

The word "automation" struck fear in the hearts of the American workingman. "The worker's greatest worry," explained a writer, "is that he will be cast upon the slag heap by a robot." The very point of automation was to eliminate labor. As *Business Week* stated flatly, "The art and science of going through as many stages of production as possible with as little human help as possible is called automation." From 1947 to 1961 employment in textiles, an industry especially susceptible to automation, declined 35 percent. Although automation offered openings to the college-trained, it took a heavy toll of unskilled laborers, farmhands, and inexperienced young manual workers who had dropped out of school; disproportionate numbers of these were black. One student of the subject claimed: "Automation is today the same kind of menace to the unskilled—that is, the poor—that the enclosure movement was to the British agricultural population centuries ago." However, employers countered that automation, while making some jobs obsolete, would create new opportunities, as indeed it did.

Much of this technological advance owed a debt to research and development, for it was the laboratories of companies like Bell Telephone and IBM that turned out many of the new products that sparked the postwar economy. Between 1953 and 1964, spending for "R & D" nearly quadrupled. Fast-spreading industries such as electronics and chemistry depended heavily on the university labs at Caltech and Stanford and along "Research Row" on the banks of the Charles in Cambridge, Massachusetts. Businessmen learned that graduate school training was a crucial source of economic growth and profit increments, and science departments in turn became enmeshed in corporation and government contracts. Some of them were for military purposes; in the late 1950's aircraft and guided missiles made the greatest use of R & D. A big chunk of investment went directly into laboratories like GE's in Schenectady and RCA's in Princeton, and only the very big firms could afford operations of these dimensions.

Most of the corporations of the postwar world bore familiar names like General Electric and United States Steel, but they had so expanded that they were different not in degree but in kind from their prewar counterparts. The giants of the 1950's, not yet the behemoths of the 1970's, did ten times the business of their predecessors in the 1920's and possessed resources vaster than the domains of many heads of state. General Motors, the world's biggest corporation, had a payroll of nearly 700,000 by the mid-1960's, and

American Telephone and Telegraph referred to its weekly board conclaves as "cabinet meetings." In 1957–1958, 574 corporations (out of a national total of 573,000) received over half of the net income of American industry. Corporations accounted too for the enlargement of the gaudy "growth industries" like chemicals and electronics.

In 1950 *Fortune* called chemicals "the premier industry of the United States," because none could match it "in dynamics, growth, earnings, and potential for the future." Since 1937, E. I. DuPont de Nemours & Co., the world leader, had doubled, Monsanto had quadrupled, Dow Chemical had expanded seven and a half times. Operated by chemists and engineers, these enterprises prospered by plowing back earnings into research, which yielded a never-ending array of new products for the consumer culture — Aerosol bombs, Dacron suits, synthetic tires, laundry detergents. In the five years after the war, DuPont tripled its nylon capacity and in 1950 began production of another synthetic fiber, Orlon, one of a series of discoveries that radically altered the textile business. The most spectacular gains came in plastics, a branch of the chemicals industry that by fashioning products such as Vinyl curtains, melamine dishes, and Teflon skillets grew a stunning 600 percent in a decade. Little wonder that when in the 1960's the secret of life was confided to Dustin Hoffman in *The Graduate,* the talisman was "plastics."

Chemicals also led all other manufacturing enterprises in direct foreign investment with 17 percent of the 1959 total. During the 1950's its overseas investment more than tripled, a slightly more rapid increase than that for American business generally. Especially remarkable was the penetration by the United States of the Canadian economy, accounting for one-third of the entire United States direct foreign investment, more than in all of Latin America. By 1957 Americans owned no less than one-half of its northern neighbor's manufacturing assets and mines and three-fourths of its oil and gas.

Nurtured by government contracts, the electronics industry came to maturity as a war baby and continued to thrive on war and rumors of war. In 1939, electronics, with total sales of less than $1 billion (mostly radios), ranked only forty-ninth in the country. By 1956, less than two decades later, it was America's number 5 industry, with $11.5 billion annual sales and a work force of 1.5 million, some ten times that of 1939. It had doubled since 1950 and was enlarging at a pace of more than $1 million a day. So avidly did electronics corporations recruit new talent that a single issue of *The New York Times* carried nearly six pages of want ads, forty-five full columns.

The favorite child of Mars, the electronics industry had flourished in World War II thanks to radar and after the war because of the demand for costly weapons systems. The $3 billion market in 1956 for military items (forty times the sales of 1947!) was twice as large as that for consumer goods like television sets and electronic kitchen ranges.

As the experience of the electronics industry indicated, if corporations played a stellar role in promoting economic growth, they had to share the limelight with government. Welfare benefits, minimum wage statutes, and farm subsidies built a base of purchasing power, and stock exchange regulation helped stabilize the securities markets. Manipulation of rediscount rates and reserve requirements regulated the money flow, and spending and taxing policies rechanneled it. Even enterprises that seemed to be "private" often rested on a government base. Some businesses got a head start in the postwar boom when the federal government disposed of its wartime holdings in shiny new plants — 50 percent of the country's machine tool facilities and aluminum capacity; 90 percent of aircraft construction, shipbuilding, and magnesium processing; and 97 percent of synthetic rubber production. Of spending for research and development at the end of the 1950's, Washington financed one-half. Consumer credit hinged on government bonds in the vaults of financial institutions, and the ex-GI's home in the suburbs depended on federal guarantees of mortgages. The government also intervened in more direct ways. In 1929 Washington's expenditures for goods and services totaled little more than 1 percent of the GNP; in 1953, they amounted to nearly 17 percent, marking the government as the nation's number 1 buyer. In 1956 alone the United States government spent more on highways than the entire worth of the economy of Norway. That year Congress took the first steps toward building a national, limited-access highway system to facilitate high-speed travel. Government had also become a major employer, with public jobs at all levels more than doubling between 1950 and 1970, when close to 13 million drew government paychecks. Uncle Sam's payroll underpinned the four most prosperous counties in the United States — Montgomery County in Maryland and Arlington and Fairfax counties in Virginia, all encapsulating bedroom communities of Washington, D.C., and Los Alamos County, which embraced New Mexico's atomic site.

High employment and the growth in productivity redounded to the benefit of large numbers of Americans. While the economy

Cars crowd the parking lot at the Crenshaw shopping center in Los Angeles. Widespread ownership of automobiles not only made it possible for industry to draw workers from a large area but was indispensable to the consumer culture.

was absorbing an increase in the civilian labor force from 54 million in 1945 to 78 million in 1970, real weekly earnings of factory employees rose 50 percent. Some workers had even attained the security of a guaranteed annual wage, a reform promoted by Walter Reuther, leader of the automobile union, and first instituted in 1955. Most industrial workers also enjoyed "fringe benefits" such as hospitalization insurance. In the 1950's the sums in private pension funds quadrupled; by 1959, they totaled $44 billion.

The distribution of income gave the American social structure the shape less of a pyramid than of a diamond, with a vastly expanded middle class. The proportion of families and unattached individuals with an annual income of $10,000 or more (in standard 1968 dollars) rose from 9 percent in 1947 to 33 percent in 1968, while that below $3000 fell from 34 percent in 1947 to 19 percent in 1968.

Nothing measured access to the middle class so well as the op-

Average Income of Families and Individuals

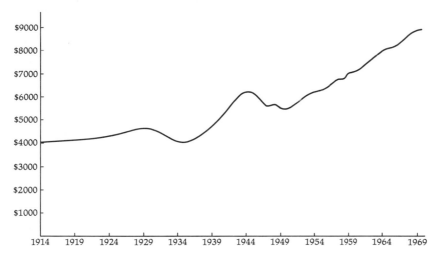

Source: From *Rich Man, Poor Man* by Herman P. Miller. Copyright © 1964 by Thomas Y. Crowell Company, Inc.

portunity to win a college diploma. In 1870 the campus had been largely the preserve of the well-to-do: Less than 2 percent of young people in the eighteen to twenty-one age group attended any institution of higher learning. The ensuing seventy years saw important gains; yet as late as 1940 only 1.5 million Americans (15 percent of their age cluster) went beyond high school, which meant that the remaining 85 percent would have virtually no chance of becoming professionals and little more of rising in the corporation or government worlds. After World War II, the situation changed dramatically. By 1960, college enrollments had increased to 3.6 million, and in the ensuing decade campus populations exploded. From the mid-1950's to 1969, registration tripled; in just one year in the 1960's the growth was greater than the total attendance in all universities in Great Britain. By 1970 five times as many Americans were on college campuses as in 1940. They comprised 40 percent of their age group, 60 percent in California, which had more college students than did France, a nation with three times as many people. And for all the alarms about dropouts, three students out of four in 1970 were graduated from high school, while in 1929 three out of four did not get beyond the eighth grade.

These developments led some enthusiasts to conclude that the United States was moving rapidly toward a classless society as a consequence of the accelerating redistribution of income. In 1955 *Fortune* asserted, "Though not a head has been raised aloft on a pikestaff, nor a railway station seized, the United States has been for some time now in a revolution," and in *America in the Sixties* the periodical's editors claimed that only a million families "still look really poor." In truth, there had been a change. The top 5 percent of the population raked in one-third of the national income in 1929, only 15 percent in 1968, and the proportion statistically defined as impoverished markedly diminished.

However, extreme disparities in income distribution continued to characterize American society. The economist Paul Samuelson wrote, "If we made an income pyramid out of child's blocks, with each portraying $1,000 of income, the peak would be far higher than the Eiffel Tower, but almost all of us would be within a yard of the ground." Most of the income readjustment since the 1920's had taken place before 1945, and in the postwar years new riches were accumulated. A study by Robert J. Lampman found that the top 1.6 percent of the adult population in 1953 held 90 percent of corporate

Unemployment Among Nonwhite Men, 1955-1963

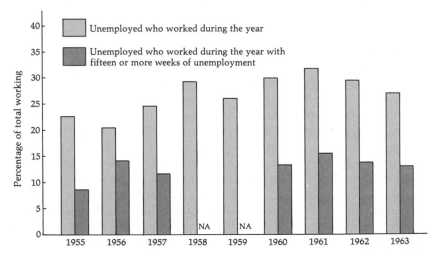

Source: Daniel Patrick Moynihan, *The Negro Family: The Case for National Action*, U.S. Department of Labor, Office of Policy Planning and Research, March 1965, p. 23.

Ben Shahn's 1948 painting *Miner's Wives* illustrates the hard times that were the lot of millions even in an affluent society. Like Jackson Pollock a beneficiary of New Deal art projects, the Russian-born Shahn was also an excellent photographer and a gifted muralist.

bonds and almost all state and local government bonds. By 1968, 153 Americans held nine-digit fortunes, including Dr. Edwin H. Land, the self-made chairman of Polaroid, and, despite steep estate taxes, one of the centimillionaires was a sixteen-year-old who had inherited a chunk of the Duke tobacco treasure. Nor did increases in income for the less well-to-do always guarantee a rise in class position. The sociologist Eli Chinoy learned that automobile workers had relinquished the "American Dream" of upward mobility and were settling instead for lateral mobility — a fancier car, a nicer house.

Moreover, millions still languished in want — Puerto Ricans in what Oscar Lewis called the "culture of poverty" in New York City, Mexican-Americans in the California lettuce fields, Indians wasting away on reservations with a death rate three times the national average, Negroes consigned to menial labor as busboys and janitors, whites in mountain hollows and lonely boarding houses. A report by the Survey Research Center in cooperation with the Federal Reserve Board concluded that in 1959 45 percent of spending units had less than $200 in liquid assets such as savings accounts. As late as the boom year of 1968, an estimated 25 million to 30 million Americans subsisted below the poverty line, three times the population of Belgium.

In the 1950's the Joint Economic Committee concluded that one-fourth of the poor were sixty-five years of age or older, a group particularly threatened by rising prices. The consumer price index (1957–1959 = 100) jumped from 62.7 in 1945 to 127.7 in 1969. Most of the increase in the 1945–1960 period came in two early spurts, during reconversion and at the outset of the Korean War, but prices continued to drift upward in the 1950's as well. Government spending, union demands (especially in service industries and municipal bureaucracies where wage boosts outran increased productivity), and monopolistic practices all drove prices up. When budget-minded administrations sought to preserve the dollar, they did so at the cost of heightened unemployment and retarded growth, and with mixed success in curbing price rises. Inflation cut cruelly into the pocketbooks of individuals who were not organized to win compensatory wage hikes and of people like pensioners who were on fixed incomes and who found it hard to absorb the spiraling costs of medical care.

Of those who lived below the "poverty line," one-fourth worked on farms at a time when many found agriculture unrewarding. From 1948 to 1956, the farmer's share of the national income fell from

The Purchasing Power of the Dollar, 1950-1965

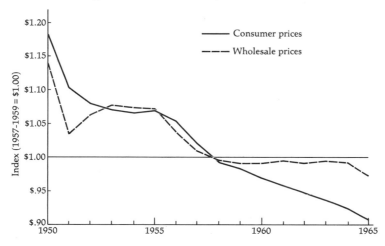

Source: U. S. Bureau of the Census, *Pocket Data Book, USA 1967.*

almost 9 percent to scarcely more than 4 percent, and as surpluses mounted, net farm income dropped from $3667 in 1946 to $2640 in 1960. Mechanization, a boon to wealthier growers, drove field hands off the land. Farm workers comprised over 40 percent of the male labor force in 1900, under 10 percent in 1960. Since tenant farmers, sharecroppers, and small growers lacked the capital to exploit technological changes or to cope with rising costs, many gave up the struggle. From 1940 to 1960, a time of prodigious population growth, the farm community declined by nine million, almost one-third. In 1935, 25 percent of the nation lived on farms; in 1969, only 5 percent did. The rich farm state of Iowa was scarred with crumbling villages that were once bustling trade centers: churches gone, the high school closed down, the bandstand in the square in ruin.

Yet these years, which carried such unhappy tidings to so many American farmers, brought piping times to others. By investing great amounts of capital to cultivate huge acreages, "corporation farmers" took advantage of a technological revolution. In 1945 for the first time the number of tractors exceeded the total of horses and mules. Mechanical pickers harvested cotton and corn, labor-saving machines spread chemical fertilizers, and airplanes dusted crops with new pesticides. As a result of such innovations, agricultural

Farm Production, 1947-1960

Source: The Life History of the United States, Volume 12, *The Great Age of
Change* by William E. Leuchtenburg and the Editors of Time-Life Books.
© 1964 Time Inc.

output per man-hour doubled in the fifteen years after the war. In
happy contrast to their ordeal in the Depression, some farmers in the
postwar years lived high on the hog. When Truman came to Dexter,
Iowa, to speak at a plowing contest in the 1948 campaign, he found
fifty private airplanes there. Soviet delegates watched popeyed while
an Iowa farmer drove up to the Coon Rapids golf links, unloaded
clubs from an electric cart, and teed off in a foursome.

Even the poverty-stricken had come a long way from the age of
Social Darwinism. Old age benefit coverage was extended from 1.9
million persons in 1950 to 9.6 million in 1959, while average monthly
benefits nearly tripled, though they were still far from generous. In
the fifteen years following the end of World War II, welfare payments sextupled, and from 1960 to 1968 they increased another two
and a half times. Over the two decades after 1940 the life expectancy
of nonwhites rose ten years, the number of Negro college students
and professionals more than doubled, and wage-earnings for blacks
increased four and a half times. Of American families with pretax

annual incomes of less than $4000 in 1959, 40 percent owned their homes. In 1964 in Harlan County, Kentucky, long regarded as a down-and-out mining district, 42 percent of the families had telephones, 59 percent owned automobiles, 67 percent TV sets, and 88 percent washing machines. In the consumer culture game, a minority of the players held the bulk of the vouchers, but most of the players had at least some vouchers to spend.

The Consumer Culture

The booming economy enabled millions of Americans to take part in the burgeoning consumer culture. With unprecedented amounts of disposable income, consumers devoted much of their time to institutions that catered to their needs and whims—shopping malls with hanging baskets of flowers and piped music, suburban department stores with civic auditoriums, supermarkets with row on row of brilliantly colored cartons. Shopping, while still often a chore, also became a kind of avocation. Husbands found release in "impulse buying," and the poet Randall Jarrell wrote of a housewife "Moving from Cheer to Joy, from Joy to All." After the advent of television in the late 1940's, millions each week turned their dials to a show that featured contestants who raced through the aisles of a supermarket competing to see who could accumulate the greatest value of goods in his shopping basket, and *Life* rejoiced at customers who wandered around a "$5 million grocery store, picking from the thousands of items on the high-piled shelves until their carts became cornucopias filled with an abundance that no other country in the world has ever known."

Foreign nations that in the 1920's had sent emissaries to Detroit to study the wizardry of America's industrial productivity now paid tribute to the magnetic consumer culture of a country "rich beyond the dreams of Marx." A Swiss department store chain, displaying a broad selection of products from the United States, admonished its customers, "Live like an American." At Uppsala in Sweden, a distinguished literary critic from Yale drew an audience of only thirty while in the next room three hundred were giving close attention to an address by his wife on the American kitchen. Yugoslavians gathered around TV sets to watch "Peyton Place," "Batman" became a big hit in Tokyo and Buenos Aires, and two avid admirers of "Bonanza" were Kenya's Tom Mboya and South Vietnam's Nguyen

Cao Ky. In Frankfurt, advertising men shamelessly borrowed a chestnut from Madison Avenue: "Ziehn wir's am Flaggenmast hoch und sehn wir wer grüsst" ("Run it up the flagpole and see if anyone salutes").

The consumer culture even made its mark on the cold war. In the competition for the allegiance of the Third World, the United States scored points when at the Jakarta trade fair in 1955 Indonesians showed more interest in an American toy train than in machine tools from Communist China. United States intelligence tried to weigh the significance of the fact that Ho Chi Minh had switched from Philip Morrises and Camels to Salems, and Soviet policy makers fretted over the popularity of rock music in Leningrad and Budapest. One of the Kremlin's first acts following Stalin's death was to re-open GUM, the State department store, and immediately after Nikita Khrushchev returned from his visit to the United States in 1959 the Russian government ordered a rapid acceleration of the out-

Land of plenty. To foreign observers, few aspects of American life were more striking than the well-stocked shelves of a supermarket. Stores like this one served as models for the burgeoning consumer societies abroad.

George Silk. LIFE Magazine. © 1951 Time Inc.

The consumer culture meets the cold war. On July 25, 1959, Vice President Richard M. Nixon and Soviet Premier Nikita Khrushchev sip Pepsi-Cola before exchanging hot words at the model kitchen of the American National Exhibition in Moscow. In America the "kitchen debate" enhanced Nixon's reputation as a Cold Warrior, but the Russian people seemed more interested in the display of new household appliances from the homeland of capitalism.

put of television sets, refrigerators, and other consumer goods, "to match the best foreign samples."

The most noteworthy face-to-face encounter between cold war leaders in the 1950's took place neither on the battlefield nor at the negotiating table but in front of the kitchen of a model ranch house at the United States exhibition in Moscow in 1959. After sipping some Pepsi-Cola, Nikita Khrushchev and Richard Nixon engaged in a shouting match about washing machines and military machines. During the next six weeks nearly 3 million Russians looked in on the kitchen, where an automatic polisher popped out of an electronic console and dishwashers careened across the floor at the press of a housewife's thumb.

When the Paris editor of *U.S. News and World Report* came home to the United States in 1960 after twelve years abroad, he was astonished at the changes that had been wrought in his absence. He marveled at such manifestations of affluence and the consumer culture as small boats featuring electronic depth finders and automatic pilots, cocktails ready-mixed in plastic envelopes, and that ultimate evidence of a society with millions of its members far removed from subsistence concerns, striped toothpaste. He had been living in an advanced Western nation where only one family in ten had a bathtub with hot running water, and he was coming home to a country where, in some sections of California, at least one family in ten owned a swimming pool in the back yard.

The economy not only turned out an abundance of goods for the American consumer but gave him more leisure to enjoy them. As recently as the "prosperous" 1920's, the average industrial employee had been granted no paid holidays and had toiled fifty-two weeks a year without vacation. By 1970, the work week for production employees in manufacturing had been reduced to a little under forty hours. One study estimated that a typical employee enjoyed each year "1,500 more free, awake hours" than his counterpart in the mid-nineteenth century. Although in many countries of the world the Saturday workday was a regular feature, some American firms had begun to experiment with a four-day week. By 1963, paid holidays had risen to eight a year (double the 1946 figure), and many employees accrued paid sick leave too. In the 1960's almost all workers could count on an annual paid vacation (which most had not received in 1940), and the typical vacation ran at least two weeks, contrasted with one week on the eve of World War II. "Trade unions that once had a hard time getting clean toilets for their members are now plugging three-week package tours in Europe," noted Robert Bendiner. When steelworkers went out on strike in 1919, one of their "radical" demands was for one day's rest in seven. In 1963 the United Steel Workers secured a contract that provided for a "sabbatical" leave for the senior half of its members of thirteen weeks every five years.

Even the pace of work seemed more easygoing, as befit what the sociologist Pitirim Sorokin called a "late sensate society." The "coffee break," which before the war would have been frowned on as soldiering on the job, became a standard institution, and no office was complete without a water cooler, which served the purposes formerly met by the cracker barrel of the general store. At construction sites and in office buildings, caterers' trucks made their rounds each day with coffee and pastry. Many workers migrated to states like Florida and California because they offered a balmier climate for the pursuit of pleasure and amenities such as lighted tennis courts when the day's labors were over. By 1950, the country was already spending one-seventh of the gross national product (twice the expenditure for rent) on pleasure, and in 1971 Merrill Lynch, Pierce, Fenner and Smith estimated the value of the leisure market at better than $150 billion a year.

Yet these developments failed to persuade all writers that the change was as fundamental as it seemed. Some employees, including numbers of the steelworkers, took advantage of their "leisure time" to swell their incomes by "moonlighting" (working at a second job), and not a few would have been readily recognized by the go-getters of Sinclair Lewis' *Dodsworth*. In *Of Time, Work and Leisure*, Sebastian De Grazia derided the "myth" that the heavily committed modern man had more leisure than his grandfather, who worked much longer hours, and in *Couples*, John Updike wrote of "a climate still *furtively* hedonist." David Riesman, the *savant nonpareil* of the new society, cautioned: "But an attenuated puritanism survives in his exploitation of his leisure. He may say, when he takes a vacation or stretches a weekend, 'I owe it to myself' — but the self in question is viewed like a car or house whose upkeep must be carefully maintained for resale purposes."

As a consequence of higher income, longer vacations, and advances in commercial aviation, middle-class Americans traveled to places that had long seemed the destinations only of the well-heeled. In July 1955, *Newsweek* commented that "the Passport Office in New York's Rockefeller Center was as jammed as a department-store white sale," and one year later *Time* noted: "In Manhattan, liners packed to the last berth with tourists edged daily from their docks into the Hudson's high slack water." Families who had once counted it an adventure to take the San Francisco ferry thought nothing of crossing the Bosporus or riding the hydrofoil from Copenhagen to Malmö. The Piazza San Marco swarmed with camera-toting tourists from Fort Wayne and Passaic, and each August the Parisians abandoned their city to the peaceful invaders from the West. By the 1960's the beaches of San Juan and Montego Bay were so crowded in February by Americans who had come to consider a winter sojourn in the

Caribbean as much their right as the familiar summer jaunt that an increasing number of Yankees were planting themselves on the more remote shores of Acapulco and Ipanema.

The traveler, who in prewar days had been compelled to put up with fly-specked tourist "cabins," bedded down in luxurious motels boasting kidney-shaped swimming pools, saunas, chuck-wagon buffets, and the inevitable television set in every air-conditioned room. For a quarter the weary driver could stretch out on his double bed, with its decorator-coordinated spread, and be jiggled out of his tensions by a relaxing machine. In Vladimir Nabokov's *Lolita*, Humbert Humbert sang the praises of "the Functional Motel—clean, neat, safe nooks, ideal places for sleep, argument, reconciliation, insatiable illicit love," of "stone cottages under enormous Chateaubriandesque trees," and of the twin-bedded "cell of paradise, with yellow window shades pulled down to create a morning illusion of Venice and sunshine when actually it was Pennsylvania and rain." So attentive did the motels become to the spiritual needs of the wayfarers that Holiday Inns introduced a "chaplain on call" service and in Shreveport even a motel chapel and a meditation garden. Yet spirituality, too, paid homage to the opulence of the consumer culture. The ubiquitous Gideon Bible in the motel drawer appeared in hues such as bittersweet, beige, walnut, and olive, and when a Playboy Hotel requested 350 Bibles in the original black (to harmonize with the black and white motif that was a Hugh Hefner trademark), the Gideon functionaries had to scour a warehouse to find enough copies of the Good Book in the required color.

Air travel, once largely confined to the wealthy, became so commonplace in the postwar world that pilots, the glamorous fly-boys of the 1930's, were put down as "bus drivers." By 1956, airlines, which in prewar years had carried only 5 percent as much passenger traffic between cities as railroads, pulled even with their rivals. Two years later, a Boeing 707 introduced the country to the greater speed and comfort of jet aircraft. Both the prop planes and the jets, with their shapely stewardesses, piped music, in-flight movies, and stabs at gourmet dining, catered to a public that was being taught to expect luxury wherever it went. Braniff even painted its planes in gorgeous colors and clad its stewardesses in Pucci bloomers. One traveler, Jean Shepherd, recounted the experience of "floating gently on a sea of barely audible Muzak, the sweet Karo Syrup of Existence. . . . Muzak rises to a crescendo and we take off. Instantly we are high over this big chunk of land, and the world has become a blurred

Kodachrome slide. . . . Silently the red velour is rolled out and baby-blue and silver *houris* are plying me with stuff to eat—which if my mother knew I was eating she would really know I have gone to hell. By God, caviar and Moët *brut* and diced lamb's-liver pâté at 8:17 A.M., over Altoona."

The vast output of industry did not begin to satisfy the demands of the American consumer, and in the 1950's the United States moved past the United Kingdom as the world's leading importer. A country with the lion's share of the earth's goods and resources now acquired more from foreign lands than any other nation. Domestic sources no longer sufficed for the multitude of customers who coveted Simcas and Jaguars, preferred Heineken to Budweiser, furnished their homes in Danish modern, and counted on buying Carnaby Street fashions at J. C. Penney's.

The American household in the postwar years adopted a style of consumption that was more sophisticated, more worldly, more diversified, one appropriate to a nation that was not only affluent but imperial. A 1969 account observed: "Thirty years ago the average Midwesterner had never heard of pizza, sukiyaki, or South African lobster tails. He had never seen a foreign car, a Vietnamese, or a reproduction of Van Gogh's *Sunflowers*. It would have surprised him to see teak furniture in a neighbor's living room, let alone African tribal masks on the walls, or Thai silk at the windows. Now such former exotica are taken for granted."

The new style revealed itself most conspicuously at the dinner table, for in a decade wine purchases doubled, and millions of Americans learned to serve Chateauneuf du Pape (or more likely, Almadén's Cabernet Sauvignon) with the boeuf Bourguignonne and a chilled Pouilly-Fuissé with the frozen halibut. Before the war, the grocer's shelves offered little more in prepared foods than mundane items such as Heinz spaghetti and Del Monte spinach; after it, the frozen food locker of the supermarket was brimful of delicacies like frogs' legs and cannelloni. To meet the expectations of different ethnic groups, one new product was labeled both "Kreplach" and "Won Ton Soup." By 1971 "fancy food" was a billion-dollar industry, and *Gourmet* magazine's circulation had reached 550,000, more than twice what it had been four years before.

Although these changes affected most classes, differentiation in consumption styles (and, of course, in income distribution) remained critical. When the lower middle class protagonist from Newark, New Jersey, of Philip Roth's novella *Goodbye, Columbus* visited the up-

Growth in Production of Prepared Foods, 1947-1958

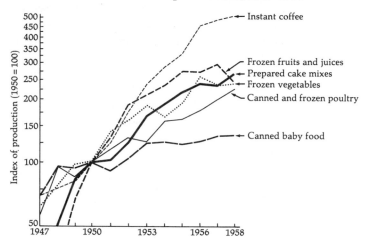

Source: Elmer Smith for Fortune Magazine, September 1959.

wardly mobile Patimkins in Briarpath Hills, he marveled at their refrigerator, which no longer held herring in cream sauce but "greengage plums, black plums, red plums, apricots, nectarines, peaches, long horns of grapes, black, yellow, red, and cherries, cherries flowing out of boxes and staining everything scarlet. And there were melons—cantaloupes and honeydews—and on the top shelf, half of a huge watermelon, a thin sheet of wax paper clinging to its bare red face like a wet lip. Oh Patimkin! Fruit grew in their refrigerator and sporting goods dropped from their trees!"

But not only the Patimkins moved into new homes. After enduring a critical housing shortage when they returned stateside in 1945, millions of GI's and their young families created a demand for shelter that both sparked the economy and sharply upgraded accommodations for millions of Americans. By 1950 over $18 billion was being invested in the construction of nonfarm, private residences. Life insurance companies erected large-scale urban projects like Stuyvesant Town and Peter Cooper Village in New York City, while national agencies such as the Federal Housing Administration and the Veterans Administration underwrote suburban developments. Washington also pumped money into public housing for lower-income groups, although much too parsimoniously and with urban renewal frequently carried on at the expense of the dislocated slum dweller. Nonetheless, during the 1950's, dwelling units were constructed at a record rate of better than a million a year, faster than the growth of new households. Of all the housing in America in 1960, one-fourth had been built during the 1950's, when for the first time in this century more Americans owned their homes (even if mortgaged) than lived in rented premises. While the well-to-do were adding amenities like air conditioning (in 1 percent of residences with electricity in 1953, in 13 percent by 1960, in 37 percent in 1968), the less prosperous were moving into dwellings with modern bathrooms; between 1940 and 1960, housing units lacking bathtub or shower fell from 39 percent to 12 percent. During these same years, the mechanization of the home advanced at a pace inconceivable in the 1920's when the process first began. Less than 1 percent of homes with wiring boasted a refrigerator in 1925; 98 percent had them in 1960; and in 1955 alone, sales of electric clothes dryers, first marketed in 1946, totaled 1.2 million, double the figure of only two years earlier.

To many American artists, the consumer culture permeated the urban landscape, and hence their conception of reality, much as trees and farmland had impressed themselves on the consciousness of Constable and Breughel. Willem de Kooning affixed a smile from a Camel ad on one of his many "women," Claes Oldenburg entitled a work *Hamburger with Pickle and Tomato Attached,* and in 1964 Andy Warhol created *Brillo.* Oldenburg even stocked a "store" with plaster replicas of familiar objects. But it was Warhol who made "pop art" the *dernier cri* with two paintings of repeated images that caught the nation's fancy—one of Campbell's soup cans, as though on a supermarket shelf; the other, as in a redundant film strip, of the love-object Marilyn Monroe.

Both critics and the public puzzled over the meaning of "pop art." Gallery-goers, unaccustomed to finding such works hanging in collections with Rembrandts and Giottos, wondered uneasily whether they were, in a phrase of the day, being "put on." Some critics saw "pop art" as a delightful way of poking fun at the severity and earnestness of abstract art. More prevalent was the view that "pop art" was a kind of social criticism, a parody of "the materialism, spiritual vacuity, and ludicrously sexualized environment of affluent America." Perhaps. Yet Warhol would soon be making ludicrously sexualized movies, and Oldenburg expressed an outspoken fondness for the objects of the consumer culture. "I am for Kool Art, 7-Up Art,

Pepsi Art, Sunkist Art," he said. "I am for the white art of refrigerators and their muscular openings and closings."

The affluent society made possible a spectacular "culture boom," which gratified uncritical admirers of the American way as much as it depressed the mordant mandarins who watched over the country's aesthetic well-being. The cold facts seemed to give the boosters all the better of it. Between 1952 and 1961, the sale of books more than doubled, to no small degree because of the "paperback revolution." The unbreakable, long-playing record, a postwar arrival, helped swell purchases of classical albums as well as of popular

4 Campbell Soup Cans, a 1962 still life by Andy Warhol, reveals how the consumer culture served the purposes of pop art. "Warhol's art uses the visual strength and vitality which are the time-tested skills of the world of advertising that cares more for the container than for the thing contained," a critic explained. "He selects examples from this commercial affluence which best evince our growing sameness."

Leo Castelli Gallery. Photograph by Rudolph Burckhardt.

discs. Americans spent greater sums on tickets to classical concerts than to baseball games, and more on records and hi-fi equipment than on all spectator sports. Yehudi Menuhin performed in Naperville, Illinois; Byron Janis in Wartburg, Iowa; and Isaac Stern at Fort Hays, Kansas; while booming, oil-rich Houston boasted a symphony orchestra that Sir Thomas Beecham conducted. Art movie theaters, a rarity in 1945, had become fixtures by the 1960's, and Americans who had never seen a foreign language film before the war talked knowingly of Bergman and Fellini. Yet for all this, many major cities lacked even one adequate book store; television huckstered hours of dross each week; and the "middlebrows" sometimes hugged art so tightly that they squeezed it to death. The critic Dwight Macdonald, who warned that "a tepid ooze of Midcult is spreading everywhere," wrote: "There seems to be a Gresham's Law in cultural as well as monetary circulation: bad stuff drives out good, since it is more easily understood and enjoyed."

The pacesetters for much of the popular culture, America's teenagers, appropriated a huge segment of the country's productive machinery to turn out goods to conform to their tastes in consumption. In 1963 in the·United States adolescents spent the staggering sum of $22 billion, twice the gross national product of Austria. They created a specialized market for a wide variety of goods from surfboards and transistor radios to *Glamour* and *Seventeen,* but especially for pop records. When Bill Haley and the Comets' "Rock Around the Clock" burst upon the country in *The Blackboard Jungle* in 1955, the national merchandising of rock culture began. By 1965, teenagers would be shelling out over $100,000,000 for forty-fives, and in 1968 people under twenty-five would spend $1.2 billion on records. In the 1960's rock would be intimately connected to the counter culture and social protest, but in the 1950's it was more tepid. For all his pelvic gyrations, Elvis Presley, a consumer culture hero with his gold lamé suits and pastel Cadillacs, neither smoked nor drank, respected his parents, and went to bed each night after saying his prayers. Dick Clark, the clean-cut emcee of the television show "American Bandstand," which 20 million watched each week to see singers lip-synch their songs and adolescents do the twist or the frug, explained, "What I'm trying to defend is my right and your right to go to a church of our choice, or buy the record of our choice."

Television exploded on the postwar world like a bomb with a delayed-action fuse. There were in 1946 fewer than 17,000 sets in use, and viewers were concentrated in a small number of cities where

Elvis the Pelvis. Born in Mississippi in 1935, Elvis Presley hit it big in 1955 with "Hound Dog" and "Blue Suede Shoes." The suggestive gyrations of his torso helped to associate rock and roll with sexual abandon and to rocket Presley to success in Hollywood films in which he sang tunes that were instantly forgettable.

they were offered a narrow choice of fare. In 1947, the fuse grew short, and in 1948, a Californian recalled: "Sometimes at night when a blind wasn't pulled all the way down we noticed mysterious blue light flickering in a living room across the street. Occasionally it was accompanied by sound of laughter or gun shots." In 1949, the bomb burst; as many as a quarter of a million sets a month were installed. A trade association ad in 1950 warned: "There are some things a son or daughter won't tell you. . . . Do you expect him to blurt out the truth—that he's really ashamed to be with the gang—because he doesn't see the same shows they see? . . . How can a little girl describe the bruise deep inside? . . . How can you deny television to your children any longer?" The following year, television went coast to coast, and 3 million at home and about as many in bars saw the Yankee-Dodger World Series in October.

By 1953 two-thirds of American families owned television; 7 million sets were manufactured in that year, compared to six thousand in 1946. Four years later, the country boasted 40 million sets and 467 TV stations. Antennas sprouted over slum tenements, and one writer reported in 1955, "In isolated rural Mississippi, we saw unpainted Erskine Caldwell shacks topped by aerials." During the mid-1960's, 94 percent of American households owned at least one TV set, and millions possessed more than one; in 1971, 90 million sets were in use. Color TV, a luxury in under 3 million homes in 1965, had been installed in 24 million (38.2 percent) by 1970.

The history of the quarter-century after World War II could readily be told in kinescopes of TV programs—the voices of gangsters at the Kefauver hearings ("I haven't got the lease idea"), Everett Dirksen's growl at the 1952 Republican convention ("Tom Dewey, we followed you before and you took us down the road to defeat"), Nixon's Checkers speech ("And you know the kids, like all kids, love the dog"), the army-McCarthy hearings ("Point of order, Mr. Chairman"), John Glenn on the launching pad at Cape Canaveral ("10-9-8-7 . . ."), and then, as though speeded up at much too intense a pace, the snarling police dogs in Birmingham, the motorcade in Dallas, the slumping body of Lee Oswald, the vociferous students on Telegraph Avenue, the howling delegates at the Cow Palace wearing "Stamp Out Huntley-Brinkley" buttons, the machine-gun fire from Vietnam, the clubs flailing at cameramen and reporters in Chicago, Nixon's inscrutable smile at the Great Wall.

The consumer culture even affected the political process. In 1952, the Eisenhower forces introduced a new wrinkle into campaigning

TV antennas frame the Statue of Liberty in New York harbor. Ownership of a television set became such a status symbol during the 1950's that it was said that some householders raised antennas to impress their neighbors before they could afford to acquire a TV. John Wayne later observed that "there sure has never been any form of entertainment so . . . available to the human race with so little effort since they invented marital sex."

by employing a Manhattan advertising firm to sell the general. Rosser Reeves, who saturated the channels with "spot" commercials for Ike, explained: "I think of a man who hesitates between two levers as if he were pausing between competing tubes of toothpaste in a drugstore. The brand that has made the highest penetration on his brain will win his choice." "Space merchants" like Reeves were inclined to exaggerate their influence, for determinants like income and ethnicity remained of critical importance in shaping electoral decisions and programmatic differences continued to be salient. But it is also true that candidates became increasingly concerned about their "image," a piece of Madison Avenue argot, and some of their audience appraised them as they assessed the rival claims of deodorants. The 1958 gubernatorial campaign in New York appeared to turn less on issues than on the degree of finesse with which the two candidates could devour blintzes and other ethnic delicacies. W. Averell Harriman, who had served with distinction as United States envoy in the leading chancelleries of Europe, lost to Nelson Rockefeller, who made a political asset out of the gusto with which he devoured bagels in the Bronx and spaghetti in the Italian sections of Buffalo and Syracuse.

"If we were to sum up the differences between elections past and present, it could be said that the United States had moved from the politics of the country store to the politics of the supermarket," wrote Karl Meyer. "In 1960," Meyer added, "our two living ex-Presidents, Herbert Hoover and Harry Truman, seemed like nostalgic remnants of the era of the country store," in contrast to the two young candidates "who stepped briskly into and out of the shopping centers. During the campaign, it often seemed as if the country were caught in a sales war between Safeway and the A & P." The highlight of the campaign in 1960 was a series of TV debates in which Nixon was said to have been put at a disadvantage because his pancake makeup failed to cover his "five o'clock shadow" and he looked like "a sinister chipmunk." In 1968 a more experienced Nixon staff would circulate passages from Marshall McLuhan warning that "politics and issues are useless for election purposes since they are too specialized and hot" for a "cool medium" like TV.

The Homogenized Society

In the 1950's critics launched a devastating attack on the consumer culture for fostering a docile, standardized nation. Wherever they looked—toward woman's place in the home or the antiseptic one-class suburb or the comatose campus—America seemed phlegmatic and routinized. One writer described the United States as " 'The Packaged Society,' for we are all items in a national supermarket—categorized, processed, labeled, priced, and readied for merchandising." In fact, the nation was livelier and more heterogeneous than these writers suggested. Nor were the 'fifties—the decade of Korea and McCarthyism, of the Montgomery bus boycott and Little Rock—an altogether tranquil time. Some of the outcry against affluence represented only another stage in the prolonged warfare of intellectuals against a prospering middle class. Yet America did pay a price for the consumer culture. It served to engender a preoccupation with private concerns and induce a complacency about public affairs that had unfortunate consequences.

Long characterized as a polyglot society, the United States increasingly became a homogeneous nation. In 1940, 26 percent of the population were first or second-generation Americans; by 1960 only 18 percent were and 95 percent were native-born. Institutions once essential for maintaining a sense of ethnic identity lost their vitality. In the 1940's, one-third of the foreign language press disappeared. To be sure, the 1950's saw a greater immigration than any decade since the 1920's, although it was only a modest 2.5 million. Puerto Ricans filled every seat on the night flights from the island until there were more of their number in New York City than in San Juan, and Mexicans crowded the *barrios* of the Southwest until Los Angeles had a larger Hispano population than Guadalajara. Still, the United States had moved a good distance from the world of Mulberry Bend and the East Side ghetto.

Commentators found the United States not only homogeneous but homogenized. The typical American, social analysts complained, had become both conformist and bland. Each morning Mr. Jones put on a standard uniform of button-down shirt, sincere tie, and charcoal-gray flannel suit, and adjusted his perpetual smile. At night he read to his children from the "Little Golden Book" of Tootle the Engine, a cautionary tale with the admonition: "Always stay on the track no matter what." One mother was informed about her son's failings: "He was doing fine in some respects but . . . his social adjustment was not as good as it might be. He would pick one or two friends to play with—and sometimes he was happy to remain by himself." Conformity watchers fretted too about the corporation wife who was told to hide any journal discussing intellectual questions when another wife paid a call, and they noticed "more and more men prowling about in sports cars in which the driver nestles well down in the prenatal position." As ardent a Yankeephile as the French Jesuit philosopher Jacques Maritain described a dentist's office with nurses who gave him the feeling that "dying in the midst of these happy smiles and the angel wings of these white, immaculate uniforms would be a pure pleasure, a moment of no consequence. . . . I left this dentist, in order to protect within my mind the Christian idea of death." (Yet, Maritain conceded, "Deep beneath the anonymous American smile there is a feeling that is evangelical in origin— compassion for man, a desire to make life tolerable.")

The evangelist Billy Graham reads from the Good Book, as he did at scores of revival meetings and on his radio and TV program, "Hour for Decision." At home and abroad, he converted thousands. The favorite clergyman of the consumer culture and of Republican Presidents, the handsome Baptist minister accepted God's call on a Florida golf course, won the Horatio Alger award, and enjoyed the privilege of free lodging at motels throughout the world.

" 'Religion' like many other things is booming in America; it is a blue chip," reported the shrewd British observer, Denis Brogan, in 1957. Five days before he was inaugurated, President-elect Eisenhower stared out of the window of his New York hotel room for several minutes absorbed in thought, then wheeled around and said to the evangelist Billy Graham, "America has to have a religious revival." One writer has observed, "Perhaps no other policy directive issued by Mr. Eisenhower during the next eight years was executed so promptly or enjoyed such widespread support." Ike's first year in office saw Les Paul and Mary Ford's "Vaya con Dios" and Frankie Laine's "I Believe" among the top ten hits. In 1954 Congress voted to add the phrase "under God" to the pledge of allegiance and in the following year made "In God We Trust" mandatory on all United States currency. Religion was merchandised like other products of the consumer culture through the mass media (TV spot commercials announced, "The family that prays together stays together") and by testimonials from satisfied users. "I love God," announced the bosomy film actess Jane Russell. "And when you get to know Him, you find He's a Livin' Doll." Book stores sold *The Power of Prayer on Plants,* the Ideal Toy Company offered a doll that, when stroked, genuflected, and jukeboxes blared "Big Fellow in the Sky."

Although many churchmen were pleased to count a full house each week, some theologians brooded about the shallow piety purveyed by men like the Reverend Norman Vincent Peale in *The Power of Positive Thinking* and the unconsidered response he won. "By and large," wrote Will Herberg, "the religion which actually prevails among Americans today has lost much of its authentic Christian (or Jewish) content." Still, a contentless creed of good fellowship, good works, and Thursday night bingo had one advantage: It diminished the sectarian discord that had so often envenomed small-town life. The "religious revival" was yet another occurrence that served to nationalize and homogenize the American people, an eventuality having benefits as well as costs.

"The Silent Generation" in American colleges in the 1950's appeared to be even more conformist and prudent than its elders. *Fortune* first detected the cautiousness of the young when it reflected that the men of the class of '49 "seem to a stranger from another generation, somehow curiously old before their time. Above everything else, security has become their goal. . . . The class of '49 wants to work for somebody else—preferably somebody big." In 1950, President A. Whitney Griswold of Yale told the graduating class, "I observe that you share the prevailing mood of the hour, which in your case consists of bargains privately struck with fate—on fate's terms." After examining a series of interviews, Riesman concluded that the typical class of '55 senior sought a place on the corporate ladder, planned which branch of the military he would enter (guided missiles was one favorite), and knew what his wife would be like at forty-five ("the Grace Kelly, camel's hair-coat type" who would do volunteer hospital work and bring culture into the home). By 1957, *Time* was reporting, "No campus is without its atrocity story of intellectual deadness," and Leslie Fiedler complained, "The young, who should be fatuously but profitably attacking us, instead discreetly expand, analyze and dissect us. How dull they are!" As late as 1962 so perceptive an observer of the young as Kenneth Keniston could write, "I see little likelihood of American students ever playing a radical role, much less a revolutionary one, in our society."

With such near-unanimity in the contemporary testimony, the historian has little choice but to accept this characterization of "the careful young men" of the 1950's, and perhaps he should. But one wonders if they may not have been given a bad rap. Even at the time, the sociologist Reuel Denney found them "about the freest generation of students in U.S. colleges in the 20th century," liberated from the "moral inflation" of the cults of the 1920's and 1930's. If they lacked the fervor of the activists of the 1960's who would succeed them, they also were without their arrogance. If they were less civic minded, they understood the value of a life style that was personal and not politicized. There was something to be said, too, for their feeling "that they have to know a lot more in their minds before they can become effectual." Besides, however quiescent the campuses were, "Silent Generation" does not characterize adequately the brawling street gangs who provided the *dramatis personae* for Leonard Bernstein's *West Side Story*, the juvenile delinquents who sent statistics on crimes of violence soaring, or all those "rebels without a cause" who made of James Dean's death a morbid remembrance.

In 1954, *McCall's* first employed the word "togetherness." So precise a term did it seem for the spirit of the 1950's that many thought that the word, first used in the seventeenth century, had been invented by the magazine. *McCall's* boasted: "From a little cloud, like a woman's hand, it has risen to blanket the consciousness of an entire nation, popping up everywhere from Macy's to the halls of Congress." "Togetherness" was variously defined as "the beat and rhythm of our times," "the tie that binds American families to their mothers," and "the only real definitive American market." The Reverend Norman Vincent Peale explained "togetherness" as the "creative mechanism which fuses the man and the woman into a team."

Publicists and educators celebrated woman's role as homemaker and helpmate and heaped scorn on feminists. In *Modern Woman: The Lost Sex*, Ferdinand Lundberg and Marynia Farnham depicted feminism as a "deep illness" caused by penis-envy; "the shadow of the phallus lay darkly" over those masculinized females who proselytized it. To erase the influence of such neurotics, they proposed to subsidize childbearing, encourage country skills like putting up preserves, and give annual prizes to the best mothers. The president of Mills College advocated a "distinctly feminine curriculum" in which post-Kantian studies would yield to the creation of paella, and the president of Stephens College, who touted his programs in interior decorating, home economics, cosmetics, and grooming, declared that for women "the college years must be rehearsal periods for the major performance" of wedlock. Their political assignment, Adlai Stevenson told Smith graduates, was to "influence man and boy" in the "humble role of housewife." For their part, women published articles with titles like "Homemaking Is My Vocation" and underwent instruction in natural childbirth. The editors of *Mademoiselle,* after analyzing hundreds of questionnaires, concluded that young women wanted to be well-rounded rather than to excel, viewed the family as "the ultimate measure of success," and looked forward to relaxed, uneventful marriages "of thoroughly barbecued bliss."

In the midst of these placid waters, stronger currents had begun to move. To the undiscerning eye, it appeared that Rosie the Riveter could not wait to bid good riddance to the war plant and resume her familiar duties at the hearthside. Yet, in fact, little noticed at the time, women's position in the job market was fundamentally shifting. Between 1940 and 1960, the proportion of working wives doubled, and of all persons who entered the labor market in the decade after 1949, three-fifths were married women. By 1960, some 40 percent of American women were employed, fully or part-time; even more striking, about the same proportion of mothers of school-age children held jobs. When the women's liberation movement erupted in the 1960's, it was in large part because, as William H. Chafe has noted, women "had already experienced profound change in their lives."

However, in the 1950's many wives worked less in order to achieve self-fulfillment than to add to the family income. The less a husband earned, the more likely it was that a wife would be employed. In the suburbs a second paycheck made it possible to turn the basement into a rumpus room. *Mademoiselle*'s survey suggested that

Dennis Brack from Black Star

The sizeable percentage of female employees in this photograph of an office at the Internal Revenue Service demonstrates that while national attention was focused on women in the home in the Eisenhower era, large numbers were holding down jobs. The photograph also suggests the growth of the white collar sector and the rapidly increasing importance of government as an employer.

young women did not view employment as a way of altering their "place." As Russell Lynes summed up their attitude: "A job is a way of meeting 'interesting' people, of keeping amused, a continuation of one's education, a way to live in Europe a year or two, but it must not be all-absorbing."

Much of the lamentation about conformity centered on the quality of life in the suburbs, for in the period after World War II the United States experienced the most extensive internal migration in its history. Scott Donaldson has listed the main influences: "practically universal car ownership, the expanding highway system, the baby boom of the forties, and most important of all, the availability of cheap homes, and cheap financing after World War II." By 1950, there were 37 million suburbanites; two decades later, the number had nearly doubled, after bulldozers plowed up the apricot groves of the Santa Clara Valley and cleared the way for ranch houses to be plunked in Long Island potato fields. As many moved to the suburbs each year as had come to the United States in the peak year of transatlantic migration. Increasingly the suburb became not just a collection of bedrooms but the hub of activities that had long been the pride of the city. The "Dallas" Cowboys played in Irving, the Minnesota Twins performed not in the Twin Cities but in Bloomington, and when the Patriots removed to Foxboro they even dropped "Boston" from their name. With more people living in suburbs in the 1960's than in cities or villages or on farms, the suburbanite became the representative American.

This great exodus had an exceptional racial characteristic; it was turning the United States into a nation of black cities and white suburbs. Analysts frequently wrote of "the flight" to the suburbs, and the movement was in fact motivated not only by the attraction of azaleas and green lawns but also by an aversion to the changing character of the city. Some whites wanted simply to escape crowded schools and foul air, but others undoubtedly left in response to the rapid influx of Negroes into the central cities. From 1940 to 1960, the number of blacks living outside the South more than doubled, in large part because of the mechanization of the cotton fields, and by 1969 only 52 percent of American Negroes still lived in Dixie (contrasted to 77 percent as late as 1940). In both North and South, the displaced persons of modern technology migrated to the city. Washington, D.C., 72 percent white in 1940, had become a predominantly black metropolis by 1960; a decade later, it had been joined by Newark, Gary, and Atlanta, and seven other cities were more than 40 percent black. Although well over a million Negroes moved to the suburbs in the two decades after 1950, the suburban population in 1970 remained more than 95 percent white.

To critics of the suburb, its racial homogeneity represented only one of its deplorable aspects. Shoddy housing developments, "conceived in error, nurtured by greed, corroding everything they touch," wrote John Keats in *The Crack in the Picture Window*, had been "vomited up" by conscienceless speculators who defaced the countryside with rows of "identical boxes spreading like gangrene." These excrescences bred "swarms of neuter drones . . . [who] cannot be said to have lives of their own." Nathan Detroit, in Frank Loesser's *Guys and Dolls*, sneered at the "Scarsdale Galahad, the breakfast-eating, Brooks Brothers type," while feature writers decried the truncated existence of people who dwelt in communities with no institutions more permanent than the supermarket and the filling station. In these misshapen matriarchies, where children

Levittown, Pennsylvania, and its counterpart on Long Island typify the suburban development in postwar America. On the lower left of the photograph one can see that part of the tract has not yet been landscaped. The picture is by Margaret Bourke-White, who began her distinguished career in photojournalism in 1927, won fame for her sensitive portraits of sharecroppers in the Great Depression, and received the American Woman of Achievement Award in 1951.

rarely saw their commuter fathers, harried mothers, it was said, were endlessly delivering children, "obstetrically once and by car forever after," to synthetic "activities." When writers were not taking suburbanites to task for insulating their children from contact with other races and classes, they were scolding them for running away from the crises of the city. One church in Old Greenwich,

Connecticut, noted John Brooks, even felt compelled to hold a symposium entitled "overcoming guilt about having deserted the urban core." "The very word, 'suburbia,'" as Donaldson observed, came to have "unpleasant overtones, suggesting nothing so much as some kind of scruffy disease."

More careful studies of "suburbia" indicated that these indictments were overdrawn. The critics, it became clear, had spun broad generalizations from a single type of suburb—the new, artificially created, one-class cluster—though there were, in fact, many different kinds. Some suburbs, like Secaucus, New Jersey, and Cicero, Illinois, had few of the attributes associated with "suburban" whereas sections such as New York City's Forest Hills and Philadelphia's Chestnut Hill within the incorporated areas of central cities had many. Suburbs like Oak Park outside Chicago were over a century old. Furthermore, one sociologist found that even in the archetypal Levittown on Long Island, residents had, by ingenious rearranging, modified the standardized boxes to reflect their own tastes. In another study, *Class in Suburbia,* William Dobriner reported that although Levittown may have been "monotonously middle class" at the outset, it rapidly acquired a more heterogeneous social mix. If blacks were still largely confined to the central cities, other ethnic groups fanned out as did Philip Roth's Jews, who "had struggled and prospered, and moved further and further west, towards the edge of Newark, then out of it, and up the slope of the Orange Mountains, until they had reached the crest and started down the other side, pouring into Gentile territory as the Scotch-Irish had poured through the Cumberland Gap."

A number of commentators asserted that changes in the structure of the economy, especially the evolution of the consumer culture, were producing a new character type. The psychoanalyst Erich Fromm wrote of the individual with a "marketing orientation" who thought acceptability hinged on "how well a person sells himself on the market, how well he gets his personality across, how nice a 'package' he is." In *White Collar,* C. Wright Mills declared: "When white-collar people get jobs, they sell not only their time and energy but their personalities as well. They sell by the week or month their smiles and their kindly gestures, and they must practice the prompt repression of resentment and aggression." William H. Whyte, Jr., in his best-seller *The Organization Man,* claimed that group-oriented Americans gave allegiance no longer to the individualistic Protestant ethic but to "an organization ethic," marked by "a belief in 'belongingness' as the ultimate need of the individual."

The most elaborate exposition of this interpretation came from the pen of David Riesman, notably in his highly influential 1950 volume *The Lonely Crowd*. In a consumption society, Riesman pointed out, characteristics honed in a scarcity order such as frugality and self-denial were no longer appropriate. What was required was "an 'abundance psychology' capable of 'wasteful' luxury consumption of leisure and of the surplus product." A child adapted in this new milieu not by internalizing traditional values but by sensitizing himself to the expectations of others, particularly peer groups but also strangers in the mass media. "Parents make him feel guilty not so much about violation of inner standards as about failure to be popular or otherwise to manage his relations with these other children," Riesman wrote. Indeed, in these changed circumstances, "parents who try, in inner-directed fashion, to compel the internalization of disciplined pursuit of clear goals run the risk of having their children styled clear out of the personality market."

Americans continued to think of their country as a citadel of individual entrepreneurs, but many more worked for organizations — corporations, government agencies, universities — than made it on their own. The proportion of self-employed (36 percent of the labor force in 1900) fell from 26 percent in 1940 to 16 percent in 1960. By the end of the 1950's some 38 percent drew their pay from organizations with more than five hundred employees, in contrast to only 28 percent in 1940. From 1950 to 1960 the employment rolls of state and local government increased 52 percent; in 1960 they accounted for nearly one-eighth of the nonagricultural work force.

In the 1950's, too, the United States evolved the world's first "service economy." The government announced in 1956 that white collar workers outnumbered blue collar workers. Most employees were engaged not in turning out tangible goods like coal and steel but in professional capacities or in distributive or promotional occupations — sales clerks, office workers, advertising personnel — to provide services to the consumer. From 1947 to 1957 the number of factory operatives fell 4 percent, clerical ranks grew 23 percent, and the salaried middle class increased 61 percent. On the TV show "What's My Line?" the panel learned to frame a critical question, "Do you deal in services?"

To social critics like C. Wright Mills this "new middle class" of white collar workers seemed menacing. The modern office reminded Mills of Herman Melville's description of a factory: "At rows of blank-looking counters sat rows of blank-looking girls, with blank, white folders in their blank hands, all blankly folding blank paper."

Indifferent or hostile to the impoverished, hungering for higher social status, the white collar people were the fulcrum of a world in which "political expression is banalized, political theory is barren administrative detail, history is made behind men's backs. Such is the political situation in which the new middle classes enact their passive role."

The work of writers like Riesman, Mills, Whyte, and Fromm sent through intellectual circles reverberations that have not yet ended. "The upper-middle-educated American became a fascinated voyeur of his own victimization," Cushing Strout has observed. "The relish with which so many academics devoured these depressing images of American society reflects a blend of self-congratulatory relief for not having 'gone into trade' and self-accusing recognition of their own fate in the struggle for tenure and grants in the affluent 'multi-versities.'" Riesman was widely misunderstood to be saying that most Americans were "other-directed" and that the "other-directed" man was more conformist than the "inner-directed" man. In fact, some sociologists and historians doubted that conformity was a new phenomenon or peculiar to America and questioned whether it was so pervasive in the United States as the faultfinders suggested. Uniformity of views clearly did not characterize the scholarly community, for though writers like Mills were disenchanted, others were more favorably disposed.

Intellectuals who had once heaped derision on the United States now sang its praises. In 1950 Samuel Eliot Morison told the American Historical Association that he was pleased to discern "a decided change of attitude towards our past, a friendly almost affectionate attitude," which he contrasted with the earlier "cynical, almost hateful" judgment. The new mood resulted in part from the fact that the dour prophecies intellectuals had made had not been fulfilled. The historian Richard Hofstadter later commented: "We were surprised by the fact that instead of having a tremendous depression after the war, which those of us who were mature in the '30s thought surely was coming, we entered upon one of the great boom periods of history." As an unanticipated by-product of this prosperity, lavish foundation grants bankrolled a good many intellectuals. One critic remarked, "They are almost never unemployed; they are only between grants." When *Partisan Review,* once a gadfly of the establishment, sponsored a symposium of intellectuals, it bore the remarkable title, "Our Country and Our Culture," nomenclature that would have seemed odd in the 1920's and would again in the 1960's. "For the first time in the history of the modern intellectual," observed one of the contributors to that symposium, the literary critic Lionel Trilling, "America is not to be conceived of as *a priori* the vulgarest and stupidest nation of the world."

In the Eisenhower years, liberals lost their dread of the mammoth corporation. It was hard to summon up the kind of hatred reformers had once felt for the Jay Goulds and direct it toward the virtuous executives who sponsored projects like the Pepsi-Cola art contest. Moreover, those who sang paeans for a pluralist social order observed that corporation leaders, unlike the despots of old, were restrained by the "countervailing power" (John Kenneth Galbraith's phrase) of government and unions. Nor could one gainsay the accomplishment of corporations in swelling the gross national product. As a consequence of all these developments, David Lilienthal, who had entered public life as a Brandeisian foe of the power companies, wrote, "Big business represents a proud and fruitful achievement of the American people," and Adolf A. Berle, Jr., who had once anatomized the uncontrolled power of the new managerial class, praised tycoons for their sense of social concern.

No longer did corporations present the image of the heartless robber barons of the 1880's or the vicious union busters of the 1930's. "The big, coldly menacing grizzlies of 1939," wrote John Brooks, became "the superbig, smiling, approval-seeking pandas of 1964." The nineteenth century's "dark Satanic mill" gave way to the bright, if antiseptic, plant in the "industrial park." IBM maintained country clubs for its employees; Richfield Oil built model homes; and American Cyanamid hired psychiatrists to minister to the emotional needs of its workers. In fact, corporations came to be criticized not because they were malevolent but because they had become too benign and were imprisoning their employees in brotherhood and "belongingness." As one reviewer summed up this argument, "The capitalist robber baron has turned out to be a love-starved aunt cramming cake into eager little mouths." The diminished animus toward corporations inevitably shifted politics in a conservative direction, for leftwing movements in the past had battened on antipathy to monopolies.

Radicalism had no significant form of political expression in the 1950's. The Progressive Party petered out after its poor showing in 1948, and in 1952 Henry Wallace resigned from the party to signify his determination to stand by his country in the Korean War. He denounced the Soviet Union, came out for massive rearmament, and approved using the atomic bomb if military necessity required it. In that year the Socialist Party drew less than one-third as many votes as the Prohibitionists, and "for all intents and purposes," wrote Irving Howe and Lewis Coser in 1957, "the American Communist Party is dead."

Those who hoped for a more militant political movement in the 1950's looked expectantly at the ranks of organized labor. The goal of a labor party on a European scale had long been the Big Rock Candy Mountain of American social democrats, and in the 1940's they eyed wistfully the nationalization experiments of British Labour. For a time, Walter Reuther, who came out of a Socialist background, contemplated creating such a party. This would have been inconceivable at the start of the Roosevelt era, but by 1945 union membership, only 3 million in 1932, had risen to nearly 15 million. In 1955, when Reuther of the Congress of Industrial Organizations and George Meany of the American Federation of Labor concluded merger negotiations, the new AFL-CIO claimed over 16 million members, and there were another 1.7 million in independent unions like the railway brotherhoods. In the late 1950's two-thirds of the production force in manufacturing was unionized. Furthermore, labor organizations had expanded their domain from wages and hours to negotiations over such a range of questions, from rest periods to health insurance to pensions, that economists spoke of "welfare bargaining."

Yet well before the merger had been carried out, Reuther recognized that there was no prospect for a vigorous labor party. After the turbulence that in 1946 cost 115 million man-days, union aggressiveness had subsided to such a point that by 1963 less time was lost to strikes than to coffee breaks. The young, class-conscious workingmen who had fought the battles of River Rouge and Flint in the 1930's had become middle-aged, enbourgeoised members of the PTA. Often the union leaders were even more removed from their working-class origins. Refractory steelworkers grumbled about the "tuxedo unionism" of their president, David J. McDonald. Dave Beck of the Teamsters could afford a stud, trainers, and jockeys. In Washington, Meany, who once plied the trade of plumber, rode in a chauffeured limousine, and the Hod Carriers Union shared the ground floor of the swank Carlton Hotel with a covey of stockbrokers. Furthermore, labor's stake in the prosperity of the weapons industries reinforced the inclination of union leaders to subdue protests that might seem to jeopardize national unity. Increasingly, social reform had a lower priority than loyalty to the government's aims in the cold war.

In part because of deficient leadership, but more as a result of changes in the structure of the labor market, union efforts to attract new recruits faltered. Although membership rolls continued to expand in the 1950's, they failed to keep pace with additions to the working force. The percentage of the nonagricultural laboring population in unions fell from 33.2 in 1955 to 28.4 in 1968. Labor was hurt by the movement of industry to the South and to other regions hostile to unionism and by shifts in the economy that reduced the number of bituminous coal miners in the 1950's from 344,000 to 149,000 and the highly unionized railroad force from 1,700,000 in 1929 to 800,000 in 1960. It was hit even harder by the rapid growth of the white collar segment. Labor organizations made little headway in signing up clerical employees, who regarded union buttons as stigmata of lower social status. By the early 1960's, unions confronted a sorrowful situation: Snooty white collar workers were composing an ever larger portion of the labor force at the same time that technological displacement was shoving union members into the ranks of the unemployed.

Through much of the 1950's, the United States lived, as the social critic Paul Goodman wrote, "in a political limbo." Serious questions, such as whether to recognize Red China, were treated as though they were beyond the bounds of decent discourse, and criticism of Eisenhower was reproved as lèse majesté if not blasphemy. The President reflected the wishes of a society that wanted a respite from public affairs, but he in turn helped to reinforce these sentiments. If the country did not agitate more vigorously for attention to pressing needs, this was partly because Eisenhower, by his own example, served to mute concern and to tranquilize the nation.

The more disaffected American intellectuals viewed Eisenhower if not as the agent of quiescence and even torpor in a homogenized society then as its representative figure. A Nebraska professor, bemoaning the passivity of the university student, observed, "The vague but comforting symbol of Eisenhower has seeped into the vacuum of this generation's mind," and Robert Lowell concluded his poem "Inauguration Day: January, 1953" by writing:

> Ice, ice. Our wheels no longer move.
> Look, the fixed stars, all just alike
> as lack-land atoms, split apart,
> and the Republic summons Ike,
> the mausoleum in her heart.

Ike. The smile and the waving hand convey the amiable reassurance that won overwhelming victory for Dwight D. Eisenhower in 1952 and approval of 69 percent polled in 1955. "Everybody ought to be happy every day," the President said. "Play hard, have fun doing it, and despise wickedness."

The Politics of Tranquility

Rarely has a public figure so suited a nation's mood as did Dwight David Eisenhower. At a time when many had wearied of partisan strife, he was a man unsullied by political experience. In 1948, he had thrown cold water on an attempt to draft him for the presidency by observing, "The necessary and wise subordination of the military to civilian power will be best sustained when life-long professional soldiers abstain from seeking high political office." Never had a general seemed so singularly lacking in the qualities associated with a martinet. His genial manner and his ready grin moved multitudes to shout, "I like Ike." So did his humble comportment. At a whistle stop he would say, "It's all a bit overwhelming to me to see a great crowd like this. My memory goes back to a barren Kansas prairie and six little boys running around barefooted in the dust. I never get over my astonishment that you want to know what I think." Yet as the victorious commander of the Allied forces in the war against fascism, the general appeared ideally qualified to bring the Korean episode to a satisfactory termination.

Eisenhower had little difficulty in overcoming his opposition in the 1952 campaign. As the favorite of the internationalist, moderate eastern seaboard wing of his party, he won the Republican nomination by subduing Robert Taft, the idol of the more nationalist, conservative hinterland. (From 1936 until 1964, Corn Belt conservatives dominated the GOP bloc in Congress but failed to win the presidential designation.) The Democrats came up with a reluctant nominee of their own in Adlai Stevenson, Illinois governor and former New Deal functionary. Although Stevenson's wit and eloquence delighted readers of the *Atlantic Monthly,* he was no match for Ike. Stevenson's admirers had a moment of hope when it was revealed that Eisenhower's running mate, Senator Richard Nixon of California, had benefited from a "millionaires' fund." But Nixon turned this to his advantage with a "soap opera" performance on television in which he told about receiving an unsolicited gift, a black and white cocker spaniel which his six-year-old daughter Tricia named Checkers. Consumption styles also seemed relevant, for Nixon's reference to his wife's simple cloth coat was offered as a measure of his probity in contrast to the mink-coated spouses of Democratic officials. Apart from Eisenhower's personal popularity, the critical development of the campaign came on October 24 in Detroit when the general promised, "I shall go to Korea." Few any longer thought the Democrats could terminate the "police action." In balloting featured by a sharply increased turnout, Eisenhower rolled up 34 million votes (55.1 percent) to Stevenson's 27 million (44.4 percent).

The 1952 elections revealed affection for Ike rather than for his party. Despite his whopping plurality, the Republicans barely won control of Congress, the Senate only by the Vice-President's tie-breaking margin. Indeed in the 1950's the GOP not once got as much as 50 percent of the total national popular vote for the House; in 1958, when Vermont sent the first Democrat to Congress in 106 years and Missouri gave Senator Stuart Symington a lopsided 66 percent, the Republican share fell to the lowest level since 1936. In 1956, Eisenhower would defeat Stevenson a second time with the slogan "Everything's booming but the guns," but the Democrats would sweep both houses of Congress—the first time since Zachary Taylor's victory in 1848 that a presidential candidate had triumphed without his party's carrying at least one house. However, Eisenhower's appeal did contribute to the nationalization of American politics. The general captured four southern states in 1952. In 1956, he added Louisiana, which had been Democratic since 1880. Since 1944, the Democrats have not been able to count on their old standby, the "Solid South."

Some hoped that when Eisenhower entered the White House he would use his enormous popularity to lead the country toward a solution of pressing social problems, but the new President had quite a different expectation. He believed that his Democratic predecessors had impaired the dignity of the office in legislative brawls and that a President who assumed the role of chief legislator was transgressing the prerogatives of Congress. "I don't feel like I should nag them," he explained. At times he carried his conviction to the point of refusing even to comment on pending bills. The political scientist Louis W. Koenig has called this conception of the presidency "the greatest retreat in the national experience since the first battle of Bull Run." Eisenhower thought of his chairman-of-the-board stance as a neutral attitude, but it inevitably had programmatic consequences. As Earl Latham has noted, "The weak-President model of the Executive office is congenial to an economic philosophy in which the major decisions are to be left in private hands." When, after the death of John Foster Dulles in 1959 and the departure, in a cloud of obloquy, of the President's trusted aide Sherman Adams, Eisenhower did take a firm hold on the reins, it was in order to diminish government action—an attempt, as Richard Rovere said, to use "mastery in the service of drift."

Election of 1952

■ Eisenhower (Republican)

□ Stevenson (Democrat)

Election of 1956

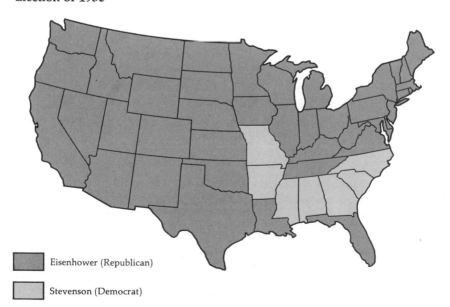

■ Eisenhower (Republican)

□ Stevenson (Democrat)

For those who had conceived of Eisenhower as leader of the GOP's liberal wing, his appointments came as a shock. To his Cabinet he named no fewer than three men with ties to General Motors — Charles E. Wilson, president of GM, as secretary of defense, and two auto distributors, Douglas McKay to the Interior Department and Arthur Summerfield as postmaster general. He filled other slots with conservatives such as George Humphrey of Mark Hanna's old company, who became secretary of the treasury. The one exception was the president of the plumbers union, Martin Durkin, chosen secretary of labor; within eight months he would give way to a businessman. "Eight millionaires and a plumber," *The New Republic* wrote, and Adlai Stevenson remarked that "the New Dealers have all left Washington to make way for the car dealers."

When Secretary Humphrey hung Andrew Mellon's portrait behind his desk, some feared that the nation was in the hands of 1920's reactionaries. Asked whether he had read Ernest Hemingway's *The Old Man and the Sea,* Humphrey responded, "Why would anybody be interested in some old man who was a failure and never amounted to anything anyway?" Humphrey's mother, it was learned, insisted on spelling Franklin Roosevelt's name with a small *r*. Secretary Wilson added to the uneasiness by saying that "what was good for our country was good for General Motors, and vice versa," and by likening the unemployed to "kennel-fed dogs." In Washington, the story circulated that the former GM executive had invented the automatic transmission so that he would have one foot free to put in his mouth. Yet though men like Humphrey and Wilson were undoubtedly conservative, most had made a separate peace with the New Deal and recognized that they could not undo developments such as industrial unionism. The President relied on these spokesmen for the "Practical Right"; of the fifty-three in the highest circle of the administration, only four were professional politicians.

Eisenhower advertised his program as "dynamic conservatism," which implied being "conservative when it comes to money and liberal when it comes to human beings." (Stevenson gibed: "I assume what it means is that you will strongly recommend the building of a great many schools to accommodate the needs of our children, but not provide the money.") By budget-cutting, the President hoped to preserve the value of the dollar through reducing inflationary pressure. Even in recessions the administration opposed deficit financing and large public works projects; Eisenhower warned against "going too far with trying to fool with our economy" and setting up "huge federal bureaucracies of the PWA or the WPA type." The President deliberately sought ways to reduce the role of the federal government in the economy by increasing opportunities for private corporations and turning national functions back to state and local governments. After the conservative Senator Taft, his former rival, explained the proposals for social legislation he was sponsoring, Ike responded, "Why, Bob, with those views you're twice as liberal as I am."

When the President attempted to apply these doctrines to natural resources, he came to grief. He did win congressional support for handing over to the adjacent states the oil-rich offshore "tidelands," which the Supreme Court had ruled belonged to the federal government. But the administration's efforts to hem in the Tennessee Valley Authority (Eisenhower actually wanted to sell it) by negotiating an arrangement with the Dixon-Yates utility syndicate embroiled it in a costly fiasco. So objectionable were the circumstances of the deal that the government wound up in the embarrassing position of suing to cancel as "contrary to public policy" the contract it had negotiated.

Outside of natural resources, the Eisenhower administration made limited attempts to turn back the clock. Although little of the New Deal or Fair Deal was dismantled, the Reconstruction Finance Corporation was liquidated, the Korean war economic controls were abruptly ended, and Secretary of Agriculture Ezra Taft Benson attempted to reduce farm subsidies. The new emphasis was apparent in the policies pursued by business-minded officials on regulatory commissions and other government agencies, often with deplorable results. When Secretary of Commerce Sinclair Weeks fired the head of the Bureau of Standards for refusing to sanction the marketing of a defective battery additive, he raised an outcry against business influence on government, and when Secretary of Health, Education and Welfare Oveta Culp Hobby opposed the free distribution to schoolchildren of the new vaccine for polio developed by Dr. Jonas Salk, the resulting furor led to her resignation.

In Eisenhower's second term, as criticism of the lack of attention to national needs mounted, the President stiffened. He vetoed two public housing measures, two anti-recession public works bills, an area redevelopment proposal, anti-pollution legislation (pollution was a "uniquely local blight"), and by the threat of the veto deterred Democrats who wanted to push Fair Deal legislation. At his behest, Congress changed a labor reform measure sponsored by Senator John F. Kennedy, as a consequence of hearings that exposed the "hoodlum empire" of Dave Beck and Jimmy Hoffa's Teamsters, into the Landrum-Griffin Act, a statute that settled some old scores with unions but left the Teamsters virtually unscathed. Intimidated by the President's insistence on budget-cutting, the Democratic leaders—Lyndon B. Johnson in the Senate and Sam Rayburn in the House—squandered the opportunities for advanced legislation provided by the big Democratic gains in the 1958 elections.

Yet Eisenhower's legislative agenda also found room for moderate reform measures, in part because the President accepted the need for a degree of government responsibility, in part because of the insistence of Democrats and pressure groups. In the Eisenhower years, Congress greatly expanded social security and unemployment compensation coverage, raised the minimum wage, authorized the construction of the St. Lawrence seaway in cooperation with Canada, and in 1953 established a Department of Health, Education and Welfare. (As secretary of the new department, Mrs. Hobby became the second woman, and first Republican of her sex, to hold a Cabinet post. The first female Cabinet member, Secretary of Labor Frances Perkins, had been appointed by Franklin D. Roosevelt in 1933.) Eisenhower did little substantial to develop federal programs in housing and education, but he did suggest that government initiative in these fields was appropriate. In sum, Eisenhower, although his actions generally ran in a contrary direction, helped encourage an important sector of "modern Republicans" to acknowledge that national responsibility for social welfare was something other than New Deal heresy.

In spite of Eisenhower's commitment to diminish the suzerainty of the federal government, Washington was playing at least as great a role at the end of Eisenhower's tenure as it had when he took office. When, on three occasions, the administration encountered recessions, it resorted, however queasily, to some of the devices associated with the New Dealers—government spending (albeit for highways that leveled the countryside), easier credit, tax cuts, depreciation allowances, and welfare payments. If Eisenhower was hardly the Keynesian some writers have described him as being, and if recovery resulted more from built-in stabilizers and inadvertent deficits than from the President's efforts, he did make clear that a Republican administration would pursue at least limited countercyclical policies in a slump. Moreover, not only did the President's attempt to decentralize authority fizzle but his campaign to slash federal spending ran into a series of obstacles—the voracious demands of military and foreign aid programs, the baleful effect on the economy of reductions in government outlays, and the unacceptable political and economic costs of denying benefits to groups such as farmers. Under Eisenhower, the federal administrative budget, which totaled $39.5 billion in 1950, a Truman year, reached $76.5 billion in 1960, and the national debt rose from $266 billion in 1953 to $286 billion in 1960. At the end of the 1959 fiscal year, Eisenhower's administration was running the highest deficit ever accumulated by an American government in peacetime.

History (or at least historians, who hold letters patent from the Muse) has judged Eisenhower more harshly than did his contemporaries. During his two terms in office, millions of Americans admired him as a man and for his emphasis on defusing the cold war while promoting the consumer culture. Although there were swelling numbers of Ikonoclasts at the end of his reign, few doubted that if Eisenhower had been a candidate in 1960 he would have won another resounding victory. However, two years later a poll of seventy-five historians placed him between Chester Arthur and Andrew Johnson. Eisenhower's achievements lay in his performance as a bringer of tranquility, a kind of peace abroad, a respite from strife at home. Yet calm bore a high price tag—the public sector shortchanged, the national estate deteriorating, the legal rights of Negroes disregarded, and an accumulation of unsolved social problems that would overwhelm his successors in the 1960's.

The Struggle for Civil Rights

The consumer culture made a profound impact on an upheaval from which it might have been thought quite remote, the campaign for Negro equality. Some of the most important battlefields of the civil rights movement would be motels, dime store eating places, and laundromats. Michael Walzer found that sit-in participants had materialistic as well as moral ends and were "willing to take risks in the name of both prosperity and virtue." At times cold war and consumer culture aspects were linked together by a single graphic incident. When the finance minister of Ghana ordered orange juice at a Howard Johnson's in Dover, Delaware, only to be told that Negroes could not drink or eat on the premises, Washington was embarrassed in its relations with the third world. The vivid display of the affluence of white society on television screens in black ghettos helped arouse anger at the maldistribution of wealth and a demand for a fairer share. To be sure, for most of the world's ghetto dwellers possession of a TV set would have seemed the ultimate luxury, but in a land of superabundance Negroes understandably felt a sense of relative deprivation. Moreover, the fact that many lived well above the subsistence level meant that increasing numbers were exposed to additional forms of discrimination when they sought to spend their cash. As a foreign observer noted, "Only people who are relatively well off in the first place worry about service and treatment at a lunch counter."

The campaign to give Negroes a central place in American society gained greatly increased momentum in the postwar era as the NAACP, the organization of aspiring middle-class Negroes, carried its brilliant strategy of ending racial discrimination through litigation to its culmination. For a generation a battery of lawyers, Negro and white, had been adroitly chipping away at the "separate but equal" doctrine in education, not by assaulting separateness but by insisting on absolute equality. The NAACP's attorneys won a series of victories in higher education, sorely trying the ingenuity of the segregationists. "You can't build a cyclotron for one student," conceded the president of the University of Oklahoma. In 1950 the court ruled that even if Texas built a separate law school for its lone Negro applicant it would not be providing equality.

With little left of the "separate but equal" doctrine on the campus, the NAACP leveled its guns directly at the principle of separateness, and not in the university but in the much more socially sensitive institution of the public school. It was conceded that in Topeka the separate black system that eight-year-old Linda Carol Brown attended was substantially equal to the white schools, but the NAACP's counsel, Thurgood Marshall, offered sociological evidence to demonstrate that segregation harmed children, both black and white, and argued that classification by race violated the Fourteenth Amendment.

On May 17, 1954, Eisenhower's new appointee, Chief Justice Earl Warren, spoke for a unanimous Supreme Court in *Brown* v. *Board of Education.* The Court, reversing *Plessy* v. *Ferguson,* stated that "in the field of public education the doctrine of 'separate but equal' has no place." To separate schoolchildren "solely because of their race," Warren averred, "generates a feeling of inferiority as to their status in the community that may affect their hearts and minds in a way unlikely ever to be undone." In one footnote, Warren cited several sociological works, adding: "And see generally Myrdal, *An American Dilemma.*" By a subsequent order the Court asked not for immediate total compliance but for action "with all deliberate speed." The border states, as well as idiosyncratic localities in Kansas and Arizona, responded readily, and large cities like Washington and Baltimore rapidly overhauled their entire school systems to end racial discrimination. The success in Washington owed much to President Eisenhower, who moved firmly in areas where federal authority was unquestionable — veterans' hospitals, navy yards in Norfolk and Charleston, as well as schools and other institutions in the District of Columbia.

But Eisenhower refused to perform the much more important task of persuading the South to abide by the Court's rulings. Skeptical of the value of coercion, fastidious about not overstepping his authority, the President would not even say that he supported the Court. "I am convinced that the Supreme Court decision *set back* progress in the South *at least fifteen years,*" he told an aide. "The fellow who tries to tell me you can do these things by *force* is just plain *nuts.*" He insisted: "No matter how much law we have, we have a job in education, in getting people to understand what are the issues here involved." Yet it was precisely the "job in education" that he would not carry out, and as Eisenhower faltered, moderates in the South who wanted to obey the law of the land were left leaderless, and racist opposition gained momentum.

Within a year, the federal courts faced a hostile phalanx in the southern press, almost all of Dixie's political leaders, and the newly formed White Citizens' Councils. In 1955 the Richmond *News Leader,* one of the country's most respected newspapers, trumpeted:

In May of 1954, that inept fraternity of politicians and professors known as the United States Supreme Court chose to throw away the established law. These nine men repudiated the Constitution, spit upon the Tenth Amendment, and rewrote the fundamental law of this land to suit their own gauzy concepts of sociology. If it be said now that the South is flouting the law, let it be said to the high court, *You taught us how.*

In eight southern states in 1955 not one Negro pupil attended school with a white child. The following year a pugnacious Southern Manifesto was signed by 101 members of Congress, including the former Rhodes Scholar and university president J. William Fulbright and every Senator from the states of the Confederacy save Lyndon Johnson of Texas and Tennessee's Estes Kefauver and Albert Gore.

Bayonet-wielding paratroopers escort Negro students at Little Rock Central High School in September 1957, after the governor of Arkansas, Orval E. Faubus, had used National Guardsmen to bar their entry. Critics of the governor gibed: "Would you want Orval Faubus to marry your daughter?"

As Anthony Lewis wrote: "The true meaning of the Manifesto was to make defiance of the Supreme Court and the Constitution socially acceptable in the South—to give resistance to the law the approval of the Southern Establishment."

Encouraged by such sentiment, Governor Orval Faubus of Arkansas in 1957 raised the most serious challenge to federal authority since the Civil War. When Little Rock, a New South city under moderate leadership, acceded to a federal court order to admit nine Negroes to Central High School, Faubus sent in the Arkansas National Guard to bar their path. One child made an unforgettable impression. Fifteen-year-old Elizabeth Eckford, neatly dressed in a white short-sleeved blouse, a cotton skirt, bobby socks, and ballet slippers, got off a bus at the corner of 14th and Park Streets carrying her notebook. Head held high, she made her way through the hostile crowd to the line of soldiers, who raised their rifles. Turned away, she walked back through the gauntlet of guardsmen, followed by jeering students and

Coretta King and Martin Luther King sit in front of the courthouse at Montgomery, Alabama, where the young Baptist minister led a successful year-long boycott against segregated buses. A year before he took over the pastorate of the Dexter Avenue church in Montgomery, King married Coretta Scott, an Antioch graduate who was studying at the New England Conservatory of Music.

adults. For thirty-five minutes she stood at the bus stop harried by the threatening crowd, until a bus came by and took her home. As the crisis built, Eisenhower had offered no guidance and had even remarked on the southern concern about "mongrelization of the race." When he conferred with Faubus at his vacation headquarters in Newport, Rhode Island, he failed to bring the governor to heel. A second attempt to secure admission for the students was frustrated when a howling mob ringed the school and refused to heed a presidential order to disperse.

With the prestige of his office at stake, Eisenhower acted straightforwardly in defense of national supremacy. He placed the Arkansas National Guard under federal authority and sent in a thousand paratroopers. On the morning of September 18, an armed detachment led Elizabeth Eckford and the other eight young blacks into the school. For a while soldiers with bayonets escorted Negro students through the corridors of Central High School. Eisenhower, who had been unwilling to sanction any force, had ended up outraging the white South by becoming the first president since Reconstruction to dispatch federal troops in support of the rights of Negroes.

Even this did not end the turmoil. Faubus shut down Little Rock's high schools altogether in 1958 and 1959, and to open the schools required still another federal court edict. Virginia, too, sanctioned closing schools to forestall integration, but a series of federal and state court decrees terminated "massive resistance" in 1959, the year the walls of segregation were breached in Florida. Still, it was only token integration. A decade after the *Brown* decision, merely 1 percent of the Negro pupils in the South went to school with white children.

Congress did even less than the President to speed integration, but the little it did was hailed as epic-making. In 1957, for the first time since 1875, Congress enacted a civil rights statute. The law authorized federal suits in support of Negroes denied the right to vote and set up a Commission on Civil Rights. A second Civil Rights Act in 1960, which overcame a southern filibuster of 125 consecutive hours, further strengthened national authority over suffrage. For his role in securing passage of these modest measures, which sidestepped the issue of segregation, Lyndon Johnson was hailed as master legislator. In truth neither Congress nor the President gave much aid to the beleaguered judges or the harried black students, and as a consequence only slow headway was made in the Eisenhower years.

Yet the courageous Negro youngsters (and their white allies on bench and school board) did help win an increasing number of Americans of all races to the cause of civil rights. As Alexander M. Bickel of Yale Law School wrote of the school clashes: "Here were grown men and women furiously confronting their enemy: two, three, a half-dozen scrubbed, starched, scared and incredibly brave colored children. The moral bankruptcy, the shame of the thing, was evident." The movement to desegregate the schools also encouraged Negroes to move on other fronts to regain the rights they had enjoyed during Radical Reconstruction but had been deprived of thereafter.

One year after the Court handed down the *Brown* decision, an episode on a Montgomery, Alabama, bus turned the civil rights movement in a new direction. On December 1, 1955, Mrs. Rosa Parks, a Negro seamstress weary from a day's work, refused to give up her seat to a white man. She was arrested and ordered to stand trial. Leaders of the Negro community met the next night in the Dexter Avenue Baptist Church; there to take up his first pastorate had recently come a young Atlantan trained in theology at Boston University, Reverend Martin Luther King, Jr. Under King's leadership, Montgomery's Negroes organized a massive boycott; for months, buses rolled nearly empty through the streets of the Cradle of the Confederacy. At first, King's Montgomery Improvement Association was willing to settle for maintaining the custom of Negroes sitting in the back of the bus so long as seats were on a first-come first-served basis, but as the months went by the whole Jim Crow system came under attack. The long boycott ended in victory when on November 13, 1956, the Supreme Court unanimously affirmed a lower court ruling invalidating Alabama's segregation statutes. In the end, Jim Crow met death through traditional methods — litigation in federal courts by an elite of NAACP attorneys — but the protest also marked the beginning of a new style of mass action led by young, indigenous black southerners.

King, who would eventually become a Nobel Peace Laureate, attracted national attention by his skillful direction of the boycott and his eloquent espousal of the doctrine of nonviolent resistance. On the night after he was indicted in Montgomery for violating Alabama's anti-boycott law, he said: "If we are arrested every day, if we are exploited every day, if we are trampled over every day, don't ever let anyone pull you so low as to hate them. We must use the weapon of love. We must have compassion and understanding for those who hate us."

King's preaching combined the rhetoric of evangelical Christianity with the lessons of Gandhi's Satyagraha campaign against the British *raj* in India, and when in 1957 the young minister founded the Southern Christian Leadership Conference (SCLC), Negro churches played old movies of the Mahatma. King sensed not only that nonviolence was an appropriate technique for a caste-ridden minority but that it could make a unique contribution to reuniting "the broken community." He assured his followers: "If you will protest courageously, and yet with dignity and Christian love, when the history books are written in future generations, the historians will have to pause and say, 'There lived a great people—a black people—who injected new meaning and dignity into the veins of civilization.'"

The passive resistance movement took on added dimensions when on February 1, 1960, four Negro freshmen from North Carolina Agricultural and Technical College—Ezell Blair, Jr., Franklin McCain, Joseph McNeill, and David Richmond—sat down at a Woolworth's lunch counter in Greensboro, North Carolina, and, having been refused service, remained in their seats. They were soon joined by other students, white and black, some fifty thousand in all, who organized similar "sit-ins" in restaurants, theaters, and laundromats, as well as "kneel-ins" in churches and "wade-ins" in pools. Although the Congress of Racial Equality (CORE) had organized a sit-in in Chicago as early as 1942, it had not succeeded in eliciting such a broad-gauged, largely spontaneous response. Well-mannered, well-groomed, the students shunned violence even when provoked by tormentors who burned them with lighted cigarettes, and their comportment impressed segregationists as well as partisans. The editor of the Richmond *News Leader* wrote:

Here were the colored students, in coats, white shirts, ties, and one of them was reading Goethe and one was taking notes from a biology text. And here, on the sidewalk outside, was a gang of white boys come to heckle, a ragtail rabble, slack-jawed, black-jacketed, grinning fit to kill, and some of them, God save the mark, were waving the proud and honored flag of the Southern States in the last war fought by gentlemen. *Eheu!* it gives one pause.

The sit-ins fundamentally transformed both the mores of public accommodation in the upper South and the structure of the civil rights movement. Before 1960 had run its course, lunch counters in 126 cities had been desegregated, and the total would reach 200 in the next year. The demonstrations had an even more consequential

long-range impact by shifting the focus of activity from the courtroom to the streets and from the prestigious NAACP to SNCC, the
Student Nonviolent Coordinating Committee, organized in April
1960 at a conference called by Martin Luther King, although the
NAACP Legal Defense Fund would continue to prove indispensable
to the students. At its birth "Snick" embraced King's philosophy of
peaceful, interracial protest, but it would soon be marching to a different drum.

The Warren Court

With the President exerting little leadership and Congress stalemated, the main engine of social action in the Eisenhower era, and
even later, turned out to be the least likely of the three branches, the
Supreme Court, under Chief Justice Earl Warren. Reformers had long
viewed this "undemocratic" institution, with its robed dignitaries
insulated from popular control, as a bulwark for reaction, and the
"Constitutional Revolution of 1937" had marked a triumph for
liberalism precisely because it had circumscribed the powers of the
High Bench. New Dealers rejoiced, and conservatives moaned, when
the Court accepted the doctrine of "judicial self-restraint." But after
Eisenhower in 1953 named California's three-time governor to the
chief justiceship, the "Warren Court" (which embraced seventeen
justices during Warren's sixteen-year tenure) astonished the nation
by intervening in areas traditionally thought to be beyond its scope.
The appointment of Warren ("biggest damfool mistake I ever made,"
Eisenhower later said) brought to the High Court a "Swedish Jim
Farley," gregarious and politically astute, who had an instinct for
governing. However, because he had opposed reapportionment,
ardently advocated the internment of Japanese-Americans during
World War II, and flayed the Truman administration for "coddling"
Reds, few in 1953 anticipated that under Warren's leadership the
Court would revamp the apportionment system and protect the
liberties of minorities and radicals. The Court's wide-ranging decisions resulted in a historic flip-flop, with conservatives denouncing
the judiciary for meddling and liberals hailing it as the instrument
of democratic change.

The Warren Court, which first kicked up a storm with the decisions putting it in the business of desegregating schools and other
social institutions, stirred another tempest over its rulings on sub-

Above the bespectacled Chief Justice of the United States, Earl Warren, stands Associate Justice William
J. Brennan, Jr. Eisenhower appointed Warren, the popular California governor,
in 1953 and named Brennan, a New Jersey judge, to the "Catholic seat" on the Supreme Court in
1956, but both quickly adopted positions well beyond those held by the President.

version. To be sure, the Supreme Court has customarily defended civil liberties from encroachment by the national government in wartime and in other periods of stress only after the main peril has passed, and the Warren Court proved no exception. Not until 1957, the year Joe McCarthy died, did it act forthrightly. On "Red Monday," June 17, Justice William J. Brennan, Jr., another Eisenhower appointee, spoke for the court in the *Jencks* opinion, which held that the accused had the right to inspect the government's files. In dissent, Justice Tom Clark protested that the decision afforded the accused "a Roman holiday for rummaging through confidential information as well as vital national secrets." Two weeks later, the Justices, on what C. Herman Pritchett called "one of the most memorable decision days in the history of the United States Supreme Court," handed down rulings in the *Yates, Watkins,* and *Sweezy* cases, modifying the *Dennis* holding and curbing legislative investigatory powers; several Communists were freed. Under a barrage of criticism, some of it fomented by the Eisenhower administration, the Court retreated in the 1958–1959 term, but as Walter F. Murphy has observed, it was "a tactical withdrawal, not a rout." By 1964 the Warren Court would be taking a bolder line when it wiped out a section of the Subversive Activities Control Act of 1950 forbidding passports to Communists as an unconstitutional denial of the right to travel.

If the Court sometimes behaved circumspectly on national security questions, it moved daringly on other civil liberties matters, often by embracing ideas earlier advanced for the Court's minority by Hugo Black and William O. Douglas. The Court greatly expanded First Amendment protection, notably in cases like *New York Times Company* v. *Sullivan,* making it all but impossible for a public figure to win a libel action. In the 1964 *Times* opinion, Justice Brennan remarked on the "profound national commitment to the principle that debate on public issues should be uninhibited, robust, and wide-open." *The New York Times* would provide the occasion for another important ruling in 1971, when the Court held that the federal government could not enjoin that newspaper or *The Washington Post* from publishing material from a classified study of Vietnam policy.

The Warren Court also gave new meaning to Fourteenth Amendment guarantees. In 1966 the High Bench enjoined the Georgia legislature from excluding Julian Bond, a properly elected black member who had angered lawmakers by voicing "sympathy and support for the men in this country who are unwilling to respond to a military draft." Two years later in *Katzenbach* v. *Morgan* the Court sanctioned federal legislation outlawing New York state's requirement that a prospective voter demonstrate literacy in English. The Court invaded a still more delicate area when it ruled on sexual and marital relations. It struck down a Connecticut statute banning the sale of contraceptives, a Virginia act outlawing racial intermarriage, and a Florida law penalizing sexual relations between whites and blacks.

Through another series of decisions, the Warren Court drastically reshaped the code of criminal justice. In 1957 it unanimously upset the conviction of a Negro in the District of Columbia for the brutal rape of a white woman because his confession had been secured only after extended grilling and he had not been promptly arraigned. Seven years later Justice Arthur Goldberg spoke for a divided Court in voiding the murder confession of Danny Escobedo, who had been denied permission to see his lawyer, a year after the Court, in *Gideon* v. *Wainwright,* ruled that a pauper must be provided with an attorney at public expense. In 1966 the Court brought this line of reasoning to a climax in the bitterly controverted *Miranda* opinion, which required police to advise a suspect of his right to remain silent and to have counsel present during interrogation.

Considerations of judicial restraint had inhibited previous courts from examining "political questions" of the sort involved in the malapportionment of legislatures, but the Warren Court was not deterred. In the 1962 case of *Baker* v. *Carr*, it insisted that Tennessee, which had not reapportioned its legislative seats since 1900, act to reflect changes in the population, especially the movement from the country to city and suburb. *Wesberry* v. *Sanders* in 1964 established the principle of "one man, one vote," and in that same year *Reynolds* v. *Sims* held that in apportioning legislative seats no allowance could be made for geographical diversity within the state. "Legislators represent people, not acres or trees," Warren stated. In a companion ruling, the Court stipulated that these guidelines be followed even when the people of the state had approved a different system in a referendum, a decision that the Court's critics viewed as a new high in arrogance.

Each departure from precedent added more recruits to the forces opposed to the Warren Court. For some, it was the cold war decisions that stuck in the craw. Congressman Rivers called the Justices "a greater threat to this Union than the entire confines of Soviet Russia." Others were so provoked by the desegregation opinions that they plastered huge "Impeach Earl Warren" posters on bill-boards along southern and western highways. Rulings on pornography offended people fretful about public morals, and they were likely to be the most distressed, too, by the Court's interdiction of Bible-reading and prayer in the schools, decisions that, to some, appeared to align the Supreme Court with all the godless elements subverting the American way of life. "They've put the Negroes in the schools," cried an Alabama Congressman, "and now they've driven God out."

Even some of the Court's defenders conceded that the Judges were often cavalier in drafting opinions and that they seemed concerned less with the legal merits of a case than with seeing that the better cause won. Anthony Lewis, Supreme Court correspondent of *The New York Times*, wrote, "A Warren opinion, characteristically, is a morn made new—a bland, square presentation of the particular problem in that case almost as if it were unencumbered by precedents or conflicting theories, as it inevitably must be. Often the framework of the argument seems ethical rather than legal." Its methods, friendly critics feared, needlessly antagonized the bar, "jeopardized acceptance of its commands," and impaired "the credibility of the judicial process." "Earl Warren," Lewis concluded, "was the closest thing the United States has had to a Platonic Guardian, dispensing law from a throne without any sensed limits of power except what was seen as the good of society." Yet he added: "Fortunately, he was a decent, humane, honorable, democratic Guardian."

The Quest for National Purpose

For all its political achievements and for all the indications that the United States was a confident, prosperous nation, many observers detected signs of an underlying anxiety. Both the cold war and the consumer culture contributed to the feeling of unease. The Soviet Union's rapid recovery from the devastation of World War II shook America's conviction of superiority, for the 1950's were punctuated by Russia's explosion of a hydrogen bomb early in the decade and its seizure of the lead in the "space race" in the latter half. Those fearful that America might fall to the number 2 spot among the world's powers sharply questioned the desirability of consumer sovereignty, which, it was said, sacrificed national needs to private indulgences. Others viewed with disfavor the value system of the consumer culture. Creative writers spoke out against what one literary critic called "the sentimental, supermarket humanism and homogenized morality of modern America." Before Eisenhower left office, public figures would be sending out search parties to rediscover the lost sense of national purpose.

Commentators found hard evidence for an "age of anxiety" in the burgeoning of psychoanalysis, the manifestations of mental illness, and the bull market in tranquilizers, often some form of meprobamate like "Miltown." In upper middle class circles in the 1950's it seemed as though almost everyone was saying, "I've got to hurry or I'll be late for my hour," and that prototypical literary character Holden Caulfield tells his story from the perspective of a period of psychiatric treatment. Admissions to mental hospitals nearly doubled between 1940 and 1956, and by the latter year mental patients occupied more hospital beds than all other patients combined. That same year Americans consumed over a billion tranquilizer pills, and during the last part of the decade one out of every three prescriptions included a tranquilizer.

The anxiety resulted in no small degree from the gains America had achieved. A people who could roam freely from place to place found it hard to establish the community stability of a more fettered society. "Opportunities for mobility and morbidity go together," wrote *Time*. And the relative emancipation from the boundaries of class and status took its toll in depriving people of a sense of certainty about what was expected of them. "Nobody truly occupies a station in life any more," observed the central figure of Saul Bellow's *Henderson the Rain King*. "There are displaced persons everywhere."

In an individualistic society, men and women often experienced a sense of isolation not only from their world but from themselves. Psychoanalysts reported an increase in a new kind of neurosis characterized by doubts that life has meaning and by an atrophying of the capacity to feel, a desperate awareness of entrapment in an empty cosmos that the theologian Paul Tillich called the fear of "nonbeing." James Jones in *From Here to Eternity* ruminated about "the song of the Great Loneliness, that creeps in like the desert wind and dehydrates the soul"; Paddy Chayefsky's *Marty*, a TV drama later made into a movie, evoked the lonesome wanting of unglamorous ordinary people; and the poet Richard Wilbur wrote, "We are this man unspeakably alone." In *The Catcher in the Rye* by J. D. Salinger,

George Tooker's *The Subway* (1950) portrays the dreadful alienation and fragmentation that many experienced in urban America. Tooker's work hangs in the permanent collections of the Museum of Modern Art, the Whitney Museum of American Art, and Dartmouth College.

who better than any other author of his time understood that dolorous rite of passage, American adolescence, Holden Caulfield revealed that he was "lonesome as hell. No kidding"; and the poet Robert Bly delineated "the loneliness hiding in grass and weeds / That lies near a man over thirty, and suddenly enters." From such an angle of vision, America would inevitably seem, as John Updike observed in his novel *The Centaur*, "a paralyzed patch of thankless alien land." "I dunno what to think of things now, Cora," confessed Rubin Flood in William Inge's drama *The Dark at the Top of the Stairs*. "I'm a stranger in the very land I was born in."

Through much of the literature of the period ran the themes of disillusion, desolation, and even disgust. The era opened in 1945 with Tennessee Williams' affecting "memory play," *The Glass Menagerie*, which included the stage direction: "The apartment faces an alley, and is entered by a fire-escape, a structure whose name is a touch of accidental poetry, for all of these huge buildings are always burning with the slow and implacable fires of human desperation." The following year came the poet Robert Lowell's *Lord Weary's Castle*, an exploration of a ruined world. In Edward Albee's drama *The Death of Bessie Smith* (1959), Nurse cried: "I am sick of everything in this stupid, fly-ridden *world*. . . . I am sick of going to bed and I am sick of waking up. . . . I am tired of my skin. . . . I WANT OUT!" That same year, William Burroughs' *Naked Lunch* reached a nadir in the imagery of decay: "Smell of chili houses and dank overcoats and atrophied testicles. . . . A heaving sea of air hammers in the purple brown dusk tainted with rotten metal smell of sewer gas." In 1963, a year when everything began to come apart, the poet Louis Simpson, in *At the End of the Open Road*, stood on a Pacific beach musing on the "same old city-planner, death." And in that year, too, the brilliant young expatriate poet Sylvia Plath, who, haunted by the horror of the Nazi extermination chambers, had written of the moon "of complete despair, I live here," took her life.

The playwrights of the theater of the absurd and the novelists of black comedy depicted a world of pointlessness, in which there was no order to history, no pattern to life, no relationship between intention and outcome. In plays like Edward Albee's *The Sand Box* and in novels such as John Barth's *The Sot-Weed Factor*, life was devoid of any meaning save what might be gained from the perception that people are helpless players in a cosmic farce. Yet if the subject of these works is Everyman, and if they have a strong kinship to those of European writers like Samuel Beckett, it is often the world of the American consumer culture they are ridiculing. *Catch-22,* Joseph Heller explained, "is about the contemporary, regimented business society," and Lenny Bruce's savage "sick humor" found targets in the Lone Ranger and the Avon Lady.

In 1957, with the publication of Jack Kerouac's *On the Road,* there burst on the bourgeois world of Eisenhower's America that disturbing phenomenon to which Kerouac gave the designation "beat." It was a term with varied resonances. "Beat" suggested the quest for beatitude, a life style of inner grace often pursued through the cult of Zen Buddhism. It appeared to refer as well to the special state of blessedness attained by those who were down and out, especially the drifters. And it reverberated too with a musical connotation, not only in the obvious synonym but in the affinity of the beat movement for the "cool jazz" of Lester Young, Stan Getz, and Gerry Mulligan, whose rhythms seemed "disengaged." In each sense of the word, the beats rejected the canons of respectability—organized religion, striving for material success, homage to the state. Lawrence Ferlinghetti, who owned the beats' hangout, the City Lights book store in San Francisco, entitled one of his poems "Tentative Description of a Dinner to Promote the Impeachment of President

Eisenhower." The "beatniks," as the squares preferred to call them, shocked the bourgeoisie in other ways, too. The "Dharma bums" helped popularize marijuana among the young and made no secret of their promiscuity. Sometimes the male camaraderie of the boys on the road found homosexual expression, as in Allen Ginsberg's *Howl and Other Poems*, which celebrated sex with "saintly motorcyclists."

In some respects, especially in their concern for self and their disengagement, the beats shared the values of the square world of the 1950's. "We're no action group, man," one explained. ". . . I stay cool, far out, alone. When I flip it's over something *I* feel, only me." The beats' oceanic compassion seemed to discourage political protest by embracing their adversaries. "We love everything—Bill Graham, the Big Ten, Rock and Roll, Zen, apple pie, Eisenhower— we dig it all," Kerouac explained. The beats even made a minor contribution to the California economy. With their beards and sandals, they became tourist bait in San Francisco, and it was possible to acquire "Beatnik kits." But however much the beats mirrored conventional society, their real significance lay in the fact that they had fired the first gun of the rebellion of the "counter culture" that would shake the 1960's.

Despite the preoccupations of writers and artists, not every commentator agreed that the postwar period was an especially anxious time. The increase in patients, it was pointed out, was less a sign of a rise in illness than of the diminished stigma attached to mental ailments and of the fact that when many more could afford professional care, fewer were willing to tolerate fear and depression. Nor was this the first era that had known stress. In the 1830's, a doctor remarked that "the population of the United States is beyond that of other countries an anxious one," and Tocqueville observed "that strange melancholy which often haunts the inhabitants of democratic countries in the midst of their abundance, and that strange disgust at life which sometimes seizes upon them in the midst of calm and easy circumstances." Yet much in the modern age was unsettling. If in Tocqueville's time the United States was a country of limitless prospects, in the 1950's Americans were coming to question the results of a century and a half of progress and to doubt that the world would continue to step to the tune of "Yankee Doodle Dandy."

On October 4, 1957, Radio Moscow reported an event that struck a savage blow at American pride. The U.S.S.R. announced that it had thrust a man-made satellite, *Sputnik I*, into orbit around the earth. A month later, *Sputnik II* circled the globe carrying a live dog of the Laika breed. Within less than two years, the Russians would plant the emblem of the hammer and sickle on the surface of the moon. The United States, the premier nation in industrial skill, the country that had unlocked the secret of the atom, had been beaten in the one area where it was certain it was supreme — technology. In truth, the United States was not so far behind as it seemed, but for many months Americans had to endure the ignominy of watching foreign observers gather at Florida's Cape Canaveral only to see United States rockets climb a foot into the air and topple over. Dismaying as this was to the nation's self-esteem, even more disturbing was the thought that Soviet armaments might soon be pointing down from the sky at Kansas rooftops. When the physicist Edward Teller was asked what American spacemen would find if they ever got to the moon, he answered, "Russians."

The *Sputnik* furor had its greatest immediate impact on the American school. The same month that Laika soared into space, Washington released a 200-page study, *Education in the U.S.S.R.*, which highlighted the disciplined training Soviet pupils received in science, mathematics, and languages. Little wonder, it was reasoned, their spacemen were ahead of ours. Critics had been telling the American public that this kind of intellectual rigor was missing from their schools, and writers like Arthur Bestor (*Educational Wastelands*) and Mortimer Smith (*The Diminished Mind: A Study of Planned Mediocrity in Our Public Schools*) now found an attentive audience for their assaults on the shortcomings of progressive education. None was more attentive than the United States Congress, which in September 1958 approved the National Defense Education Act (NDEA) to authorize government financing of programs in science, mathematics, and foreign languages. What a generation of liberals clamoring for federal aid to education had failed to achieve, the cold war accomplished almost overnight. Thanks to NDEA funds, schools acquired expensive hardware such as language laboratories, a response in part to the emphasis of the Harvard psychologist B. F. Skinner on programmed instruction. ("Any teacher who can be replaced by a machine should be," Skinner said.) The *Sputnik* crisis also led to a drastic reworking of the curriculum, with the introduction of the "new physics" of atomic structure, the "new biology" of DNA, and the "new math" of set theory, a unique contribution to the generation gap.

The United States reacted to the *Sputnik* challenge too with a massive effort to overtake the Russians in the "space race." In October 1958, the National Aeronautics and Space Administration (NASA) began its operations with funds that would climb rapidly from some $340 million in 1959 to more than $5 billion in 1965. By 1959 the country had already made the acquaintance of NASA's team of astronauts—handsome, crew-cut young fathers reared in Protestant families in small towns, with Anglo-Saxon craftsmen's names like Carpenter and Cooper and reassuring old-fashioned virtues of pluck, stamina, and technological prowess. Soon the nation would also be introduced to a new glossary—retro-rockets, A-OK, lift-off, Mission Control, T minus 2 and holding, we return you to Roger Mudd. Only a generation earlier, men had relegated stories of space travel to the comic book fantasies of a Flash Gordon or the suppertime radio of Buck Rogers, but on February 20, 1962, Lieutenant Colonel John Herschel Glenn, Jr., would orbit the globe in a five-hour voyage in which he would see three sunsets and experience nightfall over the Indian Ocean like a brilliant desert night "when there's no moon and the stars just seem to jump out at you." Glenn's message, "Cape is go and I am go," would spell success for three and a half years of exertion, but in the Eisenhower years, as failure was compounded by failure, the outlook appeared bleak.

Much of the censure for the miscarriage of the space enterprise fell on the President, who was charged with neglecting the national interest, for America's lag in the space race seemed as dangerous as it was humiliating. The U.S.S.R. was mistakenly believed to be far ahead of the United States in missiles, and, in announcing one of their space successes, the Russians crowed, "The present generation will witness how the freed and conscious labor of the people of the new socialist society turns even the most daring of man's dreams into a reality." The administration was upbraided for the low priority it had given to missile development as well as for its hostility to intellectuals and its contempt for basic research. After the success of the Soviet scientists, Postmaster General Summerfield's boast of "progress in rooting out eggheads" and Secretary of Defense Wilson's insistence that basic research is "when you don't know what you are doing" appeared especially ill advised.

Even that marvel of the country's industrial genius, the American economy, came under fire. Although the increment in the gross national product had been sizable, critics deemed the rate of growth unsatisfactory. Partly as a consequence of Eisenhower's policies, the growth rate fell from 4.3 percent in the 1947–1952 period to 2.5 percent in 1953–1960. Three "Eisenhower recessions" impeded the development of sustained advance, with a resultant loss of billions of dollars of productivity in idle machines and a rise in unemployment that neared 8 percent in Eisenhower's last year in office. By early 1961 the economy, wrote Walter Heller, was "in the position of the .300 hitter who started the season batting a weak .250, then slumped to .230."

The "sluggish" economy also had international implications. At a time when the country was already embarrassed by *Sputnik*, it was discomforting to be reminded that the Soviet rate of growth for 1950–1958 was 7.1 percent (in large part, to be sure, because Russia had started at a much lower level). Nor was worry limited to competition from cold war rivals. The European Common Market, once a ward of Uncle Sam, was jeopardizing America's world trade position, and the drain of gold to Europe led some economists to predict that in the foreseeable future the United States would have to devalue the dollar.

Dissidents objected not only that the administration's policies yielded a smaller GNP but that they reflected a distorted scale of values. Eisenhower's aversion to government spending begot, said Adlai Stevenson, "private opulence and public squalor." Crucial decisions on how to allocate resources were delegated to the shopper or to the advertiser who manipulated him. While the consumer was euchred into diverting the nation's metal resources to add tailfin excrescences on automobiles, school boards lacked the funds to erect critically needed new buildings. By Eisenhower's second term, social critics were deploring the very economy of abundance that was the President's pride. The historian Eric Goldman, with an ascetic intensity that rivaled Saint Simeon Stylites, complained, "We meander along in a stupor of fat." In *A Surfeit of Honey*, Russell Lynes grumbled, "Prosperity produces not only plenty but curiously empty values. . . . Cars get gaudier; hi-fi sets get hi-er; beer-can openers become mink-bearing."

Poets and novelists, too, raised their voices against the consumer society. Robert Lowell, in "For the Union Dead," wrote:

> . . . Everywhere,
> giant finned cars nose forward like fish;
> a savage servility
> slides by on grease.

In Thomas Pynchon's novel *V.*, Benny Profane felt bereft "in the aisles of a bright, gigantic supermarket, his only function to want," and Allen Ginsberg, in "A Supermarket in California," suffered a headache when he entered a store until he found Walt Whitman "poking among the meats in the refrigerator and eyeing the grocery boys." Rabbit, John Updike's protagonist in *Rabbit, Run*, mused ruefully on a world with no consciousness of tragedy as he watched his wife on her hospital bed absorbed by "Queen for a Day" on a rented TV set. In this "air-conditioned nightmare" (Henry Miller's term), one had to commit one's self to a deliberate act of rejection of the consumer culture. The projective poet Charles Olson, in "The Songs of Maximus," urged:

> In the midst of plenty, walk
> as close to
> bare
> .   .   .
> In the land of plenty, have
> nothing to do with it.

By the end of the decade, publicists were charging that the United States, in the catch phrase of the day, had lost its sense of national purpose. Eisenhower responded to this reproof forthrightly: He appointed a commission to ascertain what the country's aims were. In the commission's reports and in popular journals there ensued a "debate" about national purpose that resulted in more high-minded thinking than Americans had witnessed in many a year. Like Puritan divines scourging a colony of sinners, the tribunes of purpose flailed away at a people who put private pleasure ahead of national goals. Some of the scolding centered less on the quality of life in the United States than on the country's role as a world power, for critics alleged that the United States had given the consumer culture higher priority than the cold war. The failure of the Russians to match the American outpouring of consumer goods, once a source of rejoicing in the United States, was taken as evidence of Soviet dedication and the explanation for Uncle Sam's debility. Adlai Stevenson asked, "With the supermarket as our temple and the singing commercial as our litany, are we likely to fire the world with an irresistible vision of America's exalted purposes and inspiring way of life?"

A good deal of the concern about the quality of American life focused on the city, for the transition of the United States from a rural to an urban society continued at a rapid pace. Even though almost all the largest cities were losing population to the suburbs (Boston had fewer people in 1960 than in 1920), the total metropolitan agglomerations grew relentlessly. Of the population gains in the 1950's, they accounted for no less than 97 percent. In 1940, 48 percent of the nation lived in metropolitan areas; by 1969, 64.5 percent did. Flying at night, pilots who used to be able to pick out each cluster of lights that separated city from countryside found the urban areas indistinguishable; from Newport News north to New York was a single ribbon of light. It was estimated that by the year 2000, 85 percent of the country's 300 million people would live in urban centers, and many of them would be clustered in four huge concentrations whose parameters were already evident in the postwar years—"Boswash," from Boston to Washington; "Chipitts," from the Windy City to the Golden Triangle; "San San," running south from San Francisco all the way to San Diego near the Mexican border; and "JaMi," a megalopolis stretching the length of Florida's east coast, from Jacksonville to Miami.

The cities had long been the nation's nerve centers. Like powerful magnets attracting iron filings, they drew black tenant farmers to Gary's steel mills, Chicanos out of the sugar beet fields to the metropolises of California and Texas, Navaho and Zuñi to the streets of Gallup, girls from Columbus (as in Leonard Bernstein's *Wonderful Town*) to Greenwich Village, because for all they offered at least the illusion of a new beginning. Painters who once found their subject matter in the countryside—the Hudson River School, "Motif No. 1" on the New England shore—set up their easels along urban thoroughfares. Franz Kline and Frank Stella painted New York bridges; Larry Rivers designed the cover for Frank O'Hara's lengthy poem *Second Avenue*. As the artist John Ferren explained, "It is not accident that contemporary painting used lots of black and white. It didn't come from the sunlit fields—it came from white lofts in dirty buildings on dirty streets and from the inner resources of the mind. Its beginning was urban, of the city."

Yet many also viewed the city as the country's number 1 problem, indeed the very embodiment of the nation's ills. There were the festering sores of racial antagonism, the warrens of crime, the breeding places of a hundred social maladies. The fragmented life of the city, critics wrote, resulted in what the French sociologist Emile Durkheim termed *anomie,* the vacuum characterized by the absence of an accepted value system. Los Angeles was taken to be

the leading instance of a distended town lacking authentic community—"six suburbs in search of a city," one observer called it.
The metropolis, which existed only because of the achievements of
technology, seemed to have reached the point where it was throttling
the very mechanisms it needed to keep going. Passengers whisked
across the country at over 700 miles per hour were moved at a snail's
pace from the airport to their downtown destinations. And when in
1965 power failures plunged New York into darkness and trapped
hundreds in unlighted subway tunnels, some even came to doubt
whether Gotham would survive. To the gloomiest Cassandras, the
American city, like Nineveh and Tyre, seemed doomed to perish as
had the centers of other civilizations that had lost their sense of
national purpose.

Although many of the national purpose diatribes hit home, they
also included a fair amount of malarkey. It was not clear to all that a
nation ought to have a "purpose." As Britain's Prime Minister
Harold Macmillan observed, "If people want a sense of purpose,
they should get it from their archbishops." The concentration on
vulgar consumption distracted attention from the millions with low
incomes, and, as Stephan Thernstrom has noted, it was particularly
ungracious often to have "the loudest complaints against tailfins . . .
voiced by people whose own Spartan mode of transportation was a
Porsche." Nor were the critics altogether fair in their assessment of
the nature of American society in the 1950's, although they helped
establish a mode of interpretation of those times that may never be
seriously altered.

Bland, vapid, self-satisfied, banal—all true of Eisenhower's America, yet not the whole truth. The political life of the decade was un-
dernourished, but Adlai Stevenson made important contributions to
the advances of the 1960's, and both the Supreme Court and the civil
rights movement broke new ground on race. As a result of the efforts
of mayors like New Haven's Richard Lee, Ford Foundation executives such as Paul Ylvisaker, and political scientists like Robert
Wood, the country was beginning to accept the need for national
action on behalf of the cities. Those who concentrated their attention on the shortage of classrooms gave too little notice to the impressive gains in education. And although many of the by-products
of economic growth were deplorable, the soaring GNP lifted millions out of poverty.

A culture allegedly hostile to creativity, it nonetheless found room
for the inventive sculpture of David Smith, the architectural genius

of Minoru Yamasaki and Eero Saarinen, and brilliant paintings like Joseph Albers' *Homage to the Square*. During this "arid" period Ralph Ellison published *Invisible Man,* and Tennessee Williams' *A Streetcar Named Desire* had its premiere. The barbs at mass culture were often well directed, and in retrospect this has come to seem a period of little save paint-by-the-number kits, Liberace's smirk, Lassie, and the Nelson family. But the popular culture of the time also had its special pleasures—Edward R. Murrow's "See It Now," Gian Carlo Menotti's *Amahl and the Night Visitors*, Phil Silvers breaking them up as Sergeant Bilko, Rodgers and Hammerstein's *The King and I* and Loewe and Lerner's *My Fair Lady*, Bill Russell sweeping the boards, and Paul Hornung bursting off tackle on a Green Bay power sweep.

Even the value system of the 1950's had its virtues. If children raised by parents with one eye on Dr. Spock's manual were overindulged, they were also spared the mindless tyranny of some earlier kinds of upbringing. Critics were depressed by the hero of Sloan Wilson's *Man in the Gray Flannel Suit*, who rejected an offer to become a top executive so that he might spend more time with his family, but such a decision may have indicated less an attenuation of character than a sensible turning away from the go-getter striving of primitive capitalism. Yet despite all the buncombe the national purpose debate brought forth, it did serve to raise questions about the shortcomings of the consumer culture and to point the country toward different emphases in the 1960's.

The participants in the debate on national purpose looked toward the 1960 presidential campaign for new directions. Without exception, they emphasized the importance of government leadership. "It is time," said the political scientist Hans Morgenthau, "for the President to reassert his historical role as . . . the initiator of policy." But the two young candidates (the Democrat, Senator John F. Kennedy, was forty-three; the Republican, Vice-President Richard M. Nixon, forty-six) had both been identified with the unadventurous politics of the 1950's.

In 1956 alarm over Eisenhower's health after the President suffered a heart attack and ileitis had led the Republicans to unveil a "new Nixon." The Vice-President was revealed to be a man of such modest demeanor that none could confuse him with the unshaven mudslinger Herblock had made the butt of his cartoons. In his "high level" campaign that year, Nixon shunned all controversy; "I lean to the Dodgers, but my wife is a Yankee fan," he confided.

His critics were unimpressed. Nixon, said Adlai Stevenson, had "put away his switchblade and now assumes the aspect of an Eagle Scout." However, observed Stevenson, "This is a man of many masks. Who can say they have seen his real face?" In 1960, too, many who opposed the Vice-President did so less because they disagreed with his views, or even because they recalled resentfully his role in the McCarthy era, than because they thought he typified the hollow man of a synthetic society. Often Nixon appeared to be manipulating himself in order to gain a temporary advantage; in one address, he soberly explained how much preparation had to go into a spontaneous talk and stressed the importance of "seeming sincere." The question, noted one editor, was not whether the real Nixon was the old Nixon or the new Nixon but "whether there is anything that might be called the 'real' Nixon, new or old."

Kennedy, many of these same critics claimed, was a "Democratic Nixon," a man wanting in strong convictions. In view of the fact that he had not stood up to Joe McCarthy, the Massachusetts Senator opened himself to ridicule by publishing *Profiles in Courage*, a study of the valor of resolute legislators. During the McCarthy era, Kennedy, it was said, should have shown less profile and more courage. He won the 1960 nomination by defeating Minnesota's Senator Hubert Humphrey, who in a decade when moderation was the national style had boldly taken forthright positions. Kennedy's victory over him in the primaries was interpreted as further evidence that the nation would not countenance an outspoken candidate in 1960.

"The 'managerial revolution' has come to politics," wrote the television commentator Eric Sevareid, "and Nixon and Kennedy are its first completely packaged products. The Processed Politician has finally arrived." Recalling his experience in the 1930's when he had been deeply aroused by the Republic Steel massacre and the fate of the Spanish Loyalists, Sevareid added:

I can't find in the record that Kennedy or Nixon ever did, thought or felt these things. They must have been across the campus on Fraternity Row, with the law and business school boys, wearing the proper clothes, thinking the proper thoughts, cultivating the proper people. I always sensed that they would end up running the big companies in town but I'm damned if I ever thought one of them would end up running the country.

Much about the 1960 campaign served to confirm these misgivings. The public response to the four television confrontations between

Paul Schutzer. LIFE Magazine. © 1960 Time Inc.

John F. Kennedy debates Richard M. Nixon in the camera's eye. The four confrontations
in the 1960 presidential campaign, which helped determine the outcome of the election,
marked the culmination of the impact of the new medium of television on American politics.

the two candidates centered less on their ideas than on which
man was the more "telegenic." So little choice did some detect that
the veteran political writer Gerald Johnson saw the contest as "Burroughs Against IBM."

Yet during the campaign Kennedy did take up the themes of national purpose, especially by emphasizing that the cold war should

Election of 1960

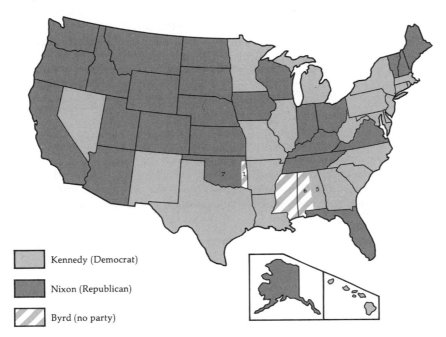

have higher priority than the consumer culture. In asserting the need to "get America moving again," he insisted that America must make a choice "between the public interest and private comfort." "I run for the Presidency because I do not want it said that in the years when our generation held political power . . . America began to slip," Kennedy declared. "I don't want historians writing in 1970 to say that the balance of power in the Nineteen Fifties and the Nineteen Sixties began to turn against the United States and against the cause of freedom."

The country gave little indication that it was in a heroic mood or that it was ready to give either candidate a decisive mandate. So evenly did the electorate distribute its ballots on election day that after a long night of television-viewing the nation was still not certain of the outcome. Kennedy's victory margin in the popular vote (two-tenths of 1 percent) was the smallest since 1880, although his edge in the Electoral College was more emphatic, 303 to 219. The first triumph of a Roman Catholic nominee was taken as proof of the country's freedom from bigotry, despite the fact that Kennedy may have lost over 4 million votes of Democrats who would not support a Catholic candidate. And the distribution of congressional seats left the pivotal conservative coalition essentially undisturbed.

Eisenhower ended his eight years in office with a symbolic act. He left behind for his successor an official paper that attempted what had never been tried so self-consciously before—to define the national goals. But in the same year that Kennedy was elected, Daniel Bell wrote in *The End of Ideology:*

> Thus one finds, at the end of the fifties, a disconcerting caesura. In the West, among the intellectuals, the old passions are spent. The new generation, with no meaningful memory of these old debates, and no secure tradition to build upon, finds itself seeking new purposes within a framework of political society that has rejected, intellectually speaking, the old apocalyptic and chiliastic visions.

For many American liberals, however, Kennedy's election offered the hope that the United States could leave behind the torpid Eisenhower years and face up to the challenge of critical public issues. Kennedy's admirers pointed out that when Martin Luther King had been jailed for taking part in a sit-in at the Magnolia Room restaurant of Rich's Department Store in Atlanta, Nixon had done nothing but Kennedy had intervened to secure his release. They noted too that Kennedy had campaigned on a platform calling for elimination of racial discrimination, federal aid to education, medical care for the aged and government action to foster economic growth. With a program embodying so much of the Fair Deal agenda, with a vigorous chief executive committed to the doctrine of a strong presidency and eager to regain a sense of national purpose, liberals looked forward with confidence to what awaited them in the 1960's.

SUGGESTED READINGS

Few historians so far have attempted to assess the quarter-century after 1945. The most judicious brief account is Carl N. Degler, *Affluence and Anxiety* (1968). Eric F. Goldman, *The Crucial Decade And After—America, 1945–1960* (1961), is a lively narrative of the Truman-Eisenhower era. A somewhat longer period is covered by John Brooks, *The Great Leap* (1966), an effervescent social history. More political in focus is Walter Johnson, *1600 Pennsylvania Avenue* (1960), which begins in 1929 and terminates in 1959. Herbert Agar, *The Price of Power* (1957), is a volume in The Chicago

History of American Civilization, edited by Daniel Boorstin. Chester E. Eisinger, ed., *The 1940's: Profile of a Nation in Crisis* (1969), compiles original sources for that decade; and Joseph Satin, ed., *The 1950's: America's "Placid" Decade* (1960), performs the same task for the succeeding ten years.

There are extended essays on each of the postwar elections through the 1968 contest in volume 4 of Arthur M. Schlesinger, Jr., and Fred L. Israel, eds., *History of American Presidential Elections* (4 vols., 1971). In the first of these essays, Richard Kirkendall analyzes the 1948 election. For the minor parties in that contest, see Karl M. Schmidt, *Henry Wallace: Quixotic Crusader* (1960), a rather uncritical view of the Progressive candidate, and V. O. Key, Jr., *Southern Politics in State and Nation* (1949), a major work which includes material on the Dixiecrats. Key also wrote *The Responsible Electorate* (1966) in support of his contention that voters are more rational than many political scientists concede. Paul David et al., *Presidential Nominating Politics in 1952* (1954), is an exhaustive five-volume study. The succeeding presidential election is dealt with in Charles A. H. Thomson and Frances M. Shattuck, *The 1956 Presidential Campaign* (1960), a Brookings monograph. Heinz Eulau, *Class and Party in the Eisenhower Years* (1962), examines the data on politics and social structure for the 1952 and 1956 elections. The Democratic candidate in both years, Adlai Stevenson, is the subject of Kenneth S. Davis's *A Prophet in His Own Country* (1957). The 1960 election is described in Theodore H. White, *The Making of the President* (1961), and in Paul T. David et al., *The Presidential Election and Transition, 1960–1961* (1961). Richard M. Dalfiume, ed., *American Politics Since 1945* (1969), is one of a number of skillfully edited collections of articles that first appeared in *The New York Times*. Angus Campbell et al., *The American Voter* (1960), a summary of the work of the Survey Research Center of the University of Michigan, has had a pervasive influence. Samuel Lubell's *The Future of American Politics* (rev. ed., 1956) and his *Revolt of the Moderates* (1956) are contributions of a hardworking journalist. For the legislation of the period, *Congressional Quarterly*'s bulky *Congress and Nation* (1965) is a mine of information. Donald R. Matthews, *U.S. Senators and Their World* (1960), dissects the upper house, while Richard Bolling, *House Out of Order* (1965), offers the perspective of an able liberal Congressman from Kansas City on the House of Representatives.

Literary developments in the beginning of this period are surveyed in John W. Aldridge, *After the Lost Generation* (1951), which deals with the war writers, and Chester E. Eisinger, *Fiction of the Forties* (1963). Howard M. Harper, Jr., *Desperate Faith* (1967), analyzes brilliantly the novels of Bellow, Salinger, Mailer, Baldwin, and Updike. Malcolm Cowley, *The Literary Situation* (1954), offers the judgments of a veteran critic. For the beats, see Lawrence Lipton, *The Holy Barbarians* (1959), and Jane Kramer, *Allen Ginsberg in America* (1969). Sidney Finkelstein, in *Existentialism and Alienation in American Literature* (1965), approaches his subject in a single-mindedly Marxist manner. Stephen Stepanchev, *American Poetry Since 1945* (1965), and M. L. Rosenthal, *The New Poets* (1967), which covers British as well as American writing since World War II, are excellent. Alvin B. Kernan, ed., *The Modern American Theater* (1967), pulls together essays on drama. Exceptionally wide-ranging is Richard Kostelanetz, ed., *The New American Arts* (1965). Barbara

Rose, *American Arts Since 1900* (1967), has a substantial section on postwar developments, which is also the subject of an anthology, Gregory Battcock, ed., *The New Art* (1966). There are important documents too in Barbara Rose, *Readings in American Art Since 1900* (1968). For architecture, see John Burchard and Albert Bush-Brown, *The Architecture of America* (1966).

Richard S. Kirkendall, ed., *The Truman Period as a Research Field* (1967), a collection of essays, is the best introduction to the Truman era. Barton J. Bernstein and Allen J. Matusow, eds., *The Truman Administration: A Documentary History* (1966), is a painstaking anthology. Another useful collection is Louis W. Koenig, ed., *The Truman Administration* (1956). The Washington correspondent Cabell Phillips has written *The Truman Presidency* (1966). For the politics of the veterans issue, see Davis R. B. Ross, *Preparing for Ulysses* (1969). Stephen K. Bailey, *Congress Makes a Law* (1950), details the legislative history of the Employment Act of 1946. Another landmark of political science is David B. Truman, *The Congressional Party* (1959), on the Eighty-first Congress. Questions of labor policy in the postwar era are aired in R. Alton Lee, *Truman and Taft-Hartley* (1966), and H. A. Millis and E. C. Brown, *From the Wagner Act to Taft-Hartley* (1950). The Fair Deal has already spawned several monographs including Allen J. Matusow, *Farm Policies and Politics in the Truman Years* (1967), and Richard O. Davies, *Housing Reform During the Truman Administration* (1966). Alonzo L. Hamby will soon publish an ambitious study of American liberalism in the Truman period. Some of his preliminary findings appeared in "The Vital Center, the Fair Deal, and the Quest for a Liberal Political Economy," *American Historical Review* (1972). For the most formidable opponent of the Fair Deal, see James T. Patterson, *Mr. Republican* (1972), the first scholarly biography of Robert Taft.

Earl Latham, *The Communist Controversy in Washington: From the New Deal to McCarthy* (1966), provides a good historical background and takes a tough-minded view of the subversion question. Latham has also edited an anthology of essential essays, *The Meaning of McCarthyism* (1965). Three important monographs on the loyalty issue in the Truman era are Alan D. Harper, *The Politics of Loyalty* (1969); Robert K. Carr, *The House Un-American Activities Committee, 1945–1950* (1952); and C. Herman Pritchett, *Civil Liberties and the Vinson Court* (1954). Richard M. Freeland adds an international dimension in *The Truman Doctrine and the Origins of McCarthyism* (1972). David A. Shannon's *The Decline of American Communism* (1959) does justice to that subject. Alistair Cooke, *A Generation on Trial* (1950), contributes a British perspective to the Hiss case. The participants in that confrontation have each written their own accounts, Whittaker Chambers' disturbing *Witness* (1952) and Alger Hiss' much thinner *In the Court of Public Opinion* (1957). Truman's firing of MacArthur is covered by Richard Rovere and Arthur M. Schlesinger, Jr., *The General and the President* (1951); J. W. Spanier, *The Truman-MacArthur Controversy and the Korean War* (1959); and Trumbull Higgins, *Korea and the Fall of MacArthur* (1960). Richard Rovere, *Senator Joe McCarthy* (1959), is superb, but Jack Anderson and R. W. May, *McCarthy: The Man, the Senator, the "Ism"* (1952), is also of value. Robert Griffith, *The Politics of Fear* (1970), is a substantial analysis of McCarthyism and the Senate. Richard Fried's forthcoming study illuminates the Democratic Party's response to McCarthyism, while Ronald J. Caridi,

The Korean War and American Politics (1968), examines the impact on the Republicans of limited war. Daniel Bell, ed., *The New American Right* (1955), later revised as *The Radical Right* (1964), is a seminal but much controverted work by prominent intellectuals in the 1950's. Richard Hofstadter, who contributed an essay to that volume, returned to the subject in *The Paranoid Style in American Politics and Other Essays* (1965). Michael Paul Rogin, *The Intellectuals and McCarthy* (1967), raises doubts about the hypotheses in the Bell volume.

The impact of the cold war on American society requires more careful attention than it has so far received, but Edward Bernard Glick, *Soldiers, Scholars, and Society* (1971), sheds light on the influence of the military. Samuel P. Huntington is the author of both *The Soldier and the State* (1957) and *The Common Defense* (1961). Two other worthwhile books are Demetrios Caraley's exploration of *The Politics of Military Unification* (1966) and Edward A. Kolodziej, *The Uncommon Defense and Congress, 1945–1963* (1966). Lawrence Wittner, *Rebels Against War* (1969), dissects the peace movement. Seymour Melman, *Pentagon Capitalism* (1970), is one of a number of books that deplore the influence of the military-industrial complex.

The most comprehensive book on the economy in this period is Harold G. Vatter, *The U.S. Economy in the 1950's* (1963). Other important studies are John Kendrick, *Productivity Trends in the United States* (1961); Walter Adams and Horace M. Gray, *Monopoly in America* (1955); Walter Adams, ed., *The Structure of American Industry* (3d ed., 1961); and A. E. Holmans, *United States Fiscal Policy, 1945–1959* (1961). John Kenneth Galbraith's most influential books are *American Capitalism* (1952), which developed the notion of "countervailing power," and *The Affluent Society* (1952; rev. ed., 1969). Many of the best analyses of the economy appear not in books but in articles, notably those published in *Fortune*, such as William B. Harris' 1957 essays on electronics and computers. Harry M. Trebing, ed., *The Corporation in the American Economy* (1970), collects articles that originated with *The New York Times*. The role of the Council of Economic Advisers is the subject of Edward S. Flash, Jr., *Economic Advice and Presidential Leadership* (1965). E. L. Dale, *Conservatives in Power* (1960), looks at Eisenhower's economic policies. Norman Macrae, *The Neurotic Trillionaire* (1970), is an incisive commentary by the deputy editor of *The Economist*. Historians have given little attention to the consumer culture, but David M. Potter, *People of Plenty* (1954), and Daniel J. Boorstin, "Welcome to the Consumption Community," *Fortune* (1967), are suggestive. The best book on the difficult question of income distribution is Herman P. Miller, *Rich Man, Poor Man* (1971). The persistence of maldistribution is emphasized by Gabriel Kolko, *Wealth and Power in America* (1962); Michael Harrington, *The Other America* (1962); Letitia Upton and Nancy Lyons, *Basic Facts: Distribution of Personal Income and Wealth in the United States* (1972), a Cambridge Institute study; and Stephan Thernstrom, "The Myth of American Affluence," *Commentary* (1969). On urban developments, see Blake McKelvey, *The Emergence of Metropolitan America, 1915–1966* (1968), and Nathan Glazer, ed., *Cities in Trouble* (1970). Jane Jacobs, *The Death and Life of Great American Cities* (1961), is stimulating even to those who do not share the author's viewpoint. A forthcoming study by Mark Gelfand presents rich detail on the relationship of the federal government to the cities. Robert C. Wood, *Suburbia: Its*

People and Their Politics (1959), is the standard work on that subject, but see too Scott Donaldson, *The Suburban Myth* (1969), and Herbert J. Gans, *The Levittowners* (1967).

Bernard Rosenberg and D. M. White, eds., *Mass Culture* (1957), is an ambitious anthology. David Manning White, ed., *Pop Culture in America* (1970), is another useful collection, as is Eric Larrabee and Rolf Meyersohn, eds., *Mass Leisure* (1958). Erik Barnouw, *The Image Empire* (1970), the third volume of his History of Broadcasting in the United States, gives a provocative, if jaundiced, view of television. David Quentin Voigt, *American Baseball, Volume II: From the Commissioners to Continental Expansion* (1970), explores baseball's coming of age. In the superabundant literature on rock, see Jerry Hopkins, *The Rock Story* (1970), Carl Belz, *The Story of Rock* (1969), and Jonathan Eisen, ed., *The Age of Rock 2* (1970).

David Riesman et al., *The Lonely Crowd* (1950), deeply affected the interpretation of national character. Riesman was a prolific writer; among his many contributions, see *Faces in the Crowd* (1952), written in collaboration with Nathan Glazer, and "The Found Generation," in *Abundance for What?* (1964). C. Wright Mills, *White Collar* (1951) and *The Power Elite* (1956), and William H. Whyte, *The Organization Man* (1956), also had a huge influence. Thomas L. Hartshorne, *The Distorted Image: Changing Conceptions of American Character Since Turner* (1968), examines the impact of Riesman and others. Clyde Kluckhohn, "The Evolution of Contemporary American Values," *Daedalus* (1958), is an important survey. Eric Larrabee, *The Self-Conscious Society* (1960), is insightful, as is D. W. Brogan, "Unnoticed Changes in America," *Harper's* (1957). Karl E. Meyer, *The New America* (1961), offers a melancholy estimate. Seymour Martin Lipset takes a longer look in "A Changing American Character," in Lipset and Leo Lowenthal, eds., *Culture and Social Character* (1961).

Among the studies of Eisenhower, Marquis Childs, *Eisenhower: Captive Hero* (1958), and Emmet John Hughes, *The Ordeal of Power* (1963), are highly critical, while Merlo J. Pusey, *Eisenhower, The President* (1956), and Arthur Larson, *Eisenhower: The President Nobody Knew* (1968), are approving. R. J. Donovan, *Eisenhower: The Inside Story* (1956), and Richard Rovere, *Affairs of State: The Eisenhower Years* (1956), are the best sources for Ike's first term. Dean Albertson, ed., *Eisenhower as President* (1963), puts together some of the important essays. Richard M. Nixon, *Six Crises* (1962), gives the viewpoint of Eisenhower's Vice-President. For the legislation of this period, James L. Sundquist, *Politics and Policy: The Eisenhower, Kennedy, and Johnson Years* (1968), is indispensable. Eisenhower's attitudes toward natural resources may be approached through E. R. Bartley, *The Tidelands Oil Controversy* (1953), and Aaron Wildavsky, *Dixon-Yates* (1962). For farm and labor policies, consult Lauren Soth, *Farm Trouble in an Age of Plenty* (1957), and Alan K. McAdams, *Power and Politics in Labor Legislation* (1964).

Most of the literature on the civil rights revolution concentrates on the period beginning with the *Brown* decision in 1954. Important studies of developments in the postwar era prior to 1954 are Clement E. Vose, *Caucasians Only* (1967), and Richard M. Dalfiume, *Desegregation of the U.S. Armed Forces* (1969). Harvard Sitkoff examines the political contours in "Harry Truman and the Election of 1948: The Coming of Age of Civil Rights in American Politics," *Journal of Southern History* (1971). Albert P. Blaustein and Clarence Clyde Ferguson, Jr., *Desegregation and the Law* (rev. ed., 1962), discusses the *Brown* decision. Benjamin Muse, *Ten Years of Prelude* (1964), and Anthony Lewis and *The New York Times, Portrait of a Decade: The Second American Revolution* (1964), are the best sources for the reverberations of the Court's decision. See, too, Robert Harris, *The Quest for Equality* (1960). *Race Relations in the USA, 1954–68* (1970), is one of the many useful Keesing's Research Reports. The leader of the Montgomery bus boycott, the Reverend Martin Luther King, Jr., states his views in *Stride Toward Freedom* (1958). C. Eric Lincoln, ed., *Martin Luther King, Jr.* (1970), is a useful anthology. J. W. Anderson, *Eisenhower, Brownell, and the Congress* (1964), presents a legislative history of the 1957 civil rights statute. Richard H. Sayler et al., eds., *The Warren Court* (1968), is an excellent anthology on the tribunal that delivered the *Brown* decision. C. Herman Pritchett, *Congress versus the Supreme Court, 1957–1960* (1961), and Walter F. Murphy, *Congress and the Court* (1962), analyze the attempt to shackle the Court. Among the many first-rate appraisals by constitutional lawyers, see Archibald Cox, *The Warren Court: Constitutional Decision As An Instrument of Reform* (1968); Herbert Wechsler, *Principles, Politics and Fundamental Law* (1961); Alexander M. Bickel, *The Supreme Court and the Idea of Progress* (1970); and Philip B. Kurland, *Politics, the Constitution, and the Warren Court* (1970).

Significant Statistics

	1900	1920	1932	1945	1960
Population	76,094,000	106,466,000	124,949,000	139,928,000	**180,684,000**
Percentage urban	39.7	51.2	NA	58.6	**69.9**
Percentage rural	60.3	48.8	NA	41.4	**30.1**
Percentage non-white	12.0	10.0	10.0	10.0	**11.0**
Life expectancy					
White	47.6	54.9	63.2	66.8	**70.6**
Nonwhite	33.0	45.3	53.7	57.7	**63.6**
Gross national product (current dollars)					
Total (billions of dollars)	17.3	88.9	58.5	213.6	**503.7**
Per capita (dollars)	231	835	468	1,526	**2,788**
Defense spending (millions of dollars)[a]	332	4,329	1,688	84,311	**51,334**
As percentage of GNP	1.9	5.0	3.0	40.0	**10.0**
Military personnel on active duty	125,923	343,302	244,902	12,123,455	**2,476,435**
Labor union membership	791,000	5,034,000	3,226,000	14,796,000	**18,117,000**
Birth rate (per 1,000 live births)	32.3	27.7	19.5	20.4	**23.7**
Advertising expenditures (millions of dollars)	542	2,935	1,627	2,874	**11,932**
Motor vehicle registrations	8,000	239,161	24,391,000	31,035,420	**73,869,000**
Persons lynched					
White	9	8	2	0	**0**
Nonwhite	106	53	6	1	**0**
High school graduates (as percentage of all persons over 16 years old)	6.4	16.8	NA	NA	**65.1**

Sources: *Historical Statistics of the United States, Colonial Times to 1957; Statistical Abstract of the United States,* 1970; and *Digest of Educational Statistics,* 1970.

[a] Includes veterans spending; excludes interest.

8

The Travail of Liberalism
American Society, 1961 to the Present

WILLIAM E. LEUCHTENBURG

At 12:51 P.M. on January 20, 1961, Chief Justice Earl Warren administered the oath of office to the thirty-fifth President of the United States, John Fitzgerald Kennedy, at a ceremony appropriate to Liberalism Ascendant. In the brilliant sunshine on snow-swept Capitol Hill, each of the elements of the New Deal tradition (notably its hospitality to diverse faiths and to intellectuals) found acknowledgment. Richard Cardinal Cushing intoned the invocation to take cognizance of the accession of the first Roman Catholic chief executive, and the benediction was read by the president of the Hebrew Union College of Cincinnati, Rabbi Nelson Glueck. Out of gratitude for the invitation to men of letters, Robert Frost wrote a verse tribute to the new administration for

> Summoning artists to participate
> In the august occasions of the state.

Kennedy's inaugural address, much admired despite its affectations, made clear that the cold war, too, was near high noon and that the tribunes of national purpose had won a convert. In his acceptance speech at Los Angeles in 1960, Kennedy had indicated a resolve to move the country away from the values of the consumer culture and toward a commitment to engagement. The "New Frontier," he explained, "sums up, not what I intend to offer the American people, but what I intend to ask of them. It appeals to their pride, not their pocketbook." During one of his TV debates he had scolded Nixon for telling Khrushchev, "You may be ahead of us in rocket thrust, but we're ahead of you in color television," for rocket thrust was more important. In his inaugural oration, the new President admonished, "Ask not what your country can do for you. Ask what you can do for your country."

The youngest man ever elected to the presidency, Kennedy emphasized that "the torch has been passed to a new generation of Americans — born in this century, tempered by war, disciplined by a hard and bitter peace, proud of our ancient heritage." In 1917, the year of his birth, his predecessor Dwight Eisenhower (at seventy the oldest man ever to occupy the White House) was already a captain in the United States army, Konrad Adenauer was chosen lord mayor of Cologne, and Nikita Khrushchev was soldiering for the czar. Kennedy appointed young men to the highest posts in the government, notably the attorney-generalship, to which he named his thirty-five-year-old brother Robert. When critics deplored the appointee's apparent lack of qualifications, the President, in a characteristic jest, said, "I don't see what's wrong with giving Bobby a little experience before he goes into law practice." President Kennedy found young people responsive to such new departures as the Peace Corps, and he helped turn their energies toward public affairs and activities like the civil rights movement.

The young judged attractive not only the "vigor" of the new administration but also its vivacious style and the welcome extended to intellectuals and to novel ideas. Of the two hundred most important posts in the government, three times as many went to men from the university world under Kennedy as under Eisenhower. If neither the President nor the First Lady were the intellectuals they were sometimes imagined to be, they did read widely, patronize the arts, and exhibit solicitude about the quality of American life. Richard Rovere observed, "Kennedy's concern with motels was not only with whether Negroes should get into them but with the *idea* of

President-elect John F. Kennedy and his wife Jacqueline look radiant as they walk through snowclad Washington on the way to Kennedy's inauguration. The society of the New Frontier seemed to some like the *Camelot* of the musical by Alan Jay Lerner and Frederic Loewe based on T. H. White's *The Once and Future King*.

motels—with their function, with the way they looked, with the strange names they bore, and with what they revealed about us." In a single short speech at the University of Wisconsin in 1959, Kennedy had quoted Goethe, Emerson, Swift, Faulkner, Tennyson, Woodrow Wilson, Lord Asquith, Artemus Ward, Finley Peter Dunne, and Queen Victoria, and when Jacqueline Kennedy accompanied the President to Paris, she visited the Jeu de Paume with Malraux and talked blithely of the Duc d'Angoulême with De Gaulle. Kennedy's summons to national service reminded some of Henry V's salutation to his forces before Agincourt in Shakespeare's drama, and some even fancied they saw in the White House circle the Arthurian idyll of Camelot.

Yet Kennedy's fondness for a dashing style also led him to admire the Green Berets, his penchant for vigorous action would result in his approving the ill-fated Cuban invasion, and Jackie's *haute couture* and *haute cuisine,* her much-copied coiffeur, and her conspicuously consuming jet set would bring to the White House the consumer culture writ large. Indeed, the sensibility of the Kennedy years frequently blended the value systems of the consumption society and the cold war, notably after the Berlin crisis fostered a craze for fallout shelters. *The New York Times* ran a two-page ad from Hammacher Schlemmer for "Shelters for Living" (one room would cost around $14,000), and in Dallas, the Lone Star Steel Company marketed a shelter with a window painted on the wall showing an outdoor scene; it even came equipped with a shade that could be pulled down at night. Before Kennedy's administration was cut short, some sixteen thousand young men would be demonstrating in Vietnam what they could do for their country.

The cold war figured too in Kennedy's economic policy. Increased military and space expenditures exercised a leavening influence on the economy, and appeal to the national interest served to exalt the administation's anti-inflation campaign. When steel magnates hiked prices, the President thundered: "In this serious hour in our nation's history, when we are confronted with grave crises in Berlin and Southeast Asia . . . , the American public will find it hard, as I do, to accept a situation in which a tiny handful of steel executives whose pursuit of private power and profit exceeds their sense of public responsibility can show such utter contempt of the interests of 185 million Americans." Browbeaten by Kennedy, the steel companies backed down, and the administration won that particular battle to maintain the price level. But business never forgave him for this dressing down or for his private utterance: "My father always told me that all businessmen were sons of bitches, but I never believed it till now."

To "get America moving again," Kennedy gave much of his attention to the sluggish economy. In part out of worry over the balance-of-payments exigency, he acted with such restraint at the outset that the Kennedy government was contemned as "the third Eisenhower administration." However, Kennedy's policies—a moderate climb in federal spending, a trade expansion act, stable interest rates—helped account for a $100 billion increment in the gross national product without an appreciable price rise. Furthermore, Kennedy became, asserted the economist Seymour Harris, "the most literate of all Presidents in his understanding of modern economics and revealed great courage in his willingness to risk political losses in putting his economics to the test of the market place." He sought to educate the country in the heresies of the New Economics and asked Congress for a multi-billion-dollar slash in taxes with the aim of deliberately augmenting a federal deficit in the expectation that this would stimulate growth. Congress bottled up the tax cut request, and the President was disappointed to find that despite the soaring GNP unemployment remained a melancholy 5.5 percent. Yet Kennedy could take satisfaction in knowing that he had brought the country out of the Eisenhower recession and started the longest sustained recovery in the nation's history.

Kennedy had less success in achieving a new frontier in social welfare. He did put through unemployment compensation, area redevelopment, public works, and manpower training legislation, as well as water pollution control and seashore acquisition programs. A raise in the minimum wage was extended to such consumer culture occupations as hotel and restaurant work. But Congress frustrated him repeatedly in his attempts to win approval for Fair Deal measures like federal aid to education and for new legislation such as his mass transit proposal. By 1963 the stalemate that had begun in 1938 was a quarter-century old, and Kennedy's biographer, James MacGregor Burns, was writing of *The Deadlock of Democracy*. Some blamed the conditions of stasis on the President. They pointed out that he enjoyed top-heavy majorities in both houses of Congress and charged that, in the columnist James Reston's words, "he didn't really know the deck on Capitol Hill." "In his relations with Congress," John Roche has contended, "Kennedy suffered from what Sören Kierkegaard once called the 'paralysis of knowledge.' He was temperamentally incapable of leading lost causes, or causes which seemed lost in a rational appraisal of the odds." Most commentators, however, conceded that he faced formidable impediments in the powerful bipartisan conservative coalition and the obdurate committee structure in Congress. Above all, he lacked a constituency for social change. As the economist George Stigler observed, "The trouble is that hardly anybody in America goes to bed angry at night." But some did go to bed hungry, and three days before his death Kennedy instructed Walter Heller, his principal economic aide, to draft battle plans for a war on poverty.

Lee Harvey Oswald's bullets left the question of Kennedy's place in history in the land of What Might Have Been. His admirers pointed out that in every area — civil rights, economic policy, foreign affairs — the young President was moving more confidently in his third year in office, and they anticipated that he would chalk up impressive achievements in his fourth year and in his second term. They remarked, too, on what he had already accomplished — his championing of civil rights and the New Economics, the defusing of the cold war, the renewed dedication to public service. But skeptics doubted that he had done much that was fundamental about the festering cities or the arms race and noted that most of his key proposals were stymied. Four days before his death, the *Congressional Quarterly* calculated that he had gained acceptance for less than one-third of his legislative program. The New Frontier, concluded the British critic Henry Fairlie, was no more than "a limited exercise in civilizing the status quo" and Kennedy "a Man of Only One Season." Still, there could be no doubt that Kennedy had, at least in some degree, gotten the country moving again and that he had made possible many of the successes, as well as some of the failures, of the Johnson administration.

The young felt a special sense of deprivation at Kennedy's death. The slain President had broken through the middle-aged complacency of the 1950's to give a feeling of hopefulness about American society and a free field to the idealism of young people. They had admired, too, the President's gallantry and the impression he conveyed of being a valorous adventurer who was, William Carleton wrote, in the romantic tradition of Achilles, Roland, Bayard, Raleigh, and Henry of Navarre. By any rational calculation, it was not the young of the 1960's but Kennedy's contemporaries, the Depression generation pushing fifty, who had grounds for grievance at being denied a leader. But as Richard Neustadt commented less

President Lyndon B. Johnson on his horse Lady M rounds up a Hereford yearling at the LBJ ranch in Texas. Johnson put the LBJ brand on all he was associated with, including his daughters — Lynda Bird Johnson and Lucy Baines Johnson. His wife, Lady Bird, had acquired her nickname as a child, and marriage made the LBJ symmetry complete.

than a year after the President's murder, "He left a broken promise, that 'the torch has been passed to a new generation,' and the youngsters who identified with him felt cheated as the promise, like the glamor, disappeared. What do their feelings matter? We shall have to wait and see."

The assassination of John F. Kennedy brought to the White House a man of unbounded ambition and prodigious skills in the craft of politics. At fifty-five, only nine years older than his predecessor, Lyndon Baines Johnson seemed to come from a different generation as well as from a dissimilar social stratum. He had been raised not in the mansion of a multimillionaire financier but on a farm in the arid mesquite country of southwest Texas. "When I was young," Johnson once told reporters, "poverty was so common that we didn't know it had a name." A state director of the National Youth Administration who was first elected to Congress in 1937 as an FDR loyalist, he had trimmed sail in the 1950's but in 1963 was determined to outdo Roosevelt as liberal lawgiver, in fact to leave an indelible brand on the whole history of the presidency. Three flags unfurled at his Texas ranch—Old Glory, the ensign of the blue bonnet state, and his personal flag with LBJ lettered in white on a blue field. Toward the government he took a proprietary interest. When on one occasion an air force officer told him he was headed for the wrong helicopter at Andrews Field, Johnson replied, "Son, all of them are mine."

Johnson's dexterity as legislative tactician enabled him to exploit to the fullest the grief and remorse following the assassination. The new President put to good use what the columnists Rowland Evans, Jr., and Robert D. Novak dubbed the Johnson Treatment: "He moved in close, his face a scant millimeter from his target, his eyes widening and narrowing, his eyebrows rising and falling. From his pockets poured clippings, memos, statistics. Mimicry, humor, and the genius of analogy made the Treatment an almost hypnotic experience and rendered the target stunned and helpless." As chief executive, he followed the course of legislation in the most minute detail. "Not a sparrow falls," said one adulatory aide, "that he doesn't know about." In less than a year, Congress enacted a quantity of bills that had been stranded in the Kennedy era—a Higher Education Facilities Act, which authorized federal assistance for the construction of campus buildings and provided federal aid to graduate centers, appropriations for mass transit, the tax cut, an anti-poverty program, and, as a memorial to Kennedy, civil rights legislation.

In February 1964, Congress defied economic orthodoxy by approving a tax cut of more than $10 billion. Johnson succeeded in part because his emphasis on consensus and budgetary prudence had mollified business leaders, although they accepted the Keynesian rationale with some trepidation. The tax cut turned out to be a brilliant success. In the next six quarters consumer spending increased an unprecedented $45 billion, the gross national product soared, and the government took in more money under the new tax schedule than it had before. During the 1960's the total of goods and services increased some 60 percent. Fears of automation diminished as the economy developed 10 million new jobs, a rate of a million a year. From 1961 to 1968, over 14 million Americans moved above the "poverty line," as the proportion of the impoverished in the nation was halved from 22 percent to 11 percent. Median annual family income, under $4000 in 1958 when Galbraith's *The Affluent Society* was published, approached $8000 when a revised edition appeared a decade later, a gain of 85 percent after allowance is made for price rises. The figures for families earning $7000 a year, measured in 1966 dollars, rose from 22 percent in 1950 to roughly 55 percent in 1966, and by 1970, 30 percent of the families in the United States took in over $13,000 annually.

Liberal economists had exhilarating proof that they could put their theories into practice with gratifying results. Daniel P. Moynihan called the tax cut outcome "perhaps the most impressive demonstration that has yet occurred . . . of the capacity of organized intelligence to forecast and direct events." This feat of social engineering, said Secretary of Labor W. Willard Wirtz, marked "the ultimate triumph of the spirit of John Maynard Keynes over the stubborn shade of Adam Smith," and the country's leading conservative economist, Milton Friedman, conceded, "We are all Keynesians now."

On January 8, 1964, in his first State of the Union message, Johnson declared "unconditional war on poverty," another program that carried on initiatives first explored by his predecessor. Kennedy had been shocked by what he had seen in West Virginia during the 1960 primary campaign. "Imagine," he said one night, "just imagine kids who never drink milk." Kennedy and his advisers had also been influenced by Michael Harrington's *The Other America*, a small book that had a big impact. "The millions who are poor in the United States tend to become increasingly invisible," Harrington wrote. It required "an effort of the intellect and will even to see them." Accounts like Harrington's, and more scholarly assessments by Robert Lampman and Leon Keyserling, indicated that in an age of affluence, one-fifth of the nation existed, as Johnson said, "on the outskirts of hope" in "inherited, gateless poverty." Blacks made up a disproportionate number of the poor, but 70 percent were whites, many of them trapped in cul-de-sacs of distress such as Appalachia.

Johnson took Kennedy's slowly emerging plan, revamped it, and drove it through Congress with a blare of trumpets and a roll of drums. Reporters for London's *Sunday Times* commented that it "was not the most daring, but it was perhaps the most bellicose program of social reform in history. It was to be a *war* on poverty. Federal funds were to be 'fired in' to pockets of poverty in what was known in Washington as 'the rifle-shot approach.' . . . He actually spoke of 'throttling want.' " The Economic Opportunity Act of 1964 (a title that suggests the endurance of nineteenth-century ideas) appropriated nearly a billion dollars for projects such as Head Start to help preschoolers, the Job Corps for dropouts, a work-study program to assist college students, a domestic peace corps — Volunteers in Service to America (VISTA) — a Neighborhood Youth Corps, basic education and work experience activities to help adults, and, what would prove to be the most controversial departure, a Community Action Program stipulating "maximum feasible participation" by the impoverished. The Public Works and Economic Development Act in 1965 would add over $3 billion more and an Appalachian Regional Development Act another $1 billion to rehabilitate that section. "We are not helpless before the iron laws of economics," the President said. Although the war on poverty was inadequately funded, it was a hopeful beginning, and the Negro novelist Ralph Ellison would call Johnson "the greatest American President for the poor and for the Negroes."

In 1964 Johnson announced a conception of his own — the "Great Society." At Ann Arbor in May, he explained that the Great Society was "a place where men are more concerned with the quality of their goals than the quantity of their goods," thus challenging the ethos of the consumer culture while the tax cut was aggrandizing it. But Johnson's prospectus went beyond the preoccupations of "qualitative liberalism." The President stated, "The Great Society rests on abundance and liberty for all. It demands an end to poverty and racial injustice, to which we are totally committed in our time."

Johnson's Great Society confronted a challenge that fall from a die-hard reactionary, Senator Barry Goldwater of Arizona. A millionaire Phoenix department store owner, Goldwater thrived on the consumer culture, but his ideas were more appropriate to the entrepreneurial individualism of frontier America. In *The Conscience of a Conservative*, published four years earlier, he had called for the abolition of the graduated income tax and the sale of TVA, and he recommended that the national government abandon most of its functions at the rate of 10 percent a year. A spokesman for the new rich of Scottsdale, the retired officer corps of San Diego, and small-town Americans in retreat, Goldwater distrusted the cosmopolitan

East, with its solicitude for society's outcasts and its fussiness about nuclear war. He expected to win the presidency by putting together a regional combination of the South and West and, by offering the nation "a choice not an echo," to bring to the polls millions of dormant conservative, nationalist voters with the appeal, "In Your Heart, You Know He's Right."

Goldwater's campaign gave Lyndon Johnson the enormous advantage of running as a social reform candidate and still seeming the less "radical" of the two. By picking Senator Hubert Humphrey of Minnesota as his running mate, Johnson quieted lingering doubts about his commitment to liberalism, and by saying, "We are not about to send American boys nine or ten thousand miles from home to do what Asian boys ought to be doing for themselves," he emerged as the peace nominee. Moderate Republicans were disturbed by Goldwater's statement at the rowdy San Francisco convention that "extremism in the defense of liberty is no vice," a declaration that appeared to give benediction to the far-right John Birch Society, which even viewed Eisenhower as a Communist agent. Goldwater's missile-rattling created unease about whether he should have his finger on the nuclear button; as the Democrats put it, "In Your Heart, You Know He Might." Blacks were antagonized by Goldwater's covert countenancing of "white backlash," and old people were troubled by his hostility to social security. On election day, Johnson sent Goldwater down to a crushing defeat by gaining a record 61.1 percent of the popular returns and every electoral vote save those of Goldwater's Arizona and five Deep South states. In Congress the Democrats swelled their margin to 155 in the House and attained a 68 to 32 edge in the Senate, enough to nullify the conservative coalition and enhance prospects for a legislative performance that would rival the New Deal.

In rolling up the most impressive record of any Congress in three decades, the "fabulous Eighty-ninth" wiped clean the legislative slate of the Fair Deal. When Congress approved a Medicare program of health insurance for the aged under Social Security, Johnson flew to Independence so that Harry Truman could witness the signing. (Congress also provided Medicaid for the indigent.) Truman saw the effectuation of another of his goals with the enactment, also in 1965, of the Elementary and Secondary Education Act, which provided more than a billion dollars in grants for low-income pupils and authorized, for the first time, assistance to children in Catholic parochial and other private schools. This departure resulted from

Election of 1964

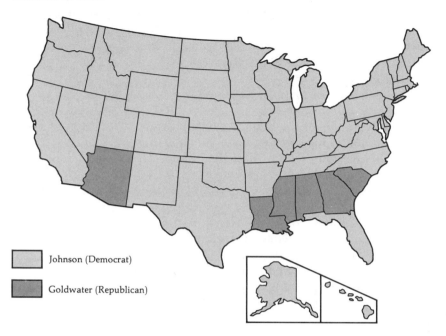

Johnson (Democrat)

Goldwater (Republican)

Kennedy's easing of fears about Catholics and the ecumenical spirit fostered by Pope John XXIII as well as from Johnson's acumen as chief legislator. Regarded by many of the literati as anti-intellectual, Johnson prided himself on being the Education President. That same year he shepherded through Congress the Higher Education Act for assistance to college students. In one year, the President claimed, Congress had done "more for the wonderful cause of education in America than all the previous 176 regular sessions of Congress did, put together."

The Eighty-ninth Congress, at Johnson's behest, also instituted reforms that went beyond the New Deal and Fair Deal. It established two new Cabinet-level departments, for Transportation and for Housing and Urban Affairs, in recognition of the railroad crisis occasioned by the ubiquitous automobile and of the fact that the United States had become a nation of cities. To carry out the Great Society's emphasis on the quality of life, legislation made provision for the beautification of highways, an abiding interest of the President's

wife, Lady Bird Johnson, and, under the sponsorship of Senator
Edmund Muskie of Maine, for the cleansing of air and rivers. Influenced by Ralph Nader's *Unsafe at Any Speed,* Congress adopted
the Highway Safety Act and the Traffic Safety Act. The lawmakers
agreed to the first important change in immigration policy since the
1920's when they ended the national origins system of quotas, which
favored Northwestern Europe, while imposing a quota on nations
in the Western Hemisphere for the first time. In response to recent
episodes such as Eisenhower's illness, a resolution subsequently
ratified as the Twenty-fifth Amendment outlined procedures in case
of presidential disability. The Housing Act of 1965 enabled Washington to supplement the rent of poor tenants and in 1966 Congress set
up a Demonstration Cities program, although neither was supported
with adequate appropriations. This was the Congress, too, that made

The Fair Deal becomes the Great Society. President Johnson, on signing the Medicare bill on July 30,
1965, at the Truman Library in Independence, Missouri, gives the pen to former President Harry
Truman, an early advocate of national health insurance. Lady Bird Johnson
and Bess Truman look on, while Vice-President Hubert Humphrey, perhaps sensing that
the euphoria will not last, eyes the President nervously.

Walter Bennett. TIME Magazine. © 1965 Time Inc.

advances in civil rights and furnished additional rounds of ammunition for the war on poverty.

"The Congress of Fulfillment" completed almost the entire agenda of twentieth-century progressivism. Under Kennedy and more markedly under Johnson, the quarter-century deadlock had been broken. The Eighty-ninth Congress, wrote one Washington reporter, "brought to a harvest a generation's backlog of ideas and social legislation." Arthur Krock observed that it had "moved the country nearer to state collectivism at the federal level than in any previous period." For those who since the Great Depression had waited in vain for another era like that of the New Deal, the first half of the 1960's was a time for rejoicing, and the Eighty-ninth Congress recalled the halcyon days of 1935. "It is the Congress of accomplished hopes," declared Speaker John W. McCormack. "It is the Congress of realized dreams."

Black and White Together

The same sanguine ebullience animated the civil rights movement, which in those years reached the apogee of its power in an ambience of brotherhood, goodwill, optimism, and euphoria. Negroes took to the streets in hundreds of cities, south and north, and frequently whites joined them:

> Black and white together
> We'll walk hand in hand.

Often they enjoyed instant success. The Justice Department toted up three hundred cities in which lunch counters were desegregated in 1963 alone. Blacks pursued equality with an unshakable determination, and sizable numbers of whites became their allies. The National Opinion Research Center at the University of Chicago reported that the proportion of whites in the North who accepted integration of neighborhoods rose from 42 percent in 1942 to 72 percent in 1963 and that those favoring school integration increased from 40 to 75 percent. Both Kennedy and Johnson committed themselves by words and deeds to the civil rights revolution, and the Supreme Court, its patience gone, announced, "The time for mere 'deliberate speed' has run out." Even in the Deep South the times they were a-changin'; more than six hundred community leaders in McComb, Mississippi, called for compliance to civil rights legislation. With so many hopeful indicators, many could sing with conviction:

> Oh, deep in my heart I do believe
> We shall overcome some day.

And "some day" would be now.

In the early 1960's, racial prejudice, as Benjamin Muse has observed, "entered the catalog of unquestioned evils—like water pollution or reckless driving." To be sure, whites were often patronizing and even expected gratitude from Negroes for helping them win rights they should have been able to take for granted. Some of the change, too, was mere tokenism. The black comedian Godfrey Cambridge announced facetiously that he had organized a "Rent a Negro" organization so that every firm could have one temporarily on display in the reception foyer. Yet even the most awkward, self-serving gestures indicated a shift in what was regarded as socially desirable.

The cold war and the consumer culture continued to be instrumental in advancing racial equality. The needs of cold war (and limited war) in the 1960's served to justify national civil rights legislation. In his civil rights message to Congress in June 1963, President Kennedy would point out that "when Americans are sent to Viet-Nam or West Berlin, we do not ask for whites only." The consumer culture proved an even more significant base than it had in the 1950's. Negroes in Birmingham and other cities made effective use of the boycott to demonstrate the importance to white merchants of black consumer buying power, estimated as equivalent in the United States to that of all the people of Canada. In San Francisco militants seeking to increase Negro employment in supermarkets created disorder by piling their shopping carts high with groceries and abandoning them at check-out counters. An important measure of advance in the 1960's was to be the increasing numbers of blacks appearing in television commercials to sing the praises of detergents. Black nationalists touted the distinctive virtues of soul food, but the political future of the black mayor of Cleveland was jeopardized by a quarrel with militants over franchises for McDonald's hamburger drive-ins.

The motel provided the locale for stirring episodes in the civil rights movement. In Florida black and white activists dove into motel swimming pools to break the taboo on integrated bathing. Attorney General Robert F. Kennedy, guidebook in hand, would point out to a congressional committee that a black tourist could not find a room in Danville, Virginia, though a dog accompanied by a white man would be taken in by at least four hostelries. When Congress responded by legislating the Civil Rights Act of 1964, it was sustained in the *Heart of Atlanta Motel* case (as well as by the Court's ruling on Ollie's Barbecue in Birmingham). The Reverend Martin Luther King, Jr., won a sympathetic response from whites by telling what it was like "when you take a cross-country drive and find it necessary to sleep night after night in the uncomfortable corners of your automobile because no motel will accept you." By the late 1960's, King would no longer face this hardship, but in the spring of 1968 in Memphis he would meet death on a motel balcony.

John Kennedy has been hailed as the first President to make the cause of racial integration his own, but he came to his final position slowly and under duress. Of his antipathy to discrimination and his support of the *Brown* decision there was no doubt. But he hesitated to advocate civil rights legislation, for he feared it would fail and would pull the rest of his program down with it. (In fact, when in 1963 he did take a strong stand in the Alabama desegregation crisis, his comfortable margin for an area development measure melted away. When thirty-nine Congressmen switched abruptly, the bill lost by five votes.) Kennedy reasoned that he would have to rely on executive action and concentrate his attention on the federal establishment.

The President used his authority as chief executive to make the national government a staging area for the civil rights movement. He put together a committee headed by Vice-President Johnson to ferret out evidence of discrimination in federal employment and in industries with government contracts. Under his brother Robert the Department of Justice enlisted a remarkable crew of dedicated men— Byron R. White (raised to the Supreme Court in 1962), Nicholas de B. Katzenbach, Burke Marshall, Ramsey Clark, and John Doar, who on one occasion in Jackson, Mississippi, would create a legend by nervily walking into a mob like Gary Cooper gunless on the streets of Dodge City. They were a tough breed. When Ed Guthman, besieged at the University of Mississippi in 1962, reported on the phone to the attorney general, "It's sorta like the Alamo," Bob Kennedy retorted, "Well, you know what happened to those fellows." The President filled high government offices with distinguished blacks—Carl Rowan as ambassador to Finland, Robert Weaver to head the Housing and Home Finance Agency, Thurgood Marshall as United States Circuit Court Justice, and the first Negro district judges ever to serve in the continental United States. In the year ending June 1963, the appointment of Negroes to top-level federal posts increased 39 percent.

However, even in the orbit of executive authority, Kennedy encountered criticism from civil rights activists. He had said during the 1960 campaign that discrimination in federally financed housing could be ended by a stroke of the pen. But not until November 21, 1962, after numerous pens were mailed to him, did he issue an order, so circumscribed and so unenthusiastically administered that it had small effect. His excellent selections for judicial posts in the North were offset when he placed segregationists on the federal bench in the South. Even the Department of Justice was accused of preferring racial peace to the enforcement of rights and of failing to live up to its pledge to protect registration workers. In Mississippi, Allen J. Matusow has noted, "SNCC's only contact with federal authority consisted of the FBI agents who stood by taking notes while local policemen beat up SNCC members." Although some of the objections failed to take into account either political constraints or the limits imposed on federal action by state sovereignty, it is clear that the national government required the prod of the civil rights movement to push it to reaching the full extent of its powers.

The new Department of Justice team got its baptism of fire when it was called to the defense of the "freedom riders" four months after Kennedy took office. That spring the Supreme Court, in *Boynton* v. *Commonwealth of Virginia,* ruled that restaurants in bus stations could not discriminate against interstate travelers. On May 14, 1961, an interracial group from the Congress of Racial Equality set out for the Deep South to test the effectiveness of the decision. In Anniston, Alabama, a mob incinerated a Greyhound bus carrying one delegation (which barely escaped), and in Birmingham the rest of the party was savagely mauled as it left a Trailways bus. When a mob seized the Montgomery bus terminal, the attorney general dispatched hundreds of federal marshals under "Whizzer" White's command. Before order was restored, the mob beat the President's personal representative, John Seigenthaler, into semi-consciousness when he tried to protect a rider. Federal authority prevented a repetition of such episodes, but it could do nothing to help the riders when Mississippi shrewdly eschewed violence and resorted instead to mass arrests.

Nevertheless, the freedom rides did spur the Justice Department to move on two different fronts. The attorney general persuaded the Interstate Commerce Commission to issue an order banning segregation in carriers and terminals, and by government edict signs stating "Waiting room for colored" came tumbling down. The Justice Department also got thirteen of the country's fifteen segregated airports to desegregate voluntarily and filed suit against the other two.

Black and white volunteers challenge Jim Crow in the cradle of the Confederacy, Montgomery, Alabama, in May 1961. After the Greyhound bus pulled into the Montgomery station, a mob of a thousand clubbed and beat the freedom riders. The Kennedy administration dispatched hundreds of marshals, but order was not restored until the governor of Alabama belatedly called out the national guard.

To channel the energy of civil rights workers in less explosive, and it was thought more constructive, directions, the attorney general encouraged a drive to register black voters in the South. By the spring of 1963, Claude Sitton was writing:

There are harbingers of a new day: voting applicants standing patiently at the courthouse door in Greenwood for hour on endless hour, a Justice Department attorney shaking hands with a Negro while a white woman shivers with rage, the songs of freedom rolling out of the little Negro churches into the blackness of the Delta night.

The Department of Justice brought more than five times as many voting rights suits in its first two years as Eisenhower had in three years. The previous administration had left Mississippi alone; the Kennedys filed nineteen suits, even in Sunflower County, home of James Eastland, the mighty segregationist chairman of the Senate Judiciary Committee.

Mississippi provided the battlefield, too, for a confrontation with federal authority even more critical than the one at Little Rock. In 1962 James H. Meredith, the grandson of a slave and a cold war veteran with eight years in the air force, attempted to enroll at the University of Mississippi. To his aid came the able state secretary of the NAACP, Medgar Evers. But in defiance of a United States Circuit Court order, sustained by the Supreme Court, Governor Ross Barnett turned Meredith away and announced a doctrine of interposition reminiscent of John C. Calhoun. President Kennedy responded by sending to the campus of Ole Miss hundreds of federal marshals and, when they proved necessary, almost thirty thousand troops, including the federalized national guard. They were met by a mob who treated the forces of the United States as though they were enemy invaders. The rioters were led by a former major general, Edwin Walker, who, ironically, had commanded the troops at Little Rock five years earlier. In a night of terror, two were killed and 375 injured, including 166 federal marshals (twenty-nine with gunshot wounds) and thirteen members of the steadfast Mississippi National Guard, among them William Faulkner's nephew. Only at such a cost was it possible for one black man to go to the university of his native state.

In 1963 the alliance of the civil rights movement and the federal government overcame the final bastion of white supremacy, Alabama. On Good Friday, April 12, Martin Luther King led a massive demonstration in Birmingham, "the Johannesburg of America." The police commissioner, Eugene "Bull" Connor, shocked the nation, and indeed the world, by employing high-pressure water hoses, ferocious police dogs, and electric cattle prods against the marchers. Despite the intervention of the Justice Department, King won only limited concessions, and when his brother's home and the movement's headquarters motel were bombed, angry blacks rioted, an omen of things to come. However, newspaper photographs and televised accounts of Birmingham motivated still more Americans to align themselves with King.

In June the civil rights forces encountered a less volatile but more dangerous enemy than Connor, the governor of Alabama, George C. Wallace. Although he was slicker than Joe McCarthy, he conveyed the same image of a punisher. Golden Gloves bantamweight champion in 1936 and 1937, he had flown in B-29 bombing missions over Japan in World War II, then entered the Alabama political ring. After being defeated by a little-known racist in his bid for the governorship in 1958, Wallace said, "John Patterson out-nigguhed me. And boys, I'm not going to be out-nigguhed again." He pledged to the people of his state that he would stand in the doorway to prevent Negroes from entering the University of Alabama. But when the President federalized the national guard, Wallace, after putting up a farcical show of resistance, gave way. No longer did any state in the union have an exclusively white school system.

Two hours after Wallace capitulated, Kennedy spoke to the nation

Bull Connor's America. In April 1963 Martin Luther King led a direct-action campaign against segregation and discrimination in Birmingham, Alabama. Eugene Theophilus Connor, Birmingham's commissioner of public safety, horrified the world by using police dogs against Negro demonstrators.

Charles Moore from Black Star

in a televised address, much of it extemporaneous, which conveyed an intensity of emotional commitment that had not been manifest before. The President stated:

If an American, because his skin is dark, cannot eat lunch in a restaurant open to the public; if he cannot send his children to the best public school available; if he cannot vote for the public officials who represent him; if, in short, he cannot enjoy the full and free life which all of us want, then who among us would be content to have the color of his skin changed and stand in his place?

Who among us would then be content with the counsels of patience and delay? One hundred years of delay have passed since President Lincoln freed the slaves, yet their heirs, their grandsons, are not fully free. They are not yet freed from the bonds of injustice; they are not yet freed from social and economic oppression. And this nation, for all its hopes and all its boasts, will not be fully free until all its citizens are free.

He warned that "the fires of frustration and discord are burning in every city," leading to actions that "threaten violence — and threaten lives." The President's words gained added meaning, tragically, when that very night Medgar Evers was murdered by a cowardly assassin in the driveway of his home. A week later, Kennedy, who had said that "the time has come for this nation to fulfill its promise," asked Congress to enact the most comprehensive civil rights law in history.

To demonstrate their enthusiasm for the proposed legislation, which Congress showed no haste to pass, more than two hundred thousand gathered in the nation's capital on August 28, 1963, for an impressive March on Washington. Mobilizer of the march was Bayard Rustin, a veteran of the civil rights movement who had organized the original Aldermaston Ban-the-Bomb protest in England and had been in the front ranks of the marchers in the Sahara to halt a French nuclear test. Highlight of the occasion was a passionate speech by Martin Luther King. "Even though we face the difficulties of today and tomorrow, I still have a dream," he said. "It is a dream chiefly rooted in the American dream." He anticipated that "one day on the red hills of Georgia, the sons of former slaves and the sons of former slave-owners will be able to sit together at the table of brotherhood." Many in Washington had feared that violence would erupt. But London's *Daily Express* was able to headline its account, "The Gentle Flood," and Russell Baker commented, "The sweetness and patience of the crowd may have set some sort of national highwater mark in mass decency." There was reason enough to fear violence, but not there. In September a chill of horror went through the nation when in Birmingham a bomb took the lives of four Negro children at Sunday school, and two months later the President, too, would be gone, his civil rights legislation not yet enacted, King's dream far short of fulfillment.

In his initial address to Congress on November 27, 1963, Lyndon Johnson, the first President from a southern state since Reconstruction, stated emphatically: "We have talked long enough in this country about equal rights. We have talked for one hundred years or more. It is time now to write the next chapter, and to write it in the books of law." By July 1964, the President, with expert assistance from Hubert Humphrey, a long-time fighter for civil rights, and Everett Dirksen, a recent convert, had guided a more ambitious version of Kennedy's bill through both houses, after breaking a southern filibuster. Dirksen, known for his grandiloquent manner of speaking as "the Wizard of Ooze," proclaimed, after Victor Hugo, "Stronger than all the armies is an idea whose time has come."

The Civil Rights Act of 1964 outlawed racial discrimination in public accommodations like restaurants, motels, soda fountains, and filling stations, required equal access to public facilities such as stadiums and swimming pools, and authorized withholding federal subsidies from recipients like schools and hospitals that continued to evince prejudice. It prohibited discrimination in voter registration and established a sixth-grade education as presumptive of literacy. For the first time in some Deep South communities, Negroes sat in "white only" sections of movies and spent the night in hotels from which they had always been excluded. "The thing that the Act reaches," said Burke Marshall, "is the official caste system in this country."

Although the voting rights section of the 1964 act was an improvement, it still left hundreds of thousands of southern Negroes without a ballot. The total of Negroes registered in Alabama had risen from 6,000 in 1947 to 110,000 in 1964, but not one was registered in counties like Lowndes and Wilcox where whites were outnumbered 4 to 1. To dramatize the plight of the disfranchised blacks, King went to Selma, Alabama. Six days after being honored in Oslo as the youngest American ever to receive the Nobel Prize, he was in a Selma jail. The imprisonment of King served only to rally Alabama's Negroes, who sang:

> Police cars are the Berlin Wall,
> Berlin Wall, Berlin Wall,

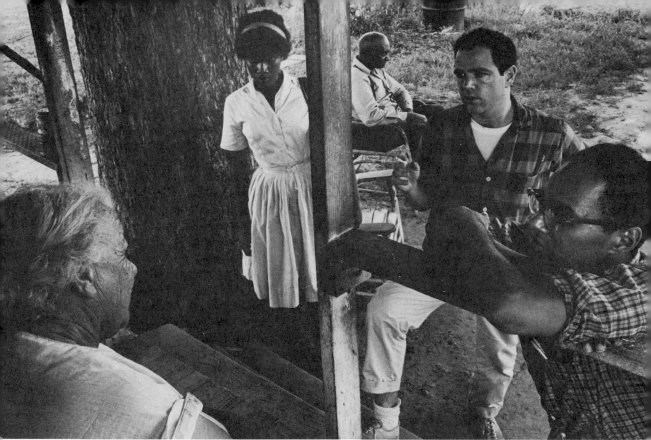

Young civil rights workers of both races urge the older generation to register to vote. These efforts, reinforcing national legislation, proved so successful that Negro registration in Mississippi rose from 22,000 in 1960 to 285,000 in 1970.

> Police cars are the Berlin Wall,
>   In Selma, Alabama.
> We're going to stand here till it falls,
>   till it falls, till it falls,
> We're going to stand here till it falls,
>   In Selma, Alabama.
> Love is the thing that'll make it fall,
>   make it fall, make it fall,
> Love is the thing that'll make it fall,
>   In Selma, Alabama.

In the spirit of militant love, King organized yet another interracial demonstration, this time a march from Selma to the Alabama capital, Montgomery.

When local authorities harassed the marchers and Governor Wallace refused to safeguard them, President Johnson came to their aid in the kind of tandem between King and the chief executive that had proved so effective before. He federalized the Alabama National Guard, and on March 15, 1965, went before Congress to deliver one of the greatest addresses ever made by a President. He compared the struggle at Selma to that at Lexington, stated that equal rights was an issue that "lay bare the secret heart of America," told the legislators that "the real hero of this struggle is the American Negro," and promised to use the full power of his office to wipe out the prejudice he had once seen scar the children he had taught in a small Mexican-American school. Because local officials had calculatedly denied suffrage to Negroes, he was submitting a bill to "establish a simple, uniform standard which cannot be used, however ingenious the effort, to flout the Constitution." "And," the President said emphatically, "we *shall* overcome." That August, Johnson put his signature on the Voting Rights Act, which authorized federal examiners to register qualified voters and suspended devices like literacy tests.

The Voting Rights Act and related measures proved spectacularly successful in expanding Negro suffrage in the South and in encouraging black officeholding. The 1965 act marked the culmination of a series of such reforms—the 1957 law, the 1960 statute, the Twenty-third Amendment, ratified in 1964, which outlawed the poll tax in federal elections. (In 1966, the Supreme Court invalidated the poll tax altogether.) Two months after a federal examiner arrived in Dallas County (Selma), the percentage of voting-age Negroes registered rose from under 10 to 60. By spring, Alabama had added 166,000 Negro registrants, and black registration in Mississippi had increased fourfold. At the end of the decade, the country had fifty Negro mayors, heading municipal governments in cities such as Cleveland, Newark, Gary, and Wichita. In 1966, a year when pundits were accentuating the power of "white backlash" in the North, the Democratic state of Massachusetts, with a population less than 3 percent black, gave a Republican, Edward W. Brooke, III, an overwhelming 61 percent of its ballots. In defeating the patrician former governor Endicott Peabody, Brooke became the first Negro elected to the United States Senate since 1881. Black representatives sat in the state capitol in George Wallace's Montgomery, as well as in Atlanta and Columbia; blacks controlled Greene County, Alabama; and, to the consternation of white supremacists, the mayor of Fayette, Mississippi, was Medgar Evers' brother, Charles.

When on August 6, 1965, President Johnson signed the Voting

Rights Act, liberals of both races felt gratification, and whites took pride in the fact that virtually every piece of national legislation Negroes had requested had been adopted. A period of tranquility loomed, for, as *Time* observed, "there was a growing sentiment that perhaps it was time for the revolution to move off the streets." To be sure, there had been rumblings — rising disaffection among SNCC workers in the South, massive boycotts to terminate de facto school segregation in the North, even moderate-scale riots in Harlem and Rochester in 1964. James Baldwin had warned that "if we do not dare everything, the fulfillment of that prophecy, recreated from the Bible in song by a slave, is upon us: 'God gave Noah the rainbow sign, no more water, the fire next time.'" But that had been in 1963, and since then the movement had achieved much. As the civil rights lawmakers gathered about the President for the bill-signing ceremony at the White House on August 6, there was an air of liberalism triumphant. Five days later the Watts area of Los Angeles burst into flame; up in smoke with it went many of the assumptions and the expectations of the civil rights movement and of American liberalism.

The Fire Next Time

The Watts explosion detonated the first of four successive "long hot summers." Before the burning and looting in Los Angeles ended, thirty-four were dead, nearly four thousand arrested, and property damage had reached at least $35 million. The uprising stunned the evangels of the Great Society because Watts, for all its deprivation, was so much better off than other Negro districts that the anti-poverty program had been aiming at raising the level of black slum dwellers elsewhere to that of Watts. With tidy bungalows along palm-lined streets and nine public swimming pools, the black section of Los Angeles bore little physical resemblance to the typical grimy tenement ghetto. The National Urban League rated Los Angeles first among sixty-eight cities for Negroes, and delegates from Africa and Asia visited the city to study its success in race relations. White reformers, who had been stressing the importance of access to the democratic process, were puzzled that such a holocaust could occur in a place where Negroes boasted a Congressman, two assembly-men, and three city councillors, and held one-quarter of the jobs in the county government. Morever, the riots revealed a depth of anti-white bitterness that in the era of brotherhood anthems few

Burn, baby, burn! When the Watts district of Los Angeles exploded in August 1965, arson and looting devastated many of the edifices of the consumer culture. Plunderers carted merchandise from stores, including a huge Safeway supermarket, then used Molotov cocktails to burn them out.

liberals recognized existed. A governor's commission headed by John McCone concluded, "The existing breach, if allowed to persist, could in time split our society irretrievably. So serious and so explosive is the situation that, unless it is checked, the August riots may seem by comparison to be only a curtain-raiser for what could blow up one day in the future."

Following a series of outbreaks in 1966, notably in Chicago, where young blacks stoned white motorists and sniped at police, the summer of 1967 saw the most intense racial violence of modern times. During five days in July, twenty-six died and some twelve hundred were wounded in Newark, New Jersey. A week later, Detroit erupted in the worst upheaval in half a century; forty-three were killed, two thousand injured, and more than four thousand fires burned out a large part of the country's fifth largest city. After flying in a helicopter over the smoking ruins, Governor George Romney said that Detroit looked like "a city that has been bombed." As in a major war, too, tanks rolled through the streets, and machine guns raked snipers' nests.

The riots raised fundamental doubts about the liberals' policy strategy. Washington had spent more per capita on anti-poverty efforts in Newark than in any other northern metropolis. But Newark had long been a dead-end town. It was the Detroit disaster that was the shocker. The Motor City had a farsighted mayor, supported by Negro voters and responsive to ghetto problems, black officeholders, expensive anti-poverty and urban renewal programs, a high-wage industry, an anti-discriminatory union in Reuther's United Automobile Workers, and the stability indicated by the fact that 45 percent of the Negro families owned their homes. As Benjamin Muse observed, "There was probably more widespread affluence among Negroes in Detroit than in any other American city."

Civil rights activists, committed to the principle of "black and white together," found one emphasis of the 1967 riots especially

The Negro Revolt, 1965-1967

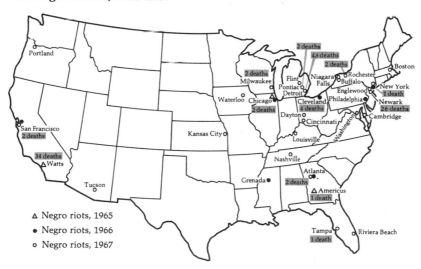

△ Negro riots, 1965
● Negro riots, 1966
○ Negro riots, 1967

Source: Reprinted by permission of The Macmillan Company, New York, and Weidenfeld and Nicolson Limited, London, from *American History Atlas* by Martin Gilbert. Cartography by Peter Kingland. Copyright © 1969 by Martin Gilbert.

perturbing, the cry of "Black Power!" The slogan first captured national attention as the unanticipated consequence of the determination of James Meredith to walk from Memphis to Jackson to inspirit Mississippi Negroes by his example. He got only ten miles across the border of his native state when, on June 6, 1966, he was shot from ambush (but not seriously wounded). On the very next day Martin Luther King and other civil rights leaders arrived in Mississippi to carry on Meredith's pilgrimage. Although Dr. King continued to stress racial integration and nonviolence, even when the marchers were stoned by white mobs and assaulted by the highway police, the young SNCC leader, Stokely Carmichael, sounded a different note when he said, "The only way we gonna stop them from whuppin' us is to take over. We been saying freedom for six years, and we ain't got nothin'. What we gonna start saying now is black power." When fifteen thousand marchers reached Jackson on June 26, many of them were shouting the new slogan, "Black Power!"

Not all who took up the chant agreed about what it meant. "At its inception in June 1966," Allen J. Matusow has noted, "black power was not a systematic doctrine but a cry of rage." By late August 1966 CORE's Floyd McKissick was explaining that "black power" implied self-determination based on six ingredients: "(1) political power; (2) economic power; (3) an improved self-image of the black man himself; (4) the development of young militant leadership; (5) the enforcement of federal laws, the abolition of police brutality; (6) the development of the black consumer bloc." In practice, black power exponents might aim at community control of the school system in northern ghettos or the election of Negro officials in the southern Black Belt. The phrase could convey little more than a plea for capital for aspiring black shopkeepers or the kind of precinct activity that the New York Irish had traditionally pursued through Tammany Hall. But increasingly "black power" acquired two features that were anathema to the civil rights activists—rejection of integration (coupled with hostility to whites) and a willingness to employ violence. Developments in the third world persuaded black nationalists in the United States that they were not a hopelessly outnumbered minority that had to accommodate to whites because they composed only 11 percent of the population. Instead, they concluded that they could afford to take a more militant stance as members of a potentially powerful community that made up two-thirds of the peoples of the earth.

Black leaders in the United States found inspiration in the successful nationhood movements in Africa. In 1960, the "African Year" when sixteen nations won their independence, Muslim luminaries welcomed the black American pilgrim Elijah Muhammad to Mecca. American black nationalists drew sustenance from Frantz Fanon's *Wretched of the Earth*, demanded instruction in Swahili in the public schools, and identified their own struggle with a worldwide process of decolonization. "At the rate things are going here," complained James Baldwin, "all of Africa will be free before we can get a lousy cup of coffee." However much they admired Africans like Nkrumah and Lumumba, most blacks recognized that they were indigenous Americans, and few save those fleeing prosecution expatriated themselves. As LeRoi Jones (who would later change his name to Imamu Amiri Baraka) wrote:

> Africa
> is a foreign place. You are
> as any other sad man here
> american.

Black nationalism, which had achieved a considerable following under Marcus Garvey in the 1920's, had recently gained new converts through the Black Muslims. Founded in 1930 by a mysterious Detroit peddler, W. Fard Muhammad, believed by his disciples to be the incarnation of Allah, The Lost-Found Nation of Islam in the Wilderness of North America flourished under his Messenger, Elijah Poole, who took the name of Elijah Muhammad. The Black Muslims preached that whites were agents of the devil, rejected Christianity as the creed of the slaveholder, denounced both the word "Negro" and Christian surnames as slavemaster's terms, and demanded territory from the United States in compensation for past wrongs in order to create a separate black nation. The order offered Negroes heightened self-esteem as well as the vision of a future society in which they would be ascendant and a hereafter when they would be resurrected first. It made greatest headway among the young black unemployed and the social outcasts of the northern ghettos, but it numbered among its adherents two prominent athletes, Jim Brown and Cassius Clay (Muhammad Ali).

Although in the early 1960's the Black Muslims probably did not have the allegiance of more than fifteen thousand fully involved members (but with several times that number of believers and sympathizers), they exerted a powerful impact on Negro thought despite, or perhaps because of, the fact that many of their doctrines mirrored those of their enemies. Like the Klansmen, they celebrated female chastity and racial immaculacy. "No nation that loves the purity of that nation desires any mixture of blood with any un-alike people," said Elijah Muhammad, adding, "We must use force, if necessary, to stop our people from destroying our race through intermarriages and intermixing." Advocates of a radical restructuring of society, they preached nevertheless a message of self-help, hard work, and sobriety that recalled the teachings of Booker T. Washington and Benjamin Franklin, and they established consumer culture ventures such as department stores, restaurants, and groceries. Outraged by racial discrimination against blacks, they fostered anti-Semitism by denouncing Jews as exploiters and the NAACP as the instrumentality of Zionists, and they preached hatred of whites. "How can Martin Luther, being the minister he claims of God, teach his people to love their enemy, when God Himself said he had set a day to deal with his enemies?" asked Elijah Muhammad. Yet the actions of the Black Muslims rarely matched their fiery rhetoric, and even opponents admired their success with the down-and-out whom the older civil rights organizations had not reached.

None of the Black Muslim leaders excited such adulation among young blacks (and apprehension among whites) as the son of an Omaha Garveyite, Malcolm Little, who, casting off his "slavemaster" final name, became better known as Malcolm X. At a time when other Negro leaders were preaching nonviolence, Malcolm asserted that a Mau Mau was required. He jeered at King's strategy. "You need somebody who is going to fight," he insisted. "You don't need any kneeling in or crawling in." In response to the March on Washington, he asked:

Who ever heard of angry revolutionists all harmonizing "We Shall Overcome . . . Suum Day . . ." while tripping and swaying along arm-in-arm with the very people they were supposed to be angrily revolting against? Who ever heard of angry revolutionists swinging their bare feet together with their oppressors in lily-pad park pools, with gospels and guitars and "I Have a Dream" speeches?

Whites were incensed by his tirades and took special offense at his chortling over President Kennedy's murder, and he came into even sharper conflict with blacks, including Elijah Muhammad, who broke with him in late 1963. On February 21, 1965, at a meeting of his new group, the Organization for Afro-American Unity, at the Audubon Ballroom in New York, three black men armed with a shotgun

Eve Arnold, Magnum

"The shining black prince," Malcolm X, addresses a meeting of Black Muslims. In 1952 he enlisted under Elijah Muhammad, leader of the Nation of Islam, and became, as Louis Lomax observed, the "St. Paul" of the Black Muslim movement. In 1964 he founded a new organization, and on February 21, 1965, at a meeting in Harlem, he was murdered.

and revolvers gunned him down. Conflicting evidence suggests that Malcolm may have been moving toward a more integrationist stance in his final days, but it is as the shining prince of black nationalism that he left his mark, notably in his posthumously published, and widely read, autobiography.

During Malcolm's lifetime, most Negroes, as devout Christians, rejected his teaching, and the civil rights movement followed Dr.

King's star, but increasing numbers of embittered blacks were finding such ideas congenial because they had lost faith in white intentions. In James Baldwin's *Another Country* (1962), one character sneered that "white people go around jerking themselves off with all that jazz about the land of the free and the home of the brave." Baldwin, far from urging the integration of Negroes into white America, judged white civilization unfit to survive. As early as July 1963, Negroes in Cambridge, Maryland, fired shotguns at whites, and that summer too *Dissent* published a symptomatic essay, "The Black Man's Burden: The White Liberal." By the fall of 1963, an element in SNCC was muttering about expelling white volunteers from the organization.

While much of the country marveled at the rapid rate of change in the South, the young civil rights workers experienced deep frustration. Albany, Georgia, and Jackson, Mississippi, both showed that a city with enough jail space could foil peaceful efforts at desegregation. Token compliance proved even more troublesome; in 1967, four hundred thousand more Negro pupils attended all-black schools in the South than in 1954 when the *Brown* decision was handed down. The gains that were made came at a fearful cost — churches and homes bombed, civil rights workers brutally beaten and even murdered. Sometimes local authorities approved or covertly collaborated, as in the sickening slayings of James Chaney, Andrew Goodman, and Michael Schwerner in Mississippi in 1964.

Despite the sacrifices of whites like Goodman and Schwerner, radicalized blacks took a growingly cynical attitude toward white liberals. Whereas most white civil rights enthusiasts viewed the March on Washington as an epiphany, SNCC militants thought of it as an occasion that the Kennedy administration had turned to its political advantage by co-opting the leadership. Blacks in SNCC remembered bitterly that the speech of their leader John Lewis had been censored and that Negroes had been insulted by a humiliating edict closing down liquor stores and bars for the day. At the Democratic national convention in 1964, the SNCC-sponsored Mississippi Freedom Democratic Party scored an important victory over racism, but since the outcome was a compromise, the MFDP claimed that white liberals had sold them out. That summer proved to be the last in which white and black volunteers in the South were able to work together.

A faction of SNCC had been skeptical of the Mississippi Summer Project of 1964 from the outset on the grounds that blacks should carry out the job of registering blacks, and their doubts were reinforced by the coverage the national press gave the project. Julius Lester, a SNCC field secretary who would later publish *Look Out Whitey! Black Power's Gon' Get Your Mama!*, recalled:

The feature stories it wrote usually went something like, "Blop-blop is a blue-eyed blonde from Diamond Junction-on-the-Hudson, New York. She is a twenty-year-old junior at Radcliffe majoring in Oriental metaphysics and its relationship to the quantum theory, when the sun is in Saggitarius [*sic*]. This summer she's living with a Negro family in Fatback, Mississippi who has never heard of the quantum theory, etc., etc., etc." All summer the articles came about white boys and white girls living with poor Negroes in Mississippi. It didn't escape the attention of Negroes that seemingly no one cared about the Negro civil rights workers who have been living and working in Mississippi for the previous three years. Didn't anyone care about Willie Peacock, born and raised on a Mississippi plantation, who couldn't get back to his town because he was an organizer for SNCC and the white people would kill him if he went to see his mother? Apparently not.

Many of the whites in the summer project sympathized with these sentiments, but that failed to heal the breach. Michael Schwerner's young wife said that if the Negro Chaney had been the only one killed there would not have been the national expressions of outrage, and after attending a memorial service for Chaney in Mississippi a Connecticut girl wrote her family:

How the Negro people are able to accept all the abuses of the whites — all the insults and injustices which make me ashamed to be white — and then turn around and say they want to love us, is beyond me. . . . As a white northerner I can get involved whenever I feel like it and run home whenever I get bored or frustrated or scared. I hate the attitude and position of the Northern whites and despise myself when I think that way. Lately I've been feeling homesick and longing for pleasant old Westport and sailing and swimming and my friends. . . . And what is making it worse is that all those damn northerners are thinking of me as a brave hero.

To blacks like Lester and Carmichael such expressions of empathy had become depreciated currency because in the North as well as in the South white America was responding too slowly.

Although the North presented many fewer legal obstacles to the struggle for equality, it also revealed the limitations of familiar approaches. When Martin Luther King attempted to desegregate housing in Chicago by employing the techniques that had been successful in southern towns, he was rebuffed by angry mobs. More than brotherhood marches, or even new statutes, were required to change the de facto pattern of Jim Crow in northern school districts or to undo the legacy of discrimination in slum societies. As Claude Brown wrote of Harlem in *Manchild in the Promised Land,* "There were too many people full of hate and bitterness crowded into a dirty, stinky, uncared-for closet-size section of a great city." To some, Detroit and Los Angeles may have seemed model communities, but Watts suffered from a dreadful transportation system and even worse police-black relations, and Detroit had a nonwhite unemployment rate triple that for whites. Anti-poverty programs raised expectations and dashed them. And though the income of Negroes had been steadily rising, the economic gap between the races remained wide, at the very time when TV commercials were rubbing noses in the disparity between the two worlds.

When blacks in the ghettos erupted, they lashed out at the institutions of the consumer culture that they felt denied them a fair share. Dynamite charges blew up supermarkets, and Molotov cocktails burned out shopping centers. The consumer culture provided adaptable weapons in the form of empty Coca Cola bottles which were filled with gasoline and rags and lit. *"Things go better with coke,"* Lester wrote sardonically. One participant in the Detroit uprising explained: "On Twelfth Street everybody was out, the whole family, Mama, Papa, the kids, it was like an outing. . . . The rebellion —it was all caused by the commercials. I mean you saw all those things you'd never been able to get—go out and get 'em. Men's clothing, furniture, appliances, color TV. All that crummy TV glamour just hanging out there." Many whites were disturbed by the way the noble aspirations of Dr. King were demeaned by the sacking of liquor stores. However, Paul Jacobs observed:

Looting in the cities can be just as much an act of politics as it is a desire for goods. It is a way in which the poor can make a representation to the society, for they have no other kind of representation; it is a way in which the black poor can express their hate of the white world for not giving them their chance to share in the goodies.

Hatred of whites became a cardinal principle of SNCC, which had been founded as a vehicle for interracial amity. When Stokely Carmichael, a twenty-five-year-old West Indian–born graduate of the Bronx High School of Science and Howard University, became chairman of SNCC in May 1966, he set about to establish black control of the organization. He insisted that blacks develop their own indigenous leadership, likened the role of whites in the movement to that of colonial administrators, and suggested that if white liberals wanted to be helpful they should work not in black communities but to eliminate racism in white communities. "If we are to proceed toward true liberation, we must cut ourselves off from white people," said a SNCC document that Carmichael played a prominent part in drafting. "We must form our own institutions, credit unions, co-ops, political parties, write our own histories." Still, in the summer of 1966 SNCC's attitude was not extreme. It credited white volunteers with gaining for Mississippi Negroes the right to vote and to demonstrate and stated, "The reason that whites must be excluded is not that one is anti-white, but because the efforts that one is trying to achieve cannot succeed because whites have an intimidating effect." However, with his lieutenant, H. Rap Brown, Carmichael was soon advancing slogans like "Off the Pigs" and "Kill the Honkies." After Brown, who took over from Carmichael in 1967, urged a black audience in Cambridge, Maryland, to "get your guns" and "burn this town down," fire consumed a large section of the community, and a similar incendiary harangue in Dayton preceded arson in that Ohio city. In 1967 too the Chicago office of SNCC asserted, "We must fill ourselves with hate for all white things." "Black traitors" were to be ostracized and, if necessary, exterminated. The Chicago faction emphasized, "We have to hate and disrupt and destroy and blackmail and lie and steal and become blood-brothers like the Mau-Mau." So far did SNCC depart from its original character that it lobbied against civil rights legislation and dropped the word "nonviolent" from its name.

By the beginning of 1967, the civil rights movement, at its greatest vantage only seventeen months before, lay on its deathbed. In January, President Johnson gave just forty-five words to civil rights in his State of the Union message, and *Harper's* published an article by C. Vann Woodward pronouncing the demise of the cause and finding "disturbing parallels" to the end of Reconstruction. The following month *The New York Times* reported:

The civil rights movement has collapsed in broad areas of the South, and is fighting what seems to be a last-ditch battle for survival in its few remaining spheres of influence. . . . Civil rights headquarters have been abandoned in many communities, and street demonstrations are now only a memory in all except a handful of Southern communities.

Soon members of the black Revolutionary Action Movement would be plotting the murder of Roy Wilkins, leader of the NAACP, and Whitney Young, executive director of the National Urban League. Carmichael enrolled in the paramilitary Black Panther Party, founded in Oakland in 1966, only to be subsequently expelled and denounced as a CIA agent by the party's Minister of Defense Huey P. Newton. Inflamed and badly schismatized by black power tactics, black militants had turned to devouring one another.

However, if in its extreme forms "black power" served to frighten whites and disjoin Negroes, the cultural emphases of black nationalism yielded a richer harvest. The demand for recognition of black culture was sometimes carried to regrettable lengths such as jerry-built curricula and exclusionist dormitories, but it also called attention to shamefully neglected areas of history. As late as 1963 the Fuller Products Company had grossed better than $10 million in the sales of bleaches and hair-straighteners to make Negroes over in the image of whites. Young blacks of the late 1960's, sporting Afros and sometimes dashikis, made clear they did not want to be alchemized into plasticized whites. The rejection of King's teachings had pernicious results, but it was evident in retrospect that white liberals had often been paternalistic and that the efforts of Negroes to suppress rage in the cause of nonviolence had been psychologically disabling. James Brown's song hit spoke for a whole generation, "Say It Loud—I'm Black and I'm Proud."

The current of cultural nationalism also coursed through other communities. Puerto Ricans demanded the incorporation of the history of the island in high school and college syllabi, and the paramilitary Young Lords seemed a duplicate of the Black Panthers. Indians advanced similar claims for attention to their heritage as well as to their economic needs, especially the problem of alienated lands. They wrote books with titles like *Custer Died for Your Sins,* succeeded in banishing offensive symbols such as Dartmouth's "Indian" football mascot, and startled the country by maneuvers such as seizing Alcatraz island, which they proposed to develop as a cultural center. (They offered to buy it from the national government for $24—"in glass beads and red cloth.") "Even the name Indian is not ours," protested a Sioux who was a candidate for the Ph.D. at Berkeley. "It was given to us by some dumb honky who got lost and thought he'd landed in India." In November 1970, two hundred Indians came to Plymouth Rock to proclaim Thanksgiving a day of national mourning. "That damned rock," said a young Mohawk. "I'd like to blow it up. It was the start of everything bad that has happened to the American Indian." But it was Mexican-Americans who, save for the Negroes, mounted the most broad-gauged campaign for recognition.

Although the word was a generation old, "Chicano" first exploded on the national consciousness as a result of strikes of migrant *obreros* in the lettuce fields and vineyards of California organized by Cesar Chavez after the founding of the National Farm Workers Association in 1963. Young militants used the term to signify that Mexican-Americans (or even all Spanish-Americans) were not a hyphenated people defined by their relationship to the Anglo world but constituted a unified nation with its own traditions and cultural identity. While separatists proclaimed the need to build a discrete society for *La Raza,* Chavez chose to work within the system with allies like Robert Kennedy and the national AFL-CIO and to appeal to a liberal public. He made clever use of the political potentialities of a consumption society by encouraging a national boycott that left grapes the forbidden fruit of college dining rooms and, after protracted struggles, he won out over the corporation farmers. The consumer culture figured in a different way in Chicano strategy when protests were mounted against the debased image of the Spanish-American projected by Frito Bandito purloining corn "cheeps" on TV commercials and, in the movie type associated with Leo Carrillo, obligingly holding John Wayne's reins as he doffs his sombrero. The cultural separatist wing of *La Causa* appealed for bilingual education in the public schools, Chicano courses and degree programs in southwestern universities, the use of *Pocho* dialect, community control in cities (where most Hispanic Americans were concentrated), and acceptance of a distinctive value system. As Ysidro Ramon Macias explained, "Rejecting the Puritan ethic of self-improvement above all else, the Chicano . . . recognizes that he is part of a brotherhood, that he has an obligation to work for the betterment of his people in whatever way he can."

While the exponents of brown power, red power, and black power captured the headlines, they met resistance among their own people. Older Mexican-Americans rejected the term "Chicano," while San Antonio's Congressman, Henry B. Gonzales, denounced "hate sheets" that threatened gringos with death and added: "I cannot accept the belief that racism in reverse is the answer for racism and discrimination; I cannot accept the belief that simple, blind, and stupid hatred is an adequate response to simple, blind, and stupid hatred." The overwhelming preponderance of black Americans honored not Eldridge Cleaver but Martin Luther King, and polls showed that integration remained the goal of most of them. There was a growing tide of black nationalism even within groups like the

Beth Bagby, Photofind, S.F.

The embattled Indian. The former site of the federal penitentiary on Alcatraz Island in San Francisco Bay is seized for "Indian land." In an ironic commentary on the consumer culture, the Indian stands by an "Apache" Chevrolet.

In the midst of a National Farm Workers Association strike (*huelga*), Cesar Chavez, union leader and the most prominent spokesman for the Chicanos, talks to Robert F. Kennedy, an early and steadfast supporter of the movement. Kennedy called Chavez "one of the heroic figures of our time."

SCLC. But prominent leaders, including Wilkins, Young, and A. Philip Randolph, reaffirmed their commitment to integration and announced, "We repudiate any strategies of violence, reprisal or vigilantism, and we condemn both rioting and the demagoguery that feeds it." Wilkins castigated black power as a "reverse Mississippi," "the father of hatred and the mother of violence," and Negro strategists pointed out that blacks had been the main victims of riots and that, as a minority group, they needed white allies. Bayard Rustin scolded the militants as conservatives masquerading as revolutionaries and as defeatists too indolent to tackle the difficult job of uniting with white workingmen. Above all, Martin Luther King, who said that "black supremacy would be equally as evil as white supremacy," continued to serve as a bridge between the races and the best hope for achieving an integrated society.

On April 4, 1968, in Memphis, that hope was tragically extinguished. Dr. King had come to the Tennessee city to lend support to a strike of predominantly black garbage workers. Criticized for staying at an expensive Holiday Inn, he checked into the cinderblock Lorraine Motel; at dusk on a balcony of that motel he fell mortally wounded, the victim of a shot fired by a disreputable drifter and ex-convict, James Earl Ray, another homicidal American loner. Within minutes after the news was flashed over transistor radios, angry blacks were on the streets. Rioters burned out twenty blocks of West Madison Street in Chicago, where Mayor Richard J. Daley ordered police, should another outbreak occur, to "shoot to kill" arsonists, "shoot to maim" looters. In Cincinnati a gang of young Negroes grabbed a white graduate student from his car and stabbed him to death; in Jacksonville white teen-agers wantonly shot a black cyclist. The worst pillaging took place in Washington, D.C., where more than seven hundred fires created an incendiary spectacle not seen since the British ignited the capital in 1814.

In the smoking ruins of the gutted cities little remained of the sanguine expectations of liberalism. At his desk in the White House, President Johnson could hear the sounds of racial turmoil that reached within two blocks of the executive mansion. He had come to office dedicated to building a national consensus, but from the steps of the Capitol a machinegun emplacement eyed the approaches to Congress. His allies in the civil rights movement, Negro and white, were appalled by the bloodshed and sickened by the looting. "Martin's memory is being desecrated," said Roy Wilkins. King's death was all but unbearable. On an Indianapolis street corner, where he broke the news to a crowd of Negroes, Robert Kennedy told the grief-stricken gathering that he understood how they felt, for he too had lost a brother at the hands of a white assassin, and, as the weeping subsided, he quoted Aeschylus: "Even in our sleep, pain which cannot forget falls drop by drop upon the heart until in despair, against our own will, comes wisdom through the awful grace of God."

The Violent Society

One month before the assassination of Dr. King and the ensuing commotion, the National Advisory Commission on Civil Disorders issued a 250,000-word report that became a critical document in the national self-examination into the causes of race riots and the pre-

After the assassination of Martin Luther King, Coretta King, her right hand clasped to her father-
less son's, leads a march in Memphis where the Negro leader was slain.
In the light coat is King's successor as head of the Southern Christian Leadership
Conference, the Reverend Ralph Abernathy, and next to him, the
Reverend Andrew Young. Behind King's widow stands the Reverend Jesse Jackson,
who, like Young, would be a spokesman for reforms within the Democratic Party.

valence of violence. The report gave no comfort to those who placed
the chief onus for the disturbances on black conspirators. "What
white Americans have never fully understood—but what the Negro
can never forget—is that white society is deeply implicated in the
ghetto," the commission stated. "White institutions created it, white
institutions maintain it, and white society condones it."

The commission, which recommended vigorous measures to heal
the festering sores of the slums, expressed alarm that the predominant
reaction of the white community had been to acquire more armament.
"In several cities," the commission found, "the principal official
response has been to train and equip the police with more sophisticated weapons." In Newark and other communities, white vigilante

bands sprang up, and the deputy editor of *The Economist*, having been told by Washingtonians that they had acquired rifles, was reminded of a passage in Gibbon about another capital: "At such a time . . . when none could trust their lives or properties to the impotence of the law, the powerful citizens were armed for safety, or offence, against the domestic enemies whom they feared or hated." Unless the spiral of neglect, outbreak, and retaliation was broken, the commission warned, it "could quite conceivably lead to a kind of urban apartheid with semi-martial law in many cities." Liberals hoped that a different lesson would be learned from the explosions. Federal Communications Commissioner Nicholas Johnson said, "A riot is somebody talking. A riot is a man crying out, 'Listen to me, mister. There's something I've been trying to tell you and you're not listening.'"

Congress acknowledged the crisis in the ghettos ambiguously. It struck out punitively, imposing stringent penalties for crossing state lines with the intent of inciting disorders, action (according to its sponsor) aimed at firebrands such as Stokely Carmichael, a "freelance insurrectionist." However, Congress attached this provision to a statute that marked another significant leap forward. The "open housing" law of 1968 banned discrimination in the sale of some 80 percent of United States housing. Furthermore, Congress approved an ambitious housing and urban development bill to expedite slum clearance and riot insurance.

Although the new legislation suggested an enduring commitment to civil rights, liberals no longer basked in the euphoria of the March on Washington era. Civil rights romantics had learned with innocent surprise that not only whites harbored prejudices or were guilty of cupidity, and they were unsure of how to cope with demands not for equity but for revenge. Confidence faltered when it became evident that the community action programs were fraught with difficulty and that meliorism would not suffice to overcome decades of neglect in the slums.

In 1965 the Johnson government circulated a memorandum, known after its author as "the Moynihan report," which angered blacks and depressed whites. In *Beyond the Melting Pot*, Daniel P. Moynihan and Nathan Glazer had argued that white racism was not the total explanation of the Negro's plight and that civil rights legislation could not expect to solve one critical problem—the pathology of black family structure and communal life. Moynihan's government study, *The Negro Family*, expounded further on how the "deterioration of the fabric of Negro society" resulted from the "deterioration of the Negro family." Although the matriarchal family structure of lower-class blacks had earlier been dissected in the classic monograph by the Negro sociologist E. Franklin Frazier and although Moynihan was sympathetic to civil rights goals, his appraisal vexed black leaders because it was understood to imply that until Negroes corrected their faults they could not claim equal treatment. White liberals were no less dismayed, for the report indicated that, in the very year of the Watts riots, "the Negro problem" was more intractable than they had thought.

Moynihan and other analysts traced the infirmity of the family structure of lower-class Negroes both to desertion by fathers and to illegitimacy, but the latter attracted the greater attention. In 1961, according to a federal government estimate, 22 percent of black infants were born out of wedlock (some 1.8 million), compared to 2.5 percent of white infants, and in 1970 the illegitimacy rate for young black girls was said to be running almost ten times that among whites, figures some blacks disputed. In "Love Child," the number 1 record of late 1968, Diana Ross and the Supremes sang of the shame of being raised with the stigma of illegitimacy and of having been abandoned by one's father. As a result, President Johnson pointed out in a speech at Howard University, "Only a minority— less than half—of all Negro children reach the age of 18 having lived all their lives with both of their parents." Blacks responded hotly that since middle-class Negro families proved as stable as white families, the predicament lay not with the shortcomings of blacks but in the failure of a white-dominated society to provide the economic opportunities that would permit Negro fathers to build secure households. Many whites, however, found it disconcerting that despite the rise in black family income since 1950, the proportion of nonwhite families headed by women had risen from 18 percent in that year to 29 percent in 1971.

If some were disheartened by the obduracy of the black ghetto, others saw in the riots and in the assassinations mortifying confirmation of their conviction that the United States was a peculiarly violent society. After the assassination of King, Senator Frank Church cried, "We are steeped in violence. It is the curse of the land." A numbing series of murders had taken the lives of so many leaders that it seemed, as Bruce Jay Friedman wrote, that "a new, Jack Rubyesque chord of absurdity has been struck in the land." "God, we even got to the point where we compared the style of the funerals," observed

David Halberstam. "We could make a calendar of the decade by marking where we were at the hours of those violent deaths." The casualty lists numbered too all those nameless unfortunates who were killed or mugged or raped. From 1960 to 1968 "offenses against persons" more than doubled, and in the large cities apartment dwellers immured themselves in buildings scrutinized by closed-circuit television and guarded by doormen and platoons of vigilantes. Yet neither violent crime nor the wave of assassinations could persuade Congress, cowed by the National Rifle Association, to enact an effective gun control law, although the gun-homicide rate in the United States was forty times that of the British Isles, the Netherlands, and Japan.

The consumer economy and popular culture thrived on the merchandising of violence. Mod audiences made a box office smash of Arthur Penn's movie *Bonnie and Clyde,* which transmogrified brutal killers into unconscious folk revolutionaries and tarried lovingly over the riddling of Bonnie's body by machine-gun bullets. The appeal of Jimi Hendrix owed much to acid rock's pulverizing volume and pitiless rhythm; Janis Joplin was described as a "volatile vial of nitroglycerine"; Bob Dylan, noted one critic, "tends to snarl his songs rather than sing them." Children were schooled in violence from their first shoot-out with toy guns to comic book gougings and mayhem. In 1966 New York's leading toy emporium announced, "On Valentine's Day nothing says 'I Love You' more heartily than a Valentine from F. A. O. Schwarz Children's World," the lead-in for a child's Valentine that unfolded to reveal a "swept-wing jet fighter . . . machine guns blazing." In the six weeks following one assassination, a survey discovered that at the times when most children were watching, TV showed 372 threats or acts of violence including 84 killings in eighty-five and a half hours. "Television," observed Alfred Hitchcock, "has brought back murder into the home where it belongs." TV cameras made a household event of the death of their favorite son, John F. Kennedy, who had won the presidency as a result of televised debates; born on the tube, he would die on the tube. And his slayer, who had but a moment's exposure to a national video audience, in turn met death in the camera's eye. Moreover, the technique of the "instant replay," indispensable for conveying "the violent world of Sam Huff," was first employed in televising a football game in December 1963, after being proved useful a few weeks earlier in filming the murder of Lee Oswald by Jack Ruby.

To be sure, the United States in the 1960's held no monopoly on

Characteristics of Major Types of Civil Strife in the United States, June 1963–May 1968[a]

Type of event	Number of events identified	Estimated number of participants	Reported number of casualties	Reported arrests
Civil rights demonstrations	369	1,117,600	389	15,379
Antiwar demonstrations	104	680,000	400	3,258
Student protests on campus issues	91	102,035	122	1,914
Anti–school integration demonstrations	24	34,720	0	164
Segregationist clashes and counter-demonstrations	54	31,200	163	643
Negro riots and disturbances	239	(200,000)	8,133	49,607
White terrorism against Negroes and rights workers	213	(2,000)	112	97

Source. Hugh Davis Graham and Ted Robert Gurr, *Violence in America: Historical and Comparative Perspectives*, a report submitted to the National Commission on the Causes and Prevention of Violence (New York: Bantam Books, 1969), p. 576.

[a] The data in the table include many estimates, all imprecise. Figures in parentheses are especially tentative.

violence, and some of the national lamentation about it reflected little more than the affinity of intellectuals for self-flagellation. As Richard Hofstadter observed, "The United States, even with its considerable record of violence, appears not as some mutant monster among the peoples of the world but rather as a full-fledged and somewhat boisterous member of the fellowship of human frailty." The death rate from civil strife in the United States ran well below the figures for the rest of the world, and violence in America did not begin to approximate that of Stalinist Russia or the more recent fratricide in Indonesia or Nigeria or Colombia. Furthermore, despite manifestations of violence, the United States enjoyed remarkable political stability. Nor was violence a new phenomenon in this country. Civil strife was actually greater in late-nineteenth-century America than in the 1960's, and, as Richard Maxwell Brown pointed out, "Violence has formed a seamless web with the most positive episodes in American history."

Nonetheless, contemporary America offered grounds enough for concern. A task force report by Hugh Davis Graham and Ted Robert Gurr for the National Commission on the Causes and Prevention of Violence concluded that, compared with other nations, "acts of collective violence by private citizens in the United States in the last 20 years have been extraordinarily numerous" and "in numbers of political assassinations, riots, politically relevant armed group attacks, and demonstrations, the United States since 1948 has been among the half-dozen most tumultuous nations in the world." While in the past violence in America had been inflicted by the powerful, in the 1960's it assumed a much more volatile mode in action by dissidents against persons or symbols of authority. And most ominous of all, month by month the violence of the Vietnam War was imperiling public safety by leading more and more Americans to question the very legitimacy of the national government.

By 1968 the conflict in Southeast Asia had become the longest war in the country's history, one of the bloodiest, and certainly the least popular. To be sure, most Americans, however much they disliked the slaughter, could not bring themselves to accept defeat. In the fall of 1965, two out of every three students supported the administration's war policy, and even in 1968, contrary to the impression given by the press, those under thirty were more hawkish than those over fifty. But to a significant minority, especially on campuses, United States intervention with all its consequences—the death and maiming of young Americans, the napalm-scarred bodies of Vietnamese children, the pulverization of villages, and the defoliation of the countryside—seemed a gross betrayal of humane, democratic values. The Vietnamese carnage, said Senator Fulbright, was "poisoning and brutalizing our domestic life. . . . The 'Great Society' has become the sick society."

To a rapidly radicalized segment of students, the hostilities demonstrated that American liberalism led inevitably to war and repression. It had been liberal Presidents who had lofted the bomb-laden planes and liberal advisers like the Rhodes Scholar Dean Rusk and ex-Harvard and MIT teachers such as McGeorge Bundy, Robert McNamara, and Walt Rostow who had egged them on. More than this, the very rationale for the commitment in Southeast Asia derived from the Wilson-FDR tradition of globalism. In truth, well before 1968 most liberals stoutly opposed the war. But radicals jeered that when orthodox methods had clearly failed (who, they asked, could any longer believe in the democratic process after Johnson's election as a peace candidate in 1964 and his subsequent betrayal?) liberals flinched from joining them in bolder acts.

Although most of the young continued to work within the system, ever-growing numbers, soured on liberalism and incensed by the war, felt alienated from the government and indeed from American society. The conflict, radicals charged, exposed the real priorities of Kennedy-Johnson progressivism, for social welfare programs were slashed in order to fund armaments. When General Hershey authorized draft boards to punish dissidents, when President Johnson dismissed thoughtful critics as "nervous Nellies," when disc jockeys seemed never to tire of spinning records in tribute to the Green Berets, it appeared to the radicals that "Amerika" had become a repressive, war-mad nation, even, in the words of James Baldwin, "the fourth Reich." A few young Americans chose prison to war, many more renounced their native land for Canada or, like Yossarian on his rubber raft in *Catch-22*, Sweden.

By word and by deed, numerous foes of the bloodletting in Vietnam and of the social order embraced violence. In an unconscious parody of the Wilsonian rhetoric of a war to end all wars, the Progressive Labor faction of Students for a Democratic Society (SDS) claimed that "to get rid of the gun it is necessary to take up the gun." H. Rap Brown, who called violence "as American as cherry pie," suggested shooting the President and his wife. Underground newspapers printed instructions on how to make Molotov cocktails, hailed motorcycle gangs such as Hell's Angels because they terrorized the Establishment, and apotheosized assassins at home and abroad. Eldridge Cleaver, who felt remorse for his deeds, wrote, "I became a rapist. . . . It seemed to me that the act of rape was an insurrectionary act. It delighted me that I was defying and trampling upon the white man's law, upon his system of values, and that I was defiling his women." In a destructive acting-out of the animus toward men in the women's liberation movement, one flower child organized SCUM (the Society for Cutting Up Men) and took the first step toward creating "a swinging groovy, out-of-sight female world" by shooting Andy Warhol, an improbable symbol of male supremacy.

Abusive discourse contravened the most elementary canons of fair play and civility, and slogans became truncheons. When war opponents created such a din that defenders of the administration's Asia policy could not be heard at a Harvard meeting, one professor exculpated them by claiming the right to shout down speakers as a fundamental civil liberty, and at the March on the Pentagon in 1967, a sign read, "Where is Oswald now that we need him?" Paul Goodman, one of the gurus of the young, regretted that instead of "*Satyagraha,* soul force, we have seen plenty of hate" in which "the confronted are *not* taken as human beings, but as pigs." Staughton Lynd, a dedicated agitator against the war, declared, "I am ashamed of a movement which calls policemen pigs. . . . I feel deeply troubled by the attitude that, since we are right, we can take away civil liberties from others which we insist on for ourselves." "Don't Trust Anyone Over Thirty" was lauded as preternatural wisdom, but Saul Bellow remarked pointedly, "In the way the young declare the obsolescence of the old, there's a kind of totalitarian cruelty, like Hitler's attitude toward Jews, or Stalin's toward kulaks."

The disposition of the young to resort to force took vivid form in April 1968, the tumultuous month of the riots following the murder of Dr. King, when militants at Columbia University seized five buildings, held three officials captive for twenty-six hours, took over the president's office, which they befouled, and, after a six-day occupation had been ended by club-swinging police, compelled the university to shut down. During that spring and over the next two years, Columbia was beset by a series of outrages including the deliberate destruction of one professor's notes on years of historical research, the burning of library books, the disruption of lectures, and the roughing-up of faculty and staff. The paroxysm in Manhattan had a forerunner in the Free Speech Movement led by Mario Savio at Berkeley in 1964, but while the melees in California were followed by a period of relatively small-scale outbreaks, the Columbia eruptions proved to be harbingers of explosions that would rock hundreds of other campuses. On some, black rebels were the main agents, notably at Cornell, where blacks brandishing guns wrung concessions from an administration that for months had seemed to be motivated by a death wish. At Cornell and at Yale, prominent faculty found it necessary to evacuate their families. Violence did not always stop with the terrorizing of students and teachers or the vandalizing of libraries. Bombs killed a faculty club custodian at the University of California, Santa Barbara, blinded a secretary at Pomona, and snuffed out a student's life at the University of Wisconsin.

As the placards at this demonstration in Harvard Yard indicate, two of the big demands at Harvard and on other campuses were a termination of Reserve Officers' Training Corps (ROTC) programs and a halt to the expansion of the university into the neighborhood.

The uprisings had contradictory results. They led to the creation of new institutions of academic governance with greater student representation, the abatement of parietal rules and *in loco parentis,* more intensive recruitment from minority groups, a diminution of the military presence on campus, and keener social responsibility on the part of administrators and trustees. But they also left a patrimony of bitterness and dangerously speeded up the politicization of the academic world. Furthermore, they had the ironic consequence of strengthening the political power of the right, which was able to exploit the disgust that many Americans felt with faculty and administrators wanting in minimal self-respect and students who cried out against repression but practiced intimidation. The combination of Berkeley and Watts cemented Governor Ronald Reagan's tenure in California, and the Columbia and Cornell fracases helped raise the Conservatives, under James Buckley, to prominence in New York.

Analysts attributed much of the campus unrest to the climate of affluence. Years before the first disturbances, David Potter had written: "Today the economy of abundance can afford to maintain a substantial proportion of the population in nonproductive status, and it assigns this role, sometimes against their will, to its younger and its elder members. It protracts the years of schooling, and it defers responsibilities for an unusually long span." Bruno Bettelheim found it "unnatural to keep a young person in dependence for some 20 years attending school" and traced the spirit of rebelliousness to "the waiting for things — for the real life to come." Affluence made possible not only a huge increase in the numbers of those consigned to the period of waiting but also the rise of the multiversity. Only two institutions had more than twenty thousand students in 1941; thirty-nine did in 1969. Although this expansion was the envy of other countries, it made the university more impersonal and bureaucratic and added to the undergraduate ranks many who had small interest in intellectual pursuits. Even the radicals recognized that they were a different breed. The Port Huron statement of the SDS, mostly written by Tom Hayden, began: "We are the people of this generation, bred in at least modest comfort, housed now in universities, looking uncomfortably to the world we inherit."

Still, if the campus tumult derived from general socioeconomic circumstances, it also ensued from particular political challenges, responses, and perceptions. Much of the resentment was aroused by specific issues, notably the Vietnam War and the draft, and the university made a vulnerable target, even when its complicity in military affairs was minor. The campus served as a base, too, for sorties on behalf of black nationalism. Shrewdly, the confrontationists sensed the recruitment value of provoking counterviolence by agents of the establishment, who proved all too willing to fall into the trap. As John W. Gardner wrote, "The student with an inclination toward violent or coercive action and the policeman with a taste for brutality are waiting for each other." But it was neither the pursuit of such exemplary goals as an end to war and racism nor the tactics of confrontation that gave the campus outbreaks their special character, but rather the way in which both were mingled with new-fashioned attitudes toward institutions and mores. The aroma of pot in the corridors of occupied buildings, the up-against-the-wall obscenity, the rhetoric of generational war, the guerrilla theater, the casual sex, the anti-privacy etiquette of communal toilets, the organization of "free universities" and "counter courses," the rebellion against grades, the emphasis on participatory democracy and "doing your own thing," all suggested the way in which the "counter culture" had permeated student activism, and this inter-relationship between violence-prone radicalism and the icon-breaking counter culture (and the indignant opposition it incited) imbued the late 1960's with their distinctive spirit.

The Greening of America

In the mid-1960's, during the same years that violence was rocking the country, there erupted that remarkable concatenation of phenomena that social analysts have denominated the "counter culture." Upper middle class white youth, and some of their elders, advanced ideas and behaved in ways that ran "counter" to much that was cherished not only by Eisenhower's America but by Kennedy-Johnson liberalism — affluence, economic growth, technology, and the institutions and value systems associated with the Protestant ethic of self-denial and sexual repression and the more modern premises of the consumer culture and the meritocracy. The situation, wrote Paul Goodman, was "very like 1510, when Luther went to Rome, the eve of the Reformation. There is everywhere protest, revaluation, attack on the Establishment."

Although the counter culture of the 1960's bore resemblances to earlier enthusiasms on the Continent like the Bohemianism of the Left Bank and the Burschenschaften of nineteenth-century Germany, no precursor in the United States ever permeated so broadly or so intensively. To be sure, the counter culture was foreshadowed by the "revolution in morals" and the critique of Puritanism and materialism in America of the 1920's and, more recently, by the beats in the 1950's. But to produce a movement of this particular nature demanded the special circumstances of the 'sixties — the emergence of a generation of young people endowed with a superabundance of worldly goods, locked into an educational system for two decades or more, cordoned off in multiversities, roiled by the draft and the Vietnam War, troubled by its prospects in a world that seemed increasingly bureaucratized and technologically driven.

The counter culture raised a challenge not just to entrenched institutions but to the whole way of thinking that had prevailed in the West since the eighteenth century. "Nothing less is required than the subversion of the scientific world view with its entrenched commitment to an egocentric and cerebral mode of consciousness," wrote Theodore Roszak. "In its place, there must be a new culture in which the non-intellective capacities of personality—those capacities that take fire from visionary splendor and the experiences of human communion—become the arbiters of the true, the good and the beautiful."

The counter culture rejected systematized knowledge, Aristotelian logic, and, at times, even reason itself. The few who bothered to consider the claims of traditional processes of cognition intimated that rules of evidence were snares devised by the power structure to trap the unwary, or advanced the curious notion of "radical truth," or touted the superior insights gained from intuition. "The sensibility epitomized by the Enlightenment," concluded the historian J. Meredith Neil in 1971, "has now become so embattled that it is very possible that its requiem has already been sung."

In spurning Western emphases on rationality, some explored the ancient mysteries of Asian or African creeds or found solace in the occult. Skinheaded, orange-garmented young people debouched on downtown streets chanting the Hare Krishna. Students pored over Tarot cards or perused the I Ching or shared Roszak's appreciation of shamanism, and in the Age of Aquarius, astrology won legions of devotees. Others became preoccupied with witchcraft and demonology, and even soap operas like "Dark Shadows" and movies such as *Rosemary's Baby* gave the devil his due. Women's lib publicists viewed the Salem witches as kindred political deviationists, and in Chicago coeds claimed to have put a curse on professors. In New York the Civil Liberties Union came to the aid of an organization that had been denied a permit to hold a witch-in in Central Park on Halloween, and when the city relented, the coven hailed the reversal as "the first Civil Rights victory for true witches ever won in modern times."

Frequently the interest in mysticism and the quest for communion found expression not in new cults but within the Christian church. The young, who had once scorned theological questions, ruminated about the death of God and the theology of hope and sought artless communication through "speaking in tongues." At church services Bach yielded to rock, when, to the accompaniment of electric guitars, mod liturgies made "a joyful noise unto the Lord." As William L. O'Neill observed:

Hare Krishna. On a street in San Francisco, a young Buddhist chants while bemused spectators look on. Buddhist teachings affected a small number of writers like Allen Ginsberg in the 1950's, but they did not make a mark on the public consciousness until the 1960's, when young converts, their heads shaven, appeared on city sidewalks.

American religious life was probably more fertile and diverse in the sixties than at any time since the nineteenth century. If all this did not quite amount to an age of faith, it certainly seemed so compared with the 1950's which now looked like merely an age of churchgoing. The old religious revival declined; religion itself did not. The established churches became more secular, unchurched youths more religious. Anti-communism excepted, the 1950's was a time when rational, scientific, and secular ideas dominated. In the sixties romantic, millennial, chiliastic, and utopian impulses undermined them.

Some of the same impulses, as well as the desire to escape the rigidities of a work-oriented society and to expand sense perception, led millions of Americans to experiment with drugs. "Tune in, turn on, drop out," urged the advance man of the drug culture, Timothy Leary, whom one writer called "the Johnny Appleseed of LSD." Frequently, drugs were associated with performing or listening to rock music, especially after San Francisco's light and sound shows gave birth to the "acid rock" of groups such as Big Brother and the Holding Company billeted in strobe-lit bivouacs like Bill Graham's Fillmore West. It required little special knowledge to understand that "Magic Carpet Ride" referred to a drug trip or that the Beatles' "Lucy in the Sky with Diamonds" spelled out LSD. Drugs penetrated deeply, too, into the literary world. Ken Kesey's *One Flew Over the Cuckoo's Nest* was partly written under the influence of LSD, and the undergraduate cult of Hermann Hesse got official sanction when Dr. Leary recommended: "Before your LSD session, read *Siddhartha* and *Steppenwolf*. The last part of *Steppenwolf* is a priceless manual." While psychedelic potions like LSD spread slowly, marijuana became increasingly commonplace at high school and college parties, and the question of whether it was harmful produced one of the less rewarding debates of modern times, in large part because it was not really about pharmacological properties but about clashing life styles. Drug use, said the Yippie leader, Jerry Rubin, "signifies the total end of the Protestant ethic: screw work, we want to know ourselves. But of course the goal is to free oneself from American society's sick notion of work, success, reward, and status and to find and establish oneself through one's own discipline, hard work, and introspection."

"Leaving the straight life behind," many people sought alternative ways of living. "Crash pads" accommodated nomads in the big cities, while communes in the New England hills or the deserts of the Southwest attempted to create enclaves hived off from the bustle of bourgeois striving. In the mid-1960's, thousands of "hippies" set up house in the Haight-Ashbury district of San Francisco or in New York's East Village. The hippie communes were but one of a number of free-form institutions aimed at breaking the barriers that isolated people from one another, themes of Paul Simon's "The Sound of Silence" and "The Dangling Conversation." To learn how to communicate and to become reacquainted with themselves, people joined encounter and sensitivity groups and spent weekends at Esalen. Rock concerts offered another way of achieving communion, for, as Benjamin DeMott wrote, "the rock experience at its most intense is an intimation of engulfment and merger, a route to a flowing, ego-transcending oneness."

The hegira of the young to Hashbury heightened concern about a widening "generation gap." The older generation was bewildered by the ragamuffin army of disheveled, unkempt "potheads" who dropped out of school and drifted from pad to pad with no visible ambition or direction, cadging handouts in Harvard Square or at Sather Gate, and the discontented young felt alienated from the conformity of their "uptight" parents. By the middle of the decade, more than half of the nation was under the critical age of thirty, and many had a keen sense of belonging to their own subculture. "From Los Angeles on down the California coast, this is an era of age segregation," wrote Tom Wolfe in "The Pump House Gang." "Surfers, not to mention rock and roll kids and the hot rodders . . . don't merely hang around together. They establish whole little societies for themselves." Apartment houses like the Sheri Plaza in Hollywood were restricted to tenants between twenty and thirty. Sometimes the generation gap took curious forms. In Duluth, the Zimmermans, a Jewish merchant family, encouraged their son's musical talent, purchased a piano on which he began to pick out songs, and supported him in college. But hardly had Robert arrived at the University of Minnesota than he insisted that he had no parents, was partly Indian, had lived a bleak childhood bouncing between foster homes and orphanages—and that his name was Bob Dylan.

Probably no dispute between the generations provoked more angry words than one that might have been thought to be trivial—hair. It gave a name to a raucous, impertinent "tribal love-rock musical," and law journals soberly discussed "Long Hair and Judicial Clippers: Can Welfare Officials Constitutionally Require Applicants to Trim Their Locks to Enhance Their Employability?" Fathers who could not be certain whether a passing pedestrian was a boy or a girl were profoundly shaken, and their demeanor was not improved by awareness that there was an irrational element in this response. For the young, long hair expressed withdrawal from the crewcut, repressed world of their parents, at least at the outset before it became a vogue. Some of the young took a covert pleasure in the discomfort they were causing; "We are the people our parents warned us against," read a sentence on a subway billboard.

The "now generation" judged little in man's history usable or even worthy of notice. The "now culture" pronounced the past irrelevant, observed Hazel W. Hertzberg in *Social Education,* because it appeared to be altogether different. "We seem to be producing a new generation every three or four years characterized by a sense of estrangement from the generations above and below it," she noted, and "in the now culture's intense focus on youth there is little conception of a life cycle which includes the very young or the 'mature' or 'old.'" Inevitably, many of the young turned away from the study of history to such ostensibly "time-free" disciplines as sociology. Artists often had a similar temporal perception. When an experimental music group referred to a "historical piece," it meant a 1965 opus. John Barth's *The Sot-Weed Factor* burlesqued the historical method, and Norman Mailer wrote, "We're in a time that's divorced from the past. There's utterly no tradition anymore."

The counter culture fostered a rebellion against almost every accepted personage and institution, some of them of ancient lineage. Neither army officers nor college administrators nor party officials nor cardinals could any longer count on the traditional patterns of deference. In Vietnam some soldiers refused assignments, and at stateside training camps underground newspapers and cabarets flourished. Even the professional competence of the military came into question. To accept the advice of the Pentagon in Southeast Asia, said Senator George McGovern, would be like asking "General Custer how to fight Indians." On college campuses the "disestablishmentarians" set up free universities that gave podiums to "existentialists without portfolio." So volatile did party identification become that in 1968 most of the electorate split tickets. Protestant churchmen wrestled with such disturbing works as Thomas J. J. Altizer's *The Gospel of Christian Atheism,* while the Catholic hierarchy confronted priests who revolted against celibacy and nuns who wore short skirts.

Some Americans departed so far from traditional beliefs that they advocated a heresy, which, far more than free love or Bolshevism, ran counter to the national creed—no growth. To stabilize population, young people wore buttons saying "Stop at 2" and suggested that the Mother of the Year was one who kept her IUD in place and adopted a child. An expanding gross national product "may, after a certain level, serve more as a sign of social deterioration than improvement," Professor Richard A. Falk of Princeton told a congressional committee. "If the United States were to double its GNP, I would think it would be a much less livable society than it is today."

Only a "no-growth economy," it was reasoned, could save man from making the earth uninhabitable by polluting his environment. John Gardner gave warning that Americans would get "richer and richer in filthier communities until we reach a final state of affluent misery—Croesus on a garbage heap." To achieve a high GNP, industry gouged the earth for raw materials, spewed its wastes into the air, and defiled rivers with its excrement. The achievements of the consumer culture seemed mixed boons. Shopping centers defaced the countryside; automobiles, the pride of the land of Henry Ford, were denounced, in Lewis Mumford's words, as "insolent chariots"; and detergents, previously acclaimed as household miracles, proved to be lethal contaminators. "The good earth, once golden, has begun to run out, as any neglected field, and we are discovering, a bit late, the consequences of fouling the only nest we have," wrote E. B. White. "To grow the perfect lawn we destroy the perfect bird. To kill the ultimate gnat we load the liver of the final fish. Even our national bird fights for survival and lays eggs that don't hatch."

Critics of the doctrine of economic growth cast an especially skeptical eye at twentieth-century technology. Some deprecated the sacrifice of technological efficiency to consumer culture trumpery — gorgeously colored telephones that did not yield a dial tone, rakishly styled automobiles that turned out to be death cars. Others objected that technological gains had unanticipated and unwelcome social consequences, as when life-saving medical advances helped bring on the population crisis. But most broadly articulated of all was the complaint that technology was dehumanizing. The protagonist of Saul Bellow's *Herzog* concluded that the modern world had drastically altered

what it means to be a man. In a city. In a century. In a mass. Transformed by science. Under organized power. Subject to tremendous controls. In a condition caused by mechanization. After the late failure of radical hopes. In a society that was no community and devalued the person. Owing to the multiplied power of numbers which made the self negligible. Which spent military billions against foreign enemies but would not pay for order at home. Which permitted savagery and barbarism in its own great cities.

Creative artists, radicals, and expositors of the counter culture all remonstrated against the imperatives of technology. In John Barth's *Giles Goat-Boy,* computers warred for control of the world, and in Stanley Kubrick's film *2001: A Space Odyssey,* Hal, the menacing computer, was lobotomized, to the applause of cinema audiences. Malcontents at Berkeley alleged that students at their multiversity were shuffled like IBM cards by administrators under Clark Kerr, who was essentially a systems manager. Radicals charged, too, that systems managers in Washington were sending men to their death in Vietnam at the behest of Pentagon computers. "The time has come," Mario Savio cried, "to put our bodies on the machine and to stop it."

Tom Wicker of *The New York Times*, who wrote that "we now have to turn away from the gods of production," warned:

Already these modern Americans submit to being sealed into gigantic toothpaste tubes and hurled through the skies at incredible speeds, literally peas in a pod, and already, for reasons no one can explain, the speed is being whipped up to supersonic levels. Already creatures of shrinking dimensions drive to work on swarming eight-lane highways, where metal monsters reduce human drivers to dollsize; and someday, if electronics prosper as predicted, the highway itself will drive the cars. Everywhere man turns, from the classroom to the supermarket to Mission Control, he is being dwarfed by his own handiwork—hapless and driven in his zip-code world, among his reactors and data banks, breathing his canned or polluted air and eating his frozen foods, even his physical security dependent—he is assured —upon the reaction time and judgment of an ABM computer. How typical and pathetic it was that when the great power failure of 1965 deprived urban Americans for a night of their greatest technological prop, human nature instinctively asserted itself in the darkness, and more children were conceived in and out of wedlock than on any other single occasion of which we have records on our ubiquitous punch cards.

In the 1960's the consumer culture underwent the most relentless criticism it had ever experienced. The value system of the consumer society, detractors asserted, was anti-human, a way of "making things nobody needs so they can afford to buy things nobody needs." FCC Commissioner Nicholas Johnson, who offered the heretical counsel that "you can easily ignore most of the products in your supermarket," denounced the view "that the primary measure of an individual's worth is his consumption of products, his sexuality, his measuring up to ideals found in packages mass-produced and distributed by corporate America." *Hair* mocked the consumer who pasted King Korn trading stamps in books one by one, and hippies rebelled against the "moneytheism" of an acquisitive society.

By rejecting the bourgeois catechism, the counter culture rediscovered the pleasures of ritual and rejoiced in festivals, from the "happenings" at the end of the 1950's to "love-ins" on the grass of Golden Gate Park to the grand *fête champêtre* at Woodstock. Allen Ginsberg wrote *How to Make a March / Spectacle*, and Harvey Cox began his book *A Feast of Fools* by quoting W. H. Auden:

> I know nothing, except what everyone knows—
> if there when Grace dances, I should dance.

To theologians like Cox, the recovery of festivity had a religious connotation, for Western culture, they believed, had robbed man of the sense of wonder and the joy of playfulness. "In losing our capacity for play and in devaluing our imaginations, we have in a very important sense lost ourselves," explained Marcia Cavell:

The death of God in our world is a death of our capacity to experience the world in a godlike way: with the full release of our creative powers, valuing our experience of people and of things for their own sakes, with that sense of ease and timelessness we have when for the moment we are set free from anxiety and self-preoccupation.

In August 1969, at Max Yasgur's farm in the Catskills, the counter culture reached a joyous climax. The Woodstock Music and Art Fair convened not in Woodstock, the Hudson Valley village that was Dylan's retreat, but at Bethel, which became a magnet for from 300,000 to 400,000 young people, "moving steadily down Route 17-B, like a busy day on the Ho Chi Minh Trail." The ostensible attraction was the music: Joan Baez, Jimi Hendrix, Crosby, Stills, Nash & Young, Country Joe & the Fish. But more remarked was the ready availability of sex and drugs. Unmolested by the police, hawkers called out "acid, mesc, hash," and for three days, sprawled on blankets in a sea of mud, merged in oceanic communion, the counter culture generation blew its mind. "No one in this country in this century had ever seen a 'society' so free of repression," wrote Andrew Kopkind. "Everyone swam nude in the lake, balling was easier than getting breakfast, and the 'pigs' just smiled and passed out the oats."

Much of the country considered the promiscuity and nudity of the Woodstock Nation peculiar to hippiedom, but in truth new attitudes toward sex antedated the rise of the counter culture and were by no means confined to the young. The postwar years witnessed a veritable revolution in public acceptance of forms of sexual depiction and vocabulary that had hitherto been proscribed. In 1948 Norman Mailer had been compelled to resort to the euphemism "fuggin" in *The Naked and the Dead,* and as late as 1953 Otto Preminger's movie *The Moon Is Blue* was denied a seal of approval because it employed the word "virgin." But by 1966, the bitchy language Elizabeth Taylor spoke in the film of Edward Albee's *Who's Afraid of Virginia Woolf?* was becoming conventional, and downtown movie houses would soon be screening fetishism, autoeroticism, and fellatio. In 1969 *Time* commented that "writers bandy four-letter words as if they had just completed a deep-immersion Berlitz course in

At the Woodstock Music and Art Fair in August 1969, some of the revelers strip down to let joy be unconfined. To admirers like Charles Reich, the Woodstock Nation showed the potentiality of the extended family. But scoffers thought it was little more than "Fort Lauderdale with marijuana and LSD." One promoter, captivated by the commercial aspects, said, "I wish I could rent Utah."

Anglo-Saxon" and observed that "today, the corner drugstore sells Fanny Hill along with Fannie Farmer."

The turning point had come in 1959, and once again the Warren Court stood front stage center. In voiding the censorship of *Lady Chatterley's Lover*, the Court, in the words of Mr. Justice Stewart, maintained that the First Amendment "protects advocacy of the opinion that adultery may sometimes be proper, no less than advocacy of socialism or the single tax." The film was based on D. H. Lawrence's novel of anal eroticism, published in its unexpurgated form by Grove Press that same year. Heartened by the Court's latitudinarianism, Grove Press in 1961 brought out Henry Miller's *Tropic of Cancer,* another under-the-counter item; it sold two and a half million copies and also won the benison of the Supreme Court. The Court did indicate there were still some constraints when in 1966 it sustained the conviction of Ralph Ginzburg, publisher of *Eros,* for promoting the circulation of his magazine in a pandering fashion; he had even applied for a mail permit from Intercourse, Pennsylvania. But the much-criticized Ginzburg decision proved to be an exception rather than a guideline.

In the 1960's almost every barrier came down. That bourgeois standby, *Cosmopolitan,* ran an article on "Low-Fidelity Wives" and printed instructions for its female readers on how to achieve an orgasm. Manufacturers turned out dolls with sexual organs, and in Jeane-Claude van Itallie's *America Hurrah* giant dolls fornicated on stage. "Billy the Kid" and "Jean Harlow" simulated an act of oral intercourse before audiences for *The Beard,* while in *Dionysus 69* a troupe invited members of the audience to disrobe and take part in a mock orgy. Some did. Bacchantic rock stars like Janis Joplin sang with a raw, sexual urgency, and at a Miami concert Jim Morrison of the Doors enticed female "groupies" by exposing himself. In 1970 the Federal Commission on Obscenity and Pornography brought the new era to a culmination by recommending wiping out all legal restrictions on the acquisition by adults of hard-core pornography.

The falling away of taboos on expression appeared to be accompanied by a radical change in sexual activity. Affluence and mobility encouraged experimentation and slackened the hold of folkways, and technology contributed the Pill, which virtually eliminated the fear of conception in premarital intercourse. Colleges made birth control devices available to single coeds; young unmarried mothers cited the model of Mia Farrow; and *Select,* a periodical for swingers, claimed a readership of one hundred thousand among a swiftly growing movement that was said to number perhaps 2 million middle-class citizens engaged in transient trysts. Sex, wrote David Riesman, had become America's last frontier. In a society where many groped for identity, "sex provides a kind of defense against the threat of total apathy," and the other-directed person "looks to it for reassurance that he is alive."

Scholars contributed to the fostering of this "erotic renaissance," and the modified value system in turn made possible a warmer welcome for advanced ideas. By the 1960's there was a more hospitable audience for the precepts of earlier sages like Wilhelm Reich and Henry Miller as well as for such latter-day evangelists as Norman O. Brown, who in *Life Against Death* celebrated the "resurrection of the body" and "erotic exuberance." In 1956 Dr. William H. Masters and Mrs. Virginia E. Johnson of Washington University in St. Louis began an eleven-year study in which they observed nearly seven hundred men and women masturbating and copulating and measured the intensity of their orgasms. "The '60's," Dr. Masters declared, "will be called the decade of orgasmic preoccupation." It was widely thought that the Pill accounted for the permutation in mood, but Edward Grossman reasoned that it was rather the altered perceptions that made the Pill possible. "The grants to set up the labs would not have been awarded, the talent to synthesize the chemistry would not have been collected, if there had not been an agreement . . . too deep to be put into words," he wrote, "a state of mind, in which sex would be separated — as far as science, will and conscience could separate it — from duty, pain and fear, from everything but pleasure."

Yet sexual liberation seems not to have been as seismic a development as some thought, or to have had all the consequences its earlier exponents claimed for it. Dr. Kinsey's successor as director of the Institute for Sex Research at Indiana University explained:

People talk more freely about sex nowadays, and young people are far more tolerant and permissive regarding sex. But we don't think there have been changes that we could truly call revolutionary. Our studies indicate that there has just been a continuation of pre-existing trends, rather than any sudden revolutionary changes. For instance, premarital intercourse has increased, but it hasn't shot up in any inflationary way; it has been on the rise ever since the turn of the century.

Moreover, the Dionysian spirit proved less emancipating than the oracles had foretold. The campus liaisons of the "unmarried marrieds," noted one report, were "familiar, predictable and slightly boring," and a student of group sex found that swingers "have now gone from Puritanism into promiscuity without passing through sensuality." So much did libertinism resemble babbittry that in the summer of 1970 in Chicago 184 couples congregated at the First National Swingers Convention. As the French critic Raoul de Roussy de Sales once remarked, "America appears to be the only country in the world where love is a national problem."

Furthermore, the uninhibited displays in book stores and on movie marquees obscured the fact that there was no national concordance on sexual mores. An opinion survey in 1969 learned that 76 percent of respondents wanted pornography outlawed, and a minority report of the President's commission protested that hardcore materials had "an eroding effect on society, on public morality, on respect for human worth, on attitudes toward family love, on culture." Reverend Dr. Billy James Hargis, leader of the Christian Crusade, charged that the new morality was "part of a gigantic conspiracy to bring down America from within." "I don't want any kid under 12 to hear about lesbians, homosexuals, and sexual intercourse," the evangelist said. "They should be concerned with tops, yo-yos and hide and seek." The division in the country revealed, as *Newsweek* wrote, "a society that has lost its consensus on such crucial issues as premarital sex and clerical celibacy, marriage, birth control and sex education; a society that cannot agree on standards of conduct, language and manners."

The lost consensus on sexual roles derived not just from the counter culture but also from the women's liberation movement, which combined new emancipationist convictions with old-fashioned reformism. In much of its program, "women's lib" requested simply the accomplishment of traditional and unexceptionable feminist objectives such as equality of opportunity. Spokesmen pointed out that for all the gains that had been achieved women comprised a smaller percentage of the college population in the 1950's than in the 1920's. Moreover, those with degrees earned only half of the median income of men with the same training. Although most women college graduates found ready employment, they continued to be consigned, disproportionately, to occupations defined as "female" like clerical work, and they encountered difficulty in rising to higher grades, in part because they had to assume nearly full responsibility for child-rearing. To put women on a par with men in the job market, feminists asked for statutes barring discrimination on the basis of sex and for the funding of child-care centers, which would make it possible for mothers to hold full-time positions and compete for advancement on an equal basis with men.

However, women's lib partisans pushed well beyond familiar goals like wage parity to demand an end to the exploitation of women as sexual objects. Opposed to having their roles defined exclusively by gender, they had been dismayed by the treatment accorded to their sex in the protest movements. When they joined their male

The placard reflects the growing bitterness in the women's liberation movement, which emerged in the mid-1960's. Such demonstrations, widely reported in the media, spread the message that women were an "oppressed class."

comrades in taking over buildings at Columbia, they were peremptorily assigned the food preparation chores, a practice in keeping with Che Guevara's manual, which pointed out that women could be useful to a guerrilla movement as cooks. Even more exasperating had been Stokely Carmichael's dictum: "The position of women in our movement should be prone." They resented, too, the way in which the consumer culture presented women, and they struck back by scribbling graffiti on offending billboards, writing letters against TV commercials, picketing the Miss America contest in Atlantic City, and burning their bras. Above all, they insisted on sovereignty over their own bodies. They regarded rape as a political act (and to cope with assailants took courses in karate) and campaigned strenuously for reform of anti-abortion laws.

Yet the latter-day sisters attracted attention less because they voiced these demands than because they threatened to rend the social fabric by destroying such stabilizing institutions as marriage, the home, and the nuclear family. Ti-Grace Atkinson staged a sit-in at a city marriage license bureau, and Susan Brownmiller remarked that it was "hard to find a woman's liberationist who is not in some way disaffected by the sound of wedding bells." Some of the feminists were frankly hostile to men. Refusing any longer to be "breeders," they spurned sexual intercourse, denounced the penis as a weapon of male imperialism, and insisted women could find fulfillment by concentrating their attention on the true center of sexual gratification, the clitoris. Anne Koedt discounted "the myth of the vaginal orgasm," Kate Millett announced she was bisexual, and Roxanne Dunbar advocated masturbation as preferable to the tyranny of heterosexuality. Nanette Rainone, producer of a liberationist radio program, said that a housewife's life was "nothingness, total nothingness," and even more moderate leaders like Betty Friedan, founder of the National Organization of Women (NOW), expressed contempt for homemaking. In her runaway best seller, *The Feminine Mystique,* she called the American home a "comfortable concentration camp."

Such conceptions encountered resistance from women as well as from men. Many wives found satisfaction in child nurture and conjugality, and a Gallup poll in 1970 revealed that two-thirds of American women thought they were fairly treated. Feminists were forced to concede that they spoke for only a minority (and these largely upper class). They attributed this to the fact that women had been brainwashed, and they sought through consciousness-raising sessions ("Do you pretend to have an orgasm?") to produce a sense of grievance. "There are few Noras in contemporary society," commented Alice Rossi, "because women have deluded themselves that a doll's house is large enough to find complete fulfillment within it." However, one woman writer protested: "You might have to go back to the Children's Crusade in 1212 A.D. to find as unfortunate and fatuous an attempt at manipulated hysteria as the Women's Liberation movement. . . . Where do they get the lunatic idea that women had rather work for a boss than stay home and run their own domain?" Other observers pointed out that women already wielded tremendous power. They owned most of the country's economic resources, spent most of its money, outlived men, and, as a tradition from the old comic strip of Maggie and Jiggs in "Bringing Up

Father" to TV programs like "The Donna Reed Show" suggested, were perceived to be the decision makers in the household. Dr. Benjamin Spock, not normally thought of as a spokesman for reaction, said with measured imagery: "If you liberate women in America one more inch, man will be completely subjugated."

Still, however ill regarded some of their contentions may have been, the women liberationists began to have an impact. In the same year that Betty Friedan's book appeared, the Civil Rights Act of 1964 forbade discrimination in employment on the basis of sex, and in 1970 the House of Representatives gave emphatic approval to the Equal Rights Amendment, which had been incarcerated in committee for nearly half a century. The long-term shift of women into the employment market made further headway too. Women took almost two-thirds of the new jobs in the 1960's, so that by 1970 over 43 percent of female adults were employed (up from 34 percent in 1950, and almost twice the figure for 1920), and the proportion of married women in the labor force was greater even than in Sweden. A number of states legalized abortion, and in New York during 1970 one child was legally aborted for every two born alive. The liberationists claimed, too, that women no longer experienced guilt over not meeting the consumer culture's expectations. The movement, asserted Mrs. Friedan, "has stopped women from feeling like freaks for not having that orgiastic bliss while waxing the floor."

Women's lib and the transit of wives from home to office had a more subtle influence in the blending of sexual roles. Social scientists concluded that when women added a second income to the family they could not continue to assume all their usual household obligations and husbands had to share in "female" tasks. This "increased overlapping of sexual spheres," William H. Chafe has noted, "represented perhaps the most significant by-product of the growth in women's economic activity." "Today we may be on the verge of a new phase in American family history," wrote the sociologist Robert Blood. "The classic differences between masculinity and femininity are disappearing as both sexes in the adult generation take on the same roles in the labor market."

The distinction between "male" and "female" blurred. Robert Oldenwald, who coined the word "unisex," wrote of *The Disappearing Sexes,* and Faubion Bowers insisted, "The time is long overdue to face what is by now a truism—the psychically androgynous nature of man." The media showed a morbid fascination with transsexuals like Christine Jorgensen and Gore Vidal's *Myra Brecken-*

ridge. Couples wore identical clothing, and when the *National Observer* assayed trends for the 1970's, it forecast, "The look will be natural, the sex indeterminate." While some women had long been wearing "mannish" garb (in the early 1930's Marlene Dietrich had shocked Hollywood by strolling Vine Street in slacks), the change in male plumage was startling. The "Peacock Revolution" saw shirts and ties take on the colors of the rainbow, and even the gray flannel suit set switched to epicene Nehru jackets. Leaders of the women's liberation movement noted with approval that gorgeously garmented, long-maned males were rejecting "the masculine mystique." "How can any man live up to that Ernest Hemingway *machismo* concept of masculinity?" Betty Friedan asked.

The new-type professional athlete indicated that *machismo* was no longer a universal ideal. The life style of the athletic performer had traditionally been that of the tobacco-spitting, no-quarter-given plug-uglies of John McGraw or St. Louis' spikes-flying, belly-sliding Gas House Gang. Now Yogi Berra huckstered hair sprays for men, Ron Swoboda wore beads, and Spider Lockhart donned a blue crushed velvet suit from Neiman-Marcus. The athlete was reflecting a change in the definition of "male," which by the mid-1960's made possible a thriving business in men's beauty salons. "The embrace of the hairnet, the whisper of the hair dryer, the provocative aroma of hair spray, all are now as routine as shaving lotion for thousands of men who only a few years ago would have recoiled in disgust at such vanities," noted *The New York Times*. Joe Pepitone grew bangs, and Jim Bouton curried a Clara Bow fringe. In a tribute to "The Frankly Beautiful New Young Gentleman," *Harper's Bazaar* admired its hero's "long, extremely tossable hair," which he brushed "with absorption," and reported that he "chooses his shampoos with the gravity of a connoisseur, and scents himself with enormous care."

This mitigation of sex differences sometimes took the form of an open avowal of homosexuality. In the 1960's the "closet queens" came out of hiding. Male homosexuals who had formerly feared ostracism or blackmail identified themselves publicly with groups like the Mattachine Society and the Pink Panthers, and the University of Minnesota was only one of a number of institutions that accorded recognition to a student homosexual association. In June 1970, militant homosexuals organized in the Gay Liberation Front marched boldly from Sheridan Square in Greenwich Village through the heart of midtown Manhattan to the Sheep Meadow in Central Park where they held a "gay-in." Flaunting brilliantly hued silk banners, the paraders, whose ranks extended fifteen blocks long, chanted, "Say it loud, gay is proud." Movie audiences hailed the tragicomic *The Boys in the Band,* which centered on a homosexual gathering, and John Schlesinger's less explicit *Midnight Cowboy.* To some, these occurrences represented a stride toward freedom for another persecuted group. Others, however, deplored the flight from heterosexuality said to be occasioned by growing female aggressiveness and regretted that the attenuation of sexual distinctions further accelerated the homogenization of American society.

The counter culture and radical politics frequently merged, and one convention in Philadelphia, called to write a new Constitution, united the gay liberation movement and the Black Panthers, Weathermen and Yippies. Conservatives preferred to treat the two phenomena as one, and, in truth, the two movements did find occasion to

Lesbians take part in a gay liberation demonstration in New York City. At times members of both sexes participated in homosexual protests and in campus homosexual organizations. Americans were familiarized with lesbianism by movies like *The Fox* and *The Killing of Sister George.*

Leonard Freed, Magnum

join forces against "the power structure." "Make love, not war" harmonized the aims of peace and sexual freedom, and in *On Liberation,* Herbert Marcuse wrote, "The new society will be one where the hatred of the young bursts into laughter and song, mixing the barricade and the dance floor, love play and heroism."

But frequently the two tendencies diverged or even conflicted. Peter and Brigitte Berger wrote of the counter culture: "The rhetoric is Rousseauean rather than Jacobin, the imagery of salvation is intensely bucolic, the troops of the revolution are not the toiling masses of the Marxist prophecy but naked children of nature dancing to the tune of primitive drums." There was a deep-seated contradiction between the privatism of doing one's own thing (especially by tripping) and a commitment to political engagement. After observing the Woodstock festival, a *Newsweek* reporter conceded that the hippie population was far larger than anyone had thought but added, "They form a new constituency whose views go beyond the anger that produces picket lines and reform drives in Congress to the turned-on indifference that sets them questing after tangerine trees and marmalade skies."

Black nationalists, radicals, and other advocates of social change found increasingly that they had essentially different perceptions from many in the counter culture. Eldridge Cleaver denounced drugs as a way of avoiding confrontation with the system and disowned the counter culture as "harmful to our cause," and the Viet Cong foreign minister, Madame Nguyen Thi Binh, complained that antiwar students in America were protracting United States involvement in Vietnam by antagonizing their elders with their bizarre life style. When homosexuals at Columbia requested a gay lounge similar to the exclusively black lounge, the Students' Afro-American Society belittled them as "social misfits," adding that blacks "don't have time to wallow in the mud with people who cannot decide if they are men or women." While the counter culture spurned work-oriented America, women's lib believed that a woman's place was in the office. It was shocked, too, by the way rock degraded women, especially the debased groupies. The name of Dr. Spock, a hero of the peace movement, was hissed at women's lib gatherings. If the counter culture often parted company with radicalism, conservatism showed some of its effects. Reporters were surprised to observe a conservative youth convention attended by long-haired, bearded delegates, and a survey learned that a good number of pot smokers backed Barry Goldwater and William Buckley.

Far more than it was ready to acknowledge, the counter culture blended with the consumer culture. While bemoaning the materialism of suburban America, the young rebels acquired expensive stereo sets, amplified the sound of electric guitars, and drove Triumphs decorated with psychedelic butterflies. Psychedelicatessens catered to the needs of drug addicts; the forty-six-store chain, Jeans West, profited from the sale of hippie clothing; and other merchants retailed accessories like love beads and Benjamin Franklin eyeglasses. One participant in the Woodstock festival, Tom Smucker, recalled:

We awoke to hear the U.S. Committee to Aid the National Liberation Front announcing over their loudspeaker: "Get Your Dry Che Guevara T-Shirts. Only Two Dollars."

The T-shirts had cost them, so I heard, about 5 or 10 per cent of that maybe, and were silk-screened earlier in New York.

"The slogan of Dr. Leary's medicine show, 'Tune in, turn on, drop out,' is fundamentally the same make-it lyric as 'There's a Ford in your future,'" wrote Frederic Morton. "Yesterday the young marrieds from Yonkers motored to the country club in their de luxe hardtop for a cocktail with prestigious friends. Today they split for the Electric Circus in their (American Motors) Rebel to freak out with fellow swingers." Arlo Guthrie's "Alice's Restaurant" may have impaled bourgeois America, but the actual Alice, who provided the locale for the song and the movie, wound up commissioning a chain of Alice's Restaurants.

The ideology of the counter culture, set forth in works such as Charles Reich's *The Greening of America* and Theodore Roszak's *The Making of a Counter Culture,* drew heavy flak. Some intellectuals were offended by the soggy ratiocination. One reviewer called Reich's best seller "a colloidal suspension of William Buckley, William Blake and Herbert Marcuse in pure applesauce." Others pointed out that in celebrating the natural, these writers were demeaning man. Reich, said Samuel McCracken, was "a humanist at odds with humanity" who held "stricter standards for man than for nature, blaming him for the bomb, excusing her of such peccadilloes as anthrax and the typhoon." Most of all, critics decried the counter culture's rejection of technology because it made no allowance for technologically dependent necessities such as modern surgery and the requirement of disciplined training to achieve surgical skills. Moreover, the counter culture was "profoundly parasitic" and intrinsically elitist. As Kenneth Keniston observed:

Historically, the Byronic romanticism characteristic of Roszak's counter culture has arisen only among the privileged classes of prosperous societies. People who *really* live in organic, tribal, symbiotic and shamanistic cultures generally can't wait to escape into the world of affluence, science and technology. It is only *after* technology has triumphed, and only for those whose lives are glutted with the goodies it provides, that the young can begin to look wistfully at the delights of shamanism.

Even intellectuals who were well disposed toward the counter culture were perturbed by its more egregious manifestations. Paul Goodman, who had done so much to encourage the young to question shibboleths, recoiled from the realization that some had carried antinomianism to the point of denying that there were any professional standards at all. Toward the end of the decade he wrote:

Suddenly I realized that they did not really believe that there was a nature of things. Somehow all functions could be reduced to interpersonal relations and power. There was no knowledge, but only the sociology of knowledge. They had so well learned that physical and sociological research is subsidized and conducted for the benefit of the ruling class that they did not believe there was such a thing as the simple truth. To be required to learn something was a trap by which the young were put down and co-opted. Then I knew that I could not get through to them. I had imagined that the world-wide student protest had to do with changing political and moral institutions, to which I was sympathetic, but I now saw that we had to do with a religious crisis of the magnitude of the Reformation in the fifteen hundreds, when not only all institutions but all learning had been corrupted by the Whore of Babylon.

Much more important than the second thoughts of intellectuals was the repugnance millions of their countrymen felt to the counter culture and the radical persuasion. The most bitter resistance to both the counter culture and the New Left came not from Wall Street but from the "hardhats." A 1969 study by Daniel Yankelovich found that the generation gap between the young and their parents was not nearly so wide as the gulf separating the attitudes of college students from young people not in college. While suburban youth was queuing up to see *The Graduate,* the sons of factory hands crowded drive-in movies to cheer John Wayne in *The Green Berets.* Campus *sans culottes* scoffed at split-level respectability, but workers who had scrimped to achieve lower middle class status and the appurtenances of the consumer culture felt a fierce protectiveness about their achievements. Admirers of the Vince Lombardi regimen of hard work and discipline, they were driven to fury by the sight of indolent hippies strung out on drugs and panhandling for their next fix. They were even more incensed by the burning of the American flag. To show their own colors, they pasted decals of Old Glory on their car windows alongside "Support Your Local Police." The tremors of the 1960's, especially war, violence, and the counter culture, were wrenching the axes of controversy away from the old simplicities of economic interest and aligning them instead with the disturbing new polarities of cultural politics.

Crescendo: The 1968 Campaign

The 1968 presidential campaign encapsulated the strains of cultural politics and violence of the mid-1960's, and raised profound concern over the viability of the American political system. As early as the summer of 1967, the cover of *United States News and World Report* had asked: "IS THE U.S. ABLE TO GOVERN ITSELF?" By February 1968, Robert F. Kennedy, noting the turn of the young from public commitment to "lives of disengagement and despair," was writing, "We seem to fulfill the vision of Yeats: 'Things fall apart, the center cannot hold; / mere anarchy is loosed upon the world.'" In the following month James Reston commented, "The main crisis is not Vietnam itself, or in the cities, but in the feeling that the political system for dealing with these things has broken down."

In 1968, the sores that had been rapidly spreading on the body politic abcessed and burst. The war in Vietnam, the breeding place of much of the infection, refused to respond to poultices, and during those twelve months 16,511 more Americans died, leaving critics of the bloodletting in a feverish rage. Unnerving, too, was the sickness at home, for race riots came unseasonably early and hard upon them the mayhem at Columbia and other universities. Only two men had the ears of both whites and blacks, both campus and ghetto, and before 1968 was half over, Martin Luther King and Robert Kennedy would be gone. By the time the fever had run its course, a President had been toppled, a presidential candidate murdered, a party convention stained with blood.

The new year had hardly begun when on January 3, 1968, Eugene McCarthy, a fervent critic of the administration's Vietnam policy, announced that he was launching an insurrection to wrest the Democratic presidential nomination from his party's chieftain, Lyndon Johnson. As the first move in this patently quixotic endeavor, he would enter New Hampshire's primary. Few took the gambit seriously. Almost everyone understood that it was impossible to deny renomination to a President who wanted to run again, let alone to an incumbent who had been elected by the biggest margin in modern history. Furthermore, McCarthy had never cut much of a figure in the Senate. Liberal colleagues complained that he was frequently missing when the going got rough, and no important legislation bore his name. To be sure, the Vietnam War had eroded much of Johnson's popularity. But Johnson appeared to have a firm grip on the party apparatus, and reports from Saigon were encouraging. On January 17, exactly two weeks after McCarthy's announcement, the President boasted that "the enemy had been defeated in battle after battle" and "the number of South Vietnamese living in areas under government protection tonight has grown by more than a million since January of last year." Small wonder that early polls gave McCarthy as little as 8 percent of the primary ballots in New Hampshire.

On the final day of January, the situation changed dramatically. Exploiting the distracted mood of the Tet (lunar new year) festivities, the Viet Cong attacked innumerable villages, sixty-four district towns, over four-fifths of the provincial capitals, a dozen United States bases, and, brazenly, the American embassy in Saigon. A bazooka blew a hole in the embassy compound, and for several hours V.C. commandos put the custody of this "impregnable" bastion in doubt. The Pentagon claimed that the enemy had suffered a devastating defeat, and in a military sense it had, for it failed to capture a single capital and it sustained terrible losses. But that was beside the point. By demonstrating that it could invade the very grounds of the United States embassy, the Viet Cong shattered confidence in the Johnson administration's claims. As McCarthy said to a gathering in Manchester, New Hampshire: "Only a few months ago we were told sixty-five percent of the population was secure. Now we know that even the American Embassy is not secure."

The Tet offensive gave a big lift to McCarthy's campaign because from the outset his strength lay in opposition to the war. He cheered anti-militarist elements by stating that, if elected, he would go to the Pentagon: "I would at least try to get diplomatic representation there." McCarthy offered himself, too, as the champion of a "new politics." "Whatever is morally necessary must be made politically possible," he declared.

As the evangel of a renascence that would foster spiritual values and innovative ideas in American politics, McCarthy had an unusual background and exceptional attributes. A devout Catholic, he had spent a nine-month novitiate at a monastery and had contemplated taking the vows of a monk. Subsequently he had taught at a Catholic college. He was close to Robert Lowell, read difficult poets like Wallace Stevens and Charles Peguy, and wrote passable verse himself. Appropriately, his favorite writer was the author of *Utopia,* Sir Thomas More. McCarthy salted his speeches and conversation with literary and historical imagery. In an address to a political gathering he alluded to the Punic Wars, and on another occasion he told a British reporter, "One of the things I object to about the

On the night of March 21, 1968, Senator Eugene McCarthy of Minnesota celebrates with young admirers his strong showing in the New Hampshire presidential primary. College students played an important role in his campaign against Lyndon Johnson, which culminated in the President's withdrawal from the race less than three weeks later.

Charles Harbutt, Magnum, from *Crisis in America,* published by Ridge Press and Holt, Rinehart and Winston

Kennedys is that they are trying to turn the Presidency into the Wars of the Roses." If introspection led him to self-doubt, it was not because he overvalued his rivals. In 1960 he had said, only half in jest, that he thought of making a run for the White House because "I'm twice as liberal as Hubert Humphrey, and twice as intelligent as Stuart Symington, and twice as Catholic as Jack Kennedy."

McCarthy's wit and learning, conjoined with his stand against the war and his moral preachments, attracted legions of young volunteers. To New Hampshire flocked over ten thousand students from more than a hundred campuses. Sensitive to the fact that counter culture styles of hair and dress might alienate New Englanders, they resolved to be "Neat and Clean for Gene." Hair trimmed, shirts laundered, chinos pressed, they went door to door in towns from Keene to Berlin, politely soliciting votes for the Senator. "What is happening," reported the Washington correspondent Mary McGrory, "is that violet-eyed damsels from Smith are pinning McCarthy buttons on tattooed mill-workers, and Ph.D.s from Cornell, shaven and shorn for world peace, are deferentially bowing to middle-aged Manchester housewives and importuning them to consider a change of Commander-in-Chief." To appeal to the Granite State's hundred thousand people of French-Canadian descent, an Amherst student translated McCarthy pamphlets into French, and two score sons of Eli went house-to-house in Berlin's factory districts speaking Yale French and distributing leaflets with titles like "*McCarthy au sujet de Vietnam*" and "*McCarthy parle des citoyens âgés*." Buoyed by the reaction to the Tet raids, reinforced by the student volunteers, McCarthy's campaign, once a forlorn gesture, reached formidable proportions. On March 12, New Hampshire Democrats gave McCarthy 42.4 percent to LBJ's 49.5 percent, and when Republican write-ins were added, Johnson's margin in "hawkish" New Hampshire fell to less than 1 percent.

The tidings from New Hampshire reached a President already sore beset. Two weeks earlier the military command in Saigon had sent him a request for 206,000 more United States troops, and even this huge increment could not assure success. When Johnson called for a full-scale policy review, he was told that victory was unachievable save at unacceptable risks. Staggered by this intelligence, he realized that if he decided to push for negotiations, the fact that he was a candidate for reelection meant any action he took would be discounted as a campaign ploy. Moreover, he could not help but recognize that he had become a divisive force in a dangerously fragmented nation. There were political considerations too. Advisers warned the President that McCarthy would trounce him in the April 2 primary in Wisconsin, where eight thousand students were in the field, fanning out from the University of Wisconsin in Dane County. One of LBJ's deputies reported, "We sent a man into Dane County to recruit for Johnson and all we've heard from him since is a few faint beeps, like the last radio signals from the beach of the Bay of Pigs." Even more ominously, four days after the New Hampshire primary Robert Kennedy had entered the race.

On the night of March 31, Johnson sounded retreat. At the end of a nationally televised address in which he announced initiatives toward a Vietnam settlement, the President raised his right arm as a signal to his wife that he would add a postcript. "I have concluded that I should not permit the Presidency to become involved in the partisan divisions that are developing in this political year," he said. "Accordingly, I shall not seek, and I will not accept, the nomination of my party for another term as your President." The McCarthy forces were jubilant. It had taken less than three months to bring down a President. Two days later, as predicted, McCarthy shellacked Johnson in the Wisconsin primary.

However, for McCarthy, the fruits of victory had soured. He had eliminated Johnson only to confront a new challenge from Robert Kennedy (as well as from the President's surrogate, Hubert Humphrey). Critics of the junior Senator from New York who had earlier taunted him for hesitating to oppose the President (placards read "BOBBY KENNEDY: HAWK, DOVE, OR CHICKEN?") reviled him as a ruthless opportunist for waiting until McCarthy's courage had shown the way. Yet if his belated candidacy incensed McCarthy's acolytes, Kennedy had a constituency that McCarthy could not reach — among admirers who viewed him as a prince of the blood, among white workingmen tempted by George Wallace, in black ghettos and Mexican-American *barrios,* in Appalachian hamlets and on Indian reservations. Such coalitions carried Kennedy to a string of primary victories. But in Oregon on May 28 McCarthy snapped the skein by chalking up the first defeat for a Kennedy after twenty-seven consecutive triumphs. The duel headed toward the moment of truth in the California primary on June 4 and Robert Kennedy toward his appointment at Samarra.

Kennedy's campaign had aroused ecstasy bordering on the dangerous, and in California the frenzy reached a peak. In Los Angeles, especially in areas of Mexican-American concentration, his motorcade could barely get through the crowded streets loud with cries of "Viva Kennedy." For weeks, clutching mobs had bloodied his hands, had stripped him of laces and cuff links; here even his shoes were removed. McCarthy hoped to counter this appeal by getting the same intense effort from young people he had elicited in New Hampshire. His daughter Mary told California students, "We do not want to go to the beach with an uneasy conscience." But abetted by his advantage in Los Angeles County, Kennedy won a clear-cut victory. On primary election night, as he prepared to leave his suite at the Ambassador Hotel in Los Angeles to go downstairs to greet his exultant campaign workers, Kennedy received word of another big success that same day in South Dakota. Indians, he was told, had voted 811 for him, 11 for McCarthy, 4 for Humphrey. "That's marvelous," he replied. "I just wish we hadn't taken Oregon away from them." To his volunteers, he remarked with quiet restraint, "I think we can end the division within the United States, the violence." Moments later, as he walked through a kitchen corridor, Kennedy was shot and mortally wounded by Sirhan Bishara Sirhan, a twenty-four-year-old Jordanian immigrant. "Not *again!*" screamed a spectator. On the wall a few feet from where he lay someone scribbled in crayon, "THE ONCE AND FUTURE KING."

As a result of the assassination, McCarthy became the legatee of the hopes of most anti-war Democrats, but not all were reconciled. In Negro neighborhoods, Samuel Lubell found a sense of irreparable loss. "I won't vote," a New Yorker said. "Every good man we get they kill." Some Kennedy Democrats tried to scrape together a candidacy for Senator McGovern as an alternative to McCarthy. Even a number of early enthusiasts found McCarthy exasperatingly aloof and indecisive. In "The Lament of an Aging Politician," McCarthy had written:

> I have left Act I, for involution
> And Act II. There mired in complexity
> I cannot write Act III.

"You know the old rules," he elaborated. "Act I states the problem. Act II deals with the complications. And Act III resolves them. I'm an Act II man. That's where I live—involution and complexity." As the day of the Democratic convention approached, he immured himself in a Benedictine retreat and seemed indifferent to the ardor of his followers. "No one doubted that Eugene McCarthy bore love in his heart—but it was an abstract love, a love for youth, a love for

Hiroji Kubota, Magnum

At a Chicago rally, a grim Humphrey contrasts with the projected image of the usually smiling, ebullient Hubert as Chicago's Mayor Richard Daley looks on. When, in Salt Lake City on September 30, 1968, Humphrey modified his support of Johnson's war policies, the lectern was no longer adorned with the vice-presidential emblem, signifying that he spoke not for the administration but on his own.

beauty, a love for vistas and hills and song," observed Theodore White. "All through the year, one's admiration of the man grew — and one's affection lessened."

Neither McCarthy nor the anti-war cause fared well at the convention. Vice-President Hubert Humphrey won the presidential nomination handily by accumulating more than twice the number of votes for McCarthy and McGovern. The peace forces did somewhat better in corraling support for a minority plank calling for "an unconditional end to all bombing in North Vietnam," but by a 3 to 2 margin the administration's plank prevailed. After the tally, the band played "Off We Go into the Wild Blue Yonder." Still, as the

Foreign Policy Association observed, "Never before in time of war against a foreign foe had so large a minority of a presidential nominating convention signified its readiness to repudiate its own leadership on so critical a question." However, to many of the disgruntled delegates, the outcome proved that America was a repressive society and that the political system no longer worked. McCarthy, the choice of the people, they claimed, had been passed over for a Johnson toady who was bulldozed through by party bosses, and the platform had turned a deaf ear to the nation's cry for peace.

In truth, the process of choosing delegates left much to be desired, although the Chicago convention had more democratic features than its critics acknowledged. It outraged the conservative Texas governor, John B. Connally, by abolishing the ancient unit rule, initiated a pathbreaking democratization of delegate selection for 1972, and refused to seat the segregationist Mississippi regulars. When half

A tune for Mars. A flutist taunts national guardsmen at the Democratic convention in Chicago in 1968. Some foes of the war used less peaceful means, but even critics of the demonstrators conceded that the violence perpetrated by the Chicago police was inexcusable.

Roger Malloch, Magnum

of the Georgia vote was allotted to insurgents led by the Negro legislator Julian Bond, Governor Lester Maddox went home in a fit of pique. The peace element had ample opportunity to state its case at Platform Committee hearings, where their spokesmen included Senators McGovern and Fulbright, and in a full-dress debate on the convention floor. The final vote may have been a rough representation of the actual divisions within the party, for although many wanted to get out of the war, fewer wished to lose it. Polls in the early spring revealed that most Americans opposed halting the bombing and that a preponderance of those interviewed opted for an invasion of North Vietnam. Those who recalled McCarthy's "victory" in New Hampshire forgot that he actually lost the state, and to a write-in candidate; moreover, a substantial portion of McCarthy's ballots came from people who wanted to escalate the fighting and who later voted for George Wallace. Humphrey never underwent the trial by combat of party primaries, but polls showed that he was the favorite of registered Democrats.

Anti-war delegates objected, too, to the "police state" atmosphere of the convention — the barbed-wire and chain-link fences cordoning off the amphitheater, Mayor Daley's ubiquitous bluecoats. Yet given the events of that spring — the carnival of violence, the assassinations of King and Kennedy — it would have been irresponsible not to have taken thorough precautions. Apprehension about the vulnerability of public men was extensive and deeply felt. Mourners alongside the tracks of Robert Kennedy's funeral train bore hand-lettered signs reading "Who Will Be The Next One?" (as well as "The Gebharts Are Sad"). To be sure, the call for a national mobilization of radicals in Chicago brought only a small turnout. Blacks were noticeably absent, and most young people drawn to the city were Gene McCarthy volunteers working within the system. But to Chicago had also come a cadre bent on savaging "the pigs" and provoking a violent incident. A subsequent investigation, the Walker Report, found that the police "were the targets of mounting provocations by both word and act" and that they "had been put on edge by widely published threats of attempts to disrupt both the city and the Convention."

However, none of these extenuating circumstances justified the sadistic behavior of the Chicago police. Even sympathetic journalists certified that Daley's minions went "berserk," and the Walker Report later described a preliminary episode at Lincoln Park as a "police riot." "The cops had one thing on their mind," wrote Jimmy Breslin.

"Club and then gas, club and then gas, club and then gas." A memorandum from a British journalist from the crack staff of the *Sunday Times* recounted:

Then at 8 p.m. it happened. Cohorts of police began to charge the crowd from a street north of the Hilton, Balbo. The kids screamed and were beaten to the ground by cops who had completely lost their cool. Some tried to surrender by putting their hands on their heads. As they were marched to vans to be arrested, they were rapped in the genitals by the cops' swinging billies.

The Walker Report concluded that there had been "unrestrained and indiscriminate police violence" and added:

That violence was made all the more shocking by the fact that it was inflicted upon persons who had broken no law, disobeyed no order, made no threat. These included peaceful demonstrators, onlookers, and a large number of residents who were simply passing through, or happened to live in, the areas where confrontations were occurring.

(The disorders had a shameful aftermath in the trial of Bobby Seale, Abbie Hoffman, and others, in which judge and defendants seemed bent on outdoing one another in making a travesty of a court of justice.)

The imbroglio left Hubert Humphrey the nominee of a party many of whose followers blamed him both for the wanton harassment in Chicago and for the prolonged conflict in Vietnam. Garrulous but ineffective, he cut a sorry figure in the first weeks of the campaign, a dreadful comedown for a man who had been the helmsman of civil rights legislation, the initiator of the Peace Corps, the sponsor of a host of social welfare measures for two decades. His very achievements led him to be too complacent about his credentials as a reformer, insufficiently alert to the needs of a new day. "People say to me, 'Whatever happened to that liberal program you stood for?'" Humphrey related. "I say to them, 'We passed it. Does that upset you?'" As the number 2 man in the Johnson administration, he wore around his neck the albatross of LBJ's Vietnam policies. Although he had developed misgivings about the war, he feared that if he advocated a different course Johnson, who held him in contempt, would punish him and that others would accuse him of disloyalty. For weeks Humphrey waffled, despite the clamor of antiwar dissidents. In Boston left-wing students howled him down, and in Seattle they jeered him noisily. No endorsement was forthcoming from Senator McCarthy, and party activists rusticated. In early

October the Vice-President had only twenty-eight sure electoral votes.

The divisive war and the disastrous Democratic convention permitted the Republicans, like Lazarus, to rise from the dead. In 1964 the GOP had been devastated, and some doubted that this party of lace curtain respectability could recover. If it did, it would not be for a long time to come, and certainly not under Richard Nixon. Two years earlier, his political career palpably finished, the former Vice-President had ranted at reporters, "You won't have Nixon to kick around any more, because, gentlemen, this is my last press conference." That week ABC televised the "Political Obituary of Richard Nixon," with Alger Hiss as one of the pallbearers. But with a tough animal instinct for survival, Nixon earned the confidence of party professionals through his faithful service in the 1966 campaign, and when the Republicans picked up forty-seven seats in the House, he received the lion's share of the credit. By the time the 1968 Republican convention got underway in Miami, a location that signified that the GOP had become an all-section party, Nixon was the front runner. At Miami, Nixon, through quieting the doubts of Senator Strom Thurmond of South Carolina and other southerners, out-pointed California's Governor Ronald Reagan so skillfully that he made his hard-fought victory look easy. Russell Baker said the convention had been "planned in advance by six bores and a sadist," but the Democratic donnybrook in Chicago put the relative calm of Miami in a favorable light.

Nixon, who had won notoriety as a divider, campaigned in 1968 as a unifier. The change reflected in part his own maturation in the 1960's, for as a New York attorney he had become more self-assured and self-controlled. But it also represented his conviction that a "silent majority" of the nation desired surcease from civil discord. In his acceptance speech, Nixon showed that his talent for pathos had lost none of its fine edge. As Eisenhower lay dying, Nixon urged, "Let's win this one for Ike." But he also struck the chord that would find a sympathetic vibration in the weeks to come. Nixon stated:

As we look at America, we see cities enveloped in smoke and flame. We hear sirens in the night. We see Americans hating each other; killing each other at home.

And as we see and hear these things, millions of Americans cry out in anguish: Did we come all this way for this? Did American boys die in Normandy and Korea and in Valley Forge for this?

Listen to the answers to these questions.

It is another voice, it is a quiet voice in the tumult and the shouting. It is the voice of the great majority of Americans, the forgotten Americans, the nonshouters, the nondemonstrators.

In capitalizing upon the yearning for domestic tranquility, Nixon's "low-profile" campaign singularly suited the public mood in 1968. The Republicans sensed that the country had heard more than enough about its shortcomings (at Miami John Wayne delivered "an inspirational reading" of "Why I Am Proud to Be an American") and of the need to smash the State. By making Nixon a present of the law and order issue, the zealots of the New Politics committed a grave tactical error. Robert Kennedy had understood the advisability of presenting himself as the former "chief law-enforcement officer of the United States," a tough Eliot Ness who had cracked down on the Mafia and put Jimmy Hoffa behind bars and who would "bring an end to this violence." But many insurgents viewed the demand for "law and order" as nothing but a code phrase for racism. Often it was. Yet most of those who wanted an end to burning cities did not wish to halt gains for blacks, and the anxiety about the destruction and disunity had to be spoken to. In the end the conviction that a healing emollient was required determined the outcome of the election, for millions shared the sentiment on the sign held aloft by an Ohio girl in the closing days of the campaign: "BRING US TOGETHER AGAIN."

While Nixon sought to take advantage of what political analysts called the "social issue" by offering himself as a harmonizer, the American Independence Party candidate, George Wallace, made headway by catering to the resentments of his followers. "If any demonstrator ever lays down in front of my car," Wallace cried, "it'll be the last car he'll ever lay down in front of." A Harris poll learned that more than half of the nation shared Wallace's view that "liberals, intellectuals, and long-hairs have run the country for too long." Attacking the "pointy-head," bearded "intellectual morons" who "don't know how to park a bicycle straight," the Alabama governor promised, "When I get to Washington I'll throw all these phonies and their briefcases into the Potomac." He rallied, too, those who believed, as one conservative said, that as a result of the Social Security Act "breeding children as a cash crop has become a way of life for many women." New York City alone had a million on its welfare rolls by the end of 1968, and indignation at the tax burden and at what was thought to be a mendicant style of life was mounting. Merle Haggard's "Welfare Cadilac," aimed at cheaters who thrived on government checks, became a big hit, as did his "Okie from Muskogee" on pot smokers and long-hairs, and "The Fightin' Side of Me," which chewed out "squirrely guys who don't believe in fightin'" for their native land. When Nixon invited endorsements from Nashville's Silent Majority singers, he found that almost everyone was for Wallace.

Wallace profited from the disapproval of demonstrators, the counter culture, and the Welfare State, but his audiences identified him chiefly as the most prominent opponent of racial integration. In his inaugural address in 1963, Governor Wallace had said, "I draw the line in the dust and toss the gauntlet before the feet of tyranny, and I say, 'Segregation now . . . segregation tomorrow . . . and segregation forever.'" President Kennedy soon forced him to back down, but his state remained a bastion of white supremacy. When in September 1963 a bomb blasted a Negro church, Martin Luther King wired him: "The blood of four little children . . . is on your hands. Your irresponsible and misguided actions have created in Birmingham and Alabama the atmosphere that has induced continued violence and now murder." But in 1964 Wallace aroused alarm over the power of "white backlash" by rolling up 34 percent of the vote in the Wisconsin Democratic primary, 30 percent in Indiana, 43 percent in Maryland. He did especially well in working-class districts that had been the mortar of the Roosevelt coalition; in Gary, he took every white precinct. Wallace's strong run challenged the liberal expectation that as politics became increasingly nationalized the South would become more like the North and suggested instead that the North was becoming more like the South. The correspondent Douglas Kiker wrote: "It is as if somewhere, sometime a while back, George Wallace had been awakened by a white, blinding vision: they all hate black people, all of them. They're all afraid, all of them. Great God! That's it! They're all Southern! The whole United States is *Southern!*"

As Wallace invaded the North in 1968 to test the assumption that it shared the predilections of the former Confederacy, he found white working-class neighborhoods, particularly those bordering on black ones, markedly hospitable. He appealed to transplanted Appalachian hilljacks, to Polish and other "newer" ethnic groups, and generally to blue collar laborers who believed that blacks were getting away with murder—like the Brooklyn members of SPONGE, the Society for the Prevention of Negroes Getting Everything. To the dismay of

UAW leaders, key locals reported Wallace had the edge on the major party candidates. Some were drawn as much by his pugnacious style as by his content. He was attractive, said the political scientist David Derge, to the "kind of guy the Tuesday night bowling league might choose to represent them with a group of unfriendlies." Although many of his ideas were conservative, Wallace, who won Tom Watson's millworker ward in Augusta, frequently sounded a Populist note. He asserted that the major parties were "owned by the Eastern Establishment" and in a jab at Nixon remarked, "I can't afford to sun myself on Key Biscayne." "On November 5," he declared, "they're going to find out there are a lot of rednecks in this country."

Well before the November 5 election, it had become clear that the Governor would have to be reckoned with. Wallace moved steadily upward in the polls from 9 percent in the spring to 16 percent in June to 21 percent by mid-September. If he had maintained that rate of increase until November 5, he would have denied any candidate a majority in the Electoral College, and the nerve-fraying year of 1968 would have ended with the presidential succession in doubt for weeks, even months. At that pace he would have finished ahead of Humphrey, who would have suffered the humiliation of coming in third. In late September Humphrey was running fifteen points behind Nixon in the Gallup survey and was only seven points ahead of Wallace.

However, at precisely that juncture Humphrey's fortunes took a decided turn for the better. He advanced his own cause when on September 30 in Salt Lake City he indicated he would no longer be LBJ's vassal. His lectern divested of the vice-presidential seal, Humphrey announced that he would "stop the bombing of North Vietnam as an acceptable risk for peace." It was a guarded speech, with conditions attached, but he made it without the President's approval, and the address heartened anti-war Democrats. By late October, even Gene McCarthy managed a feeble endorsement: "I believe the Vice-President is a man who can be relied upon to tell the difference between the pale horse of death and the white horse of victory. I am not sure that Mr. Nixon can make that distinction."

Humphrey also benefited from the contrast between his running mate, Senator Edmund Muskie of Maine, who exuded quiet good sense, and the vice-presidential nominees of his rivals. Wallace's most damaging blunder was his choice of General Curtis LeMay, former air force chief of staff and Warfare State potentate as chairman of the board of Networks Electronic, to fill out his ticket. LeMay, who had launched the fire raids against Japan in World War II and who favored bombing North Vietnam "back to the Stone Age," was held to be the model for the general in *Dr. Strangelove.* At a disastrous press conference, he stated, "We seem to have a phobia about nuclear weapons." Such indiscretions permitted Humphrey to tag Wallace and LeMay the "bombsy twins." Nixon's teammate, Governor Spiro Agnew, reinforced the image of the Republicans as the party of well-to-do WASPs. He even said, "We the Establishment." Agnew made artless ethnic allusions to a "fat Jap" and to "Polacks," aroused recollections of McCarthyism by calling Humphrey "squishy-soft" on communism, and illustrated the callousness of the Old Guard by remarking that "if you've seen one city slum, you've seen them all." So often did he goof that at one stop he was greeted by a sign: "APOLOGIZE NOW, SPIRO. IT WILL SAVE TIME LATER."

By mid-October, Democratic voters were flocking back to FDR's party like the swallows returning to Capistrano. More Americans regarded themselves as Democrats than as Republicans, and, with Agnew to rekindle memories of Herbert Hoover and Joe McCarthy, the old pulls of party identification began to reassert themselves. Unions did such a herculean job of counteracting the Wallace temptation and of mobilizing their members behind Humphrey that the Alabama governor eventually received only 15 to 18 percent of the votes of unionists. But the biggest boost came on October 31, less than a week before election day, when Johnson announced, "I have now ordered that all air, naval, and artillery bombardment of North Vietnam cease." For a brief interval it seemed that peace was in the offing, and the shift of voters, especially women, to Humphrey picked up speed. Over the final weekend of the campaign, the Vice-President pulled even. However, when the South Vietnamese spiked the understanding, the movement reversed, and Humphrey's remarkable upsurge fell just short of success.

Nixon scored a 301 to 191 victory over Humphrey in the Electoral College, but his edge in pivotal states was razor-thin and his popular margin less than seven-tenths of 1 percent. His 43.4 percent of the popular vote was the smallest share for a winner since Wilson's in 1912. Despite an increment in the electorate of over 4 million, he received 2.3 million fewer ballots than he had in 1960. The Democrats also demonstrated their residual strength by retaining control of both houses of Congress. Wallace polled 9.9 million, 4.1 million from the North and West, and 46 electoral votes. His 13.5 percent of the popular vote was the best showing for a third party in forty-

Election of 1968

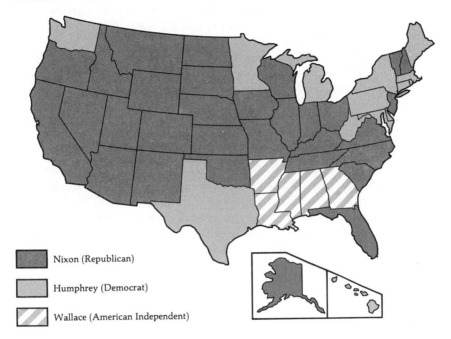

Nixon (Republican)

Humphrey (Democrat)

Wallace (American Independent)

four years, but it netted him only five states, all in the South (plus the ballot of a Nixon elector in North Carolina who defected to him).

Every four years pundits proclaimed the death of the Roosevelt coalition, but in 1968 the Democrats once again ran most strongly in the great cities, none of which went Republican, and among less well-to-do workers, unionists, and blacks, albeit in diminished proportions. Income cleavages remained the most salient determinants of voting, but with reduced force. Humphrey prevailed over Nixon among manual laborers by only a 50 to 35 ratio. The Democratic component of the nonwhite vote also fell off from the spectacular 94 percent of 1964, but it still totaled an impressive 85 percent. Petersburg, Virginia's black third ward, gave Humphrey 1,092, Nixon 17, Wallace 3. Nixon, who got 32 percent of the Negro vote in 1960, received only 12 percent in 1968. However, a smaller proportion of blacks in the North and West went to the polls, and this falloff proved critical. The erosion of the Roosevelt coalition was just large enough to cost Humphrey the victory.

Roosevelt had been able to take for granted one large electoral cluster—the South—but 1968 made clear how far the "Solid South" had disintegrated in presidential politics. Humphrey carried only a single state in the ex-Confederacy, LBJ's Texas, and this narrowly, with an increased turnout by Mexican-Americans and blacks tipping the balance. Of his meager 31 percent of the popular vote in Jefferson Davis' old realm, over two-thirds came from Negroes. (Nixon and Wallace divided the remainder of Dixie's ballots almost evenly.) Although the South was no longer a one-party preserve, sectionalism persisted, for Humphrey's domain lay almost wholly in the Northeast, while Nixon fell only four states short of capturing the entire trans-Mississippi West.

So after all the tumult of the 'sixties, Richard Milhous Nixon, the quintessential man of the 'fifties, entered the White House. The forces of radical change had been frustrated, largely because, as Richard Scammon pointed out, most of the electorate was composed of "the unyoung, the unblack, and the unpoor." Thwarted too was George Wallace, for racism failed to sway most white voters, and the deadlock he hoped to precipitate never eventuated. Of all the extraordinary developments of 1968, perhaps least expected was the durability of characters and institutions in the face of defiant challenge.

In the 1968 campaign, the consumer society and pop culture had come into their own. The son of a grocer, Dick Nixon had operated a hamburger stand, Nixon's Snack Shack, while serving in the navy in the South Pacific and, after law school, had tried to launch an enterprise to market packaged orange juice. His main rival for the Republican nomination, the former film star Ronald Reagan, had once been "the voice of the Chicago Cubs." The father of Nixon's campaign manager, John Mitchell, had been part owner of one of the first trading stamp companies. In the 1950's Nixon's running mate, Spiro Agnew, the son of a restaurant proprietor, had managed a supermarket. "The Drugstore Liberal," Hubert Humphrey, who had worked in his father's pharmacy, had begun with a decided disadvantage; appropriately, he had chosen as his first agency the advertising firm that had coined Avis Rent A Car's slogan, "We're only Number Two. We have to try harder." (His chief Democratic opponent, Eugene McCarthy, had been publicized by the same company that huckstered Hertz Rent A Car.) Nixon, the former Whittier College benchwarmer, had taken great pride in winning the endorsement of Bart Starr, quarterback of the Green Bay Packers. Humphrey had called a press conference to announce that he was

The Duke gives them a piece of his mind. A red-white-and-blue American, John Wayne addresses the
Republican national convention in Miami Beach in 1968, the same year that he starred
as Rooster Claghorn in *True Grit,* a role that won him an Academy Award. A year earlier, he had
directed *Green Berets* because he believed ''we're helping a
brave little country defend herself against a ruthless Communist invasion.''

being backed by Diana Ross of the Supremes. The third-party candidate, Governor Wallace, married to a former dime-store clerk, had enjoyed the ardent support of a young lady who had been imploring TV viewers to join "the Dodge rebellion" and had given consideration to selecting as his vice-presidential nominee "Colonel" Harland Sanders, the "finger-lickin' good" fried chicken impresario.

Foreign journalists, often hypercritical of American society in the 1960's, found themselves impressed by the bloodless transfer of authority. Although there was "dramatic and even melodramatic" violence in the United States in 1968, noted the British observer Henry Fairlie, "it is politically illiterate — ignorant and impatient — to refuse to acknowledge that the American political system took the strain. It may not have produced the result that one wanted. But there was a peaceable change of government." Another British writer, Louis Heren, Washington correspondent of the *Times* of London, concluded:

Some of the onlookers standing in the freezing cold as Nixon was sworn in remembered the bitter divisions, the loss of confidence, and the fear that the country was coming apart. Yet at the end of the year the presidential election was held, and there was no violence as 69 million Americans went to the polls. The enormous power of the presidency passed peacefully from one man to another.

The Center Holds

The inauguration of Richard Nixon as thirty-seventh President brought a decided change in the climate of public affairs. To the White House came a man determined to pursue the kinds of policies associated on the European Continent with Center parties. During the 1968 campaign one of his more conservative speech writers, Richard Whalen, had been distressed to find that Nixon was not interested in right-wing ideology, or indeed in the validity of any ideas; rather he wanted to position himself "athwart the technically determined 'center' of the electorate." In office he proved no less preoccupied with "the pragmatic splitting of differences along a line drawn through the middle of the electorate." To further this end and to take advantage of the revulsion against the excesses of the mid-sixties, he sought also to lower the temperature of political controversy. As Eisenhower incarnated much of the 1950's, as Kennedy quickened concern in the 1960's, so Nixon fostered the spirit of moderation of the 1970's.

The new President began his administration in a temperate manner that deliberately contrasted with the frenetic mood of the Johnson era. In his inaugural address, he stated:

America has suffered from a fever of words; from inflated rhetoric that promises more than it can deliver; from angry rhetoric that fans discontents into hatreds; from bombastic rhetoric that postures instead of persuading.

We cannot learn from one another until we stop shouting at one another—until we speak quietly enough so that our words can be heard as well as our voices.

Nixon's centrist politics and muted style seemed particularly well suited to winning the allegiance of "Middle America." The columnist

At his inauguration in January 1969, Richard Nixon gets a hug from the out-going President, Lyndon Johnson. In the front row Chief Justice Earl Warren applauds, while among Nixon's Cabinet appointees in the background are Melvin Laird, John Mitchell, and William Rogers.

Elliott Erwitt, Magnum

Joseph Kraft coined the phrase to describe "the great mass of some 40,000,000 persons who have recently moved from just above the poverty line to just below the level of affluence," but it came to connote something else, the vast United States interior that provided a ballast of common sense not to be found on either seaboard. The phrase thus incorporated three different notions, none precisely defined—an income group, a geographic location (although "Middle Americans" could also be found in Baltimore and Oakland), and a state of mind. Middle America was where the white petite bourgeoisie lived, people who went to 8 A.M. mass or to vespers, enlisted in the army, boosted their town, and were "damned sick and tired of listening to all this nonsense about how awful America is." To its denigrators in the universe of *The New York Review of Books,* Middle America suggested what George Babbitt's Zenith conveyed to intellectuals in the 1920's or Squaresville to the 1950's. But Nixon understood that "as the champion of the good, God-fearing burghers of Heartland U.S.A.," as *Newsweek* called him, he could count on a large following among those who looked back on the 'sixties with dismay.

Neither a politics of the center nor a state of tranquility came easily. In his attitudes on civil rights, in his Supreme Court appointments, and in forging an economic program, Nixon swerved in a conservative direction, although in each area he was brought back closer to the middle of the road. Some of his initiatives in Asia were sharply divisive, and his Vice-President polarized sentiment. The Nixon administration felt the impact of a politicized counter culture and was shaken by spasms of violence. Yet Nixon partly offset his rightward lurches with more unorthodox policies. Before his first three years were over, he had become the champion of costly welfare programs, had frozen prices and wages, and had shaken hands with Mao in Peking. The persistence of turmoil proved less characteristic than a condition of relative quiescence. By preempting Democratic positions and by bringing a respite from the tumultuous 1960's, Nixon appropriated so much center ground that he left his opposition in disarray.

The electoral and legislative situation also worked toward moderation. Having been elected by so narrow a margin, Nixon could claim no mandate and was well advised to tread lightly. Since he had received less than 44 percent of the vote, he knew he would have to find substantial additional support to gain reelection if the 1972 contest turned out to be a two-way race. Sometimes this inclined him to the right to pick off followers of George Wallace, although he had to keep in mind that the Wallace movement contained a populistic element. At other times he gravitated to the left to attract independents and progressive Democrats. The thorny situation on Capitol Hill made the latter course especially prudent. Not since the disputed election of 1876 had a presidential candidate won for the first time while the opposition party gained control of the House of Representatives. The Senate, also under Democratic dominance, was in an ornery mood. Having been badgered by Lyndon Johnson as majority leader and President over a long period, that august body was determined to assert its independence. To chalk up a record of legislative achievement, Nixon needed to adjust to the disposition of the Democratic majority in both houses.

Nixon contributed rather unexpectedly to the politics of moderation by advancing propositions and employing language that indicated he held larger views than adversaries had credited to him. Under the tutelage of his adviser on urban affairs, Daniel Patrick Moynihan, who gave him a copy of Lord Blake's biography of Disraeli, he persuaded himself for a time that like the Victorian Prime Minister he could achieve social reforms where a liberal Democrat would fail. After a hardline campaign in 1970 yielded indifferent returns in the midterm congressional elections, he blossomed forth in his January 1971 State of the Union message as the leader of a "New American Revolution" that, in a catchphrase of the Left, would give "power to the people," "a revolution as profound, as far-reaching, as exciting as that first revolution 200 years ago." Some of his White House aides were embarrassed by the President's overblown rhetoric, and not much came of most of his specific recommendations, but liberals were agreeably surprised by his stance.

The President created the biggest stir by proposing a sweeping overhaul of the welfare system through guaranteeing a national minimal level of support. In place of the controversial Aid to Dependent Children program, the Family Assistance Plan would give a family of four with no income $1600 a year ($2460 when food stamps were added), a big rise from Mississippi's $468 and more than welfare families were receiving in nineteen other states, predominantly Southern. In addition the plan might double the total of eligible beneficiaries through helping the "working poor." To allay conservative misgivings, Nixon insisted that every head of household on the welfare rolls, save for mothers with preschool children, work or register for job training. "There is no reason why

one person should be taxed so that another can choose to live idly,"
he asserted. Critics objected to forcing welfare recipients to labor
at substandard pay and protested that the FAP minimum was too
low; the congressional Black Caucus demanded $6500. When Con-
gress adjourned in the fall of 1972, it still had not approved the program. Yet Nixon's "great leap forward," as Moynihan, one of its
chief authors, called it, markedly shifted the fulcrum of debate. As a
putative Disraeli, the President claimed, "Tory men with liberal
principles are what has enlarged democracy in this world."

The movement to preserve the environment could count substantial
gains, only partly due to Nixon's influence. Of all his appointments,
none seemed so regrettable as that of Walter J. Hickel to be secretary
of the interior. A loud outcry greeted news of the choice, for the
self-made millionaire governor of Alaska was alleged to be close to
oil interests and said he opposed "conservation for conservation's
sake." But Hickel rapidly won over his assailants. He joined in a
successful effort to preserve the Everglades from a destructive jet-
port, halted oil drilling in the Santa Barbara Channel after a devastating blowout, persuaded the Justice Department to prosecute the
Chevron Oil Company for befouling the Gulf of Mexico, encouraged
suits against corporations charged with poisoning waters with mer-
cury, banned billboards on United States government lands, helped
defend whales and alligators from predators, and held up construction of the trans-Alaska oil pipeline that jeopardized the tundra of
his state. Nixon approved, or at least tolerated, Hickel's actions and
he included in his 1970 State of the Union message an environmental
protection program.

However, on the main ecological issue of Nixon's first two years—
the supersonic transport plane—the environmentalists scored a
notable victory over the President's opposition. Nixon was one of
many who thought that American prestige was at stake in the construction of the mammoth conveyance that might dominate air
traffic in the future. Opponents objected that the expensive project
was an example of distorted priorities and threatened the quality of
life on earth and in the upper atmosphere. At first their cause seemed
hopeless. In 1969 when the Wisconsin Democrat, Senator William
Proxmire, sought to kill government funding for the SST, the administration had no trouble in overwhelming him, 58 to 22. Yet so
rapidly did the tide of opinion change that in December 1970 the
Senate, under Proxmire's leadership, voted down the SST, a heartening performance to those who believed it was possible to work
within the system.

Liberal Democrats like Proxmire accounted for much of the modest legislative portfolio of Nixon's first term, but the administration had a hand too. Few of the Great Society arrangements were scrapped, and new schemes were undertaken. Congress increased social security benefits, voted nearly $3 billion for medical training, and enacted the first comprehensive regulation of campaign spending since the Corrupt Practices Act of 1925. It balanced accounts on the era of McCarthyism by repealing the part of the McCarran Internal Security Act of 1950 that authorized setting up detention camps for subversives in times of national emergency. Legislation granting eighteen-year-olds the right to vote in federal elections was followed by the Twenty-sixth Amendment, ratified in June 1971, extending the privilege to state and local elections; the two measures enfranchised 11.5 million youths. The assumption that advertisers could manipulate the consumer culture at will received a setback when Congress banned cigarette advertising on television and radio. On January 1, 1971, viewers of the bowl games got their last glimpse of Marlboro Country. Nixon's "Second American Revolution" fell far short of fulfillment, but on the eve of the 1972 election Congress approved a path-breaking revenue-sharing plan that allotted funds to the fifty states. Although the legislative record in the four years after Nixon's 1968 victory did not approach that of Lyndon Johnson's "fabulous 89th," Congress was productive enough to give some substance to Nixon's claims for a centrist emphasis.

When he tried to cope with the unruly economy, however, Nixon's policy of moderation foundered, largely because the President inherited difficulties that were not amenable to middling measures. Lyndon Johnson bequeathed his successor not only an ugly war but rampant inflation that was a by-product of that war. Liberal economists had been proud of the fact that they had achieved expansion without cheapening the dollar, for, as Paul Samuelson said, "Creeping inflation is the malaria of the modern mixed economy." But after Johnson abruptly escalated Vietnam expenditures without calling for a tax rise to siphon off purchasing power, he came to grief. The injection of war spending into an already booming economy shot prices up—3 percent in 1967, 5 percent in 1968. As a consequence, real earnings of industrial workers, which had soared in the first half of the decade, slowed to a halt. His predecessor's policies left Nixon unpalatable alternatives: permit inflation to continue or take action to curb it but at the cost of rising unemployment. Shortly before Nixon's inauguration, his choice for chairman of the Council of Economic Advisers, Paul W. McCracken, remarked, "There is some kind of malevolent law about the rhythm of political life that puts some of us here when it is hard to be a hero."

In shaping economic policy, as in other aspects of his administration, the new President set out on what to him was a centrist course but to others was a veer to the right. While putting the economy through "slowing pains," as he phrased it, Nixon tried to avoid a full-blown recession with a high rate of joblessness, for he remembered that the final downturn under Eisenhower had cost him the election in 1960. However, Nixon was no less determined to arrest inflation, in part because he believed that by penalizing thrift it sapped the nation's character. And to check rising prices he was prepared to bring about a higher level of unemployment than Johnson had been willing to tolerate.

The President's "game plan," as the anti-inflation program of the country's Number 1 football fan was labeled, proposed to keep government intervention to a minimum. During World War II Nixon had worked for ten months as a small-fry bureaucrat for the Office of Price Administration in a shabby Washington building left over from the first world war, and he had come out of that lonely experience with a deep distaste for the New Dealers and their ways. When it was suggested in 1969 that he clamp a lid on prices, he said, "Controls. Oh my God, no! I was a lawyer for the OPA during the war and I know all about controls. They mean rationing, black markets, inequitable administration. We'll never go for controls." Nor would he sanction more modest approaches. He rejected both an "incomes policy" of federal guideposts on wages and prices and "jawboning" to use the prestige of his office to shame corporations and unions into line, since neither met the fundamental problem of excess demand. Instead, Nixon resorted to two-pronged action — fiscal and monetary. He pruned the federal budget, and he encouraged the Federal Reserve System to act in accordance with the theory of the University of Chicago economist, Milton Friedman, who claimed that prices could be leveled by adjusting the money supply. Convinced that fine tuning would be sufficient to contain inflation, he carried out both activities in a spirit of "gradualism."

Nixon's strategy plunged the country into the recession he had hoped to escape. After the Federal Reserve tightened the money supply in the last half of 1969, interest rates reached their highest peaks in at least a century, and investors staggered under the worst bear market since the Great Depression. The Dow-Jones average, at 985 on December 3, 1968, a month after Nixon's election, tumbled to 631 on May 26, 1970—the biggest decline in more than three decades. In June 1970 the country saw the worst business failure in its history when the Penn Central Railroad went bankrupt. Real gross national product declined in 1970 for the first time since 1958, and as the recession ate into tax receipts the government began to run an unanticipated deficit. Unemployment, at a low 3.3 percent when Nixon took office, climbed to 6 percent by the end of 1970, and each point sacrificed another 800,000 jobs, including positions in prestige industries such as aerospace.

In spite of the slowdown, prices kept going up. The 5.3 percent rise in 1970 was the most precipitous since the Korean War year of 1951. In a society of highly organized economic units, policies based on the assumption of a free market miscarried. Walter Heller gave the name "Nixonomics" to this unhappy compound of lagging output and soaring prices. "Nixonomics," explained the chairman of the Democratic National Committee, Lawrence O'Brien, "means that all the things that should go up—the stock market, corporate profits, real spendable income, productivity—go down, and all the things that should go down—unemployment, prices, interest rates—go up."

His game plan a bust, Nixon decided to revamp it before the whistle blew for the second half. Especially after Arthur F. Burns took over as chairman of the Federal Reserve Board, the tight money emphasis was scuttled, although some thought Burns should have been even more unrestrained. "Gradualism" and voluntarism having failed, Nixon began "jawboning" the steel industry and took to task the construction unions, thereby alienating hardhats who supported him on the war. Concluding that economic decline was a greater evil than inflation, the President turned cautiously to fiscal policies that would stimulate employment. On January 4, 1971 he told the ABC news correspondent, Howard K. Smith, "I am now a Keynesian." (For such a longtime foe of liberal economic doctrine to take up this heresy was, said Smith, "a little like a Christian crusader saying, 'All things considered, I think Mohammed was right.' ") Yet the administration still would not countenance wage-price guideposts, let alone controls, and as late as June 1971, when top-level policy makers held a weekend "summit conference" at the President's retreat in Camp David, Maryland, the anti-control faction prevailed.

Despite the new tactics, Nixon lost ground. Unemployment reached 6.2 percent in May 1971 and hovered at about that point for months thereafter. Prices rose another 4 percent in 1971, only a small improvement on the previous year. To Nixon's distress, the United States ran an acutely adverse trade deficit; in 1971 imports exceeded exports for the first time since 1893. Confidence in the President's program buckled, in Washington and in the nation. When administration experts predicted that the country would soon turn the corner, a union leader responded, "Paul McCracken on the economy is getting to sound more and more like General Westmoreland on Vietnam." The President's new secretary of the treasury, the handsome Texas Democrat John Connally, decided a more aggressive policy was required, and other advisers agreed. In July, shortly after Nixon made the startling announcement that he would visit China, McCracken said, "There may come a time for an economic 'trip to Peking.' " When the President's counselors met again at Camp David in mid-August, the activists carried the day.

On the night of August 15, 1971, a month after he divulged that he would call on Mao, Nixon performed another somersault. He announced he was freezing wages, prices, and rents for ninety days. In addition he asked for tax cuts to stimulate business, slapped a surcharge on most imports, and paved the way for the devaluation of the dollar, which took place in December. All of the President's original game plan — gradualism, resistance to an incomes policy, objection to intruding into the private sector, hostility to controls — had been jettisoned. He even referred to his turnabout as a "new economic plan," terminology resembling that hitherto associated with Leninist Russia. An Office of Emergency Preparedness issued edicts that recalled OPA directives, although its docket included unfamiliar items such as a complaint against a marijuana dealer who kited prices.

In mid-November the emergency freeze gave way to long-term thaw. Phase II aimed to hold annual price rises to 2.5 percent and aggregate wage increases to 5.5 percent, although exceptions were made for special cases like the sensational Oakland pitcher Vida Blue. Critics of the administration protested that the controls were manifestly unfair since neither profits nor dividends were restrained and the worker had to stretch his paycheck to meet items that were not controlled — taxes, credit, and supermarket produce like fruits and vegetables. In March 1972 the AFL-CIO walked out of the Pay Board in protest. Unemployment continued at a high rate, and industrial capacity was one-quarter unused. But Nixon could claim somewhat better results from braking inflationary expectations. In July 1972 the administration reported an encouraging decline in the rate of price rises coupled with the biggest gain in real GNP for any quarter since late 1965. Nixon had still not discovered how to combine stable price levels with full employment, but he had succeeded in reducing the political penalties for his earlier failures and in disclosing himself to be both flexible and forceful.

The "new, new Nixon" confounded some of his persistent critics. He exhibited a skill in foreign affairs that to many was a revelation, and if his performance on domestic matters was less imposing, he showed greater hospitality to novel ideas than had been anticipated. In a curious way his reputation as "Tricky Dick," the low-level politician who had never accomplished much beyond getting Alger Hiss, helped him. "Everybody is saying that Mr. Nixon is doing better than they expected," wrote James Reston, "which proves the success of past failures." As President, this "shy, lonely, much-wounded, ambitious, courageous and deeply patriotic man," in Allen Drury's words, seemed a bigger man than he had before. He gave an impression of self-confidence and composure that had been missing in the tense, scowling Cold Warrior of the 1950's.

Yet some expressed skepticism about the President's serene demeanor, for it was achieved by such an effort at self-control that he almost seemed programmed. "There is an extraordinary lack of affect about Nixon," observed Bruce Mazlish in his "psychohistorical" study of the President. "If Nixon did visit Dr. Arnold Hutschnecker as a 'psychotherapist,' I suspect the going must have been very tough for the doctor. Nixon's opaque quality becomes in itself a subject for investigation; it directs our attention to the time when the young Nixon must have 'switched off' his emotions (or was he born with the tendency?)." The President recognized that he constantly kept himself in check, never let himself out of his sight. "I have a fetish about disciplining myself," he acknowledged.

This self-command helped Nixon dissipate much of the animus against him, but it did not inspire a great deal of affection. "The Presidency makes some men father figures," commented a Washington correspondent. "But not Richard Nixon. He is a brother-in-law figure." When he used expressions like "the lift of a driving dream," as he had during the campaign, he moved out of character, and when he tried to establish easy relationships, he stumbled. The man the country saw on its television screens was rigid, his face jowly, his eyes hooded, his gestures mechanical, his smile wooden. Reclusive, solitary, wary, he walled himself off even from his Cabinet and appeared remote from the concerns of ordinary citizens, especially those who had not made it and never would. To be sure, fewer liberals continued to think of him, as Philip Roth did in *Our Gang*, as

Hiroji Kubota, Magnum, from *Crisis in America*,
published by Ridge Press and Holt, Rinehart and Winston

The President gestures in the mechanical manner that encouraged speculation about whether
there was a "real" Nixon. The political scientist James Barber wrote that he was an
"active-negative type" with an "unclear and discontinuous self-image" engaged in "continual self-examination and effort to construct a Richard Nixon."

"Trick E. Dixon." "He is no longer viscerally hated," said a Democratic Congressman, but neither was he "viscerally loved." His
foes held this against him too. One liberal journalist, Paul Hoffman,
complained, "He has re-made himself into someone so bland, so
colorless, so devoid of passion that even those who disagree with
him most cannot rouse enough emotion to hate him."

People who cherished the Camelot era feared that Nixon would
usher in "four years of Lawrence Welk," and from the outset his administration was analyzed for its cultural as well as its political significance. Indeed, to the President's critics the two had a symbiotic
relationship. A chief executive who put catsup on his cottage cheese
and listened to Mantovani and Kostelanetz records would naturally
shape his political appeal to Middle America. As Vice-President
Agnew told a banquet audience after the inauguration, "We're all

middlebrows here." At the inauguration ceremonies the Reverend Billy Graham offered a prayer, and the evangelist, whom I. F. Stone called Nixon's "smoother Rasputin," led off the White House series of religious services. "It's a measure of the capital's social life under the Nixons," noted a disgruntled reporter, "that the one 'in' invitation is to the White House Sunday prayer meetings."

The President's family brought back memories of the bland 1950's. As First Lady, Pat Nixon exhibited few of the impulses of her predecessors to beautify the national estate or to aid the disadvantaged. Their daughters, Tricia and Julie, seemed to come out of a stylized magazine ad from the age of Eisenhower. In Gore Vidal's *An Evening with Richard Nixon,* "the two daughters are rolled into view; large cutie-pie dolls on wheels." When Julie married the cleancut, boyish David Eisenhower, the former President's grandson, it was inevitable that the ceremonies would be performed by the Reverend Norman Vincent Peale, the representative clerical figure of the 'fifties.

"The marketing managers of Nixon, Inc.," in Richard Whalen's phrase, also derived from the consumer culture of the Eisenhower period. One disenchanted aide, who dismissed the "suburban cronies" on the White House staff as "the Hot Shoppes vote," pointed out that Nixon's press officer had earlier wielded a pole to fend off the hippopotamus on the Jungle Ride at Disneyland. Predominantly good gray technicians, the President's associates well suited a government that aimed less to solve problems than to manage them. The key responsibility for running the domestic policy operation fell to Harry R. Haldeman and John Ehrlichman, two former "advance men." Eagle Scouts, Christian Scientists, total abstainers from alcohol and tobacco, these college roommates were so indistinguishable that they were called the "Rosenkrantz and Guildenstern" of the administration. Nixon's original Cabinet, all white, all male, all Republican, "suggests cool competence rather than passion or brilliance," wrote *Time.* "There are no blooded patricians in the lot, just strivers who have acted out the middle-class dream."

Nixon's accession to office signaled a shift in the public mood toward retrenchment and tranquility. After the spring of 1968, riots in black ghettos tapered off. No one fully understood why the long hot summers ended (at least for a time), but black leaders apparently concluded that burning their own neighborhoods was self-destructive and fighting beefed-up police forces foolhardy. In the strife-torn universities, too, the high tide of violence had ebbed. The fall

semester of 1970 opened quietly. At Columbia's Low Plaza, political
placards had vanished, and Berkeley's Sproul Hall reported all quiet
on the Western front. In the spring of 1970 the peace of the Yale
campus was shattered by outcries over the trial in New Haven of
Black Panthers accused of torture and murder. But that fall a Saturday afternoon political rally drew a small turnout because most of
Yale's undergraduates were more interested in cheering their football
team on against Dartmouth; Bobby Seale had given way to Boola
Boola. Early in 1971 Mel Elfin, Washington Bureau Chief of *Newsweek*, commented:

Today, the sirens in the night no longer wail as urgently as they once did.
An uneasy but palpable calm has settled over the cities and the campuses.
Voices have been lowered and, if the President has not succeeded in bring-
ing us together, at least things are no longer falling apart. The center has held.

The President played an important part in promoting domestic
tranquility. Even some of his liberal opponents found his low-key
manner an agreeable relief from LBJ's bombast. In contrast to his
Democratic forerunners in the 1960's, he promised neither a New
Frontier nor a Great Society, and since little was expected of him
there was less possibility of disappointment. Furthermore, the President made one notable contribution to peace in America—winding
down the war in Vietnam. He reduced troop levels there, which at
their peak had reached 543,000, to 39,000 by September 1, 1972. Reform of selective service greatly lessened anxiety for young men
with higher numbers in the lottery. The peace movement approved
his decision to terminate production of biological weapons and his
role in carrying on the Strategic Arms Limitation Talks (SALT)
with Soviet Russia and in negotiating the historic treaty limiting
land- and sea-based missiles. Nixon's journeys to Peking and Moscow, a far cry from his former image of Cold Warrior extraordinary, encouraged hopes for a détente.

The campus stillness resulted from such external causes but also
from internal reexaminations. Nixon's policies helped to defuse the
war issue, and a slowdown in the economy, which sharply diminished employment opportunities, turned energies toward job seeking and professional training. Some students were inactive not because they accepted the system but because they felt exhausted and
disillusioned after a period of hyperactivity. But the calm also
emanated from second thoughts about many of the assumptions of
the 1960's, especially with respect to the efficacy of violence. The

U.S. Troops in South Vietnam, 1965-1972

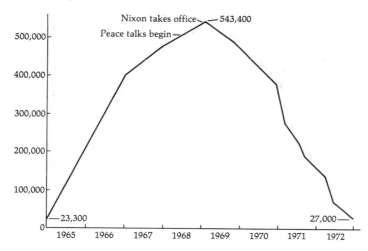

Source: © 1972 by The New York Times Company. Reprinted by permission.

conduct of radicals encountered increasing criticism from those who had long favored fundamental social change. Supreme Court Justice William O. Douglas, whose tolerance of iconoclasm had brought calls for his impeachment, denounced "radicals of the left" for employing disruptive courtroom tactics that struck "at the very heart of Constitutional government." Students who had sanctioned the resort to violence recoiled when a bomb factory in a Greenwich Village townhouse exploded in March 1970, killing three Weathermen, including one of the leaders of the 1968 Columbia uprising, and when the bombing of the Army Mathematics Research Center at the University of Wisconsin five months later resulted in the death of a graduate student. Even some of the conspirators reconsidered. In the manifesto "New Morning—Changing Weather," Bernadine Dohrn asserted that the Greenwich Village disaster "forever destroyed our belief that armed struggle is the only real revolutionary struggle. It is time for the movement to go out into the air, to . . . risk calling rallies and demonstrations."

After the nerve-jangling dissonance of the 1960's, young Americans in the early 1970's reached back toward the 1950's, which, to the surprise of some who had lived through that decade, were perceived as a time of innocent pleasure. The 'sixties had written off

the 'fifties as moribund, but at least a few in the 'seventies thought
of the age of Eisenhower as a lively era before it became fashionable
to take dope, look cool, and dig groups like the Grateful Dead.
"Everybody in the sixties was into a death trip," said one girl. In
the spring of 1971 a wave of nostalgia for the 1950's swept the
campuses. Students packed auditoriums to join Buffalo Bob in singing "It's Howdy Doody Time," watched kinescopes of "Hopalong
Cassidy" and "Sergeant Preston of the Yukon," and staged "sock
hops" at which greased-haired young men in pegged pants danced
with pony-tailed coeds to "golden oldies" like "Teen Angel" and
"Sealed with a Kiss." Nostalgia often fused with romanticism. Acid
rock made way for the sweet sounds of James Taylor and Neil Young,
and groups like Creedence Clearwater Revival identified with the
pristine countryside. In a return to the never-never land of Sigmund
Romberg, the White House even dressed its police force in Grau-
starkian regalia. Whereas the romantics of the counter culture wanted
to refashion the world, romanticism in the 1970's implied a sentimental attachment to the past and a deliberate rejection of the
politicized adolescence of the 'sixties.

The *Mein Kampf* of the new romanticism was Erich Segal's teary
novella, *Love Story,* which by the late spring of 1971 had sold
450,000 hardback and 9 million paperback copies, and as a motion
picture had already grossed more than any production since *Gone
with the Wind.* In campus bookstores it climbed past *The Greening
of America* to take over the Number 2 spot on the best seller list;
Number 1 was David Reuben's *Everything You Always Wanted to
Know About Sex (But Were Afraid to Ask).* To the true believers of the
counter culture, the success of *Love Story* heralded the arrival of
Thermidor, and they responded by abusing Segal as "the Lawrence
Welk of literature" and a "venal reactionary" who turned out "garbage." The film, grumbled a reviewer, was an "exploitation movie,
cashing in on crying the way other movies cash in on sex." To Segal's
detractors, *Love Story* not only raised questions of aesthetic sensibility
but was a political event. "Segal's not the point," one of his critics
explained. "It's what he stands for. He stands for a return to Eisenhower morality, commercialized emotion, political insensitivity, the
whole Middle America schmeer." Segal, under such heavy fire that
he was counseled to take a leave of absence from his teaching position at Yale, said, "God, it's crazy! If I were a homosexual or wanted
by the FBI, the same people who attack me would protect me.
They're killing me because I'm straight."

In this circumambience of nostalgia and romanticism, the counter culture lost much of its exuberance. Campus bookstores found themselves overstocked with volumes by Marcuse and Jerry Rubin. Bob Dylan, a married man with children, accepted an honorary degree from Princeton and aged visibly on his thirtieth birthday. At thirty-five, Abbie Hoffman got a haircut. Hippie society had actually come to grief before the Nixon era. Haight-Ashbury began to disintegrate when "speed" (methedrine) took over in 1967, the same year that Linda Rea Fitzpatrick, a runaway from a suburban Connecticut home, was raped and murdered in the East Village. In both Hashbury and Manhattan, there were too many scary trips, too many cases of hepatitis, too many foul-ups in communal living. Some in the counter culture blamed the collapse on a repressive society, but others accepted the onus. *Easy Rider* concluded: "We blew it."

Experimentation in consciousness expansion had become a bad scene. More than a few grammar school pupils were taking barbiturates, and numbers of highschoolers were mainlining. "With the same openness that some students hurl Frisbees and do homework on the major lawn of the City College campus," reported *The New York Times*, "others congregate there to buy and use heroin." London worried about its enormous drug problem, but there were only about three thousand known addicts in all of Great Britain, compared to one hundred thousand in New York City alone, concentrated in the Harlem slums but spreading to more prosperous sections. To finance their habit, drug users resorted to muggings, which became a rising threat even in college dorms. The State University of New York at Buffalo was compelled to close down the recreation area of the student union, a center of drug traffic. Communities were horrified by the mounting casualty lists of teenagers who had "OD'd," and the rock world was shaken by the deaths from narcotics of Janis Joplin and Jimi Hendrix, both at the age of 27.

Only four months after the celebration of the Age of Aquarius at Woodstock in August 1969, the world of rock festivals turned sour. At the Altamont Speedway near San Francisco, where three hundred thousand were drawn to a free concert by Mick Jagger and the Rolling Stones, hundreds required treatment for bad trips, including one stoned youth who injured himself by jumping off a freeway overpass. Hired to keep order (for $500 in beer), the Hell's Angels went amok; they struck people with weighted pool cues and, to the horror of onlookers, stabbed and stomped to death a gun-wielding black eighteen-year-old from Berkeley, one of four deaths that day. Despite the lesson of Altamont, Louisiana's "Celebration of Life," which in July 1971 endeavored to offer "a living example of an alternative life style," employed as security guards members of New Orleans motorcycle gangs, who chain-whipped festival goers. That same month, just as Dionne Warwick had concluded singing "What the World Needs Now Is Love, Sweet Love," rock fans, many of them high on drugs, brought the Newport Jazz Festival to a halt by a four-hour rampage that resulted in three hundred being treated at a hospital. Within an astonishingly short period, the exhilaration of the rock culture had been subdued—Joplin, Hendrix, Jim Morrison gone, the Beatles splintered. In New York in the spring of 1971, Fillmore East and the Electric Circus closed down, and, bitter irony, in San Francisco Fillmore West was sold to the consumer culture anaconda, Howard Johnson's.

To the dismay of the Woodstock Nation, the consumer culture prevailed, often by co-opting or absorbing its opponents. General Motors, manufacturers of the Olds, responded to the generation gap by advertising its cars as "Youngmobiles," and soft drink vendors announced that the young were part of "the Pepsi generation." "Every time I turn on the television I see movie stars with long hair—Peter Fonda, Dennis Hopper," said Abbie Hoffman. "The youth cult has been taken over by Warner Brothers." The music of the 1960's found its way into singing commercials when Opel promised to "light your fire," and, with consummate gall, Amoco gasoline used folk rhythms to claim that its product advanced the cause of ecology. Women's lib also served the purposes of the consumer culture. Department stores hired female Santas (as well as black ones), and by advancing the slogan, "You've come a long way, baby, to get where you've got to today," Virginia Slims sold billions of cigarettes. Even the religiosity of the "Jesus freaks" proved marketable. Tin Pan Alley hailed "Jesus Christ Superstar," and a radio blurb announced: "Hi kids, it's me, Jesus. Look what I'm wearing on my wrist. It's a wristwatch with a five-color picture of me on the dial and hands attached to a crimson heart."

Nor had the counter culture persuaded most Americans to abandon traditional values. A University of Michigan psychologist pointed out that most of the younger generation of the 1970's had not experienced directly the "youth rebellion" of the previous decade. "The majority have not gone to college, have not smoked pot, have not demonstrated against the war, and probably still stick to the main principles of the old morality," he noted. Despite the "sexual revolu-

Photographs like this one (of Nixon and Chou En-lai eating with chopsticks in Shanghai in February 1972) had an impact on the United States. The President's visit encouraged chopstick-wielding in Chinese restaurants in America and led to a fad of $130 "people's suits" so that Fifth Avenue dowagers could look like Chinese peasants.

tion" of the 1960's, half of the country's newlyweds in the early 'seventies had not engaged in premarital relations, and for all the interest in alternatives to monogamy, marriage continued to be a thriving institution. A four-year study of suburban adolescents by a team of Chicago psychiatrists "found more of a bridge than a gap between the generations," a 1969 summary reported. "The typical American boy still seems to have more in common with Penrod than with Holden Caulfield or Alexander Portnoy." In 1970, the people of Muncie, Indiana (the "Middletown" dissected by the sociologists Robert and Helen Lynd), had not wavered in their belief in "the Calvinist notion of the virtue of work," a writer stated, and a sociologist concluded that the community's credo was "the importance of work, of enterprise, of upward mobility, of material rewards."

In the summer of Nixon's first term came a climactic event that thrilled Americans who retained their faith in such qualities and that captivated much of the world. On July 16, 1969, Apollo 11 blasted off for the moon. Four days later Neil A. Armstrong and Colonel Edwin E. Aldrin, Jr., set their lunar module down on the Sea of Tranquility while Lieutenant Colonel Michael Collins maneuvered the command vessel. "The Eagle has landed," Armstrong told Mission Control Center in Houston, a report that, as one writer commented, "sounded like a message in a Resistance broadcast from London." At 10:56 P.M. EDT, Sunday, July 20, 1969, Neil Armstrong became the first earthling to set foot on the moon. "That's one small step for [a] man, one giant leap for mankind," he said. "Buzz" Aldrin soon joined him in gathering moon rocks and other scientific data, and the two frolicked about like schoolboys let out of class. Together they unveiled a plaque, signed by the Apollo 11 crew and President Nixon, that proclaimed: "HERE MEN FROM THE PLANET EARTH FIRST SET FOOT UPON THE MOON JULY 1969, A.D. WE CAME IN PEACE FOR ALL MANKIND." A few minutes later, the White House put a telephone call through to the moon, and as the world's television screens showed Nixon's visage with those of the two astronauts on the moon's surface, the President said, "For one priceless moment in the whole history of man, all the people on this earth are truly one — one in their pride in what you have done and in our prayers that you will return safely to earth."

Not everyone joined in the applause for the great odyssey. The Nobel laureate Harold Urey asserted that the endeavor was not a scientific undertaking but pyramid-building. Critics pointed out that the astronauts were returning to an earth plagued by festering social ills, and argued that the vast sums Apollo 11 cost would have been better spent in solving terrestrial problems. Some doubted that twentieth-century civilization ought to be exported to other parts of the universe. "If there are people up there," said one teenage girl, "I hope they can stand us." Still others saw the lunar landing not as a triumph for "all mankind" but as a delayed consequence of the cold war, beginning with President Kennedy's resolve to outrace the Russians and ending with the flagstaff of the Stars and Stripes planted on the resistant surface of the moon.

Even the fantastic achievement of televising live color pictures of the moon walk to one billion viewers 240,000 miles away found nay-

Tranquility Base, the Moon. During the Apollo 11 mission, Neil Armstrong snapped this shot of his fellow astronaut, Buzz Aldrin, alongside the solar wind instrument before the lunar module as they walked on the surface of the moon. The American flag leaves no doubt about which nation was winning this phase of the space race.

sayers. Admirers marveled both at the advanced technology and at the openness of a society that was willing to permit the world to witness an experiment in which the possibility of tragic failure was highly conceivable. But the telecast, it was said, added to the public relations nature of the proceedings. In the *Saturday Review*, Robert Lewis Shayon wrote:

Wherever explorers go in the future accompanied by television cameras, they will be actors, making their nebulous exits and entrances for the benefit of multi-planetary audiences. Nowhere will there ever again be pure events (if ever there were); everything hereafter will be stage-managed for cosmic Nielsens, in the interest of national or universal establishments.

Many, perhaps most, in Nixon's America had few such doubts, for the voyage to the moon offered reassurance that the institutions and the beliefs the counter culture had mocked were essential to worthy achievements. Apollo 11, said Eric Hoffer, marked the "triumph of the squares." Although the leader of the expedition bore the same surname as the hero of the 1930's radio serial, "Jack Armstrong, All-American Boy," he emphasized that he was not an adventurer but an organization man. "I think if historians are fair, they won't see this flight like Lindbergh's," Armstrong commented. "They'll recognize that the landing is only one small part of a large program." *Time* concluded:

The astronauts themselves were paragons of Middle American aspiration. Redolent of charcoal cookouts, their vocabularies an engaging mix of space jargon and "gee whiz," the space explorers gave back to Middle America a victory of its own values. It was little noted, except in Middle America where such things still matter, that among Neil Armstrong's extraterrestrial baggage was a special badge of his college fraternity, Phi Delta Theta.

For Nixon, the successful moon expedition provided otherworldly assistance to his strategy of offering himself as the exponent of middle-class ideals. He had shared in the glory through his transspatial phone call, and when the returning astronauts were plucked out of the Pacific and set down aboard the *Hornet*, Richard Nixon was on the deck of the carrier waiting to greet them. Even though he had contributed nothing to the exploit, the trip to the moon made more credible his claims for a stable social order that rewarded men of energy and perseverance. Like the astronauts, he would guide the ship of state through the perils of a dangerous universe to a safe destination on a sea of tranquility.

However, if Nixon's emphases helped turn America away from violence, political extremism, and the counter culture, much of the spirit of the 1960's persisted, at least in attenuated forms. Even Neil Armstrong indulged in hippie lingo; his move into lunar orbit "was like perfect." George Wallace sported sideburns, and a week after J. Edgar Hoover was buried, the acting director of the FBI announced that his agents could grow beards and wear colored shirts and that he would try to recruit women, blacks, and Indians. Most important, the country came to accept a level of violence that hitherto would have seemed intolerable. Authorities described as "peaceful" an academic year in which institutions such as Kansas University were rocked by explosions and others like Rutgers were nearly paralyzed by false bomb threats.

Not even crime could be relied upon to maintain the pristine character of the American way of life. Murder, arson, banditry, once the domain of a reporter on the police beat, moved into the political and cultural commentary. When mass slayings were uncovered near Yuba City, California, a nationally syndicated columnist lost little time in comparing them to the Mylai massacre in Vietnam. In another California mass murder, the killer left a note identifying himself with Tarot, ecology, and radical politics. A message signed "Knight of Wands, Knight of Cups, Knight of Pentacles, Knight of Swords" warned: "Today World War 3 will begin as brought to you by the People of the Free Universe. From this day forward anyone and/or company of persons who misuses the natural environment or destroys same will suffer the penalty of death." Whereas a bank holdup by a Jesse James or a John Dillinger had been triggered by a straightforward desire for loot, similar heists in contemporary America were sometimes motivated by eagerness to advance the Revolution. The savage ritual murder of the actress Sharon Tate and her jet set companions by a band of young people associated with the hippie pads of Hashbury, desert communes, drugs, rock, sex, hints of race war, and hatred of sybaritic society suggested the degree to which crime had become connected with a complex cultural politics, even if a Weatherman leader had not confirmed the relationship by applauding the deed. It was symptomatic that San Quentin's death row housed simultaneously Charles Manson and Sirhan Sirhan.

Nixon and his circle tended to exploit the more conservative aspects of cultural politics. The administration's policies, predominantly centrist and temperate, gravitated in a more rightward direction to take advantage of certain characteristics of the middle of the electorate. Since the ranks of Middle America were swelled by unionists and ethnic groups who had benefited from the New Deal, Nixon sometimes adapted by offering social reforms that approximated the orientation of the Democrats rather than the position of Barry Goldwater. Yet the middle range of the voting public included not a few who were receptive to the argument that the Democrats were friends of the blacks but not of the white blue collar worker, of Chicanos but not of Polish-Americans, were indulgent toward campus violence, soft on crime, profligate with welfare funds, and indifferent to the expansion of communism overseas. To win voters like those in Minneapolis who elected a police detective as their mayor, the Republicans frequently concentrated not on moving toward the center with regard to social issues but on stressing the themes of law and order and national honor. Democrats like Adlai E. Stevenson III might respond by wearing American flags in their lapels, but Republicans knew that when the Archie Bunkers drove to work their cars often bore bumper stickers reading "SPIRO IS MY HERO."

While Nixon played the part of the Grand Unifier who counseled a lowering of voices, his Vice-President took on the rowdy role of "the Great Polarizer." In the spring of 1970 he declared, "I intend to be heard above the din even if it means raising my voice." No one doubted him after his performance of the preceding year. To a commencement audience at Ohio State in June 1969 he said:

A society which comes to fear its children is effete. A sniveling, hand-wringing power structure deserves the violent rebellion it encourages. If my generation doesn't stop cringing, yours will inherit a lawless society where emotion and muscle displace reason.

That fall, at a time when protests against the Vietnam war were being organized in Washington, he railed against the "spirit of national masochism . . . encouraged by an effete corps of impudent snobs who characterize themselves as intellectuals," and he denounced political leaders who promoted peace demonstrations as "ideological eunuchs." In Las Vegas he leveled his sights at *Easy Rider* and the Jefferson Airplane. But he created the greatest uproar when he attacked network television commentators as "a tiny and closed fraternity of privileged men" who reflected the biases of the Eastern seaboard. "Gresham's Law seems to be operating in the network news," he observed. "Bad news drives out good news. . . . One minute of Eldridge Cleaver is worth ten minutes of Roy Wilkins."

Agnew's invective nettled liberals, delighted the Old Guard, and disconcerted Republican moderates. Liberals professed to regard him as a dim-witted bumbler and joked about the appearance of the Vice-President's face on Mickey Mouse wristwatches. They belittled his addiction to pretentious alliteration — "pusillanimous pussyfooting," "vicars of vacillation," "nattering nabobs of negativism" — and noted that he had been a faithful reader of the "Increase Your Word Power" section of *Reader's Digest*. But Agnew was no dunce. He had an instinctive touch for the spot that would make his critics cry with rage, and he revealed an unexpected talent for self-mockery. ("I told the President I was appearing here, and he said I could only give my name, rank and serial number." Or: "The President has just ordered that I be issued my own plane. It's Air Force Thirteen . . . and it's a glider.") Agnew was invaluable for attracting southerners; Senator Strom Thurmond of South Carolina praised him as "next to John C. Calhoun, the greatest Vice President in the history of America." Even so, some GOP leaders were troubled by Agnew's hardshell conservatism and his divisive style and doubted that their party would benefit from his activities in the long run. Republicans should not try to "polarize anything," confided one party chieftain. "We want to broaden the base of the party, not narrow it." Still, Agnew's sharp-tongued sallies threw Democrats on the defensive and had the considerable advantage of permitting Nixon, who had once served a similar purpose for Eisenhower, to seem by contrast a dignified, self-composed statesman.

Occasionally, however, Nixon joined Agnew in focusing political debate on the newer cultural questions of disparate life styles. Even the nurture of children became politicized. Nixon scoffed at the "Spock-marked" generation, and Agnew fulminated against the progeny of "affluent, permissive, upper-middle class parents who learned their Dr. Spock and threw discipline out the windows." He told guests at a Fort Lauderdale fund-raising dinner:

They are the children dropped off by their parents at Sunday school to hear the modern gospel from a "progressive" preacher more interested in fighting pollution than fighting evil — one of those pleasant clergymen who lifts his weekly sermons out of old newsletters from a National Council of Churches that has cast morality and theology aside as "not relevant" and set as its goal on earth the recognition of Red China and the preservation of the Florida alligator. Today, by the thousands — without a cultural heritage, without a set of spiritual values, and with a moral code summed up in that idealistic injunction "Do your own thing," Junior — his pot and Portnoy secreted in his knapsack—arrives at college and finds there a smiling and benign faculty even less demanding than his parents.

The administration's views found their way into both political campaigns and public policy. In 1970 the Vice-President reminded his admirers that he had been "travelling the length of this land . . . to heip elect men to public office who will lean hard against the trend toward permissiveness." Agnew complained, "The decree that infants should be fed on demand and not on schedule has been elevated to dogma up to age 30." When the President subsequently vetoed a bill for a national system of day care centers, he announced that he was against committing "the vast moral authority of the national government to the side of communal approaches to child-rearing over against the family-centered approach."

The Nixon forces exploited the political potentialities of the sexual revolution too. In 1967 Congress had voted funds to pay a presidential commission to read dirty books and decide what ought to be done about them. When in 1970 the commission issued its report opposing punitive action, Nixon denounced the conclusions as "morally bankrupt" and Agnew assured campaign audiences, "As long as Richard Nixon is President, Main Street is not going to turn into Smut Alley." The following year the President, in placing the question of abortion on military bases under state jurisdiction, seized the occasion to say that he could not square "abortion on demand" with his "personal belief in the sanctity of human life—including the life of the yet unborn." After Republican Senator Charles E. Goodell broke with the Nixon administration over its Vietnam policies, the Vice-President castigated him not as a turncoat but as the "Christine Jorgensen of the Republican party," an allusion to the male nurse whose sex had been transformed by an operation. (Similarly, at Wallace rallies the Alabama governor would reply to long-haired hecklers by feigning confusion as to their sex.) Agnew managed to link the cultural upheaval to political persuasion by charging that the erosion of decency had "been abetted by a political hedonism that permeates the philosophy of the radical liberals." Indeed, he said, "a paralyzing permissive philosophy pervades every policy they espouse."

The President's social and economic policies also often bore a conservative stamp. In appealing to groups in the center who wanted stability, he by-passed those who asserted that the urban crisis required more rapid change. He addressed himself hardly at all to the deterioration of the black ghetto. Nixon's Cabinet overweighted the business interest—it included a Chicago banker, an auto manufacturer, and three men who had profited from construction—and spokesmen for other elements had few friends in court. The leader of the liberal wing of the administration, HEW Secretary Robert Finch, lost out when the President bowed to pressure from the American Medical Association on a crucial appointment; and after Hickel criticized the administration for hostility to the young, Nixon fired him. The President grasped that Disraeli had sponsored social reforms, but he knew even better that the Prime Minister had been a Tory. He vetoed health, education, and welfare legislation, a measure to expand public works, and appropriations for hospital construction. Nor did he make much headway on those proposals he did favor. Nixon seemed to lose interest in projects once he had announced them, and he could never work up the enthusiasm for the "New American Revolution" that he did for the SST. Congress procrastinated on programs like the Family Assistance Plan in part because of the President's preoccupation with foreign policy and near indifference to domestic concerns.

Nixon's conduct of foreign affairs frequently proved inflammatory. Although his phased withdrawal of troops from Vietnam helped to bank the fires of dissent, he earned the animosity of the peace forces by making Lyndon Johnson's war his own, especially after he called Nguyen Van Thieu one of the world's five greatest statesmen. Four years after he claimed that he had a plan for ending the conflict, the fighting was still going on, at a cost in Nixon's first three years of 15,000 additional American lives. Furthermore, he periodically undertook new military initiatives—the Cambodian invasion in 1970, the venture in Laos in 1971, the saturation bombing of North Vietnam in 1972—that excited angry protests.

As early as the fall of Nixon's first year, discontent with his Southeast Asian policies exploded into massive demonstrations. A "moratorium" on October 15, 1969, attracted what was said to be the biggest turnout in the nation's history, with perhaps a million participants across the country, and on November 15 a mobilization in Washington, D.C., drew hundreds of thousands in a witness against the war. One homemade placard read, "all too long i dwelt with those who hate peace," and another sign said simply, "MY FRIEND JIMMY SILVERSTEIN IS DEAD: AUG. 16, 1969 VIETNAM WAR." But the antiwar forces could not maintain the momentum of that autumn. By the beginning of 1970, Nixon's combination of rebuffs to their endeavors and continuing troop withdrawals appeared to have succeeded in deflating his opposition. In mid-April, the Vietnam Moratorium Committee closed its Washington office with the announcement that the age of the large-scale peace rally was at an end.

Less than two weeks later, Nixon destroyed this uneasy equilibrium. On April 29, 1970, United States troops crossed the border of Cambodia. To millions of war-weary Americans, the news that a conflict they thought nearly over had been expanded was shocking enough. But the President's justification in a televised address on April 30 made the situation far worse. In language more appropriate to Armageddon, he asserted:

We will not be humiliated. We will not be defeated. . . . If when the chips are down, the world's most powerful nation . . . acts like a pitiful, helpless giant, the forces of totalitarianism and anarchy will threaten free nations and free institutions throughout the world.

At a time when he was sending young men to their death, he asked pity for his own plight. "I would rather be a one-term president and do what I believe was right than to be a two-term president at the cost of seeing America become a second-rate power," he declared. Before the week was out, infuriated students were on a rampage— from campuses in the big coastal cities to those in small Midwestern towns like Kent, Ohio.

On the night after Nixon's speech, students at Kent State University hurled bottles at police cars and smashed store windows, and on the following night they firebombed the ROTC building. Governor James Rhodes responded by imposing martial law and dispatching units of the national guard to Kent. On Monday, May 4, violence renewed. Students threw rocks and other projectiles at the guardsmen, who replied with barrages of gas. Then suddenly, without warning or any direct provocation, guardsmen opened fire with their M-1 rifles. Four students fell dead; eleven were wounded, one paralyzed by a bullet in his spine. None of the four was a radical: one of the two young men slain ranked second in his ROTC class; the two girls killed were walking to class. A report by the President's Commission on Campus Unrest subsequently condemned the casual issuance of live ammunition to guardsmen and denounced the "indiscriminate firing" as "unnecessary, unwarranted and inexcusable." But it also added, "Those who wreaked havoc on the town of Kent, those who burned the ROTC building, those who attacked and stoned National Guardsmen and all those who urged them on

The avuncular evening newsman Walter Cronkite reports to millions of Americans on yet another shattering development. The map in the background indicates that the story comes from Kent, Ohio, where on May 4, 1970, four college students were slain.

and applauded their deeds share the responsibility for the deaths and injuries of May 4."

Reports of the massacre at Kent State reached campuses already overheated by Nixon's speech on Cambodia and sent temperatures to the boiling point. Resentment was heightened by word from Mississippi that on May 15 highway patrolmen killed two and wounded eleven black students at Jackson State College. During May the lid blew off on campuses in every part of the nation, including many that had been unscathed in 1968. Students sacked the treasurer's office at the University of South Carolina, scores were injured in riots at the University of Maryland, a half-million-dollar fire blazed at Colorado State, and in a melee at the University of New Mexico three students were stabbed. In what President William J. McGill of Columbia called "the most disastrous month of May in the history of American higher education," hundreds of colleges and universities went on strike for a day or shut down for the rest of the semester.

Faculty members, administrators, and unaffiliated liberals and radicals took part in many demonstrations, and numbers of antiwar protesters once more congregated in Washington. "The country is virtually on the edge of a spiritual—and perhaps even a physical—breakdown," asserted Mayor John Lindsay of New York. The Nixon administration, he said, had so bisected the nation that "for the first time in a century, we are not sure there is a future for America."

Shaken by the realization that he had badly miscalculated, Nixon sought to make amends. He agreed to talk to six Kent State students who had come to Washington, and he conferred with the presidents of eight universities. But he remained disturbed. Before dawn on May 9, unable to sleep, he got out of bed, dressed, and, accompanied only by his valet and Secret Service men, left the White House in a limousine. At 5 A.M., student demonstrators at the Lincoln Memorial were startled to find themselves face-to-face with the President of the United States. "I know you think we are a bunch of sons-of-bitches," he said, but he hoped they would recognize that he and his advisers also wanted peace. In a rambling monologue he urged them to see the world while they were young; among the places he suggested they might visit was Indochina. His desire to communicate, undoubtedly deeply felt, got nowhere because Nixon had come to talk but not to listen and because he did not know how to reach this new generation. When he chatted with students who had come three thousand miles from California to show their concern about the war, he asked them how they liked surfing; and when he spoke to undergraduates from Syracuse, shut down by a strike against his policies, he wanted to know whether the Big Orange would be able to field a powerful football team. Still, his extraordinary caper suggested the extent of his concern and his readiness to be conciliatory.

The President's propitiatory mood reflected awareness that rumblings about his aloofness were rife within his administration as well as on the campuses. A number of highly ranked Republicans had doubted for some time the wisdom of Nixon's calculated display of disdain toward those who advocated a termination of the war. In November 1969, when hundreds of thousands had gathered in Washington for the peace mobilization, the White House had let it be known that the President was preoccupied with the telecast of the Ohio State–Purdue game. Cabinet officers resented the "Berlin Wall" that "the Germans," Ehrlichman and Haldeman, put between them and the chief executive. Both sets of grievances came together in a well-publicized letter Wally Hickel sent to Nixon. The President, his secretary of the interior recommended, ought to make himself more accessible to youth and to members of his Cabinet, while Agnew's abrasive alliteration should be heard less. Nixon was nettled by Hickel's epistle, but for a time he seemed responsive. He asked G. Alexander Heard, the president of Vanderbilt University, to serve as liaison with the universities and appointed a nine-member commission to study campus violence.

Nixon's inclination to placate his critics proved short-lived, in no small part because many Americans applauded his Cambodian policy and thought the Kent State undergraduates had "got what they were asking for." On May 8, when antiwar students from New York City colleges gathered in the financial district, wrench-wielding, helmeted construction workers set upon the long-haired protesters and bludgeoned them while the police looked on. Shouting "All the way, U.S.A.," they marched on City Hall and raised the flag Mayor Lindsay had ordered lowered to half-staff in mourning for the Kent victims.

Bolstered by groups like the hardhats, Nixon resumed a more aggressive stance in the fall 1970 campaign, and periodically thereafter he took steps that provoked further ill feeling. In April 1971, demonstrators were back in Washington, this time because of the invasion of Laos in the first part of the year. On that occasion hundreds of Vietnam veterans, some on crutches, flung away their Purple Hearts, Silver Stars, and campaign ribbons. That month, too, Nixon created bitterness by intervening in the case of First Lieutenant William L. Calley, Jr., convicted of the premeditated murder of unarmed South Vietnamese civilians at the hamlet of Mylai but regarded as a martyr by the Right, especially in the South. This series of actions threatened to impair Nixon's centrist strategy since much of the country wanted to withdraw from Southeast Asia and was sickened by Calley's deed. In fact, Nixon came out of these episodes stronger than before. When in the spring of 1972 he ordered Haiphong harbor mined, there were new outbursts of campus violence but only a small number of antiwar demonstrators turned up in Washington. His willful meddling in the Calley case earned political dividends, for it promoted the Southern strategy devised by John Mitchell, Nixon's 1968 campaign manager and strong man of his administration.

Brusque, self-confident, domineering, Mitchell had been called "El Supremo" by younger Republican workers during the campaign, and in the Nixon government he became top counselor on a

In May 1970 construction workers demonstrate in New York City to show their support of the Nixon administration's policies in Vietnam. The march was organized by the president of the Building and Construction Trades Council, Peter J. Brennan, who in November 1972 was named Secretary of Labor.

wide range of policy questions. A British journalist commented that he "looked like Judge Jeffreys, the hanging judge of the Bloody Assizes, and in his case looks were not altogether misleading." As Nixon's attorney general he alarmed liberals by claiming the right to wiretap without court order and advocating preventive detention for recalcitrant criminal suspects. In 1970 Congress acceded to Mitchell's request to authorize "no-knock" searches and mandatory prison sentences. He initiated a number of prosecutions that critics charged, not always persuasively, were repressive in intent—against

"the Chicago Eight" for the 1968 disruptions; against the anti-war priest, Philip Berrigan, and others for allegedly hatching a plot to kidnap Henry Kissinger; and against Daniel Ellsberg, accused of filching the Pentagon papers. An arch-conservative Wall Street lawyer, Mitchell was naturally inclined to push the administration toward the right. But he was also convinced that in such an orientation lay Nixon's best prospects for reelection. Hence he embarked on a Southern strategy to woo Wallace's following below the Mason-Dixon line and those in the North troubled by the breakdown of law and order and especially by black militancy.

One of Mitchell's young aides, Kevin Phillips, spelled out the Administration's battle plan, perhaps indiscreetly, in *The Emerging Republican Majority*. Phillips reasoned that Nixon could win reelection by ignoring those few regions still attracted to liberalism—the Northeast, Minnesota, the Pacific Northwest—and forgetting about black and Latin voters. The Republicans could become the new majority party if they appealed to conservative sentiments in the suburbs, among Catholic ethnic workingmen, and in the increasingly Republican South. The richest rewards would be found in "the Sunbelt," ranging from Nixon's Florida residence in Key Biscayne across the Southwest to his San Clemente compound on the shores of the Pacific.

Mitchell's Southern strategy and Nixon's conservative bent determined their disposition toward the Supreme Court. By promising to put law-and-order judges on the bench, the President appealed to those Wallace enthusiasts who shared his view that *Miranda* and other decisions had "tipped the balance against the peace forces in this country, and strengthened the criminal forces." He soon had four posts to fill, the most open to any first-term president since Harding. President Johnson had nominated Abe Fortas to succeed Earl Warren as Chief Justice, but the attempt miscarried when Fortas' association with a fraudulent stock operator was revealed. (Fortas subsequently resigned from the Court.) Nixon thus gained the opportunity to designate his own choice for Chief Justice, a "strict constructionist." Given the President's determination to reverse the prevailing philosophy of the Court, his selection of Warren Earl Burger to replace Earl Warren was, as Bruce Mazlish suggested, a striking, if perhaps unconscious, play on words. A Minnesotan with long judicial experience, Judge Burger easily won Senate approval.

However, in his effort to put someone in the seat vacated by Fortas, Nixon came to grief, largely because of his relentless pursuit of the

Southern strategy. To repay his campaign obligation to the diehard Republican Senator from South Carolina, Strom Thurmond, Nixon named a conservative South Carolinian, Judge Clement F. Haynsworth, Jr. Labor and civil rights groups mobilized opposition to Haynsworth, and charges of conflict-of-interest improprieties led seventeen Republicans, including the minority leader and assistant minority leader, to join in denying confirmation. On November 21, 1969, the Senate rejected Haynsworth, 55 to 45. He was the first nominee to the Supreme Court to suffer this fate since John J. Parker in 1930, who, oddly, had once been Haynsworth's mentor on the same federal circuit.

The maladroit Mitchell then turned up the name of G. Harrold Carswell of Tallahassee, another Court of Appeals judge from the Deep South. It seemed inconceivable that the President could be humiliated by a second turndown, but the Senate became convinced that Carswell was third-rate. Law school professors, including nine of fifteen at the University of Florida in Carswell's home state, insisted that he was not nearly distinguished enough for a seat once held by Louis Brandeis and Felix Frankfurter. This did not faze the Old Guard Republican Senator from Nebraska, Roman Hruska, who said of Carswell: "Even if he were mediocre, there are lots of mediocre judges and people and lawyers. They are entitled to a little representation, aren't they?" The majority of the Senate, including thirteen Republicans, did not think so, and on April 8, 1970, the nomination failed. Not since Grover Cleveland had a President been rebuffed twice in a row, and Nixon and Mitchell were furious. "I understand the bitter feeling of millions of Americans who live in the South," Nixon declared. "They have my assurance that the day will come when judges like Carswell and Haynsworth can and will sit on the High Court." After his angry outburst against the Senate, Nixon repaired some of the damage he had inflicted upon himself by appointing a respected Northern conservative, Judge Harry Blackmun. So closely did Blackmun's views dovetail with those of his longtime friend, Burger, that he and the Chief Justice were soon being called "the Minnesota Twins."

Neither Nixon nor Mitchell, who professed such concern about the integrity of the Supreme Court, had yet finished showing their contempt for it. Special care was demanded to replace the Court's two most esteemed members, Hugo Black and John Harlan. But the President and the attorney general decided once more on two lackluster nominees, one a California woman with a reputation for toughness,

the other a Little Rock attorney known for his role in litigation against desegregation. The American Bar Association's judiciary committee, which had put its stamp of approval on both Haynsworth and Carswell, found neither of the new candidates to be qualified. Recognizing that he faced certain defeat if he persisted with these nominations, Nixon gave up and named instead Lewis F. Powell, Jr., of Virginia, the highly regarded former president of the ABA, and Assistant Attorney General William H. Rehnquist, a Goldwater Republican from Arizona. (Rehnquist had earlier discounted his chances: "I'm not from the South, I'm not a woman, and I'm not mediocre.") In the end, the President wound up with four relatively conservative judges who would shape jurisprudence for many years to come; and, by trying and failing to appoint a Deep South justice, he won the gratitude of loyalists of the Lost Cause.

The Southern strategy also affected Nixon's performance on racial issues, which illuminated the pitfalls in a policy of centrism. "There are those who want instant integration and those who want segregation forever," he said. "I believe that we need to have a middle course between those two extremes." This sounded like a sensible way to strike a happy medium, but in practice it frequently meant that Negroes who had been waiting so long for recognition of their constitutional rights were expected to wait still longer or be viewed as "extreme." Critics feared that blacks would pay the penalty for the administration's desire for quiescence when it was revealed that the President's adviser, Pat Moynihan, had recommended an attitude of "benign neglect" toward the issue of race. Often, too, Nixon's interest in knitting the nation together took shape in obsequiousness toward the mores of the white South.

Mitchell's Southern strategy jolted civil rights advocates when in June 1969 the Department of Justice, in sharp contrast to its position in the Kennedy-Johnson era, came out against extension of the Voting Rights Act of 1965. In the name of sectional equity, the department proposed to eliminate the sanctions that, by placing election procedures in much of the South under federal supervision, had enfranchised nearly a million blacks. Instead it would substitute a uniform national statute. The provisions of Mitchell's bill, protested the Ohio Republican Congressman William McCulloch, "sweep broadly into those areas where the need is least and retreat from those areas where the need is greatest. . . . The Administration creates a remedy for which there is no wrong and leaves grievous wrongs without adequate remedy. I ask you, what kind of civil rights bill is that?'' The House went along with Mitchell, but when the Senate balked, the 1965 law was reenacted in essentially its original form.

To the dismay of integrationists, Mitchell's attitude prevailed throughout the government. Talk of encouraging "black capitalism" did not advance much beyond the rhetorical stage. The "Philadelphia Plan" to require construction unions on federal projects to admit blacks was better conceived, but had modest results. So half-hearted was enforcement of civil rights legislation that the United States Civil Rights Commission reprimanded the administration three times in one year. If Mitchell's experience as bond salesman had engendered any empathy for the lot of urban blacks, he never showed it. But he was able to impress his viewpoint even on HEW, although Secretary Robert Finch was regarded as the most liberal figure in the President's circle. Within a year after Nixon entered the White House, mutiny brewed. Half of Mitchell's "line attorneys" in the Justice Department were in a rebellious mood, and HEW functionaries were hopping mad. However, the implacable Mitchell won out, and the top HEW official in charge of enforcing integration guidelines was fired.

The symptomatic episode took place in Mississippi during the first summer of the new administration. In August 1969 Secretary Finch and the head of Mitchell's civil rights division shocked integrationists by asking a federal court to postpone the date scheduled for desegregating Mississippi school districts. Appalled by this turnaround in federal policy, the NAACP's legal arm asked to have the United States switched from plaintiff to defendant on the grounds that it was now in league with white racists. "The United States Government," the NAACP Fund's attorney said, "for the first time has demonstrated that it no longer seeks to represent the rights of Negro children." The Court of Appeals granted the government the reprieve it sought, but that October the Supreme Court in *Alexander* v. *Holmes* ruled unanimously (in Chief Justice Burger's first big decision) that Mississippi schools must be desegregated "at once."

In large part as a result of such stipulations by the federal courts, the Nixon years saw a rapid acceleration in desegregating schools, despite the rhetoric of the Southern strategy. The proportion of Negro students in all-black schools dropped strikingly from 68 percent in 1968 to 18 percent in 1970. Much of the advance represented the culmination of forces set in motion by the courts and by the Johnson administration, especially after HEW established guidelines in 1966. But the Nixon administration made important contributions too. Sometimes it moved aggressively, as when it filed suit against the entire state of Georgia to require an end to dual school systems. More often it acted quietly; the White House refused even to take credit for gains. The achievement of Nixon lay, as John Osborne has written, "in cozening the White South" into thinking he would forestall an inevitable process and thereby lowering resistance to the dismantling of the Jim Crow apparatus, which had finally begun to move at more than deliberate speed.

Moynihan, in a memorandum to the President in March 1970, pointed to the "extraordinary progress" that Negroes had been making in other fields as well. Over the past four years, black enrollment in colleges had increased 85 percent; registration had soared from 27,000 in 1930 to 434,000 in 1968. An American Negro had a better chance of going to college than did a German youth. Median family income for blacks was higher than for British whites. By 1968, 21 percent of nonwhite families were in the above $10,000-a-year bracket (compared to 3 percent in 1947). They were now full-fledged members of the consumer culture, although these increments were frequently due to the fact that families had more than one breadwinner. Over that same 1947–1968 period, the proportion of nonwhite families receiving under $3000 annually (in dollars of the same purchasing power) declined from 60 percent to 23 percent. In many areas integration had moved well beyond tokenism. It was hard to believe that an enterprise like major league baseball had been all-white in 1945; on one occasion in the recent period the Pittsburgh Pirates fielded an all-black nine. Four years after George Wallace stood in the doorway, the University of Alabama had nearly three hundred black students.

In spite of these accomplishments, black Americans viewed the Nixon administration with dismay. "For the first time since Woodrow Wilson," said the chairman of the board of the NAACP, "we have a national administration that can be rightly characterized as anti-Negro." The attainments to which Moynihan and others pointed with pride had largely been consummated in the Johnson years, not under Nixon. In fact, the Nixon recession halted economic improvement and resulted in a rise in black unemployment, especially for inner city youths. Most important, blacks understood that while Nixon would continue to move along some of the paths cleared by his predecessors, he would not run risks to blaze new trails. In particular, he would not act against de facto segregation in housing, North or South, nor would he approve expedients like busing to bring about racial balance in the schools.

Once again, external forces pushed the Nixon administration to a more centrist position, but not for long. In April 1971, in the Charlotte, North Carolina, school case, the Burger Court ruled, again 9 to 0, that cities must bus pupils out of their neighborhoods if this was necessary to bring about greater integration. For a time, the administration went along; HEW included busing provisions in its desegregation guidelines for Austin, Texas, and Nashville, Tennessee. But the busing issue proved to be, quite literally, explosive. So fierce was white resistance in communities like Denver, Colorado, and Pontiac, Michigan, that school buses were firebombed. In March 1972 Nixon startled Congress by asking it to impose a moratorium on busing orders by the federal courts while Congress devised legislation that would sharply restrict busing for purposes of racial balance. (He also asked for $2.5 billion to improve education in impoverished school districts.) The House acceded to Nixon's basic proposal, and it required a determined Senate filibuster led by the Democrat, Walter Mondale of Minnesota, and the Republican, Jacob Javits of New York, to forestall full compliance with the President's anti-busing recommendations.

Nixon's racial policies had one important political aim: to outflank George Wallace. The main threat to the President's election in 1972 lurked in the prospect that Wallace would deprive him of indispensable votes on the right, whether he ran as a third-party candidate or, less likely, as the Democratic nominee. In the 1972 primaries the Alabama governor carried out his promise to "rattle the eye teeth of the Democratic party." He swept through primaries in the South, and ran a strong second in Northern states like Pennsylvania and Indiana. But on May 15, while campaigning in Maryland, Wallace was shot several times at close range by Arthur Bremer, a Milwaukee white described as "a confident loner." Again the consumer culture provided the venue. As Martin Luther King met death on a motel balcony and Robert Kennedy in a hotel kitchen corridor, Wallace was shot at a shopping center in Laurel. However, indicative of the muted violence of the Nixon era, Wallace survived, although the bullets left him paralyzed. On the following day, he demonstrated his political prowess by winning both the Maryland and the Michigan primaries, but he was too ill to continue in the race. Wallace's departure left Nixon with a monopoly of the right. His only concern was the possibility that the Democrats would name a strong candidate who could out-duel him for the crucial center.

To Nixon's relief, the Democrats turned not to the center but to the left, for Wallace's bid inadvertently facilitated the capture of the Democratic presidential nomination by a longshot, the liberal, antiwar Senator from South Dakota, George McGovern. By his powerful showing in the early primaries, Wallace contributed to the elimination of the frontrunner, Senator Edmund Muskie of Maine, who in January had pulled even with Nixon in the polls. With Muskie's popularity put in doubt by Wallace and by a hostile press and with Muskie forced to share middle ground with Humphrey, McGovern was able to win enough votes from the party's left sector to capture a series of contests in divided fields. After the ineffectual Muskie had been removed and Wallace rendered *hors de*

At the 1972 national convention, key figures in the Democratic Party unite. From left to right stand vice-presidential nominee Thomas Eagleton, Senator Hubert Humphrey, Congresswoman Shirley Chisholm, presidential nominee George McGovern, Senator Henry Jackson, Senator Edmund Muskie, and the former governor of North Carolina, Terry Sanford, president of Duke University.

combat, McGovern clinched the nomination by surviving a head-on confrontation with Humphrey in California. "Quite frankly, I am not a 'centrist' candidate," McGovern said. His constituency lay among the young veterans of the New Politics who had enlisted under Eugene McCarthy and Robert Kennedy four years earlier, newly enfranchised college students, minorities, and the welfare poor.

Much of the nation had only an indistinct impression of the Democratic nominee. "He appeared something of a hick, from South Dakota—or was it North?" noted his biographer. "Whichever it was, McGovern surely looked the part: a slow-talking, stiff-jointed rube in a shiny Sears Roebuck suit." As a speaker, he rarely electrified audiences. Washington correspondents reported: "His eyes go flat and lifeless on television. His voice struggles for passion and sounds like grace at a Rotary lunch." Yet McGovern had compiled an impressive record—Ph.D. in American history at Northwestern, professor at Dakota Wesleyan, Congressman, director of Food for Peace, United States Senator. A World War II bomber pilot who had earned the Distinguished Flying Cross, he had become one of the first opponents of the Vietnam War, and as an advocate of social reform, he was known as "the Prairie Populist." Above all, he had a reputation for integrity. "George is the most decent man in the Senate," Robert Kennedy once told a visitor. "As a matter of fact, he's the only one."

McGovern conceived of his effort as nothing less than a religious crusade. The son of a "hell-fire, come-to-Jesus" fundamentalist preacher, he modeled himself on the Social Gospel minister Walter Rauschenbusch and for a time had studied for the Methodist ministry. He had begun his campaign by pledging to appeal to "the better angels" of the national spirit, and one of his advisers likened him to Luther and Zwingli. At the Democratic convention, he borrowed a theme from an old hymn to urge, "Come Home, America." Some were moved by these evangelical entreaties. "Saint George will slay the dragon," placards read. But others felt that McGovern did not cope well with issues such as economic controls that could not be framed in scriptural terms and thought that beneath his quiet diffidence they detected an alarming self-righteousness.

Well before the Democratic convention, McGovern's crusade had run into difficulty in his own party. In the California primary, Humphrey riddled McGovern's proposal to give $1000 each year to everyone "from the poorest migrant workers to the Rockefellers," tax it back from the rich, and redistribute it to the needy. Humphrey showed that the proposition had not been thought through and denounced his rival as a radical who would tax the workingman to benefit those on welfare rolls. The former Vice-President also hit out at McGovern's intention to cut $30 billion from the Pentagon budget, a plan that worried large numbers of Americans whose livelihood depended on the Warfare State and upset those who suspected McGovern was an isolationist bent on reducing the United States to a second-class power. After the California primary, a poll found that 40 percent of Democrats who had voted for Humphrey preferred Nixon to McGovern.

The Democratic convention gave much of the nation its first look at McGovern's New Politics, and not all were pleased with what they saw. As chairman of his party's reform commission, McGovern had promoted changes in the rules that required increased representation for the young, women, and minorities, and these innovations paved the way for his nomination. The Miami convention was notably more peaceful than that four years earlier because, it was said, those who had been demonstrating outside in Chicago were now inside the convention as delegates. But many in the party, and in the country, found quota systems menacing and, since quotas were fixed only for a few selected groups, viewed them as elitism masquerading as democracy. Moreover, the reforms resulted in the displacement of many of the party's veteran leaders, notably when Mayor Daley and his contingent were unseated. Union leaders, mainstays of the Roosevelt coalition but vexed by the counter culture and often hawkish on the war, were so outraged that George Meany ordered AFL-CIO unions to be neutral in the forthcoming campaign. As one labor leader grumbled, "There is too much hair and not enough cigars at this convention."

The political neophytes, especially the minority pushing for planks like abortion law reform, reinforced the impression that McGovern was the candidate of the counter culture. In fact, he had been raised with a reverence for the Puritan ethic and preferred small town America to the big city. His views on cultural political issues like abortion, legalized marijuana, and amnesty for draft dodgers and deserters were fairly orthodox. Yet he had written a blurb for *The Greening of America* (which he thought contained nothing he had not learned from his father and in Sunday School forty years before), and his whole campaign was based on the belief that the center would not hold. Three years earlier, Richard Scammon had warned,

At a press conference in Custer, South Dakota, on July 25, 1972, George McGovern announces he stands "1,000 percent" behind his running mate, Thomas Eagleton, who has just revealed that in the recent past he had been hospitalized for nervous ailments and had received shock treatment. Several days later, Eagleton's name was erased from the ticket.

"If the Democratic image in the 1970s is basically one of a party oriented away from the center, toward beard and sandal rather than toward crew cut and bowling shoe, then it seems very likely that President Nixon and the Republicans will establish a dominant position in American politics."

McGovern capped his predicament by his handling of "the Eagleton affair." At the Miami convention, he appeared to have made a shrewd choice in picking as his running mate the likeable United States Senator from Missouri, Thomas Eagleton, a Catholic with good links to organized labor. But two weeks later, on July 25, Eagleton announced that he had been hospitalized three times for nervous illnesses and had twice received electric-shock therapy. "I am 1000 percent for Tom Eagleton and I have no intention of dropping him from the ticket," McGovern affirmed. Within a week, following an outcry in the press and a malicious column by Jack

Anderson, McGovern had forced Eagleton out. He then began an embarrassing search for a substitute that, after a series of turndowns, resulted in the selection of R. Sargent Shriver, a member of the Kennedy clan who had run the Peace Corps and the War on Poverty and was acceptable to Mayor Daley. McGovern had encountered unusual bad luck, and those who criticized his staff work and blamed him for inconsistency failed to apply the same measuring rod to Nixon. But the episode led to questioning of McGovern's judgment, his fidelity, his decisiveness, and of his most valuable asset, his integrity. Young idealists were disillusioned, and party regulars had added cause to defect. Asked if he would back McGovern, the Rhode Island state chairman replied that he was behind him "1000 percent."

The tribulations of the Democrats and McGovern's posture as a candidate of the left gave Nixon an insurmountable advantage. He became the favorite not just of Republicans but of all those independents and Democrats who had been distressed by the life styles of the 1960's. At their national convention, the Republicans put on display screen stars who embodied the certitudes of an earlier America—John Wayne, Jimmy Stewart, Glenn Ford, and Pat Boone—and the predominantly male gathering adopted a platform that paid tribute to women for their "great contribution . . . as homemakers and mothers." Many in the Roosevelt coalition still approved of social legislation and distrusted the GOP as the party of big business, but they were disturbed even more by the notion that McGovern was associated with runaway change. Eager to terminate American involvement in Vietnam, they were unwilling to accept blame for genocide. Forced to choose, they preferred Julie Eisenhower to Jane Fonda.

McGovern's strength as a candidate for the nomination proved a weakness in his race against Nixon. In the primaries, his uncompromising stands had won him the admiration of the left spectrum of his party. But when he offered undiluted observations during the presidential contest, saying that he would "crawl" to Hanoi and that it was better to "beg than bomb," he alienated the center of the electorate, where most of the votes lay. His attempts to shift direction and move toward the center were also fraught with peril. By wooing Mayor Daley and Lyndon Johnson, he tarnished his reputation as an advocate of party reform and a foe of the war. When he abandoned his scheme for $1000 "Demogrants" and said he would name the conservative Wilbur Mills as Secretary of the Treasury, he raised doubts about the depth of his commitment to income redistribu-

Julie Nixon Eisenhower speaks at a $1000-a-plate fund-raising candlelight dinner at the Alameda Plaza Hotel in Kansas City's Country Club Plaza. Women campaigners played an important part in the 1972 race, but women's lib advocates seemed less effective than traditionalists like the President's daughter.

tion. As a consequence, McGovern was thrown on the defensive and the main issue became not Nixon's vulnerable record but McGovern's character. Nixon was even able to run a "noncampaign" in which he almost never appeared at a partisan gathering, a situation admirably tailored to proving that he was the bringer of a politics of tranquility, however ill-suited to educating the public on the principal issues.

To the very end, McGovern persevered in his moral crusade

against Nixonism, but in a losing cause. He received an unexpected boon when intruders were caught red-handed at the Democratic National Committee headquarters in the Watergate, a hotel-apartment-office complex in Washington. Details were murky, but newspapers linked the raiders to the "Disneyland Mafia" of University of Southern California graduates in the White House circle and even to John Mitchell, who had managed Nixon's reelection campaign before his wife compelled him to resign. (Martha feigned innocence about the whole matter. "Why do they keep asking me about the Watergate affair?" she asked. "I never had any Watergate affair.") McGovern said the President headed "the most morally corrupt Administration in the history of the United States," and compared Nixon to Hitler in his conduct of foreign affairs. But since McGovern did not have the nation's confidence, his attacks seemed shrill, especially because the incumbent was no longer perceived as "Tricky Dick" but as "the President." Moreover, two weeks before the election, Henry Kissinger's announcement, "Peace is at hand," served to distract attention from the Watergate controversy. Although some expressed skepticism about Kissinger's statement, Nixon was able to face the electorate as a chief executive who had convinced two-thirds of the American people that he would be "better able to move the world closer to peace."

Nixon won a resounding victory with 45.9 million votes to McGovern's 28.4 million. His 60.8 percent of the popular vote gave him a greater share than that won by any presidential candidate save Lyndon Johnson. He swept to a 521 to 17 electoral triumph, losing only Massachusetts and the largely black District of Columbia; his electoral total came within two votes of matching FDR's all-time high. For Nixon, the results, which reached him on the tenth anniversary of his stormy "last" press conference when he had called an end to his career, climaxed a remarkable comeback. The "Great American Loser," he had twice come close to being dropped from the Eisenhower ticket, had succumbed to Kennedy in 1960, had been beaten in California in 1962, and had narrowly missed defeat in 1968. Now he had run better than Ike or any other nominee in the history of the Republican Party.

On the presidential line, Nixon opened gaping holes in the New Deal coalition. The Southern strategy paid off when the Republican candidate swept the entire region "from the Potomac to the Pedernales," a section that had been solidly Democratic as late as 1944. He took a majority of the urban vote, including cities like Cleveland, of ballots cast by blue collar families, of Catholic voters, and of Italian

Election of 1972

Nixon (Republican)

McGovern (Democrat)

neighborhoods (which had given him just 37 percent in 1968). Only black, low-income, and Jewish voters remained in the FDR alliance, although Nixon doubled his percentage in Jewish precincts in four years. The biggest disappointment for McGovern was the perform-ance of young Americans. They gave almost half their ballots to Nixon and did not go to the polls in nearly the proportion of older voters.

Once again the center had held, in no small degree because Nixon had captured 65 percent of the votes of middle-income Americans who composed more than half of the electorate. The dimensions of the McGovern disaster sent Democratic politicians scurrying back to the center and caused second thoughts about the quota system. Farther to the left, Benjamin Spock's People's Party polled an abysmal 74,000. The candidate of the right, Representative John G. Schmitz, who had accepted the American Party's nomination after Wallace was shot, fared little better. Congressman from Nixon's California district, Schmitz said he had joined the John Birch Society to get the middle-of-the-road vote in Orange County. He castigated

McGovern as the favorite of "Hanoi and the Manson family," but he aimed most of his barbs at Nixon, who had become a Keynesian and had banqueted with Chou. "I'm not opposed to his visiting China," Schmitz remarked. "I'm only opposed to his coming back." Schmitz received a mere 1.1 million ballots and no electoral vote, far below Wallace's 9.9 million ballots and 46 electoral votes in 1968.

Yet for Nixon and the Republicans, the returns also had disquieting aspects. Despite the President's landslide victory, the Democrats maintained control of both houses of Congress; incredibly, they even picked up a net of two seats in the Senate. Nixon became the first President to begin two terms with an opposition Congress. The unprecedented ticket splitting confirmed that the country still was inclined toward the Democrats and supported Nixon less out of enthusiasm for him or his party than from distrust of McGovern. In fact, millions of Americans were so put off by the two candidates that they did not vote; turnout sank to the lowest percentage since 1948. Nixon's success suggested "the emerging Republican majority" that Kevin Phillips had foreseen, and in areas like the upper South it did seem that the Democratic hold had been broken. But in much of the nation the results indicated less a realignment than a transitory rebellion against a candidate who was not thought to be presidential timber. Fittingly, the consumer culture provided the stage for McGovern's final bow. After the defeated candidate checked out of his motel suite in Sioux Falls, South Dakota, on the day after the election, the marquee at the Holiday Inn read, "It's Over."

The verdict of the electorate implied that when the United States celebrated its two-hundredth anniversary in 1976 Richard Nixon would preside over the national stock-taking. For some Americans, especially intellectuals inspired by the departures of the 1960's, this was a dismaying prospect. Henry Adams once observed that contemplating the movement between fixed points in the line of Presidents from Washington to Grant had caused him to lose faith in the conception of inevitable progress; and for reformers the transition from Franklin D. Roosevelt to Nixon vividly highlighted the tribulations of liberalism since 1945. Some had apocalyptic fears —that the Nixon administration would eradicate the First Amendment, that America would become a fascist society, that the United States was doomed to decay as had other civilizations. Nixon himself in his 1972 State of the Union address had said: "I think of what happened to Greece and Rome and you see what is left—only the pillars. . . . The United States is now reaching that point." Such a fate, some felt, was only what the country deserved. "God punishes imperial nations," declared the theologian Harvey Cox, and he would punish America. To critics at home and abroad, Uncle Sam seemed to be on his last legs. In Britain, travel posters urged, "See America While It Lasts."

The Jeremiahs had too little faith. The most extreme expressions of concern about Nixon's triumph bordered on hysteria. As Garry Wills remarked sardonically, "The apocalypse has better taste than to associate itself with American elections." More important, the doom-watchers conceded too little to the accomplishments of the years of the consumer culture and the cold war. If it would be too much to say, with Macaulay, "We have heard nothing but despair and seen nothing but progress," the progress had been substantial enough to make the voices of gloom seem strident. The most poignant fears of 1945 had not been realized. The country had not only escaped a recurrence of the Great Depression but had achieved a trillion-dollar economy, a feat that a British economist called "the most momentous news-story so far in the history of the world." By 1972 more than half of American families enjoyed an annual income of over $10,000. Twice since 1945 the United States had gone to war. Yet the dreaded nuclear holocaust had not eventuated, and shortly after Nixon's reelection, James Reston wrote: "It is probably fair to say that there is less danger and fear of a major clash between the nuclear powers than at any other time since the start of the cold war." As a consequence of Supreme Court decisions, the civil rights movement, presidential leadership, and congressional action, the political system had been markedly democratized and Negroes had made the greatest gains of any time in this century.

"The major advances in civilization," Alfred North Whitehead once pointed out, "are processes which all but wreck the societies in which they occur." In the United States, the disorders of the quarter-century after World War II resulted in large part from a willingness to face up to problems too long ignored. As Eugene McCarthy said in his farewell address to his followers in Chicago in 1968, "I think we can say that we were willing to open the box and to see what America was." Each achievement served to awaken new expectations and make the nation more aware of unexplored shortcomings. But as Herbert von Borch wrote in *The Unfinished Society*, "American society possesses virtually inexhaustible capacities for self-redress." There could be little doubt that this capability for self-renewal would be sorely tested in the years that remained of the unfinished century.

SUGGESTED READINGS

Historians have, curiously, given more probing attention to the 1960's than to the decade and a half immediately after the war. David Burner, Robert D. Marcus, and Thomas R. West, *A Giant's Strength: America in the 1960s* (1971), is a judicious appraisal. William L. O'Neill, *Coming Apart* (1971), views the same decade disapprovingly. Ronald Berman, *America in the Sixties* (1968), is an excellent intellectual history. For essays and documents of the period, see Edward Quinn and Paul J. Dolan, eds., *The Sense of the Sixties* (1968); Herbert Mitgang, ed., *America at Random* (1970); Murray Friedman, ed., *Overcoming Middle Class Rage* (1971); Walt Anderson, ed., *The Age of Protest* (1969); and Patrick Gleeson, ed., *America, Changing . . .* (1968). The publications of *Congressional Quarterly* and of *Facts on File* are invaluable.

There is ampler coverage of national elections in the 1960's than for any prior decade. Theodore H. White contributed *The Making of the President, 1964* (1965) and *The Making of the President, 1968* (1969). For the 1964 contest, there is also available Harold Faber, ed., *The Road to the White House* (1965), a study by the staff of *The New York Times,* and Milton C. Cummings, ed., *The National Election of 1964* (1966). Lewis Chester, Godfrey Hodgson, and Bruce Page, *An American Melodrama* (1970), is a fascinating account by a team of British journalists who covered the 1968 campaign. Richard M. Scammon and Ben J. Wattenberg, *The Real Majority* (1970), explodes some popular myths about the electorate. Samuel Lubell, *The Hidden Crisis in American Politics* (1970), should be read in conjunction with Frederick G. Dutton, *Changing Sources of Power* (1971).

As a campaign biography, James MacGregor Burns, *John Kennedy* (2nd ed., 1961), is in a class by itself. Arthur M. Schlesinger, Jr., *A Thousand Days* (1965), and Theodore C. Sorensen, *Kennedy* (1965), are accounts by members of the slain President's White House staff. Louise Fitz Simons, *The Kennedy Doctrine* (1972), is much more critical. Helen Fuller, *Years of Trial* (1962), and Hugh Sidey, *John F. Kennedy, President* (1963), offer contemporary estimates by Washington correspondents; and Tom Wicker, *Kennedy without Tears* (1964), presents another journalist's views shortly after the President's death. Aida Di Pace Donald, ed., *John F. Kennedy and the New Frontier* (1966), is a well-edited anthology. James MacGregor Burns, *The Deadlock of Democracy* (1963), attempts to explain Kennedy's difficulties with Congress. Among the rapidly appearing monographs on the Kennedy years are Grant McConnell, *Steel and the Presidency — 1962* (1963), and Jim F. Heath, *John F. Kennedy and the Business Community* (1969).

Eric Goldman, *The Tragedy of Lyndon Johnson* (1969), comes from a historian who served in LBJ's administration. Most of the estimates of Johnson are by journalists; among the best are Robert Novak and Rowland Evans, *Lyndon B. Johnson, The Exercise of Power* (1966), and Hugh Sidey, *A Very Personal Presidency: Lyndon Johnson in the White House* (1968). Perceptive accounts by foreign journalists include Louis Heren, *No Hail, No Farewell* (1970), and Michael Davie, *LBJ: A Foreign Observer's Viewpoint* (1966). The purport of Marvin E. Gettleman and David Mermelstein's *The Great Society Reader* (1967) is indicated by its subtitle: "The Failure of American Liberalism." Among the extensive writings on welfare and poverty, see Chaim I. Waxman, *Poverty: Power and Politics* (1968); Richard M. Elman, *The Poorhouse*

State (1966); and Ben B. Seligman, ed., *Poverty as a Public Issue* (1965). For government and politics in the Johnson years, *Congress and the Nation,* vol. 2 (1969), is very helpful.

The change in the nature of Negro protest in the 1960's is well detailed in Benjamin Muse, *The American Negro Revolution: From Nonviolence to Black Power, 1963–1967* (1969), and Allen J. Matusow, "From Civil Rights to Black Power: The Case of SNCC, 1960–1966," in Barton J. Bernstein and Matusow, eds., *Twentieth Century America: Recent Interpretations* (1969). August Meier and Elliott Rudwick, eds., *Black Protest in the Sixties* (1970), is an excellent anthology of *New York Times* materials. W. Haywood Burns, *The Voices of Negro Protest in America* (1963), ends before "Black Power" became a rallying cry; so too does Bradford Daniel, ed., *Black, White and Gray* (1964). Martin Luther King, Jr., *Why We Can't Wait* (1964), is an eloquent statement published the same year as Charles Silberman's thoughtful *Crisis in Black and White* and Howard Zinn's *SNCC: The New Abolitionists.* James W. Silver, *Mississippi: The Closed Society* (1964), and Frank E. Smith, *Congressman from Mississippi* (1964), both relate the experiences of courageous white liberals. Donald R. Matthews and James W. Prothro, *Negroes and the New Southern Politics* (1966), is an important study by political scientists. Among the many articles on the riots, see Joseph Boskin, "The Revolt of the Urban Ghettos, 1964–1967," *Annals of the American Academy* (1969). Robert Conot, *Rivers of Blood, Years of Darkness* (1968), probes the meaning of Watts. Lee Rainwater and William Yancey, *The Moynihan Report and the Politics of Controversy* (1967), deals with an issue that divided the scholarly community. Matt S. Meier and Feliciano Rivera, *The Chicanos* (1972), is a history of Mexican-Americans. Edward Simmen, ed., *The Chicano: From Caricature to Self-Portrait* (1971), and Wayne Moquin with Charles Van Doren, eds., *A Documentary History of the Mexican Americans* (1971), give multifaceted views. Stan Steiner has written on Mexican-Americans in *La Raza* (1970) as well as on *The New Indians* (1968). Oscar Lewis, *La Vida* (1966), is a classic account of Puerto Rican acculturation.

Hugh Davis Graham and Ted Robert Gurr, *The History of Violence in America* (1969), is an important study that may be supplemented by an anthology, Thomas Rose, ed., *Violence in America* (1969). Henry Fairlie, "The Distemper of America: A Minority Report on Violence in the United States," *Interplay* (1969), is skeptical of some of the orthodox views. Richard Hofstadter's sensitive, wide-ranging "Reflections on Violence in the United States," in Hofstadter and Michael Wallace, eds., *American Violence: A Documentary History* (1970), is one of the last pieces written by this exceptional historian whose brilliant career was tragically cut short. Daniel Bell and Irving Kristol, eds., *Confrontation* (1969), and Nathan Glazer, *Remembering the Answers* (1970), deal with the campus uprisings. Seymour Lipset and Sheldon Wolin, eds., *The Berkeley Student Revolt* (1965), covers the first major campus outbreak, and Jerry Avorn et al., *Up Against the Ivy Wall* (1968), chronicles the Columbia tempest a few years later.

The standard works on the counter culture are Theodore Roszak, *The Making of a Counter Culture* (1969), and Charles Reich, *The Greening of America* (1970). Samuel McCracken's review of Reich's book in *Change* (1971) is devastating. Herbert Marcuse states his case in *An Essay on Liberation*

(1969). Daniel Bell, "Sensibility in the 60's," *Commentary* (1971), is penetrating, and Seymour Martin Lipset, "New Perspectives on the Counter-Culture," *Saturday Review* (1971), suggests that not everything about that phenomenon is new. Kenneth Keniston, the most astute observer of youth, has written *The Uncommitted* (1965) and *Young Radicals* (1968), as well as such essays as "To Heal Our Society's Deep Rifts," *Journal* (1970). Hazel W. Hertzberg, "The Now Culture: Some Implications for Teacher Training Programs," *Social Education* (1970), is discerning on the time perspective of the young. For the movement to Haight-Ashbury and the East Village, see Lewis Yablonsky, *The Hippie Trip* (1968), and John Robert Howard, "The Flowering of the Hippie Movement," *The Annals of the American Academy* (1969). Among the more enlightening articles on the counter culture are Marcia Cavell, "Visions of a New Religion," *Saturday Review* (1970); Daniel Seligman, "A Special Kind of Rebellion," *Fortune* (1969); Peter L. Berger and Brigitte Berger, "The Blueing of America," *New Republic* (1970); and Anthony Scaduto, "'Won't You Listen to the Lambs, Bob Dylan?'" *The New York Times Magazine* (Nov. 28, 1971).

William H. Chafe, *The American Woman* (1972), traces the history of women from 1920 to 1970. For supplementary material, consult Robert J. Lifton, ed., *The Woman in America* (1965), and Robin Morgan, ed., *Sisterhood Is Powerful* (1970). Carl N. Degler "Revolution Without Ideology: The Changing Place of Women in America," *Daedalus* (1964), is a trenchant appraisal. Articles on more recent developments include Helen Dudar, "Women's Lib: The War on 'Sexism,'" *Newsweek* (Mar. 23, 1970), and Susan Brownmiller, "'Sisterhood Is Powerful,'" *The New York Times Magazine* (Mar. 15, 1970).

The first writings on an incumbent administration are often ephemeral, but the literature on the Nixon years is of a much higher order. Garry Wills, *Nixon Agonistes* (1970), is a stimulating, although often tendentious, study. Mark Harris, *Mark the Glove Boy* (1964), deals with Nixon before he became President. Bruce Mazlish, *In Search of Nixon* (1972), is a "psychohistorical inquiry." Among the more useful contributions by journalists are Rowland Evans, Jr., and Robert D. Novak, *Nixon in the White House: The Frustration of Power* (1971); Paul Hoffman, *The New Nixon* (1970); and Mel Elfin, "The President at Midpassage," *Newsweek* (Jan. 25, 1971). The *New Republic*'s columnist, John Osborne, has written *The Nixon Watch* (1970), *The Second Year of the Nixon Watch* (1971), and *The Third Year of the Nixon Watch* (1972). Allen Drury, *Courage and Hesitation: Inside the Nixon Administration* (1972), and Richard J. Whalen, *Catch the Falling Flag* (1972), are by worried conservatives. Gore Vidal, *An Evening with Richard Nixon* (1972), is occasionally amusing, more often tasteless. Leonard Silk, *Nixonomics* (1972), is a witty explanation of "How the Dismal Science of Free Enterprise Became the Black Art of Controls." Nixon's Democratic opponent in 1972 is the subject of Robert Sam Anson, *McGovern* (1972). David S. Broder, *The Party's Over* (1972), expresses distress over "The Failure of Politics in America," while a much more approving view of the state of the nation may be found in Arnold Beichman, *Nine Lies About America* (1972). For the new decade, see The Editors of The National Observer, *The Seventies* (1970), and Leonard Freedman, ed., *Issues of the Seventies* (1970).

Significant Statistics

	1900	1920	1932	1945	1960	1970
Population	76,094,000	106,466,000	124,949,000	139,928,000	180,684,000	**203,185,000**
Percentage urban	39.7	51.2	NA	58.6	69.9	**73.5**
Percentage rural	60.3	48.8	NA	41.4	30.1	**26.5**
Percentage non-white	12.0	10.0	10.0	10.0	11.0	**11.1**
Life expectancy						
White	47.6	54.9	63.2	66.8	70.6	**71.7**
Nonwhite	33.0	45.3	53.7	57.7	63.6	**64.6**
Gross national product (current dollars)						
Total (billions of dollars)	17.3	88.9	58.5	213.6	503.7	**976.8**
Per capita (dollars)	231	835	468	1,526	2,788	**4,807**
Defense spending (millions of dollars)[a]	332	4,329	1,688	84,311	51,334	**78,013**
As percentage of GNP	1.9	5.0	3.0	40.0	10.0	**9.0**
Military personnel on active duty	125,923	343,302	244,902	12,123,455	2,476,435	**3,065,508**
Labor union membership	791,000	5,034,000	3,226,000	14,796,000	18,117,000	**20,752,000**
Birth rate (per 1,000 live births)	32.3	27.7	19.5	20.4	23.7	**18.2**
Advertising expenditures (millions of dollars)	542	2,935	1,627	2,874	11,932	**19,600**
Motor vehicle registrations	8,000	239,161	24,391,000	31,035,420	73,869,000	**108,977,000**
Persons lynched						
White	9	8	2	0	0	**0**
Nonwhite	106	53	6	1	0	**0**
High school graduates (as percentage of all persons over 16 years old)	6.4	16.8	NA	NA	65.1	**78.4**

Sources: *Historical Statistics of the United States, Colonial Times to 1957; Statistical Abstract of the United States,* 1970; and *Digest of Educational Statistics,* 1970.
[a] Includes veterans spending; excludes interest.

Notes on the Contributors

RICHARD M. ABRAMS, Professor of History at the University of California, Berkeley, received his Ph.D. from Columbia University in 1962. His publications include *The Issue of Federal Regulation in the Progressive Era* (1963), *Conservatism in a Progressive Era* (1964), *The Shaping of Twentieth-Century America* (2nd ed., 1971, edited with Lawrence W. Levine), *Issues of the Populist and Progressive Eras, 1892–1912* (1969), and several journal articles.

STANLEY COBEN, Professor of History at the University of California, Los Angeles, received his Ph.D. from Columbia University in 1961. In addition to numerous journal articles, he has edited *Problems in American History* (2 vols., 3rd ed., 1972, with Richard Leopold and Arthur S. Link) and written *A. Mitchell Palmer, Politician* (2nd ed., 1971) and *The Democratic Heritage* (1971, with Arthur S. Link).

ROBERT H. FERRELL, Professor of History at Indiana University, received his Ph.D. from Yale University in 1951. He has authored or co-authored journal articles and books, notably *Peace in Their Time* (1952), *American Diplomacy in the Great Depression* (1957), *The American Secretaries of State and Their Diplomacy* (with Samuel Flagg Bemis), and *American Diplomacy: A History* (rev. ed., 1969).

OTIS L. GRAHAM, JR., Associate Professor of History at the University of California, Santa Barbara, received his Ph.D. from Columbia University in 1966. In addition to journal articles, he has authored or edited several books, including *An Encore for Reform* (1967), *The Great Campaigns: Reform and War, 1900–1928* (1971), and *The New Deal* (1971).

WILLIAM E. LEUCHTENBURG, De Witt Clinton Professor of History at Columbia University, received his Ph.D. from Columbia University in 1951. His books include *The Perils of Prosperity, 1914–1932* (1958), *Franklin D.*

Roosevelt and the New Deal, 1932–1940 (1963), and *The Growth of the American Republic* (2 vols., 6th ed., 1969, with Samuel Eliot Morison and Henry Steele Commager).

DAVID F. TRASK, Professor of History and Chairman of the History Department at the State University of New York, Stony Brook, received his Ph.D. from Harvard University in 1958. He has written numerous journal articles and authored or edited many books, including *The United States in the Supreme War Council: American War Aims and Inter-Allied Strategy, 1917–1918* (1961) and *Victory Without Peace: American Foreign Relations During the Twentieth Century* (1968).

SAMUEL F. WELLS, JR., Associate Professor of History at the University of North Carolina, Chapel Hill, received his Ph.D. from Harvard University in 1967. He has authored several articles and the forthcoming *The Tenuous Entente: Anglo-American Strategy and Diplomacy, 1904–1914*.

Index